CIMA

Paper P3

Performance Strategy

Study Text

CIMA

PUBLISHING

PUBLISHING

Published by: Kaplan Publishing UK

Unit 2 The Business Centre, Molly Millars Lane, Wokingham, Berkshire RG41 2QZ

Acknowledgements

The CIMA Publishing trade mark is reproduced with kind permission of CIMA.

Notice

The text in this material and any others made available by any Kaplan Group company does not amount to advice on a particular matter and should not be taken as such. No reliance should be placed on the content as the basis for any investment or other decision or in connection with any advice given to third parties. Please consult your appropriate professional adviser as necessary. Kaplan Publishing Limited and all other Kaplan group companies expressly disclaim all liability to any person in respect of any losses or other claims, whether direct, indirect, incidental, consequential or otherwise arising in relation to the use of such materials.

British Library Cataloguing in Publication Data

A catalogue record for this book is available from the British Library

ISBN: 978-0-85732-977-6

Printed and bound in Great Britain.

Contents

Paper Introduction

Acknowledgements

Every effort has been made to contact the holders of copyright material, but if any here have been inadvertently overlooked the publishers will be pleased to make the necessary arrangements at the first opportunity.

How to Use the Materials

These Official CIMA learning materials brought to you by CIMA Publishing and Kaplan Publishing have been carefully designed to make your learning experience as easy as possible and to give you the best chances of success in your *'Performance Strategy'* exam.

The product range contains a number of features to help you in the study process. They include:

- a detailed explanation of all syllabus areas;

- extensive 'practical' materials;

- generous question practice, together with full solutions;

- an exam preparation section, including a suggested approach on how to tackle the pre-seen information, both before and during the exam..

This Study Text has been designed with the needs of home-study and distance-learning candidates in mind. Such students require very full coverage of the syllabus topics, and also the facility to undertake extensive question practice. However, the Study Text is also ideal for fully taught courses.

This main body of the text is divided into a number of chapters, each of which is organised on the following pattern:

- *Detailed learning outcomes* expected after your studies of the chapter are complete. You should assimilate these before beginning detailed work on the chapter, so that you can appreciate where your studies are leading.

- *Step-by-step topic coverage.* This is the heart of each chapter, containing detailed explanatory text supported where appropriate by worked examples and exercises. You should work carefully through this section, ensuring that you understand the material being explained and can tackle the examples and exercises successfully. Remember that in many cases knowledge is cumulative: if you fail to digest earlier material thoroughly, you may struggle to understand later chapters.

- *Activities*. Some chapters are illustrated by more practical elements, such as comments and questions designed to stimulate discussion.

- *Question practice*. The test of how well you have learned the material is your ability to tackle exam style questions. Make a serious attempt at producing your own answers, but at this stage do not be too concerned about attempting the questions in exam conditions. In particular, it is more important to absorb the material thoroughly by completing a full solution than to observe the time limits that would apply in the actual exam.

- *Solutions*. Avoid the temptation merely to 'audit' the solutions provided. It is an illusion to think that this provides the same benefits as you would gain from a serious attempt of your own. However, if you are struggling to get started on a question you should read any introductory guidance provided at the beginning of the solution, where provided, and then make your own attempt before referring back to the full solution.

Having worked through the chapters you are ready to begin your final preparations for the examination. The final three chapters of this Study Text provide you with the guidance you need. They include the following features:

- How to use the pre-seen information and prepare for the exam.

- Guidance on how to tackle the exam itself.

- An exam standard set of pre-seen information, with detailed analysis and example requirements and answers.

- Revision questions. These are exam standard and should be tackled in exam conditions, especially as regards the time allocation.

- Solutions to the revision questions.

- A sample paper that you can attempt under exam conditions, along with the relevant answers.

You should plan to attempt the sample paper just before the date of the real exam. By this stage your revision should be complete and you should be able to attempt the sample paper within the time constraints of the real exam.

If you work conscientiously through the official CIMA Study Text according to the guidelines above you will be giving yourself an excellent chance of exam success. Good luck with your studies!

Icon Explanations

Definition – these sections explain important areas of knowledge which must be understood and reproduced in an exam environment.

Key Point – identifies topics which are key to success and are often examined.

Supplementary reading – indentifies a more detailed explanation of key terms, these sections will help to provide a deeper understanding of core areas. Reference to this text is vital when self studying.

Test Your Understanding – following key points and definitions are exercises which give the opportunity to assess the understanding of these core areas.

Illustration – to help develop an understanding of particular topics. The illustrative exercises are useful in preparing for the Test your understanding exercises.

Exclamation Mark – this symbol signifies a topic which can be more difficult to understand, when reviewing these areas care should be taken.

Study technique

Passing exams is partly a matter of intellectual ability, but however accomplished you are in that respect you can improve your chances significantly by the use of appropriate study and revision techniques. In this section we briefly outline some tips for effective study during the earlier stages of your approach to the exam. Later in the text we mention some techniques that you will find useful at the revision stage.

Planning

To begin with, formal planning is essential to get the best return from the time you spend studying. Estimate how much time in total you are going to need for each subject you are studying. Remember that you need to allow time for revision as well as for initial study of the material. You may find it helpful to read "Pass First Time!" second edition by David R. Harris ISBN 978-1-85617-798-6. This book will provide you with proven study techniques. Chapter by chapter it covers the building blocks of successful learning and examination techniques. This is the ultimate guide to passing your CIMA exams, written by a past CIMA examiner and shows you how to earn all the marks you deserve, and explains how to avoid the most common pitfalls. You may also find "The E Word: Kaplan's Guide to Passing Exams" by Stuart Pedley-Smith ISBN: 978-0-85732-205-0 helpful. Stuart Pedley-Smith is a senior lecturer at Kaplan Financial and a qualified accountant specialising in financial management. His natural curiosity and wider interests have led him to look beyond the technical content of financial management to the processes and journey that we call education. He has become fascinated by the whole process of learning and the exam skills and techniques that contribute towards success in the classroom. This book is for anyone who has to sit an exam and wants to give themselves a better chance of passing. It is easy to read, written in a common sense style and full of anecdotes, facts, and practical tips. It also contains synopses of interviews with people involved in the learning and examining process.

With your study material before you, decide which chapters you are going to study in each week, and which weeks you will devote to revision and final question practice.

Prepare a written schedule summarising the above and stick to it!

It is essential to know your syllabus. As your studies progress you will become more familiar with how long it takes to cover topics in sufficient depth. Your timetable may need to be adapted to allocate enough time for the whole syllabus.

Students are advised to refer to the notice of examinable legislation published regularly in CIMA's magazine (Financial Management), the students e-newsletter (Velocity) and on the CIMA website, to ensure they are up-to-date.

The amount of space allocated to a topic in the Study Text is not a very good guide as to how long it will take you. For example, the material relating to Section A 'Basic Mathematics' and Section C 'Summarising and Analysing Data' each account for 15% of the syllabus, but the latter has more pages because there are more illustrations, which take up more space. The syllabus weighting is the better guide as to how long you should spend on a syllabus topic.

Tips for effective studying

(1) Aim to find a quiet and undisturbed location for your study, and plan as far as possible to use the same period of time each day. Getting into a routine helps to avoid wasting time. Make sure that you have all the materials you need before you begin so as to minimise interruptions.

(2) Store all your materials in one place, so that you do not waste time searching for items around your accommodation. If you have to pack everything away after each study period, keep them in a box, or even a suitcase, which will not be disturbed until the next time.

(3) Limit distractions. To make the most effective use of your study periods you should be able to apply total concentration, so turn off all entertainment equipment, set your phones to message mode, and put up your 'do not disturb' sign.

(4) Your timetable will tell you which topic to study. However, before diving in and becoming engrossed in the finer points, make sure you have an overall picture of all the areas that need to be covered by the end of that session. After an hour, allow yourself a short break and move away from your Study Text. With experience, you will learn to assess the pace you need to work at.

(5) Work carefully through a chapter, making notes as you go. When you have covered a suitable amount of material, vary the pattern by attempting a practice question. When you have finished your attempt, make notes of any mistakes you made, or any areas that you failed to cover or covered more briefly.

(6) Make notes as you study, and discover the techniques that work best for you. Your notes may be in the form of lists, bullet points, diagrams, summaries, 'mind maps', or the written word, but remember that you will need to refer back to them at a later date, so they must be intelligible. If you are on a taught course, make sure you highlight any issues you would like to follow up with your lecturer.

(7) Organise your notes. Make sure that all your notes, calculations etc can be effectively filed and easily retrieved later.

Structure of subjects and learning outcomes

Each subject within the syllabus is divided into a number of broad syllabus topics. The topics contain one or more lead learning outcomes, related component learning outcomes and indicative knowledge content.

A learning outcome has two main purposes:

(a) To define the skill or ability that a well prepared candidate should be able to exhibit in the examination

(b) To demonstrate the approach likely to be taken in examination questions

The learning outcomes are part of a hierarchy of learning objectives. The verbs used at the beginning of each learning outcome relate to a specific learning objective e.g.

"**Evaluate** the proposed strategy to introduce information technology on to the production line."

The verb **'evaluate'** indicates a level five learning objective.

These verbs are outlined in the first chapter of the text.

PAPER P3
PERFORMANCE STRATEGY

Syllabus overview

Two key issues underpin Paper P3 – what risks does the organisation face and how can those risks be managed and controlled? The scope of the paper includes both financial and non-financial risks. The management strategies covered extend to the use of financial instruments, and more general strategies of risk identification and management, involving establishing and monitoring appropriate systems of internal control. With the growing importance of 'new' sources of risk, the paper pays particular attention to risks arising from governance, ethical and social/environmental issues.

Syllabus structure

The syllabus comprises the following topics and study weightings:

A	Management Control Systems	10%
B	Risk and Internal Control	25%
C	Review and Audit of Control Systems	15%
D	Management of Financial Risk	35%
E	Risk and Control in Information Systems	15%

Assessment strategy

There will be a written examination paper of three hours, plus 20 minutes of pre-examination question paper reading time. The examination paper will have the following sections:

Section A – 50 marks
A maximum of four compulsory questions, totalling fifty marks, all relating to a pre-seen case study and further new un-seen case material provided within the examination.

(**Note:** The pre-seen case study is common to all three of the strategic level papers at each examination sitting i.e. paper E3, P3 and F3).

Section B – 50 marks
Two questions, from a choice of three, each worth twenty five marks. Short scenarios will be given, to which some or all questions relate.

P3 – A. MANAGEMENT CONTROL SYSTEMS (10%)

Learning outcomes
On completion of their studies students should be able to:

Lead	Component	Indicative syllabus content
1. evaluate control systems for organisational activities and resources.	(a) evaluate appropriate control systems for the management of an organisation; (b) evaluate the appropriateness of an organisation's management accounting control systems; (c) evaluate the control of activities and resources within an organisation; (d) recommend ways in which identified weaknesses or problems associated with control systems can be avoided or solved.	• The ways in which systems are used to achieve control within the framework of an organisation (e.g. contracts of employment, policies and procedures, discipline and reward, reporting structures, performance appraisal and feedback). [4] • The application of control systems and related theory to the design of management accounting control systems and information systems in general (i.e. control system components, primary and secondary feedback, positive and negative feedback, open and closed-loop control). [5] • Structure and operation of management accounting control systems (e.g. identification of appropriate responsibility and control centres within the organisation, performance target setting, avoiding unintended behavioural consequences of using management accounting controls). [5] • Variation in control needs and systems dependent on organisational structure (e.g. extent of centralisation versus divisionalisation, management through strategic business units). [5] • Assessing how lean the management accounting system is (e.g. extent of the need for detailed costing, overhead allocation and budgeting, identification of non-value adding activities in the accounting function). [5] • Cost of quality applied to the management accounting function and "getting things right first time". [5]

P3 – B. RISK AND INTERNAL CONTROL (25%)

Learning outcomes
On completion of their studies students should be able to:

Lead	Component	Indicative syllabus content
1. evaluate types of risk facing an organisation.	(a) discuss ways of identifying, measuring and assessing the types of risk facing an organisation, including the organisation's ability to bear such risks; (b) evaluate risks facing an organisation.	• Types and sources of risk for business organisations: financial, commodity price, business (e.g. from fraud, employee malfeasance, litigation, contractual inadequacy, loss of product reputation), technological, external (e.g. economic and political), and corporate reputation (e.g. from environmental and social performance or health and safety) risks. [2] • Fraud related to sources of finance (e.g. advance fee fraud and pyramid schemes). [6] • Risks associated with international operations (e.g. from cultural variations and litigation risk, to loss of goods in transit and enhanced credit risk). (**Note:** No specific real country will be tested). [2], [11] • Quantification of risk exposures (impact if an adverse event occurs) and their expected values, taking account of likelihood. [3] • Information required to fully report on risk exposures. [3] • Risk map representation of risk exposures as a basis for reporting and analysing risks. [3]
2. evaluate risk management strategies and internal controls.	(a) discuss the purposes and importance of internal control and risk management for an organisation; (b) evaluate risk management strategies; (c) evaluate the essential features of internal control systems for identifying, assessing and managing risks; (d) evaluate the costs and benefits of a particular internal control system.	• Purposes and importance of internal control and risk management for an organisation. [4] • Issues to be addressed in defining management's risk policy. [3] • The principle of diversifying risk. (**Note:** Numerical questions will not be set). [3] • Minimising the risk of fraud (e.g. fraud policy statements, effective recruitment policies and good internal controls, such as approval procedures and separation of functions, especially over procurement and cash). [6] • The risk manager role (including as part of a set of roles) as distinct from that of internal auditor. [3] • Purposes of internal control (e.g. safeguarding of shareholders' investment and company assets, facilitation of operational effectiveness and efficiency, contribution to the reliability of reporting). [4] • Elements in internal control systems (e.g. control activities, information and communication processes, processes for ensuring continued effectiveness etc). [4]

Learning outcomes On completion of their studies students should be able to: Lead	Component	Indicative syllabus content
		• Operational features of internal control systems (e.g. embedding in company's operations, responsiveness to evolving risks, timely reporting to management). [4] • The pervasive nature of internal control and the need for employee training. [4] • Costs and benefits of maintaining the internal control system. [4]
3. evaluate governance and ethical issues facing an organisation.	(a) discuss the principles of good corporate governance, particularly as regards the need for internal controls; (b) evaluate ethical issues as a source of risk to the organisation and control mechanisms for their detection and resolution.	• The principles of good corporate governance based on those for listed companies (the Combined Code), e.g. separation of chairman and CEO roles, appointment of non-executive directors, transparency of directors' remuneration policy, relations with shareholders, the audit committee. Other examples of recommended good practice may include The King Report on Corporate Governance for South Africa, Sarbanes-Oxley Act in the USA, The Smith and Higgs Reports in the UK, etc). [8] • Recommendations for internal control (e.g. The Turnbull Report). [8] • Ethical issues identified in the CIMA Code of Ethics for Professional Accountants, mechanisms for detection in practice and supporting compliance. [7]

P3 – C. REVIEW AND AUDIT OF CONTROL SYSTEMS (15%)

Learning outcomes
On completion of their studies students should be able to:

Lead	Component	Indicative syllabus content
1. discuss the importance of management review of controls.	(a) discuss the importance of management review of controls.	• The process of review (e.g. regular reporting to management on the effectiveness of internal controls over significant risks) and audit of internal controls. [9] • Major tools available to assist with a review and audit process (e.g. audit planning, documenting systems, internal control questionnaires, sampling and testing). [10]
2. evaluate the process and purposes of audit in the context of internal control systems.	(a) evaluate the process of internal audit and its relationship to other forms of audit; (b) produce a plan for the audit of various organisational activities including management, accounting and information systems; (c) recommend action to avoid or solve problems associated with the audit of activities and systems; (d) recommend action to improve the efficiency, effectiveness and control of activities; (e) discuss the relationship between internal and external audit work.	• Role of the internal auditor and relationship of the internal audit to the external audit. [9] • Relationship of internal audit to other forms of audit (e.g. value-for-money audit, management audit, social and environmental audit). [9] • Operation of internal audit, the assessment of audit risk and the process of analytical review, including different types of benchmarking, their use and limitations. [10] • Particular relevance of the fundamental principles in CIMA's Ethical Guidelines to the conduct of an impartial and effective review of internal controls. [7] • Detection and investigation of fraud. [6] • The nature of the external audit and its process, including the implications of internal audit findings for external audit procedures. [9]
3. discuss corporate governance and ethical issues facing an organisation.	(a) discuss the principles of good corporate governance for listed companies, for conducting reviews of internal controls and reporting on compliance; (b) discuss the importance of exercising ethical principles in conducting and reporting on internal reviews.	• The principles of good corporate governance for listed companies, for the review of the internal control system and reporting on compliance. [8] • Application of the CIMA Code of Ethics for Professional Accountants to the resolution of ethical conflicts in the context of discoveries made in the course of internal review, especially section 210. [7]

P3 – D. MANAGEMENT OF FINANCIAL RISK (35%)

Learning outcomes
On completion of their studies students should be able to:

Lead	Component	Indicative syllabus content
1. evaluate financial risks facing an organisation.	(a) evaluate financial risks facing an organisation.	• Sources of financial risk, including those associated with international operations (e.g. hedging of foreign investment value and trading (e.g. purchase prices and sales values). [11] • Transaction, translation, economic and political risk. [12] • Quantification of risk exposures, their sensitivities to changes in external conditions and their expected values. [13]
2. evaluate alternative risk management tools.	(a) evaluate appropriate methods for managing financial risks; (b) evaluate the effects of alternative methods of risk management; (c) discuss exchange rate theory and the impact of differential inflation rates on forecast exchange rates; (d) recommend risk management strategies and discuss their accounting implications.	• Minimising political risk (e.g. gaining government funding, joint ventures, obtaining local finance). [11] • Operation and features of the more common instruments for managing interest rate risk: swaps, forward rate agreements, futures and options. (*Note:* Numerical questions will not be set involving FRA's, futures or options. See the note below relating to the Black Scholes model). [13] • Operation and features of the more common instruments for managing currency risk: swaps, forward contracts, money market hedges, futures and options. (*Note:* The Black Scholes option pricing model will not be tested numerically, however, an understanding of the variables which will influence the value of an option should be appreciated). [12] • Simple graphs depicting cap, collar and floor interest rate options. [13] • Theory and forecasting of exchange rates (e.g. interest rate parity, purchasing power parity and the Fisher effect). [12] • Principles of valuation of financial instruments for management and financial reporting purposes (IAS 39), and controls to ensure that the appropriate accounting method is applied to a given instrument. [14] • Quantification and disclosure of the sensitivity of financial instrument values to changes in external conditions. [14] • Internal hedging techniques (e.g. netting and matching). [12], [13]

Learning outcomes
On completion of their studies students should be able to:

Lead	Component	Indicative syllabus content
1. evaluate the benefits and risks associated with information-related systems.	(a) advise managers on the development of information management (IM), information systems (IS) and information technology (IT) strategies that support management and internal control requirements; (b) evaluate IS/IT systems appropriate to an organisation's needs for operational and control information; (c) evaluate benefits and risks in the structuring and organisation of the IS/IT function and its integration with the rest of the business; (d) recommend improvements to the control of IS; (e) evaluate specific problems and opportunities associated with the audit and control of systems which use IT.	• The importance and characteristics of information for organisations and the use of cost-benefit analysis to assess its value. [15] • The purpose and content of IM, IS and IT strategies, and their role in performance management and internal control. [15], [16] • Data collection and IT systems that deliver information to different levels in the organisation (e.g. transaction processing, decision support and executive informative systems). [15] • The potential ways of organising the IT function (e.g. the use of steering committees, support centres for advice and help desk facilities, end user participation). [16] • The arguments for and against outsourcing. [16] • Methods for securing systems and data back-up in case of systems failure and/or data loss. [17] • Minimising the risk of computer-based fraud (e.g. access restriction, password protection, access logging and automatic generation of audit trail). [17] • Risks in IS/IT systems: erroneous input, unauthorised usage, imported virus infection, unlicensed use of software, theft, corruption of software, etc. [17] • Risks and benefits of Internet and Intranet use by an organisation. [17] • The criteria for selecting outsourcing/facilities management partners and for managing ongoing relationships, service level agreements, discontinuation/change of supplier, hand-over considerations. [16] • Controls which can be designed into an information system, particularly one using IT (e.g. security, integrity and contingency controls). [17] • Control and audit of systems development and implementation. [17] • Techniques available to assist audit in a computerised environment (computer-assisted audit techniques e.g. audit interrogation software). [17]

AREA UNDER THE NORMAL CURVE

This table gives the area under the normal curve between the mean and a point Z standard deviations above the mean. The corresponding area for deviations below the mean can be found by symmetry.

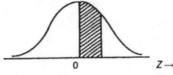

$Z = \dfrac{(x - \mu)}{\sigma}$	0.00	0.01	0.02	0.03	0.04	0.05	0.06	0.07	0.08	0.09
0.0	.0000	.0040	.0080	.0120	.0159	.0199	.0239	.0279	.0319	.0359
0.1	.0398	.0438	.0478	.0517	.0557	.0596	.0636	.0675	.0714	.0753
0.2	.0793	.0832	.0871	.0910	.0948	.0987	.1026	.1064	.1103	.1141
0.3	.1179	.1217	.1255	.1293	.1331	.1368	.1406	.1443	.1480	.1517
0.4	.1554	.1591	.1628	.1664	.1700	.1736	.1772	.1808	.1844	.1879
0.5	.1915	.1950	.1985	.2019	.2054	.2088	.2123	.2157	.2190	.2224
0.6	.2257	.2291	.2324	.2357	.2389	.2422	.2454	.2486	.2518	.2549
0.7	.2580	.2611	.2642	.2673	.2704	.2734	.2764	.2794	.2823	.2852
0.8	.2881	.2910	.2939	.2967	.2995	.3023	.3051	.3078	.3106	.3133
0.9	.3159	.3186	.3212	.3238	.3264	.3289	.3315	.3340	.3365	.3389
1.0	.3413	.3438	.3461	.3485	.3508	.3531	.3554	.3577	.3599	.3621
1.1	.3643	.3665	.3686	.3708	.3729	.3749	.3770	.3790	.3810	.3830
1.2	.3849	.3869	.3888	.3907	.3925	.3944	.3962	.3980	.3997	.4015
1.3	.4032	.4049	.4066	.4082	.4099	.4115	.4131	.4147	.4162	.4177
1.4	.4192	.4207	.4222	.4236	.4251	.4265	.4279	.4292	.4306	.4319
1.5	.4332	.4345	.4357	.4370	.4382	.4394	.4406	.4418	.4430	.4441
1.6	.4452	.4463	.4474	.4485	.4495	.4505	.4515	.4525	.4535	.4545
1.7	.4554	.4564	.4573	.4582	.4591	.4599	.4608	.4616	.4625	.4633
1.8	.4641	.4649	.4656	.4664	.4671	.4678	.4686	.4693	.4699	.4706
1.9	.4713	.4719	.4726	.4732	.4738	.4744	.4750	.4756	.4762	.4767
2.0	.4772	.4778	.4783	.4788	.4793	.4798	.4803	.4808	.4812	.4817
2.1	.4821	.4826	.4830	.4834	.4838	.4842	.4846	.4850	.4854	.4857
2.2	.4861	.4865	.4868	.4871	.4875	.4878	.4881	.4884	.4887	.4890
2.3	.4893	.4896	.4898	.4901	.4904	.4906	.4909	.4911	.4913	.4916
2.4	.4918	.4920	.4922	.4925	.4927	.4929	.4931	.4932	.4934	.4936
2.5	.4938	.4940	.4941	.4943	.4945	.4946	.4948	.4949	.4951	.4952
2.6	.4953	.4955	.4956	.4957	.4959	.4960	.4961	.4962	.4963	.4964
2.7	.4965	.4966	.4967	.4968	.4969	.4970	.4971	.4972	.4973	.4974
2.8	.4974	.4975	.4976	.4977	.4977	.4978	.4979	.4980	.4980	.4981
2.9	.4981	.4982	.4983	.4983	.4984	.4984	.4985	.4985	.4986	.4986
3.0	.49865	.4987	.4987	.4988	.4988	.4989	.4989	.4989	.4990	.4990
3.1	.49903	.4991	.4991	.4991	.4992	.4992	.4992	.4992	.4993	.4993
3.2	.49931	.4993	.4994	.4994	.4994	.4994	.4994	.4995	.4995	.4995
3.3	.49952	.4995	.4995	.4996	.4996	.4996	.4996	.4996	.4996	.4997
3.4	.49966	.4997	.4997	.4997	.4997	.4997	.4997	.4997	.4997	.4998
3.5	.49977									

PRESENT VALUE TABLE

Present value of $1, that is $(1+r)^{-n}$ where r = interest rate; n = number of periods until payment or receipt.

Periods	Interest rates (r)									
(n)	1%	2%	3%	4%	5%	6%	7%	8%	9%	10%
1	0.990	0.980	0.971	0.962	0.952	0.943	0.935	0.926	0.917	0.909
2	0.980	0.961	0.943	0.925	0.907	0.890	0.873	0.857	0.842	0.826
3	0.971	0.942	0.915	0.889	0.864	0.840	0.816	0.794	0.772	0.751
4	0.961	0.924	0.888	0.855	0.823	0.792	0.763	0.735	0.708	0.683
5	0.951	0.906	0.863	0.822	0.784	0.747	0.713	0.681	0.650	0.621
6	0.942	0.888	0.837	0.790	0.746	0.705	0.666	0.630	0.596	0.564
7	0.933	0.871	0.813	0.760	0.711	0.665	0.623	0.583	0.547	0.513
8	0.923	0.853	0.789	0.731	0.677	0.627	0.582	0.540	0.502	0.467
9	0.914	0.837	0.766	0.703	0.645	0.592	0.544	0.500	0.460	0.424
10	0.905	0.820	0.744	0.676	0.614	0.558	0.508	0.463	0.422	0.386
11	0.896	0.804	0.722	0.650	0.585	0.527	0.475	0.429	0.388	0.350
12	0.887	0.788	0.701	0.625	0.557	0.497	0.444	0.397	0.356	0.319
13	0.879	0.773	0.681	0.601	0.530	0.469	0.415	0.368	0.326	0.290
14	0.870	0.758	0.661	0.577	0.505	0.442	0.388	0.340	0.299	0.263
15	0.861	0.743	0.642	0.555	0.481	0.417	0.362	0.315	0.275	0.239
16	0.853	0.728	0.623	0.534	0.458	0.394	0.339	0.292	0.252	0.218
17	0.844	0.714	0.605	0.513	0.436	0.371	0.317	0.270	0.231	0.198
18	0.836	0.700	0.587	0.494	0.416	0.350	0.296	0.250	0.212	0.180
19	0.828	0.686	0.570	0.475	0.396	0.331	0.277	0.232	0.194	0.164
20	0.820	0.673	0.554	0.456	0.377	0.312	0.258	0.215	0.178	0.149

Periods	Interest rates (r)									
(n)	11%	12%	13%	14%	15%	16%	17%	18%	19%	20%
1	0.901	0.893	0.885	0.877	0.870	0.862	0.855	0.847	0.840	0.833
2	0.812	0.797	0.783	0.769	0.756	0.743	0.731	0.718	0.706	0.694
3	0.731	0.712	0.693	0.675	0.658	0.641	0.624	0.609	0.593	0.579
4	0.659	0.636	0.613	0.592	0.572	0.552	0.534	0.516	0.499	0.482
5	0.593	0.567	0.543	0.519	0.497	0.476	0.456	0.437	0.419	0.402
6	0.535	0.507	0.480	0.456	0.432	0.410	0.390	0.370	0.352	0.335
7	0.482	0.452	0.425	0.400	0.376	0.354	0.333	0.314	0.296	0.279
8	0.434	0.404	0.376	0.351	0.327	0.305	0.285	0.266	0.249	0.233
9	0.391	0.361	0.333	0.308	0.284	0.263	0.243	0.225	0.209	0.194
10	0.352	0.322	0.295	0.270	0.247	0.227	0.208	0.191	0.176	0.162
11	0.317	0.287	0.261	0.237	0.215	0.195	0.178	0.162	0.148	0.135
12	0.286	0.257	0.231	0.208	0.187	0.168	0.152	0.137	0.124	0.112
13	0.258	0.229	0.204	0.182	0.163	0.145	0.130	0.116	0.104	0.093
14	0.232	0.205	0.181	0.160	0.141	0.125	0.111	0.099	0.088	0.078
15	0.209	0.183	0.160	0.140	0.123	0.108	0.095	0.084	0.079	0.065
16	0.188	0.163	0.141	0.123	0.107	0.093	0.081	0.071	0.062	0.054
17	0.170	0.146	0.125	0.108	0.093	0.080	0.069	0.060	0.052	0.045
18	0.153	0.130	0.111	0.095	0.081	0.069	0.059	0.051	0.044	0.038
19	0.138	0.116	0.098	0.083	0.070	0.060	0.051	0.043	0.037	0.031
20	0.124	0.104	0.087	0.073	0.061	0.051	0.043	0.037	0.031	0.026

Cumulative present value of $1 per annum, Receivable or Payable at the end of each year for n years $\frac{1-(1+r)^{-n}}{r}$

Periods (n)	Interest rates (r)									
	1%	2%	3%	4%	5%	6%	7%	8%	9%	10%
1	0.990	0.980	0.971	0.962	0.952	0.943	0.935	0.926	0.917	0.909
2	1.970	1.942	1.913	1.886	1.859	1.833	1.808	1.783	1.759	1.736
3	2.941	2.884	2.829	2.775	2.723	2.673	2.624	2.577	2.531	2.487
4	3.902	3.808	3.717	3.630	3.546	3.465	3.387	3.312	3.240	3.170
5	4.853	4.713	4.580	4.452	4.329	4.212	4.100	3.993	3.890	3.791
6	5.795	5.601	5.417	5.242	5.076	4.917	4.767	4.623	4.486	4.355
7	6.728	6.472	6.230	6.002	5.786	5.582	5.389	5.206	5.033	4.868
8	7.652	7.325	7.020	6.733	6.463	6.210	5.971	5.747	5.535	5.335
9	8.566	8.162	7.786	7.435	7.108	6.802	6.515	6.247	5.995	5.759
10	9.471	8.983	8.530	8.111	7.722	7.360	7.024	6.710	6.418	6.145
11	10.368	9.787	9.253	8.760	8.306	7.887	7.499	7.139	6.805	6.495
12	11.255	10.575	9.954	9.385	8.863	8.384	7.943	7.536	7.161	6.814
13	12.134	11.348	10.635	9.986	9.394	8.853	8.358	7.904	7.487	7.103
14	13.004	12.106	11.296	10.563	9.899	9.295	8.745	8.244	7.786	7.367
15	13.865	12.849	11.938	11.118	10.380	9.712	9.108	8.559	8.061	7.606
16	14.718	13.578	12.561	11.652	10.838	10.106	9.447	8.851	8.313	7.824
17	15.562	14.292	13.166	12.166	11.274	10.477	9.763	9.122	8.544	8.022
18	16.398	14.992	13.754	12.659	11.690	10.828	10.059	9.372	8.756	8.201
19	17.226	15.679	14.324	13.134	12.085	11.158	10.336	9.604	8.950	8.365
20	18.046	16.351	14.878	13.590	12.462	11.470	10.594	9.818	9.129	8.514

Periods (n)	Interest rates (r)									
	11%	12%	13%	14%	15%	16%	17%	18%	19%	20%
1	0.901	0.893	0.885	0.877	0.870	0.862	0.855	0.847	0.840	0.833
2	1.713	1.690	1.668	1.647	1.626	1.605	1.585	1.566	1.547	1.528
3	2.444	2.402	2.361	2.322	2.283	2.246	2.210	2.174	2.140	2.106
4	3.102	3.037	2.974	2.914	2.855	2.798	2.743	2.690	2.639	2.589
5	3.696	3.605	3.517	3.433	3.352	3.274	3.199	3.127	3.058	2.991
6	4.231	4.111	3.998	3.889	3.784	3.685	3.589	3.498	3.410	3.326
7	4.712	4.564	4.423	4.288	4.160	4.039	3.922	3.812	3.706	3.605
8	5.146	4.968	4.799	4.639	4.487	4.344	4.207	4.078	3.954	3.837
9	5.537	5.328	5.132	4.946	4.772	4.607	4.451	4.303	4.163	4.031
10	5.889	5.650	5.426	5.216	5.019	4.833	4.659	4.494	4.339	4.192
11	6.207	5.938	5.687	5.453	5.234	5.029	4.836	4.656	4.486	4.327
12	6.492	6.194	5.918	5.660	5.421	5.197	4.988	7.793	4.611	4.439
13	6.750	6.424	6.122	5.842	5.583	5.342	5.118	4.910	4.715	4.533
14	6.982	6.628	6.302	6.002	5.724	5.468	5.229	5.008	4.802	4.611
15	7.191	6.811	6.462	6.142	5.847	5.575	5.324	5.092	4.876	4.675
16	7.379	6.974	6.604	6.265	5.954	5.668	5.405	5.162	4.938	4.730
17	7.549	7.120	6.729	6.373	6.047	5.749	5.475	5.222	4.990	4.775
18	7.702	7.250	6.840	6.467	6.128	5.818	5.534	5.273	5.033	4.812
19	7.839	7.366	6.938	6.550	6.198	5.877	5.584	5.316	5.070	4.843
20	7.963	7.469	7.025	6.623	6.259	5.929	5.628	5.353	5.101	4.870

Formulae

Annuity

Present value of an annuity of £1 per annum receivable or payable for n years, commencing in one year, discounted at r% per annum:

$$PV = \frac{1}{r}\left[1 - \frac{1}{[1+r]^n}\right]$$

Perpetuity

Present value of £1 per annum, payable or receivable in perpetuity, commencing in one year, discounted at r% per annum:

$$PV = \frac{1}{r}$$

Growing Perpetuity

Present value of £1 per annum, receivable or payable, commencing in one year, growing in perpetuity at a constant rate of g% per annum, discounted at r% per annum:

$$PV = \frac{1}{r-g}$$

1

CIMA verb hierarchy – Strategic level exams

Chapter learning objectives

CIMA VERB HIERARCHY

CIMA place great importance on the choice of verbs in exam question requirements. It is thus critical that you answer the question according to the definition of the verb used.

1 CIMA verb hierarchy – Strategic level

In strategic level exams you will mainly meet verbs from levels 3, 4 and 5. Examiners have commented on many occasions that they ask a level 5 verb and get a level 2 response. It is vital that the higher level verbs are understood and responded to. Very occasionally you will also see level 1 and 2 verbs but these should not account for more than 5–10% of the marks in total.

Level 3 – APPLICATION

How you are expected to apply your knowledge

VERBS USED	DEFINITION
Apply	Put to practical use.
Calculate	Ascertain or reckon mathematically.
Demonstrate	Prove with certainty or exhibit by practical means.
Prepare	Make or get ready for use.
Reconcile	Make or prove consistent/compatible.
Solve	Find an answer to.
Tabulate	Arrange in a table.

Level 4 – ANALYSIS

How you are expected to analyse the detail of what you have learned.

VERBS USED	DEFINITION
Analyse	Examine in detail the structure of.
Categorise	Place into a defined class or division.
Compare and contrast	Show the similarities and/or differences between.
Construct	Build up or compile.
Discuss	Examine in detail by argument.
Interpret	Translate into intelligible or familiar terms.
Prioritise	Place in order of priority or sequence for action.
Produce	Create or bring into existence.

Level 5 – EVALUATION

How you are expected to use your learning to evaluate, make decisions or recommendations.

VERBS USED	DEFINITION
Advise	Counsel, inform or notify.
Evaluate	Appraise or assess the value of.
Recommend	Propose a course of action.

2 Further guidance on strategic level verbs that cause confusion

Verbs that cause students most confusion at this level are as follows:

Level 3 verbs

- **The verb "to apply"**

  Given that all level 3 verbs involve application, the verb "apply" is rare in the real exam. Instead one of the other more specific verbs is used instead.

- **The verb "to reconcile"**

  This is a numerical requirement and usually involves starting with one of the figures, adjusting it and ending up with the other.

  For example, in a bank reconciliation you start with the recorded cash at bank figure, adjust it for unpresented cheques, etc, and (hopefully!) end up with the stated balance in the cash "T account".

- **The verb "to demonstrate"**

  The verb "to demonstrate" can be used in two main ways.

  Firstly it could mean to prove that a given statement is true or consistent with circumstances given. For example, the Finance Director may have stated in the question that the company will not exceed its overdraft limit in the next six months. The requirement then asks you to demonstrate that the Director is wrong. You could do this by preparing a cash flow forecast for the next six months.

  Secondly you could be asked to demonstrate **how** a stated model, framework, technique or theory **could be used** in the particular scenario to achieve a specific result – for example, how a probability matrix could be used to make a production decision. Ensure in such questions that you do not merely describe the model but use it to generate the desired outcome.

Level 4 verbs

- **The verb "to analyse"**

  To analyse something is to examine it in detail in order to discover its meaning or essential features. This will usually involve breaking the scenario down and looking at the fine detail, possibly with additional calculations, and then stepping back to see the bigger picture to identify any themes to support conclusions.

  For example, if asked to analyse a set of financial statements, then the end result will be a set of statements about the performance of the business with supporting evidence. This could involve the following:

  (1) You could break down your analysis into areas of profitability, liquidity, gearing and so on.

  (2) Under each heading look at key figures in the financial statements, identifying trends (e.g. sales growth) and calculating supporting ratios (e.g. margins).

  (3) Try to explain what the figures mean and why they have occurred (e.g. why has the operating margin fallen?)

  (4) Start considering the bigger picture – are the ratios presenting a consistent message or do they contradict each other? Can you identify common causes?

  (5) Finally you would then seek to pull all this information together and interpret it to make some higher level comments about overall performance.

  The main error students make is that they fail to draw out any themes and conclusions and simply present the marker with a collection of uninterpreted, unexplained facts and figures.

- **The verb "to discuss"**

  To discuss something is very similar to analysing it, except that discussion usually involves two or more different viewpoints or arguments as the context, rather than a set of figures, say. To discuss viewpoints will involve looking at their underlying arguments, examining them critically, trying to assess whether one argument is more persuasive than the other and then seeking to reach a conclusion.

  For example, if asked to discuss whether a particular technique could be used by a company, you would examine the arguments for and against, making reference to the specific circumstances in the question, and seek to conclude.

- **The verb "to prioritise"**

  To prioritise is to place objects in an order. The key issue here is to decide upon the criteria to use to perform the ordering. For example, prioritising the external threats facing a firm could be done by considering the scale of financial consequences, immediacy, implications for the underlying business model and so on.

  The main mistake students make is that they fail to justify their prioritisation - why is this the most important issue?

Level 5 verbs

- **The verb "to evaluate"**

  To evaluate something is to assess it with a view to placing a value on it. In many respects "evaluate" should be seen as a higher level version of "analyse" and "discuss" and could include qualitative and quantitative factors within your criteria. Your resulting arguments will need to be prioritised and weighed against each other to form a conclusion.

  For example, suppose you are asked to evaluate a proposed strategy in paper E3. At its simplest your answer could contain a series of arguments for and against the strategy. Each argument should be discussed to assess its importance. The arguments can then be weighed up against each other to form a conclusion. You are thus evaluating the factors within each argument and then evaluating the arguments against each other.

  With such questions many students struggle to generate enough points or arguments. Part of the solution is to produce mental checklists when studying the paper concerned. These give criteria to use for valuing the matter at hand. With the above example on strategy evaluation, criteria could include any of the following:

  – Are there any useful calculations – e.g. NPV, impact on profit?

  – Does the strategy resolve any major threats faced by the firm?

  – Does the strategy capitalise on the firm's strengths or do weaknesses need resolving first?

  – Does the strategy enhance the firm's competitive strategy?

  – Does the strategy lead to a better "fit" with the environment?

  – What are the risks and are they acceptable?

  – What are the implications for different stakeholders and would it be acceptable to them?

  – What are the resource implications – how feasible if the strategy?

Use of such a checklist will ensure you have enough points to pass.

In some questions you may have to do more preliminary work before you can evaluate. For example, if asked to evaluate a firm's approach to change management you would start by identifying what type of approach they are taking (referencing to different models of change management) before you can evaluate it.

- **The differences between the verbs "to evaluate", "to advise" and "to recommend"**

All three level 5 verbs involve a mixture of identifying relevant issues, analysing them, evaluating them and then finishing with some form of conclusion. Some writers see this as a three step approach:

(1) **What?** Identify relevant issues.

(2) **So what?** Why are the issues relevant? How significant are they?

(3) **What now?** What response is required by the firm being considered?

The difference between the level 5 verbs lies in where the main emphasis is in these three steps. With "advise" and "recommend" the examiner will be looking for more detail in step 3. Recommendations in particular could involve formulating a plan of action that includes both short- and longer-term aspects.

Recommended reading

For further reading on the verb hierarchy see 'It ain't what you do, it's...' (February 2010) written by David Harris, a former examiner and now consultant to CIMA. This article can be found on the CIMA website www.cimaglobal.com.

2

Risk

Chapter learning objectives

Lead	Component
B1. Evaluate types of risk facing an organisation.	(b) Evaluate risks facing an organisation.
B2. Evaluate risk management strategies and internal controls.	(a) Discuss the purposes and importance of internal control and risk management for an organisation.

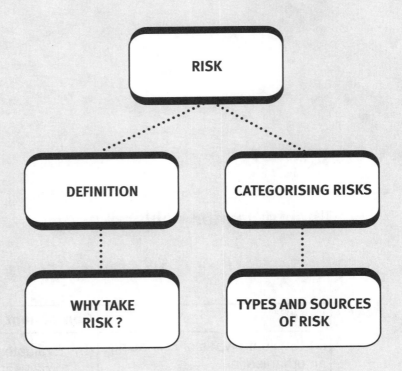

1 What is risk?

- Risk in business is the chance that future events or results may not be as expected.

- Risk is often thought of as purely bad (pure or **'downside'** risk), but it must be considered that risk can also be good – the results may be better than expected as well as worse (speculative or **'upside'** risk).

- Businesses must be able to identify the principal sources of risk if they are to be able to assess and measure the risks that the organisation faces.

  Risks facing an organisation are those that affect the achievement of its overall objectives, which should be reflected in its strategic aims. Risk should be managed and there should be strategies for dealing with risk.

Risk and uncertainty

The term 'risk' is often associated with the chance of something 'bad' happening, and that a future outcome will be adverse. This type of risk is called '**downside**' **risk** or **pure risk**, which is a risk involving the possibility of loss, with no chance of gain.

Examples of pure risk are the risk of disruption to business from a severe power cut, or the risk of losses from theft or fraud, the risk of damage to assets from a fire or accident, and risks to the health and safety of employees at work.

Not all risks are pure risks or down-side risks. In many cases, risk is two-way, and actual outcomes might be either better or worse than expected. **Two-way risk** is sometimes called **speculative risk**. For many business decisions, there is an element of speculative risk and management are aware that actual results could be better or worse than forecast.

For example, a new product launch might be more or less successful than planned, and the savings from an investment in labour-saving equipment might be higher or lower than anticipated.

Risk is inherent in a situation whenever an outcome is not inevitable. **Uncertainty**, in contrast, arises from ignorance and a lack of information. By definition, the future cannot be predicted under conditions of uncertainty because there is insufficient information about what the future outcomes might be or their probabilities of occurrence.

In business, uncertainty might be an element in decision-making. For example, there might be uncertainty about how consumers might respond to a new product or a new technology, or how shareholders might react to a cut in the annual dividend. Uncertainty is reduced by obtaining as much information as possible before making any decision.

Why incur risk ?

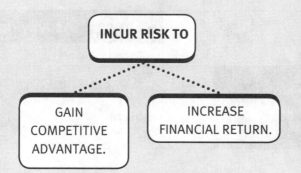

- To generate higher returns a business may have to take more risk in order to be competitive.

- Conversely, not accepting risk tends to make a business less dynamic, and implies a 'follow the leader' strategy.

- Incurring risk also implies that the returns from different activities will be higher – 'benefit' being the return for accepting risk.

- Benefits can be financial – decreased costs, or intangible – better quality information.

- In both cases, these will lead to the business being able to gain competitive advantage.

For some risks there is a market rate of return e.g. quoted equity – where a shareholder invests in a company with the expectation of a certain level of dividend and capital growth. However, for other risks there may not be a market rate of return e.g. technology risk – where a company invests in new software in the hope that it will make their invoice processing more efficient. The important distinction here is that the market compensates for the former type of risk, but might not for the latter.

Benefits of taking risks

Consider the following grid in terms of the risks a business can incur and the benefits from undertaking different activities.

		Activity risk	
		Low	High
Ability to gain competitive advantage	Low	2 Routine	4 Avoid
	High	1 Identify and develop	3 Examine carefully

Focusing on low-risk activities can easily result in a low ability to obtain competitive advantage – although where there is low risk there is also only a limited amount of competitive advantage to be obtained. For example, a mobile telephone operator may produce its phones in a wide range of colours. There is little or no risk of the technology failing, but the move may provide limited competitive advantage where customers are attracted to a particular colour of phone.

Some low-risk activities, however, will provide higher competitive advantage – when these can be identified. If these can be identified, then the activity should be undertaken because of the higher reward. For example, the mobile phone operator may find a way of easily amending mobile phones to make them safer regarding the electrical emissions generated. Given that customers are concerned about this element of mobile phone use, there is significant potential to obtain competitive advantage. However, these opportunities are few and far between.

High-risk activities can similarly generate low or high competitive advantage. Activities with low competitive advantage will generally be avoided. There remains the risk that the activity will not work, and that the small amount of competitive advantage that would be generated is not worth that risk.

Other high-risk activities may generate significant amounts of competitive advantage. These activities are worth investigating because of the high returns that can be generated. For example, a new type of mobile phone providing, say, GPS features for use while travelling, may provide significant competitive advantage for the company; the risk of investing in the phone is worthwhile in terms of the benefit that could be achieved.

The point is, therefore, that if a business does not take some risk, it will normally be limited to activities providing little or no competitive advantage, which will limit its ability to grow and provide returns to its shareholders.

2 CIMA's risk management cycle

Risk management should be a proactive process that is an integral part of strategic management.

This perspective is summarised in **CIMA's risk management cycle**, illustrated below:

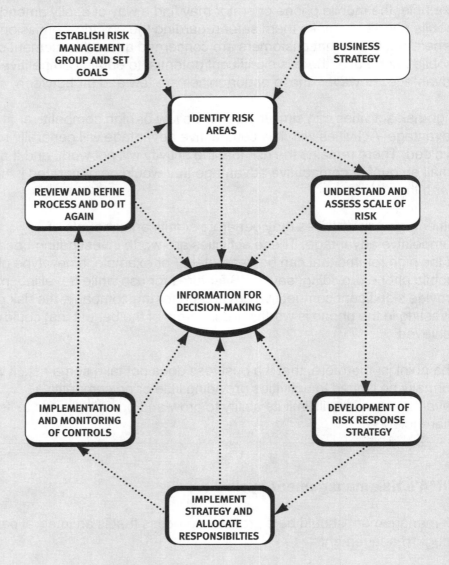

Source: Chartered Institute of Management Accountants (2002), Risk Management: A Guide to Good Practice, CIMA.

The risk management cycle is a very important tool for your exam.

3 Types and sources of risk for business organisations

Identifying and categorising risks

- Many organisations categorise risks into different types of risk. The use of risk categories can help with the process of risk identification and assessment.

- There is no single system of risk categories. The risk categories used by companies and other organisations differ according to circumstances. Some of the more commonly-used risk categories are described below.

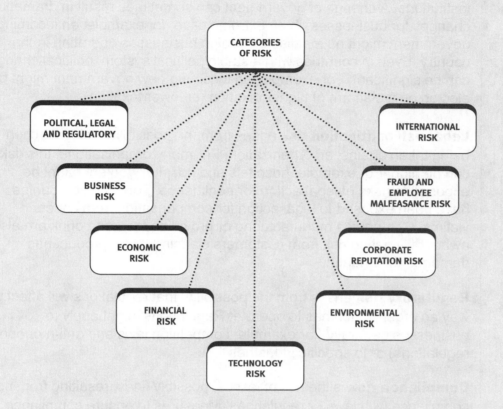

Political, legal and regulatory

These are the risks that businesses face because of the regulatory regime that they operate in. Some businesses may be subject to very strict regulations, for example companies that could cause pollution, but even companies that do not appear to be in a highly regulated industry have some regulatory risk. For example, all companies are subject to the risk of employment legislation changing or customers bringing litigation.

This risk can be broken up into different types:

Political risk	Risk due to political instability. Generally considered to be external to the business.
Legal/litigation risk	Risk that litigation will be brought against the business.
Regulatory risk	Risk of changes in regulation affecting the business.
Compliance risk	Risk of non-compliance with the law resulting in fines/penalties, etc.

More on political, legal and regulatory risks

Political risk depends to a large extent on the political stability in the country or countries in which an organisation operates, and the political institutions. A change of government can sometimes result in dramatic changes for businesses. In an extreme case, for example, an incoming government might nationalise all foreign businesses operating in the country. Even in countries with a stable political system, political change can be significant. For example, an incoming new government might be elected on a platform of higher taxation (or lower taxation).

Legal risk or **litigation risk** arises from the possibility of legal action being taken against an organisation. For many organisations, this risk can be high. For example, hospitals and hospital workers might be exposed to risks of legal action for negligence. Tobacco companies have been exposed to legal action for compensation from cancer victims. Companies manufacturing or providing food and drink are also aware of litigation risk from customers claiming that a product has damaged their health.

Regulatory risk arises from the possibility that regulations will affect the way an organisation has to operate. Regulations might apply to businesses generally (for example, competition laws and anti-monopoly regulations) or to specific industries.

Compliance risk is the risk of losses, possibly fines, resulting from non-compliance with laws or regulations. Measures to ensure compliance with rules and regulations should be an integral part of an organisation's internal control system.

Business risk

Business risk is the risk businesses face due to the nature of their operations and products. Some businesses for instance are reliant on a single product or small range of products, or they could be reliant on a small key group of staff. The risks can be considered in different categories:

Strategic risk	Risk that business strategies (e.g. acquisitions/product launches) will fail.
Product risk	Risk of failure of new product launches/loss of interest in existing products.
Commodity price risk	Risk of a rise in commodity prices (e.g. oil).

Product reputation risk	Risk of change in product's reputation or image.
Operational risk	Risk that business operations may be inefficient or business processes may fail.
Contractual inadequacy risk	Risk that the terms of a contract do not fully cover a business against all potential outcomes.
Fraud and employee malfeasance	Considered separately later.

More on business risks

Business risks for a company are risks arising from the nature of its business and operations. Some businesses are inherently more risky than others.

- **Strategic risks** are risks arising from the possible consequences of strategic decisions taken by the organisation. For example, one company might pursue a strategy of growth by acquisitions, whilst another might seek slower, organic growth. Growth by acquisition is likely to be much more high-risk than organic growth, although the potential returns might also be much higher. Strategic risks should be identified and assessed at senior management and board of director level.

- **Product risk** is the risk that customers will not buy new products (or services) provided by the organisation, or that the sales demand for current products and services will decline unexpectedly. A new product launched on to the market might fail to achieve the expected volume of sales, or the take-up will be much slower than expected. For example, the demand for 'third generation' (3G) mobile communications services has been much slower to build up than expected by the mobile telephone service providers, due partly to the slower-than-expected development of suitable mobile phone handsets.

- **Commodity price risk**. Businesses might be exposed to risks from unexpected increases (or falls) in the price of a key commodity. Businesses providing commodities, such as oil companies and commodity farmers, are directly affected by price changes. Equally, companies that rely on the use of commodities could be exposed to risks from price changes. For example, airlines are exposed to the risk of increases in fuel prices, particularly when market demand for flights is weak, and so increases in ticket prices for flights are not possible.

- **Product reputation risk**. Some companies rely heavily on brand image and product reputation, and an adverse event could put its reputation (and so future sales) at risk. Risk to a product's reputation could arise from adverse public attitudes to a product or from adverse publicity: this has been evident in Europe with widespread hostility to genetically-modified (GM) foods. There could also be a risk from changes in customer perceptions about the quality of a product. For example, if a car manufacturer announces that it is recalling all new models of a car to rectify a design defect, the reputation of the product and future sales could be affected.

- **Operational risk** refers to potential losses that might arise in business operations. It has been defined broadly as 'the risk of losses resulting from inadequate or failed internal processes, people and systems, or external events' (Basel Committee on Banking Supervision). Operational risks include risks of fraud or employee malfeasance, which are explained in more detail later. Organisations have internal control systems to manage operational risks.

- **Contractual inadequacy risk** may arise where a business has negotiated contracts and other business transactions without adequate consideration of what may happen if things don't go according to plan. For example, a builder may have a fixed completion date to complete the construction of a house. If he does not complete on time, he may have to pay compensation to the house purchaser. Similarly, there is also a risk that the purchaser does not have the funds when payment is due. This risk may be mitigated by having terms in the contract as to what rights he will have in such circumstances. Clearly, if the builder does not consider either or both of these possibilities when agreeing to build the house, then there is an unidentified and unquantified risk of loss.

Economic risk

This is the risk that changes in the economy might affect the business. Those changes could be inflation, unemployment rates, international trade relations or fiscal policy decisions by government. Again, this risk is considered to be external to the business.

The 'credit crunch'

In 2008 there was global banking crisis which then led to what has since been called a 'credit crunch' and, for some countries, recession. This section looks at the causes of the banking crisis and its knock-on effects.

Contributory factor 1: US sub-prime mortgage lending

In 2001 the US faced recession, due partly to the events of 9/11 and the Dot com bubble bursting, so the US government was keen to stimulate growth. As part of this in 2003 the Federal Reserve responded by cutting interest rates to 1% - their lowest level for a long time.

Low interest rates encouraged people to buy a house backed by a mortgage, resulting in house prices rising due to the increased demand for housing. As house prices began to rise, mortgage companies relaxed their lending criteria and tried to capitalise on the booming property market. This boom in credit was also fuelled by US government pressure on lenders to grant mortgages to people who, under normal banking criteria, presented a very high risk of default. These were the so called 'sub–prime mortgages', with many borrowers taking out adjustable rate mortgages that were affordable for the first two years.

This 'sub-prime market' expanded very quickly and by 2005, one in five mortgages in the US were sub-prime. Banks felt protected because house prices were continuing to rise so if someone defaulted the bank would recover its loan.

In 2006 inflationary pressures in the US caused interest rates to rise to 4%. Normally 4% interest rates are not particularly high but, because many had taken out large mortgages, this increase made the mortgage payments unaffordable. Also many homeowners were coming to the end of their 'introductory offers' and faced much higher payments. This led to an increase in mortgage defaults.

As mortgage defaults increased the boom in house prices came to an end and house prices started falling. In some areas the problem was even worse as there had been a boom in the building of new homes, which occurred right up until 2007. It meant that demand fell as supply was increasing causing prices to collapse. Banks were no longer able to recover their loans when borrowers defaulted. In many cases they only ended up with a fraction of the house value.

Contributory factor 2: 'Collateralised debt obligations' or CDOs

Normally if a borrower defaults it is the lending bank or building society that suffers the loss. As a result they are very diligent to verify the credit worthiness of potential borrowers and whether they have the income and security to repay loans. However, in the US, mortgage lenders were able to sell on mortgage debt in the form of CDOs to other banks and financial institutions. This was a kind of insurance for the mortgage companies. It meant that other banks and financial institutions shared the risk of these sub-prime mortgages.

Using the income from their mortgage book as security, banks sold CDO bonds with a three-tier structure:

(1)   Tier 1 was "senior" or "investment grade" and supposed to be very low risk but with a low return.

(2)   Tier 2 was the "mezzanine tranche" and had medium risk and medium return

(3)   Tier 3 was the "equity tranche" and had highest risk and return.

As money was received on mortgages, it was used to pay the Tier 1 bond holders their interest first, then Tier 2 and finally Tier 3, so if borrowers defaulted, then Tier 3 holders would suffer first and so on, like a waterfall effect.

Unfortunately losses were so great that Tier 3 and Tier 2 and in some cases Tier 1 investors were affected. At the very least, the value of Tier 1 bonds fell due to the perceived risks.

Contributory factor 3: Debt rating organisations

The CDO bonds were credit-rated for risk, just like any other bond issues. Maybe because these sub-prime mortgage debts were bought by 'responsible' banks like Morgan Stanley and Lehman Brothers, or maybe because they didn't fully understand the CDO structures, risk agencies gave risky Tier 1 debt bundles AAA safety ratings. Normally AAA would denote extremely low risk investments.

This encouraged many banks and financial institutions to buy them, not realising how risky their financial position was. The trillions of dollars of sub-prime mortgages issued in the US had thus become distributed across the global markets ending up as CDOs on the balance sheets of many banks around the world.

Many commentators have seen this factor as an example of regulatory failure within the financial system.

Contributory factor 4: Banks' financial structure

Unlike most other commercial enterprises, banks are very highly geared with typically less than 10% of their asset value covered by equity. A drastic loss of asset value can soon wipe out a bank's equity account and it was this risk which led some banks to start selling their asset–backed securities on to the market.

However, the sellers in this restricted market could not find buyers; as a result, the values at which these "toxic assets" could be sold fell and many banks around the world found themselves in a position with negative equity.

Contributory factor 5: Credit default swaps

As an alternative (or in addition) to using CDOs, the mortgage lenders could buy insurance on sub-prime debt through credit default swaps or CDSs.

For example, AIG wrote $440 billion and Lehman Brothers more than $700 billion-worth of CDSs. These were the first institutions to suffer when the level of defaults started to increase.

Warren Buffett called them "financial weapons of mass destruction".

Contributory factor 6: Risk-takers

There is a school of thought that the risk-takers were taking risks they didn't understand. Some risks can be easily understood, however, others are far more complicated.

Implication 1: the collapse of major financial institutions

Some very large financial institutions went bust and others got into serious trouble and needed to be rescued. For example,

- In September 2008 Lehman Brothers went bust. This was the biggest bankruptcy in corporate history. It was 10 times the size of Enron and the tipping point into the global crash, provoking panic in an already battered financial system, freezing short-term lending, and marking the start of the liquidity crisis.

- Also in September 2008 the US government put together a bail out package for AIG. The initial loan was for $85bn but the total value of this package has been estimated at between 150 and 182 billion dollars.

- In the UK the Bank of England lent Northern Rock £27 billion after its collapse in 2007.

Implication 2: the credit crunch

Banks usually rely on lending to each other to conduct every day business. But, after the first wave of credit losses, banks could no longer raise sufficient finance.

For example, in the UK, Northern Rock was particularly exposed to money markets. It had relied on borrowing money on the money markets to fund its daily business. In 2007, it simply couldn't raise enough money on the financial markets and eventually had to be nationalised by the UK government.

In addition to bad debts, the other problem was one of confidence. Because many banks had lost money and had a deterioration in their balance sheets, they couldn't afford to lend to other banks. Even banks that had stayed free of the problem began to suspect the credit worthiness of other banks and, as a result, became reluctant to lend on the interbank market.

The knock on effect was that banks became reluctant to lend to anyone, causing a shortage of liquidity in money markets. This made it difficult for firms to borrow to finance expansion plans as well as hitting the housing market.

Many companies use short-term finance rather than long-term. For example, rather than borrowing for, say, 10 years a company might take out a two year loan, with a view to taking out another two year loan to replace the first, and so on. The main reason for using this system of "revolving credit" is that it should be cheaper – shorter-term interest rates are generally lower than longer-term. The credit crunch meant that these firms could not refinance their loans causing major problems.

Implication 3: government intervention

Many governments felt compelled to intervene, not just to prop up major institutions (e.g. Northern Rock and AIG mentioned above) but also to inject funds into the money markets to stimulate liquidity.

Efforts to save major institutions involved a mixture of loans, guarantees and the purchase of equity.

Usually, central banks try to raise the amount of lending and activity in the economy indirectly, by cutting interest rates. Lower interest rates encourage people to spend, not save. But when interest rates can go no lower, a central bank's only option is to pump money into the economy directly. That is quantitative easing (QE). The way the central bank does this is by buying assets – usually financial assets such as government and corporate bonds – using money it has simply created out of thin air. The institutions selling those assets (either commercial banks or other financial businesses such as insurance companies) will then have "new" money in their accounts, which then boosts the money supply.

In February 2010 the Bank of England announced that the UK quantitative easing programme, that had cost £200m, was to be put on hold.

The end result was that many governments found themselves with huge levels of debt with the corresponding need to repay high levels of interest as well as repay the debt.

Implication 4: recession and "austerity measures"

The events described above resulted in a recession in many countries. Despite the falling tax revenues that accompany this, some governments would normally try to increase government spending as one measure to boost aggregate demand to stimulate the economy.

However, the high levels of national debt have resulted in governments doing the opposite and making major cuts in public spending.

Implication 5: problems refinancing government debt

In 2010/2011 some countries tried to refinance national debt by issuing bonds:

- A problem facing the Spanish government at the end of 2010/2011 was the need to raise new borrowing as other government debt reached maturity. Spain successfully sold new bonds totalling nearly €3 billion on 12/1/11 in what was seen as a major test of Europe's chances of containing the debt crisis gripping parts of the region. This was in addition to the Spanish government cutting spending by tens of billions of euros, including cuts in public sector salaries, public investment and social spending, along with tax hikes and a pension freeze.

- The problem of refinancing is more severe for countries whose national debt has a short average redemption period (Greece is about 4 yrs) but much less of a problem where the debt is long dated (e.g. the UK where the average maturity is about 14 yrs).

For others they needed help from other countries and the International Monetary Fund (IMF).

- Greece received a €110 billion rescue package in May 2010.
- At the end of 2010 Ireland received a bailout from the EU, the UK and the IMF. The total cost is still being debated but could be as high as €85 billion.

Financial risk

Financial risk is a major risk that affects businesses and this risk is studied in much more depth in later chapters of this text.

Financial risk is the risk of a change in a financial condition such as an exchange rate, interest rate, credit rating of a customer, or price of a good.

The main types of financial risk are:

Credit risk	Risk of non-payment by customers.
Political risk	Risk arising from actions taken by a government that affect financial aspects of the business.
Currency risk	Risk of fluctuations in the exchange rate.
Interest rate risk	Risk that interest rates change.
Gearing risk	Risk in the way a business is financed (debt vs. equity) (sometimes this is considered part of interest rate risk).

More on financial risks

Financial risks relate to the possibility of changes in financial conditions and circumstances. There are several types of financial risk. More will be seen on these risks in chapter 11.

- **Credit risk.** Credit risk is the possibility of losses due to non-payment by debtors. The exposure of a company to credit risks depends on factors such as:
  - the total volume of credit sales
  - the organisation's credit policy
  - credit terms offered (credit limits for individual customers and the time allowed to pay)
  - the credit risk 'quality' of customers: some types of customer are a greater credit risk than others
  - credit vetting and assessment procedures
  - debt collection procedures.
    - **Currency risk.** Currency risk, or foreign exchange risk, arises from the possibility of movements in foreign exchange rates, and the value of one currency in relation to another.
    - **Interest rate risk.** Interest rate risk is the risk of unexpected gains or losses arising as a consequence of a rise or fall in interest rates. Exposures to interest rate risk arise from:
      - borrowing
      - investing (to earn interest) or depositing cash.
    - **Gearing risk.** Gearing risk for non-bank companies is the risk arising from exposures to high financial gearing and large amounts of borrowing.

Technology risk

Technology risk is the risk that technology changes will occur that either present new opportunities to businesses, or on the down-side make their existing processes obsolete or inefficient.

More on technology risk

Technology risk arises from the possibility that technological change will occur. Like many other categories of risk, technology risk is a two-way risk, and technological change creates both threats and opportunities for organisations.

There are risks in failing to respond to new technology, but there can also be risks in adopting new technology. An example of over-investing in new technology was the so-called 'dot.com boom' in the late 1990s and early 2000s. For a time, there was speculation that Internet-based companies would take over the markets of established 'bricks and mortar' companies.

To varying degrees, established companies invested in Internet technology, partly as a protective measure and partly in order to speculate on the growth of Internet commerce. (Whereas most established companies survived the collapse of the 'dot.com bubble' in 2001 – 2002, many 'dot.com' companies suffered financial collapse.)

Environmental risk

Environmental risk is the risk that arises from changes in the environment such as climate change or natural disasters. Some businesses may perceive this risk to be low, but for others, for example insurance companies, it can be more significant. Insurance companies have to take environmental risks into account when deciding policy premiums, and unusual environmental circumstances can severely alter the results of insurance businesses.

More on environmental risk

Environmental risk arises from changes to the environment:

*   over which an organisation has no direct control, such as global warming
*   for which the organisation might be responsible, such as oil spillages and other pollution.

To ensure their long-term survival, some companies should consider the sustainability of their businesses. When raw materials are consumed, consideration should be given to ensuring future supplies of the raw material. For example, companies that consume wood and paper should perhaps show concern for tree planting programmes, and deep-sea fishing businesses should consider the preservation of fishing stocks.

The Japanese tsunami

The Japanese tsunami of 2011 illustrates very well the fact that some risks can be understood and others are far more complicated.

The Japanese have some of the best flood defence systems in the world, being on the edge of a plate system and regularly experiencing tremors. However, even the best defence system is built with a risk factor included – using probabilities and modelling by water engineers.

While it is not possible to prevent a tsunami, in some particularly tsunami-prone countries some measures have been taken to reduce the damage caused on shore. Japan has implemented an extensive programme of building tsunami walls of up to 4.5 m (13.5 ft) high in front of populated coastal areas. Other localities have built floodgates and channels to redirect the water from incoming tsunami. However, their effectiveness has been questioned, as tsunami are often higher than the barriers. For instance, the Okushiri, Hokkaidō tsunami which struck Okushiri Island of Hokkaidō within two to five minutes of the earthquake on July 12, 1993 created waves as much as 30 m (100 ft) tall – as high as a 10-story building. The port town of Aonae was completely surrounded by a tsunami wall, but the waves washed right over the wall and destroyed all the wood-framed structures in the area. The wall may have succeeded in slowing down and moderating the height of the tsunami, but it did not prevent major destruction and loss of life.

On 11 March, 2011 a 10-meter tsunami slammed into the Japanese city of Sendai killing hundreds and sweeping away everything in its wake. The wall of water was triggered by the country's biggest ever earthquake. Cars, lorries and boats bobbed like toys as a wave of debris spread over huge swathes of north-eastern Japan.

An after effect of the tsunami was the malfunctioning of a nuclear plant in Fukushima, north of Tokyo, where the reactor's cooling system overheated. Other nuclear power plants and oil refineries had been shut down following the 8.9 magnitude quake. Engineers opted to cover the plant in concrete, the technique used at Chernobyl 25 years ago, however this failed and experts have since tried to plug the leak using an absorbent polymer. An exclusion zone of 30 kilometres has been advised by the Japanese government, which will be long-term. It is thought the crack in reactor number two is one source of leaks that have caused radiation levels in the sea to rise to more than 4000 times the legal limit. Food products and water supplies have been affected.

Scientists in Europe are convinced this scenario could happen closer to home. They have been working on an early warning system for countries surrounding the Mediterranean Sea. The region along the Turkish coast in the Eastern Mediterranean is considered the most vulnerable.

In these scenarios, engineers have tried to learn from the past and estimate what might happen in the future. However, with the best will in the world it is sometimes impossible to ascertain all the implications of a single event, such as a tsunami.

Fraud risk

Fraud risk (a type of operational business risk) is the vulnerability of an organisation to fraud. Some businesses are more vulnerable than others to fraud and as a result have to have stronger controls over fraud. Fraud risk is a risk that is considered controllable by most businesses.

More on fraud risk

Fraud risk is the vulnerability of an organisation to fraud. The size of fraud risk for any organisation is a factor of:

- the probability of fraud occurring, and
- the size of the losses if fraud does occur.

For example, a bank will be subject to much higher fraud risk than a property investment company due to the desirability of money and the potential value that theft could achieve; it is unlikely that someone will steal a building from an investment company.

Fraud risk should be managed, by:

- fraud prevention: ensuring that the opportunities to commit fraud are minimised
- fraud detection and deterrence: detection measures are designed to identify fraud after it has occurred. If employees fear that the risk of detection is high, they will be deterred from trying to commit fraud.

The management of fraud risk should be an element of an organisation's internal control system.

Corporate reputation risk

Reputation risk is for many organisations a down-side risk as the better the reputation of the business the more risk there is of losing that reputation. A good reputation can be very quickly eroded if companies suffer adverse media comments or are perceived to be untrustworthy.

This could arise from:

- environmental performance
- social performance
- health & safety performance.

More on corporate reputation risk

Many large organisations are aware of the potential damage to their business from events affecting their 'reputation' in the opinion of the general public or more specific groups (such as existing customers or suppliers).

Some organisations succeed in being perceived as 'environmental-friendly', and use public relations and advertising to promote this image.

For many organisations, however, reputation risk is a down-side risk. The risk can be particularly significant for companies that sell products or services to consumer markets. There have been cases where a company's reputation has been significantly affected by:

- employing child labour in under-developed countries or operating 'sweat shops' in which employees work long hours in poor conditions for low pay
- causing environmental damage and pollution
- public suspicions about the damage to health from using the company's products
- investing heavily in countries with an unpopular or tyrannical government
- involvement in business 'scandals' such as mis-selling products
- management announcements about the quality of the product a company produces.

Managing reputation risk can be complicated by the fact that many of these factors lie outside the control of the organisation. For example, many companies outsource production to third parties who operate in countries where labour costs are cheaper. Such arrangements can work well, although major multinational corporations have had their reputations tarnished by being associated with third parties who used dubious employment or environmental policies in order to keep costs down.

Employee malfeasance risk

Malfeasance means doing wrong or committing an offence. Organisations might be exposed to risks of actions by employees that result in an offence or crime (other than fraud). This, like fraud risk, is a type of operational business risk.

More on employee malfeasance

Examples of employee malfeasance are:

- deliberately making false representations about a product or service in order to win a customer order, exposing the organisation to the risk of compensation claims for mis-selling

- committing a criminal offence by failing to comply with statutory requirements, such as taking proper measures for the safety and protection of employees or customers.

Risks from illegal activities by employees should be controlled by suitable internal controls, to ensure that employees comply with established policies and procedures.

Risks in international operations

International businesses are subject to all the risks above but also have to consider extra risk factors, which could be due to the following:

Culture A UK business may fail in a venture overseas because it does not adapt to the overseas culture. Good knowledge of local culture can, however, give companies an advantage.

Litigation There is a greater danger of litigation risk in overseas operations as the parent company management may not understand the legislation well and therefore have more risk of breaching it.

Credit	There is often a greater difficulty in controlling credit risk on overseas sales. Chasing debts is more difficult and expensive.
Items in transit	There is a greater risk of losses or damage in transit if companies are transporting goods great distances
Financial risks	These include foreign exchange risks, and will be considered in more detail in a later chapter.

More on risks in international operations

Companies that engage in international operations could face substantial risks in addition to country risk.

- There could be significant **cultural differences** between the various countries in which the company operates. There could be a risk that products, services and business practices that are acceptable in one country will be unacceptable in another. Failure to understand a national or local culture could mean that a company will fail to succeed in establishing its business.

- A lack of understanding of local legislation could expose an organisation to **litigation risk**. When legal action is initiated in a different country, a company has to appoint lawyers to represent them and rely on their advice on the appropriate and necessary steps to take.

- When a company exports goods to other countries, there could be **risks that the goods will be held up or lost in transit**, and the loss might not always be covered by insurance. For example, goods might be held up in customs due to inadequate import documentation.

- When a customer in another country buys goods on credit, the exporter is exposed to credit risk. However, the **credit risk is often greater**, because in the event of non-payment by the customer, legal action might be more difficult to arrange (and more expensive) and the prospects of obtaining payment might be much lower.

Test your understanding 1 – ZXC

The ZXC company manufactures aircraft. The company is based in Europe and currently produces a range of four different aircraft. ZXC's aircraft are reliable with low maintenance costs, giving ZXC a good reputation, both to airlines who purchase from ZXC and to airlines' customers who fly in the aircraft.

ZXC is currently developing the 'next generation' of passenger aircraft, with the selling name of the ZXLiner. New developments in ZXLiner include the following:

- Two decks along the entire aircraft (not just part as in the Boeing 747 series) enabling faster loading and unloading of passengers from both decks at the same time. However, this will mean that airport gates must be improved to facilitate dual loading at considerable expense.

- 20% decrease in fuel requirements and falls in noise and pollution levels.

- Use of new alloys to decrease maintenance costs, increase safety and specifically the use of Zitnim (a new lightweight conducting alloy) rather than standard wiring to enable the 'fly-by-wire' features of the aircraft. Zitnim only has one supplier worldwide.

Many component suppliers are based in Europe although ZXC does obtain about 25% of the sub-contracted components from companies in the USA. ZXC also maintains a significant R&D department working on the ZXLiner and other new products such as alternative environmentally friendly fuel for aircraft.

Although the ZXLiner is yet to fly or be granted airworthiness certificates, ZXC does have orders for 25 aircraft from the HTS company. However, on current testing schedules the ZXLiner will be delivered late.

ZXC currently has about €4 billion of loans from various banks and last year made a loss of €2.3 billion.

Required:

Identify the sources of risk that could affect ZXC, and evaluate the impact of the risk on the company.

Exam questions may ask candidates to address novel situations that are outside their experience. In addition to reading the text, candidates should refer to the business press on a regular basis.

4 Chapter summary

```
                    ┌──────────────────────┐
                    │        RISK          │
                    └──────────────────────┘
```

RISK

DEFINITION
- Chance that future events/results may not be as expected
- Downside or upside

CATEGORISING RISKS

WHY TAKE RISK ?
- Gain competitive advantage
- Increase returns

TYPES AND SOURCES OF RISK
- Political, legal and regulatory
- Business
- Economic
- Financial
- Technology
- Environmental
- Corporate reputation
- Fraud
- Employee malfeasance
- International operations

Test your understanding answers

Product/market risk

This is the risk that customers will not buy new products (or services) provided by the organisation, or that the sales demand for current products and services will decline unexpectedly.

For ZXC, there is the risk that demand for the new aircraft will be less than expected, either due to customers purchasing the rival airplane or because airports will not be adapted to take the new ZXLiner.

Commodity price risk

Businesses might be exposed to risks from unexpected increases (or falls) in the price of a key commodity.

Part of the control systems of the ZXLiner rely on the availability of the new lightweight conducting alloy Zitnim. As there is only one supplier of this alloy, then there is the danger of the monopolist increasing the price or even denying supply. Increase in price would increase the overall cost of the (already expensive) ZXLiner, while denial of supply would further delay delivery of the aircraft.

Product reputation risk

Some companies rely heavily on brand image and product reputation, and an adverse event could put its reputation (and so future sales) at risk.

While the reputation of ZXC appears good at present, reputation will suffer if the ZXLiner is delayed significantly or it does not perform well in test flights (which have still to be arranged). Airline customers, and also their customers (travellers) are unlikely to feel comfortable flying in an aircraft that is inherently unstable.

Currency risk

Currency risk, or foreign exchange risk, arises from the possibility of movements in foreign exchange rates, and the value of one currency in relation to another.

ZXC is currently based in Europe although it obtains a significant number of parts from the USA. If the €/$ exchange rate became worse, then the cost of imported goods for ZXC (and all other companies) would increase. At present, the relatively weak US$ is in ZXC's favour and so this risk is currently negligible.

Interest rate risk

Interest rate risk is the risk of unexpected gains or losses arising as a consequence of a rise or fall in interest rates. Exposures to interest rate risk arise from borrowing and investing.

As ZXC do have significant bank loans, then the company is very exposed to this risk.

Gearing risk

Gearing risk for non-bank companies is the risk arising from exposures to high financial gearing and large amounts of borrowing.

Again, ZXC has significant amounts of bank loans. This increases the amount of interest that must be repaid each year.

Political risk

Political risk depends to a large extent on the political stability in the countries in which an organisation operates, the political institutions within that country and the government's attitude towards protectionism.

As ZXC operates in a politically stable country this risk is negligible.

Legal risk or litigation risk

The risk arises from the possibility of legal action being taken against an organisation.

At present this risk does not appear to be a threat for ZXC. However, if the ZXLiner is delayed any further there is a risk for breach of contract for late delivery to the HTS company.

Regulatory risk

This is the possibility that regulations will affect the way an organisation has to operate.

In terms of aircraft, regulation generally affects noise and pollution levels. As the ZXLiner is designed to have lower noise and pollution levels than existing aircraft then this risk does not appear to be a threat to ZXC.

Technology risk

Technology risk arises from the possibility that technological change will occur or that new technology will not work.

Given that ZXC is effectively producing a new product (the ZXLiner) that has not actually been tested yet, there is some technology risk. At worse, the ZXLiner may not fly at all or not obtain the necessary flying certificates.

Economic risk

This risk refers to the risks facing organisations from changes in economic conditions, such as economic growth or recession, government spending policy and taxation policy, unemployment levels and international trading conditions.

Demand for air travel is forecast to increase for the foreseeable future, so in that sense there is a demand for aircraft which ZXC will benefit from. The risk of product failure is more significant than economic risk.

Environmental risk

This risk arises from changes to the environment over which an organisation has no direct control, such as global warming, to those for which the organisation might be responsible, such as oil spillages and other pollution.

ZXC is subject to this risk – and there is significant debate concerning the impact of air travel on global warming. At the extreme, there is a threat that air travel could be banned, or made very expensive by international taxation agreements, although this appears unlikely at present.

Risk management

Chapter learning objectives

Lead	Component
B1. Evaluate types of risk facing an organisation.	(a) Discuss ways of identifying, measuring and assessing the types of risk facing an organisation, including the organisation's ability to bear such risks (b) Evaluate risks facing an organisation.
B2. Evaluate risk management strategies and internal controls.	(a) Discuss the purposes and importance of internal control and risk management for an organisation (b) Evaluate risk management strategies.
D1. Evaluate financial risks facing an organisation.	(a) Evaluate financial risks facing an organisation.

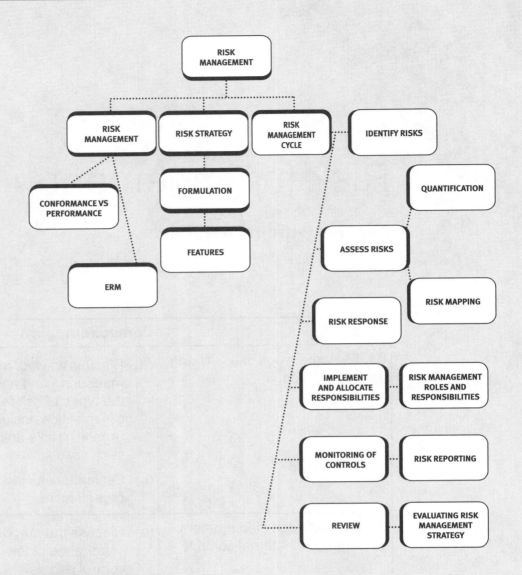

1 Risk management

Risk management is defined as:

'the process of understanding and managing the risks that the organisation is inevitably subject to in attempting to achieve its corporate objectives'

CIMA Official Terminology

- The traditional view of risk management has been one of protecting the organisation from loss through conformance procedures and hedging techniques – this is about avoiding the **downside** risk.

- The new approach to risk management is about taking advantage of the opportunities to increase overall returns within a business – benefiting from the **upside** risk.

- The following diagram shows how risk management can reconcile the two perspectives of conformance and performance (as discussed previously in chapter 2).

Source: IFAC (1999) Enhancing Shareholder Wealth By Better Managing Risk

Enterprise Risk Management (ERM)

Enterprise risk management is the term given to the alignment of risk management with business strategy and the embedding of a risk management culture into business operations.

It has been defined as:

'A process, effected by an entity's board of directors, management and other personnel, applied in strategy setting and across the enterprise, designed to identify potential events that may affect the entity, and manage risk to be within its risk appetite, to provide reasonable assurance regarding the achievement of entity objectives.'

Committee of Sponsoring Organisations of the Treadway Commission (COSO) (2003)

Risk management has transformed from a 'department focused' approach to a holistic, co-ordinated and integrated process which manages risk throughout the organisation.

The key principles of ERM include:

- consideration of risk management in the context of business strategy

- risk management is everyone's responsibility, with the tone set from the top

- the creation of a risk aware culture

- a comprehensive and holistic approach to risk management

- consideration of a broad range of risks (strategic, financial, operational and compliance)

- a focused risk management strategy, led by the board (embedding risk within an organisation's culture).

The COSO ERM Framework is represented as a three dimensional matrix in the form of a cube which reflects the relationships between objectives, components and different organisational levels.

- The four objectives (strategic, operations, reporting and compliance) reflect the responsibility of different executives across the entity and address different needs.

- The four organisational levels (subsidiary, business unit, division and entity) emphasise the importance of managing risks across the enterprise as a whole.

- The eight components must function effectively for risk management to be successful.

The eight components are closely aligned to the risk management process addressed previously, and also reflect elements from the COSO view of an effective internal control system:

- **Internal environment:** This is the tone of the organisation, including the risk management philosophy and risk appetite (see later in this chapter).

- **Objective setting:** Objectives should be aligned with the organisation's mission and need to be consistent with the organisation's defined risk appetite.

- **Event identification:** These are internal and external events (both positive and negative) which impact upon the achievement of an entity's objectives and must be identified.

- **Risk assessment:** Risks are analysed to consider their likelihood and impact as a basis for determining how they should be managed.

- **Risk response:** Management selects risk response(s) to avoid, accept, reduce or share risk. The intention is to develop a set of actions to align risks with the entity's risk tolerances and risk appetite.

- **Control activities:** Policies and procedures help ensure the risk responses are effectively carried out.

- **Information and communication:** The relevant information is identified, captured and communicated in a form and timeframe that enables people to carry out their responsibilities.

- **Monitoring:** The entire ERM process is monitored and modifications made as necessary.

Benefits of effective ERM include:

- enhanced decision-making by integrating risks

- the resultant improvement in investor confidence, and hence shareholder value

- focus of management attention on the most significant risks

- a common language of risk management which is understood throughout the organisation

- reduced cost of finance through effective management of risk.

Risk management and shareholder value

Ernst and Young (2001) have developed a model of shareholder value in which

Shareholder value = Static NPV of existing business model + Value of future growth options

which more simply put is 'the sum of the value of what a company does now and the value of what they could possibly do in the future'.

Good risk management allows businesses to exploit opportunities for future growth while protecting the value already created. By aligning risk management activity to what the shareholders consider vital to the success of the business, the shareholders are assured that what they value is protected.

Ernst and Young identify four stages:

(a) Establish what shareholders value about the company – through talking with the investment community and linking value creation processes to key performance indicators.

(b) Identify the risks around the key shareholder value drivers – the investment community can identify those factors that will influence their valuation of the company. All other risks will also be considered, even if not known by investors.

(c) Determine the preferred treatment for the risks – the investment community can give their views on what actions they would like management to take in relation to the risks. The risk/reward trade-off can be quantified by estimating the change in a company's market valuation if a particular risk treatment was implemented.

(d) Communicate risk treatments to shareholders – shareholders need to be well informed, as a shared vision is important in relation to the inter-related concepts of risk management and shareholder value.

The exam

The frameworks and diagrams in this chapter are a useful starting point for an exam question, but all entities have to deal with risks in an appropriate manner and so guidance cannot be definitive.

2 Risk management strategy

Formulation of a risk strategy

- For many businesses the specific formulation of a risk strategy has been a recent development.

- In the past a formal strategy for managing risks would not be made but rather it would be left to individual managers to make assessments of the risks the business faced and exercise judgement on what was a reasonable level of risk.

- This has now changed: failure to properly identify and control risks has been identified as a major cause of business failure (take Barings Bank as an example).

A framework for board consideration of risk is shown below:

Formulating a risk management strategy

A risk management strategy needs to be developed to ensure that the risk exposures of the organisation are consistent with its risk appetite. At the very least, the risk management capability within the organisation should be sufficient to:

- review its internal control system, at least annually (and whether it is adequate),

- ensure that controls are properly implemented, and

- monitor the implementation and effectiveness of controls.

However, the investment by the organisation in risk strategy should be largely determined by the performance requirements of its business objectives and strategy.

- **Risk appetite** can be defined as the amount of risk an organisation is willing to accept in pursuit of value. This may be explicit in strategies, policies and procedures, or it may be implicit. It is determined by:
  - **risk capacity** – the amount of risk that the organisation can bear, and
  - **risk attitude** – the overall approach to risk, in terms of the board being risk averse or risk seeking.

- The way that the organisation documents and determines the specific parts of its risk strategy will have to link to the business strategy and objectives.

- Overall the risk management strategy is concerned with trying to achieve the required business objectives with the lowest possible chance of failure. The tougher the business objectives, however, the more risks will have to be taken to achieve them.

- **Residual risk** is the risk a business faces after its controls have been considered (see later in this chapter for more details).

More on risk appetite

To bring risk management into line with strategic management, an organisation should define the amount of risk it is prepared to take in the pursuit of its objectives. This willingness to accept risk can be stated in a mixture of quantitative and qualitative terms. For example:

- The board of directors might state how much capital they would be prepared to invest in the pursuit of a business objective and how much loss they would be willing to face in the event that results turn out badly.

- Risk can also be stated qualitatively, for example in relation to the organisation's reputation.

In practice, in a large organisation, there will be different levels of risk appetite for different operations or different profit centres/investment centres within the business.

Risk appetite factors

The factors, or business strategies, which could affect the risk appetite of the board of a company include:

Nature of product being manufactured	A high risk of product failure in certain products (e.g. aircraft) must be avoided due to the serious consequences of such an event. This will, out of necessity, limit the risk appetite of the board with regard to these specific products. For other products the risk of failure will be less (e.g. a fizzy drink having small changes from the normal ingredients – customers may not even notice the difference). Additionally if a business is taking significant risks with part of its product range it may be limited in the risk it can take with other products.
The need to increase sales	The strategic need to move into a new market will result in the business accepting a higher degree of risk than trying to increase sales or market share in an existing market. At that stage the business will appear to have a higher risk appetite.
The background of the board	Some board members may accept increased risk personally and this may be reflected in the way they manage the company.
Amount of change in the market	Operating in a market place with significant change (e.g. mobile telephones) will mean that the board have to accept a higher degree of risk. For example, new models of phone have to be available quickly.
Reputation of the company	If the company has a good reputation then the board will accept less risk – as they will not want to lose that good reputation.

Features of a risk management strategy

In a CIMA and IFAC (International Federation of Accountants) joint report in 2004 – Enterprise Governance – the following key features of a risk management strategy were identified:

- Statement of the organisation's attitude to risk – the balance between risk and the need to achieve objectives.

- The risk appetite of the organisation.

- The objectives of the risk management strategy.

- Culture of the organisation in relation to risk (and the behaviour the organisation expects from individuals with regard to risk-taking).

- Responsibilities of managers for the application of risk management strategy.

- Reference should be made to the risk management systems the company uses (i.e. its internal control systems).

- Performance criteria should be defined so that the effectiveness of risk management can be evaluated.

An alternative risk management process

The Institute of Risk Management (IRM) developed a risk management process containing three elements:

(1) **Risk assessment** is composed of the analysis and evaluation of risk through the process of identification, description and estimation.

The purpose of risk assessment is to undertake risk evaluation. Risk evaluation is used to make decisions about the significance of risks to the organisation and whether each specific risk should be accepted or treated.

(2) **Risk reporting** is concerned with regular reports to the board and to stakeholders setting out the organisation's policies in relation to risk and enabling the effective monitoring of those policies.

(3) **Risk treatment** (risk response) is the process of selecting and implementing measures to modify the risk.

Following risk treatment therefore will be residual risk reporting.

3 Identifying, measuring and assessing risks

Chapter 2 examined the different types of risks faced by an organisation. It is key, however, that businesses can identify the risks they face and evaluate the effect of the risks on the business. Some risks will be relatively easily borne by businesses, but others will be more difficult and more serious in their implications.

Risk identification

- The risk identification process will often be controlled by a **risk committee** or risk management specialists (see later in this chapter).

- The risks identified in the process should be recorded in a **risk register**, which is simply a list of the risks that have been identified, and the measures (if any) that have been taken to control each of them.

- There are a variety of methods that can be used by businesses to identify the risks that they face:

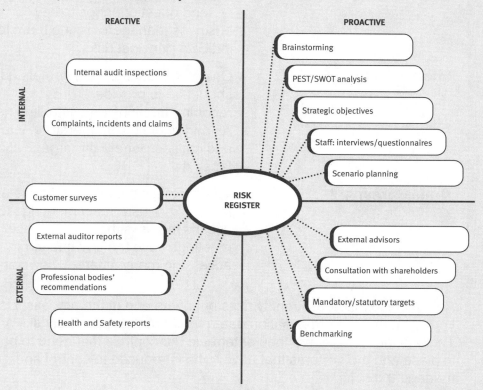

More on risk identification

Some of the common methods of risk identification include:

PEST/SWOT analysis	PEST (Political, Economic, Social, Technological) and SWOT (Strengths, Weaknesses, Opportunities, Threats) are very well known and familiar business analysis tools. These models can be used to assess risks by providing a framework to identify and think about the risks in the organisation.

External advisors	Companies may employ external risk consultants who will advise on key risks and processes that can be used to limit and control those risks. Consultants have access to other businesses and as a result may have pools of knowledge not available internally.
Interviews/questionnaires	The company may conduct interviews or send questionnaires to key business managers asking them to indicate principal risks.
Internal audit	One of the functions of internal audit should be to provide recommendations on controlling risk. As part of their work therefore, internal audit assess where the organisation faces risk.
Brainstorming	The business may decide to use more informal brainstorming meetings to assess the risks they face. These meetings have the advantage of accessing many different viewpoints.

Any of these methods identify risks but at the end of the process it is important that the organisation determines what its principal risks are. These principal risks will then determine the controls that need to be put in place and the systems that have to be introduced to control and manage the risks.

Quantification of risk exposures

Quantification of risk is important in understanding the extent and significance of the exposure. This can be done by measuring the impact of the risk factor (such as exchange rates) on the total value of the company, or on any individual item such as cash flow or costs.

- Risks that are identified should be measured and assessed. The extent to which this can be done depends on the information available to the risk manager.

- In some companies, particularly in the banking and insurance industries, many risks can be measured statistically, on the basis of historical information.

- In many other situations, the measurement and assessment of risk depends on management judgement.

Some quantitative techniques include:

- expected values and standard deviation
- volatility
- value at risk (VaR)
- regression analysis
- simulation analysis

Expected values and standard deviation

- Some risks can be measured by the use of expected values.

  Expected value = Σ prob X

  where prob = probability, X = outcome

Expected value of risk

When statistical estimates are available for the probabilities of different outcomes, and the value of each outcome, risk can be measured as an expected value of loss or gain.

Expected value of loss = $p \times L$

Where:

p is the probability that the outcome will occur

L is the loss in the event that the outcome does occur.

Example

The finance director of a company has to prepare an assessment of credit risk for a report to the board. The company has annual credit sales of $12 million, and customers are given 60 days, (two months,) credit. Experience shows that:

- irrecoverable debts written off amount to 1.5% of total annual credit sales
- 10% of irrecoverable debts written off are subsequently recovered by legal action.

Required:

(a) What is the credit risk exposure of the company?

(b) What is the expected loss each year due to credit risk?

Solution

(a) The total exposure to credit risk can be expressed either as the total annual credit sales ($12 million) or the exposure to unpaid debts at any point in time ($12 million × 2/12 = $2 million).

(b) For a full year the expected value of loss is = $12 million × 1.5% × 90% = $162,000.

The standard deviation is a measure of the dispersion of the possible values of a given factor, such as cash flow, from the expected value or mean. Thus the standard deviation provides a measure of volatility – the greater the standard deviation, the greater the risk involved.

Volatility

- Another way of assessing risk might be looking at potential volatility. For example, a company might calculate an expected value based on a range of probabilities but also assess the potential variation from that expected outcome (range or standard deviation).

Test your understanding 1 – Volatility

The following are the forecast purchases of raw materials in a future month:

£200,000	30% probability
£250,000	50% probability
£300,000	20% probability

Calculate the upside and downside volatility from expected purchases.

Value at risk

VaR is based on the assumption that investors care mainly about the probability of a large loss. The VaR of a portfolio is the maximum loss on a portfolio occurring within a given period of time with a given probability (usually small).

- Calculating VaR involves using three components: a time period, a confidence level and a loss amount or percentage loss.

- Statistical methods are used to calculate a standard deviation for the possible variations in the value of the total portfolio of assets over a specific period of time.

- Making an assumption that possible variations in total market value of the portfolio are normally distributed, it is then possible to predict at a given level of probability the maximum loss that the bank might suffer on its portfolio in the time period.

- A bank can try to control the risk in its asset portfolio by setting target maximum limits for value at risk over different time periods (one day, one week, one month, three months, and so on).

- VaR may be calculated as standard deviation × Z-score (where the Z-score can be found from the normal distribution tables).

Example of VaR

Suppose a UK company expects to receive $14 million from a US customer. The value in pounds to the UK company will depend on the exchange rate between the dollar and pounds resulting in gains or losses as the exchange rate changes. Assume that the exchange rate today is $1.75/£ and that the daily volatility of the pound/dollar exchange rate is 0.5%.

Calculate the

(a) 1-day 95% VaR

(b) 1-day 99% VaR.

The value of the $14 million today is £8 million ($14 million ÷ $1.75/£) with a daily standard deviation of £40,000 (0.5% × £8 million).

(a) The standard normal value (Z) associated with the one-tail 95% confidence level is 1.645 (see Normal Distribution tables). Hence, the 1-day 95% VaR is 1.645 × £40,000 = £65,800. This means that we are 95% confident that the maximum daily loss will not exceed £65,800. Alternatively, we could also say that there is a 5% (1 out of 20) chance that the loss would exceed £65,800.

(b)   The standard normal value (Z) associated with the one-tail 99% confidence level is 2.326 (see Normal Distribution tables). Hence, the 1-day 99% VaR is 2.326 × £40,000 = £93,040. Thus, there is a 1% (1 out of 100) chance that the loss would exceed £93,040.

Given the 1-day VaR, we can easily calculate the VaR for longer holding periods as:

n day Var = 1 day Var × √n

Thus, we can calculate the 5-day 95% VaR as:

5 day 95% VaR = 1 day 95% VaR × √5 = £147,129

There is a 5% chance that the company's foreign exchange loss would exceed £147,129 over the next 5 days.

Similarly, the 30-day 99% VaR would be:

1 day 99% VaR × √30 = £509,601

Notice that for a given confidence level, the VaR increases with the holding period. Thus, the longer the holding period, the greater the VaR.

More on value at risk (VaR)

The Basel committee established international standards for banking laws and regulations aimed at protecting the international financial system from the results of the collapse of major banks. Basel II established rigorous risk and capital management requirements to ensure each bank holds reserves sufficient to guard against its risk exposure given its lending and investment practices. Regulators require banks to measure their market risk using a risk measurement model which is used to calculate the Value at Risk (VaR).

However, the global financial crisis has identified substantial problems with banks governance procedures in terms of understanding operational risk and applying risk measurement models like VaR. This has been emphasised by the number of banks that have failed or required government support – Northern Rock and Bradford and Bingley in the UK; Bear Sterns and Washington Mutual in the US amongst others.

> ### Test your understanding 2 – Value at risk
>
> A bank has estimated that the expected value of its portfolio in two weeks' time will be $50 million, with a standard deviation of $4.85 million.
>
> **Required:**
>
> Calculate and comment upon the value at risk of the portfolio, assuming a 95% confidence level.

Regression analysis

This can be used to measure a company's exposure to various risk factors at the same time. This is done by regressing changes in the company's cash flows against the risk factors (changes in interest rates, exchange rates, prices of key commodities such as oil). The regression coefficients will indicate the sensitivities of the company's cash flow to these risk factors.

The drawback with this technique is that the analysis is based on historical factors which may no longer be predictors of the company in the future.

Simulation analysis

This is used to evaluate the sensitivity of the value of the company, or its cash flows, to a variety of risk factors. These risk factors will be given various simulated values based on probability distributions, and the procedure is repeated a number of times to obtain the range of results that can be achieved.

The mean and standard deviation are then calculated from these results to give an expected value and measure of the risk.

This technique can be complex and time-consuming to carry out, and is limited by the assumptions of the probability distributions.

Other methods of measuring or assessing the severity of an identified risk include:

- scenario planning – forecasting various outcomes of an event;

- decision trees – use of probability to estimate an outcome;

- sensitivity analysis – used to ask 'what-if?' questions to test the robustness of a plan. Altering one variable at a time identifies the impact of that variable.

Drawbacks of the quantification of risk

Once a risk has been quantified, there is a problem – whether anyone really knows what it means. Unless you are a trainee or qualified accountant (or similar) this is unlikely, hence risks are often left unquantified.

Risk mapping

A common qualitative way of assessing the significance of risk is to produce a '**risk map**'.

- The map identifies whether a risk will have a significant impact on the organisation and links that into the likelihood of the risk occurring.

- The approach can provide a framework for prioritising risks in the business.

- Risks with a significant impact and a high likelihood of occurrence need more urgent attention than risks with a low impact and low likelihood of occurrence.

- Risks can be plotted on a diagram, as shown below.

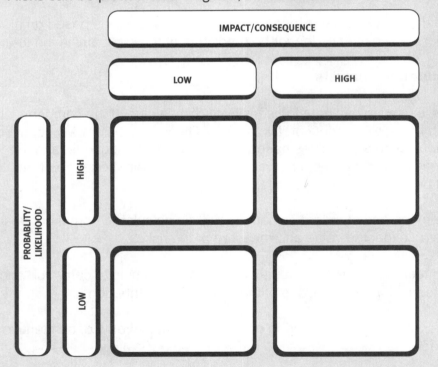

More on risk mapping

The potential loss from an adverse outcome is a function of:

- the probability or likelihood that the adverse outcome will occur, and
- the impact of the outcome if it does occur.

When an initial review is carried out to identify and assess risks, the assessment of both probabilities and impact might be based on judgement and experience rather than on a detailed statistical and numerical analysis.

- In an initial analysis, it might be sufficient to categorise the probability of an adverse outcome as 'high', 'medium' or 'low', or even more simply as 'high' or 'low'.
- Similarly, it might be sufficient for the purpose of an initial analysis to assess the consequences or impact of an adverse outcome as 'severe' or 'not severe'.

Each risk can then be plotted on a risk map. A risk map is simply a 2 × 2 table or chart, showing the probabilities for each risk and their potential impact.

Example

The following simple risk map might be prepared for a firm of auditors:

	Impact/consequences	
	Low	**High**
High	New audit regulations for the profession	Loss of non-audit work from existing clients
Low	Increases in salaries above the general rate of inflation	Loss of audit clients within the next two years.

Probability/likelihood

Using a risk map

A risk map immediately indicates which risks should be given the highest priority.

- High-probability, high-impact risks should be given the highest priority for management, whether by monitoring or by taking steps to mitigate the risk.

- Low-probability, low-impact risks can probably be accepted by the organisation as within the limits of acceptability.

- High-probability, low-impact risks and low-probability, high-impact risks might be analysed further with a view to deciding the most appropriate strategy for their management.

For each high-probability, high-impact risk, further analysis should be carried out, with a view to:

- estimating the probability of an adverse (or favourable) outcome more accurately, and

- assessing the impact on the organisation of an adverse outcome. This is an area in which the management accountant should be able to contribute by providing suitable and relevant financial information.

Test your understanding 3 – Restaurant

Suggest a risk that could be included in each quadrant for a restaurant.

4 Risk response strategy

So far we have considered the types of risk a company could be exposed to and the way it may choose to assess, measure and bear those risks. The next area is to look at the formulation of a strategy to respond to those risks, the general methods that can be used to treat risks and the implementation of such strategy.

The management of risks involves trying to ensure that:

- Exposure to severe risks is minimised.

- Unnecessary risks are avoided.

- Appropriate measures of control are taken.

- The balance between risk and return is appropriate.

The estimate of the potential loss for each risk should be compared with the acceptable risk limit for the company. If the risk is greater than the acceptable limit, the next stage in risk management is to consider how the risk should be managed or controlled, to bring it down in size.

Risk treatment (management) methods

Assuming that the business does want to manage its risks in some way a number of methods can be used. These methods will limit the risks, and the overall risk management strategy may define how the risks will be managed and the way these methods will interact.

Avoid risk

- A company may decide that some activities are so risky that they should be avoided.

- This will always work but is impossible to apply to all risks in commercial organisations as risks have to be taken to make profits.

Transfer risk

- In some circumstances, risk can be transferred wholly or in part to a third party.

- A common example of this is insurance. It does reduce/eliminate risks but premiums have to be paid.

Pool risks

- Risks from many different transactions can be pooled together: each individual transaction/item has its potential upside and its downside. The risks tend to cancel each other out, and are lower for the pool as a whole than for each item individually.

- For example, it is common in large group structures for financial risk to be managed centrally.

Diversification

- Diversification is a similar concept to pooling but usually relates to different industries or countries.

- The idea is that the risk in one area can be reduced by investing in another area where the risks are different or ideally opposite.

- A correlation coefficient with a value close to -1 is essential if risk is to be nullified.

Managing risk by diversification

The syllabus refers specifically to the principle of diversifying risk, but states that numerical questions will not be set. It will therefore be useful to look in more detail at the effect of diversification on risk.

- Risk can be reduced by diversifying into operations in different areas, such as into Industry X and Industry Y, or into Country P and Country Q.

- Poor performance in one area will be offset by good performance in another area, so diversification will reduce total risk.

- Diversification is based on the idea of 'spreading the risk'; the total risk should be reduced as the portfolio of diversified businesses gets larger.

- Diversification works best where returns from different businesses are negatively correlated (i.e. move in different ways). It will, however, still work as long as the correlation is less than +1.0.

- Example of poor diversification – swimming costumes and ice cream – both reliant on sunny weather for sales.

- Spreading risk relates to portfolio management as an investor or company spreads product and market risks.

- The most common form of diversification attempts to spread risk according to the **portfolio** of companies held within a group based more on links within the supply chain.

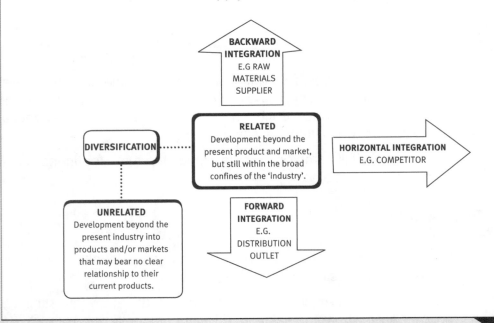

Spreading risk by portfolio management

Within an organisation, risk can be spread by expanding the portfolio of companies held. The portfolio can be expanded by integration – linking with other companies in the supply chain, or diversification into other areas.

This is development beyond the present product and market, but still within the broad confines of the 'industry'.

- **Backward integration** refers to development concerned with the inputs into the organisation, e.g. raw materials, machinery and labour.

- **Forward integration** refers to development into activities that are concerned with the organisation's outputs such as distribution, transport, servicing and repairs.

- **Horizontal integration** refers to development into activities that compete with, or directly complement, an organisation's present activities. An example of this is a travel agent selling other related products such as travel insurance and currency exchange services.

Unrelated diversification

This is development beyond the present industry into products and/or markets that may bear no clear relationship to their present portfolio. Where appropriate an organisation may want to enter into a completely different market to spread its risk.

Problems with diversification:

- If diversification reduces risk, why are there relatively few conglomerate industrial and commercial groups with a broad spread of business in their portfolio?

- Many businesses compete by specialising, and they compete successfully in those areas where they excel.

- Therefore, it is difficult for companies to excel in a wide range of diversified businesses. There is a possible risk that by diversifying too much, an organisation might become much more difficult to manage. Risks could therefore increase with diversification, due to loss of efficiency and problems of management.

- Many organisations diversify their operations, both in order to grow and to reduce risks, but they do so into related areas, such as similar industries (e.g. banking and insurance, film and television production, and so on) or the same industry but in different parts of the world.

- Relatively little advantage accrues to the shareholders from diversification. There is nothing to prevent investors from diversifying for themselves by holding a portfolio of stocks and shares from different industries and in different parts of the world.

Test your understanding 4 – Diversification

Evaluate whether it is always a good business strategy for a listed company to diversify to reduce risk.

Risk reduction

- Even if a company cannot totally eliminate its risks, it may reduce them to a more acceptable level by a form of internal control.

- The internal control would reduce either the likelihood of an adverse outcome occurring or the size of a potential loss.

- The costs of the control measures should justify the benefits from the reduced risk.

- More will be seen on internal controls in chapter 5.

Hedging risks

- Hedging will be considered in detail when financial risk is examined in later chapters.

- The concept of hedging is reducing risks by entering into transactions with opposite risk profiles to deliberately reduce the overall risks in a business operation or transaction.

Risk sharing

- A company could reduce risk in a new business operation by sharing the risk with another party.

- This can be a motivation for entering into a joint venture.

Risk management using TARA

An alternative way of remembering risk management methods is via the mnemonic '**TARA**':

Transference. In some circumstances, risk can be transferred wholly or in part to a third party, so that if an adverse event occurs, the third party suffers all or most of the loss. A common example of risk transfer is insurance. Businesses arrange a wide range of insurance policies for protection against possible losses. This strategy is also sometimes referred to as **sharing**.

Avoidance. An organisation might choose to avoid a risk altogether. However, since risks are unavoidable in business ventures, they can be avoided only by not investing (or withdrawing from the business area completely). The same applies to not-for-profit organisations: risk is unavoidable in the activities they undertake.

Reduction/mitigation. A third strategy is to reduce the risk, either by limiting exposure in a particular area or attempting to decrease the adverse effects should that risk actually crystallise.

Acceptance. The final strategy is to simply accept that the risk may occur and decide to deal with the consequences in that particularly situation. The strategy is appropriate normally where the adverse effect is minimal. For example, there is nearly always a risk of rain; unless the business activity cannot take place when it rains then the risk of rain occurring is not normally insured against.

Risk mapping and risk responses

Risk maps can provide a useful framework to determine an appropriate risk response:

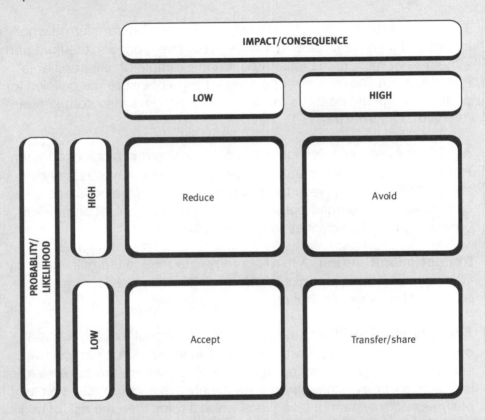

Test your understanding 5 – Twinkletoes

You are the management accountant of a large private company, Twinkletoes. Twinkletoes manufactures a high volume of reasonably priced shoes for elderly people. The company has a trade receivables ledger that is material to the financial statements containing four different categories of account. The categories of account, and the risks associated with them, are as follows:

(i) small retail shoe shops. These accounts represent nearly two thirds of the accounts on the ledger by number, and one third of the receivables by value. Some of these customers pay promptly, others are very slow;

(ii) large retail shoe shops (including a number of overseas accounts) that sell a wide range of shoes. Some of these accounts are large and overdue;

(iii) chains of discount shoe shops that buy their inventory centrally. These accounts are mostly well-established `high street' chains. Again, some of these accounts are large and overdue; and

(iv) mail order companies who sell the company's shoes. There have been a number of large new accounts in this category, although there is no history of irrecoverable debts in this category.

Receivables listed under (ii) to (iv) are roughly evenly split by both value and number. All receivables are dealt with by the same managers and staff and the same internal controls are applied to each category of receivables. You do not consider that using the same managers and staff, and the same controls, is necessarily the best method of managing the receivables ledger.

Twinkletoes has suffered an increasing level of irrecoverable debts and slow payers in recent years, mostly as a result of small shoe shops becoming insolvent. The company has also lost several overseas accounts because of a requirement for them to pay in advance. Management wishes to expand the overseas market and has decided that overseas customers will in future be allowed credit terms.

Management has asked you to classify the risks associated with the receivables ledger in order to manage trade receivables as a whole more efficiently. You have been asked to classify accounts as high, medium or low risk.

Required:

(a) Classify the risks relating to the four categories of trade receivables as high, medium or low and explain your classification.

Note: More than one risk classification may be appropriate within each account category.

(b) Describe the internal controls that you would recommend to Twinkletoes to manage the risks associated with the receivables ledger under the headings: all customers, slow paying customers, larger accounts, and overseas customers.

5 Risk reporting

Risk reports now form part of UK annual reports. It is an important disclosure requirement. (Examples of these are available on larger companies websites. Candidates are encouraged to read some.)

Managers of a business, and external stakeholders, will require information regarding the risks facing the business. A risk reporting system would include:

- A systematic review of the risk forecast (at least annually).

- A review of the risk strategy and responses to significant risks.

- A monitoring and feedback loop on action taken and assessments of significant risks.

- A system indicating material change to business circumstances, to provide an 'early warning'.

- The incorporation of audit work as part of the monitoring and information gathering process.

Risk reports should show:

- the **gross risk** = an assessment of risk before the application of any controls, transfer or management responses, and

- the **net risk** (or **residual risk**) = an assessment of risk, taking into account the controls, transfer and management responses

to facilitate a review of the effectiveness of risk responses.

An example of gross and net risk assessments, utilising the risk map (impact / likelihood matrix) is shown below:

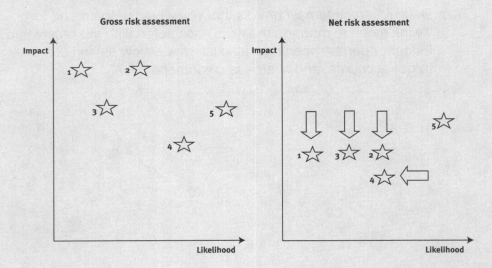

If the residual risk is considered to be too great then the company will need to:

- not expose itself to the risk situation; or
- put in place better controls over the risk.

The amount of residual risk a company can bear is ultimately a management decision.

- It is possible to measure that residual risk, possibly as a proportion of profit/capital/turnover, in order to help management make that judgement.

Residual risk

Risk reports should show:

- the **gross risk** = an assessment of risk before the application of any controls, transfer or management responses, and
- the **net risk** (or **residual risk**) = an assessment of risk, taking into account the controls, transfer and management responses

to facilitate a review of the effectiveness of risk responses.

An example of gross and net risk assessments, utilising the risk map (impact / likelihood matrix) is shown below:

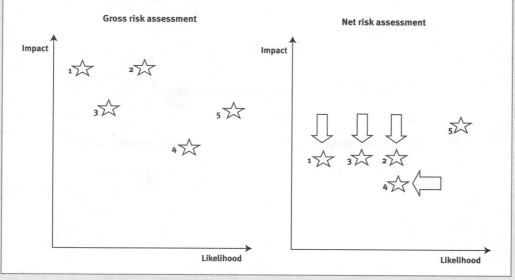

Ability to bear risk

One approach to assessing the ability to bear a risk is to consider the financial consequences of the risk, in relation to:

- the organisation's profits
- return on capital employed
- the organisation's expenditure budget (not-for-profit organisations).

For example, suppose that the financial consequences of a particular risk have been estimated as a potential loss of $200,000. For an organisation making annual profits of, say, $200 million, this might seem relatively insignificant. On the other hand, for an organisation with annual profits of just $250,000, say, the risk would be much more significant.

An organisation might establish policy guidelines as to the maximum acceptable residual risk for any individual risk, or set risk limits to the maximum acceptable loss on particular operations.

6 Evaluating risk management strategy

Once the company has established its risk strategy and decided in what areas it will reduce its risks and the methods it will use to achieve the desired reductions, the strategy should be evaluated.

The purpose of the evaluation is two-fold, as shown below:

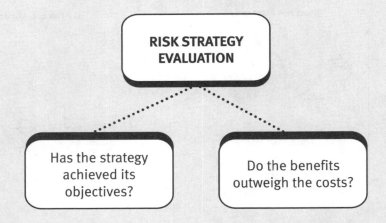

Has the strategy been successful?

Within the risk management strategy, targets should be included to enable the company to assess whether the risk strategy objectives have been achieved. For example, a company might set a target for risk of faulty products at a set number or percentage level and then formulate a risk strategy to achieve that level. In order to assess this a control mechanism will need to be set up. The basic control idea is that the company compares the actual results with a required target, and assesses whether the target has been achieved. If not, the reasons must be investigated and action taken, including possibly a re-assessment of the risk strategy.

Do benefits outweigh costs?

- The costs and benefits of risk measures such as internal controls can be evaluated, and a cost-benefit comparison carried out.

- The benefits from risk controls should preferably be measured and quantified, although some benefits (such as protecting the company's reputation) might have to be assessed qualitatively.

- The evaluation process should be based on the principle that the benefits from a control measure should not exceed the benefits that it provides.

  - For example, a company could be very concerned about theft of petty cash and therefore introduce controls limiting the cash held to £25 and also requiring daily reconciliations of the cash balance by the financial controller, with observation by a member of the internal audit department.

  - This control would probably reduce theft, but would be very expensive for the company to operate and as a result the costs would exceed the benefits. The controls set up must be proportionate to the potential losses that could occur if the risk results in losses.

Cost-benefit example

A manufacturing company is concerned about the rate of rejected items from a particular process. The current rejection rate is 5% of items input, and it has been estimated that each rejected item results in a loss to the company of $10. 600 items go through the process each day.

It is estimated that by introducing some inspection to the process, the rejection rate could be reduced fairly quickly to 3%. However, inspections would result in an increase of costs of $70 per day.

Required:

How should this control through inspection be evaluated?

Solution

The example is a simple one, but it is useful for suggesting an approach to risk management and control evaluation.

What is the objective of the control?

Answer: To reduce losses from rejected items from the process, initially from 5% to 3% of input.

What is the expected benefit?

Answer: A reduction in rejects by 2% of input, from 5% to 3%. The reduction in rejects each day is (2% × 600) 12. Since each reject costs $10, the total daily saving is $120.

What is the expected cost of the control?

Answer: $70 per day. Therefore the control appears to be worthwhile in achieving the objective.

Is the control effective?

Answer: This should be established by monitoring actual results. For example, if the control costs $70 each day, but succeeds in reducing the rejection rate from 5% to just 4% (a reduction of 1%), the benefits would be only $60 each day and the control would not be cost-effective (unless the savings are more than $10 per unit).

7 Risk management roles and responsibilities

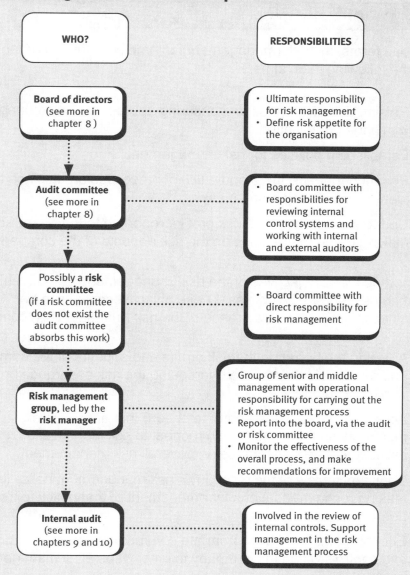

If the company being considered is divisional there may be a **risk officer** for each division who will help to identify and manage tactical and operational level risks.

All **employees** have a role and responsibility for risk too. You should be **aware** of possible risks (through policies issued and training given) and you should be **audible** if you believe a risk needs to be managed (by reporting it to your manager or by whistleblowing).

Roles of the risk committee

In broad terms, the risk (management) committee within an organisation has the following main aims:

- Raising risk awareness and ensuring appropriate risk management within the organisation.

- Establishing policies for risk management.

- Ensuring that adequate and efficient processes are in place to identify, report and monitor risks.

- Updating the company's risk profile, reporting to the board and making recommendations on the risk appetite of the company.

Supporting these objectives of the risk (management) committee, there are many secondary objectives. These objectives may also be contained in the terms of reference of the risk (management) committee.

- Advising the board on the risk profile and appetite of the company and as part of this process overseeing the risk assurance process within the company.

- Acting on behalf of the board, to ensure that appropriate mechanisms are in place with respect to risk identification, risk assessment, risk assurance and overall risk management.

- Continual review of the company's risk management policy including making recommendations for amendment of that policy to the board.

- Ensuring that there is appropriate communication of risks, policies and controls within the company to employees at all management levels.

- Ensuring that there are adequate training arrangements in place so management at all levels are aware of their responsibilities for risk management.

- Where necessary, obtaining appropriate external advice to ensure that risk management processes are up to date and appropriate to the circumstances of the company.

- Ensuring that best practices in risk management are used by the company, including obtaining and implementing external advice where necessary.

Risk manager activities

Typical activities carried out by a risk manager include:

- Provision of overall leadership for risk management team.

- Identification and evaluation of the risks affecting an organisation from that organisation's business, operations and policies.

- Implementation of risk mitigation strategies including appropriate internal controls to manage identified risks.

- Seeking opportunities to improve risk management methodologies and practices within the organisation.

- Monitoring the status of risk mitigation strategies and internal audits, and ensuring that all recommendations are acted upon.

- Developing, implementing and managing risk management programmes and initiatives including establishment of risk management awareness programmes within the organisation.

- Maintaining good working relationships with the board and the risk management committee.

- Ensuring compliance with any laws and regulations affecting the business.

- Implementing a set of risk indicators and reports, including losses, incidents, key risk exposures and early warning indicators.

- Liaising with insurance companies, particularly with regards to claims, conditions and cover available.

- Depending on specific laws of the jurisdiction in which the organisation is based, working with the external auditors to provide assurance and assistance in their work in appraising risks and controls within the organisation.

- Again, depending on the jurisdiction, producing reports on risk management, including any statutory reports (e.g. Sarbanes-Oxley (SOX) reports in the US).

Northern Rock

A failure of risk management

Perhaps the most interesting example of risk and control was the case of Northern Rock. In September 2007 Northern Rock plc was a top five UK mortgage lender, on the FTSE 100 index with over £100 billion in assets. Northern Rock raised over 70% of the money it used in its growing mortgage lending business from banks and other financial institutions. Following the global credit crunch that resulted from the crisis in the US sub-prime (high risk) mortgage sector, banks stopped lending to each other and Northern Rock could not raise sufficient cash to cover its liabilities.

A bank run (the first on a UK bank for 150 years) on Northern Rock by its customers led to the government providing 'lender of last resort' funding and guarantees for the bank's depositors totalling about £20 billion. The result has been a 90% fall in the bank's share price, a deteriorating credit rating and a loss of reputation. The CEO has resigned and several directors have also left the board.

Northern Rock had a formal approach to risk management, including liquidity, credit, operational and market risk, fully described in its Securities and Exchange Commission filings. Northern Rock's assets were sound so there was no significant credit risk. Market risk was also well managed in terms of interest rate and foreign exchange exposure. However, despite formal procedures and a demonstrated compliance with regulations, there was an assumption by managers that access to funds would continue unimpeded. The US sub-prime crisis led to liquidity risk materialising, causing the Northern Rock problems. The consequence was also the loss of reputation that followed press reports which blamed the bank's management for not having a contingency plan to cover the possibility of disruption to its funding, an operational risk. It is likely that the board of Northern Rock failed in both monitoring liquidity risk and in monitoring the effectiveness of the existing controls.

The lesson of Northern Rock is that we need to move beyond the tick-box approach to compliance and that good governance requires a more insightful approach to risk management and internal control.

Risk in a retail chain

The group has 480 stores and sales of £1.5 billion. Risk management was part of the internal audit function. The internal auditor/risk manager said that the motivation for risk management was to 'establish best practice in corporate governance'. However, he commented that the business recently had 'problems with its fundamental controls' when 'senior management were looking at refinancing so took their eye off the ball'.

The process commenced with a brainstorming by the internal audit team of 'risk drivers' to identify what could go wrong and what controls could be put in place to address risks. The internal audit team held interviews with all managers to determine a measure of the effectiveness of these controls on a scale from 1 to 5. The threat of the control gap was identified and recommendations were made. This list looked like a risk register, although the group did not call it that. The internal auditor/risk manager did not see value in a risk register but rather saw risk management as high level.

The Risk Management Committee (RMC) meets every 2 months, comprising all business (executive) directors. The list given by the internal audit team to RMC showed the monetary value of a 'fundamental control breakdown', from which was deducted the monetary value arising from controls implemented to give a 'residual risk' (i.e. the risk after controls) to which was assigned a probability. These values were admittedly subjective. The RMC consider the risk maps, which showed the percentage probability of a threat arising and the residual monetary risk after taking account of controls. The whole process has been centrally driven, with a concern for 'high level' risks. The big risks identified through this process were: supply chain, suppliers, people management, rebates, cost base, key processes, property management, market share, product offering and pricing, brand management, strategic management, integration and change, systems and business continuity.

The most recent development is a Key Control Improvement Plan (KCIP) that provides recommendations to address the risks. It summarises each risk (the example of supply chain failure was given) and the 'mitigating factors' (i.e. controls) and what still needs to be done.

The Audit Committee (AC) of the Board has four non-executive directors, the external auditors, the finance director and the internal auditor/risk manager and monitors progress in relation to the risk maps. The risk maps also drive the audit plan which is agreed on by the AC, business directors and RMC.

The 'big nasties' are picked off, for example, purchase ordering and goods received, new stores, margins. Results are provided to the RMC and AC where the value of the report is greater than £250,000. Internal audit now had more exposure to decision-makers, as the risk management role had given them a high profile. In the future, the internal auditor/risk manager wants to implement a Risk Intelligence Report to provide early warning of risks, by looking at key performance indicators to identify what the business should be concerned with. He also wanted to introduce a Risk Management Marketing Plan to help communicate risk and to pass on the responsibility to other managers with senior managers making presentations to RMC. The internal auditor/risk manager expects it to take another 2 years to establish risk management in the organisation. More 'bottom up' controls need to be introduced and risk management needs to be embedded at the cultural level.

Risk in an engineering consultancy

This organisation is privately owned with 3,500 employees. A review of its financial performance had revealed that the estimated cost of project over-runs, non-productive time and contractual penalties incurred was about 2% of annual turnover. This represented an opportunity loss of about £3 million per annum against reported profits of about £5 million.

However, the main driver behind risk management was to address the rapidly increasing premium for professional indemnity that had increased premiums to several million pounds and had seen its excess increase from £5,000 to £500,000 per annum over the last few years. The organisation had appointed a risk manager; adopted an offshore 'captive' insurer and implemented a management development programme to improve the skills of all its managers. This had included a substantial content on risk awareness.

One of the ways in which it was helping its managers to understand risk was to undertake risk assessments as part of every project bid and to reflect each risk in pricing. During contract negotiations, each risk could be discussed between the lead consultant and the client when the value of the risk could be discussed in terms of the control devices that could be put in place by the client to reduce the risk and hence reduce that component of the project price that reflected the risk.

It was anticipated that this collaboration between consultant and client would reduce risk and lead to a more profitable outcome for both parties.

Test your understanding 6 – Gastrotime

Gastrotime is a company that owns and runs a number of restaurants. A risk assessment is being carried out, and one element in this process is to assess the risks facing individual restaurants in the group. As management accountant, you have been sent to one of these restaurants to interview the manager.

The restaurant manager supplies you with the following information:

(1) There are 40 tables in the restaurant, which opens in the evenings but not at lunchtime.

(2) The manager tries to arrange reservations so that there are two sittings at each table each day, an early-evening and a late-evening sitting.

(3) The restaurant is operating beneath full capacity. Actual capacity is 60% for the early evening sittings and 75% for the late evening sittings.

(4) Each table seats four people, and the average number of guests per table is 3.2.

(5) The average income from each customer in the restaurant is $40. The direct cost of a meal averages $6 for food and $4 for drinks.

(6) The restaurant opens 300 days each year.

The restaurant manager is concerned about the quality of the food, and estimates that about 1 in 100 customers complain about the food they have been served, and send it back to the kitchen. However, he does not think that the food quality is so bad that it affects customers and damages the restaurant's reputation. He would, however, like to improve the standards of cuisine as a matter of professional pride.

You discuss the possible reasons why the restaurant is not full every day. The restaurant manager comments that on many occasions, tables are booked for a time that makes only one sitting possible at the table for the evening, rather than two. He also admits that there have been several problems with poor service, which he is trying to resolve. A number of customers have informed him that they would not be eating at the restaurant again in view of the service they had received.

Required:

Use appropriate methods to identify and evaluate the risks facing this restaurant.

Test your understanding 7 – Azure Ltd

Azure Ltd was incorporated in Sepiana on 1 April 2004. In May, the company exercised an exclusive right granted by the government of Pewta to provide twice weekly direct flights between Lyme, the capital of Pewta, and Darke, the capital of Sepiana.

The introduction of this service has been well advertised as 'efficient and timely' in national newspapers. The journey time between Sepiana and Pewta is expected to be significantly reduced, so encouraging tourism and business development opportunities in Sepiana.

Azure operates a refurbished 35-year-old aircraft which is leased from an international airline and registered with the Pewtan Aviation Administration (the PAA). The PAA requires that engines be overhauled every two years. Engine overhauls are expected to put the aircraft out of commission for several weeks.

The aircraft is configured to carry 15 First Class, 50 Business Class and 76 Economy Class passengers. The aircraft has a generous hold capacity for Sepiana's numerous horticultural growers (e.g. of cocoa, tea and fruit) and general cargo.

The six-hour journey offers an in-flight movie, a meal, hot and cold drinks and tax-free shopping. All meals are prepared in Lyme under a contract with an airport catering company. Passengers are invited to complete a 'satisfaction' questionnaire which is included with the in-flight entertainment and shopping guide. Responses received show that passengers are generally least satisfied with the quality of the food – especially on the Darke to Lyme flight.

Azure employs ten full-time cabin crew attendants who are trained in air-stewardship including passenger safety in the event of accident and illness. Flight personnel (the captain and co-pilots) are provided under a contract with the international airline from which the aircraft is leased. At the end of each flight the captain completes a timesheet detailing the crew and actual flight time.

Ticket sales are made by Azure and travel agents in Sepiana and Pewta. On a number of occasions Economy seating has been over-booked. Customers who have been affected by this have been accommodated in Business Class as there is much less demand for this, and even less for First Class. Ticket prices for each class depend on many factors, for example whether the tickets are refundable/non-refundable, exchangeable/non-exchangeable, single or return, mid-week or weekend, and the time of booking.

Azure's insurance cover includes passenger liability, freight/baggage and compensation insurance. Premiums for passenger liability insurance are determined on the basis of passenger miles flown.

Required:

(a) Identify and explain the risks facing Azure Ltd.

(b) Advise how the risks identified in (a) could be managed and maintained at an acceptable level by Azure Ltd.

Test your understanding 8 – Risk and control

SPM is a manufacturer and distributor of printed stationery products that are sold in a wide variety of retail stores around the country. There are two divisions: Manufacturing and Distribution. A very large inventory is held in the distribution warehouse to cope with orders from retailers who expect delivery within 48 hours of placing an order.

SPM's management accountant for the Manufacturing division charges the Distribution division for all goods transferred at the standard cost of manufacture which is agreed by each division during the annual budget cycle. The Manufacturing division makes a 10% profit on the cost of production but absorbs all production variances. The goods transferred to Distribution are therefore at a known cost and physically checked by both the Manufacturing and the Distribution division staff at the time of transfer.

The customer order process for SPM's Distribution division is as follows:

- SPM's customer service centre receives orders by telephone, post, fax, email and through a new on-line Internet ordering facility (a similar system to that used by Amazon). The customer service centre checks the creditworthiness of customers and bundles up orders several times each day to go to the despatch department.

- All orders received by the despatch department are input to SPM's computer system which checks stock availability and produces an invoice for the goods.

- Internet orders have been credit checked automatically and stock has been reserved as part of the order entry process carried out by the customer. Internet orders automatically result in an invoice being printed without additional input.

- The despatch department uses a copy of the invoice to select goods from the warehouse, which are then assembled in the loading dock for delivery using SPM's own fleet of delivery vehicles.

- When SPM's drivers deliver the goods to the customer, the customer signs for the receipt and the signed copy of the invoice is returned to the despatch office and then to the accounts department.

- SPM's management accountant for the Distribution division produces monthly management reports based on the selling price of the goods less the standard cost of manufacture. The standard cost of manufacture is deducted from the inventory control total which is increased by the value of inventory transferred from the manufacturing division. The control total for inventory is compared with the monthly inventory valuation report and while there are differences, these are mainly the result of write-offs of damaged or obsolete stock, which are recorded on journal entry forms by the despatch department and sent to the accounts department.

Due to the size of inventory held, a physical stocktake is only taken once per annum by Distribution staff, at the end of the financial year. This has always revealed some stock losses, although these have been at an acceptable level. Both internal and external auditors are present during the stocktake and check selected items of stock with the despatch department staff. Due to the range of products held in the warehouse, the auditors rely on the despatch department staff to identify many of the products held.

Required:

(a) Evaluate any weaknesses in the risk management approach taken by SPM's Distribution division and how this might affect reported profitability.

(b) Recommend internal control improvements that would reduce the likelihood of risk.

Test your understanding 9 – Risk management

The operations division of ABC, a listed company, has responsibility to maintain and support the sophisticated computer systems used for call centres and customer database management which the organisation's retail customers rely on as much of their sales are dependent on access to these systems, which are accessed over the Internet.

Although there is no risk management department as such, ABC has a large number of staff in the operations division devoted to disaster recovery. Contingency plans are in operation and data are backed up regularly and stored off-site. However, pressures for short-term profits and cash flow have meant that there has been a continuing under-investment in capital equipment, which one manager was heard to comment as being 'a little like Railtrack'.

A review of disaster recovery found that although data were backed up there was a real risk that a severe catastrophe such as fire or flood would have wiped out computer hardware and although data back-up was off-site, there was no proven hardware facility the company could use. While managers have relied on consequential loss insurance, they appear to have overlooked the need to carry out actions themselves to avoid or mitigate any possible loss.

Required:

(a) Advise the board as to the main business issue for ABC and the most significant risks that ABC faces.

(b) Advise the board as to its responsibilities for risk management and recommend a risk management system for ABC that would more effectively manage the risks of losing business continuity.

(c) Evaluate the likely benefits for ABC of an effective risk management system for business continuity.

8 The exam

The models and frameworks detailed in this chapter are a starting point for the exam, however, candidates need to be able to use their common sense in order to relate this material to exam questions.

9 Chapter summary

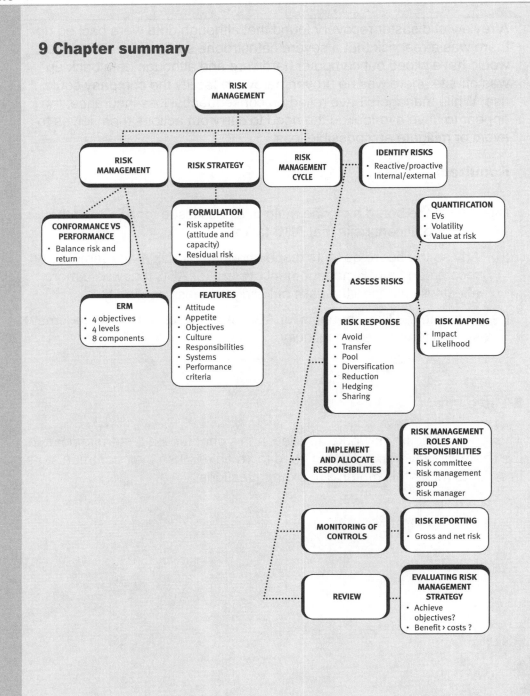

Test your understanding answers

Test your understanding 1 – Volatility

The expected value of purchases is:

	£
£200,000 × 0.3	60,000
£250,000 × 0.5	125,000
£300,000 × 0.2	60,000
	245,000

The volatility therefore is:

Downside (£300,000 – £245,000)	£55,000
Upside (£245,000 – £200,000)	£45,000

The volatility is the possible amount away from the expected value.

Test your understanding 2 – Value at risk

At the 95% confidence level the value at risk = 1.65 × 4.85 = $8 million (1.65 is the normal distribution value for a one-tailed 5% probability level – this can be taken from the normal distribution tables).

There is thus a 5% probability that the portfolio value will fall to $42 million or below.

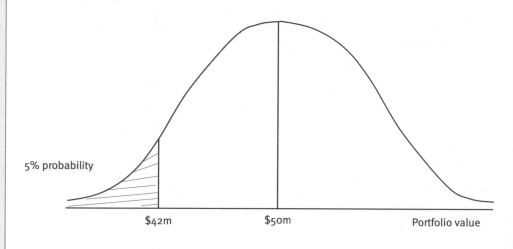

For a restaurant:

		Impact/consequences	
		Low	**High**
Probability/likelihood	**High**	A staff member is taken ill and cannot work	Head chef resigns
	Low	Ingredient prices rise sharply	Several customers suffer from food poisoning

Each suggestion could arguably be in a different quadrant, depending on the restaurant. These are just suggestions.

Arguments for and against diversification:

For

- Reduces risks and enables company to give more predictable return to investors.

- Attracts investors who want low risk investments.

Against

- Management may not understand all the businesses that the company operates in – increases the risk.

- It is not necessary to diversify for investors – they can diversify themselves by investing in a number of different companies.

- New business areas can attract risks – for instance going into a new country may increase the risk of not understanding a company culture.

Twinkletoes

(a) **Classification of risks for receivables**

   (i) **Small retail shoe shops**

      Despite the fact that individual accounts in this category have small balances, the category as a whole is significant to Twinkletoes because of the total amounts owed (one-third of total receivables), the rising level of irrecoverable debts and the adverse effect of slow payers on cash flow. It is likely that most of these accounts individually are low risk because customers pay promptly and the amounts are small. Accounts that are significantly overdue may be classified as medium risk, but probably only if they are substantial accounts because all entities must expect to experience a small number of small irrecoverable debts. If, however, a large number of accounts are significantly overdue, they may be classified as high risk.

   (ii) **Large retail shoe shops**

      Some of these accounts are large and overdue and may therefore be classified as medium or high risk. However, as the total value of such accounts is around 22% of total receivables and the total value of the overdue accounts may be small in relation to total receivables, the classification should probably only be medium risk. The classification for accounts that are not overdue may be low risk

      Overseas accounts. Whilst these might at first appear to be at risk because the accounts are being lost, they represent a small proportion of accounts by both number and value (customers currently pay in advance). This means that they may be viewed as low risk.

   (iii) **Chains of shoe shops**

      As with the large shoe shops, large and overdue accounts might be classified as medium or high risk. However, 'high street' chains of well-established shops are less likely to become insolvent than less well-established entities and therefore represent a lower risk. This means that the classification may be low risk, even for accounts that are large and overdue.

(iv) **Mail order companies**

New accounts generally represent an increased risk of irrecoverable debts and a large number of new accounts increases this risk. However, there is no history of irrecoverable debts in this category at all so the new accounts may therefore be classified as medium risk. Existing accounts within this category may be classified as low risk because there is no history of irrecoverable debts.

(b) **Internal controls**

(i) **All customers**

I would recommend that:

-   credit checks be performed when new customers seek credit, and that cash in advance or on delivery is required where large orders are placed by new customers;

-   credit limits be set for all customers based on the length of the relationship with the customer, the volume of sales and their payment history;

-   payment terms be set (say, 30 days for local customers, 45 days for overseas customers);

-   insurance be taken out against the risk of irrecoverable debts.

These controls will help ensure that accounts do not become overdue, damaging the company's cash flow and increasing the risk of irrecoverable debts.

(ii) **Slow paying customers**

I would recommend that:

-   dedicated staff are assigned to chase slow payers regularly for outstanding amounts and to ensure that a `stop' is put on accounts that are significantly overdue;

-   legal action is taken against those customers owing large amounts for long periods for which there are no good reasons.

(iii) **Larger accounts** – large shops, chains of shops and mail order companies

I would recommend that:

-   dedicated staff are assigned to manage the relationship with larger customers, particularly the mail order companies.

(iv) Overseas customers

I would recommend that:

— overseas customers be allowed a credit period of say, 45 days in order to permit the required bank transfers to take place;

— overseas customers be required to pay in the currency used by Twinkletoes (except perhaps for large orders which may be backed by government guarantees) or in a stable currency which does not fluctuate significantly against the currency used by Twinkletoes.

Test your understanding 6 – Gastrotime

Risk identification

The risks facing the restaurant will be identified and assessed by considering their possible causes and consequences.

Risk	Possible causes	Consequences
Failure to achieve full capacity	Poor service	Lack of bookings/reservations
Failure to achieve full capacity	Booking system	Only one sitting each day at some tables
Fall in sales income	Fewer customers at each table	Lower profit
Fall in income	Lower average spending per customer	Lower profit
Food returned to the kitchen	Poor quality cuisine	Cost of replacing the meal

An initial assessment of these risks can be entered on a risk map. Without further information, the assessment is as follows:

Impact/consequences

Probability/ likelihood		Low	High
	High	Poor food, food returned to kitchen	Poor service, lost customers. Lost capacity, only one sitting at tables
	Low		Drop in average number of customers per table. Fall in average spending per customer

Evaluation of risks

Workings

(1) **Current capacity: reservations (bookings)**

		Maximum capacity bookings	Current capacity bookings	
Early sitting	(40 tables × 300 days)	12,000	(60%)	7,200
Late sitting	(40 tables × 300 days)	12,000	(75%)	9,000
Total		24,000		16,200

(2) **Capacity, number of customers**

	Maximum annual bookings	Current annual bookings
Reservations / bookings	24,000	16,200
Current customers / table	3.2	3.2
Maximum customers / table	4.0	4.0
Annual numbers at 3.2 customers / table	76,800	51,840
Annual numbers at 4.0 customers / table	96,000	64,800
Difference in customer numbers	19,200	12,960

The effect of failure to achieve maximum capacity for reservations

The failure to achieve maximum capacity for bookings could be due to either poor service affecting the business reputation, or to a booking system that allows some tables to be used for only one sitting each day.

There is insufficient information to assess the effect on bookings of each of these factors individually.

However, the current maximum number of bookings each year, assuming two sittings each day, is 24,000. Actual volume is currently 16,200 bookings, which is 7,800 less.

If we assume that an average table has 3.2 customers, each providing a contribution of $30 per head ($40 − $6 − $4), the potential shortfall in annual profit is:

7,800 bookings × 3.2 customers × $30 contribution = $748,800

This would therefore appear to be a serious risk.

Effect of lower customer numbers per table

Each customer provides the restaurant with an average contribution of $30.

If the restaurant were able to reach a capacity of 4 customers per table, it would have 12,960 extra customers each year at the current level of bookings, and additional profit of $388,800.

However, the risk that has been identified is the risk that the average number of customers per table will fall.

At the current level of bookings per year, a fall in the average number of customers per table would reduce profits by $486,000 (16,200 bookings × $30) for a fall in the average by 1.0 customers/table. A fall in the average from 3.2 to, say, 3.0, would therefore result in a fall in profits of $97,200 ($486,000 × 0.2).

Effect of lower spending per customer

The gross contribution from each customer is 75% of sales income ($30/$40).

Assuming that this contribution/sales ratio would apply at all levels of customer spending, a fall of $1 in the average spending by customers for each meal would result in a fall in annual profit:

- at current customer levels, of 51,840 × $1 × 75% = $38,880.
- at maximum bookings capacity, of 76,800 × $1 × 75% = $57,600.

Cost of food returned to the kitchen:

Assuming that when food is returned to the kitchen, it is replaced, the maximum cost of replacement is $6 on each occasion.

If 1% of customers send back their food, the annual cost at current customer levels is 1% × 51,840 × $6 = $3,110.

Unless there is also a knock-on effect that results in lower customer bookings (which does not appear to be the case), this is a comparatively low risk.

Test your understanding 7 – Azure Ltd

(a) Risks facing Azure Ltd.

(b) Processes for managing.

Rights to operate

(a) All terms and conditions of the rights to operate, which provide assurance that Azure is a going concern for the time-being, must be met. For example, twice-weekly flights may be a 'guaranteed' minimum.

Terms and conditions attached to the rights may threaten Azure's operational existence if, for example, there are any circumstances under which the rights could be withdrawn. For example, if the standard of service falls below a minimum specified level.

(b) Accept at the present level (as one that has to be borne) but, bear in mind (e.g. when making strategic decisions) the impact that management's actions could have on any renewal of the rights.

Relevant terms and conditions should be communicated to all staff so they are clear about the importance of their areas of responsibility.

Competition

(a) Although at the moment there appears to be none (as the rights are exclusive), any competition in the future could reduce profitability (e.g. if the rights were to become non-exclusive or an indirect service between Sepiana and Lyme should be established).

(b) Monitor the progress of applications for flights to destinations which could provide transit to Lyme.

Reduce the risk by increasing the reliability and reputation of Azure's service, improving comfort, etc (e.g. by increasing leg room and air-conditioned lounges).

Age of aircraft

(a) The age of the aircraft (35 years) is likely to have a bearing on fuel consumption and other costs (e.g. repairs and maintenance).

(b) Azure should manage its cash flows and borrowing capability (e.g. bank loan facility) to carry out ongoing operating repairs as and when needed.

Engine overhaul

(a) If the lease is a finance lease it is likely that Azure will have to bear the costs of the overhaul – which may have a detrimental effect on cash flows.

The service would need to be suspended while the engine is being overhauled unless an alternative is planned for.

(b) As above, Azure should budget its financial resources to meet the costs of the overhaul, the timing of which can be planned for.

The lease agreement with the airline should provide that an equivalent aircraft be available.

Leased asset

(a) Azure operates with just one leased asset which may be withdrawn from service:

- in the interests of passenger safety (e.g. in the event of mechanical failure);

- for major overhaul;

- if Azure defaults on the lease payments.

(b) Azure should enter into a contractual arrangement (e.g. may be included within the terms of an operating lease) for a replacement aircraft in the event that the aircraft be grounded.

Azure should carry adequate insurance cover for remedying and/or providing compensation to customers for significant disruptions to the scheduled service.

Fuel prices

(a) Increases in fuel prices (a major operational cost) will reduce profitability.

(b) Fuel surcharges should be included in the flights' price structure so that significant increases can be passed on to the customers.

Hedging against the effect of energy price (and exchange rate) risks through forward contracts.

Weather

(a) Weather conditions may delay or cancel flights. Actual and potential customers may choose not to plan trips if the flight *schedule* is so unreliable that they expect to face disruptions and uncertain journey times.

(b) Manage the impact of the risk/modify the business activity. For example, as any form of travel may be hazardous if weather conditions are so bad as to disrupt the flight schedule, there should be air-conditioned facilities in which travellers can relax before their journey.

Horticultural cargo

(a) Certain produce may be prohibited from import (e.g. due to the risk of spread of disease). Azure may face fines for carrying banned produce.

- Growers may seek to hold Azure liable for:
    - produce which perishes (e.g. if successive flights are cancelled);
    - impounded goods.

(b) Contracts with growers should clearly state items of produce that cannot be carried.

Azure's operational controls should include verification checks on produce carried.

Azure should have adequate insurance cover against claims for damaged/lost cargo.

Economy

(a) With significantly less demand for Business Class than for Economy (which gets over-booked) and even less for First Class, the service is operating at well below capacity (economy is only 54% of seating capacity).

Azure may not be recouping fixed operating costs in the long run, making the service uneconomical.

(b) Keep demand for the classes of tickets under review and respond to the excess of supply over demand for Economy seating (and demand shortfall for First and Business Class seats). For example:

- charge higher prices for economy on peak flights;
- offer larger discounts for advance bookings on First and Business Class seats;
- introduce a loyalty scheme for frequent users which offers 'preferred customer' seat upgrades.

Service levels

(a) Azure's schedule is described as 'efficient and timely'. If the level of service delivered does not meet expectations it is unlikely that a regular customer base will be established.

(b) Azure should benchmark the timeliness of its service, against a comparable airline service operating under similar weather conditions.

On-board services

(a) Passengers are expressing dissatisfaction with meals provided, especially on the 'return' flight from Darke. The food prepared in Lyme may be stale or contaminated by the time it is served.

Passengers may be deterred from using this flight if they are subject to the risk of illness.

(b) Azure should consider:
  - changing caterer in Lyme;
  - a contract with a caterer in Darke;
  - expert advice (e.g. of a chef) on preserving the quality of meals for long-haul flights.

Passenger safety

(a) Penalties for non-compliance with safety regulations (e.g. maintenance checks on life jackets, etc) may be incurred if inspection logs are not kept.

Azure may face lawsuits for personal injury or illness (e.g. deep vein thrombosis 'DVT'),

(b) Staff training should be on-going with regular safety drill procedures (e.g. in evacuation procedures and the use of life-rafts).

Safety procedures must be demonstrated before take-off on every flight and passengers referred to safety information, including how to reduce the risk of DVT, provided with each seat.

Air stewards/Cabin crew safety

(a) Azure will have difficulty recruiting and maintaining the services of appropriately qualified cabin crew if it does not have sufficient regard for their health and safety.

(b) Flight personnel rotas should ensure, for example, that:
  - pilots take 'ground leave' between flights;
  - there is adequate 'cover' when crew are sick or taking leave.

Emergency

(a) A serious accident (e.g. fire), collision or breakdown may threaten operations in both the short- and longer-term.

(b) Accept at the present level, but taking all practicable safety checks now implemented in the airline industry to ensure that Azure is not exposed to preventable risks. For example:

- x-ray screening of checked-in baggage;

- security screening of cabin baggage and passengers, etc.

Flight personnel

(a) Azure may not be able to service the flight in the event of non-supply of flight personnel by the international airline (e.g. due to strike action).

(b) The agreement with the airline should indemnify Azure for all costs and losses incurred if flights are cancelled due to non-availability of flight personnel.

Flight tickets

(a) Tickets are sold by more than one party (Azure and travel agents) and at more than one location. Also, pricing is complex, with a range of tariffs depending on many factors. This increases the risk that:

- revenue may be lost if passengers are undercharged or ticket sales unrecorded; and

- flights may be over-booked, with consequent loss of customer goodwill.

The configuration of the aircraft does not currently meet the current demand profile of passengers and under the terms an operating lease may not be changeable.

(b) Strict controls must be exercised over:

- unused tickets;

- ticket pricing;

- real-time reservations; and

- ticket refund and exchange transactions.

Commence negotiations with the international airline for an amendment to the current lease terms allowing flexibility in the seating arrangements.

Tutorial note: Candidates are not expected to have specific knowledge of the airline industry. However, marks will be awarded for relevant comments, for example, concerning quotas for landing/take-off slots and IATA's levy. The preceding answer is not exhaustive. For example, that the aircraft is flying for only 24 hours a week is a risk as this is a low capacity at which to operate for the recovery of overheads.

Test your understanding 8 – Risk and control

(a) Risk management is the process by which organisations systematically identify and treat upside and downside risks across the portfolio of all activities with the goal of achieving organisational objectives. Risk management increases the probability of success, reduces both the probability of failure and the uncertainty of achieving the organisation's objectives. The goal of risk management is to manage, rather than eliminate risk. This is most effectively done through embedding a risk culture into the organisation.

For SPM's Distribution division, there is a risk of stock losses through theft, largely due to the lack of separation of duties. This lack of separation occurs because the Distribution Division:

- enters all orders to the computer;
- selects all stock from the warehouse;
- despatches all goods to customers;
- receives the signed paperwork evidencing delivery;
- writes off stock losses due to damage and obsolescence;
- carries out and to a large extent controls the annual physical stocktake.

This lack of separation of duties could result in stock losses or theft that is not identified or not recorded and any stock losses or theft may be disguised during the stocktake due to the expertise of the Distribution division which the auditors appear to rely on.

These stock losses or theft may not be accurately recorded and the reported profits of SPM may overstate profits if physical inventory does not match that shown in the accounting records. Stock of stationery is easy to dispose of and losses can easily happen due to error or carelessness, for instance through water damage, dropping and so on. The possibility of theft of stock which can readily be sold in retail stores is also high and the consequences of not identifying stock losses or theft might be severe over a period of time. There is a risk that inventory records may substantially overstate the physical stock. There is a serious limitation of accounting here as it relies on computer records and a stocktake process that may be severely impaired and hence there may be hidden losses not reflected in SPM's reported financial statements.

Fraud is dishonestly obtaining an advantage, avoiding an obligation or causing a loss to another party. Those committing fraud may be managers, employees or third parties, including customers and suppliers. There are three conditions for fraud to occur: dishonesty, opportunity and motive. If stock theft is occurring, the weakness in systems due to the lack of separation of duties provides an opportunity. Personnel policies and supervision may influence dishonesty and employment or social conditions among the workforce may influence motive.

As for all other risks, a risk management strategy needs to be developed for fraud. This strategy should include fraud prevention; the identification and detection of fraud and responses to fraud.

Existing risk treatment does not appear to be adequate due to the lack of separation of duties, the possibility of fraud and the reliance of internal and external auditors on the Distribution division's staff.

(b) The main recommendation is for the separation of duties in SPM's distribution division. The customer service centre should process all customer orders, even though this may mean transferring staff from the despatch department. It may be more effective to use a document imaging system to reduce paperwork by the conversion of orders into electronic files that are capable of being read by computer programs and transferred to the despatch department. Further separation can be carried out by signed paperwork evidencing delivery being sent to the accounts department and for all write offs of stock losses due to damage or obsolescence to be carried out by the accounts department. Finally, the reliance on Distribution staff for stocktaking needs to be reduced and accountants and internal auditors need to play a more prominent role in physical counting and reconciling to computer records.

The second recommendation is for greater emphasis on controls to prevent dishonesty. These include pre-employment checks, scrutiny of staff by effective supervision, severe discipline for offenders and strong moral leadership. Motive can be influenced by providing good employment conditions, a sympathetic complaints procedure, but dismissing staff instantaneously where it is warranted.

Test your understanding 9 – Risk management

(a) A review of disaster recovery had identified a lack of hardware back-up as costs had been continually deferred from year to year to maintain current profits. This has an effect on business continuity for both ABC and its retail customers. Insurance is only one type of risk treatment and ABC has overlooked the need to address business continuity more proactively and comprehensively.

The pressure on short-term profits and cash flow is important to recognise but the short-term view may lead to medium- and long-term problems if under-investment continues. This needs to be the focus of a risk management exercise to properly assess, evaluate, report and treat the business continuity risk.

Although a severe catastrophe may have a small likelihood of occurrence, the impact will be severe and insurance cover is unlikely to be adequate as ABC will not have taken adequate steps to mitigate the loss. Customer awareness of the risk is likely to result in customers moving their business elsewhere. Public disclosure or a severe catastrophe will have a major impact on the reputation of ABC and on ABC's share price.

(b) The board is responsible for maintaining a sound system of internal control to safeguard shareholders' investment and the company's assets. When reviewing management reports on internal control, the board should consider the significant risks and assess how they have been identified, evaluated and managed; assess the effectiveness of internal controls in managing the significant risks, having regard to any significant weaknesses in internal control; consider whether necessary actions are being taken promptly to remedy any weaknesses and consider whether the findings indicate a need for more exhaustive monitoring of the system of internal control.

Risk management is the process by which organisations systematically identify and treat upside and downside risks with the goal of achieving organisational objectives. The goal of risk management is to manage, rather than eliminate risk. Initially, there needs to be a commitment from the board and top management in relation to risk management generally and business continuity in particular, even if this means a short-term detrimental impact on profitability. The board of ABC, through the audit committee, needs to be more involved in the risk management process. Individual responsibilities for risk management need to be assigned and sufficient resources need to be allocated to fund effective risk management for business continuity.

ABC needs to identify its appetite for risk, and a risk management policy needs to be formulated and agreed by the board. The risk management process needs to identify and define risk, which needs to be assessed in terms of both likelihood and impact. For ABC, the risks have been clearly defined: a loss of business continuity caused by a major catastrophe and the consequent loss of reputation this would involve.

The likelihood of fire, flood, terrorist or criminal activity and so on needs to be assessed, particularly in terms of the risk avoidance processes that are already in place. For example, ABC needs to evaluate whether there has been flooding in the area before, whether water pipes run near the computer facility, whether fire prevention measures are in place, whether firewalls are in place and have been tested so as to reduce the likelihood of attack via the Internet. An assessment of probability of these and other catastrophes should be made. Although these may be low probability events, the impact on the business of any such catastrophe will be severe.

Risk evaluation determines the significance of risks to the organisation and whether each specific risk should be accepted or treated. It should be emphasised that these risks cannot be accepted but do need to be treated. Risk treatment (or risk response) is the process of selecting and implementing measures to reduce or limit the risk. The existing contingency plans need to be examined in detail. While data appear to be backed up regularly and stored off-site, there seems to be inadequate back-up for hardware. Risk treatment will involve deciding the most cost-effective method by which to manage the risk. A preferred solution given the reliance of ABC's customers on the system is to have a remote site equipped with a second system that data can be restored onto. While this is the most expensive option there may be business benefits in having two sites. A second solution may be to outsource the back-up facility so that ABC contracts with a third party to have a system available if one is needed. A third option is to negotiate with suppliers as to the availability of other sites and the replacement of equipment on a short notice basis. Finally, insurance coverage needs to be reviewed and the mitigation decided in consultation with ABC's insurers. The present method of risk management that relies only on off-site data back-up is inadequate to assure business continuity.

As business continuity is so important, the board and audit committee need to be involved in the decision-making process about risk treatment. There needs to be regular risk management reporting to assess the control systems in place to reduce risk; the processes used to identify and respond to risks; the methods used to manage significant risks and the monitoring and review system itself. Reporting should take place to business units, senior management, internal audit, the board and the audit committee.

(c) The benefits of effective risk management for ABC include the maintenance of profitability in the medium- and longer-term and the avoidance of sudden losses if business continuity is impeded. The major benefit for ABC in such a case is the avoidance of profit warnings and major exceptional items. Additional benefits may include more cost-effective insurance cover and reduced premium cost. If the recommendations are adopted, despite the increased costs that will almost necessarily be incurred, the board of ABC will have greater degree of assurance that business continuity will be safeguarded in the event of a catastrophe, will continue to satisfy its customers and will maintain its reputation with customers, the public and investors.

Internal control

Chapter learning objectives

Lead	Component
B2. Evaluate risk management strategies and internal controls.	(a) Discuss the purposes and importance of internal control and risk management for an organisation.
	(b) Evaluate risk management strategies.
	(c) Evaluate the essential features of internal control systems for identifying, assessing and managing risks.
	(d) Evaluate the costs and benefits of a particular internal control system.

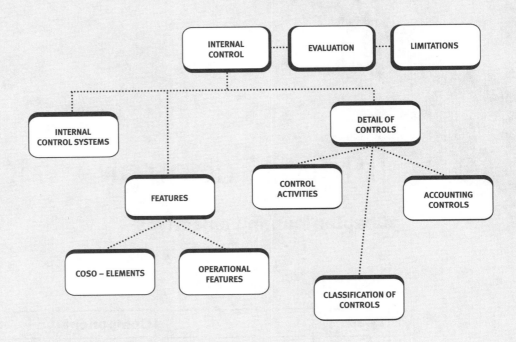

1 Internal control systems

- In order to manage their risks, businesses need to set up internal control systems.

- These internal controls apply across all parts and activities of a business.

Definition

There are a number of different definitions of internal control systems, but all have similar features. One definition is:

'The whole system of controls, financial and otherwise, established by the management in order to carry out the business of the enterprise in an orderly and efficient manner, ensure adherence to management policies, safeguard the assets, prevent and detect fraud and error and secure as far as possible the completeness and accuracy of the records.'

An internal control system can be thought of as a *system for management to control certain risks and therefore help businesses achieve their objectives.*

Internal controls and risk management

- Internal controls can be considered as part of the risk reduction method of responding to risk.

- The need for a robust system of internal control and risk management is seen as a major element of good corporate governance.

- In the UK for example, the Corporate Governance Code requires the board of directors to review the system of internal control in their organisation, and satisfy themselves that a suitable system is in place.

Objectives of internal control

A definition of an internal control system included:

Definition	Commentary
...the orderly and efficient conduct of its business, including adherence to internal policies'	There will be systems in place to ensure that all transactions are recorded (so the business is conducted in an orderly manner) through to following policies such as provision of good customer service.
...the safeguarding of assets'	Assets in this case include buildings, cars, cash, etc. (e.g. those things that can be touched) through to other assets including the intellectual property of the company (e.g. those things which cannot be touched but are still an asset of the business).
...the prevention and detection of fraud and error'	This will include fraud an error at the operational level through to the strategic level (e.g. off balance sheet finance or the adoption of incorrect or suspect accounting policies (think of Enron).
...the accuracy and completeness of the accounting records and ...'	Again, ensuring that all transactions are recorded – so liabilities are not 'hidden' and assets are not overstated.
...the timely preparation of financial information.'	Reporting deadlines in many jurisdictions are quite strict (60 days in the US for some reports) hence the need to ensure information is available to produce those reports in a timely fashion.

The main point to note here is that the internal control system encompasses the **whole business**, not simply the financial records.

2 The Turnbull Report

In October 2005, the Financial Reporting Council issued 'Internal Control - Revised Guidance for Directors on the Combined Code', known more commonly as the Turnbull Report (originally published in 1999). The report covered the importance of internal control in companies. An extract is detailed below.

The importance of internal control and risk management

(1) A company's system of internal control has a key role in the management of risks that are significant to the fulfilment of its business objectives. A sound system of internal control contributes to safeguarding the shareholders' investment and the company's assets.

(2) Internal control facilitates the effectiveness and efficiency of operations, helps ensure the reliability of internal and external reporting and assists compliance with laws and regulations.

(3) Effective financial controls, including the maintenance of proper accounting records, are an important element of internal control. They help ensure that the company is not unnecessarily exposed to avoidable financial risks and that financial information used within the business and for publication is reliable. They also contribute to the safeguarding of assets, including the prevention and detection of fraud.

(4) A company's objectives, its internal organisation and the environment in which it operates are continually evolving and, as a result, the risks it faces are continually changing. A sound system of internal control therefore depends on a thorough and regular evaluation of the nature and extent of the risks to which the company is exposed. Since profits are, in part, the reward for successful risk-taking in business, the purpose of internal control is to help manage and control risk appropriately rather than to eliminate it......

Responsibilities

(15) The board of directors is responsible for the company's system of internal control. It should set appropriate policies on internal control and seek regular reassurance that will enable it to satisfy itself that the system is functioning effectively. The board must further ensure that the system of internal control is effective in managing those risks in the manner which it has approved...

(16) All employees have some responsibility for internal control as part of their accountability for achieving objectives. They, collectively, should have the necessary knowledge, skills, information, and authority to establish, operate and monitor the system of internal control. This will require an understanding of the company, its objectives, the industries and markets in which it operates, and the risks it faces.

Elements of a sound system of internal control

(19) An internal control system encompasses the policies, processes, tasks, behaviours and other aspects of a company that, taken together:

- facilitate its effective and efficient operation by enabling it to respond appropriately to significant business, operational, financial, compliance and other risks to achieving the company's objectives. This includes the safeguarding of assets from inappropriate use or from loss and fraud and ensuring that liabilities are identified and managed;

- help ensure the quality of internal and external reporting. This requires the maintenance of proper records and processes that generate a flow of timely, relevant and reliable information from within and outside the organisation;

- help ensure compliance with applicable laws and regulations, and also with internal policies with respect to the conduct of business.

(20) A company's system of internal control will reflect its control environment which encompasses its organisational structure. The system will include:

- control activities;

- information and communications processes; and

- processes for monitoring the continuing effectiveness of the system of internal control.

(21) The system of internal control should:

- be embedded in the operations of the company and form part of its culture;

- be capable of responding quickly to evolving risks to the business arising from factors within the company and to changes in the business environment; and

- include procedures for reporting immediately to appropriate levels of management any significant control failings or weaknesses that are identified together with details of corrective action being undertaken.

(22) A sound system of internal control reduces, but cannot eliminate, the possibility of poor judgement in decision-making; human error; control processes being deliberately circumvented by employees and others; management overriding controls; and the occurrence of unforeseeable circumstances.

(23) A sound system of internal control therefore provides reasonable, but not absolute, assurance that a company will not be hindered in achieving its business objectives, or in the orderly and legitimate conduct of its business, by circumstances which may reasonably be foreseen. A system of internal control cannot, however, provide protection with certainty against a company failing to meet its business objectives or all material errors, losses, fraud, or breaches of laws or regulations.

('Internal Control – Revised Guidance for Directors on the Combined Code' – Financial Reporting Council – October 2005)

3 Features of internal control systems

COSO model of internal control

In 1992 COSO (Committee of Sponsoring Organisations) stated that effective internal control systems consist of five integrated elements.

Control environment

The control environment can be thought of as management's **attitude**, **actions** and **awareness** of the need for internal controls.

If senior management do not care about internal controls and feel that it is not worthwhile introducing internal controls then the control system will be weak.

Management can try to summarise their commitment to controls in a number of ways:

- Behave with integrity and ethics (corporate governance will be considered in the next session).

- Maintain an appropriate culture in the organisation.

- Set up a good structure – for example, an independent internal audit function, and have segregation of duties.

- Set proper authorisation limits.

- Employ appropriately qualified staff and conduct staff training.

When auditors assess the control systems of business for the audit, if the environment is poor they will place no reliance on any detailed control procedures.

Risk assessment

Risk assessment (as discussed in chapter 3) feeds directly into the internal control system. A risk assessment must be performed and should identify:

- **Controllable risks** – for these risks internal control procedures can be established.

- **Uncontrollable risks** – for these risks the company may be able to minimise the risk in other ways outside the internal control environment. Uncontrollable risks could be risks that are caused by the external environment that the company operates in. For example, the best internal control processes in the world cannot reduce the risk of inflation or the economy going into recession.

Control activities

Once controllable risks have been identified, actual specific control activities can be undertaken to reduce those risks. There is a huge variety of control activities that companies can adopt at all levels of management and in all parts of the organisation.

Due to the need to adapt and change control systems, most companies use a variety of different control processes to ensure that the business achieves its objectives.

The typical processes that could be used are:

- having a defined **organisation structure.** All staff need to understand how their role fits in with the rest of the organisation to aid their understanding of the job. They need to know who to report to on a daily basis and also points of contact when they need to deal with other departments or divisions;

- having **contracts of employment** with individuals at all levels. Contracts of employment guide an employees behaviour. Typically they include hours of work, job title, salary and pension entitlements, holiday, data protection rules through to codes of dress. A major control within the contract of employment is the section on disciplinary action where it is outlined what constitutes a disciplinary procedure and the resulting event which will usually include dismissal;

- establishing **policies**, and subsequently procedures to ensure the policies are followed. Organisations typically have policies on health and safety, travel expenses, dignity at work, etc. Procedures might include the setting up of an audit department to ensure that the policies are adhered to;

- setting up a suitable **discipline and reward system**. Discipline has already been mentioned, however, rewards can also control an individuals behaviour. If an employee knows that there is a month-end bonus for meeting a particular sales target then most if not all of their actions will be focussed on that outcome. The objective is performance and conformance. However, if rewards are not structured correctly they can lead to 'dysfunctional behaviour' which is covered later in the chapter;

- ensuring a system of **performance appraisal and feedback**. Appraisals are usually at least an annual event (perhaps more often whilst an employee is being trained). During the appraisal the manager and employee should have an opportunity to discuss whether the job is being performed satisfactorily, whether previous objectives have been met, and what any future objectives are. An employees behaviour is controlled via an appraisal since they know that their manager will be watching their work in order that a discussion can be held. It is an opportunity for the manager and employee to feedback on any issues that concern them or activities which may have been performed well.

Information and communication

In order for managers to operate the internal controls, they need information and therefore a good information system must be set up. The information provided to managers must be:

- Timely.

- Accurate (and therefore reliable).

- Understandable.

- Relevant to the actions being taken.

Computer systems have led to increased quality of information being provided to managers but the systems must be integrated into the business strategies if they are to provide what managers need.

Information systems and information management are a specific part of this syllabus because they are so important to the successful running and control of business. These topics are covered in more detail in other chapters.

Monitoring

The company may have produced a very good internal control system but it must be monitored. If the system is not monitored it will be very difficult to assess whether it is out of control and needs amendment. Internal control systems are also dynamic in that they need to evolve over time as the business evolves.

The internal audit function is often the key monitor of the internal control system. Internal auditors will examine the controls and control system, identify where controls have failed so that the failures can be rectified, and also make recommendations to management for new and improved systems. More will be seen in later chapters on internal audit.

Elements of an internal control system

COSO identify five elements of an effective control system.

(1) Control environment

This is sometimes referred to as the 'tone at the top' of the organisation. It describes the ethics and culture of the organisation, which provide a framework within which other aspects of internal control operate. The control environment is set by the tone of management, its philosophy and management style, the way in which authority is delegated, the way in which staff are organised and developed, and the commitment of the board of directors.

The control environment has been defined by the Institute of Internal Auditors as: 'The attitude and actions of the board and management regarding the significance of control within the organisation. The control environment provides the discipline and structure for the achievement of the primary objectives of the system of internal control.

The control environment includes the following elements:

– Management's philosophy and operating style.

– Organisational structure.

– Assignment of authority and responsibility.

– Human resource policies and practices.

– Competence of personnel.

(2) **Risk assessment**

There is a connection between the objectives of an organisation and the risks to which it is exposed. In order to make an assessment of risks, objectives for the organisation must be established. Having established the objectives, the risks involved in achieving those objectives should be identified and assessed, and this assessment should form the basis for deciding how the risks should be managed.

The risk assessment should be conducted for each business within the organisation, and should consider, for example:

- **internal factors,** such as the complexity of the organisation, organisational changes, staff turnover levels, and the quality of staff
- **external factors,** such as changes in the industry and economic conditions, technological changes, and so on.

The risk assessment process should also distinguish between:

- **risks that are controllable:** management should decide whether to accept the risk, or to take measures to control or reduce the risk
- **risks that are not controllable:** management should decide whether to accept the risk, or whether to withdraw partially or entirely from the business activity, so as to avoid the risk.

(3) **Control activities**

These are policies and procedures that ensure that the decisions and instructions of management are carried out. Control activities occur at all levels within an organisation, and include authorisations, verifications, reconciliations, approvals, segregation of duties, performance reviews and asset security measures. These control activities are commonly referred to as internal controls.

(4) **Information and communication**

An organisation must gather information and communicate it to the right people so that they can carry out their responsibilities. Managers need both internal and external information to make informed business decisions and to report externally. The quality of information systems is a key factor in this aspect of internal control.

(5) Monitoring

The internal control system must be monitored. This element of an internal control system is associated with internal audit, as well as general supervision. It is important that deficiencies in the internal control system should be identified and reported up to senior management and the board of directors.

COSO model applied to fraud prevention

The main elements of an internal control system should be in place for dealing with fraud. In general terms, managing the risks of fraud is similar to the management of other types of risk and consists of the following elements:

- **Control environment**. Management should show an active interest in the prevention and detection of fraud. There should also be a fraud policy statement on how to respond to suspicions of fraud, to ensure that timely and effective action is taken in a consistent manner, and that management responsibilities are clear. For example, should initial suspicions be reported to the line manager in whose area of operations the suspected fraud is taking place, or should the matter be reported to senior accounts management for investigation?

- **Risk recognition and assessment**
    - Identify risk areas. Management should identify those areas that are vulnerable to fraud risk.
    - Activities where the risks might be high include cash handling and payments, purchasing and payroll.

- **Assess the scale of the risk**. The scale of the risk depends on the probability of fraud and the size of potential losses if fraud occurs. It also depends on the measures that are already in place to prevent fraud, and their apparent effectiveness. The scale of the risk to be considered is the 'residual risk' after allowing for the existing control measures.

- **Control activities and procedures**. The responsibility for the management of each risk to specific individuals. Specific controls are suggested below.

- **Information: monitoring and reporting**. Information should be provided regularly to management so that they can monitor performance with respect to efficiency and effectiveness in achieving targets, economy and quality. Effective monitoring can detect certain types of fraudulent activity. A company might use internal auditors to investigate a problem, after line management have established the basic facts. Any risk of continuing fraud should be dealt with if possible, for example by halting further payments or changing operating procedures until the matter is resolved.

- **Monitoring activities and correcting deficiencies**
  - Identify the need for revised controls. The adequacy of existing controls should be evaluated. Where appropriate, the need for specific additional controls should be identified, to reduce or eliminate the risk of fraud.

  - Implement the revised controls.

  - Monitor the implementation of the revised controls, to assess their effectiveness. One way of doing this is to carry out an internal audit investigation.

'The risk management cycle should be treated as an iterative process. If the implementation of revised controls is not sufficient to eliminate the threat of fraud, then the cycle must begin again' (HM Treasury).

Operational features of internal control systems

There are considered to be three features of a sound internal control system:

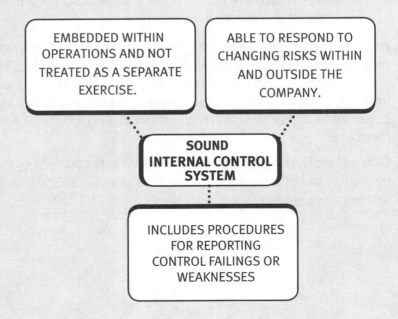

EMBEDDED WITHIN OPERATIONS AND NOT TREATED AS A SEPARATE EXERCISE.

ABLE TO RESPOND TO CHANGING RISKS WITHIN AND OUTSIDE THE COMPANY.

SOUND INTERNAL CONTROL SYSTEM

INCLUDES PROCEDURES FOR REPORTING CONTROL FAILINGS OR WEAKNESSES

More on sound internal control systems

The Turnbull guidance described three features of a sound internal control system:

- Firstly, the principles of internal control should be **embedded** within the organisation's structures, procedures and culture. Internal control should not be seen as a stand-alone set of activities and by embedding it into the fabric of the organisation's infrastructure, awareness of internal control issues becomes everybody's business and this contributes to effectiveness.

- Secondly, internal control systems should be capable of **responding quickly** to evolving risks to the business arising from factors within the company and to changes in the business environment. The speed of reaction is an important feature of almost all control systems. Any change in the risk profile or environment of the organisation will necessitate a change in the system and a failure or slowness to respond may increase the vulnerability to internal or external trauma.

- Thirdly, sound internal control systems include **procedures for reporting** immediately to appropriate levels of management any significant control failings or weaknesses that are identified, together with details of corrective action being undertaken. Information flows to relevant levels of management capable and empowered to act on the information are essential in internal control systems. Any failure, frustration, distortion or obfuscation of information flows can compromise the system. For this reason, formal and relatively rigorous information channels are often instituted in organisations seeking to maximise the effectiveness of their internal control systems.

4 The detail of controls

As discussed in the COSO model of internal control, specific control activities will be undertaken to reduce risks. Some examples of organisational controls include:

Segregation of duties

Most accounting transactions can be broken down into three separate duties: authorisation or initiation of the transaction, the handling of the asset that is the subject of the transaction, and the recording of the transaction. This reduces the risk of fraud and the risk of error.

For example, in the purchases system, the same individual should not have responsibility for:

- Making a purchase;
- Making the payment;
- Recording the purchase and payment in the accounts.

If one individual had responsibility for all of these activities they could record fictitious purchases (for personal use) and pay themselves for transactions that had not occurred, which is fraudulent.

Also segregation of duties makes it easier to spot unintentional mistakes.

Physical controls

Physical controls are measures and procedures to protect physical assets against theft or unauthorised access and use. They include:

- using a safe to hold cash and valuable documents;
- using a secure entry system to buildings or areas within;
- dual custody of valuable assets, so that two people are required to obtain access;
- periodic inventory checks;
- hiring security guards and using closed-circuit TV cameras.

Authorisation and approval

Authorisation and approval controls are established to ensure that a transaction must not proceed unless an authorised individual has given his approval, possibly in writing.

For **spending transactions**, an organisation might establish **authorisation limits**, whereby an individual manager is authorised to approve certain types of transaction up to a certain maximum value.

Management control

Controls are exercised by management on the basis of information they receive.

- **Top level reviews.** The board of directors or senior management might call for a performance report on the progress of the organisation towards its goals. For example, senior management might review a report on the progress of the organisation toward achieving its budget targets. Questions should be asked by senior management, prompting responses at lower management levels. In this way, top level reviews are a control activity.

- **Activity controls**. At departmental or divisional level, management should receive reports that review performance or highlight exceptions. Functional reviews should be more frequent than top-level reviews, on a daily, weekly or monthly basis. As with top-level reviews, questions should be asked by management that initiate control activity. An example of control by management is the provision of regular performance reports, such as variance reports, comparing actual results with a target or budget.

Supervision

Supervision is oversight of the work of other individuals, by someone in a position of responsibility. Supervisory controls help to ensure that individuals do the tasks they are required to and perform them properly.

Organisation

Organisation controls refer to the controls provided by the organisation's structure, such as:

- the separation of an organisation's activities and operations into departments or responsibility centres, with a clear division of responsibilities

- delegating authority within the organisation

- establishing reporting lines within the organisation

- co-ordinating the activities of different departments or groups, e.g. by setting up committees or project teams.

Arithmetic and accounting

Controls are provided by:

- recording transactions properly in the accounting system

- being able to trace each individual transaction through the accounting records

- checking arithmetical calculations, such as double-checking the figures in an invoice before sending it to a customer (sales invoice) or approving it for payment (purchase invoice) to make sure that they are correct.

Personnel controls

Controls should be applied to the selection and training of employees, to make sure that: suitable individuals are appointed to positions within the organisation; individuals should have the appropriate personal qualities, experience and qualifications where required; individuals are given **suitable induction and training**, to ensure that they carry out their tasks efficiently and effectively.

Staff should also be given **training** in the purpose of controls and the need to apply them. Specific training about controls should help to increase employee awareness and understanding of the risks of failing to apply them properly.

Remember that any controls you recommend in the exam should **cost less than the benefits** they bring. For example, you would not recommend the hiring of a security guard at £35,000 per annum to watch over the petty cash tin which held £100.

Test your understanding 1 – Types of control

Recommend the types of control that a company could put in place for the following risks:

(1) Shoplifting from a retail business.

(2) Goods being sent to customers but not invoiced.

(3) Poor quality supplies being purchased.

(4) Incorrect prices being charged.

Classification of controls

Controls can be understood as falling within three broad categories:

- Financial controls;
- Non-financial quantitative controls;
- Non-financial qualitative controls.

Financial controls

- These controls express financial targets and spending limits.
- Examples include
    - budgetary control
    - controls over sales, purchases, payroll and inventory cycles.

Sales cycle

Objectives of controls

The objectives of controls in the sales cycle are to ensure that:

- sales are made to valid customers
- sales are recorded accurately
- all sales are recorded
- cash is collected within a reasonable period.

Below is a summary of the sales cycle, showing examples of possible risks and the related controls:

Process	Risks	Control procedures
Receive an order.	Orders may be taken from customers that are unable to pay or unlikely to pay for a long time.	All new customers subject to credit check.
Goods are despatched to customer.	Incorrect goods may be sent to customers leading to loss of goodwill.	Pick goods using a copy of the customer's order.
Invoice is raised.	Invoices may be missed, incorrectly raised or sent to the wrong customer.	Checked that all goods delivered notes (GDNs) match an invoice.

Sale is recorded.	Invoiced sales may be inaccurately recorded.	Customer statements sent out (customers let you know if error).
Cash received.	Customer may not pay for goods.	Review aged debt listing and investigate (customer underpaid).
Cash recorded.	Cash received may be stolen.	Regular banking/physical security over cash (i.e. a safe).
Receive an order.	Orders may not be recorded accurately.	Confirm order back to customer (or) get all orders in writing.
	Orders may be taken from customers that are unable to pay or unlikely to pay for a long time = financial loss.	All new customers subject to credit check. Perform regular credit checks on existing customers. Credit limit check before order is accepted.
	Orders cannot be fulfilled and therefore customer goodwill is lost (and possibly the customer).	Check inventory system before issuing order. Automatic re-ordering system linked to customer order system.
Goods are despatched to customer.	Goods may not be despatched for orders made.	Use sequentially numbered customer order pads. Send a copy to the warehouse where they are filed numerically and sequence is checked to ensure that all are there (none missing).
	Incorrect goods may be sent to customers leading to loss of goodwill or goods may not be in inventory.	Pick goods using a copy of the customer's order. Get the copy signed by the picker as correct. When GDN is raised check it matches with the customer order (staple together and file). Get the customer to sign a copy of the GDN and return to the company. Use sequentially numbered GDNs, file a copy numerically and check that they are all there.

Invoice is raised.	Invoices may be missed, incorrectly raised or sent to the wrong customer.	Copy of sequentially numbered GDN sent to invoicing dept, stapled to copy of the invoice, checked all GDNs are there and having invoice to match.
	Credit notes may be raised incorrectly, missed or to cover cash being mis-appropriated.	On copy of the invoice sign as agreed to original order and GDN, signed as agreed to customer price list, signed as agreed it adds up properly.
		Credit notes to be allocated to invoice it relates.
		Authorised by manager and sequence check done on a regular basis.
Sale is recorded.	Invoiced sales may be inaccurately recorded, missed or recorded for the wrong customer.	Review receivables ledger for credit balances (paid for goods but no debtor recorded).
		Perform a receivables ledger reconciliation (check info in individual ledger matches that in nominal).
		Computer controls.
		Double check back to invoice.
		Perform receivables ledger control account reconciliation.
		Customer statements sent out (customers let you know if error).

Cash received.	Incorrect amounts may be received.	Agree cash receipt back to the invoice.
	Customer may not pay for goods.	Review receivables ledger for credit balances (customer overpaid).
		Review aged debt listing and investigate (customer underpaid).
		Review aged debt listing regularly, phone when overdue by 30 days, another letter at 45 days final letter threatening legal action at 60 days.
		Refer receivable to solicitor.
Cash recorded.	Cash maybe incorrectly recorded or recorded against the wrong customer account.	Customer statements.
		Perform a bank reconciliation.
		Customer statements.
	Cash received may be stolen.	Regular banking/physical security over cash (i.e. a safe).
		Reconciliation of banking to cash receipts records.
		Segregation of duties.

Bank and cash controls

Bank and cash

Objectives of controls

The objectives of controls over bank and cash are to ensure that:

- cash balances are safeguarded

- cash balances are kept to a minimum

- money can only be extracted from bank accounts for authorised purposes.

Below is a summary showing examples of possible risks to cash and bank accounts and the related controls:

| Cash is stolen from the premises. | Safes/strongroom/locked cashbox with restricted access. |

Tills emptied regularly.

| Money is taken from bank accounts for unauthorised purposes (i.e. stolen). | Restricted list of cheque signatories. |

Regular bank reconciliations reviewed by person with suitable level of authority.

Risks	**Control procedures**
Cash is stolen from the premises.	• Safes/strongroom/locked cashbox with restricted access.
	• Security locks.
	• Swipe card access.
	• Key access to tills.
	• Night safes.
	• Imprest system.
	• Use of security services for large cash movements.
	• People making bankings vary routes and timings.
	• Tills emptied regularly.
	• Frequent bankings of cash and cheques received.
Money is taken from bank accounts for unauthorised purposes (i.e. stolen).	• Restricted list of cheque signatories.
	• Dual signatures for large amounts.
	• Similar controls over bank transfers and on-line banking, e.g. secure passwords and pin numbers.
	• Cheque books and cheque stationery locked away.
	• Regular bank reconciliations reviewed by person with suitable level of authority.

Non-financial quantitative controls

- These controls focus on targets against which performance can be measured and monitored.

- Examples include
    - balanced scorecard targets
    - TQM quality measures

- It is important that a feedback loop exists:
    - performance target (standard) set
    - actual result recorded
    - compared with target
    - control action taken (if required).

Non-financial qualitative controls

- These form the day-to-day controls over most employees in organisations.

- Examples include
    - management control methods (such as organisation structure, contracts of employment)
    - physical controls
    - project management.

The Bribery Act

The Bribery Act is a type of non-financial control. It came in to force in the UK on 1st July 2011 and it is designed to bring the UK in line with international norms on anti-corruption legislation. It will make it a criminal offence to give or receive a bribe. It will also introduce a corporate offence of failing to prevent bribery.

The Serious Fraud Office will be able to prosecute both domestic and foreign companies, providing they have some presence in the UK. Bribes committed in the UK and abroad could be prosecuted under the Act.

Some experts have argued the new law could put British companies at a disadvantage as it goes further than similar legislation in other jurisdictions.

Individuals will face up to 10 years in prison and an unlimited fine if found guilty of committing bribery.

For example, a former court worker became the first person to be convicted under the Bribery Act 2010. He was jailed for six years having been convicted of bribery and misconduct in a public office after admitting that he received a bribe in his role as an administrative officer at a Magistrates' Court. The administrative officer pleaded guilty for requesting and receiving a £500 bribe to "get rid" of a speeding charge and to misconduct in public office for other similar offences. He was sentenced to three years for bribery and six years for misconduct in a public office, to be served concurrently.

5 Evaluation of an internal control system

Developing an adequate control system

The first step in designing an adequate control system is to ascertain the objectives of the system in question. For example, the system may be human resources and their objectives are many, but include sourcing, recruiting, training and retaining quality staff.

Secondly, research should be conducted regarding the current systems in place (if any) and communication with employees (questionnaires and interviews for example) would help to collate useful information.

Inputs to the process should be identified to check whether they meet the intended objective (or create the desired output). For example, the objective of retaining quality staff will not be met if , say, an appraisal process is not carried out whereby well-trained but unhappy staff repeatedly leave the company.

In order to work out whether the system currently works, the company should have a comparator set up, for example, a target labour turnover indicator. If this is met or surpassed then action should be taken since it demonstrates that the current system, in say HR, of retaining a certain level of staff, is not working.

In this example, the control system appears to work – it has identified a problem with labour turnover, however, it has also identified a problem in the HR process. This now needs to be resolved.

New controls can be implemented, such as regular appraisals – giving an employee a forum to discuss their job satisfaction, or setting up a new policy on staff welfare which might include an open-door policy, a whistleblowing policy or even just a suggestion box.

These new processes now also need controls putting in place. Again indicators that will be acted on are required. Appraisals need to be done for all staff on, say, a yearly basis. The number of suggestions put in the suggestion box needs to be logged and a record kept of the number which have been actioned.

A responsible individual then needs to ascertain whether these extra controls have led to a reduction in the number of leavers and whether this is now at a satisfactory level. If not, then further corrective action needs to be taken.

Costs v benefits

The internal control system of the business is no different to other business activities – the benefits of maintaining the system must outweigh the costs of operating it. As part of the monitoring process therefore management must consider the costs and benefits.

However, it can be difficult to quantify those costs and benefits as they are often not direct cash costs.

Costs of an internal control system will include:

- time of management involved in the design of the system
- implementation:
  - costs of IT consultants to implement new software
  - training all staff in new procedures
- maintenance of system:
  - software upgrades
  - monitoring and review.

Benefits are to be found in the reduction of the risks and achievement of business objectives.

Limitations of internal control systems

Warnings should be given regarding over-reliance on any system, noting in particular that:

- A good internal control system cannot turn a poor manager into a good one.
- The system can only provide reasonable assurance regarding the achievement of objectives – all internal control systems are at risk from mistakes or errors.
- Internal control systems can be by-passed by collusion and management override.
- Controls are only designed to cope with routine transactions and events.
- There are resource constraints in provision of internal control systems, limiting their effectiveness.

Test your understanding 2 – Race discrimination

Design a control system that addresses the risk of race discrimination in the work place.

Test your understanding 3 – Call centre

A credit card company has a call centre. Cardholders with queries or complaints call the centre by telephone, where they are dealt with by the first junior operator to respond to the call. The junior operators are required to deal with the customer's query or complaint if they can, and to refer more complicated problems to a senior operator.

When customers have a valid complaint about items incorrectly included in their monthly statement, the account details must be corrected, and inappropriate interest charges must be cancelled.

The costs of the centre are high, but the board of directors and senior management believe that providing a high quality service is essential to maintain the reputation of the company's brand name and the continued support of its customers.

Required:

As a person newly appointed to the role of manager of the call centre:

(a) Identify the components of an internal control system.

(b) Identify the main risks within the call centre and recommend the controls that should be implemented with respect of those risks.

Test your understanding 4 – Cliff

Day-to-day internal controls are important for all businesses to maximise the efficient use of resources and profitability.

Your firm has recently been appointed as auditor to Cliff, a private company that runs a chain of small supermarkets selling fresh and frozen food, and canned and dry food. Cliff has very few controls over inventory because the company trusts local managers to make good decisions regarding the purchase, sale and control of inventory, all of which is done locally. Pricing is generally performed on a cost-plus basis.

Each supermarket has a stand-alone computer system on which monthly accounts are prepared. These accounts are mailed to head office every quarter. There is no integrated inventory control, sale or purchasing system and no regular system for inventory counting. Management accounts are produced twice a year.

Trade at the supermarkets has increased in recent years and the number of supermarkets has increased. However, the quality of staff that has been recruited has fallen. Senior management at Cliff are now prepared to invest in more up-to-date systems.

Required:

(a) Describe the problems that you might expect to find at Cliff resulting from poor internal controls.

(b) Make FOUR recommendations to the senior management of Cliff for the improvement of internal controls, and explain the advantages and disadvantages of each recommendation.

Test your understanding 5 – SPD

SPD has been approached by Q, a specialist manufacturer of extremely expensive high performance cars. Q is in the process of developing a new car that will be one of the fastest in the world. The car will be designed to be driven on public roads, but the owners of such cars often take them to private race tracks where they can be driven at very high speeds.

Q has designed an electronics system to enable an average driver to drive the car safely at high speed. The system will monitor the engine, brakes and steering and will compensate for errors that could cause a crash. The system will, for example, sense that the car is about to skid and will compensate for that. The electronics system will be based on a circuit board that Q wishes to have built by SPD.

Building Q's circuit board will pose a number of challenges for SPD. The circuit board will be subject to a great deal of vibration when the car is driven at speed. The cars are expected to last for a very long time and so there could be problems if the circuit boards deteriorate with age. The circuit board will be installed in an inaccessible part of the car where it will be difficult to inspect or maintain.

Many of the components on the board will be manufactured by SPD, but some crucial components will be supplied by a third party that has already been selected by Q.

Required:

Discuss controls that should be in place to reduce the risks faced by SPD if they accept an order from Q.

Test your understanding 6 – Rhapsody Company

Rhapsody Co supplies a wide range of garden and agricultural products to trade and domestic customers. The company has 11 divisions, with each division specialising in the sale of specific products, for example, seeds, garden furniture, agricultural fertilizers. The company has an internal audit department which provides audit reports to the audit committee on each division on a rotational basis.

Products in the seed division are offered for sale to domestic customers via an Internet site. Customers review the product list on the Internet and place orders for packets of seeds using specific product codes, along with their credit card details, onto Rhapsody Co's secure server. Order quantities are normally between one and three packets for each type of seed. Order details are transferred manually onto the company's internal inventory control and sales system and a two part packing list is printed in the seed warehouse. Each order and packing list is given in a random alphabetical code based on the name of the employee inputting the order, the date and the products being ordered.

In the seed warehouse, the packets of seeds for each order are taken from specific bins and despatched to the customer with one copy of the packing list. The second copy of the packing list is sent to the accounts department where the inventory and sales computer is updated to show that the order has been despatched. The customer's credit card is then charged by the inventory control and sales computer. Irrecoverable debts in Rhapsody are currently 3% of the total sales.

Finally, the computer system checks that for each charge made to a customer's credit card account, the order details are on file to prove that the charge was made correctly. The order file is marked as completed confirming that the order has been despatched and payment obtained.

Required:

In respect of sales in the seeds division of Rhapsody Co

(a) identify and evaluate weaknesses in the sales system.

(b) provide a recommendation to alleviate each weakness.

Test your understanding 7 – Bassoon Ltd

Bassoon Ltd runs a chain of shops selling electrical goods all of which are located within the same country.

It has a head office that deals with purchasing, distribution and administration. The payroll for the whole company is administered at head office.

There are 20 staff at head office and 200 staff in the company's 20 shops located in high streets and shopping malls all over the country.

Head office staff (including directors) are all salaried and paid by direct transfer to their bank accounts.

The majority of the staff at the company's shops are also paid through the central salary system, monthly in arrears. However, some students and part time staff are paid cash out of the till.

Recruitment of head office staff is initiated by the department needing the staff who generally conduct interviews and agree the terms and conditions of employment. Bassoon has an HR manager who liaises with recruitment agencies, places job adverts and maintains staff files with contracts of employment, etc.

Shop managers recruit their own staff.

Shop staff receive a basic salary based on the hours worked and commission based on sales made.

The company has a fairly sophisticated EPOS (electronic point of sale) till system at all shops that communicates directly with the head office accounting system.

All staff when making a sale have to log on with a swipe card which identifies them to the system, and means that the sales for which they are responsible are analysed by the system and commissions calculated.

Store managers have a few 'guest cards' for temporary and part time staff, who generally do not receive commissions.

Store managers and regional supervisors are paid commissions based on the performance of their store or region. Directors and other head office staff usually receive a bonus at Christmas, depending on the company's performance. This is decided on by the board in consultation with departmental managers and put through the system by the payroll manager.

The payroll manager is responsible for adding joiners to the payroll and deleting leavers as well as for implementing changes in pay rates, tax coding and other deductions and for making sure that the list of monthly transfers is communicated to the bank.

The computerised payroll system is a standard proprietary system which is sophisticated enough to incorporate the commission calculations mentioned above which are fed in directly from the EPOS system.

The company employs an IT manager who is responsible for the maintenance of all IT systems and installing new hardware and software.

Required:

Identify the risks inherent in the payroll system at Bassoon Ltd and recommend any changes which you think are appropriate.

6 Chapter summary

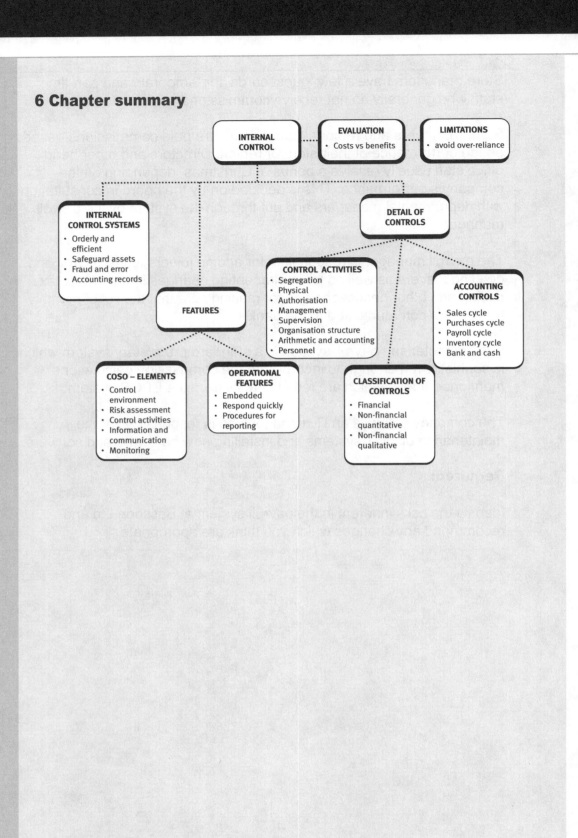

Test your understanding answers

Test your understanding 1 – Types of control

(1) **Shoplifting**

- CCTV cameras in the shop.
- Security tagging of products.
- Stock reconciliations to detect theft.
- Employment of security guards.

(2) **Goods not invoiced**

- Reconcile goods despatch notes to invoices.
- Check sequences of goods despatch notes and invoices.
- Segregation of duties between despatch and invoicing.
- Reconcile stock movement and sales figures.

(3) **Poor quality supplies**

- Inspection of all goods when received.
- Approval of suppliers who can supply high quality.

(4) **Incorrect prices**

- Arithmetic checks on invoices.
- Computer system control to ensure that every invoice is priced on current price levels.
- Authorisation of staff who can change price levels.

Test your understanding 2 – Race discrimination

Controls that should be in place to overcome the risk of race discrimination include an 'equality and diversity policy' which can include:

Training

All new employees should be made aware, during the induction process, of their rights and responsibilities with regards to equality and avoiding unlawful discrimination. The relevant policies should be available to all employees via Human Resources and will often be found on a company's intranet.

The company should provide additional written guidance to those likely to be involved in recruitment, selection, training or other relevant decision making, and the Human Resources team should provide direct advice whenever appropriate.

Employee responsibilities

Every employee should be required to assist the company to meet its commitment to provide equal opportunities in employment and avoid unlawful discrimination.

Employees should be held personally liable as well as, or instead of, the company for any act of unlawful discrimination. Employees who commit serious acts of harassment may be guilty of a criminal offence.

Acts of discrimination, harassment, bullying or victimisation against employees or customers should be disciplinary offences and be dealt with under the company's disciplinary procedure. Discrimination, harassment, bullying or victimisation may constitute gross misconduct and could lead to dismissal without notice.

Resolving concerns

If it is considered that someone may have been unlawfully discriminated against, they may use the company's grievance procedure to make a complaint. If the complaint involves bullying or harassment, they should also refer to the company's Dignity at Work Policy (if they have one).

The company should take any complaint seriously and seek to resolve any grievance which it upholds. The employee should not be penalised for raising a grievance, even if the grievance is not upheld, unless the complaint is both untrue and made in bad faith.

Monitoring and review

The policy should be monitored periodically by the company to judge its effectiveness and be updated in accordance with changes in the law. The company should also take steps to monitor the ethnic, gender and age composition of the existing workforce and of applicants for jobs, and the number of people with disabilities within these groups. The company should consider and take any appropriate action to address problems which may be identified as a result of the monitoring process.

The company cannot lawfully use what is referred to as "positive discrimination" in the selection of employees for recruitment or promotion, but should use appropriate lawful methods such as seeking to widen the pool of applicants, in order to address the under-representation of any group within particular types of job.

Test your understanding 3 – Call centre

(a) **Tutorial note:** A full solution is not given here, because a suitable answer is to reproduce the five elements of an internal control system identified by COSO:

- control environment
- risk assessment
- control activities (internal controls)
- information and communication
- monitoring.

(b) The controls within the call centre should relate to the major risks that have been identified. The main risks might be:

- dealing with customer queries or complaints incorrectly, and against the customer's interests (for example, failing to cancel interest charges when a complaint is justified)
- dealing with customer queries or complaints inefficiently
- by error or intentionally, reducing the balance on the customer's account by too much
- not being able to trace the details of a customer's previous call, in cases where the customer calls again to continue with a complaint
- unauthorised access to customer account details.

Suitable controls that should be in place might be as follows:

- All employees in the call centre should understand the importance of handling customer queries efficiently and correctly (i.e. treating the customer fairly, and resolving queries effectively).

- Organisation controls. There should be clear rules about how customer queries should be handled, and when they should be referred to a more senior person. If letters are sent to customers, there should be rules about who has the authority to sign the letters in the company's name.

- Operators should be supervised, to ensure that they are dealing with calls properly. Supervisors might listen in to calls at random, to carry out checks.

- The rules about authorisation of refunds to customers and the cancellation of interest charges should be applied properly. Authorisations to refund money should be signed at an appropriate level of seniority within the centre.

- Suitable individuals should be recruited as operators. For example, they should have a suitable 'manner' and 'voice' on the telephone.

- There should be a training system in place for training new junior operators and for grooming junior operators for a more senior position.

- Operators should have ready access to a set of operating rules and procedures.

- There should be an audit trail for calls, and all telephone calls should be recorded. Recorded calls should be retained for a suitable period of time.

- There should be controls over physical access to the call centre operations room, to prevent unauthorised access. The efficiency of the operators should be monitored by means of performance targets or efficiency standards. Performance reports should be sent regularly to the call centre manager.

- There might be some segregation of duties, to ensure that the individual who gives refunds to customers is not also responsible for updating the customer's account. This might provide a check on errors. (It is not clear in this situation whether the possibility of fraud exists, except through unauthorised access to customer account records).

Test your understanding 4 – Cliff

(a) Problems expected at Cliff: poor internal control

    (i) I would expect the company to experience some level of over-ordering, leading to reduced profitability as a result of inventory going past its `best before' date.

    (ii) Inventory that is not well-controlled in a supermarket may result in a breach of health and safety regulations which may result in fines or even closure of the supermarkets.

    (iii) I would expect there to be stock-outs leading to the potential loss of business to other supermarkets.

    (iv) I would expect there to be inefficiencies as a result of a lack of central ordering system resulting from quantity discounts not being obtained.

    (v) All of the problems noted above are likely to be exacerbated where local managers or staff are either inexperienced or possibly dishonest – the question states that poorer quality staff have been recruited recently.

    (vi) Supermarket inventory is very easily pilfered either by staff or customers even where it is well-controlled. The lack of regular inventory counts in particular means that pilferage is very easy to hide.

    (vii) I would expect there to be a lack of understanding in the business as a whole as to the availability of new products, products with high margins or other areas in which profitability might be improved.

(b) Four recommendations, explanation of advantages and disadvantages: improvements to internal control

Recommendation 1: that an integrated system be introduced across all supermarkets that links sales, purchases and inventory records.

Advantages

This would provide the company with an overall view of what inventory is held at any particular time, enable it to order centrally and reduce the scope for pilferage. It would result in reduced stock-outs and reduced inventory obsolescence.

Disadvantages

This would require considerable capital investment in hardware, software and training. It would also take control away from local managers which would almost certainly cause resentment.

Recommendation 2: the imposition of regular, or continuous inventory counting procedures together with the prompt update of inventory records for discrepancies found and investigation of the reason for the discrepancies.

Advantages

This would further reduce the possibility of stock-outs and provide evidence of over-ordering, which would enable purchasing patterns to be refined.

Disadvantages

There are costs in terms of staff time and, again, a certain level of resentment among staff who may feel that they are being `spied on', or that they are no longer trusted. Training would also be required and additional administrative work would need to be undertaken by local managers

Recommendation 3: that management accounts are produced on at least a quarterly basis, that figures relating to each supermarket are provided to head office on a monthly basis, and that an analysis is undertaken by head office on the performance of individual supermarkets and inventory lines.

Advantages

This would enable the company to determine which supermarkets are performing better than others. It would also enable the company to identify those inventory lines that sell well and those that are profitable.

Disadvantages

The production of more regular and detailed information will be time consuming. Local managers may feel that they are unable to service the particular needs of their customers if decisions are made on a global basis; customers may feel the same way.

Recommendation 4: that sales price decisions are made by head office.

Advantages

This would enable the company to experiment with the use of 'loss leaders', for example, and to impose a degree of consistency across supermarkets to prevent inappropriate pricing decisions being taken by local managers.

Disadvantages

Again, loss of control at a local level is likely to result in resentment and the possible loss of good staff. What sells well in one supermarket may not do so in another. To the extent that head office have less experience of local conditions than local staff, it is possible that inappropriate pricing decisions may be made by head office.

Test your understanding 5 – SPD

Reputation risk could be managed by actively warning drivers of the system's limitations. That could involve insisting that Q signs an acknowledgement that the system cannot prevent all crashes. This document should be kept in a safe place at SPD for future reference if need be. The warning could be repeated in the owner's handbook which should be signed for by the driver, and, again, a copy should be kept at SPD.

Any promotional material published by Q should stress that the system is designed to enable drivers to be even safer when driving within their limits but that responsibility for any failure cannot be accepted by SPD.

SPD could insist that the circuit board is designed to "fail safe" conditions. It could have a diagnostic routine programmed into it which will check that it is functioning correctly whenever it is switched on. In the event that this routine fails the circuit board will immobilise the engine. A contract drawn up by their solicitors would be required to absolve SPD of any blame for failure.

SPD should ask Q to accept responsibility for the work done by the third party and get this put in writing. Again a solicitor would need to deal with this. Any lost business due to delays or failures to meet delivery deadlines should be compensated. SPD will also have to insist on its own quality control procedures over this component. That may involve having the right to request details of the technical specification of the part and the subsequent testing of it on a regular basis.

Test your understanding 6 – Rhapsody Company

Tutorial note: It is not recommended that you lay out answers to examination questions in a tabular format such as that shown below. Full sentences and paragraphs will ensure that you explain points in enough detail to earn full marks.

Weakness	Evaluation of weakness	Recommendation
Recording of orders		
Orders placed on the Internet site are transferred manually into the inventory and sales system. Manual transfer of order details may result in information being transferred incompletely or incorrectly, for example, order quantities may be incorrect or the wrong product code recorded.	Customers will be sent incorrect goods resulting in increased customer complaints.	The computer systems are amended so that order details are transferred directly between the two computer systems. This will remove manual transfer of details limiting the possibility of human error.
Control over orders and packing lists		
Each order / packing list is given a random alphabetical code. While this is useful, using this type of code makes it difficult to check completeness of orders at any stage in the despatch and invoicing process.	Packing lists can be lost resulting either in goods not being despatched to the customer (if the list is lost prior to goods being despatched) or the customer's credit card not being charged (if lost after goods despatched but prior to the list being received in the accounts department).	Orders/packing lists are controlled with a numeric sequence. At the end of each day, gaps in the sequence of packing lists returned to accounts are investigated.

Obtaining payment

The customer's credit card is charged after despatch of goods to the customer, meaning that goods are already sent to the customer before payment is authorised.

Rhapsody Co will not be paid for the goods despatched where the credit company rejects the payment request. Given that customers are unlikely to return seeds, Rhapsody Co will automatically incur a bad debt.

Authorisation to charge the customer's credit card is obtained prior to despatch of goods to ensure Rhapsody Co is paid for all goods despatched.

Completeness of orders

The computer system correctly ensures that order details are available for all charges to customer credit cards. However, there is no overall check that all orders recorded on the inventory and sales system have actually been invoiced.

Entire orders may be overlooked and consequently sales and profit understated.

The computer is programmed to review the order file and orders where there is no corresponding invoice for an order, these should be flagged for subsequent investigation.

Test your understanding 7 – Bassoon Ltd

Tutorial note: It is not recommended that you lay out answers to examination questions in a tabular format such as that shown below. Full sentences and paragraphs will ensure that you explain points in enough detail to earn full marks.

Risks	Recommendation
Cash paid to part time staff (easier to misappropriate cash).	Apply the payroll system to all employees.
No control over the appointment of head office staff the HR Manager deals with (may recruit unnecessary staff).	Head office staff should be approved by the board.
No control over shop staff, the shop manager recruits own staff.	Should be approved by head office.
Guest cards, could be anybody and they could steal a card to access till at a later date to steal money.	A control system to monitor guest cards so management know who has a specific card.
Lack of segregation of duties, the payroll manager is responsible for all processing.	Split the responsibilities up, maybe get a manager to review the payroll manager's work.
In the question it states the IT manager is responsible for systems, but doesn't state there is restricted access.	Place passwords on the system and change them on a regular basis.

5

Management control systems

Chapter learning objectives

Lead	Component
A1. Evaluate control systems for organisational activities and resources.	(a) Evaluate appropriate control systems for the management of an organisation.
	(b) Evaluate the appropriateness of an organisation's management accounting control systems
	(c) Evaluate the control of activities and resources within an organisation.
	(d) Recommend ways in which identified weaknesses or problems associated with control systems can be avoided or solved.

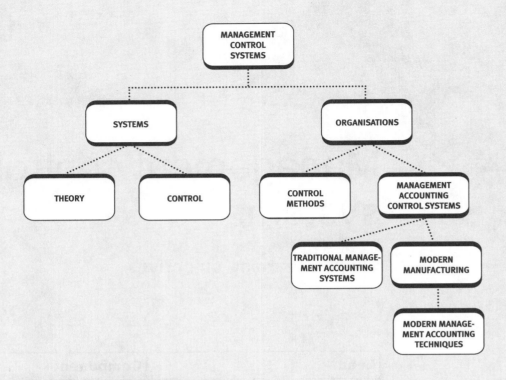

1 Organisations as systems

This section has been covered in your earlier studies and is here as a reminder.

- An organisation is a system in which people combine to carry out the purpose for which the organisation exists.
- Control makes an organisation function in a way that should enable it to meet its objectives.

Systems and their characteristics

- A system is a set of interacting components that operate together to accomplish a purpose.

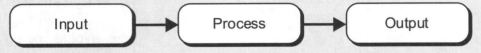

- There are inputs to a process which converts those inputs to outputs.
- All systems have these characteristics but some systems have other characteristics as well.

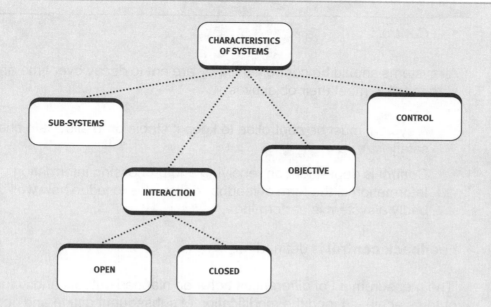

Systems theory

Systems theory is assumed knowledge from your earlier studies.

Definitions

- *Sub-systems*

Within a system there will usually be sub-systems. For example, if a company is a system, then the finance department is a sub-system. Within the finance department will be a sub-sub-system such as the management accounting system, and so on.

- *Closed systems*

These are systems that accept no input from the environment, are self-contained and cannot respond to change. These do not exist in business.

- *Open systems*

These are systems which accept inputs from their environment and provide output to the environment. They react to their environment, e.g. a company.

- *Objective*

A system must have an objective to function correctly. For example, a company's objective might be to maximise shareholder wealth. The objective allows the system to be monitored or controlled.

- *Control*

All systems should be controlled if they are not to decay over time and start to fail to meet their objectives.

- A system must be controlled to keep it stable or to allow it to change safely.
- Control is dependent on receiving and processing information. Information in the form of feedback allows us to judge how well or badly a system is performing.

Feedback control is defined as:

'The measurement of differences between planned outputs and actual outputs achieved, and the modification of subsequent action and / or plans to achieve future required results.' This is the more common type of control system.

Feedforward control is defined as:

'The forecasting of differences between actual and planned outcomes and the implementation of actions before the event to prevent such differences.'

Examples of a feedforward control system could be found in a budgeting system. A cash budget might predict that an overdraft will be required in a particular month. This could be organised in advance thereby avoiding any unauthorised overdraft charges. Or it may be that an adverse material price variance has arisen for several months in a row. Without feedforward control, this variance would continue. On investigation it may be due to the general price of the goods rising (feedback), and therefore the standard should be altered for future periods (feedforward). Therefore future prices paid are now compared to a more up to date standard. The action of changing the standard is an example of feedforward control. (Even better, the company should have anticipated the price rise and altered its standard already.)

Managers often spend more time on considering feedback. This is mainly because it is certain and can be quantified. Feedforward controls are often uncertain and accountants typically do not like dealing with the unknown. Changes will be continual and take up much management time which managers think might be better spent on other issues. Also frustrations will set in when management think they have resolved an issue only for the environment to change yet again and more time be required on the issue.

Any good manager should spend their time looking at the future of the business and consider the outside world, in conjunction with learning from aspects of the companies historic performance. Any manager who ignores feedforward control will contribute to the downfall of a company.

Primary feedback could be reported to line management in the form of control reports, comparing actual and budgeted results. If the variances are small or can be corrected easily then the information may not be fed back to anyone higher in the organisation.

Secondary feedback is where feedback is sent to a higher level in an organisation and can lead to a plan being reviewed and possibly changed; for example, the revision of a budget after large variances were discovered due to price changes over time.

Negative feedback is feedback taken to reverse a deviation from standard. This could be by amending the inputs or process so that the system reverts to a steady state; for example, a machine may need to be reset over time to its original settings.

Positive feedback is feedback taken to reinforce a deviation from standard. The inputs or process would not be altered.

Open loop systems are where there is scope within the control mechanism for outside involvement; for example, a manager might decide what action should be taken from, say, three options.

Closed loop systems are where the control action is automatic, for example, the thermostat on a central heating system.

Systems within an organisation

The company that you work for is a system incorporating many sub-systems, sub-sub-systems and so on. Materials, labour, machines and finance are inputs into a process, say food manufacture, which produces outputs, which in this case would be food.

The accounts department within this company is an example of a sub-system. The accounts department has inputs – labour, IT, etc. which process information to output the management and financial accounts amongst other things.

Within the accounts department itself there will be sub-systems. For example, there will probably be a system in place for operating the receivables ledger. Particular staff will be responsible for inputting certain data regarding sales and cash received, the computer will process it, and one of the outputs – aged receivables, might be used as an input to another process – debt collection, where that department has its own processes.

This shows that there are many, many systems within a company and all of them will be linked.

Without control a company will perform very badly. For example, if customers knew there were no controls to identify they hadn't paid (the aged receivables list), or that debt collectors wouldn't chase the debt, then customers would buy goods with no intention of payment and the company would certainly go bust. This could be said of many of the controls in all organisations – they are there to ensure that the companies objectives will be met, which is often profit maximisation.

The airline industry

British Airways (BA) promotes itself as a world leading airline, providing a quality service. It has not performed well in the past and was criticised for operating almost as a closed system.

In 1980 fuel prices for BA and its competitors increased by 70% per annum and many unprofitable routes were dropped. In 1984 the Civil Aviation Authority issued a white paper demanding a reduction in BA's routes which lead to several routes being provided by competitors. BA was accused of being reactionary to these events which appeared to take it by surprise.

The business model for airlines was fairly similar. Pricing reflected little competition and the only real differentiators between airlines were around reputation, largely a result of airline safety records. Having little competition leads to complacency and BA could be accused of this, operating as though it was almost in a closed system with little regard for what was happening in the outside world.

Around 1985 the Ryan family identified a gap in the market for a low cost European airline (Ryanair) and initially challenged BA and Aer Lingus to offer a low cost Dublin to London flight. Ryanair's passenger numbers increased from 5,000 to 82,000 in a year taking most of its custom from BA.

When applying the management control model to a conventional airline such as BA, primary control would be exercised through cost control over employment costs, fuel prices, the cost of acquiring aircraft, maintenance expenses, etc. Much of this would be performed via budgets and variance analysis which is a form of feedback control.

Secondary control can be exercised, typically through changing objectives or standards, such as varying prices, altering financial and non-financial targets. This is a example of feedforward control - where the future is considered and targets and objectives are altered so that changes in the future business environment are factored into the business model.

Amending the predictive model is a form of learning from past experience. If for example certain routes are more profitable and some less profitable or unprofitable, resources are shifted towards the more profitable routes and unprofitable ones are closed. This is what BA did - feedback had been received indicating they would not meet their objectives and so feedforward control was exercised by making changes for the future. One of these changes was when BA launched their own low cost airline 'Go' in 1998.

Ryanair and Easyjet responded by cutting their prices further, selling seats for the price of £1 plus taxes and charges, and BA decided from its feedback that they could not compete. In 2001 they sold Go due to its inability to compete with Ryanair and Easyjet on this low cost basis. (Also to some extent Go conflicted with BA's objective of being a higher quality airline and customers were confused.)

The introduction of low cost airlines such as EasyJet and Ryanair has changed the business model for airlines completely. Some of the changes introduced have been:

- Selling seats via the Internet rather than through travel agents. BA followed Ryanair's lead.

- Yield management with variable prices depending on capacity utilisation. Most airlines do this these days.

- Using lower cost, out-of-town airports. BA still differentiates by using central airports and charging for the convenience.

- No printed tickets, seat allocations, or free meals and drinks. Although many airlines offer these facilities at an extra charge.

- No exceptions policies to reduce the cost of handling exceptions (e.g. no flexibility for passengers who arrive late).

- Fast turnaround times for aircraft to improve utilisation.

These changes have reduced costs (inputs); changed processes such as turnaround times and yield management for pricing; and the predictive model (most certainly that of BA) that perceived that customers would only book through travel agents, fly from central airports, demand seat allocations and meals, etc., has been dramatically altered.

EasyJet and Ryanair have focused on the short-haul market which has grown as a result of lower prices, rather than compete head-on with the major long-haul airlines. It is the latter market segment that has been significantly affected by the reduction in international travel over recent years. Consequently, the profit declines in the major airlines are contrasted with the generally successful performance of the low cost airlines, although in the last few years even these airlines have begun to come under increasing competitive pressure from each other and Ryanair's financial performance has deteriorated.

BA has since had many other challenges to overcome – frequent strikes by their cabin crew despite being the highest paid staff in the world, reduced flyers after September 11th and increasing fuel prices. To counter this, feedforward control has been used and BA has been 're-engineered' to some extent – this has included cost cutting, consolidation of the airline industry and alliances between some of the major operators to share routes, new livery (which wasn't very successful), and cabin restructuring to offer fewer first-class seats and more World Traveller (economy) seats. It appears that BA are much more forward thinking than they used to be and are faring as well as many other major long-haul airlines in these times of recession. However, they paid a big price back in the 1980's for not assessing the outside environment, listening to their customers and missing an opportunity to become an early provider of a low cost airline. If they had spent more time using feedforward control this might have been avoided.

2 Control in organisations

It is necessary to consider how management control systems operate and to ensure that businesses achieve their objectives.

- **Management control** is defined as 'the process of guiding organisations into viable patterns of activity in a changing environment'.

- **Management control systems** are defined as 'the processes by which managers attempt to ensure that their organisation adapts successfully to its changing environment'.

These definitions are both about adapting to changing environments and therefore management control systems must be a variety of open systems that change over time.

If the control systems are to be successful, management must always be monitoring the way the system operates and how the system could be changed to improve its performance.

At the highest level, one way of controlling a business is by controlling directors' remuneration.

3 Directors' remuneration

Remuneration is defined as payment or compensation received for services or employment and includes basic salary, bonuses and any other economic benefits.

Behavioural impact

Whatever remuneration package is determined, it is essential to ensure that the directors' objective is to do a good job for the stakeholders of the company.

The remuneration package should be motivational, not too small or too easily earned. The remuneration committee should design a package that attracts, retains and motivates the director. This should take in to account the market rate i.e. comparable companies remuneration packages.

Components of the directors' remuneration package

- Basic salary – covering the job itself, the skills required, the directors' performance, their contribution to company strategy and market rates;

- Performance-related pay – remuneration dependent on the achievement of some performance measure. This could be short-term e.g. a bonus paid to the director at the end of the accounting year for achieving a certain level of profit or earnings per share, or long-term e.g. executive stock options. Stock/share options are contracts that allow the director to buy shares at a fixed price. If the share price rises above the exercise price the director can sell the shares at a profit. This encourages the director to manage the company in such a way that the share price increases, therefore share options are believed to align the directors' goals with those of the shareholders. Problems arise when the directors' actions are solely focussed on the share price to the exclusion of other stakeholder objectives. Also, if the share price rises too much the director could be tempted to sell their shares and retire, which defeats the objective of trying to tie the director in to the company for the long-term.

- Pension contributions – the remuneration committee should consider the pension consequences of increases in basic salary;

- Benefits in kind – are various non-wage compensations e.g. a company car, or health insurance.

Share (stock) options

Bonuses to directors based on the current year's profit can lead to short termism, in that the directors will maximise the current year's profit by not investing in new products and not developing existing ones (these costs would reduce the current year's profit). Not investing in new products and not developing existing ones will adversely affect future profits and may threaten the long-term existence of the business.

It is argued that share options are an effective way of paying directors and of avoiding short-termism, as the value of a share should be a reflection of the long-term profitability of the company.

Until recently, there has been no charge in the company's profit and loss account for share options, so the shareholders are not aware of the value of the options granted to the directors. However, share options can be very valuable to directors. Excluding the cost of share options from the financial statements understates directors' remuneration.

The grant date is the date when the employee and employer enter into an agreement that will entitle the employee to receive an option on a future date, provided certain conditions are met.

The service date is the date or dates on which the employee performs the services necessary to become unconditionally entitled to the option.

The vesting date is the date when the employee, having satisfied all the conditions becomes unconditionally entitled to the option.

The exercise date is when the option is taken up.

Normally, the option is granted at the market price of the shares at the grant date (e.g. 250p a share). If, at the exercise date of, say, 30 June 2010, the value of the shares is 290p, the director will buy the shares from the company for £2,500,000 and immediately sell them in the market for £2,900,000, making a gain of £400,000. If the value of the shares is less than 250p on 30 June 2010, the director will not purchase the shares (as he/she would make a loss), so the director's gain on the option will be zero.

Interestingly, most directors of UK listed companies buy and sell the shares at the exercise date (30 June 2010 in this case). Only a small minority of directors buy the shares at the option price and continue to hold them.

Share options as a measure of long-term profitability

The 'theory' of share options is that the share price on 30 June 2010 will be based on the company's long term profitability, so if the company is doing well, the share price will be higher and the director's profit on buying the shares (and subsequently selling them) will be higher. So the director's gain on selling the shares will reflect the director's success in increasing the long-term profits and hence the share price of the company.

To a certain extent, this 'theory' is correct in that the share price tends to increase if the company's profitability increases. However, share price movements also depend on other factors, such as the general price movement of other shares and investors' views about the future profitability and growth in the particular type of trade the company is in. For instance, in late 1999 and early 2000 there was an enormous increase in the value of telecom and dot.com shares, yet many of these companies had never made a profit. Thus, the increase in the share price did not depend on the profitability of the companies, and it could be argued that the prices of these shares increased because this was a fashionable sector of the market in which to invest. At the same time as the increase in value of telecom and dot.com shares there was a substantial fall in the value of other shares, including well-known retailers. Sometimes, share prices were falling, despite the fact that the companies profits were increasing. So, it can be seen that the increase in the share price of a company may be more related to market conditions than its long-term profitability. Thus, awarding options on shares may not be a very effective way of paying directors, as the change in the share price may have little to do with profitability of the company and the directors' contribution to increasing those profits.

Regarded as a way of boosting productivity and employee retention, share options have become less popular since the economy turned bearish. Fuelled in the late 90s by dot com promises of untold future wealth, option holding employees had little or no prospect of realising any value. When the economy suffered, staff became more interested in staying in progressive, well-paid jobs with quantifiable packages, so there has been less reason to implement schemes. (Some employers had been accused of using share options for employees as a way to pay salaries of less than the market rate.)

Microsoft recently ended its own option scheme. It decided to grant shares instead (not options on shares), explaining this practice is recorded on balance sheets, giving analysts a better view of the company's financial state and workers a tangible incentive.

To compound matters, the International Accounting Standards Board proposes firms put the cost of share-based awards through the income statement.

Remuneration policy – The Sage Group plc

The following is an extract of the Remuneration Report (2011) of The Sage Group plc:

'Remuneration Policy

The Remuneration Committee, in setting the remuneration policy, recognises the need to be competitive in an international market. The Committee's policy is to set remuneration levels which ensure that the executive directors are fairly and responsibly rewarded in return for high levels of performance. Remuneration policy is designed to support key business strategies and to create a strong, performance orientated environment. At the same time, the policy must attract, motivate and retain talent... The Remuneration Committee considers that a successful remuneration policy must ensure that a significant part of the remuneration package is linked to the achievement of stretching corporate performance targets... generating a strong alignment of interest with shareholders... Around 75% of each executive's total compensation value is delivered through performance-related incentives, and is therefore 'at risk' if stretching performance targets are not reached...

Performance Share Plan (PSP)

The Committee established the PSP as the Group's main long-term equity incentive to drive financial and market performance... The individual limit on award levels under the Plan is 300% of salary. PSP awards will normally have a maximum value of 210% of salary. This represents a 'core' award to the value of 140% of salary, which, if maximum EPS (earnings per share) growth is attained, and TSR (total shareholder return) performance is ranked upper quartile against the comparator group, could rise to 210% of salary...

A sliding scale based on EPS is used. 25% of the award vests at the end of the period if the increase in EPS exceeds RPI (retail prices index) by 9% over the period; 100% of the award vests at that time only if RPI is exceeded in that period by 27%...

Awards are also subject to a TSR 'multiplier' whereby the level of vesting based on EPS achievement is adjusted according to TSR performance over the same three year period compared with a group of international software and computer services companies.' (These include Adobe Systems, Cap Gemini, Microsoft, Oracle, SAP amongst others.)

The Report goes on to detail audited information including outstanding awards granted to each director under the PSP. For example, the Chief executive Officer's details were:

	Awarded 1 Oct 2010 number	Awarded during the year number	Vested during the year number	Lapsed during the year number	Awarded 30 Sept 2011 number	Vesting date
G S Berruyer	361,647	–	(95,167)	(266,480)	–	3 March 2011
	745,649	–	–	–	745,649	3 March 2012
	507,280	–	–	–	507,280	4 March 2013
	–	737,795	–	–	737,795	10 March 2014
Total	1,614,576	737,795	(95,167)	(266,480)	1,990,724	

- ' The market price of a share on 10 March 2011, the date of the awards made in the year ended 30 September 2011 was 272.1p.

- The market price of a share on 3 March 2011, the date the above awards vested in the year ended 30 September 2011 was 280.8p. The market price of a share on 3 March 2008, the date on which these awards were granted was 202.25p.'

As you will be able to calculate from the illustration, the awards are well-worth receiving if company performance meets the targets set. The targets are reasonably straightforward, there being only two – EPS and TSR; however, the calculation of the award does become reasonably complicated.

The time period for tie-in is 3 years which is in line with the UK stock exchange listing rules/the UK Corporate Governance Code, whereby directors should get a reasonable time to prove themselves but not so long that the company cannot refresh the Board should it wish to.

Performance target setting

One factor within any discussion of control systems is that there must be some standards of performance if the system is to operate successfully. The standards of performance allow the feedback loops discussed earlier to work.

- An effective control system must incorporate a feedback loop such as:
  - performance target (standard) set
  - actual result recorded
  - compared with target
  - control action taken (if required).

- If managers are to be controlled successfully then the standards set must be sufficiently varied to ensure that the manager works in the best interests of the company. The standards set can be:
  - **Financial:** These would be based on information supplied by the management accounting system and are often financial ratios, but they have the problem of being historic-looking and short-term.

  - **Non-financial:** These are measures that consider other factors such as customer perception, research and development, production efficiency or staff satisfaction. These measures are very important to help managers focus on long-term future performance.

Behavioural implications of management accounting control systems

When structuring the control system, companies must take account of the behavioural aspects of setting performance targets and standards. As with any control reporting system, there is a risk of unintended behavioural consequences.

A basic assumption should be that if a manager's performance is judged according to success or failure in achieving one or more specific targets or budget figures, the main concern of the manager will be to succeed in achieving the target. Missing a specific target would be a sign of failure. The focus of managers on performance targets will be even greater if the reward system is based on achieving them.

Focusing on performance targets or the profits or return on investment for the responsibility centre might have the following consequences:

- If the manager's performance targets are budget targets, he will **concentrate on budgeted results** to the exclusion of longer-term considerations and objectives.

- If the manager's performance targets are exclusively financial targets, the manager will **ignore non-financial considerations**.

- If the manager's performance is judged exclusively by profit or return, he might be tempted to **ignore the risks**, and take high-risk decisions in the hope of boosting profits. The risk exposures from such decisions might not be justified by the size of the expected profits.

- The manager will be more concerned about the results of his own centre rather than those of the organisation as a whole. As a consequence, the manager might make decisions that are damaging to the interests of the organisation because they will improve the performance of his own centre.

- Responsibility centre managers might get into **disputes** with each other **about transfer prices**. Transfer prices for inter-divisional transactions do not affect the profits of the organisation as a whole, but do affect the profits of each of the profit centres or investment centres involved. Arguments about transfer prices could result in a refusal by profit centre managers to co-operate with each other, and decisions to sell to or buy from the external market, when its inter-divisional transactions would benefit the organisation more.

- If the targets set for responsibility centre managers are too ambitious, the control system could be **demotivating**, when it should provide an incentive or motivation to improve performance. A criticism of ideal standard costs, for example, is that they are unattainable. If ideal standard costs are set (or if budget targets are too challenging) managers might be discouraged by the adverse performance reports he receives.

- When performance targets are financial targets, there might be opportunities for a centre manager to **manipulate short-term costs or profits**, for example by recognising revenue early or deferring costs to a later period.

- When managers participate in setting their own budget for the next financial year, and they are judged according to whether they succeed in keeping expenditure within budget limits, there will be a strong temptation to build '**padding**' or '**slack**' into the budget expenditure estimates. In other words, the manager might try to budget for more expenditure than is actually needed, to that it will be much easier to meet budget targets (and be rewarded accordingly).

Management accounting control systems

- A **management accounting control system** can be defined as an information system that helps managers to make planning and control decisions.

- All management accounting control systems differ as the circumstances of businesses always differ and the systems are designed to meet the needs of the business.

Designing a management accounting control system

- Even though the systems differ between businesses there are common factors that should be considered in the design of the systems.

There are a number of things to be considered when establishing the structure of management accounting control systems:

Organisational structure

Organisations operate through a variety of organisational forms, such as:

- functional

- divisional

- matrix

- network

The form of structure that is adopted will determine the type of control processes implemented throughout the business.

Organisational structures

Functional structure

Functional structures are usually found in smaller organisations, or within individual divisions in a larger organisation with a divisional structure. They are organised by department .e.g. production, purchasing, sales, accounts.

Advantages include:

- Decisions are easier to co-ordinate as there is only one point of contact;

- The quality of decisions should be higher due to the managers' skills and expertise;
- This structure might be cheaper due to the reduced number of managers compared to other structures;
- Decisions can be taken more quickly;
- Policies and procedures can be standardised more easily company-wide.

Disadvantages include:

- Growth is limited;

Managers may become over worked and control lost as the company grows.

Divisional structure

Where the functionally structured business grows by diversification into new products or new markets, a functional structure will be inappropriate, and the divisional structure based on products, services or geographical areas is likely to be adopted.

Each division is responsible for its own functions in relation to a related group of products. Thus, each division may be regarded as a Strategic Business Unit (SBU). In this organisation:

- corporate strategic planning takes place at central board level
- divisional planning is concerned with developing a portfolio of products
- operational planning is at the functional level within divisions.

Advantages of a divisional structure include:

- Greater awareness of local issues by managers;
- Makes diversification easier;
- Avoidance of excessive workload for top management;
- Helps in the allocation of management responsibility;
- Increased motivation for divisional management;
- Faster decision-making;
- Controls, performance measurement and accountability are more specific to the division.

Disadvantages of a divisional structure include:

- Loss of control by top management;
- Lack of goal congruence;
- Loss of divisional motivation due to management charges and transfer pricing;
- Difficulty in measuring the divisions success due to its lack of independence from the rest of the company.

Matrix structure

The matrix structure is a two-dimensional structure combining both a functional and divisional structure, for example product, service or geographical divisions and functional areas, in order to capitalise on combinations of expertise that exist in the organisation, but which are stifled by normal hierarchical structures.

An example might include a food manufacturer who supplies to food retailers such as Tesco and Sainsbury. These food retailers may be such important customers that the food manufacturer assigns, say, an account manager to each of Tesco and Sainsbury.

Advantages of this structure include:

- It should improve communication within the company;
- It allocates management responsibility for end-results and not just processes;
- It allows inter-disciplinary co-operation, mixing skills and expertise;
- It should keep the customer happy via a specific point of contact in case of any queries or problems.

Disadvantages include:

- Conflicts between functional or account managers can arise;
- Employees with two or more managers are more likely to become stressed;
- The more complex structure can be more costly due to the number of 'managers' there will be;
- The company structure can become very complex with confusion over roles.

Network structure

Network structures exist where an organisation depends on relationships with other external organisations. There are a number of other important forms of networks:

- Outsourcing and strategic alliances.

- Networks of experts which come together for a particular project.

- Teleworking, where individuals are based in different locations but work together through the use of information technology. For example, Kaplan Publishing employ writers of their material who live all over the UK. They work mainly from home (meeting occasionally at events such as the CIMA conference) but use the internet, intranet, telephone, webcam and tools such as Skype to keep in touch on a daily basis.

- One-stop-shops, where a group of organisations are co-ordinated centrally so that there is one contact point for the customer with the aim of providing a comprehensive and seamless service.

- Service networks, where the members of the network provide services to customers through any other members of the network.

An example of a network structure includes the writing of this text book - Kaplan Publishing wrote the book in conjunction with the CIMA examiner and Elsevier (another publishing company). This was a network of experts on the subject of Performance Strategy who came together for the purpose of writing this text book.

Advantages of this structure include the wider availability of experts for the project.

However, disadvantages can include poor communication and feedback due to the geographical dispersion of the experts.

Responsibility accounting

- A key aspect of management accounting control systems is that the information presented must be given to the managers who are responsible for it.

- Responsibility accounting tries to ensure that managers are only held responsible for activities that are under their control. This is known as the **principle of controllability**.

- If managers are appraised on factors outside their control, they will become demotivated.

Performance measures for investment centres might be:

- return on investment (ROI)

- residual income, and

- economic value added or EVA®.

The **return on investment** (ROI) for an investment centre is similar to the return on capital employed (ROCE) for an organisation as a whole. It is calculated for a particular period as follows:

$$ROI = \frac{\text{Profit before interest and tax}}{\text{Operations management capital employed}} \times 100$$

(CIMA Official Terminology)

Residual income is a measure of the profitability of an investment centre after deducting a notional or imputed interest cost. This interest cost is a notional charge for the cost of the capital invested in the division.

Residual income = Accounting profit – Notional interest on capital

(1) Accounting profit is calculated in the same way as for ROI.

(2) Notional interest on capital = the capital employed in the division multiplied by a notional cost of capital or interest rate. The selected cost of capital could be the company's average cost of funds (cost of capital). However, other interest rates might be selected, such as the current cost of borrowing, or a target ROI.

Economic value added (EVA®) is discussed later in the chapter.

Traditional management accounting systems

The traditional management accounting systems that have been employed by businesses have included techniques such as:

- Standard costing, budgeting and variance analysis.

- Overhead allocation: labour hour and machine hour costing systems.

- Capital investment appraisal (such as NPV, IRR, ARR).

- Transfer pricing.

- Rewards and appraisal based on financial/management accounts.

These methods have all been considered in your earlier studies.

Criticisms of traditional management accounting systems.

Despite their continuing popularity in many businesses, all these methods have been criticised for a number of reasons:

- Systems are often too formal. They produce routine pre-set information whereas managers require more on-demand adaptable information.

- Some assumptions they make are questionable, for example treating labour costs as a variable cost when in the short-term they are really a fixed cost.

- The systems are very cumbersome (for example, budgets are time-consuming) and produce information of little value.

- Traditional systems view many costs as production costs, when in reality they are overhead costs of businesses.

- The systems may not take account of the business strategy. They tend to focus on low cost, hence not assisting a business that wants to differentiate itself and produce very high quality.

More on criticisms of traditional systems

Management accounting techniques have increasingly failed to provide management with the key information they need to make decisions, because the simplistic techniques of the past have no place in the modern industrial and commercial environment. In particular, reporting systems based on detailed inventory valuations do not provide information of value to IT-intensive and capital-intensive organisations.

Traditional management accounting is essentially short-term in outlook and focused largely on short-term profit maximisation. Management, in contrast, should be thinking of the longer-term as well as the short-term and about non-financial as well as financial factors.

There are other criticisms of management accounting systems:

- Management accounting reporting systems can be too formal and based on routine performance reports for each control period. With modern IT systems, managers expect access to up-to-date information on demand, rather than having to wait until the formal reports are prepared.

- Some assumptions in management accounting are unrealistic. For example, it is unrealistic to treat direct labour costs as a variable cost. Most labour costs are fixed because, unless they work overtime, employees are usually paid a fixed amount each week or month for a given number of hours of attendance.

- Many cost accounting systems are too cumbersome, and involve a lot of work to produce information of questionable value.

- Traditional cost accounting systems focus on direct production costs. Overheads might be absorbed into cost at a rate per direct labour hour or as a percentage of direct labour cost (absorption costing) or treated as a period charge and written off as expenditure in the income statement (marginal costing). However, in a modern manufacturing and commercial environment, the largest proportion of costs are indirect costs. Management accounting control systems therefore need to provide management with more information about overhead costs, with a view to understanding how they are incurred and how they can be controlled.

- Commercial organisations might pursue a strategy of being the lowest-cost, lowest price producer in the market. Alternatively, they might seek to differentiate their products (or services) in order to charge higher prices. Management accounting systems that focus on cost reduction might be suitable for a low-cost producer, but do not necessarily provide the information to assist managers in companies that seek to differentiate themselves. Quality of product or service, for example, can be a key issue.

Beyond budgeting

It has been argued that the entire budgeting process is limiting and unsuitable for business planning and control, and budgeting systems should be abandoned.

The argument for abolishing budgets, referred to as **'beyond budgeting'**, was put forward by Hope and Fraser (Management Accounting, December 1997).

Their criticisms of budgeting are:

- Budgets are a **commitment**. They therefore act as a **constraint** on doing anything different. However, in a fast-changing business environment, budgets are based on assumptions that will soon become out-of-date. It would be much better to measure performance against challenging but achievable strategic targets, rather than detailed short-term targets.

- Traditional budgets are seen as a **mechanism for top-down control** by senior management. It strengthens the chain of command, when organisations should be empowering individuals in the 'front line'.

- Traditional budgets **restrict flexibility** because individuals feel they are expected to achieve the budget targets. This is a deterrent to continual improvement (and so is inconsistent with TQM).

- Budgeting **reinforces the barriers between departments**, instead of encouraging a sharing of knowledge across the organisation.

- Budgets are **bureaucratic**, **internally-focused** and **time-consuming**. What is needed is a flexible approach, with managers looking forward and at the business environment, and not wasting their time on needless formal planning exercises.

Modern manufacturing methods

- The concept of being competitive in industry has changed significantly in recent years, the accepted truths of efficiency have been changed fundamentally due to a number of factors.

- As a result of the change in the manufacturing environment the type of information and control systems that must be employed by the organisation have altered.

Traditional manufacturing

- standardisation of product
- long production runs
- 'acceptable' level of quality
- slow product development

Modern manufacturing

- globalisation
- competition
- JIT and TQM
- 'intelligent machines'

Traditional aims of a manufacturing organisation.

Aims in the past may have included the following:

(1) Standardisation of product, the product must be capable of being made in a continuous process, in the past this has meant that each unit of a batch of products must be identical.

(2) Long production runs, to minimise downtime when changing machinery it made sense to produce many items of a single design before re-calibrating machinery.

(3) Producing to an acceptable level of quality, the level being that which the market would accept in relation to the savings made from mass manufacture.

(4) Relatively slow product development to ensure that investment in new products and machinery were fully amortised.

Each was a logical extension of the benefits arising from mass production, but in hindsight appear unacceptable.

Major impacts on manufacturing philosophy.

In recent years the impact of 'globalisation' has led to the reduction in trade barriers and the improvement of trade links. This means that competition is not only from local companies but from around the globe. In order to compete industry has had to change the manner in which it does business. The main competition has come from Japan and other East Asian economies where the approach to manufacturing was quite different. These included the use of the following techniques and philosophies such as, just-in-time (JIT), total quality management (TQM) and value analysis (economic value added (EVA)). Finally, manufacturing has been affected by the introduction of computerisation. This has had two key impacts:

(1) The introduction of 'intelligent' machines that are capable of doing a range of different jobs without constant labour supervision. This is best illustrated by considering such technological advances as Computer Aided Design (CAD), Computer Aided Manufacture (CAM), Computer Integrated Manufacture (CIM) and Flexible Manufacturing Systems (FMS). These were all covered in your earlier studies.

(2) The vastly improved ability of computers to track and record all aspects of the workplace due to faster processing and dramatically reduced cost of installation. The difficulty does not lie with how to collect data, that is now cheap and relatively easy to do. Instead the question is what data do we collect and how do we use it.

What is world-class manufacturing?

It is simply a level of competence in a number of areas that allows the company to compete with the best in the world. These areas include:

- Cost.
- Quality.
- Customer focus.
- Flexibility.

Just-in-time (JIT)

- This is a technique for the organisation of work flows, to allow rapid, high-quality, flexible production whilst minimising manufacturing waste and stock levels.

- It was originally considered as a stock control system, but it is rather more involved than this.

- The JIT system can be applied to both production and purchasing.

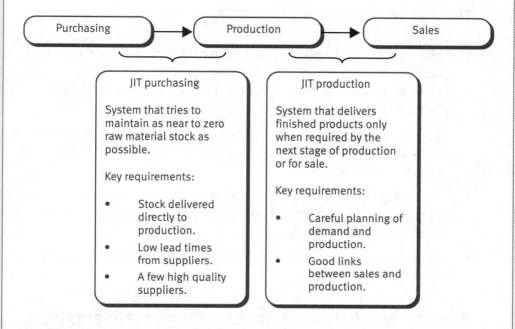

Conditions for successful JIT adoption

JIT systems were first introduced in Japan but have become more popular in the UK. They are not applicable for all businesses as a number of conditions must be present:

- Stable high volume of demand.

- Co-ordination of daily production programmes of supplier and consumer.

- Co-operation of supplier who has to be reliable on both delivery and quality.

- Suitable factory layout.

- Reliable transport system.

If these conditions are not present or cannot be created then JIT will not work. The technique has probably been most successfully employed by the motor industry, where car manufacturers have developed by finding key suppliers and locating the suppliers in very close proximity to the production facilities. They have even developed IT links to suppliers to ensure good co-ordination between the car manufacturer and the supplier.

Operational requirements of JIT

The operational requirements for JIT are as follows:

- High quality and reliability. JIT relies on getting things right first time, and preventing scrap or re-working. Hold-ups due to poor quality slow down the delivery of the product or service to the customer and reduce throughput.

- Speed of throughput. Throughput in a manufacturing operation must be fast, so that customer orders can be met by production rather than out of inventory.

- Flexibility. In order to respond immediately to customer orders ('just-in-time'), production must be flexible, and in small batch sizes. The ideal batch size is 1.

- Lower cost. Lower inventory, faster throughput and better quality will drive down costs.

Problems with traditional management accounting systems

Traditional cost and management accounting systems do not help managers to implement a JIT approach, and can actually encourage decisions that are contrary to the JIT philosophy.

- In absorption costing, profits are increased by producing more output in each period, regardless of whether the additional output is sold. Profits are increased because higher output increases the over-absorption of overheads. A profit centre manager can therefore boost his performance by producing more without having to worry about whether the output is sold.

- With marginal costing, an increase in production without any matching increase in sales does not affect profit. This is because overheads are not absorbed into product costs. From a JIT perspective, however, increases in inventory are undesirable and costly. Consequently the 'message' provided by marginal costing is misleading.

- Traditional accounting systems regard greater productivity as a 'good thing'. From a JIT point of view, however, improvements in productivity do not give any benefit if the consequence is higher output without higher sales.

The JIT philosophy and management accounting control systems

Management accounting systems within a JIT environment must be capable of producing performance and control information consistent with the JIT philosophy. Information must therefore be produced that directs management attention to the following issues.

- **Elimination of waste.** Waste occurs with any activity that does not add value. Examples of waste are:
    - Overproduction, i.e. producing more than is immediately needed by the next stage in the process.

    - Waiting time or non-productive time.

    - Movement and transport of goods. Moving items around a plant does not add value. Waste can be reduced by changing the physical layout of the factory floor to minimise the movement of materials.

    - Waste in the process. Waste and re-working of items do not add value and hold up throughput.

    - Defective finished goods are 'quality waste', and are a significant cause of waste in many operations, resulting in sales returns and customer complaints.

    - Inventory is wasteful. The target should be to reduce inventory.

- **Set-up reductions**. 'Set-up' is the collection of activities carried out between completing work on one job or batch of production and getting the process or machine ready to take the next batch. Set-up time is non-productive time. An aim in JIT is therefore to reduce set-up times, for example by pre-preparing some set-up tasks that can be done in advance, or by carrying out some tasks whilst the machines are running that were previously not done until the machines had stopped (i.e. during set-up time).

- **Continuous improvement**. The aim is to do things well, and then try to do them even better. The ideal target in JIT is to meet demand immediately with perfect quality and no waste. In practice, this ideal is never achieved. However, the JIT philosophy is that an organisation should work towards the ideal, and continuous improvement is both possible and necessary. The Japanese term for continuous improvement is 'kaizen'.

Total quality management (TQM)

TQM was covered in your earlier studies. You may remember that TQM is a business philosophy aimed at:

- minimising errors (ideally to zero) as the cost of getting things right the first time is always less than the costs of correction; and

- maximising customer satisfaction such that every customer's expectations are met or exceeded.

To achieve this philosophy a TQM firm should have an appropriately installed quality culture and very good systems that are documented and adhered to by all staff. It's fundamental features include:

- Prevention of errors before they occur;

- Continual improvement;

- Real participation by all;

- Commitment of senior management.

Costs of quality

Recognising the costs of quality is vital to any continuous improvement process. The costs associated with quality can be seen to fall into four categories:

Prevention costs: these are the costs of avoiding or reducing defects and failures. It includes the design and development of quality control equipment and the maintenance of the equipment. It could also include the cost of setting up 'quality circles' – a small group of employees who meet on a regular basis to discuss quality issues and to develop solutions to problems arising.

Any company adhering to a TQM philosophy will also incur the costs and management time involved in meeting ISO 9000 – a series of quality standards published in 2000. Companies registering for ISO accreditation have to submit to regular, external inspections. ISO 14001 is also becoming increasingly common – a standard for environmental performance.

Although costs are involved here, the advantage of achieving ISO status should be increased reputation and future sales and therefore profits.

Appraisal costs: these are the costs of assessing the actual quality achieved. They include the costs of goods inwards inspection, and the monitoring of the production output.

Internal failure costs: these are the costs arising within the organisation when the predetermined specifications are not met. They include the cost of reworking or rectifying the product, the net cost of scrap, downtime of machinery due to quality problems.

External failure costs: these are the costs of inadequate quality that are incurred once the product has been sold. They include dealing with customer complaints, warranty claims costs of repairing or replacing returned faulty goods.

Elements of TQM

The main elements of TQM that are necessary for a successful implementation are:

Meeting needs/expectations of customers

The viewpoint of the customer should always be considered. Quality issues must be addressed from the customer perspective so that the customer appreciates the quality of the product and service levels.

Right first time

The aim of TQM is zero defects and therefore quality has to be built into the production process. It is not good enough simply to spot a defective product before it goes to the customer – there should be no defective products being produced.

To achieve this, product design should have a number of features:

- Simple to produce.
- Durable.
- Functional.
- Standardised components and parts.

Prevention

This links to getting things right first time. The aim of the business should be to prevent errors occurring and therefore the company should develop processes and systems that are strictly followed in production to prevent errors and faults occurring. In the long run prevention of errors should result in cost savings.

Continuous improvement

Businesses should always be looking to improve their performance. All staff should be encouraged to look for areas where improvements are possible and make those improvements. Suggestions of all staff are considered and a reward system that supports continuous improvement needs to be introduced.

Value analysis

This is the reduction of costs into value added and non-value added activities. Value added activities will increase the overall worth of a product by increasing their saleability in some way. Therefore any part of the production process is value adding to a greater or lesser extent.

Non-value added activities add no value to the product and hence the elimination of these activities will have no adverse impact on the product, but will lead to cost savings.

A success story

Corning Inc is the world leader in speciality glass and ceramics. This is partly due to a TQM approach. In 1983 the CEO announced a $1.6 billion investment in TQM. After several years of intensive training and a decade of applying the TQM approach, all of Corning's employees had bought into the quality concept. They knew what was meant by 'continual improvement', 'empowerment', 'customer focus', 'management by prevention', and they witnessed the companies profits soar.

TQM failure

British Telecom launched a TQM program in the late 1980's. This resulted in the company getting bogged down in its quality processes and bureaucracy. The company failed to focus on its customers and later decided to dismantle the TQM program. This was at great cost to the company and they have failed to make a full recovery.

4 Modern management accounting techniques

The new manufacturing methods such as JIT and TQM have required questioning traditional techniques such as variance analysis. New management accounting techniques have been introduced as a result.

Situation	Technique(s)
JIT and TQM environments	• Throughput accounting • Backflush accounting • Costs of quality • Non-financial performance indicators
Large overhead costs	• Activity-based costing (ABC) • Activity-based budgeting (ABB)
Focus on longer-term strategic issues	• Non-financial performance indicators • Balanced scorecard • Strategic management accounting (SMA)

It is essential to remember that there is no unique ideal management accounting control system; and the most suitable accounting system varies according to circumstances.

Throughput accounting

Throughput is defined as sales less material costs. Labour costs are treated as a fixed cost in a period. In a throughput accounting system, information is given to managers on the throughput of the factory. Managers then can work at removing any constraints to throughput and any bottlenecks in the system.

Constraints might include:

* No skilled staff.
* Uncompetitive selling prices.
* Poor product quality.
* Unreliable material supplies.

Bottlenecks are parts of the production process where demand outstrips supply. A bottleneck will cause a build-up of stock before that point as the bottleneck fails to keep pace with the inputs to the process.

If the constraints and bottlenecks can be reduced or eliminated then throughput will improve.

Reporting throughput

A typical profit statement could show:

Sales	X
Less: Materials	(X)
Throughput	X
Less: Other factory expenses	(X)
Less: Other costs	(X)
Operating profit	X

The typical performance measures might be:

- Return per factory hour = Throughput ÷ time in 'bottleneck' resource.

- Return per factory hour ÷ Cost per factory hour (if this is > 1 the business will be making a profit).

Backflush accounting

Backflush accounting is defined as a 'cost accounting system that focuses on the output of an organisation and then works backwards to attribute costs to stock and cost of sales'. It is a method of accounting that is used successfully within JIT environments.

In the backflush system there is a very simple approach to stock valuation as it basically does not maintain work in progress accounts. The costing system has very few 'trigger points', such as stores issues and completion of production, and costs are only allocated at these points.

The key concepts are:

- Charge completed production with the standard cost of actual production.
- Write off the balance.
- No WIP account is maintained.

The system works very well provided that stock levels are low, but it does not allocate proper costs to WIP. As a result it relies on WIP levels being low, which they should be in a JIT environment.

Economic Value Added (EVA)

Economic value added (EVA®) is a measure of performance developed by Stern Stewart, a US management consultancy firm. The basic concept of EVA is that the performance of a company as a whole, or of investment centres within a company, should be measured in terms of the value that has been added to the business during the period.

- EVA attempts to measure the true economic profit that has been earned.
- It is a measure of performance that is directly linked to the creation of shareholder wealth.
- Economic profit is defined as NOPAT – the net operating profit after tax.
- The cost of the capital employed is the economic value of the business assets multiplied by the business cost of capital = (cost of funding, both debt capital and share capital).

EVA = NOPAT minus Capital charge

Capital charge = Economic value of business assets × Cost of capital (%).

There are similarities between EVA and residual income, because both are calculated by subtracting a capital charge from a reported profit figure. Both are based on the view that management decisions will be based on increasing this net 'profit' figure in order to improve performance.

The major difference between EVA and residual income is that:

- residual income is calculated using accounting profit and an accounting value for capital employed

- EVA is calculated using an estimated value for economic profit and an estimated economic value of capital employed.

Economic profit and economic value of capital employed are estimated by making adjustments to accounting profit and accounting capital employed.

Non-financial performance indicators

Non-financial measurement is increasingly common in most organisations. These are typically methods by which performance can be measured and monitored in order to achieve improvement in financial results.

Given the limitations of financial reports, performance measurement through a Balanced Scorecard-type approach Kaplan and Norton, 2001) has become increasingly popular. Targets are set to cover a variety of aspects of business performance (in the Balanced Scorecard, measures cover customer, internal business process, and learning and growth dimensions as well as the more traditional financial measures). As for all systems of internal control, it is important to set targets, measure actual results, compare actual results with target and take corrective action. Performance may then be judged relative to:

- Improvements over time (i.e. trend);

- Achievement of targets;

- Benchmark comparisons with world-class organisations, competitors or industry averages.

Although these are beyond the scope of this syllabus, students should recognise:

- Balanced Scorecard – or a similar non-financial performance measurement system

- Activity-Based Management – both costing and budgeting

- Total Quality Management – whether through a sophisticated system such as Six Sigma or by recognising the cost of quality or through the ISO 9000 generic standards or a system such as the European Foundation for Quality Management (EFQM) Business Excellence model.

Non-financial performance management (which can be contrasted with performance measurement) requires accountants to have a better understanding of the operational activities of the business and build this understanding into control systems design; target setting; connecting control systems with business strategy and focusing on the external environment within which the business operates.

The maxim 'what gets measured gets done' is true of both financial and non-financial performance evaluation, and hence both are powerful forms of control. However, these two broad categories of control need to be considered in more detail through the variety of forms of control that are available to organisations.

Johnson and Kaplan (1987) also criticised the excessive focus on financial performance measures. The limitations of financial measures are largely due to their focus on short-term financial performance. Financial measures are usually recognised as lagging indicators, they inform us about performance after it has happened. By contrast, non-financial measures (which are quantitative but expressed in non-monetary terms) are leading indicators of performance. They inform us about what is happening now in the business, and give a good indication of what the likely future financial performance will be.

Non-financial indicators can provide better targets and predictors for the firm's long-term profitability goals. These targets can be used effectively for control purposes, through feedback and feed forward processes. As well as monitoring target achievement, indicators can also be shown as trends, to determine whether performance is improving or deteriorating over longer time periods than is usually disclosed in financial reports. Finally, non-financial indicators can be benchmarked to internationally-recognised 'best practice', to competitor organisations and to industry averages. This is to some extent a return to the operations-based measures that were the origin of management accounting systems.

Examples of non-financial performance measurement include performance on research and development, marketing and promotion, distribution, quality, production cycle time, waste, human resources and customer relations, all of which are vital to a company's long-term performance.

In order to achieve the aims of JIT and TQM, managers have had to look at non-financial performance measures as well as financial ones. For example, TQM does not accept wastage and failures in production and therefore there need to be performance measures ensuring that wastage is monitored. These might be:

- Wastage rates.
- Rectification rates.

- In a JIT environment it will be necessary to monitor lead times and quality of input so that the raw materials can be ordered in the right quantity and at the right time.

- Non-financial measures are also often associated with forward thinking organisations. They can tell managers of problems that might occur in the future - for example, high numbers of defective products indicate higher rectification costs, and possibly a loss of customer satisfaction.

Balanced scorecard

The development of the Balanced Scorecard by Kaplan and Norton has received extensive coverage in the business press and is perhaps the best known framework for non-financial indicators. It presents four different perspectives and complements traditional financial indicators with measures of performance for customers, internal processes and innovation/improvement. These measures are grounded in an organisation's strategic objectives and competitive demands. Kaplan and Norton (2001) argued that the Scorecard provided the ability to link a company's long-term strategy with its short-term actions, emphasising that meeting short-term financial targets should not constitute satisfactory performance when other measures indicate that the long-term strategy is either not working or not being implemented well. Kaplan and Norton did not specify particular measures, but argued that the measures chosen must be those that are relevant to each particular business, its strategy, competitive position, nature of industry, etc. Performance measures need to mirror operational complexity, but must be kept simple to be understood.

Some examples are detailed below.

Financial perspective	<ul><li>Return on investment</li><li>Economic value added (EVA)</li><li>Profit target</li><li>Operating cash flow target</li><li>Cost reduction target</li><li>Profit target</li></ul>
Customer perspective	<ul><li>Target for new customers</li><li>Target for retention of existing customers or repeat orders</li><li>Percentage of orders met within X days</li><li>Percentage of orders delivered on time</li><li>Market share target</li><li>Target for customer satisfaction (quantifiable measure of satisfaction)</li></ul>

Internal business perspective	<ul><li>Percentage of tenders accepted by customers</li><li>Percentage of items produced that have to be re-worked</li><li>Production cycle time</li></ul>
Innovation and learning perspective	<ul><li>Number of new products launched</li><li>Target for employee productivity</li><li>Percentage of total revenue coming from new products</li><li>Revenue per employee</li><li>Time from identifying a new product idea to market launch</li></ul>

Research continues to show that most companies tend to make decisions primarily on financial monitors of performance. Boards, financiers and investors place overwhelming reliance on financial indicators such as profit, turnover, cash flow and return on capital. Managers tend to support the view that non-financial performance information should only be used internally.

There are dysfunctional consequences of non-financial performance measures. The following unintended consequences of performance measurement have been identified:

- Tunnel vision: the emphasis on quantifiable data at the expense of qualitative data.

- Sub-optimisation: the pursuit of narrow local objectives at the expense of broader organisation-wide ones.

- Myopia: the short-term focus on performance may have longer term consequences.

- Measure fixation: an emphasis on measures rather than the underlying objective.

- Misrepresentation: the deliberate manipulation of data so that reported behaviour is different from actual behaviour.

- Misinterpretation: the way in which the performance measure is explained.

- Gaming: an employee can pursue a particular performance standard when that is what is expected of him/her, even though s/he knows that this is not in the organisation's best interests in terms of its strategy.

- Inflexibilty: performance measurement can inhibit innovation and lead to paralysis of action.

Problems with the balanced scorecard

Advocates of a balanced scorecard approach might argue that a balanced scorecard reduces the value and purpose of a traditional budgeting system, which focuses exclusively on revenues, costs and profits over the budget period. However, a balanced scorecard approach can have its own problems.

Kaplan and Norton argued in favour of a balanced scorecard approach over traditional budgeting (and setting financial targets) because:

- accounting figures are unreliable and are easily manipulated;

- changes in the business and market environment do not show up in the financial results of a company until much later. Factors other than financial performance must therefore be targeted.

There is a risk, however, that when performance targets are selected for each of the four perspectives:

- the targets for the different perspectives could be contradictory and inconsistent with each other;

- non-financial performance targets could become an end in themselves, rather than a means towards the overall financial objective of maximising shareholder wealth or shareholder returns.

Strategic management accounting (SMA)

'The preparation and presentation of information for decision-making laying particular stress on external factors.'

CIMA Official Terminology

- SMA is linked with business strategy and maintaining or increasing competitive advantage. The achievement of objectives requires the 'linking' of strategic planning to short-term operational planning.

- Lord (1996) characterised SMA as:
  - Collection of competitor information (such as pricing, costs and volume).

  - Exploitation of cost reduction opportunities (a focus on continuous improvement and non-financial performance measures).

  - Matching the accounting emphasis with the firm's strategic position.

Lean organisations and lean accounting

- Lean manufacturing is a philosophy of management based on cutting out waste and unnecessary activities.

- Organisations can become 'lean and mean' if they can get rid of their unnecessary 'fat'.

- Two elements in lean manufacturing are JIT and TQM.

Lean management accounting

- Provides information to control and improve the value stream (focus on value streams rather than traditional departmental structures).

- Provides information for performance measurement and cost reporting purposes (non-financial measures, continuous improvement and techniques such as target and lifecycle costing).

- Provides relevant cost information for financial reporting purposes (only that which is required, eliminating non-value added information (via implementing techniques such as backflush accounting)).

- Ensures that management are provided with statements that are:
    - instantly accessible through an IT system, and
    - simple to read.

More on lean accounting

'Lean accounting is a range of methods and techniques that provide accounting, control and measurement within companies that embrace lean, world-class manufacturing principles. Underlying the methods of lean accounting are profound changes from the traditional approach to accounting, control and measurement.

An organisation that is seriously committed to the implementation of lean methods must also make radical changes to its measurement and control systems … Financial accounting methods are stripped of their inherent waste, bureaucracy and complexity. The new view is to focus on the company's business processes and to include accounting functions that are totally integrated with operations. Then accounting becomes a value added service.' (Quotation from the website of an association of US world class manufacturing companies)

Example

In a batch manufacturing organisation, a traditional cost accounting system tracks inventory transactions of large batches of material as they progress through production from one process to the next. It attempts to identify the 'value added' at each stage or process, as the extra costs of direct materials, direct labour and production overhead.

If an organisation adopts a lean manufacturing approach, and reduces inventory values towards zero, all the work that goes into cost accounting in order to measure inventory values and profits becomes a waste of effort and time. What is the point of building up production costs, stage by stage through the production process, if similar figures for inventory values (= zero, or almost zero) and costs of production could be obtained simply by recording total costs incurred in each period?

Recording accounting transactions, from a management accounting perspective (which is not the same as a financial accounting or internal control perspective) is of dubious value. 'Once you get to lean, those transactions become waste.'

Suggestions for lean management accounting include:

- eliminating variance reports

- reducing the number of cost centres in an organisation

- eliminating detailed labour reports (efficiency and utilisation reports).

5 Problems with modern management accounting

Modern management accounting techniques are not perfect. All of the techniques discussed above are open to criticism. Some of the criticisms levied include:

- JIT – Some big manufacturers have been accused of holding smaller suppliers to ransom by dictating the way they operate. The big customer expects the small supplier to forego other work to undertake their order immediately. Meanwhile the prices paid for the goods supplied might be quite low, but the smaller company reluctantly accepts this in order to keep the business in the hope that they can grow on the back of it. The ethics of this relationship have been questioned.

- TQM – The idea of 'continual' improvement can be hard to ensure. Management often have other important issues to deal with and in many companies TQM is put aside for long periods of time.

- Balanced scorecard – The criticism of the balance scorecard is that management are asked to meet so many different objectives (some of which might be conflicting) that they lose all perspective. There is a risk that the maximisation of shareholder wealth might be forgotten.

Test your understanding 1 – Control mechanisms

The management accountant of a motor vehicle dealership has completed the monthly management accounts of the Bury dealer and has identified that the branch is underperforming. Sales are falling, profit margins are dropping and customer satisfaction is also reducing.

In the branch the salesmen seem to have a significant amount of autonomy and tend to play the different new and used car sales managers off against each other. The salesmen get commission based on sales value not profit margins.

There have also been situations where customers have walked away from deals because of the attitude of the sales staff, commenting that they do not appear to value their customers. Morale in the branch is low, indicated by high staff turnover.

Required:

Recommend control mechanisms that the new general manager could put in place to improve the performance of the dealership.

Test your understanding 2 – MAC

MAC Limited has a management accounting system which has not changed for the past twenty years. The reports produced from it are in a standard format for all departments and are available two weeks after the month end. The reports are in great detail, compiled from internal and external data (some of which is paid for).

Required:

What factors should be considered in the design of a good management accounting control system?

Test your understanding 3 – Responsibility centres

To set up a control system it is important to define what is within the control of the different managers.

Required:

Describe a cost centre, a revenue centre, a profit centre and an investment centre, and state how each of these could be measured for success?

Test your understanding 4 – An entity

An entity has five revenue generating divisions that are supported by a central IT unit. The IT unit is a cost centre and the five revenue generating divisions are each charged 20% of its running costs. The IT manager is struggling to meet data processing commitments for the five divisions while remaining within budget.

Required:

Evaluate the suggestion that the IT unit costs should be passed on to the divisions in a manner that reflects the work done for each, and that the IT unit should be reorganised as a profit centre.

Test your understanding 5 – ROI

A group of companies is divided into two autonomous operating divisions. The group cost of capital is 15%. In ROI calculations, the capital employed is taken as the figure at the beginning of the year. All fixed assets are depreciated on a straight-line basis.

If no new capital expenditure transactions take place, the forecast results for next year are:

Division	Capital employed at beginning of year	Net profit for year (after depreciation)
	£000	£000
P	410	130
R	570	132

Division P could invest £38,000 now in a new asset so as to increase net profit by £11,500 per annum for five years. The asset is not expected to have any scrap value.

Required:

(a) Describe the risks inherent in the use of ROI as a performance measure for the manager of Division P.

(b) Advise how these risks may be mitigated.

Test your understanding 6 – JIT

X plc is a food manufacturer. It currently operates an Economic Order Quantity (EOQ) stock system. Management have recently been to a workshop where Just In Time (JIT) was discussed. They are now considering implementing JIT.

Required:

(a) Identify the risks that might arise if X plc moved to a JIT system.

(b) Recommend controls that could be put in place to reduce these risks.

Test your understanding 7 – Control system

Smile Training is a training organisation specialising in training sales and marketing executives and purchasing executives for a number of professional examinations. The company has four regional offices, but its main operations are in the capital city, where it also has its head office and administration team. The CEO of Smile Training is himself an experienced trainer, who takes a personal interest in each of the trainers employed by the company. He believes that the key to profitability is to deliver successful training programmes to a standard level of a high quality.

There is a risk to the company's reputation and business from unsatisfactory training programmes. The CEO is aware of several different problems that have affected quality. He has been told that many trainers employed by the company also do some training work for other organisations at weekends and during evenings, although these organisations are not direct competitors of Smile Training. There have also been instances where a trainer has failed to turn up for a course, subsequently claiming to have been ill but unable to contact head office at short notice. Although much of the feedback from students is favourable, there are occasions when a course has been unpopular and the level of complaints has been high.

You are the management accountant of Smile Training. During a recent meeting of the risk management committee which you attended, the consensus view of the meeting was that the risks from poor quality training were unacceptably high and getting worse. You expressed the view that quality could be improved within the framework of a control system for the management of the organisation. The CEO is interested in your views, and has asked for a report on the subject.

Required:

Discuss the features of a control system you would recommend for managing the organisation, explaining how you think that each of your recommendations should help to improve training quality standards and reduce the risk from poor quality.

Test your understanding 8 – Types of control

What types of control do you experience during your day at work?

Test your understanding 9 – MACS

MOVE is a transport company that operates train and bus services. Both services rely on large subsidies from the government, and profitability is low.

The train services are mainly long-distance services across the country. MOVE provides the trains, but pays another national rail service company for the hire of the rail network that it uses (tracks, signalling equipment and railway stations). There are several train service companies such as MOVE that make use of the same network. These companies also pay hire charges.

The bus services are national express services that operate between major cities and towns. MOVE owns or leases its buses, and pays a rental to local government authorities for the bus stations that it uses.

The company's senior management have set performance targets for each division that attempt to balance financial and non-financial targets, and short-term and longer-term objectives. Both divisions are given annual profit targets. Both divisions also have targets for the volume of passengers. This is expressed as a target for the number of passenger-miles carried as a percentage of full capacity. The railway services division also has a minimum target for the percentage of train services operated that reach their destination on time. This is regarded by the government as a key target of performance for all train services that it subsidises. MOVE's managers are rewarded with an annual bonus for achieving or exceeding their targets.

The management accounting system is based at the company's head office. Monthly control reports for each division show the full cost of each service operated, and the profit or loss of each service, compared with the budget.

Required:

(a) Discuss the factors to consider in deciding whether the management accounting system of MOVE should be re-located out of head office, and replaced by two separate management accounting systems in each of the divisions.

(b) Discuss the behavioural problems that might arise with the bonus system.

(c) The Finance Director believes that the current full costing system is inadequate for management's requirements, and that it would be more appropriate to introduce an activity based costing (ABC) scheme. Evaluate whether an ABC scheme might be appropriate for the company.

(d) Many of the costs incurred by MOVE are regarded as fixed costs. The marketing director has therefore argued that the main focus of monthly management control reports should be on revenues, and not costs. Discuss, giving your reasons whether you agree or disagree with this view.

Test your understanding 10 – MAP

MAP is a manufacturer of automotive products and a supplier to some of the major motor vehicle assembly plants. It operates in a just-in-time (JIT) environment and uses sophisticated manufacturing technology for efficient production. MAP has adopted a lean manufacturing philosophy and has extended this to lean management accounting. The company's emphasis is on the elimination of waste and cost control in both manufacturing and support functions and generating continual incremental improvements in all that it does.

MAP uses a strategic enterprise management system (SEM) which integrates strategic, financial and operational information and is linked to MAP's executive information system (EIS) which enables senior managers to evaluate information about the organisation and its environment. The EIS incorporates a drill down facility to move from summarised to more specific and detailed operational and financial information.

MAP is organised around production, sales, design and accounting functions that are brought together in a number of semi-autonomous work groups. Each work group is focused on several similar products. Each MAP employee has a matrix reporting relationship, to its work group and to the functional hierarchy (production, sales, design and administration).

Although it is committed to waste reduction, MAP recognises that standardisation in its manufacturing is essential for the maintenance of quality and customer satisfaction. It has carried this philosophy over into its support functions where it has established a strategic planning process focused on short-term profits and shareholder value, and policies and procedures for most support activities including human resource management (recruitment, training and appraisal, etc.). There is also a profit-sharing bonus scheme linked to MAP's overall performance.

The accounting-based control systems used by MAP include capital investment appraisal using discounted cash flow techniques with high hurdle rates for all decisions to increase manufacturing capacity. Budgets are extensively used as methods of controlling costs and ensuring that revenue targets are achieved. The chief executive relies on the finance director for accounting advice and the finance director is committed to capital investment and budget techniques. A suite of non-financial performance measures is also used to measure, for example quality, on-time delivery, production efficiency, customer satisfaction and employee morale.

The chief executive of MAP is an engineer by profession, a dominating individual, with a controlling interest in the company. He is obsessed with reducing waste and cutting costs to improve reported profits and most of the changes in philosophy, production technology, IT systems and reporting have been introduced by him. The chief executive uses the EIS to focus on work groups that need to improve their performance or that of their group of products. However, the management hierarchy is relatively flat and most managers are in staff positions rather than supervising production operations.

MAP is in a relatively stable business and its technological lead has assured it of long contractual relationships with its customers. It is a risk-averse business, evidenced by its strict controls, sophisticated information system and the hands-on role of the chief executive.

The culture of MAP is one of technological excellence and commitment to customer service although the perspective taken by employees is a long-term one. A team culture and commitment to working together is fostered by the work team structure and their relative autonomy from day-to-day management. Consequently, there is a relatively low staff turnover and generally high morale. The teams tend to carry out healthy competition between each other to see which team can produce the best performance each month.

However, surveys have shown that staff tend to be unhappy about the methods by which targets are set and believe that these are too demanding, which in turn affects their profit-related bonuses. They are also unhappy about the strict control over expenses and the way in which some of the non-financial performance measures are calculated. Many employees think that MAP has become too obsessive about cost and waste reduction.

Over the last year, the chief executive has become increasingly concerned as to whether he can rely on some of the capital investment appraisals, budget reports and non-financial performance measurement information he has been receiving.

Required:

(a) Evaluate the limitations of capital investment appraisal techniques, budgets and non-financial performance measures as methods of management control in MAP.

(b) Evaluate the effectiveness of MAP's risk management strategy in relation to its approach to management control.

Test your understanding 11 – Budgets

A social services department in the public sector is funded by government with a fixed budget each year to cover its operating costs, which are primarily salaries. The department is referred clients who have problems such as inadequate welfare benefits, poor housing, anti-social behaviour of children and mental health problems. The department is staffed by experienced social workers who are overworked and there are long waiting lists of clients whose problems have neither been investigated nor resolved.

Due to the pressure of work, in terms of both the volume of work and the effect on social workers who regularly deal with difficult situations, there is significant absenteeism due to illness, a high staff turnover and recruitment is a continuous process. However, the social workers are hardworking and dedicated and the culture in the department is one of providing excellent client service despite the inadequate resources they have. Social workers are only really concerned with satisfying their clients and resolving the underlying problems rather than with financial reports or measures of efficiency.

The department maintains a control system that incorporates budget versus actual reporting of expenditure and the analysis of variances. There are also a set of non-financial performance indicators that measure actual performance against targets in relation to waiting times for clients, the cost per service (average time spent by staff advising and assisting clients), client satisfaction with the service received and the percentage of client problems that have been resolved. Actual spending in most periods is less than budget due to vacancies following staff turnover and actual performance is lower than the targets set by senior management.

Required:

(a) Evaluate the limitations of budgetary systems, variance analysis and non-financial performance measures in the social services department;

(b) Recommend the internal controls which management should consider implementing in the social services department and the advantages of those controls.

Test your understanding 12 – Non-financial performance

Over the past few years, there have been a number of high profile financial scandals surrounding the reporting of company performance, and the associated role of accountants. As a consequence, organisations have been urged to consider future practice carefully. Some feel that an overemphasis by a company on market expectations and profitability may be detrimental to its long term well-being. Such thinking has implications for the objectives of a company and the range of performance measures used both externally and internally.

Required:

Discuss the disadvantages of using only profit related performance measures.

Test your understanding 13 – Balanced scorecard

It has been said that 'the Balanced Scorecard translates mission and strategy into objectives and measures, organised into four perspectives: financial, customer, internal business process and finally learning and growth'. Kaplan and Norton developed the Balanced Scorecard as a means of combining financial control measures with non-financial measures.

Required:

Critically evaluate the usefulness of the Balanced Scorecard in assisting organisations, both profit-motivated and not-for-profit, to achieve improvements in their operational performance.

6 Chapter summary

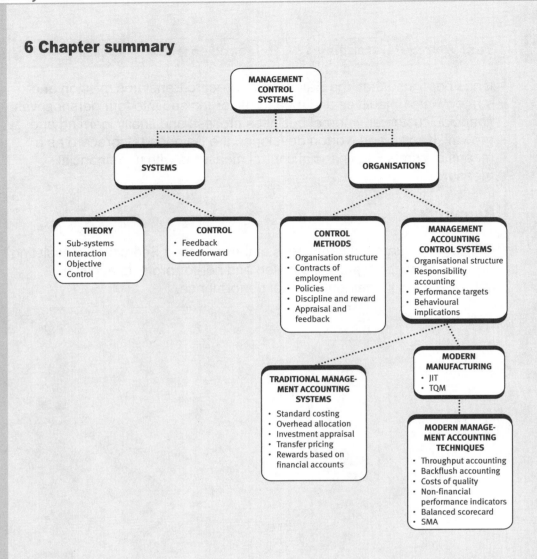

Test your understanding answers

Test your understanding 1 – Control mechanisms

Organisation structure

The new general manager could introduce clear reporting lines and structures to prevent salesmen playing managers off against each other. This would also clarify responsibilities for the managers, hopefully encouraging them to take more active control.

Contracts of employment

If possible, the contractual terms could be revised to pay commission on both sales and profit and not purely on sales.

Policies set

The new general manager could introduce more formal policies for decisions on car sales. For example, the manager could have firmly set authority limits for salesmen and managers to ensure that cars are sold profitably.

The manager could also introduce management accounting systems that provide clear information to managers about the cost of cars and acceptable target margins to aim to achieve.

Discipline and reward systems

The company needs to develop a fair discipline and reward system for the staff that motivates the salesman to sell cars profitably. The system should also reward customer service, however, as this is poor. Special bonuses for very good service or rewards for an employee of the month are possibilities.

Performance appraisal/feedback

A formal appraisal system could be set up for salesmen where they discuss their performance with their manager on a monthly basis. At these meetings their performance level could be discussed but the salesmen could also be encouraged to give ideas to help the company, for which they are rewarded if these are implemented.

Tutorial note: It is not essential to structure your answer using the five control methods – but you may find these headings help you generate ideas.

Output requirements

- The system must produce the output that the managers want. If a system does not provide the necessary information, managers will make poor decisions and will fail to control the business properly. The output should be linked to:
    - the objectives of the control system it supports; and
    - the objectives of the organisation as a whole.

Response required

- The information must be presented to managers such that they can deal with it appropriately. For example, the information could be presented in an exception report which the managers know they have to act upon.

Timing of information

- Information must be given to managers at the appropriate time for them to act on it. Some information will be presented daily, for example stock levels in retail stores so that managers can re-stock, or monthly, such as management accounts, or perhaps even on an on-demand basis, for example information about competitor actions.

Sources of information

- The data sources for the information must be defined so that the system can process the data into information.

Processing

- The actions that management are taking will define the information and therefore the processing that will be required for that information.

Cost-benefit analysis

* The system must provide the information to managers in a cost-effective way. This means that the benefits of the information must exceed the costs of producing it. The most common technique used for a cost benefit analysis is Net Present Value which you will have covered in your earlier studies and in Financial Strategy. Often the costs of the system are tangible and relatively easily identified. The benefits, however, are often intangible and can cause problems in quantifying e.g. what is the value of faster decision-making? Also, the timeframe over which the benefits are generated may be difficult to estimate.

Test your understanding 3 – Responsibility centres

Cost centres	Managers are only held responsible for the costs of their particular part of the operations. Performance reports might compare actual costs with expected costs i.e. a budget, for the actual activity level in a period. Variance analysis would be performed and relevant variances investigated.
Revenue centres	Managers are only responsible for revenue generation and control. Typically this would be the sales department. Again budgets and sales variances would probably be used for measurement.
Profit centres	Managers have control of both costs and revenues and therefore have control of profits. This might be the case in a division. Again, budgets and variances would be used in conjunction with ratios such as gross or net profit margin and costs as a % of revenue.
Investment centres	In an investment centre, managers have responsibility for profit and the capital employed in a centre. The manager can make investment decisions. Investment centre managers can be monitored by looking at **return on capital employed, residual income** and **economic value added** (ROI, RI, EVA).

Test your understanding 4 – An entity

Under the current system, the IT unit is treated as a cost centre, and actual costs are compared with budget. Presumably, the unit manager receives variance reports, and is expected to try to control costs when adverse variances occur.

There does not appear to be any distinction between variable costs and fixed costs in the IT unit budget, which suggests that all the unit's costs are treated as fixed costs. This might be inappropriate. Actual costs are likely to vary to some extent with the volume of work carried out by the unit.

Since the unit manager is expected to keep total expenditure within the budget limit, he will be reluctant to take on new work for the five divisions, because the extra work would mean higher costs and therefore larger adverse expenditure variances. It might be in the interests of the company, however, that some of this extra work should be done.

From the information available, it would appear that the costs of the IT unit are not analysed in much detail. However, there could be some control benefit in trying to distinguish between the costs of operating, for example, the mainframe services and the costs of system design and programming.

If the costs of the IT unit are driven to some extent by usage and workload, the current system of recovering IT costs as an overhead charge to the five divisions seems inadequate. The divisions should be charged for the IT services on the basis of usage, especially if these costs are quite significant.

Unless the divisions are charged for IT services on the basis of usage, there is no reason why the divisional managers should not continue to demand additional IT services, regardless of the value they obtain from them, because they are not charged extra for the services.

The current system is therefore a poor system for the control of IT costs and the usage of IT resources, and a more suitable system should be devised.

Advantages of treating the IT unit as a profit centre

Charge for services provided

If the IT unit is treated as a profit centre, it will charge each of the divisions for the services it provides. The charges will be treated as income of the IT unit and costs for the client division.

The IT unit manager might be motivated to offer more services to the divisions, provided that the divisions want them, because this should increase the revenue and the profits of the IT unit. This should remove the problem in recent years that the IT unit has been reluctant to do more work in order to limit the size of its adverse expenditure variances.

Better cost control

Since different charges would be made for mainframe services and systems development and programming services, the IT unit manager will be encouraged to study costs within the IT unit more closely, to make sure that all the unit's activities are profitable.

The potential advantages to the IT unit of becoming a profit centre are therefore that the system would encourage the unit manager to think more about providing additional services and monitoring and controlling costs.

Responsible use of IT services

Treating the IT unit as a profit centre could also have benefits for the company as a whole. The divisional managers should think more carefully before asking for additional IT services, because they will be charged for them. Divisional managers will look at the value of the IT services they receive in relation to their cost.

It is appropriate that users of IT services should be charged directly according to usage of the services, instead of being charged indirectly through an overhead absorption rate.

Check on the quality of service provided

If the divisional managers are charged for their use of UT, they might look at the quality of the service they receive, as well as the quantity, because they should show a greater concern about getting value for money. The IT unit manager will have to make sure that his centre is providing a service of suitable quality; otherwise he will risk 'losing business'.

If the IT unit is unable to operate at a profit, the company might be able to save money and still maintain the quality of IT services by outsourcing its IT operations. Treating the IT unit as a profit centre will help to focus management attention on such possibilities.

Disadvantages of treating the IT unit as a profit centre

Disputes on transfer pricing

Since the IT unit does all its work for other divisions in the company, there will almost certainly be disputes about the transfer prices for mainframe services and systems development and programming services. Transfer prices might be based on charges for similar services in the external market, but it is not clear whether comparable market prices could be obtained, given the close working relationship between the IT unit and the five divisions.

Purchasing IT services externally

Divisional managers might want to obtain IT services on the external market, if they can obtain them at a lower price. Allowing the divisions to buy IT services externally might not be in the best interests of the company.

Lack of information on IT costs

There is no information about how significant IT costs are. If IT costs are a large proportion of head office costs, it is probably appropriate to treat the IT unit as a profit centre, to encourage a more considered use of IT resources and greater efficiency and economy. On the other hand, if IT unit costs are fairly small, the costs of establishing the unit as a profit centre, negotiating transfer prices and reporting on profit performance might not be justified by the potential control benefits.

Test your understanding 5 – ROI

(a) **Calculations:**

ROI

Current ROI $= \dfrac{£130}{£140} = 31.71\%$

New ROI $= \dfrac{£130 + £11.5}{£410 + £38} = 31.58\%$

However *RI:*

Currently	£130	–	(15% × £410)	=	£68.5
New	£141.5	–	(15% × £448)	=	£74.3

Comments:

Based upon the ROI the manager will reject the asset purchase since it reduces his divisional ROI. The manager will not look beyond this short-term result and see that the asset could bring a long-term benefit to the division.

As the RI results show the project should be accepted.

The risk of using ROI is that it encourages a short-term focus with managers not wishing to take any decisions that reduce their ROI for the present time period.

Additionally the manager will focus solely on the results for their own division, and will not look to see if the decision could benefit the company as a whole.

(b) Ways in which these risks of dysfunctional decision making may be mitigated:

- Investment decisions could be made at a company level, hence removing the distorting perspective of investment centre managers.
- Investment decisions could be made based up on residual income targets as opposed to ROI (though this has other adverse consequences for performance evaluation).

Test your understanding 6 – JIT

(a) Risks of introducing JIT

- Reliability of suppliers.
- Quality of supplies essential to process.
- Key and highly trained staff may be poached by competitors.
- Reliance on information systems to co-ordinate production and purchasing.
- Fluctuations in demand.

(b) Controls required

- Strong relationships with suppliers.
- Contractual terms instigated in the event of supplier delays.
- Preferred supplier policies for all inputs.
- Pay premium to ensure quality.
- Appraisal and reward structures to retain and motivate key staff.
- Information system controls, such as system back-ups, contingency planning, network controls.
- Forecasting methods.

(**Tutorial note:** This answer is only a plan. To earn 'recommend' marks for (b) you would need to fully explain each suggestion, describing how it could reduce risk.)

Test your understanding 7 – Control system

The key issue

The key issue facing Smile Training appears to be the need to achieve a consistently high standard of training. The risks to this objective come largely from the abilities, behaviour and attitudes of some of the trainers. Improving and sustaining training performance should be achievable through the application of organisation and management controls, discipline and incentives, in a suitable balance or mix.

Trainers need to understand clearly what is expected of them, and there should be controls for recognising when they fail to achieve the required standards and for dealing with the problem. At the same time, trainers should be given incentives to perform well, so that they are motivated to deliver high-quality and successful training programmes.

Poor trainers

Some individuals are naturally better at training than others. The current recruitment and selection process for trainers should seek to ensure that individuals will be employed only if they appear to have the potential to perform well. However, mistakes can be made in the selection process, and individuals might be employed as trainers when they are not well-suited to the job.

My recommendation is that when trainers are initially employed, they should be given a probationary period of employment. If the individual does not perform to a satisfactory standard during the probationary period, the contract of employment can be terminated.

Working for other organisations

The practice of working for other organisations is clearly undesirable and should not be permitted. Unfortunately, such practices appear to be common, suggesting that they are permitted by the trainers' contracts of employment. My recommendation is that when new trainers are recruited to the company, there should be a term in the contract prohibiting them from working for any other organisation whilst they are a employee of Smile Training, except with the express permission of their manager. Basic salaries paid to trainers should be adjusted if necessary in recognition of this restriction.

Policies and procedures

Trainers should be required to operate in accordance with policies and procedures that help to ensure high-quality training. A variety of measures might be appropriate. Some are suggested below, but others should also be applied.

- There is a problem with trainers occasionally failing to turn up for a training course, and later claiming to have been ill. The problems that arise due to non-attendance might be reduced by installing an emergency 'hot line' at head office, and implementing a procedure that all trainers must contact head office on this line as soon as they are aware that they will not be able to run a course, or might be late in arriving at the course. This should give head office some time to arrange emergency cover.

- There should be regular 'refresher' training programmes for the trainers, to help them to develop their training skills.

- Training standards could be brought to a similar standard if all trainers are required to use a common set of course notes and displays for courses on the same subject. All trainers should then be required to use the notes and displays, to deliver courses of a consistent content.

Performance appraisal and feedback

There should be a system of performance appraisal for trainers within Smile Training. Management need to be kept regularly informed about how well or badly trainers are performing, so that they can take control measures when appropriate. Individual trainers should also be given regular feedback on their performance, so that they are aware of any strengths or weaknesses in their work. There should also be a formal system of performance review, possibly carried out annually, in which trainers discuss their performance throughout the period with their manager, and consider measures for development and improvement in the future.

Performance and appraisal feedback could be based on questionnaires that students are asked to complete at the end of each course. In addition, since the training programmes lead to examinations, performance can be monitored by the examination pass rates of the students.

Reporting structures

Trainers should report to a line manager. It is possible that at the moment all trainers report directly to you as CEO. If so, there is a risk that management control is insufficient due to a shortage of management time. I recommend that the management reporting structure should be reviewed, to make sure that each trainer has clear lines of reporting to a manager and is accountable to that manager for his or her work and performance.

Discipline and reward

Encouraging good performance from employees often requires a suitable balance between discipline and incentive. Appropriate disciplinary action should be taken when a trainer performs badly in the training room, or is in breach of his or her employment contract or fails to comply with established policy or procedures.

At the same time, trainers should be given an incentive to perform well. The most appropriate form of incentive might well be a cash bonus arrangement of a share option or share award scheme. I recommend that if such a scheme does not already exist, an investigation should be undertaken with a view to designing and introducing a scheme in the near future. If an incentive scheme does exist, I recommend that an investigation should be carried out into how successful or otherwise it has been, with a view to recommending improvements if necessary.

Test your understanding 8 – Types of control

Assuming you are a trainee management accountant, controls you come across each day might include:

- Budgets

- Variances

- IT controls such as passwords and user log ins

- Reconciliations

- Locks on doors

- Contract of employment regarding hours of work and codes of conduct

- Process manuals

- Pre-numbered forms

- Air-conditioning temperature control

Many other controls could be identified.

Test your understanding 9 – MACS

(a) **Factors to consider regarding the move of the management accounting systems**

As a guiding principle, the management accounting system should identify the responsibility and control centres within the organisation, and ensure that control information is provided to (and is continually available to) the managers of those responsibility centres.

It is not clear from the question whether decision-making is centralised at head office, or whether most decisions are delegated to management at a divisional level. The management structure of the organisation should affect the structure of the management accounting system.

Another principle of a management accounting system is that it should be based on the decision-making structure. This is because management accounting information is a major source of information to assist management with decision-making, and it is appropriate that the information system should be under the control of the managers who use the information most for making decisions.

A factor in deciding whether to operate with one management accounting system or two separate systems is whether the two divisions share much information, or whether their information needs are largely different. If they do not share common information, it is easier to decentralise the information systems and operate them separately. However, if the management accounting system is divided into two parts, there must be a supplementary system that enables management at head office to extract information from both systems, to provide control reports at a company level.

Since the management accounting information of each division has to be consolidated for reporting at head office level, the file and database structures of each division will have to be similar.

Finally, if MOVE's directors are contemplating a de-merger of the company, or selling one of its divisions, there is a strong argument for separating the information systems, so that a de-merger or sell-off would be administratively easier to accomplish.

(b) **Behavioural problems**

In a bonus incentive scheme individuals who will benefit from the scheme should be motivated to achieve or exceed performance targets on which their bonuses will be calculated. However, managers will almost certainly focus on the bonus performance targets to the exclusion of other considerations.

Unless the performance targets on which the bonus scheme are carefully devised, there is a risk of unexpected behavioural consequences, with managers making decisions that were not intended when the scheme was devised, and that might be damaging to the business. An example is the use of annual profit targets for a bonus scheme, particularly when sales growth is not strong and opportunities for improving profits through higher sales are limited.

When a business operation's costs are largely fixed costs, management will often seek to increase profits by reducing discretionary 'fixed cost' spending. With train and bus services, the risk might be a decision to cut back spending on repairs and maintenance, or the cleaning of trains and carriages. Cutting expenditure in certain areas will improve profits in the short-term, but could have adverse longer-term consequences through the reduction in quality and public perception of the service. Another behavioural problem might be the use of the punctuality target for the railway services.

If the division's managers are rewarded for achieving a target for the percentage of services operated that arrive on time, there might be a temptation to cancel services where delays have become inevitable. Cancelling services means that the service does not operate, and so will not affect the punctuality statistics.

(c) Benefits of current system

The current management accounting system appears to identify the costs of operating each bus service or railway service, and the profitability of each service. From the information available, it appears that many costs are related to the provision of services. Costs such as track rental charges, bus station rental charges and repairs and maintenance costs would appear to be related to service provision. If this is the case, the current focus on service profitability is probably appropriate, because providing train and bus services are the major activities driving overhead costs.

Benefits of ABC scheme

There may be other activities which the Finance Director believes is a driver of overhead costs, such as ticket sales. However, it is not clear what these are, and the Finance Director should be asked to state more specifically how an ABC system would be of benefit in the case of MOVE.

(d) In agreement with the marketing director's view

When many costs are fixed, revenue maximisation becomes a key aspect of performance. The Marketing Director is almost certainly correct in expressing the view that control reports should give emphasis to revenues.

Disagreeing with the marketing director's view

However, the view of the Marketing Director that control reports should focus on revenues to the exclusion of costs may be incorrect. There are two reasons for this.

(i) Some costs are variable and others are directly attributable to particular rail or bus services. For example, fuel costs are a variable cost of bus services. The cost of drivers is a directly attributable cost of both bus and rail services. Performance reporting should provide management information about the contribution from services, and the contribution after deducting directly attributable costs. This will provide more information than just revenue about the profitability and viability of each service.

(ii) Management need to know what their costs are and whether revenues are sufficient to cover costs. The company relies on subsidies, which means that operating costs exceed revenues before subsidies. Senior management need to be aware of the size of this shortfall, which means that reporting costs is essential, at least at a senior management reporting level.

Test your understanding 10 – MAP

(a) The behavioural effects of accounting controls need to be understood by managers. Resistance to change is a common reaction, particularly where there are conflicts between the values of dominant managers and the culture of the organisation, which seems to be the case in MAP. These tensions are likely to lead to unintended consequences for MAP.

Despite the usefulness of capital investment techniques, the assumption has been that future cash flows can be predicted with some accuracy. Despite the apparent sophistication of techniques (particularly DCF), capital investment decisions are often made subjectively and then justified after the event by the application of financial techniques to subjectively 'guessed' cash flows which can be easily manipulated through sensitivity analysis in order to meet hurdle rates for ROI, payback or internal rate of return.

One of the most common dysfunctional consequences of budgeting is the creation of 'slack' resources. Budget expectations perceived to be unfair or exploitative, as in MAP, are not internalised by employees and can lead to lower motivation and performance. Similarly, the manipulation of data or its presentation to show performance in the best possible light is another common behaviour, particularly where performance is linked to rewards, as in MAP's bonus scheme. Dysfunctional behaviours include smoothing performance between periods; selective bias and focusing on particular aspects of performance at the expense of others; gaming, or producing the desired behaviour although this is detrimental to the organisation; filtering out undesirable aspects of performance and 'illegal' acts to bypass organisational accounting rules.

In non-financial performance measurement, there are similar dysfunctional consequences where targets are perceived to be too stretching, as is the case in MAP. Tunnel vision emphasises quantified results over qualitative performance. Sub-optimisation involves a focus on narrow local objectives rather than organisation-wide ones. Myopia is a focus on short-term performance rather than long-term consequences.

Measure fixation emphasises measures rather than the underlying objective. Misrepresentation involves the deliberate manipulation of data with the aim to mislead. Misinterpretation is providing an inaccurate explanation about reported performance. Ossification inhibits innovation and leads to paralysis of action.

(b) A risk management strategy should include the risk profile of the organisation, that is the level of risk it finds acceptable; the risk assessment and evaluation processes the organisation practices; the preferred options for risk treatment; the responsibility for risk management and the reporting and monitoring processes that are required. MAP has been identified as a risk-averse organisation. Its management control systems are aimed at reducing risk through continual attention to waste and cost control and focusing on work groups and products that need to be improved. The central role of the chief executive is critical in this process.

However, there is a significant risk that is overlooked by the chief executive's approach. This risk is a result of the tensions between cybernetic and non-cybernetic forms of control and the possible dysfunctional consequences that follow from MAP's use of capital investment appraisal, budgets and non-financial measurement. MAP's chief executive lives in a world dominated by the economic-rational perspective, while MAP's employees are as much social as rational actors. There are tensions between the values of the chief executive and the culture of the organisation.

The team culture in MAP and the socialisation pressures in the work groups are a clan that produces a power base of its own, less evident but capable of compensating for the dominating influence of the chief executive. There is suggestion of resistance to the chief executive's targets and his short-term focus on waste and cost reductions. The chief executive has raised concerns about the quality of financial and non-financial data he has been receiving and this may be due to a variety of techniques adopted by employees to show the results in a better light than they actually are. It is quite possible that data in capital investment evaluations have been massaged, that budgetary slack exists and that financial and non-financial performance is smoothed, biased, subject of gaming and so on. MAP's risk management strategy is not perfect and some of the 'hard' controls may need to be relaxed in favour of a greater balance with 'soft' controls and seeking greater participation by employees in strategy, target-setting and performance measurement and adopting a focus that is not just short-term in nature. Continuing on the current path has the risk of increased employee dissatisfaction and greater resistance to and obfuscation of the system of management control.

Test your understanding 11 – Budgets

(a) Budgets are used as forecasts of future events, as motivational targets and as standards for performance evaluation. Budgets provide a control mechanism through both feed forward and feedback loops. A major difficulty in budgeting is predicting the volume of activity, particularly in a public sector or not-for-profit organisation where client demand cannot be controlled but where the funding provided by government for service delivery is limited. Budgets are not effective in controlling what the social workers do.

The 'Beyond Budgeting' movement has criticised the limitations of budgets and proposes targets based on stretch goals linked to performance against world-class benchmarks and prior periods. It enables decision making and performance accountability to be devolved to line managers and a culture of personal responsibility which leads to increased motivation, higher productivity and better customer service. This is likely to be a better model for a social services department, particularly given the spending below budget, which is most likely linked to the below target performance against non-financial measures.

Variance analysis involves comparing actual performance against plan, investigating the causes of the variance and taking corrective action to ensure that targets are achieved. Properly calculated, variations can identify poor budgeting practice, lack of cost control or variations in the usage or price of resources that need to result in corrective action. However, variance analysis is likely to be of little value in a social services department as costs, especially salary costs, are fixed and the volume of activity bears little relationship with budget costs. The cause of lower spending than budget is the inability to fill staff vacancies quickly.

Non-financial measures are better predictors of long-term performance and operational measures of performance may provide better control, especially in a public or not-for-profit organisation where financial results are unhelpful, other than as an expense limit that cannot be exceeded. Non-financial performance management requires a better understanding of the operational activities of the organisation and this understanding needs to be incorporated into control systems design.

Performance measurement through a balanced scorecard-type approach has become increasingly common in most organisations. The measures used by the social services department include client and efficiency measures. The waiting list, client satisfaction and resolution of problem measures are likely to be valued by both managers and social workers. However, in the efficiency measure used, the calculation of cost per service is also unlikely to be meaningful as resources are fixed but work pressures high, and it is unlikely that professional social workers would be influenced by measures of efficiency such as this.

Importantly, there is an absence in the non-financial measures used by the department of any improvement or staff-related measures. Given the circumstances described in the scenario, measures of absenteeism, staff turnover, staff satisfaction and vacancies may be important predictors of future performance and are important indicators of action management should undertake to resolve the internal problems in the department.

(b) An internal control system includes all the financial and non-financial controls, policies and procedures adopted by an organisation to assist in achieving organisational objectives; to provide reasonable assurance of effective and efficient operation; compliance with laws and regulations; safeguarding of assets; prevention and detection of fraud and error; the accuracy and completeness of the accounting records and the timely preparation of reliable financial information. A sound system of internal control provides reasonable, but not absolute, assurance that a company will not be hindered in achieving its business objectives, or in the orderly and legitimate conduct of its business, or by circumstances which may reasonably be foreseen.

The major risks identified in this scenario are financial risk if budgets are overspent; risk to clients and risk to employees. Internal controls need to be based on a risk assessment and the cost/benefit of controls.

Financial controls are essential to ensure that spending is contained within budget. However, continual spending below budget also identifies a problem. Recruitment activity needs to be improved to use available funds to replace social workers who have left, as this money is effectively lost by the department and contributes to below target performance on non-financial measures.

Non-financial performance measures are also important, subject to the comments made in Section (b). Additional measures need to be implemented to cover staffing and the reasons for below target performance need to be ascertained as there may either be operational problems, perhaps caused by shortages of staff, or the targets may be unrealistically high.

Non-financial qualitative controls influence behaviour to ensure that it is legally correct, co-ordinated and consistent throughout the organisation; linked to objectives; efficient and effective; fair and equitable. These controls include formal and informal structures; rules, policies and procedures; physical controls; strategic plans; incentives and rewards; project management and personnel controls.

Qualitative controls need to be emphasised in the social services department. Rules, policies and procedures are important elements of internal control as they guide behaviour. There is a trade-off between a longer waiting list for clients awaiting services and providing effective services to clients. Policies and procedures are based on prior experience and establish the most effective standards of service and procedures to be followed to ensure that each case is handled fairly, equitably and effectively.

Personnel controls are particularly important to ensure that social workers are properly recruited, trained and socialised into the organisation. Support needs to be provided to staff to help them cope with the volume and stress they face in their work. This has important health and safety considerations and improved controls might reduce staff turnover and absenteeism. Controls are also necessary over recruitment to improve the filling of vacancies which has led to lower than budget spending and probably contributes to the pressure on staff.

Test your understanding 12 – Non-financial performance

The main disadvantages of using only profit-related performance measures

Often there is an emphasis on the profit figure for private companies; this should mean that profit-based measures are the most useful measures of company performance. An example of this would be when a shareholder reads the annual reports of a plc. However, profit-based measures should only be used alongside other measures, as the use of these measures to run a business on their own has a number of disadvantages, as follows:

- They are only a snapshot of a single point in time; as such they ignore trends and other factors that may be crucial for the business to succeed.

- Profit is an accounting measure, which can result in a different decision being made than if an economic approach were used. For example in the valuation of intangibles.

- Profit is open to manipulation by creative accounting, and can also be manipulated, for example in the case of profit-related bonuses.

- Profit does not really tie in very well with strategic thinking; longer term strategic thinking should use both financial and non-financial performance measures.

- They encourage short-term thinking, for example the annual profit figure in the financial reports. For example in training the best policy long-term would be investment but short term it costs money so would lower the profit figure.

- The profit measure does not consider the cash position of a business; there have been many instances where profitable companies have failed as a result of not having adequate liquidity.

- Profit-based measures cannot be used in all businesses, for example non-profit making companies.

- To measure the performance of products/services measures like net profit are used; however, these ignore the capital assets used in the production of the good/service. This means that the net assets are ignored. These should be considered, as there could be opportunity costs if the assets are not been managed properly or could be used better elsewhere. Also they represent cash if they were sold, especially in situations where cash is in short supply.

- Overall objectives will not be aligned. For example, a manager may pursue an increase in profit at the expense of other divisions within the organisation.

- Not all functions within an organisation are financial, for example marketing and HR. Functions such as these are often cost not profit centres, and so the profit measure is of little value to these departments.

- Shareholders are not the only stakeholders in an organisation. These other stakeholders may have little or no use for the profit measures as a measurement of performance.

- A conflict of objectives can occur as the short-term views of shareholders will sometimes conflict with the long-term plans for the company.

Test your understanding 13 – Balanced scorecard

The balanced scorecard approach (BSC) is an approach to the provision of information to management to assist strategy formulation and achievement. It emphasises the need to provide the user with a set of information that addresses all relevant areas of performance in an objective and unbiased fashion. The information provided may include both financial and non-financial elements, and cover areas such as profitability, customer satisfaction, internal efficiency and innovation.

It was developed as a result of the perception that traditional financial measures of performance were not sufficient in terms of providing control. Also they were too focused on the procedures and cycles of the financial control system, that the information was usually too late, too aggregated and too distorted to be of value in management planning, control and decision-making processes. This in turn led to managers focusing on the wrong issues and making inappropriate short-term decisions because the systems were too simple and led to inaccurate product and service costs.

Businesses must use knowledge and information as a vital resource for gaining competitive advantage. So management accounting control information must provide the breadth of meaningful information required. The BSC approach attempts to address this by looking at four perspectives in order to provide operational control so that the organisation's mission and objectives can be met. These perspectives are financial, customer, internal, and learning and growth. They are balanced in the sense that managers are required to think in terms of all four perspectives to prevent improvements being made in one area at the expense of another.

Financial perspective

The financial perspective is still relevant to both profit and non-profit organisations. It asks the question how do we create value for the organisation's owners – in profit-making organisations this will be couched in terms of shareholder value and return, in the not-for-profit sector it will be in terms of efficiency allowing the available resources to be put to best use to add value to society. It covers the traditional measures such as growth, profitability, and shareholder value but targets should be set by talking to the 'owners' directly.

Financial measures alone cannot guide an organisation to add future value. They are a historical record that does not supply data on how future long-term capability and relationships with customers or users and suppliers can be developed.

Customer perspective

This asks the question – what do existing and new customers value from us? It will give rise to targets that matter to customers in the case of the profit-making sector and users in the non-profit sector. These could include cost, quality, delivery, handling, service attributes, etc.

In this perspective the BSC identifies items such as customer satisfaction, customer retention, market share, customer account profitability and new customers won. It is concerned with identifying in which market segment the organisation is engaged and how they may be measured.

It is obviously vital that a profit-motivated organisation obtains customer feedback in respect of their product or service. Also a not-for-profit organisation needs to know what its users or members feel about its services. Such organisations (clubs or charities for example) will have obligations to provide appropriate service levels which will be measured against established targets.

Internal business process perspective

This perspective asks the question what processes must we excel at to achieve our financial and customer objectives and it aims to improve internal processes and decision making. It relates to the efficiency and linkages within the internal value chain.

The organisation must assess how it goes about delivering products and/or services and what impacts these processes have on creating value for customers. In turn these generate financial returns for the profit orientated organisation or better service delivery effectiveness in the not-for-profit sector.

This perspective is linked to the customer perspective in both types of organisation. It provides an external customer focus to internal processes so that external service can be improved by looking at internal processes. An example might be members of a tennis club wanting a better booking-in service; this might be achieved by looking at how the reception operates and records bookings or whether the club's website can be extended to show unallocated courts or allow an online booking system. A driver might want improved performance from his or her car, so the internal business process perspective would result in changes to the engine and suspension to meet the customer needs.

Learning and growth perspective

The question is posed: can we continue to improve and create future value? This considers the organisation's capacity to maintain and grow its position through the acquisition of new skills and the development of new products or services.

Comparing the customer and internal perspectives may reveal gaps between what the customer wants and what the processes can deliver. The learning and growth perspective is concerned with closing that gap. These measures may include staff developing new skills.

Both profit and not-for-profit organisations will benefit from learning from the past (both successes and failures) and this perspective will ensure that they do so. So another aspect of this perspective is to enable processes to improve over time leading to improved customer satisfaction.

Whilst the BSC approach is an appropriate mechanism to achieve overall improvements in shareholder value or effectiveness (in the not-for-profit sector), there may be some problems that arise:

- There may be conflicting measures (e.g. research funding and cost reduction naturally conflict). It is often difficult to determine the balance that will achieve the best results.

- Appropriate measures have to be devised but the number of measures also has to be agreed. The impact of the results can sometimes be swamped in a sea of information because there is no summary control measure, merely an amalgamation of a variety of diverse measures.

- Measurement is only useful if it initiates appropriate action and most managers will be unfamiliar with some of the measures that do not fall within their usual area of expertise.

- The data can be difficult to interpret due to their quantity and sometimes complexity.

The BSC approach, to be successfully implemented, needs commitment from senior management and sometimes changes to the organisation's culture. The organisation will need to be recognised as a bundle of inter-related processes rather than separate, independent departments, and staff would need to recognise the need to add value and think in the long term rather than the short term.

Fraud

Chapter learning objectives

Lead	Component
B1. Evaluate types of risk facing an organisation.	(b) Evaluate risks facing an organisation.
B2. Evaluate risk management strategies and internal controls.	(b) Evaluate risk management strategies.

Specific areas of indicative syllabus content of relevance here are the following:

- Fraud related to sources of finance (e.g. advance fee fraud and pyramid schemes) and management fraud

- Minimising the risk of fraud (e.g. fraud policy statements, effective recruitment policies and good internal controls, such as approval procedures and separation of functions, especially over procurement and cash)

- Detection and investigation of fraud

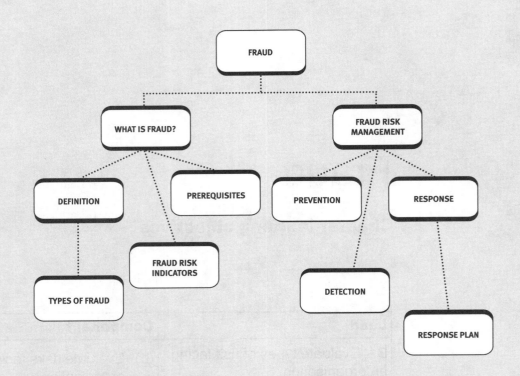

1 What is fraud ?

Fraud can be defined as

> 'dishonestly obtaining an advantage, avoiding an obligation or causing a loss to another party'.

Fraud or error

Fraud is a crime, but does not have a precise legal definition. The term 'fraud' refers to an intentional act by one or more individuals among management, those charged with governance, employees or third parties, involving the use of deception to obtain an unjust or illegal advantage. (International Standard of Auditing 240 *The Auditor's Responsibility to Consider Fraud in an Audit of Financial Statements*).

A distinction is made between:

- fraud, which is deliberate falsification, and
- errors, which are unintentional mistakes.

Different types of fraud

Examples of fraud include:

- the theft of cash or other assets

- false accounting: this includes concealing or falsifying accounting records with a view to personal gain or providing false information that is misleading or deceptive

- crimes against consumers or clients, e.g. misrepresenting the quality of goods; pyramid trading schemes; selling counterfeit goods

- employee fraud against employers, e.g. payroll fraud; falsifying expense claims; theft of cash

- crimes against investors, consumers and employees, e.g. financial statement fraud

- crimes against financial institutions, e.g. using lost and stolen credit cards; fraudulent insurance claims

- crimes against government, e.g. social security benefit claims fraud; tax evasion

- crimes by professional criminals, e.g. money laundering; advance fee fraud

- e-crime by people using computers, e.g. spamming; copyright crimes; hacking.

Pyramid schemes

Pyramid schemes are also known as multi-level plans and network marketing plans. Although the law on these schemes varies between countries, as a general rule some pyramid schemes are legitimate and some are illegal.

The nature of a pyramid scheme is for the originator of the scheme to offer other people the opportunity to become a distributor for a product or service, which could range in size and value from vitamins to car leases. The distributor is given the opportunity to sell the product or service from home, in return for a commission.

In addition, a person who becomes a distributor is encouraged to sign up other people as distributors, and in return receives a commission for each new distributor they persuade to join the scheme.

The concept of the pyramid is that the originator of the scheme signs up a few distributors, who then sign up new distributors themselves. These new distributors in turn sign up more distributors, who then sign up more distributors.

Each new distributor signing up to the scheme is asked to make a payment, for an initial amount of products to sell, or for marketing material. Sometimes, new distributors might be persuaded to pay to go on a training course in the product or service.

If a pyramid scheme is intended primarily to sell the product or service to outside customers, it could well be legal. In the UK, for example, these schemes are legal provided they comply with certain regulations.

However, **these schemes are illegal** if their primary purpose is to sign up new distributors rather than to sell products or services to external customers.

When distributors earn money mainly by signing up more distributors, the pyramid selling scheme is illegal (in many countries) because there is a limit to the number of new distributors. At some stage, there will be no more distributors willing to sign up to the scheme. The distributors at the bottom of the pyramid will have spent money buying inventory and/or marketing material, with very little prospect of getting any money back. The scheme is then likely to be wound up, possibly with many commissions still unpaid, having made a large amount of money for its originator.

Advance fee fraud

This is a fraud in which a victim is persuaded to become involved in an apparent scheme to get money out of another country with the promise of a huge reward. Having become an accomplice in this scheme, the victim is then persuaded to make payments to overcome a series of problems that 'unexpectedly' arise in gaining access to the money.

In a typical advance fee fraud, an individual working for a company receives a letter, fax or e-mail from a person claiming to be an 'official' in a government department or government agency in another country. The letter states that the person, for a reason that is explained, would like to transfer money out of the country but cannot do so for legal reasons or because of exchange control regulations.

The fraudster asks the intended victim to help by providing blank paper with a company letterhead and personal bank details. The fraudster claims that the company stationery will be used to create an invoice for a fictitious contract, and when this invoice is paid the money will then be paid into the victim's bank account. In return for his assistance, the victim is offered a large portion of the money, typically 30% or so.

By responding to the letter and supplying headed paper and bank details, the victim is hooked. The fraudster then sends a number of official-looking documents to the victim, to testify to the authenticity of the scheme that the victim is being asked to join.

There is a sense of urgency, and having to claim the money 'now' before it is too late. The victim is also sworn to secrecy. In most cases, the victim is also asked to go to the country concerned, or to a country near it. The scheme apparently moves forward to the point when the money is with the central bank of the country concerned, waiting for final approval to transfer it abroad, into the victim's bank account.

The victim starts losing money when a problem arises with the transfer of the money. The reasons for the problem might be that:

- a transaction fee has to be paid to the bank, or

- a local tax must be paid before the money can be sent abroad, or

- a local official is demanding a payment (a bribe) before he will agree to authorise the transfer of the money, or

- legal fees have to be paid before the lawyers will sign a document for the transfer of money to go ahead.

The fraudster persuades the victim to make the payment. Being so close to getting a large amount of money in return, the victim is far too involved to refuse. Several 'problems' with transferring the money might arise, one after another, and the victim might make several payments, before the nature of the fraud finally becomes apparent.

Fraud risk indicators

Test your understanding 1

From your own business knowledge, suggest some warning signs that would indicate an organisation is exposed to fraud risk.

Prerequisites for fraud

- A major reason why people commit fraud is because they are allowed to do so.

- The likelihood that fraud will be committed will be decreased if the potential fraudster believes that the rewards will be modest, that they will be detected or that the potential punishment will be unacceptably high.

- Therefore, a comprehensive system of control is needed to reduce the opportunity for fraud and increase the likelihood of detection.

There are three prerequisites for fraud to occur:

- **Dishonesty** on the part of the perpetrator.
- **Opportunity** for fraud to occur.
- **Motive** for fraud.

More on prerequisites

Three conditions that are generally present when fraud exists are:

- an ability to rationalise the fraudulent action and hence act with **dishonesty** – virtually anyone can justify almost any dishonest or illegal action that they undertake. A sense that the action is tolerated (e.g. by leaving a control weakness uncorrected) or any grievance is relatively small might be sufficient to overcome the perpetrator's conscience.

- a perceived **opportunity** to commit fraud – this can cover a vast range of circumstances, from the board of directors (whose position almost always gives some opportunity to publish fraudulent statements) to members of staff or the general public who think that the system might be weak.

- a **motive**, incentive or pressure to commit fraud – this can range from the members of the board wishing to maximise the value of their performance-related remuneration packages to greed on the part of a dishonest employee or third party.

All three factors generally exist within all organisations and at all levels.

2 Fraud risk management strategy

In common with any other type of risk, a risk management strategy needs to be developed for fraud. This strategy should include:

- Fraud prevention.
- Fraud detection.
- Fraud response.

Fraud prevention

The aim of preventative controls is to reduce opportunity and remove temptation from potential offenders. Prevention techniques include the introduction of policies, procedures and controls, and activities such as training and fraud awareness to stop fraud from occurring.

Some specific examples of fraud prevention include:

- An anti-fraud culture;
- Risk awareness;
- Whistleblowing;
- Sound internal control systems.

Test your understanding 2 – Causes of fraud

Recommend to management the major causes of fraud and the major controls that should be in place to reduce fraud.

Fraud detection

A common misbelief is that external auditors find fraud. This is actually rarely the case – in fact their letters of engagement typically state that it is **not their responsibility** to look for fraud. Most frauds are discovered accidentally, or as a result of information received (whistleblowing).

Some methods of discovering fraud are:

- Performing regular checks, e.g. stocktaking and cash counts.
- Warning signals or fraud risk indicators (see previous section). For example:
    - Failures in internal control procedures
    - Lack of information provided to auditors
    - Unusual behaviour by individual staff members
    - Accounting difficulties.
- Whistleblowers.

More on fraud detection

The risks of fraud can be reduced by suitable internal controls, properly applied. However, the internal auditor should be on the look-out for possible fraud in carrying out audit work, and should look for evidence of suspicious circumstances.

- **Failures in internal control procedures**. The risk of fraud is high when internal controls are ignored or by-passed. For example, expenditures might be made without proper authorisation or without proper documentation. In a computer system, there might be evidence of unauthorised 'hacking' into the system. There might be an 'all-powerful' individual in the department, whose work is not checked by anyone else or who appears to over-ride some internal controls.

- **Lack of information**. The auditor might be suspicious when there is an absence of documentation, and staff are unhelpful or evasive when questioned.

- **Unusual behaviour by individual staff members**. Warning signs might be members of staff who arrive first in the morning and leave last in the evening, and do not take holidays, or members of staff who keep an area of the office for their exclusive use and do not share files with others.

- **Accounting difficulties**. The auditor might be concerned if the work of the accounts department is continually behind schedule, and there is a backlog of work waiting to be done. Within the ledger accounts themselves, there might be large balances in suspense accounts, the causes of which the accounts staff have been unable to identify.

The legal position of the whistleblower

The legal position of the whistleblower is covered within the Public Interest Disclosure Act 1998.

The Act ensures that as a whistleblower you are protected from victimisation if the you meet all the following:

- You are a worker (employee, agency worker, or training with employers)

- You are revealing information of the right type: a **'qualifying disclosure'**

- You reveal information to the right person and in the right way: this makes it a **'protected disclosure'**.

Qualifying disclosures

To be protected you need to reasonably believe that malpractice is happening, has happened, or will happen. The malpractice can take the form of:

- Criminal offences
- Failure to comply with a legal obligation
- Miscarriage of justice
- Threats to health and safety
- Damage to the environment.

Protected disclosure

For a disclosure to a prescribed person to be protected you must:

- Make the disclosure in good faith
- Reasonably believe that the information is substantially true
- Reasonably believe that you are making the disclosure to the right 'prescribed person'.

In certain circumstances disclosures can be made to others:

- To your legal adviser
- To a government minister if you are a public sector worker
- To a professional body or in extreme circumstances the media (but in this case stricter rules apply).

Fraud response

- The fraud response plan sets out the arrangements for dealing with suspected cases of fraud, theft or corruption.
- It provides procedures for evidence-gathering that will enable decision-making and that will subsequently be admissible in any legal action.
- The fraud response plan also has a deterrent value and can help to restrict damage and minimise losses to the organisation.

The organisation's response to fraud may include:

- Internal disciplinary action, in accordance with personnel policies.
- Civil litigation for the recovery of loss.
- Criminal prosecution through the police.

Responsibilities

Within the response plan responsibilities should be allocated to:

- **Managers**, who should take responsibility for detecting fraud in their area.

- **Finance Director**, who has overall responsibility for the organisational response to fraud including the investigation. This role may be delegated to a **fraud officer** or internal security officer.

- **Personnel** (Human Resources Department), who will have responsibility for disciplinary procedures and issues of employment law and practice.

- **Audit committee**, who should review the details of all frauds and receive reports of any significant events.

- **Internal auditors**, who will most likely have the task of investigating the fraud.

- **External auditors**, to obtain expertise.

- **Legal advisors**, in relation to internal disciplinary, civil or criminal responses.

- **Public relations**, if the fraud is so significantly large that it will come to public attention.

- **Police**, where it is policy to prosecute all those suspected of fraud.

- **Insurers**, where there is likely to be a claim.

Elements of a fraud response plan

Any organisation's fraud response plan should include the following:

(1) **Purpose of the fraud response plan**
   - Set out arrangements for dealing with suspected cases of fraud

(2) **Corporate policy**

(3) **Definition of fraud**

(4) **Roles and responsibilities**
   - (see above)

(5) **The response**
   - Reporting suspicions
   - Establishing an investigation team
   - Formulating a response

(6) **The investigation**
- Preservation of evidence
- Physical evidence
- Electronic evidence
- Interviews
- Statements from witnesses and suspects

(7) **Organisation's objectives with respect to fraud**
- Internal report
- Civil response
- Criminal response

(8) **Follow up action**
- Lessons learned
- Management response

Taken from CIMA "Fraud Risk Management: A guide to good practice" (2008)

Investigation of fraud

When a fraud comes to light, internal auditors might be asked to investigate it. The purpose of investigating a fraud should be to:

- Establish the facts.
- Establish how the fraud occurred and initially went undetected. Were the internal controls weak or inadequate? Or were the internal controls by-passed or not properly applied?
- Consider whether anyone else might have been involved in the fraud.
- Establish or estimate the size of the loss.

The investigator should look at all relevant documents and files, listen to recorded telephone conversations and read the fraudster's e-mails. Individuals working with the fraudster should be interviewed, such as colleagues, supervisor and manager.

Great care must be taken to ensure that evidence is gathered and maintained in a manner that could be used in any criminal proceedings that the company institutes. The company might also have to defend allegations of unfair dismissal or defamation by an employee who claims they have been wrongly accused.

As a result of an investigation, an auditor should make recommendations about the system. These are likely to be that, if the risk of losses is high, either:

- the existing internal controls are not sufficient to limit the risk; new controls or stronger controls should therefore be introduced, or

- the existing internal controls should be sufficient to limit the risk, but were applied inadequately or were ignored in the past; measures should therefore be taken to ensure that the controls are properly applied in the future.

Reputation risk

If a fraud becomes public knowledge it can affect a company's reputation. The control systems within the company will be considered weak which will worry investors. The share price may fall (dependent on the size of the fraud and the investors opinion of it). Future investors will be wary and it may prevent the company from raising future finance.

(In the past companies have adopted two different attitudes to the disclosure of fraud – admit to it, or hide it. Hiding fraud is unethical. Also, often the press find out and the consequences are worse than they would have been if the company had come clean in the first place.)

Litigation risk

If fraud has been identified by the company and they take the case to court, then the perpetrator may deny the accusations resulting in a long and drawn out court case which can be costly for the company. (Often companies consider settling out of court to avoid large court costs and media attention.) However the evidence may be insufficient for a court to find the perpetrator guilty and in some cases the perpetrator might counter-sue for loss of their own reputation. If the company is large and of public interest, this will probably be covered in the press, which may be detrimental to the company's reputation and share price once again.

Test your understanding 3 – Fraud

Discuss the elements of a fraud risk management strategy.

XYS is a company manufacturing and selling a wide range of industrial products to a large number of businesses throughout the country. XYS is a significant local employer, with 2,000 people working out of several locations around the region, all linked by a networked computer system.

XYS purchases numerous components from 500 local and regional suppliers, receiving these into a central warehouse. The company carries about 20,000 different inventory items, placing 15,000 orders with its suppliers each year.

The Accounts Payable Department of XYS has five staff who process all supplier invoices through the company's computer system and make payment to suppliers by cheque or electronic remittance.

Required:

Explain the risk of fraud in Accounts Payable for a company like XYS and how that risk can be mitigated.

3 Chapter summary

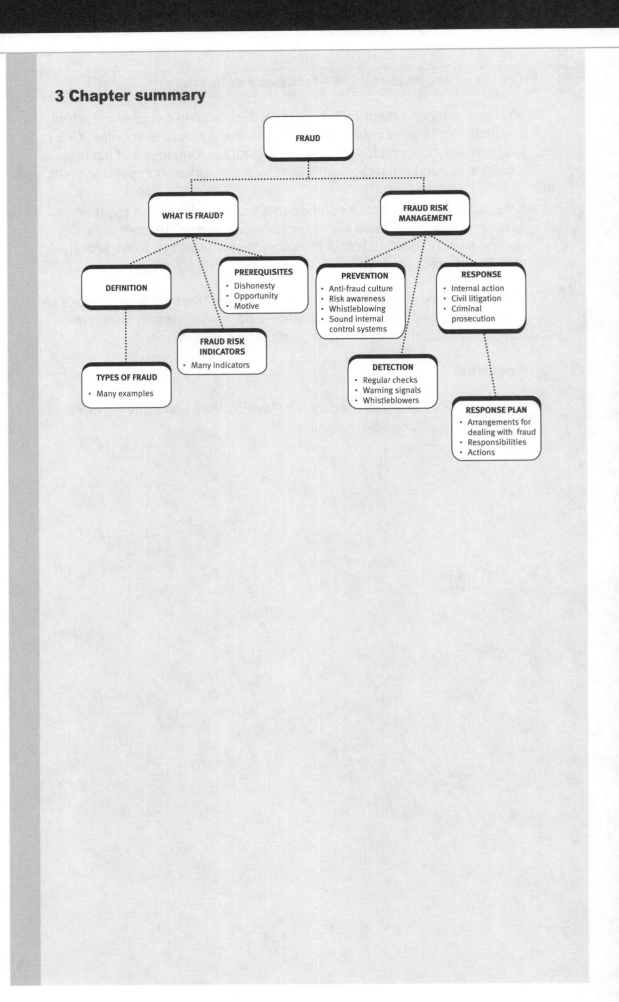

Test your understanding answers

Test your understanding 1

- Absence of an anti-fraud culture.

- Failure of management to implement a sound system of internal controls.

- Lack of financial management expertise and professionalism, lack of review of management reports and lack of review of significant cost estimates.

- Strained relationships between management and internal or external auditors.

- Lack of supervision of staff.

- Inadequate recruitment processes.

- Dissatisfied employees with access to desirable assets.

- Unusual staff behaviour.

- Personal financial pressures of key staff.

- Discrepancy between earnings and lifestyle.

- Low salary levels of key staff.

- Employees working unsocial hours unsupervised.

- Lack of job segregation and independent checking of key transactions.

- Alteration of documents and records.

- Photocopies of documents, replacing originals.

- Missing authorisations.

- Poor physical security of assets.

- Poor access controls to physical assets and IT security systems.

- Large cash transactions.

- Management compensation highly dependent on meeting aggressive performance targets.

- Significant pressure on management to obtain additional finance.

- Complex transactions.

- Complex legal ownership and/or organisational structure.

- The organisation operating in a declining business sector and facing possible business failure.

- Rapid technological change which may increase potential for product obsolescence.

Test your understanding 2 – Causes of fraud

Fraud is dishonestly obtaining an advantage, avoiding an obligation or causing a loss to another party. Those committing fraud may be managers, employees or third parties, including customers and suppliers.

Fraud risk arises out of errors or events in transaction processing or other business operations where those errors or events could be the result of a deliberate act designed to benefit the perpetrator.

There are three conditions for fraud to occur: dishonesty, opportunity and motive. Controls to prevent dishonesty include pre-employment checks; scrutiny of staff by effective supervision; severe discipline for offenders and strong moral leadership.

Opportunity can be reduced by the separation of duties, controls over inputs, processing and outputs and by the physical security of assets, especially cash.

Motive can be influenced by providing good employment conditions, a sympathetic complaints procedure, but dismissing staff instantaneously where it is warranted.

A major reason why people commit fraud is because they are allowed to do so. The likelihood of fraud will be decreased if the potential fraudster believes that the rewards will be modest, or that the chance of detection or punishment will be unacceptably high. Therefore, a comprehensive system of controls is needed to reduce the opportunity for fraud and increase the likelihood of detection.

Test your understanding 3 – Fraud

As for all other risks, a risk management strategy needs to be developed for fraud. This strategy should include fraud prevention - the identification and detection of fraud, and responses to fraud.

The existence of a fraud strategy is itself a deterrent. This can be achieved through an anti-fraud culture and the maintenance of high ethical standards throughout the organisation – risk awareness among employees through training and publicity, a whistle-blowing policy that encourages staff to raise the alarm about fraud and sound internal control systems.

The identification of fraud is often a result of performing regular checks during internal audits. There may be warning signals such as late payments, backlogs of work, holidays not being taken, extravagant lifestyles, missing audit trails, etc. Whistleblowers sometimes identify the existence of fraud. Little fraud is discovered by external auditors. The response to any suspicion of fraud is that an investigation team should be put in place.

Responses to fraud may be internal disciplinary, civil or criminal proceedings and this will influence the method of evidence collection. The fraud response plan should reinforce the organisation's commitment to high standards and its approach to those who fail to meet those standards. Individual responsibilities should be allocated to managers for management of the investigation, response (personnel, police, etc.) and other follow-up action (such as publicity, legal, insurance).

Test your understanding 4 – Fraud and mitigation

Computer systems provide a particular opportunity for fraud, although this requires dishonesty by employees, opportunity to commit fraud, and motive. Accounts Payable in particular presents the opportunity for unscrupulous suppliers to claim payment for goods not delivered or services not supplied, or to overcharge. It also provides the opportunity for employees to redirect payments to themselves or third parties rather than to the intended supplier, either alone or in concert with third parties.

Some controls are preventative to limit or prevent an event from occurring. This could include physical access control over the computer system, selection and training of staff, separation of duties between invoice and payment processing or authorisation levels for invoices and payments. Other controls are detective: they identify events that have already occurred, through, for example, the reconciliation of invoices to a supplier statement. Internal audit, based on risk identification and assessment procedures have an important role to play in detective controls. Finally, corrective controls correct events after they have occurred (e.g. recovering overpayments from suppliers, or seeking recompense from employees under a fraud response plan).

It is particularly important that strong controls exist over programme alterations to accounts payable software, physical and logical access controls to accounts payable systems, authorisation levels for invoices and payments and control over forms such as cheques and electronic bank remittances.

The risk of fraud can be reduced through fraud prevention, identification and response policies. Fraud prevention requires an anti-fraud culture and risk awareness which is part of the control environment; sound control systems; and an effective whistle-blowing policy.

Fraud can be identified through regular internal audit checks, warning signals such as late payments, work backlogs, untaken annual leave, and the lifestyle of staff where it is incommensurate with their salary. Fraud response should include disciplinary action under human resource policies, civil litigation for recovery and criminal prosecution.

7

Ethics

Chapter learning objectives

Lead	Component
B3. Evaluate governance and ethical issues facing an organisation.	(b) Evaluate ethical issues as a source of risk to the organisation and control mechanisms for their detection and resolution.
C2. Evaluate the process and purposes of audit in the context of internal control systems.	(c) Recommend action to avoid or solve problems associated with the audit of activities and systems.
C3. Discuss corporate governance and ethical issues facing an organisation.	(b) Discuss the importance of exercising ethical principles in conducting and reporting on internal reviews.

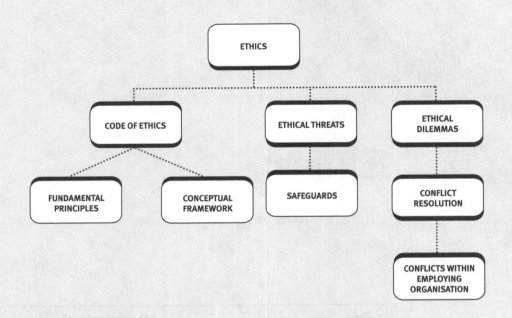

1 Code of ethics

As Chartered Management Accountants, students throughout the world have a duty to observe the highest standards of conduct and integrity, and to uphold the good standing and reputation of the profession. They must also refrain from any conduct which might discredit the profession. Members and registered students must have regard to these guidelines irrespective of their field of activity, of their contract of employment or of any other professional memberships they may hold.

The Institute promotes the highest ethical and business standards, and encourages its members to be good and responsible professionals. Good ethical behaviour may be above that required by the law. In a highly competitive, complex business world, it is essential that CIMA members sustain their integrity and remember the trust and confidence which is placed on them by whoever relies on their objectivity and professionalism. Members must avoid actions or situations which are inconsistent with their professional obligations. They should also be guided not merely by the terms but by the spirit of this Code.

CIMA members should conduct themselves with courtesy and consideration towards all with whom they have professional dealings and should not behave in a manner which could be considered offensive or discriminatory.

CIMA has adopted a code of ethics based on the IFAC (International Federation of Accountants) code of ethics which was developed with input from CIMA and the global accountancy profession. The CIMA Code of Ethics is freely available on CIMA's website – cimaglobal.com > Standards and ethics > Code of ethics.

If a member cannot resolve an ethical issue by following this code or by consulting the ethics support information on CIMA's website, he or she should seek legal advice as to both legal rights and any obligations (s)he may have.

The code of ethics is in three parts:

- Part A establishes the fundamental principles of professional ethics and provides a conceptual framework for applying those principles.

- Parts B and C illustrate how the conceptual framework is to be applied in specific situations:
  - Part B applies to professional accountants in business.
  - Part C applies to professional accountants in public practice.

Fundamental principles

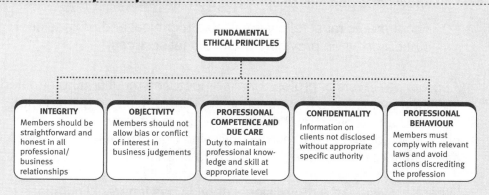

More on fundamental ethical principles

Integrity

Integrity implies fair dealing and truthfulness.

Members are also required not to be associated with any form of communication or report where the information is considered to be:

- materially false or to contain misleading statements

- provided recklessly

- incomplete such that the report or communication becomes misleading by this omission.

Objectivity

Accountants need to ensure that their business/professional judgement is not compromised because of bias or conflict of interest.

However, there are many situations where objectivity can be compromised, so a full list cannot be provided. Accountants are warned to always ensure that their objectivity is intact in any business/professional relationship.

Professional competence and due care

There are two main considerations under this heading:

(1) Accountants are required to have the necessary professional knowledge and skill to carry out work for clients.

(2) Accountants must follow applicable technical and professional standards when providing professional services.

Appropriate levels of professional competence must first be attained and then maintained. Maintenance implies keeping up to date with business and professional developments, and in many institutes completion of an annual return confirming that continuing professional development (CPD) requirements have been met.

Where provision of a professional service has inherent limitations (e.g. reliance on client information) then the client must be made aware of this.

Confidentiality

The principle of confidentiality implies two key considerations for accountants:

(1) Information obtained in a business relationship is not disclosed outside the firm unless there is a proper and specific authority or unless there is a professional right or duty to disclose.

(2) Confidential information acquired during the provision of professional services is not used to personal advantage.

The need to maintain confidentiality is normally extended to cover the accountant's social environment, information about prospective clients and employers and also where business relationships have terminated. Basically there must always be a reason for disclosure before confidential information is provided to a third party.

The main reasons for disclosure are when it is:

(1) permitted by law and authorised by the client

(2) required by law, e.g. during legal proceedings or disclosing information regarding infringements of law

(3) there is professional duty or right to disclose (when not barred by law), e.g. provision of information to the professional institute or compliance with ethical requirements.

Professional behaviour

Accountants must comply with all relevant laws and regulations.

There is also a test whereby actions suggested by a third party which would bring discredit to the profession should also be avoided.

An accountant is required to treat all people contacted in a professional capacity with courtesy and consideration. Similarly, any marketing activities should not bring the profession into disrepute.

Conceptual framework approach

- The circumstances in which management accountants operate may give rise to specific threats to compliance with the fundamental principles.

- It is impossible to define every situation that creates such threats and specify the appropriate mitigating action.

- A conceptual framework that requires a management accountant to identify, evaluate and address threats to compliance with the fundamental principles, rather than merely comply with a set of specific rules which may be arbitrary, is, therefore, in the public interest.

2 Ethical issues as sources of risk

- As stated above, CIMA's code of ethics has a 'threats and safeguards' approach to resolving ethical issues.

- If identified threats are other than clearly insignificant, a management accountant should apply safeguards to eliminate the threats or reduce them to an acceptable level such that compliance with the fundamental principles is not compromised.

Ethical threats

Although it is impossible to define all the situations that could create a threat to the fundamental principles, the code does identify five categories of common threat:

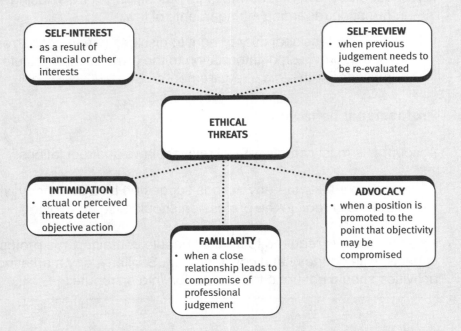

More on ethical threats

Categories of threat identified in the code are:

Self-interest threats can occur as a result of your own or your close family's interests – financial or otherwise. These threats often result in what is commonly called a 'conflict of interest' situation. Working in business, a self-interest threat could result from concern over job security, or from incentive remuneration arrangements. For those in practice it might be the possibility of losing a client or holding a financial interest in a client.

Examples of circumstances that may create self-interest threats for a management accountant in business include:

- Holding a financial interest in, or receiving a loan or guarantee from the employing organisation.

- Participating in incentive compensation arrangements offered by the employing organisation.

- Inappropriate personal use of corporate assets.

- Concern over employment security.

- Commercial pressure from outside the employing organisation.

Self-review threats occur when you are required to re-evaluate your own previous judgement.

An example of a circumstance that creates a self-review threat for a management accountant in business is determining the appropriate accounting treatment for a business combination after performing the feasibility study that supported the acquisition decision.

Familiarity threats can be present when you become so sympathetic to the interests of others as a result of a close relationship that your professional judgement becomes compromised. Sometimes this can result from long association with business contacts who influence business decisions, long association with colleagues, or from accepting gifts or preferential treatment from a client.

Examples of circumstances that may create familiarity threats for a management accountant in business include:

- Being responsible for the employing organisation's financial reporting when an immediate or close family member employed by the entity makes decisions that affect the entity's financial reporting.

- Long association with business contacts influencing business decisions.

- Accepting a gift or preferential treatment, unless the value is trivial and inconsequential.

Intimidation threats occur when you are deterred from acting objectively by actual or perceived threats. It could be the threat of dismissal over a disagreement about applying an accounting principle or reporting financial information, or it could be a dominant personality attempting to influence the decision making process.

Examples of circumstances that may create intimidation threats for a management accountant in business include:

- Threat of dismissal or replacement of the management accountant in business or a close or immediate family member over a disagreement about the application of an accounting principle or the way in which financial information is to be reported.

- A dominant personality attempting to influence the decision-making process, for example with regard to the awarding of contracts or the application of an accounting principle.

Advocacy threats can be a problem when you are promoting a position or opinion to the point that your subsequent objectivity is compromised. It could include acting as an advocate on behalf of an assurance client in litigation or disputes with third parties. In general, promoting the legitimate goals of your employer does not create an advocacy threat, provided that any statements you make are not misleading.

When furthering the legitimate goals and objectives of their employing organisations, management accountants in business may promote the organisation's position, provided any statements made are neither false nor misleading. Such actions generally would not create an advocacy threat.

Safeguards

Safeguards can be viewed as a control mechanism for detecting and resolving ethical issues.

They fall into three broad categories:

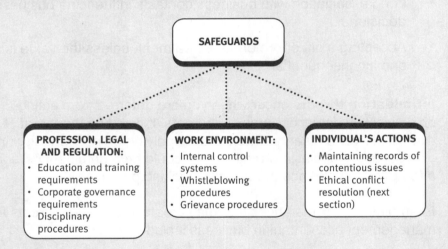

More examples of safeguards

Safeguards created by the **profession, legislation or regulation** include, but are not restricted to:

- Educational, training and experience requirements for entry into the profession.

- Continuing professional development requirements.

- Corporate governance regulations.

- Professional standards.

- Professional or regulatory monitoring and disciplinary procedures.

- External review by a legally empowered third party of the reports, returns, communications or information produced by a professional accountant.

Safeguards in the **work environment** include, but are not restricted to:

- The employing organisation's systems of corporate oversight or other oversight structures.

- The employing organisation's ethics and conduct programs.

- Recruitment procedures in the employing organisation emphasising the importance of employing high calibre competent staff.

- Strong internal controls.

- Appropriate disciplinary processes.

- Leadership that stresses the importance of ethical behaviour and the expectation that employees will act in an ethical manner.

- Policies and procedures to implement and monitor the quality of employee performance.

- Timely communication of the employing organisation's policies and procedures, including any changes to them, to all employees and appropriate training and education on such policies and procedures.

- Policies and procedures to empower and encourage employees to communicate to senior levels within the employing organisation any ethical issues that concern them without fear of retribution (whistleblowing).

- Consultation with another appropriate professional accountant (a second opinion).

- Disclosure or refusal of gifts and hospitality.

3 Example threats and safeguards

Ethical threat	Safeguard
Conflict between requirements of the employer and the fundamental principles For example, acting contrary to laws or regulations or against professional or technical standards. (Intimidation threat)	• Obtaining advice from the employer, professional organisation or professional advisor. • The employer providing a formal dispute resolution process. • Legal advice.
Preparation and reporting on information Accountants need to prepare / report on information fairly, objectively and honestly. However, the accountant may be pressurised to provide misleading information. (Intimidation threat)	• Consultation with superiors in the employing company. • Consultation with those charged with governance. • Consultation with the relevant professional body.
Having sufficient expertise Accountants need to be honest in stating their level of expertise – and not mislead employers by implying they have more expertise than they actually possess. Threats that may result in a lack of expertise include time pressure to carry out a duty, being provided with inadequate information or having insufficient experience.	• Obtaining additional advice / training. • Negotiating more time for duties. • Obtaining assistance from someone with relevant expertise.
Financial interests Situations where an accountant or close family member has financial interests in the employing company. Examples include the accountant being paid a bonus based on the financial statement results which he is preparing, or holding share options in the company. (Self-interest threat)	• Remuneration being determined by other members of management. • Disclosure of relevant interests to those charged with governance. • Consultation with superiors or relevant professional body.

Inducements – receiving offers	
Refers to incentives being offered to encourage unethical behaviour. Inducements may include gifts, hospitality, preferential treatment or inappropriate appeals to loyalty. Objectivity and/or confidentiality may be threatened by such inducements. (Self-interest threat)	• Do not accept the inducement! • Inform relevant third party such as a senior manager.
Inducements – giving offers	
Refers to accountants being pressurised to provide inducements to junior members of staff to influence a decision or obtain confidential information. (Intimidation threat)	• Do not offer the inducement!
Confidential information	
Accountants should keep information about their employing organisation confidential unless there is a right or obligation to disclose, or they have received authorisation from their client. However, the accountant may be under pressure to disclose this information as a result of legal processes such as anti-money laundering / terrorism – in this situation there is a conflict between confidentiality and the need for disclosure.	• Disclose information in compliance with the relevant statutory requirements, e.g. money laundering regulations.

Whistleblowing	
Situations where the accountant needs to consider disclosing information, where ethical rules have been broken.	• Follow the disclosure requirements of the employer, e.g. report to those responsible for governance. Otherwise disclosure should be based on the assessment of: legal obligations, whether members of the public will be adversely affected, gravity of the matter, likelihood of repetition, reliability of the information and reasons why employer does not want to disclose.

Disciplinary committee decisions

The following are illustrations of the workings of a professional institute disciplinary committee to illustrate how an institute will seek to uphold the ethical standards of all members.

Case 1

A formal complaint was submitted to the disciplinary committee that the defendant has:

"…in the course of carrying out professional work or otherwise he has committed any act or default likely to bring discredit on himself, the Institute or the profession of accountancy".

This complaint arose because the defendant breached an Anti-Social Behaviour Order by distributing correspondence relating to parking in a given area which he was prohibited from doing.

In mitigation for his action it was noted that the defendant's professional work had not been affected by this action, and no criticism had been made of his professional competence. The origins of this incident are founded by good intentions; namely, the defendant's passionate wish to improve road safety in the road where he lives.

Decision: The central issue is whether such conduct constitutes a breach of the institute's code of behaviour. It clearly does so; such conduct, which is a breach of the criminal law, inevitably brings discredit of a professional kind with it, regardless of how commendable may have been the original motives of improving road safety.

The disciplinary tribunal considered exclusion from the membership as an appropriate penalty.

Case 2

A student member of the institute was convicted this year of inflicting grievous bodily harm, and in an application for student membership, failed to declare his conviction in the previous year for common assault.

Decision: Reprimanded. (The reprimand was for withholding information from their application form. The police would have dealt with the conviction.)

You may find it useful to review further CIMA disciplinary committee decisions which can be found on their website.

CIMA's Financial Management magazine has a section on ethical dilemmas each month.

4 Ethical dilemmas and conflict resolution

What is an ethical dilemma ?

- A dilemma will only occur if there are two or more interests at stake, even if it is only an ethical duty to oneself.

- An ethical dilemma exists when one or more principles of the code are threatened.

- You may have discovered something unethical, illegal or fraudulent going on where you work, or perhaps you feel that you have been asked to do something that compromises your professional integrity.

- Conflicts of interest and confidentiality issues are also ethical problems.

- In general, ethical issues should be dealt with by taking actions (called safeguards) to reduce them to a level where they are no longer significant or of any consequence.

Ethical conflict resolution

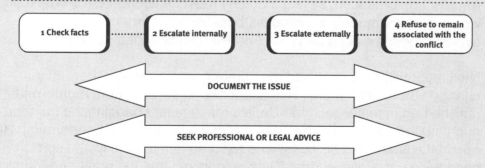

CIMA recommends the following process for addressing situations of ethical conflict:

- Gather all facts and relevant information.

- Ascertain the ethical issues involved and identify the fundamental principles related to the matter in question.

- Escalate concern internally, i.e. to direct management.

- Escalate issue further to your manager's boss, the Board or a non-executive director (following any internal grievance or whistleblowing procedure).

- Seek advice from CIMA.

- Report externally to auditors or relevant trade / regulatory body.

- Remove yourself from the situation.

Throughout the process, document the steps you take to resolve the issue. For example, raise your concern in writing and keep copies of relevant correspondence. This will allow you to demonstrate how you dealt with the problem should you ever need to do so.

Ethics and CIMA

Going downhill fast

Danielle Cohen shares the true story of a CIMA member who contacted the institute's ethics helpline for advice. His problem stemmed from allowing what seemed, on the face of it, a minor issue to snowball into a job-threatening situation.

Andrew was the management accountant of a small firm that was part of a plc. His boss, Chris, was the firm's CEO. Several months ago Chris has approached him with a query about the month-end figures that Andrew has produced, saying that they must be wrong. At the time there was a certain amount of confusion, because their firm had just taken over another small company, so Andrew adjusted them as instructed.

Next month Chris questioned the numbers again, and Andrew duly changed them once more. This happened at several more month-ends until he began to suspect that Chris's reasons for changing the numbers might not be valid – and that the business was simply not performing. He raised the issue with his boss, who assured him that he would sort everything out. Relieved that Chris recognized that the matter needed to be dealt with, Andrew dropped it.

At the end of the firm's financial year, Chris announced that he had, as promised, found a solution to the problem of the ongoing adjustments. Unfortunately, this was very different from what Andrew was expecting. Chris proposed that he own up to the discrepancies, admit that they were the result of a simple error and then resign to prevent any further questions from being asked. In return for carrying the can, Andrew would receive a glowing reference – on the understanding, of course, that he kept quiet about the whole affair.

Shocked and unsure about what to do, Andrew contacted CIMA's ethics helpline. He had gone from accepting a small month-end adjustment to his figures to finding himself about to lose a job. Our guidance to Andrew was that he should consider taking the problem to more senior people in the group, since raising it with Chris wasn't an option. Andrew had some concerns about the possible repercussions of doing this, particularly because Chris was well respected in the group, and he was worried that his version of events would not be believed. The lack of an internal grievance or whistle blowing procedure made it hard for him to predict how his case would be handled.

Given all these factors, Andrew questioned whether quitting was an acceptable solution. A good reference had been promised, but was this pledge worth anything coming from Chris? And how would he explain to any future employer why he had left? And what would happen if a colleague were to complain to CIMA about his lack of competence? If this were to happen, he could potentially lose his membership. Even worse, lying to accept responsibility that wasn't his would be another breach of CIMA's code of ethics. If discovered, this would also have consequences for his membership.

After further discussion, Andrew identified a potential ally (a financial controller) at group level. He arranged a meeting through a trusted colleague in order to minimize the chances of discovery by Chris.

We suggested that Andrew should speak to the institute's legal advice line for expert guidance on his legal obligations and employment rights, and also to the whistle-blowing advice line for free, confidential, independent advice on raising his concerns.

Andrew spoke to the financial controller and Chris was eventually forced to resign. But Andrew's ongoing compliance with his boss's wishes was enough to have tarnished his reputation. A few months later he resigned of his own accord.

Andrew's case is a reminder of how crucial it is to use your professional judgment, heed the warning signs and establish the facts at the first sign of an ethical dilemma. Armed with these and CIMA's code of ethics, you can decide whether or not you need to act and, if so, what that action should be.

So how exactly do you know when an ethical dilemma is an ethical dilemma? As Oscar Wilde observed: 'Morality, like art, means drawing a line someplace.' When the amount of money is not material, the report is only for internal purposes or when no one else seems to think there's an issue, how can you be sure where that line is?

Taking time to consider the situation from all angles will help you to know for sure. In the code of ethics, the line is where a threat to our fundamental principles is anything more than trivial. Although the changes that Andrew made to the numbers in that first month might not have been material, the pattern that they established was. If he had stood up to Chris the first time he was asked to adjust the figures, the situation might never have developed.

Danielle Cohen is CIMA's ethics manager.
This article appeared in Financial Management, November 2007.

Test your understanding 1 – Trainee

You manage a number of trainee accountants whom the company sponsors through training at their first attempt at each paper. In June you employed a final level student who told you during her interview that she did not sit her final exams in May but was sitting them for the first time in November that year. She had actually sat the exams but was worried that she would fail, tarnishing her record with the company, and also she would not get financial support for her re-sit. She passed the May exams.

Required:

What action would you take in this matter?

5 Conflicts within employing organisation

- The syllabus makes specific reference to the importance of exercising ethical principles in conducting and reporting on internal reviews.

- There may be times, however, when a professional accountant's responsibilities to an employing organisation and their professional obligations to comply with the fundamental principles are in conflict.

- Ordinarily, a professional accountant in business should support the legitimate and ethical objectives established by the employer and the rules and procedures drawn up in support of those objectives.

- Nevertheless, where compliance with the fundamental principles is threatened, a professional accountant in business must consider a response to the circumstances.

Pressures that may be faced

A professional accountant may be put under pressure by managers, directors or other individuals to:

- act contrary to law or regulation

- act contrary to technical or professional standards

- facilitate unethical or illegal earnings management strategies

- lie to, or otherwise intentionally mislead (including misleading by remaining silent) others, in particular:
    - the auditors of the employing organisation

    - regulators

- Issue, or otherwise be associated with, a financial or non-financial report that materially misrepresents the facts, including statements in connection with, for example:
    - the financial statements

    - tax compliance

    - legal compliance

    - reports required by securities regulators.

Safeguards to be applied

The significance of threats arising from such pressures, such as intimidation threats, should be evaluated. If they are other than clearly insignificant, safeguards should be considered and applied as necessary to eliminate them or reduce them to an acceptable level. Such safeguards may include:

- obtaining advice where appropriate from within the employing organisation, an independent professional advisor or a relevant professional body.

- the existence of a formal dispute resolution process within the employing organisation.

- seeking legal advice.

Test your understanding 2 – HFD

HFD is a registered charity with 100 employees and 250 volunteers providing in-home care for elderly persons who are unable to fully take care of themselves. The company structure has no shareholders in a practical sense although a small number of issued shares are held by the sponsors who established the charity many years previously. HFD is governed by a seven-member Board of Directors. The Chief Executive Officer (CEO) chairs the board which comprises the chief financial officer (CFO) and five independent, unpaid non-executive directors who were appointed by the CEO based on past business relationships. You are one of the independent members of HFD's board.

The CEO/Chair sets the board agendas, distributes board papers in advance of meetings and briefs board members in relation to each agenda item. At each of its quarterly meetings the Board reviews the financial reports of the charity in some detail and the CFO answers questions. Other issues that regularly appear as agenda items include new government funding initiatives for the client group, and the results of proposals that have been submitted to funding agencies, of which about 25% are successful. There is rarely any discussion of operational matters relating to the charity as the CEO believes these are outside the directors' experience and the executive management team is more than capable of managing the delivery of the in-home care services.

The Board has no separate audit committee but relies on the annual management letter from the external auditors to provide assurance that financial controls are operating effectively. The external auditors were appointed by the CEO many years previously.

HFD's Board believes that its corporate governance could be improved by following the principles applicable to listed companies.

Required:

Explain the aspects of CIMA's ethical principles and the conceptual framework underlying those principles which you would consider relevant to continuing in your role as an independent member of HFD's Board.

Test your understanding 3 – SPQ

As a CIMA member, you have recently been appointed as the Head of Internal Audit for SPQ, a multinational listed company that carries out a large volume of Internet sales to customers who place their orders using their home or work computers. You report to the Chief Executive although you work closely with the Finance Director. You have direct access to the Chair of the audit committee whenever you consider it necessary.

One of your internal audit teams has been conducting a review of IT security for a system which has been in operation for 18 months and which is integral to Internet sales. The audit was included in the internal audit plan following a request by the Chief Accountant. Sample testing by the internal audit team has revealed several transactions over the last three months which have raised concerns about possible hacking or fraudulent access to the customer/order database. Each of these transactions has disappeared from the database after deliveries have been made but without sales being recorded or funds collected from the customer. Each of the identified transactions was for a different customer and there seems to be no relationship between any of the transactions.

You have received the draft report from the internal audit manager responsible for this audit which suggests serious weaknesses in the design of the system. You have discussed this informally with senior managers who have told you that such a report will be politically very unpopular with the Chief Executive as he was significantly involved in the design and approval of the new system and insisted it be implemented earlier than the IT department considered was advisable. No post-implementation review of the system has taken place.

You have been informally advised by several senior managers to lessen the criticism and work with the IT department to correct any deficiencies within the system and to produce a report to the Audit Committee that is less critical and merely identifies the need for some improvement. They suggest that these actions would avoid criticism of the Chief Executive by the Board of SPQ.

Required:

Explain the ethical principles that you should apply as the Head of Internal Audit for SPQ when reporting the results of this internal review and how any ethical conflicts should be resolved.

(CIMA P3 exam November 2005)

Test your understanding 4 – Assistant financial controller

You work for a large company as the assistant financial controller. One of your duties is to reconcile the sales ledger each month. Every month it does not agree and you feel sure it is associated with irrecoverable debts being written off in the individual customer accounts but not included in the nominal ledger. You consider the differences to be material and have brought this to the attention of the financial controller but he seems unwilling to act.

Required:

What action would you take in this situation?

Test your understanding 5 – Erasmus

You are the newly-appointed financial controller of Erasmus, a fully owned subsidiary of the Think Group. The following matters have come to your attention:

(1) Your assistant, a newly-qualified Management Accountant, is heavily in debt to a junior member of the finance staff, who has a considerable amount of personal wealth in spite of his fairly junior position in the company.

(2) The CEO of the company was in the habit of making accounting adjustments to the financial statements prepared by the finance director in order to 'smooth out variances' if actual performance was not going to plan.

(3) A member of your department, another Management Accountant, recently made significant errors in completing the sales tax returns to the tax authorities, which resulted in a fine and interest charges for an underpayment of the sales tax liability.

Required:

Discuss how you would deal with each of these three problems in order to bring about an improvement in the ethical standards in the systems of management. Indicate any problems you might expect to arise when you attempt to bring about change.

Test your understanding 6 – Five ethical situations

In all of the ethical situations below, the people involved are qualified members of CIMA.

- A applies for a job and enhances his CV by indicating he obtained first time passes in all his examinations, although he actually failed three exams at the first attempt.

- B is the management accountant in C Ltd. B is paid a bonus based on the profits of C Ltd. During accounts preparation B notices an error in the inventory calculation which has the effect of overstating profits. B decides to take no action as this would decrease the bonus payable.

- D is responsible for the purchase of computer equipment in E Ltd. Quotes from three suppliers have been received for installation of new hardware; one supplier, F Co, has promised a 10% discount payable to D if their quote is accepted.

- G is preparing the management accounts in H Ltd. Part of the information presented to him indicates that H Ltd entered into an illegal agreement with I Ltd to fix price increases in the goods H and I supply. H and I together supply 90% of the total market. The price setting enabled H and I to obtain higher than expected profits for their sales.

- J is preparing the management accounts for K Ltd. L, the senior management accountant, has instructed J to omit the negative overhead variance from the accounts on the grounds that they show an 'unacceptable loss' with the inclusion of the variance.

Required:

(a) Explain how professional codes of ethics address possible conflicts of interest facing accountants.

(b) For each of the situations above:
   (i) Identify and explain the ethical threat to the accountant.
   (ii) Discuss the ethical safeguards available to overcome that threat.

6 Chapter summary

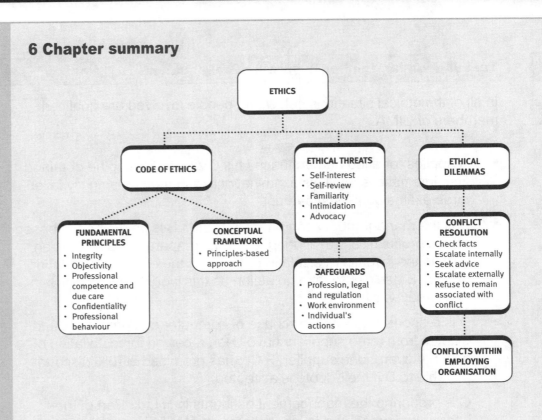

Test your understanding answers

Test your understanding 1 – Trainee

The main ethical issue here is again integrity.

The new employee has not behaved with integrity by lying, and also doing so with the deliberate attempt to further her career, and to defraud the company of her examination and tuition fees. This must be taken seriously as it could also suggest she may not behave with integrity in other areas.

Possible actions include:

- The employee should be disciplined through the formal corporate disciplinary channels such as a formal written warning.

- Depending on how seriously this is viewed, the company could consider dismissal and possibly reporting to CIMA.

Test your understanding 2 – HFD

CIMA's Code of Ethics for Professional Accountants makes clear that an accountant's responsibility is more than satisfying the needs of a client, s/he must also act in the public interest. It is irrelevant whether or not the CIMA member is paid for his/her services, which are still expected to comply with the ethical principles.

There are 5 fundamental principles in the Code of Ethics: integrity, objectivity, professional competence and due care, confidentiality and professional behaviour.

Of particular relevance to HFD are objectivity, and professional competence and due care. Objectivity may be impeded due to bias because of his/her appointment by the CEO or the influence of the CEO or other persons on the board who may align themselves with the CEO.

The demands of professional competence and due care means that the accountant must look beyond the narrow agenda set by the CEO to a broader perspective than financial statements to non-financial risks (mainly in relation to the charities operation) and the adequacy of internal controls (as it is insufficient to rely wholly on the external auditor's annual management letter).

The conceptual framework underlying CIMA's ethical principles requires accountants to risk manage their own position in relation to the work they are performing and in so doing to identify, evaluate and mitigate any risks they face. The main risks faced by an accountant include those relating to self-interested behaviour, self-review, advocacy, familiarity and intimidation.

The major threats faced in relation to HFD are familiarity and intimidation. The accountant has been appointed to the board as a result of some prior business relationship which may affect his/her objectivity. The CEO/Chair of HFD also appears to be a dominating individual and the accountant may be intimidated by this individual, resulting in the accountant's views not being presented accurately and/or forcefully.

The accountant as board member needs to identify and evaluate the risks of familiarity and/or intimidation that s/he faces, and ensure that s/he takes appropriate action (ultimately resignation from the board) to maintain his/her independence and objectivity.

Test your understanding 3 – SPQ

The fundamental principles that relate to the work of accountants as internal auditors are integrity (acting honestly and avoiding misleading statements); objectivity (impartiality and freedom from conflicts of interest); professional competence and due care; confidentiality; professional behaviour and the avoidance of conduct that might bring discredit to CIMA; and technical competence (the presentation of information fully, honestly and professionally).

Most of these principles apply in the present case. If the evidence justifies it, integrity and objectivity require that it be brought to the audit committee's attention. However, professional and technical competence requires that the Head of Internal Audit be confident in the audit findings before doing so.

CIMA's Ethical Guidelines describe the process for resolving ethical conflicts. Accountants working in organisations may encounter situations which give rise to conflicts of interest, ranging from fraud and illegal activities to relatively minor situations. An ethical conflict is not the same as an honest difference of opinion.

CIMA members should be constantly conscious of, and be alert to factors which give rise to conflicts of interest. In the present case, the ethical conflict is the real or perceived pressure placed on the Head of Internal Audit not to embarrass the Chief Executive. There is also the question of divided loyalty to the Chief Executive, to the audit committee, and to the Head of Internal Audit's professional responsibilities as a CIMA member.

Although it has not been suggested to the Head of Internal Audit that the matter not be reported, there is a suggestion that the report be softened and that work carry on behind the scenes to improve the system.

However, it is important that a draft report be produced and submitted for comment before it is sent to the audit committee. This presents the opportunity for other views to be aired. One course of action may be to discuss the matter with the Finance Director to determine his/her view and with the Chief Executive to determine that person's reactions to the draft audit report.

When faced with ethical conflicts, members should:

- Follow the organisation's grievance procedure.
- Discuss the matter with the member's superior and successive levels of management, always with the member's superior's knowledge (unless that person is involved).

Discussion with an objective adviser or the professional body may be useful to clarify the issues involved and alternative courses of action that are available, without breaching any duty of confidentiality. Throughout, the member should maintain a detailed record of the problem and the steps taken to resolve it.

If an ethical conflict still exists after fully exhausting all levels of internal review, the member may have no recourse on significant matters other than to resign and report the matter to the organisation. Except when seeking advice from CIMA or when legally required to do so, communication of information regarding the problem to persons outside the employing organisation is not considered appropriate.

Test your understanding 4 – Assistant financial controller

The main ethical issue involved here is integrity. It would not be appropriate for an accountant to assist someone with a potentially fraudulent act, or to allow misleading information to be presented to others.

There is also a potential issue of objectivity. If you are placed under pressure by the financial controller this would mean you have a conflict of interest between your personal prospects and the requirement to behave with integrity.

The possible actions could include:

- Informing the financial controller of your concern and also formally asking the financial controller to address it.

- Informing the financial controller that you are going to bring the matter to the attention of perhaps the financial director or the audit committee.

- It would be very unusual to report the matter externally even if fraud were suspected as this might breach the rules of confidentiality. Usually external reporting would only be made with legal advice.

Test your understanding 5 – Erasmus

(1) Indebtedness of the assistant to the junior staff member

This situation might call into question the independence and objectivity of the assistant in carrying out his work within the finance function. It could also threaten my own position, if it were generally known that a member of my staff is receiving financial assistance from a junior colleague.

The position of the assistant is difficult, because he is presumably unable to repay the debt immediately, and he might be unaware of the fact that he has put the internal audit section into an embarrassing position.

I should discuss the position with him, and explain the problem that it has caused. He should be reminded of CIMA's ethical guidelines about the need to maintain objectivity and independence. I should find out how quickly he plans to repay the debt. If this will not happen quickly, I should ask whether he might be able to obtain a loan to repay the debt. (The company might possibly be willing to provide a loan for such a purpose.)

If the assistant is unable to agree to my suggestion, I should have to consider recommending that he should be moved to another position where his independence and objectivity would not be compromised.

(2) CEO's accounting adjustments

It is my responsibility to provide the CEO with financial information that is competently and accurately prepared. The CEO presumably shares the financial information with his board colleagues and the board of the parent company. I need to consider whether any adjustments made by the CEO to financial statements that I prepare will bring my integrity into question.

I should resist attempts by the CEO to amend financial results to make them seem better than they actually are. It would be particularly worrying if figures have been altered in order to improve the financial rewards for the CEO. On the other hand, some prudent adjustments to the figures might be justifiable.

I should discuss the situation with the finance director and the CEO, and establish whether the CEO intends to continue altering financial statements in the future, and his reasons for doing so. If the situation cannot be resolved, I should have to consider my position within the company. I should not remain in a position where I know that my integrity is being compromised.

(3) Errors in the sales tax returns

CIMA members have an ethical duty to carry out their work with professional competence. Technical competence means that the staff in my department should understand the necessary rules in relation to the tax work they do. Ignorance is no excuse for mistakes, and a repetition of the errors – and the fine – must be avoided.

I need to ensure that the staff who carry out specialist tasks are competent to carry them out. Training should be provided if required. Suitable instructions and guidance should also be available for reference.

Test your understanding 6 – Five ethical situations

(a) There are a number of possible threats to fundamental ethical principles which lead to conflicts of interest affecting accountants in their work. Professional codes of ethics aim to enable the accountant to understand how to resolve these conflicts of interest.

Conflicts of interest and their resolution are explained in the conceptual framework to the code of ethics. A framework is needed because it is impossible to define every situation where threats to fundamental principles may occur or the mitigating action required. Different assignments may also create different threats and mitigating actions – again it is not possible to detail all the assignments an accountant undertakes. The framework helps to identify threats – using the fundamental ethical principles as guidance. This approach is preferable to following a set of rules which may not be applicable in a particular case.

Once a material threat has been identified, mitigating activities will be performed to ensure that compliance with fundamental principles is not compromised.

Where conflicts arise in the application of fundamental principles, the code of ethics provides guidance on how to resolve the conflict.

The conceptual framework:

- provides an initial set of assumptions, values and definitions which are agreed upon and shared by all those subject to the framework.

- is stated in relatively general terms so it is easy to understand and communicate.

- recognises that ethical issues may have no 'correct' answer.

- provides the generalised guidelines and principles to apply to any situation.

(b) **Situation 1**

Ethical threat – dishonesty

Accountants need to be honest in stating their level of expertise – and not mislead employers by implying they have more expertise than they actually possess. In this situation, A is implying he was better at studying for his exams than his actual exam success rate. This may make the potential employer view A more favourably, or enable A to meet a recruitment criteria of 'first time passes only' for success in obtaining the job.

Ethical safeguards

It is difficult to stop provision of incorrect information in this instance. However, A should be following the fundamental ethical principle of integrity in applying for the job. Alternatively, the potential employer could ask all applicants to confirm that information provided is accurate as a condition of employment. Any errors or omissions found later could act as initial grounds for disciplinary action.

Situation 2

Ethical threat – overstatement of profits and salary

B's bonus is determined by the same accounts that B is working on. The threat is that B will overstate profits in some way to ensure that the bonus payable is as high as possible. Again, accountants should act with integrity and honestly, although these ideals conflict in this case with B's remuneration.

Ethical safeguards

The main safeguard will be to ensure that someone other than B determines the amount of B's bonus (and checks the accounts produced) – or that the bonus is not linked to the accounts that B is preparing. This removes the conflict of interest.

Situation 3

Ethical threat – receipt of bribes / gifts

D stands to gain 10% of a contract price by accepting the quote from F rather than another company. This means D's objectivity may be breached because he will be favourably impressed by the quote from F. There is also an issue of confidentiality because presumably D will want to keep the payment 'secret' from E Ltd so his employer does not know of the inducement.

Ethical safeguard

From D's point-of-view, the obvious ethical safeguard is not to accept the bribe. This removes the objectivity issue leaving D free to choose the best system rather than the one with the most financial advantage to him. Alternatively, D can inform the senior management and/or board of E Ltd, provide the relevant information on the three quotes, and let the board make the final decision. Should the board choose F then again D should not accept the bribe.

Situation 4

Ethical threat – price fixing

In most situations, G would keep the affairs of his client confidential, and would be acting with integrity in taking this action. However, there is a conflict as H and I appear to have been acting illegally; increasing their profits at the expense of their customers. G can either choose to keep quiet about the situation or disclose the information to relevant third parties, effectively 'blowing the whistle' on H and I.

Ethical safeguards

G could report to the ethics committee or audit committee in H, should the company have either of these committees. As long as some appropriate action was taken, then this relieves G from external reporting obligations. External disclosure should only be made after taking into account various issues such as the gravity of the matter, the number of people affected and the likelihood of repetition. As many people are affected and repetition seems likely then external disclosure is likely to be appropriate.

Situation 5

Ethical threat – incorrect financial information

Accountants need to be able to prepare information honestly and with objectivity. However, in this situation, J is being pressured into producing information which will be incorrect, simply to show K Ltd in a better light. The instruction provides a conflict with J's integrity because he wants to follow the instructions of L but may not be able to do so because this would be dishonest.

Ethical safeguards

J needs to consult with other people apart from L in an attempt to determine the correct course of action. J can consult with any committee charged with governance (e.g. the audit committee or ethics committee) or if necessary take advice from his professional body. If after these discussions, the situation cannot be resolved, J may have to consider resignation.

Corporate governance

Chapter learning objectives

Lead	Component
B3. Evaluate governance and ethical issues facing an organisation.	(a) Discuss the principles of good corporate governance, particularly as regards the need for internal controls.
C1. Discuss the importance of management review of controls.	(a) Discuss the importance of management review of controls.
C3. Discuss corporate governance and ethical issues facing an organisation.	(b) Discuss the principles of good corporate governance for listed companies, for conducting reviews of internal controls and reporting on compliance.

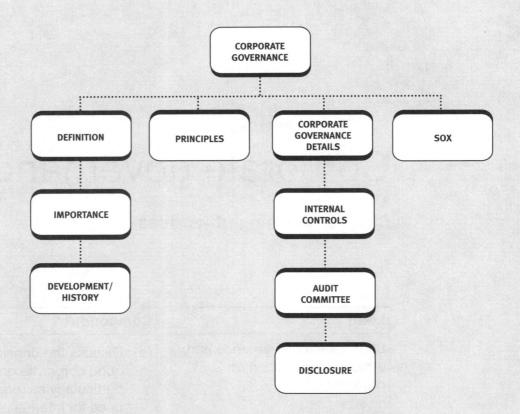

1 What is corporate governance?

Corporate governance has been defined in many different ways, but generally it can be described as:

'the system by which companies are directed and controlled in the interest of shareholders and other stakeholders'.

There are different codes and practices around the world but they tend to cover similar areas:

- The role of the board of directors.
- The reliability of financial reports and the relationship between the company and its auditors.
- The interest of the company's shareholders in the company.

Importance of corporate governance

- In most developed countries, listed companies are required to operate systems of corporate governance laid down either by statute or by professional organisations (such as the Securities and Exchange Commission (SEC) in the US or the Financial Services Authority (FSA) in the UK).
- The requirements are often given the support of the stock exchanges, in that they are built into listing rules.

- The development of corporate governance codes is closely associated with the UK, hence this is a model to discuss best practice.

- The UK Corporate Governance Code follows a principles-based approach (see next section), and is endorsed by the London Stock Exchange. The US system has been much more legislative with the introduction of the Sarbanes-Oxley Act of 2002 (to be discussed later in this chapter).

- It should be appreciated that corporate governance has links to risks and internal controls. Whilst good corporate governance cannot stop company failure or prevent companies failing to achieve their objectives, it is a major help, and well-run companies tend to achieve their objectives in a less risky way. As a result it is part of risk reduction.

Development of corporate governance

- Governance regulations have developed largely as a result of a series of corporate failures in the 1980s and early 1990s.

- The corporate governance themes that began to emerge from these collapses were:
  - poorly-run companies, especially companies with a board of directors dominated by a single chairman/chief executive figure, and companies with 'greedy' or 'fat cat' directors (demonstrating the agency problem of a company failing to operate in the best interests of its shareholders)

  - poor financial reporting, raising questions about auditing and internal control systems, and

  - an apparent lack of interest by the major investment institutions in the performance of the companies in which they invested.

- More recently the UK Corporate Governance Code has been developed further in accordance with the 2008–09 global financial crisis.

Company collapses

Several issues or problems appear to emerge when there is a corporate governance 'scandal' and a company has collapsed.

- The company has not been well-run by its board of directors.

- In many cases, there has been an individual who has dominated the board and exerted excessive influence on decision-making by the board. In many cases, this individual held the positions of both chairman of the board and chief executive officer.

- A board of directors might have lacked sufficient breadth of knowledge and experience to appreciate the problems the company was in and the risks it faced.

- Companies were being run in the interests of the executive directors, who received high remuneration packages and generous bonuses, but the rewards were not being given for the achievement of objectives that were in the best interests of the shareholders. The interests of the directors were not properly aligned with those of the shareholders.

- Financial reporting was unreliable and the published accounts did not seem to give any indication of the true financial position of the company. In some cases there was a suspicion that the auditors were not sufficiently independent of the company and so not fulfilling their responsibilities adequately. Alternatively, the auditors were accused of doing their job badly or of being misled by the company's directors and management. (In 2002 audit firm Arthur Andersen collapsed from the consequences of its involvement in the Enron scandal.)

- Whenever a company collapsed unexpectedly, there have been suspicions that the internal control system was ineffective. There usually appears to have been inadequate risk management generally.

- Questions have also been asked about major institutional shareholders, and whether they could have done more to identify problems in companies and persuade or force the directors to make improvements.

Maxwell Communications Corporation

Robert Maxwell was born in to extreme poverty in Czechoslovakia in 1923. By the time of his death (accident or murder was never established) in 1991 he was a media mogul, having built a publishing empire that spanned the world. In the weeks that followed his death however, news emerged of the state of his company's finances.

After the Second World War he set up Pergamon Press publishing scientific journals. It became very profitable and he turned his attention to politics, later becoming a Member of Parliament for the Labour Party. His relationship with the Party was an uneasy one since anyone who criticised him was confronted in the courts. This was when signs emerged of his dishonesty.

In 1969, Maxwell agreed a takeover bid for Pergamon by Leasco (an American financial and data processing group). The profits of Pergamon were questioned by Leasco and eventually talks fell apart as a Department of Trade and Industry (DTI) enquiry ensued. Inspectors found that the profits depended on transactions with Maxwell family private companies. The DTI concluded that Maxwell 'is not a person... who can be relied upon to exercise proper stewardship of a publicly quoted company'.

In 1980 Maxwell took over the troubled British Printing Corporation renaming it Maxwell Communications Corporation. In 1984 he bought Mirror Group Newspapers (MGN) and Macmillan publishers, which put his company further into debt. In 1991 he floated MGN as a public company desperate to raise cash that would save the Group from bankruptcy (with debts over £2 billion). After Maxwell's death it transpired that he had taken money from the pension funds to keep the companies afloat and boost the share price.

Enron

In December 2001, US energy trader Enron collapsed. Enron was the largest bankruptcy in US history. Even though the United States was believed by many to be the most regulated financial market in the world, it was evident from Enron's collapse that investors were not properly informed about the significance of off-balance sheet transactions. US accounting rules may have contributed to this, in that they are concerned with the strict legal ownership of investment vehicles rather than with their control. By contrast, International Accounting Standards follow the principle of 'substance over form'. There were some indications that Enron may have actively lobbied against changing the treatment in US financial reporting of special purpose entities used in off-balance sheet financing. Overall, there was a clear need for greater transparency and trust in reporting.

The failure of Enron also highlighted the over-dependence of an auditor on one particular client, the employment of staff by Enron who had previously worked for the auditors, the process of audit appointments and re-appointments, the rotation of audit partners and how auditors are monitored and regulated.

As a consequence of the failure of Enron and WorldCom, the United States has introduced Sarbanes-Oxley legislation to address many of the criticisms of reporting and auditing practice. In their comments on the failure of Enron, the Association of Certified Chartered Accountants recommended the need for global financial markets to have a global set of principles-based financial reporting standards and a global code of corporate governance, arguing that legalistic, rules-based standards encourage creative, loophole-based practice.

Former chief executive Kenneth Lay died in 2006 before he could stand trial. Enron's former chief financial officer Andrew Fastow was sentenced in late 2006 to six years in prison for stealing from Enron and devising schemes to deceive investors about the energy company's true financial condition. Lawyers have to date won settlements totalling $US 7.3 billion from banks including JPMorgan Chase, Bank of America, Citigroup, etc.

Barings Bank

Barings Bank was Britain's oldest bank, having existed for 200 years before it collapsed as a result of uncontrolled derivatives trading by Nick Leeson in the bank's Singapore office.

The collapse of Barings Bank in 1995 was caused by Nick Leeson, a 26-year-old dealer who lost £800 million in unauthorised dealings in derivatives trading from his base in Singapore. Leeson suppressed information on account '88888' which he used for trading between 1992 and 1995, which management was unaware of. The losses wiped out the Bank's capital.

As only a small amount of money (a margin) is needed to establish a derivatives position, it is possible to face financial obligations beyond an organisation's ability to pay. Therefore, strict controls are needed. There are many risk management and control lessons to be learned from the failure of Barings.

Barings had placed Nick Leeson in charge of both the dealing desk and the back office. The back office records, confirms and settles trades made by the front office and provides the necessary checks to prevent unauthorised trading and minimise the potential for fraud and embezzlement. In this dual position, Leeson was able to relay false information back to London.

An internal audit report in August 1994 concluded that Leeson's dual responsibility for both the front and back office was an excessive concentration of powers and warned of the risk that Leeson could override controls. The internal auditors' responsibility was to make sure the directors were aware of the risk they were facing by not implementing the separation of duties. However, directors did not implement these recommendations. Their response was that there was insufficient work for a full-time treasury and risk manager. There was also a lack of supervision of Leeson by Barings' managers, either in Singapore or London.

Senior managers of Barings had a superficial knowledge of derivatives, did not understand the risks of the business, did not articulate the bank's risk appetite or implement strategies and control procedures appropriate to those risks.

When the Singapore exchange made margin demands on Barings, large amounts of cash had to be paid out but still no steps were taken by the London head office to investigate the matter. Eventually, the amounts required were so great that Barings were forced to call in receivers. The trading positions taken out by Leeson were unhedged and the cost of closing out the open contracts was US$1.4 billion.

The information in this case study comes from the Report of the Board of Banking Supervision (BoBS) Inquiry into the Circumstances of the Collapse of Barings.

Worldcom

WorldCom filed for bankruptcy protection in June 2002. It was the biggest corporate fraud in history, largely a result of treating operating expenses as capital expenditure.

WorldCom (now renamed MCI) admitted in March 2004 that the total amount by which it had misled investors over the previous 10 years was almost US$75 billion (£42 billion) and reduced its stated pre-tax profits for 2001 and 2002 by that amount.

WorldCom stock began falling in late 1999 as businesses slashed spending on telecom services and equipment. A series of debt downgrades had raised borrowing costs for the company, struggling with about US$32 billion in debt. WorldCom used accounting tricks to conceal a deteriorating financial condition and to inflate profits.

Former WorldCom chief executive Bernie Ebbers resigned in April 2002 amid questions about US$366 million in personal loans from the company and a federal probe of its accounting practices. Ebbers was subsequently charged with conspiracy to commit securities fraud, and filing misleading data with the Securities and Exchange Commission (SEC). Scott Sullivan, former chief financial officer, pleaded guilty to three criminal charges.

The SEC said WorldCom had committed 'accounting improprieties of unprecedented magnitude' – proof, it said, of the need for reform in the regulation of corporate accounting.

Parmalat

In December 2003, Italian dairy-foods group Parmalat, with 36,000 employees in 30 countries, went into bankruptcy protection with US$ 8–10 billion of vanished assets. The company was 51% owned by the Tanzi family.

Parmalat defaulted on a US$185 million bond payment that prompted auditors and banks to scrutinise company accounts. Thirty-eight per cent of Parmalat's assets were supposedly held in a bank account in the Cayman Islands but no such account ever existed. Letters received from the bank by auditors were forgeries.

Parmalat has been one of the largest financial frauds in history. The company falsified its accounts over a 15-year period. This was not identified by two firms of auditors, Grant Thornton and Deloitte Touche Tohmatsu. At least 20 people have been involved in the fraud, including members of the Tanzi family, the chief financial officer, board members and the company's lawyers. Calisto Tanzi the founder and chief executive was arrested on suspicion of fraud, embezzlement, false accounting and misleading investors.

Tanzi admitted that he knew the accounts were falsified to hide losses and the falsified balance sheet was used to enable Parmalat to continue borrowing. He also confessed to misappropriating US$620 million, although prosecutors believe it could be as much as US$1 billion.

Equitable Life

During the 1960s to 1980s the 242-year-old Equitable Life had sold thousands of policies with guaranteed returns, some as high as 12%. The company ran into problems in 2000 when it closed to new business after years of excessive returns to special policy holders had left the company with no money to absorb a deterior-ation in the value of its stock market investments. It had a 'black hole' in its finances estimated at £4.4 billion because it had been paying out more to policy holders than it held in reserves. Equitable lost a case in the House of Lords in 2000 that led to a further deterioration in its financial position of £1.5 billion.

A report by Lord Penrose published early in 2004 said that the former management was primarily culpable for Equitable's near collapse, aided by the failure of regulators to identify the mutual insurer's financial position. The autocratic former Chief Executive and chief actuary Roy Ranson was blamed for keeping regulators and the board of Equitable in the dark about the precarious state of Equitable's financial position throughout the 1990s. The Penrose report also said that there had been weaknesses in the way that insurance companies were supervised throughout that period. The 'light touch' approach to regulation had not been changed to meet the requirements of an increasingly sophisticated and risky investment industry.

The Penrose report said that management had been dominated by 'unaccountable' actuaries, a board of non-executives who had no idea what was going on at the company they were charged with overseeing and a regulator that failed to act as any kind of protector for policy holders.

Lord Penrose said, "The board at no stage got fully to grips with the financial situation faced by the Society. Information was too fragmented [and], their collective skills were inadequate for the task".

2 Principles of good corporate governance

Since Hampel's work in 1998 the Financial Reporting Council (FRC) has issued several editions of the Code to incorporate the findings from subsequent reports and reviews. The latest edition came into force for accounting periods starting on or after 29 June 2010 - 'Financial Reporting Council - The UK Corporate Governance Code June 2010'.

The Listing Rules of the London Stock Exchange now require each listed company to state in its annual report:

* How it has applied the principles of the UK Corporate Governance Code.

* Whether or not it has complied with the provisions of the Code throughout the accounting period.

Although there are some legal requirements relating to corporate governance, the main approach is that listed companies are required to 'comply or explain' with the provisions of the Code. This is referred to as a principles-based approach.

Other countries around the world have based their own corporate governance principles upon either the UK or the US principles, which has led to several other similar approaches. e.g. the King Report in South Africa, which will be detailed later.

The principles of the UK Corporate Governance Code relate to the following areas:

- Leadership.
- Effectiveness.
- Accountability.
- Remuneration.
- Relations with shareholders.

Leadership

Every company should be headed by an effective board which is collectively responsible for the long-term success of the company.

There should be a clear division of responsibilities at the head of the company between the running of the board and the executive responsibility for the running of the company's business. No one individual should have unfettered powers of decision.

The chairman is responsible for leadership of the board and ensuring its effectiveness on all aspects of its role.

As part of their role as members of a unitary board, non-executive directors should constructively challenge and help develop proposals on strategy.

Roles of Chairperson and Chief Executive Officer (CEO)

The chairman of the board is responsible for managing the board of directors and for leadership of the board ensuring its effectiveness. The chief executive officer is responsible for the executive management team (and as executives, the executive director's report to the CEO).

In order to reduce the risk of domination of the board by a single powerful individual, the Code states that:

- There should be a clear division of responsibilities between running the board (the role of the chairman) and the executive responsibility for the running of the company's business (the role of the CEO).
- The roles of chairman of the board and CEO should not be held by the same individual.

The Code recommends that the chief executive officer should not go on to become the board chairman of the same company. The concern is that a former CEO who moves on to become chairman will be tempted to interfere with the work of the new CEO (who might well want to change many things that the former CEO had done).

The chairman has a duty to achieve a culture of openness and debate, and to ensure that adequate time is given to discussion.

The board is responsible for the long-term success of the company.

Non-Executive Directors (NEDs)

Non-executive directors should scrutinise the performance of management in meeting agreed goals and objectives and monitor the reporting of performance. They should satisfy themselves on the integrity of financial information and that financial controls and systems of risk management are robust and defensible. They are responsible for determining appropriate levels of remuneration of executive directors and have a prime role in appointing and, where necessary, removing executive directors, and in succession planning.

The board should appoint one of the independent non-executive directors to be the senior independent director to provide a sounding board for the chairman and to serve as an intermediary for the other directors when necessary. The senior independent director should be available to shareholders if they have concerns which contact through the normal channels of chairman, chief executive or other executive directors has failed to resolve or for which such contact is inappropriate.

The chairman should hold meetings with the non-executive directors without the executives present. Led by the senior independent director, the non-executive directors should meet without the chairman present at least annually to appraise the chairman's performance and on such other occasions as are deemed appropriate.

Where directors have concerns which cannot be resolved about the running of the company or a proposed action, they should ensure that their concerns are recorded in the board minutes. On resignation, a non-executive director should provide a written statement to the chairman, for circulation to the board, if they have any such concerns.

Effectiveness

The board and its committees should have the appropriate balance of skills, experience, independence and knowledge of the company to enable them to discharge their respective duties and responsibilities effectively.

There should be a formal, rigorous and transparent procedure for the appointment of new directors to the board.

All directors should be able to allocate sufficient time to the company to discharge their responsibilities effectively.

All directors should receive induction on joining the board and should regularly update and refresh their skills and knowledge.

The board should be supplied in a timely manner with information in a form and of a quality appropriate to enable it to discharge its duties.

The board should undertake a formal and rigorous annual evaluation of its own performance and that of its committees and individual directors.

All directors should be submitted for re-election at regular intervals, subject to continued satisfactory performance.

Board effectiveness

An effective board of directors is essential for good corporate governance. The Code lists several provisions relating to the effectiveness of the board. These include:

- The board and its committees should have the appropriate balance of skills, experience, independence and knowledge of the company to enable them to discharge their respective duties and responsibilities effectively.

- There should be a formal, rigorous and transparent procedure for the appointment of new directors to the board.

- All directors should be able to allocate sufficient time to the company to discharge their responsibilities effectively.

- All directors should receive induction on joining the board and should regularly update and refresh their skills and knowledge.

- The board should be supplied in a timely manner with information in a form and of a quality appropriate to enable it to discharge its duties.

- The board should undertake a formal and rigorous annual evaluation of its own performance and that of its committees and individual directors.

- All directors should be submitted for re-election at regular intervals, subject to continued satisfactory performance.

Audit committee

The board should establish an audit committee of at least three, or in the case of smaller companies two, independent non-executive directors. In smaller companies the company chairman may be a member of, but not chair, the committee in addition to the independent non-executive directors, provided he or she was considered independent on appointment as chairman. The board should satisfy itself that at least one member of the audit committee has recent and relevant financial experience.

The audit committee's role is:

- to monitor the integrity of the financial statements of the company and any formal announcements relating to the company's financial performance, reviewing significant financial reporting judgements contained in them;

- to review the company's internal financial controls and, unless expressly addressed by a separate board risk committee composed of independent directors, or by the board itself, to review the company's internal control and risk management systems;

- to monitor and review the effectiveness of the company's internal audit function;

- to make recommendations to the board, for it to put to the shareholders for their approval in general meeting, in relation to the appointment, re-appointment and removal of the external auditor and to approve the remuneration and terms of engagement of the external auditor;

- to review and monitor the external auditor's independence and objectivity and the effectiveness of the audit process, taking into consideration relevant UK professional and regulatory requirements;

- to develop and implement policy on the engagement of the external auditor to supply non-audit services, taking into account relevant ethical guidance regarding the provision of non-audit services by the external audit firm, and to report to the board, identifying any matters in respect of which it considers that action or improvement is needed and making recommendations as to the steps to be taken.

The terms of reference of the audit committee, including its role and the authority delegated to it by the board, should be made available. A separate section of the annual report should describe the work of the committee in discharging those responsibilities.

The audit committee should review arrangements by which staff of the company may, in confidence, raise concerns about possible improprieties in matters of financial reporting or other matters. The audit committee's objective should be to ensure that arrangements are in place for the proportionate and independent investigation of such matters and for appropriate follow-up action.

The audit committee should monitor and review the effectiveness of the internal audit activities. Where there is no internal audit function, the audit committee should consider annually whether there is a need for an internal audit function and make a recommendation to the board, and the reasons for the absence of such a function should be explained in the relevant section of the annual report.

The audit committee should have primary responsibility for making a recommendation on the appointment, re-appointment and removal of the external auditor. If the board does not accept the audit committee's recommendation, it should include in the annual report, and in any papers recommending appointment or re-appointment, a statement from the audit committee explaining the recommendation and should set out reasons why the board has taken a different position.

The annual report should explain to shareholders how, if the auditor provides non-audit services, auditor objectivity and independence is safeguarded.

Directors' re-election

All directors of FTSE 350 companies should be subject to annual election by shareholders. All other directors should be subject to election by shareholders at the first annual general meeting after their appointment, and to re-election thereafter at intervals of no more than three years. Non-executive directors who have served longer than nine years should be subject to annual re-election. The names of directors submitted for election or re-election should be accompanied by sufficient biographical details and any other relevant information to enable shareholders to take an informed decision on their election.

Accountability

The board should present a balanced and understandable assessment of the company's position and prospects.

The board is responsible for determining the nature and extent of the significant risks it is willing to take in achieving its strategic objectives. The board should maintain sound risk management and internal control systems. The board should establish formal and transparent arrangements for considering how they should apply the corporate reporting and risk management and internal control principles and for maintaining an appropriate relationship with the company's auditor.

Financial and business reporting

The Combined Code includes as a main principle: 'The board should present a balanced and understandable assessment of the company's position and prospects.' In the annual report:

- the directors should explain their responsibility for preparing the accounts

- the directors should include in the annual report an explanation of the basis on which the company generates or preserves value over the longer-term and the strategy for delivering the objectives of the company

- the directors should report in annual and half-yearly financial statements that the business is a going concern.

These requirements, simple though they might seem, go to one of the core issues in corporate governance, and in the US, the Sarbanes-Oxley Act takes a more rigorous approach to individual responsibilities for the accuracy of the published accounts.

Risk management and internal control

The board should, at least annually, conduct a review of the effectiveness of the company's risk management and internal control systems and should report to shareholders that they have done so. The review should cover all material controls, including financial, operational and compliance controls.

Remuneration

Levels of remuneration should be sufficient to attract, retain and motivate directors of the quality required to run the company successfully, but a company should avoid paying more than is necessary for this purpose. A significant proportion of executive directors' remuneration should be structured so as to link rewards to corporate and individual performance.

There should be a formal and transparent procedure for developing policy on executive remuneration and for fixing the remuneration packages of individual directors. No director should be involved in deciding his or her own remuneration.

Remuneration

The performance-related elements of executive directors' remuneration should be stretching and designed to promote the long-term success of the company.

The remuneration committee should judge where to position their company relative to other companies. But they should use such comparisons with caution in view of the risk of an upward ratchet of remuneration levels with no corresponding improvement in performance.

They should also be sensitive to pay and employment conditions elsewhere in the group, especially when determining annual salary increases.

Levels of remuneration for non-executive directors should reflect the time commitment and responsibilities of the role. Remuneration for non-executive directors should not include share options or other performance-related elements. If, exceptionally, options are granted, shareholder approval should be sought in advance and any shares acquired by exercise of the options should be held until at least one year after the non-executive director leaves the board. Holding of share options could be relevant to the determination of a non-executive director's independence.

The remuneration committee should carefully consider what compensation commitments (including pension contributions and all other elements) their directors' terms of appointment would entail in the event of early termination. The aim should be to avoid rewarding poor performance. They should take a robust line on reducing compensation to reflect departing directors' obligations to mitigate loss.

Notice or contract periods should be set at one year or less. If it is necessary to offer longer notice or contract periods to new directors recruited from outside, such periods should reduce to one year or less after the initial period.

The board should establish a remuneration committee of at least three, or in the case of smaller companies two, independent non-executive directors. In addition the company chairman may also be a member of, but not chair, the committee if he or she was considered independent on appointment as chairman. The remuneration committee should make available its terms of reference, explaining its role and the authority delegated to it by the board . Where remuneration consultants are appointed, a statement should be made available of whether they have any other connection with the company.

The remuneration committee should have delegated responsibility for setting remuneration for all executive directors and the chairman, including pension rights and any compensation payments. The committee should also recommend and monitor the level and structure of remuneration for senior management. The definition of 'senior management' for this purpose should be determined by the board but should normally include the first layer of management below board level.

The board itself or, where required by the Articles of Association, the shareholders should determine the remuneration of the non-executive directors within the limits set in the Articles of Association. Where permitted by the Articles, the board may, however, delegate this responsibility to a committee, which might include the chief executive.

Shareholders should be invited specifically to approve all new long-term incentive schemes (as defined in the Listing Rules) and significant changes to existing schemes, save in the circumstances permitted by the Listing Rules.

Disclosure of directors' remuneration

The Companies Act 2006 and the Directors' Remuneration Report Regulations 2002 introduce a regulatory aspect to directors' remuneration. Essentially, there are two major elements to this legislation for listed companies:

- The board must submit a remuneration report to the shareholders every year (which is likely to be included in the annual report and accounts), and shareholders should be invited to vote on this report at the annual general meeting of the company. However, the vote is advisory only, and the company is not obliged to change its policy if the shareholders vote against it.

- The report must also provide extensive details about the remuneration of individual directors. (The disclosure requirements are more extensive than those in the UK Listing Rules, which the Companies Act amendment effectively replaced.)

Executive Share Options (ESOPs)

Executive share options (ESOPs) have been blamed for almost every business scandal that has made the headlines in the past decade.

An ESOP is part of a manager's remuneration package. The features generally involve the following:

- Each eligible manager is granted an allocation of options as part of his or her annual remuneration. The number of options will generally be decided by the remuneration committee, comprising non-executive directors.

- The options themselves will normally have a striking price that is equal to, or slightly higher than, the share price at the date the options are granted.

- There is usually a vesting period of a few years that must pass before the options can be exercised. If the manager resigns or leaves the company during that period then the options will lapse.

- The options can normally be exercised on a specific date at the end of the vesting period.

(The vesting period and the fact that the options must be exercised on a very specific date make them more difficult to value than the more typical traded options that can be bought and sold by third parties.)

There are two main reasons why shareholders might be keen to reward their directors with options.

- If the directors hold large numbers of options then they will have a financial incentive to maximise the share price. Provided the share price exceeds the exercise price at the relevant date the directors can exercise their options and buy shares for less than their market value. They will then either retain those shares as an investment (acquired at a bargain price, so providing an attractive return) or resell them at a guaranteed capital gain. If the share price does not rise during the vesting period then the directors will receive little or no value and so they will have a direct financial stake in delivering an increased share price.

- An investment opportunity that would be attractive to the shareholders because the potential returns are high might be unacceptable to the directors because they will be exposed to the risks of it going wrong and the loss of their jobs. For example, a new product that fails might have a very limited impact on shareholders' total investment portfolios but could end the careers of the directors who were responsible for recommending that it should proceed. Thus, if the shareholders really wish to align the directors' interests with their own they need to find some way to encourage the directors to accept the risks that they would choose to accept for themselves and ESOPS provide the answer.

If the directors hold large numbers of options then they will have an economic interest in accepting risky investment opportunities that they might otherwise be inclined to reject. If the investment succeeds and the share price rises then their options will be worth far more at the exercise date and they will not be exposed to any specific loss (at least on their options) if the investment fails and the share price plummets.

Thus, ESOPs give the shareholders the reassurance that the directors will wish to work hard to increase the share price and also accept realistic risks provided the potential return is high enough. They will also encourage the directors to take a long-term view and to remain with the company rather than move elsewhere and lose their options.

Directors should only be permitted to hold share options of any kind if they are honest and upright individuals. Clearly, many company directors are both but there will always be a few dishonest individuals in every walk of life. For example, in the past directors have purchased call options with their own money and then manipulated the share price by distorting the financial statements so that the options could be exercised at a massive profit. It was felt that company directors had too much of an incentive to cheat and manipulate when they held options and so it became illegal for them to own them.

In the late 1980s company directors were being accused of taking excessive salaries and bonuses and steps were taken to reduce the amounts being paid. In the USA a law was passed to restrict remuneration to $1m per annum. Shareholders were nervous that such a limit would give directors very little incentive to work hard and so ESOPs were used as a way round the restriction. It is extremely difficult to value the options granted under ESOPs and this meant that they were not accounted for in the total disclosed in the financial statements.

Major scandals such as Worldcom in the 1990s and the recent Credit Crunch have been blamed on the pressures created by the possibility of directors earning huge amounts from any manipulation of the share price, timed to coincide with the exercise date of ESOP options.

Relations with shareholders

There should be a dialogue with shareholders based on the mutual understanding of objectives. The board as a whole has responsibility for ensuring that a satisfactory dialogue with shareholders takes place.

The board should use the AGM to communicate with investors and to encourage their participation.

Relations with shareholders

The chairman should ensure that the views of shareholders are communicated to the board as a whole. The chairman should discuss governance and strategy with major shareholders. Non-executive directors should be offered the opportunity to attend scheduled meetings with major shareholders and should expect to attend meetings if requested by major shareholders. The senior independent director should attend sufficient meetings with a range of major shareholders to listen to their views in order to help develop a balanced understanding of the issues and concerns of major shareholders.

The board should state in the annual report the steps they have taken to ensure that the members of the board, and, in particular, the non-executive directors, develop an understanding of the views of major shareholders about the company, for example through direct face-to-face contact, analysts' or brokers' briefings and surveys of shareholder opinion.

At any general meeting, the company should propose a separate resolution on each substantially separate issue, and should, in particular, propose a resolution at the AGM relating to the report and accounts.

The company should ensure that all valid proxy appointments received for general meetings are properly recorded and counted.

The chairman should arrange for the chairmen of the audit, remuneration and nomination committees to be available to answer questions at the AGM and for all directors to attend.

The company should arrange for the Notice of the AGM and related papers to be sent to shareholders at least 20 working days before the meeting.

3 Corporate governance and internal controls

The **board** is responsible for:

- maintaining a sound system of internal control,
- reviewing the effectiveness of internal controls, and
- reporting to shareholders that this review has been carried out.

It is the responsibility of **management** to:

- identify and evaluate the risks faced by the company, for consideration by the board
- design, operate and monitor a suitable system of internal control.

Turnbull Report

This is the most specific report regarding the requirements for internal control. (See Internal Control: Guidance for Directors on the Combined Code 1999 and revised 2005)

The Turnbull Report requires that internal controls should be established using a **risk-based approach**. Specifically a company should:

- Establish business objectives.
- Identify the associated key risks.
- Decide upon the controls to address the risks.
- Set up a system to implement the required controls, including regular feedback.

In establishing this structure the Turnbull Report summarises the way that businesses should be controlled (and also how this examination paper links the topics of risk and control).

In addition, the Turnbull Report addresses the responsibilities of directors and management in relation to risk and control, as discussed above.

Turnbull went on to suggest that directors should review internal controls under the five headings identified by COSO in 1992:

- Control environment.
- Risk assessment.

- Control activities.

- Information and communication.

- Monitoring.

The Turnbull Report went on to suggest that internal audit makes a significant and valuable contribution to a company.

More on reviewing the effectiveness of internal controls

Management is accountable to the board for monitoring the system of internal control. The board has a responsibility for reviewing its effectiveness.

To review the effectiveness of the internal control system, the board should not rely on the existence of suitable embedded internal control processes. It should also receive regular reports on risks and controls, in addition to carrying out an annual assessment.

When reviewing reports on internal control, the board should:

- consider the significant risks and how they have been identified, evaluated and managed

- assess the effectiveness of the internal controls for managing each significant risk

- consider whether any controls are weak and action is necessary to strengthen them.

'Should the board become aware at any time of a significant failing or weakness in internal control, it should determine how the failing or weakness arose and re-assess the effectiveness of management's ongoing processes for designing, operating and monitoring the system of internal control' (Turnbull Report).

The annual assessment of the system of internal control should consider:

- the changes since the assessment carried out in the previous year

- the scope and quality of management's ongoing monitoring of risks and of the system of internal control

- the extent and frequency of the communication of the results of this monitoring to the board

- the extent and frequency of internal control weaknesses and failing that have been identified during the year

- the effectiveness of the company's public reporting processes.

More on board's statement on internal control

The annual report should provide sufficient meaningful and high-level information to enable the shareholders to understand the main features of the company's risk management processes and system of internal control.

At the very least, the board should disclose:

- that there is an ongoing process for identifying, evaluating and managing the significant risks faced by the company

- that this process has been in place throughout the year

- that the process is regularly reviewed by the board, and

- that it accords with the Turnbull Guidance.

The statement should include an acknowledgement by the board that it is responsible for the company's system of internal control and for reviewing its effectiveness.

The board should also summarise the process by which it reviewed the effectiveness of the control systems, whether that review was conducted directly or through, say, an audit committee.

4 Corporate governance and the audit committee

Audit committees were first required under the Cadbury Code (and are now required by the UK Corporate Governance Code) in response to criticisms of the relationship between the directors and the auditors.

It was felt that the auditors were not sufficiently independent of the board of directors and that, as a result, the auditors were not providing their monitoring and reporting role as they should be.

Particular criticisms of the relationship were about:

- Remuneration of the auditors – decided by the directors.

- Appointment of the auditors – at the discretion of the directors in practice.

- Reports of the auditors – received by the directors.

- The directors had the power to give other lucrative work to auditors.

To address these concerns, audit committees were to be established.

- Audit committees are made up of non-executive directors (at least one of which should have recent relevant financial experience) and have formal terms of reference.

- The audit committee should meet at least three times per year, and also at least once a year have a meeting with the auditors without the presence of any executive directors.

Responsibilities of an audit committee

The responsibilities of the audit committee would typically include:

- Review of the financial statements, and any interim reports produced.

- Review of the company's system of internal financial controls.

- Discussion with the auditors about any significant matters that arose on the audit.

- Review of the internal audit programme and significant findings of the internal auditors.

- Recommendations on the appointment and removal of the auditors.

- The setting of the audit fee in discussion with the auditors.

- Review of the audit report and any management letter provided by the external auditors.

- Review all the company's internal control and risk management systems (unless this is delegated to a separate risk committee).

- Ensure that a system is in place for whistleblowing.

Audit committee and financial reporting

The key roles of the audit committee are 'oversight', 'assessment' and 'review' of other functions and systems in the company.

The audit committee should review the significant financial reporting issues and judgements in connection with the preparation of the company's financial statements. Management is responsible for preparing the financial statements and the auditors are responsible for preparing the audit plan and carrying out the audit.

The audit committee needs to satisfy itself that the financial statements prepared by management and approved by the auditors are acceptable. It should consider:

- the significant accounting policies that have been used, and whether these are appropriate

- any significant estimates or judgements that have been made, and whether these are reasonable

- the method used to account for any significant or unusual transactions, where alternative accounting treatments are possible
- the clarity and completeness of the disclosures in the financial statements.

The committee should listen to the views of the auditors on these matters. If it is not satisfied with any aspect of the proposed financial reporting, it should inform the board.

Audit committee and internal control

In relation to internal controls, the audit committee should:

- review the company's internal **financial** controls
- review **all** the company's internal control and risk management systems, unless the task is taken on by a separate risk committee or the full board
- give its approval to the statements in the annual report relating to internal control and risk management
- receive reports from management about the effectiveness of the control systems it operates
- receive reports on the conclusions of any tests carried out on the controls by the internal or external auditors.

Audit committee and internal audit

The audit committee should monitor and review the effectiveness of the company's internal audit function. If the company does not have an internal audit function:

- the committee should consider annually whether there is a need for an internal audit function and make a recommendation to the board, and
- the reasons for the absence of an internal audit function should be explained in the relevant section of the annual report.

Where a company does have an internal audit function, the audit committee has an important role in preserving the independence of the internal audit function from pressure or interference.

The audit committee should:

- approve the appointment or termination of appointment of the head of internal audit

- ensure that the internal auditor has direct access to the board chairman and is accountable to the audit committee

- review and assess the annual internal audit work plan

- receive a report periodically about the work of the internal auditor

- review and monitor the response of management to the findings of the internal auditor

- monitor and assess the role and effectiveness of the internal audit function within the company's overall risk management system.

Audit committee and external auditors

The audit committee is responsible for oversight of the company's relations with its external auditors. The audit committee should:

- have the primary responsibility for making a recommendation to the board on the appointment, re-appointment or removal of the external auditors

- 'oversee' the selection process when new auditors are being considered

- approve (though not necessarily negotiate) the terms of engagement of the external auditors and the remuneration for their audit services

- have annual procedures for ensuring the independence and objectivity of the external auditors

- review the scope of the audit with the auditor, and satisfy itself that this is sufficient

- make sure that appropriate plans are in place for the audit at the start of each annual audit

- carry out a post-completion audit review.

5 Disclosure of corporate governance

A schedule attached to the UK Corporate Governance Code sets out the requirements for the disclosure of corporate governance arrangements.

Test your understanding 1 – UK listed company

The following are extracts from the corporate governance guidelines issued by a UK listed company:

(i) All auditors' fees, including fees for services other than audit, should be fully disclosed in the annual report. In order to ensure continuity of standards the same audit partner, wherever possible, should be responsible for a period of at least three years.

(ii) The board shall establish a remuneration committee comprising 50% executive directors, and 50% non-executive directors. A non-executive director shall chair the committee.

(iii) The chairman of the company may also hold the position of CEO, although this shall not normally be for a period of more than three years.

(iv) The annual report shall fully disclose whether principles of good corporate governance have been applied.

(v) No director shall hold directorships in more than 20 companies.

(vi) Directors should regularly report on the effectiveness of the company's system of internal control.

Required:

Discuss the extent to which each of points (i) – (vi) is likely to comply with corporate governance systems such as the UK Code.

6 International developments

Sarbanes-Oxley Act

The US financial world was rocked by a number of very serious financial scandals around 2000/2001, the most well known of which were Enron and Worldcom. The problems of Enron and Worldcom brought into question US accounting practices (for example, by exploiting loopholes in US accounting, Enron did not show its problems on its statement of financial position) and also the corporate governance exercised by directors. In order to restore confidence in the results of US companies the Sarbanes-Oxley Act was introduced.

- The SOX legislation is extremely detailed and carries the full force of the law behind it.

- The Act also includes requirements for the Securities and Exchange Commission (SEC) to issue certain rules on corporate governance.

- It is relevant to US companies, directors of subsidiaries of US listed businesses and auditors who are working on US listed businesses.

Differences to the UK Code

Overall the two main differences between SOX and the UK Code are:

(i) Enforcement

The UK Code is a series of voluntary codes (a **'principles-based** approach') whereas SOX takes a robust legislative approach which sets out clear personal responsibility for some company directors with a series of criminal offences that are punishable by fines (both company and its officers) or lengthy jail sentences (a **'rules-based** approach').

(ii) Documentation

SOX creates a much more rigorous demand for evidencing internal controls and having them audited.

Key points of SOX

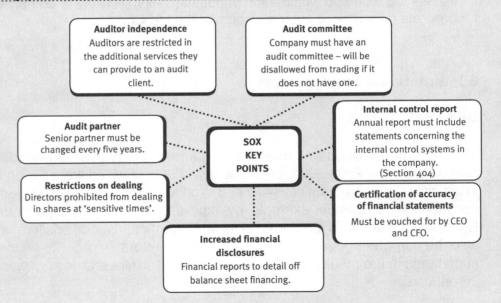

Auditor independence
Auditors are restricted in the additional services they can provide to an audit client.

Audit committee
Company must have an audit committee – will be disallowed from trading if it does not have one.

Audit partner
Senior partner must be changed every five years.

SOX KEY POINTS

Internal control report
Annual report must include statements concerning the internal control systems in the company.
(Section 404)

Restrictions on dealing
Directors prohibited from dealing in shares at 'sensitive times'.

Certification of accuracy of financial statements
Must be vouched for by CEO and CFO.

Increased financial disclosures
Financial reports to detail off balance sheet financing.

UK Code vs. SOX

Certification of accuracy the financial statements

SOX gives personal responsibility for the accuracy of the firm's financial statements to its principal executive officer (CEO) and the chief financial officer (Finance Director), who must provide a signed certificate to the Securities and Exchange Commission (SEC) vouching for the accuracy of the statements signed by the two officers above. It is a criminal offence to file defective financial statements.

The CEO and CFO must also hand back any bonuses for previous years if the financial statements need to be amended due to defective financial statements.

This is a far more specific requirement than the UK Code that only provides for a statement about the responsibility of the board for preparing financial statements and a going concern statement.

Increased financial disclosures

Whilst the UK Code focuses more on directors and their accountability to shareholders SOX includes a number of provisions for greater or more rapid disclosure of financial information:

* In its financial reports the company must disclose details about its off balance sheet transactions and their material effects.

* Material changes should be disclosed on a rapid and current basis i.e. new off balance sheet transactions, loss of a major customer or a one-off writing down charge.

Internal control report

Companies need to include a report on 'internal control over financial reporting' in their annual report. This must:

* Include a statement of management's responsibility for adequate control systems.

* Identify the framework to evaluate internal control.

* Provide an assessment of the effectiveness of internal control and any material weakness.

Again this follows the UK Code quite closely regarding the board's responsibilities and the role of the audit committee in reporting on the effectiveness of financial controls.

Audit committee

In the same way as the UK Code, SOX requires companies to comply with certain audit committee requirements. However, the US stock exchanges are prohibited from listing any firm that does not comply.

As per the Combined Code the committee should:

- Be independent (in the UK NEDs).
- Have responsibility for appointing and compensating auditors.
- Oversee the auditors.
- Establish whistleblower procedures regarding questionable accounting or audit matters.

Unlike the UK Code, however, SOX goes much further in restricting auditors and non-audit work. A number of specific non-audit activities are explicitly prohibited.

Whilst the UK Code discourages auditors carrying out non-audit work, an explanation of how companies safeguard auditor independence in the annual report is usually sufficient if additional work is carried out.

SOX also requires a compulsory rotation of the lead audit partner working on a corporate client.

International corporate governance

King Report – South Africa

The King Report on Corporate Governance in South Africa provides an integrated approach to corporate governance in the interest of all stakeholders, embracing social, environmental and economic aspects of organisational activities. It therefore takes, to some extent at least, a broader stakeholder model of governance. The King Report relies heavily on disclosure as a regulatory mechanism.

The South African changes emphasised increasing the accountability and independence of boards, noting that delegation to committees does not absolve the board of its responsibilities.

The King Report philosophy is that in presenting financial information, openness and substance is more important than form. Internal control is part of the risk management process for which the board is responsible. The internal audit function has its main focus on risk and control.

The King Committee on Corporate Governance developed the King Report on Corporate Governance for South Africa, 2002 (King II). King II acknowledges that there is a move away from the single bottom line (that is, profit for shareholders) to a triple bottom line, which embraces the economic, environmental and social aspects of a company's activities.

Other international developments

In 1995 the Canadian Institute of Chartered Accountants through the Criteria of Control Committee (that has become known as 'CoCo') published Guidance for Directors – Governance Processes for Control. This emphasised the role of the board in understanding the principal risks facing companies and ensuring a proper balance between risks incurred and the potential returns to shareholders.

In France, the Vienot Report in 1995 proposed that boards should not simply aim to maximise share values but to safeguard the prosperity and continuity of the business.

In Australia, the Australian Stock Exchange has a Corporate Governance Principles and Recommendations. There is also a series of standards that have been issued by Standards Australia relating to governance, risk and control. AS8000 of 2003 covers Good Governance Principles, supported by a number of practical handbooks. AS8000 covers best practice for the Board charter, Board protocol, a statement of matters reserved for the Board, Board delegations of authority, letters of appointment for board members, and a code of conduct for board members.

(1) In 2004, the OECD published their principles of Corporate Governance (OECD, 2004). The principles were:

(2) Ensuring the basis for an effective corporate governance framework by promoting transparent and efficient markets, being consistent with the rule of law and clearly articulating the division of responsibilities among different authorities.

(3) Protecting and facilitating the exercise of the rights of shareholders.

(4) Ensuring the equitable treatment of all shareholders, who should have the opportunity to obtain effective redress for violation of their rights.

(5) The rights of shareholders is established by law and active co-operation between companies and shareholders should be encouraged in creating wealth, jobs and the sustainability of financially sound enterprises.

(6) Ensuring timely and accurate disclosure on all material matters regarding the financial situation, performance, ownership and governance of the company.

(7) The strategic guidance of the company, effective monitoring of management by the board and the board's accountability to the company and its shareholders.

Test your understanding 2 – Disclosure

Download from the Internet a company annual report of your choosing and review the disclosures for corporate governance.

Test your understanding 3 – Naseby plc

Naseby plc is a large UK listed company in the retailing sector. Over the past one or two years, the company has been losing market share to competitors, and the share price has fallen from about £5 two years ago to £2.80 now.

The chairman has arranged a meeting with representatives of an institutional investment organisation, and is aware that two matters for discussion will be the role of the non-executive directors and reviewing the effectiveness of risk management systems.

Required:

Prepare some briefing notes for this meeting, in which you:

- explain the role of the non-executive directors, and
- advise how the effectiveness of the risk management systems of the company should be reviewed.

Test your understanding 4 – JKL

JKL is a profitable but small FTSE 500 company in a technology-related service industry with annual sales of £150 million. Its gearing is 50% of total assets, secured by a mortgage over its main site. The industry is highly competitive but there are major barriers for entry to new competitors and the long-term future of JKL is considered by industry analysts to be sound.

The Board comprises a non-executive chairman, a chief executive who has a large shareholding, an executive finance director, operations director and marketing director and a non-executive director with wide knowledge of the industry and who retired from the company 3 years ago. There is only one committee of the board. The audit committee consists of the chairman, non-executive director and finance director.

There is no internal audit function in JKL but the external auditors are relied on to report on any weaknesses in control and their letter of engagement authorises them to carry out work over and above the financial audit in relation to internal control. The external auditors have always given a 'clean' audit report to the company and have reported that internal controls within JKL are sound. There is no formal risk management process in place in JKL although board meetings routinely consider risk during their deliberations.

The chairman and chief executive both believe that compliance with corporate governance reforms will not benefit JKL and is likely to be too costly. This is disclosed in JKL's Annual Report.

Required:

Write a report to the Chairman

(a) evaluating the key reforms and best practice in:

   – corporate governance

   – risk management that have taken place over the last few years and which affect JKL; and

(b) with reasons, which (if any) of those reforms should be adopted by the company.

Test your understanding 5 – HFD

HFD is a registered charity with 100 employees and 250 volunteers providing in-home care for elderly persons who are unable to fully take care of themselves. The company structure has no shareholders in a practical sense although a small number of issued shares are held by the sponsors who established the charity many years previously. HFD is governed by a seven-member Board of Directors. The Chief Executive Officer (CEO) chairs the board which comprises the chief financial officer (CFO) and five independent, unpaid non-executive directors who were appointed by the CEO based on past business relationships. You are one of the independent members of HFD's board.

The CEO/Chair sets the board agendas, distributes board papers in advance of meetings and briefs board members in relation to each agenda item. At each of its quarterly meetings the Board reviews the financial reports of the charity in some detail and the CFO answers questions. Other issues that regularly appear as agenda items include new government funding initiatives for the client group, and the results of proposals that have been submitted to funding agencies, of which about 25% are successful. There is rarely any discussion of operational matters relating to the charity as the CEO believes these are outside the directors' experience and the executive management team is more than capable of managing the delivery of the in-home care services.

The Board has no separate audit committee but relies on the annual management letter from the external auditors to provide assurance that financial controls are operating effectively. The external auditors were appointed by the CEO many years previously.

HFD's Board believes that its corporate governance could be improved by following the principles applicable to listed companies.

Required:

(a) Recommend how HFD's Board should be restructured to comply with the principles of good corporate governance.

(b) Explain the aspects of CIMA's ethical principles and the conceptual framework underlying those principles which you would consider relevant to continuing in your role as an independent member of HFD's Board.

7 Chapter summary

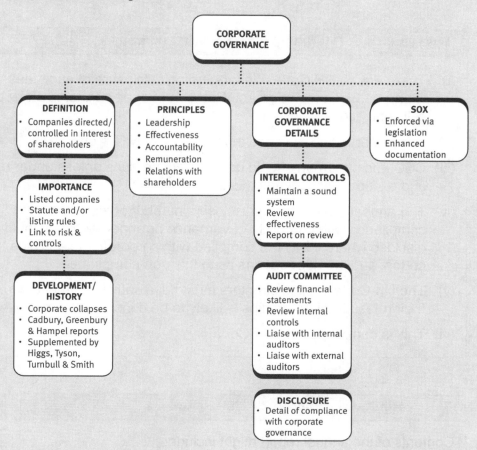

CORPORATE GOVERNANCE

DEFINITION
- Companies directed/controlled in interest of shareholders

IMPORTANCE
- Listed companies
- Statute and/or listing rules
- Link to risk & controls

DEVELOPMENT/HISTORY
- Corporate collapses
- Cadbury, Greenbury & Hampel reports
- Supplemented by Higgs, Tyson, Turnbull & Smith

PRINCIPLES
- Leadership
- Effectiveness
- Accountability
- Remuneration
- Relations with shareholders

CORPORATE GOVERNANCE DETAILS

INTERNAL CONTROLS
- Maintain a sound system
- Review effectiveness
- Report on review

AUDIT COMMITTEE
- Review financial statements
- Review internal controls
- Liaise with internal auditors
- Liaise with external auditors

DISCLOSURE
- Detail of compliance with corporate governance

SOX
- Enforced via legislation
- Enhanced documentation

Test your understanding answers

Test your understanding 1 – UK listed company

(i) There are no UK Code rules regarding disclosure of audit fees. This is part of the Companies Act. Rotation of audit partner is an 'auditor' self-regulation guideline.

(ii) Remuneration committees must consist of NEDs only.

(iii) CEO and chairman should be separate persons unless under rare and exceptional circumstances.

(iv) The annual report should disclose a number of aspects of compliance with corporate governance arrangements. It should also disclose where it has not complied with corporate governance codes, and provide reasons as to this non-compliance.

(v) The UK Code implies directors must have sufficient time to carry out their roles. 20 directorships is likely to be considered excessive.

(vi) This is correct per the UK Code.

Test your understanding 2 – Disclosure

Contents of the annual report might include:

- a statement of how the board operates, including a high level statement of which types of decisions are to be taken by the board and which are to be delegated to management;

- the names of the chairman, the deputy chairman (where there is one), the chief executive, the senior independent director and the chairmen and members of the board committees;

- the number of meetings of the board and those committees and individual attendance by directors;

- where a chief executive is appointed chairman, the reasons for their appointment (this only needs to be done in the annual report following the appointment);

- the names of the non-executive directors whom the board determines to be independent, with reasons where necessary;

- a separate section describing the work of the nomination committee, including the process it has used in relation to board appointments and an explanation if neither external search consultancy nor open advertising has been used in the appointment of a chairman or a non-executive director;

- any changes to the other significant commitments of the chairman during the year;

- a statement of how performance evaluation of the board, its committees and its directors has been conducted;

- an explanation from the directors of their responsibility for preparing the accounts and a statement by the auditors about their reporting responsibilities;

- an explanation from the directors of the basis on which the company generates or preserves value over the longer term (the business model) and the strategy for delivering the objectives of the company;

- a statement from the directors that the business is a going concern, with supporting assumptions or qualifications as necessary;

- a report that the board has conducted a review of the effectiveness of the company's risk management and internal controls systems;

- a separate section describing the work of the audit committee in discharging its responsibilities;

- where there is no internal audit function, the reasons for the absence of such a function;

- where the board does not accept the audit committee's recommendation on the appointment, re-appointment or removal of an external auditor, a statement from the audit committee explaining the recommendation and the reasons why the board has taken a different position;

- an explanation of how, if the auditor provides non-audit services, auditor objectivity and independence is safeguarded;

- a description of the work of the remuneration committee as required under the Large and Medium-Sized Companies and Groups (Accounts and Reports) Regulations 2008 including, where an executive director serves as a non-executive director elsewhere, whether or not the director will retain such earnings and, if so, what the remuneration is;

- the steps the board has taken to ensure that members of the board, in particular the non-executive directors, develop an understanding of the views of major shareholders about their company.

The following information should be made available (which may be met by placing the information on a website that is maintained by or on behalf of the company):

- the terms of reference of the nomination, audit and remuneration committees, explaining their role and the authority delegated to them by the board;

- the terms and conditions of appointment of non-executive directors;

- where performance evaluation has been externally facilitated, a statement of whether the facilitator has any other connection with the company; and

- where remuneration consultants are appointed, a statement of whether they have any other connection with the company.

The board should set out to shareholders in the papers accompanying a resolution to elect or re-elect directors:

- sufficient biographical details to enable shareholders to take an informed decision on their election or re-election;

- why they believe an individual should be elected to a non-executive role; and

- on re-election of a non-executive director, confirmation from the chairman that, following formal performance evaluation, the individual's performance continues to be effective and to demonstrate commitment to the role.

The board should set out to shareholders in the papers recommending appointment or reappointment of an external auditor. If the board does not accept the audit committee's recommendation, a statement from the audit committee should be disclosed explaining the recommendation, and a statement from the board should be disclosed setting out reasons why they have taken a different position.

Test your understanding 3 – Naseby plc

To: The Chairman, Naseby plc

From: Management accountant

Briefing notes

Role of non-executive directors

Non-executive directors have the same legal responsibilities to the company as executive directors.

The board collectively has responsibility for the success of the company and:

- provides entrepreneurial leadership within a framework of prudent and effective controls that enable risk to be assessed and managed

- sets the company's strategic aims

- ensures that the company has sufficient resources to meet its objectives

- reviews management performance

- sets the company's values and standards

- ensures that the company's obligations to its shareholders and others are understood and met.

In addition, NEDs have a role in the following areas:

- Strategy: constructively challenging and helping to develop proposals on strategy.

- Performance: scrutinising the performance of managers in meeting agreed goals and objectives.

- Risk: satisfying themselves that financial controls and systems of risk management are robust and defensible.

- People: deciding the remuneration of executive directors and having a prime role in the appointment or removal of directors and in succession planning.

Since the institutional investor organisation wishes to discuss NEDs, it might be expected that there is dissatisfaction with the actual performance of the NEDs in one or more of these areas. The meeting will almost certainly cover the actual role of the NEDs in these areas, and there might be a suggestion that the NED representation on the board needs changing and/or strengthening.

Note A problem for NEDs is that they have two contradictory responsibilities:

- working with executive director colleagues to develop strategy
- policing executive directors and managers, through monitoring performance, the effectiveness of internal control and risk management and even succession planning.

Reviewing the effectiveness of risk management systems

There are several elements to a review of the effectiveness of risk management systems.

- The risk management system needs to be identified. Ideally, the elements of the system should be documented.
    - Who is responsible for identifying the risks facing the company?
    - How frequently are risks re-assessed?
    - What, currently, are the main risks facing the company?
- How are risks evaluated? Are they evaluated in quantitative terms (severity of impact, probability of occurrence) or in descriptive, qualitative terms?
- Following the identification and evaluation of risks, what measures are taken to manage the risks? Are there formal company policies on risk management? Are individual managers given responsibility for managing particular risks? What methods are used to reduce or contain risks?
- Is there a system in place for assessing the cost of risk control measures and the likely benefits from the control measures? In other words, is cost-benefit analysis carried out? Does the system ensure that the most appropriate risk management methods are adopted? Are alternative methods of risk management considered?

The answers to these questions should provide information about whether the company has an effective system for identifying risks and planning for the control of the risks.

A review of the effectiveness of risk management systems should also consider how the policies, plans and procedures are applied in practice.

- How does the company review its actual risks and their significance, compared to the expected risks? Are there procedures for evaluating actual risks retrospectively? A retrospective assessment of risks should enable management and the board to assess the effectiveness of the risk identification and evaluation processes.

- Does the company review whether the planned risk management measures have been implemented properly?

- How does the company assess the actual costs and the actual benefits of the risk management measures taken?

At the meeting, the institutional investor organisation might want to know how the risk management system operates, and what the experience of the company has been with its formal risk management reviews.

It might also want reassurance that strong-minded NEDs contribute to the review of risk management, and that the process of review is not dominated by the executive directors.

Test your understanding 4 – JKL

Report

Dear Chairman,

Introduction

You have asked me to report on the key reforms in corporate governance and risk management that have taken place recently which affect JKL and to recommend (with reasons), which (if any) of those reforms should be adopted by JKL.

This report addresses the following issues: corporate governance, in particular non-executive directors and the audit committee; and risk management, internal control and internal audit. The recommendations are contained at the end of this report.

Corporate governance

Corporate governance in most of the western world is founded on the principle of enhancing shareholder value. Major corporate collapses have been a feature of recent business history in the United Kingdom and elsewhere, and the publicity surrounding these collapses and the actions of institutional investors have raised corporate governance to prominence. The emergence of corporate governance can be seen as a result of regulatory action in response to past failings; changing financial markets including the desire of institutional investors to be more active and the dependence of an ageing population on pensions and savings which have been affected by declining confidence in stock markets.

The main principles of corporate governance are in relation to directors, the remuneration of directors, accountability and audit, relations with shareholders, and in particular with institutional shareholders and disclosure. The 'comply or explain' approach requires listed companies to disclose how they have applied the principles in the Corporate Governance Code and to either comply with the Code or to explain any departure from it. Under the Code, board effectiveness can be summarised as the effective splitting of the roles of chairman and chief effective; the role of non-executive directors and the role of remuneration, nomination and audit committees of the board. In JKL, the roles of chairman and chief executive are split but JKL does not comply with recommendations in relation to non-executive directors or the audit committee. I shall deal with each of these in turn.

Non-executive directors

The board should include a balance of executive and non-executive directors, and in particular 'independent' non-executives. It is recommended that a smaller company (outside FTSE 350) should have at least two independent non-executive directors. The notion of independence precludes non-executives from having recently been an employee of, or in a material business relationship with the company; receiving performance-related pay or a pension; having family ties or cross directorships; representing a substantial shareholder, or having been a board member for an excessive period of time.

Non-executive directors should be independent in judgement and have an enquiring mind. They need to be accepted by management as able to make a contribution; to be well informed about the company and its environment and be able to have a command of the issues facing the business. Non-executives need to insist that information provided by management is sufficient, accurate, clear and timely.

There should be a formal, rigorous and transparent procedure for the appointment of new directors to the board. Levels of remuneration should be sufficient to attract, retain and motivate directors of the quality required to run the company successfully. All directors should receive induction on joining the board and should regularly update and refresh their skills and knowledge. The board should undertake a formal and rigorous annual evaluation of its own performance and that of its committees and individual directors.

Audit committee

The Code states that the board of smaller companies (below FTSE350) should establish an audit committee of at least two members, who should all be independent non-executive directors. At least one member of the audit committee should have recent and relevant financial experience.

The audit committee has a role to act independently of management to ensure that the interests of shareholders are properly protected in relation to financial reporting and internal control. The main role and responsibilities of the audit committee should include monitoring the integrity of the company's financial statements; reviewing the company's internal control and risk management systems; monitoring and reviewing the effectiveness of the internal audit function; making recommendations to the board for the appointment, re-appointment and removal of the external auditor and approving the terms of engagement and remuneration of the external auditor, including the supply of any non-audit services; reviewing and monitoring the external auditor's independence and objectivity and the effectiveness of the audit process.

There should be no less than three audit committee meetings each year held to coincide with key dates in the financial reporting and audit cycle as well as main board meetings. JKL's audit committees should have, as part of its terms of reference, the responsibility to assess risk management and internal control within JKL. Each of these is considered in turn.

Risk management

Risk management is the process by which organisations systematically identify, evaluate, treat and report risk with the goal of achieving organisational objectives. Risk management increases the probability of success, reduces both the probability of failure and the uncertainty of achieving the organisation's objectives.

A risk management strategy should include the risk profile of the organisation, that is the level of risk it finds acceptable; the risk assessment and evaluation processes the organisation practices; the preferred options for risk treatment; the responsibility for risk management and the reporting and monitoring processes that are required. Resources (money, experience and information, etc.) need to be allocated to risk management.

The benefits of effective risk management include being seen as profitable and successful with fewer surprises, predictable results without profit warnings or reporting major exceptional items. Being seen to have a system of risk management is also likely to be reflected in reputation and credit rating.

JKL has no clear risk management system in place and while the board considers risk, it does not do so systematically. Consequently, there may be risks faced by JKL that it has not recognised.

Internal control

The Code incorporates what is known as the Turnbull Guidance, which recommends the adoption by a company's board of a risk-based approach to establishing a sound system of internal control and reviewing its effectiveness.

The board should acknowledge that it is responsible for the company's system of internal control and for reviewing its effectiveness. It should also explain that the system is designed to manage rather than eliminate the risk of failure to achieve business objectives, and can only provide reasonable but not absolute assurance against material mis-statement or loss. The board's statement on internal control should disclose that there is an ongoing process for identifying, evaluating and managing the significant risks faced by the company, that it has been in place for the year and up to the date of approval of the annual report and accounts, and that it has been regularly reviewed by the board and conforms to the Turnbull Guidance.

Reviewing the effectiveness of internal control is one of the board's responsibilities, which needs to be carried out on a continuous basis. The Board should regularly review reports on internal control – both financial and non-financial – for the purpose of making its public statement on internal control. When reviewing management reports on internal control, the board should consider the significant risks and assess how they have been identified, evaluated and managed; assess the effectiveness of internal controls in managing the significant risks, having regard to any significant weaknesses in internal control; consider whether necessary actions are being taken promptly to remedy any weaknesses and consider whether the findings indicate a need for more exhaustive monitoring of the system of internal control.

For risk management and for the board's assessment of the adequacy or otherwise of internal control, an internal audit function should be considered.

Internal audit

Internal audit is an independent appraisal function established within an organisation to examine and evaluate its activities and designed to add value and improve an organisation's operations. The main role of internal audit is to provide assurance that the main business risks are being managed and that internal controls are operating effectively.

The need for an internal audit function will depend on the scale, diversity and complexity of business activities and a comparison of costs and benefits of an internal audit function. Companies that do not have an internal audit function should review the need for one on an annual basis. Changes in the external environment, organisational restructuring or adverse trends evident from monitoring internal control systems should be considered as part of this review. An internal audit may be carried out by staff employed by the company or be outsourced to a third party.

In the absence of an internal audit function, management needs to apply other monitoring processes in order to assure itself and the board that the system of internal control is functioning effectively. The board will need to assess whether those processes provide sufficient and objective assurance.

Recommendations

JKL's single non-executive director is not, under the Code, considered to be independent. It is recommended that JKL appoint two independent non-executive directors to the board.

In JKL, the audit committee currently consists of the chairman, non-executive director and finance director. It is recommended that the two newly appointed independent non-executives (recommended above) be appointed and that both the chairman and the finance director attend, but not be members of the audit committee.

The audit committee should review JKL's risk management system and put in place an appropriate policy and system that reflects the risks faced.

JKL's internal controls appear to be adequate based on the external auditor's report; however, it is recommended that JKL's board specifically consider the adequacy of the external audit report in reviewing the effectiveness of internal control in JKL.

The audit committee should also consider the outcomes of the recommended risk management system before accepting the adequacy of internal controls.

This report does not recommend the appointment of internal auditors separate to the external audit function. However, once the board has implemented a risk management system and assessed the adequacy of internal controls, the value of internal audit function should be reassessed.

Test your understanding 5 – HFD

(a) Good corporate governance requires that a company be headed by an effective board with a clear division of responsibilities between running the board and running the company /charity with no individual having unfettered decision-making power. There should be a balance of executive and non-executive directors so that no individual or group can dominate the board. There should be a formal and rigorous process for the appointment of directors who should receive induction training. Information should be supplied in a timely manner to board members so that the board can discharge its duties. The board should then evaluate its performance both individually and collectively each year.

These principles do not seem to be applied for HFD as it is dominated by the chief executive who also acts as chair and appears to dominate the board through his appointment of non-executive directors and his control over the agenda. To meet the principles of good corporate governance, HFD should:

- Separate the roles of chief executive and chairman with the chairman being a non-executive director.

- Ensure that all directors are independent of influence by the chief executive. Positions should be advertised with interviews being conducted, perhaps initially by an independent person. Appointments should be for a defined period, after which directors should stand for re-election.

- Provide induction training to new board members in the goals and operations of the charity.

- Annually evaluate the performance of each director and the board as a whole.

- Accountability and audit principles of good corporate governance require that a board should be able to present a balanced and understandable assessment of the company's position and prospects, should maintain a sound system of internal control and maintain an appropriate relationship with the company's auditors.

- HFD's Board does not seem to be able to make a balanced and understandable assessment of the company's position and prospects, given the narrow confines of what the CEO/Chair allows it. The CEOs relationship with the external auditors is not appropriate.

- To meet the principles of good corporate governance, HFD should:

  - Set an agenda for board meetings that encompasses a wide variety of strategic matters including the charity's strategy, operations, risk management, internal controls and not be limited to financial reports and proposals for funding.

  - Consider meeting more frequently than quarterly.

  - Obtain an independent assessment of the company's internal controls by appointing a firm to act as (outsourced) internal auditor.

  - Affirm the reporting relationship of the external auditors to the board as a whole, and not to the CEO. The external auditors may need to be changed if they are unwilling to accept this changed relationship.

Although it is good practice, it is not necessary to have a separate audit committee, but if not, the functions of the audit committee should be carried out by the full board itself.

The disclosure principle requires that a company's annual report contains a high level statement of how the board operates and the decisions taken by the board and management, details of board members, meetings, performance evaluation, etc. HFD should provide adequate disclosure of board functioning in its annual report to make this aspect of the charity transparent.

(b) CIMA's Code of Ethics for Professional Accountants makes clear that an accountant's responsibility is more than satisfying the needs of a client, he/she must also act in the public interest. It is irrelevant whether or not the CIMA member is paid for his/her services, which are still expected to comply with the ethical principles.

There are 5 fundamental principles in the Code of Ethics: integrity, objectivity, professional competence and due care, confidentiality and professional behaviour.

Of particular relevance to HFD are objectivity, and professional competence and due care. Objectivity may be impeded due to bias because of his/her appointment by the CEO or the influence of the CEO or other persons on the board who may align themselves with the CEO.

The demands of professional competence and due care means that the accountant must look beyond the narrow agenda set by the CEO to a broader perspective than financial statements to non-financial risks (mainly in relation to the charities operation) and the adequacy of internal controls (as it is insufficient to rely wholly on the external auditor's annual management letter).

The conceptual framework underlying CIMA's ethical principles requires accountants to risk manage their own position in relation to the work they are performing and in so doing to identify, evaluate and mitigate any risks they face. The main risks faced by an accountant include those relating to self-interested behaviour, self-review, advocacy, familiarity and intimidation.

The major threats faced in relation to HFD are familiarity and intimidation. The accountant has been appointed to the board as a result of some prior business relationship which may affect his/her objectivity. The CEO/Chair of HFD also appears to be a dominating individual and the accountant may be intimidated by this individual, resulting in the accountant's views not being presented accurately and/or forcefully.

The accountant as board member needs to identify and evaluate the risks of familiarity and/or intimidation that s/he faces, and ensure that s/he takes appropriate action (ultimately resignation from the board) to maintain his/her independence and objectivity.

Review and audit

Chapter learning objectives

Lead	Component
C1. Discuss the importance of management review of controls.	(a) Discuss the importance of management review of controls.
C2. Evaluate the process and purposes of audit in the context of internal control systems.	(a) Evaluate the process of internal audit and its relationship to other forms of audit. (b) Produce a plan for the audit of various organisational activities including management, accounting and information systems. (c) Recommend action to avoid or solve problems associated with the audit of activities and systems. (d) Recommend action to improve the efficiency, effectiveness and control of activities. (e) Discuss the relationship between internal and external audit work.
C3. Discuss corporate governance and ethical issues facing an organisation.	(b) Discuss the importance of exercising ethical principles in conducting and reporting on internal reviews.

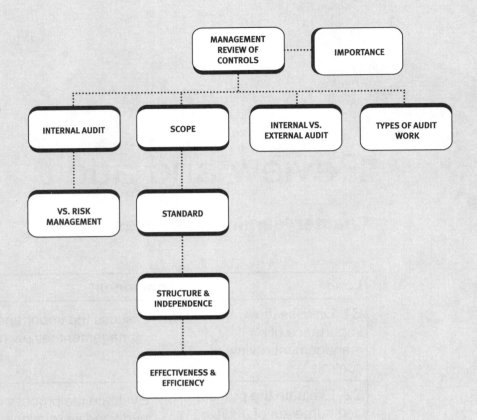

1 Management review of controls

The UK's Turnbull committee says that a review of internal controls should be an integral part of management's role. The board or committees should actively consider reports on control issues. In particular they should consider:

- The identification, evaluation and management of all key risks facing the organisation;

- The effectiveness of internal control – financial, operational, compliance and risk management controls;

- Communication to employees of risk objectives with targets and performance indicators;

- The action taken if any weakness is found.

The report goes on to recommend that the board should consider:

- The nature and extent of the risks which face the organisation;

- The threat of those risks occurring;

- The organisation's ability to reduce the probability and consequences of the risk, and to adapt to any changing risks;

- The costs and benefits of any controls implemented.

An effective internal control system should keep management properly informed about the progress of the organisation (or lack of it) towards the achievement of its objectives. Management and supervisors have a responsibility for monitoring controls in the area of operations for which they are responsible. Internal control might also be monitored by an internal audit function.

What is internal audit ?

Internal auditing is an independent and objective assurance activity designed to add value and improve an organisation's operations. It helps an organisation accomplish its objectives by bringing a systematic approach to evaluating and improving the effectiveness of risk management, control, and governance processes. Internal auditing improves an organisation's effectiveness and efficiency by providing recommendations based on analyses and assessments of data and business processes.

Internal auditing provides value to governing bodies and senior management as an objective source of independent advice.

The scope of internal auditing within an organisation is broad and may involve topics such as the efficacy of operations, the reliability of financial reporting, deterring and investigating fraud, safeguarding assets, and compliance with laws and regulations.

Internal auditing frequently involves measuring compliance with the entity's policies and procedures. However, internal auditors are not responsible for the execution of company activities; they advise management and the Board of Directors (or similar oversight body) regarding how to better execute their responsibilities.

An internal audit function therefore acts as an internal control, to ensure that the internal control system is operating effectively.

Risk management vs. internal audit

Risk management

- A risk management team would be considered to own the entire risk management process.

- They would be ultimately responsible for all aspects of this process including identification and maintenance of the company's risk register, assessment, prioritisation, treatment of risks and establishment of controls to manage these risks.

- The team would lead the company in developing a risk response strategy and would act in an advisory capacity supporting all areas of the business.

- Provision of training and development by risk staff would facilitate operational managers' ability to identify risks in their area of work and devise controls by which to manage them.

Internal audit

- The role of internal audit is that of monitoring and reviewing the effectiveness of the controls implemented by operational managers.

- In the context of risk management their key activity is in the testing and evaluation of the risk controls (hence ensuring that **those who design controls should not test them**).

- In a wider context the internal audit department can carry out special investigations as directed by management, and can assist the organisation in review of the efficient use of resources.

- Internal audit teams can provide support and assistance to senior management in a range of projects, some of which may fall outside the risk management arena.

- They are often able to contribute to the work of operational teams in identifying risks due to their extensive knowledge of the business, but this is not their primary responsibility.

In summary, risk management identify risks or problems, management devise controls which they think will prevent the risk or problem and the auditors check that the control works. If it doesn't, then it is still a problem and management will implement further or different controls which audit will check again. And so the process goes on until the risk or problem is minimised to the satisfaction of management i.e. it is within the companies attitude to risk.

There are three different parties involved in the process review – risk management, managers and auditors, to ensure independence and the best solution for the company.

Factors affecting the need for internal audit

There are a number of factors that affect the need for an internal audit department:

Factor	Comment
The scale, diversity and complexity of the company's activities	The larger, the more diverse and the more complex a range of activities is, the more there is to monitor (and the more opportunity there is for certain things to go wrong).
The number of employees	As a proxy for size, the number of employees signifies that larger organisations are more likely to need internal audit to underpin investor confidence than smaller concerns.
Cost/benefit considerations	Management must be certain of the benefits that will result from establishing internal audit and they must obviously be seen to outweigh the costs of the audit.
Changes in the organisational structures, reporting processes or underlying information systems	Any internal (or external) modification is capable of changing the complexity of operations and, accordingly, the risk.
Changes in key risks could be internal or external in nature	The introduction of a new product, entering a new market, a change in any of the PEST/PESTEL factors or changes in the industry might trigger the need for internal audit.
Problems with existing internal control systems.	Any problems with existing systems clearly signify the need for a tightening of systems and increased monitoring.
An increased number of unexplained or unacceptable events.	System failures or similar events are a clear demonstration of internal control weakness.

Where there is no internal audit department management needs to apply other monitoring processes in order to assure itself and the board that the system of internal control is functioning as intended. In these circumstances, the board will need to assess whether such procedures provide sufficient and objective assurance.

2 Scope and standard of internal audit work

Scope of internal audit work

The internal audit department will typically have the following scope and objectives as prescribed by the management of the business:

(Do not treat this as a comprehensive list of all the areas that the internal auditor considers, as management may prescribe different functions to meet the needs of their company).

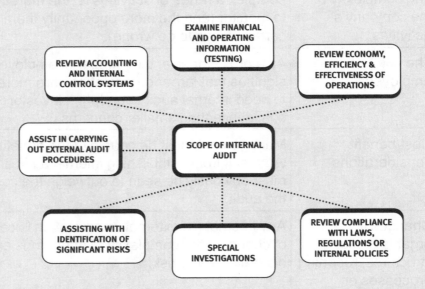

More on scope of internal audit work

Work area	Comment
Reviewing accounting and internal control systems (financial audit)	This is the traditional view of internal audit. The internal auditor checks the financial controls in the company, possibly assisting or sharing work with the external auditor. The internal auditor would comment on whether appropriate controls exist as well as whether they are working correctly. In this work, the internal auditor does not manage risk, but simply reports on controls.
Examining financial and operating information	Internal auditors ensure that reporting of financial information is made on a timely basis and that the information in the reports is factually accurate.

Reviewing the economy, efficiency and effectiveness of operations	This is also called a value for money (VFM) audit (see more later in this chapter). The auditor checks whether a particular activity is cost-effective (economical), uses the minimum inputs for a given output (efficient) and meets its stated objectives (effective).
Reviewing compliance with laws and other external regulations	This objective is particularly relevant under corporate governance codes where the internal auditor will be carrying out detailed work to ensure that internal control systems and financial reports meet stock exchange requirements.
Special investigations	Investigations into other areas of the company's business, e.g. checking the cost estimates for a new factory, or investigating suspected fraud.
Assisting with the identification of significant risks	In this function, the internal auditor does start to work on risks. The auditor may be asked to investigate areas of risk management, with specific reference on how the company identifies, assesses and controls significant risks from both internal and external sources.
Assisting in carrying out external audit procedures	The internal audit team may work closely with the external auditors and provide information that can be utilised in the external audit. There is an obvious benefit to the company from this in the form of a reduction in the audit fee.

Standard of internal audit work

The internal audit function would be expected to carry out their work to a high professional standard. To achieve this the audit function should be well managed and have clear and appropriate procedures for carrying out its work.

It would be expected that:

- There is a formal plan of all audit work that is reviewed by the head of audit and the board/audit committee.
- The audit plans should be reviewed at least annually.

- Each engagement should be conducted appropriately:
  - Planning should be performed.
  - Objectives should be set for the engagement.
  - The work should be documented, reviewed and supervised.
  - The results should be communicated to management.
  - Recommendations for action should be made.

- The progress of the audit should be monitored by the head of internal audit, and if recommendations that the head feels are appropriate are not acted on, the matters should be brought to the attention of the board.

Standards of internal audit work

Internal auditors can follow the same standards as external auditors. However, there are also International Standards for Internal Audit issued by the Internal Auditing Standards Board (IASB) of the Institute of Internal Auditors.

- **Attribute standards** deal with the characteristics of organisations and the parties performing internal auditing activities.
- **Performance standards** describe the nature of internal auditing activities and provide quality criteria for evaluating internal auditing services.

Attribute standards for internal audit

Objective of standard	Explanation
Independence	The internal audit activity should be independent, and the head of internal audit should report to a level within the organisation that allows the internal audit activity to fulfil its responsibilities. It should be free from interference when deciding on the scope of its assurance work, when carrying out the work and when communicating its opinions.
Objectivity	Internal auditors should be objective in carrying out their work. They should have an impartial attitude, and should avoid any conflicts of interest. For example, an internal auditor should not provide assurance services for an operation for which he or she has had management responsibility within the previous year.

Professional care	Internal auditors should exercise due professional care and should have the competence to perform their tasks. They should have some knowledge of the key IT risks and controls, and computer-assisted audit techniques.

Performance standards for internal audit

Area of work	Explanation
Managing internal audit	• The head of internal audit should manage the internal audit activity to ensure that it adds value to the organisation. • The head of internal audit should establish risk-based plans to decide the priorities for internal audit work, consistent with the organisation's objectives. • The internal audit plan should be reviewed at least annually. • The head of internal audit should submit the plan of work to senior management and the board for approval. Independence is maintained by the internal auditor/audit committee being able to decide the scope of internal audit work without being influenced by the board/senior management.
Risk management	• The internal audit department should identify and evaluate significant risk exposures and contribute to the improvement of risk management and control systems. It should evaluate risk exposures relating to governance, operations and information systems, and the reliability and integrity of financial and operating information, the effectiveness and efficiency of operations, safeguarding of assets, compliance with laws, regulations and contracts. Independence is maintained by the internal auditor being given access to information on all these areas and being able to report freely on any errors or omissions found.

Control	• The internal audit department should help to maintain the organisation's control system by evaluating the effectiveness and efficiency of controls, and by promoting continuous improvement. Independence is again maintained by ensuring full provision of information and independent reporting lines (via the audit committee).
Governance	• The internal audit department should assess the corporate governance process and make recommendations where appropriate for improvements in achieving the objectives of corporate governance. Independence is maintained by the internal auditor being able to report breaches of corporate governance code without fear of dismissal.
Internal audit work	• Internal auditors should identify, analyse, evaluate and record sufficient information to achieve the objectives of the engagement. • The information identified should be reliable, relevant and useful with regard to the objectives of the engagement. • The auditors' conclusions should be based on suitable analysis and evaluation. • Information to support the conclusions of the auditors should be recorded. Independence is maintained by the internal auditor being able to show that normal standards of internal audit work have been followed; there has been no pressure to 'cut corners' either from senior management or because the internal auditor decided to carry out the work to a lower standard.

Communicating results	• Internal auditors should communicate the results of their engagement, including conclusions, recommendations and action plans.
	• The results should be communicated to the appropriate persons.
	Independence is maintained by the internal auditor being able to communicate to a committee or person separate from the board who also has the power to take appropriate action on the internal auditors' reports.

3 Structure, independence and effectiveness of internal audit

Structure and independence of internal audit

To ensure that the internal audit function provides an objective assessment of control systems and their weaknesses, there should be measures in place to protect the independence of the internal audit department.

- The internal auditors should be independent of executive management (but have direct access to the highest level of management if required) and should not have any involvement in the activities or systems that they audit (free from operational responsibility).

- The head of internal audit should report directly to a senior director.

- In addition, however, the head of internal audit should have direct access to the chairman of the board of directors, and to the audit committee, and should be accountable to the audit committee.

- The audit committee should approve the appointment and termination of appointment of the head of internal audit.

- In large organisations the internal audit function will be a separate department.

- In a small company it might be the responsibility of individuals to perform specific tasks even though there will not be a full-time position.

- Some companies outsource their internal audit function, often to one of the large accountancy firms.

- The internal auditor will review the accounting and control systems, perform testing of transactions and balances, review the 3E's, implementation of corporate policies, carry out special investigations, and assist the external auditors where necessary.

- They should be technically competent and exercise due professional care by planning, supervising and reviewing any work performed. Documentation should be kept, results communicated to management and recommendations made.

Outsourcing internal audit

In common with other areas of a company's operations, the directors may consider that outsourcing the internal audit function represents better value than an in-house provision. Local government authorities are under particular pressure to ensure that all their services represent 'best value' and this may prompt them to decide to adopt a competitive tender approach.

Advantages of outsourcing internal audit

- Greater focus on cost and efficiency of the internal audit function.

- Staff may be drawn from a broader range of expertise.

- Risk of staff turnover is passed to the outsourcing firm.

- Specialist skills may be more readily available.

- Costs of employing permanent staff are avoided.

- May improve independence.

- Access to new market place technologies, e.g. audit methodology software without associated costs.

- Reduced management time in administering an in-house department.

Disadvantages of outsourcing internal audit

- Possible conflict of interest if provided by the external auditors.

- Pressure on the independence of the outsourced function due to, for example, a threat by management not to renew contract.

- Risk of lack of knowledge and understanding of the organisation's objectives, culture or business.

- The decision may be based on cost with the effectiveness of the function being reduced.

- Flexibility and availability may not be as high as with an in-house function.

- Lack of control over standard of service.

- Risk of blurring of roles between internal and external audit, losing credibility for both.

Minimising these risks

Some general procedures to minimise risks associated with outsourcing the internal audit function will include:

- Controls over acceptance of internal audit contracts to ensure no impact on independence or ethical issues.

- Regular reviews of the quality of audit work performed.

- Separate departments covering internal and external audit.

- Clearly agreed scope, responsibilities and reporting lines.

- Performance measures, management information and risk reporting

- Procedure manuals for internal audit.

Ethical threats to independence

Situations could occasionally arise in which an auditor, especially an internal auditor, might be asked to behave (or might be tempted to behave) in a way that conflicts with ethical standards and guidelines.

Conflicts of interest could relate to unimportant matters, but they might also involve fraud or some other illegal activity.

Examples of such ethical conflicts of interest are as follows:

Threat	Example
There could be pressure from an overbearing supervisor, manager or director, adversely affecting the accountant's integrity.	The auditor is asked not to report adverse findings. The threat could be made more personal, e.g. by indicating that the auditor's employment will be terminated if disclosure is made.
An auditor might mislead his employer as to the amount of experience or expertise he has, when in reality the expert advice of someone else should be sought.	The auditor wants to retain his position within the internal audit department or gain respect because of the apparent experience that they have.

An auditor might be asked to act contrary to a technical or professional standard. Divided loyalty between the auditor's superior and the required professional standards of conduct could arise.	An auditor is told to ignore the incorrect application of an accounting standard or the incorrect reporting of directors' remuneration.

Resolution of ethical conflicts of interest

Conflict resolution has been covered earlier.

Effectiveness and efficiency of internal audit

The work of an internal audit department should be monitored to assess effectiveness in the broader context of the company's risk management systems.

The internal audit process must provide benefits in excess of its cost.

- The **efficiency** of internal audit can be assessed by comparing actual costs and output against a target, such as:
    - the cost per internal audit day
    - the cost per audit report
    - the number of audit reports produced.

- The **effectiveness** of internal audit needs to be measured in a way that indicates the extent to which it provides assurance to management, the audit committee and the board about the effectiveness of the system of internal control.
    - This can be done by identifying evidence of improvements in internal control.

4 Internal and external audit

To a large extent, the work of internal auditors and external auditors is similar, and overlaps. It is therefore important that their efforts should complement each other, rather than duplicate each other.

Comparison of internal to external audit

	External audit	Internal audit
Role required by:	Statute, for limited companies.	Directors and shareholders, usually in larger organisations.
Appointed by:	Shareholders or directors.	Directors, via the Chief Internal Auditor (CIA).
Reports to:	Shareholder (primary duty) and management (professional responsibility).	Directors, via the CIA.
Reports on:	Financial statements.	Internal controls mainly.
Forms opinions on:	True and fair view and proper presentation.	Adequacy of ICS as a contribution to the economic, efficient and effective use of resources.
Scope of assignment:	Unlimited, to fulfil statutory obligation.	Prescribed by directors.

Relationship of internal audit to external audit

The audit plan of the external auditors should be drawn up taking into consideration the work of internal audit, and the extent to which the external auditors can rely on the findings of the internal auditors in reaching their audit opinion.

Factors that the external auditor should consider include:

* the status of internal audit within the organisation

* the scope of the internal audit function

* whether management act on the recommendations of the internal auditor

* the technical competence of the internal auditors

* whether the objectives of the internal audit work are aligned with that of the external auditor

* whether the work of the internal audit function appears to have been planned, supervised, reviewed and documented with due professional care.

Note that there is no particular expectation that the external auditor will be able to rely on the work done by internal audit. The duties of both sets of auditors will differ and hence the work of internal audit may be of very little relevance to the external auditor.

However, in some instances, the external auditors do rely on the internal auditors work if areas of the external auditors audit program have been covered (and the factors mentioned above can be met). Providing the testing performed meets the scope and quality level that the external auditor requires, then the external auditor will place 'some' reliance on the work already performed by internal audit, and consequently reduce the amount of further testing required in order to state an opinion.

However, the external auditors would not place 'total' reliance on the internal auditors work. (They would effectively need to audit the internal auditors work by testing it in part before they could rely on it.)

For example, internal audit might know that during the annual external audit purchase compliance tests are performed to ensure that, say, all purchases are backed up by an order, the order is authorised, etc. The sample normally taken by the external auditor might be, say, 20 transactions. Internal audit could choose to perform this work during the course of the year and present their findings to the external auditor when they arrive to perform the annual audit. The external auditors would then check the internal auditors work by re-performing the compliance tests on a few transactions, say, 3 of the 20. Providing no errors were found, the external auditors would then perform their own, new compliance tests on a reduced number of, say, 5 transactions.

More testing will have been performed since both internal and external audit have been involved, giving a higher assurance level (or lower risk).

Also, this 'sharing' of work can lead to a reduced external audit fee, because some of the testing has been done internally at a reduced cost.

More on external audit

External audit can be defined as a periodic examination of the books of accounts and records of an entity carried out by an independent third party (the auditor), to ensure that they have been properly maintained, are accurate and comply with established concepts, principles, accounting standards, legal requirements and give a true and fair view of the financial state of the entity.

The external auditors' main responsibility is to form an opinion on whether the company's financial statements give a true and fair view.

Differing perspectives on systems and controls

External auditors need to review systems and controls:

- to assess whether the systems are such that the risk of material misstatement in the financial statements is reduced

- if they are to rely on the operation of controls in a system so that the extent of the procedures which they carry out will be reduced, they will need to test those controls and document their findings
    - if the external auditors discover weaknesses in systems and controls, they will report their findings to those charged with governance in their management letter.

Internal auditors:

- may be given an assignment to review systems and controls and to report to management about their effectiveness.
    - the nature of the work carried out by internal audit in these circumstances will be very similar to that performed by the external auditors (covered in the following chapter).

Differing perspectives on fraud

The **external auditor** is responsible for identifying material misstatements in the financial statements in order to ensure that they give a true and fair view. By definition then, the external auditor is responsible for detecting any material fraud that may have occurred as this will lead to a material misstatement.

However, they have no specific responsibility with regard to immaterial fraud. As with immaterial errors, if they identify them they will be reported to those charged with governance, but there is no duty to identify them.

In order to have a chance of detecting fraud the auditor must maintain an attitude of professional scepticism when performing their work which involves keeping an open mind to the possibility of fraud occurring.

Internal auditors may be given an assignment:

- to assess the likelihood of fraud, or if a fraud has been discovered,

- to assess its consequences and

- to make recommendations for prevention in the future.

Test your understanding 1 – SHD

SHD is a property development company involved in multiple development projects across the country. In the last year a member of the finance department has established an expenses fraud through the use of a false supplier. Invoices are raised in the name of this supplier on a monthly basis for miscellaneous materials to the various development sites. These invoices are paid directly via the accounts payable system without going to the site project managers.

This fraud has increased the variable costs of construction projects by 15% in the last year, a point which has been identified by the external auditors in their recent audit. The auditors approached the management accountant for further information on the cost increase.

Required:

Discuss the differing views of external auditors and internal auditors to this increase in variable costs.

Test your understanding 2 – Snarl plc

The new finance director of Snarl plc, a listed company, is looking for ways of reducing running costs. He thinks that it should be possible to reduce the costs of the annual audit. The company has an internal audit section, and the finance director believes that the external auditors should place more reliance on the work of internal audit. This should reduce the amount of work needed for the external audit, and so reduce the external audit fee.

Required:

He raises this idea in a conversation with you, and asks for your views. Explain the points you would make in response.

5 Types of audit work

As there are many risks and many controls within a business, there will be many different types of audit that can be performed. All types will essentially ensure the same thing – that the companies processes are being adhered to.

Some different types of audit work are discussed below, but the list is not exhaustive.

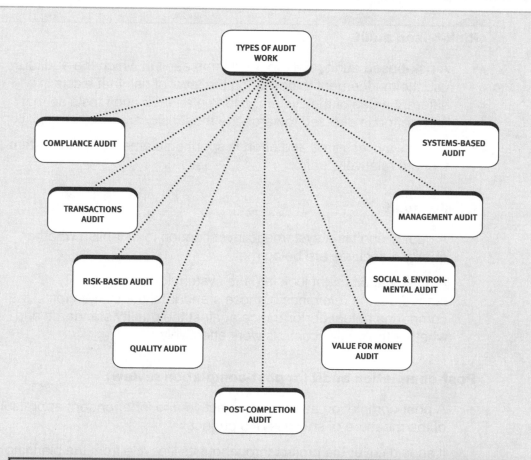

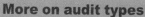

More on audit types

Compliance audit

- Compliance audits check the implementation of written rules, regulations and procedures.

- They were used originally for financial transactions, because the government (tax authorities) needed assurance that the financial figures were correct.

- The concept of compliance has been extended to other areas, such as regulatory inspections and quality audits, where there is a requirement to verify that activities are being performed in strict compliance with approved standards and procedures.

Transactions audit

- A transactions audit involves the checking of a sample of transactions against documentary evidence.

- This method can be used where controls are weak or where transactions are high risk.

Risk-based audit

- A risk-based audit refers to a systems audit in which the auditors use their judgement to decide on the level of risk that exists in different areas of the system, and to plan their audit tests so that more effort is directed towards the most risky areas.

- In this way, less time and effort is spent on elements of the system that are relatively 'safe'.

Quality audit

- A quality audit is a systematic investigation to establish whether quality objectives are being met.

- A quality audit might look into the system for setting quality standards, the relevance of those standards, the system for comparing actual performance against the quality standards and whether the quality controls work effectively.

Post-completion audit (or post-completion review)

- A post-completion audit is an objective and independent appraisal of the measure of success of a project.

- It should cover the project throughout its lifecycle from the planning and implementation stages through to performance after commissioning.

- The review should take place at some time after the project or process has been completed or is being used. Review should not be too soon, where the project or process hasn't been given a chance to 'bed in'. But it should also not be too late where important feedback and learning has not been applied on later projects.

- Its objective is to provide feedback as to the success of a project or otherwise, and acts as a learning tool for future projects.

- Projects are often assessed on three criteria: time, cost and quality. Was the project implemented on time? Did the project come in on budget? Was the project delivered at the expected quality level, or more commonly, did it solve the original issue that prompted the project?

- Post-completion audits are often performed by internal audit, as long as they are not involved in the original design of the project itself. The auditor will source the documentation which stated the original objectives of the project, and then follow the process carried out to ensure that all activities led to the successful completion of these objectives – in an economical, efficient and effective way. If the objectives were not met, why not? And what should be done about it?

The latter four types of audit work will now be considered in more detail.

Value for money audit

An area that internal auditors have been getting increasingly involved in is value for money audits. These have been replaced in terminology more recently by 'best value' audits, but many of the principles remain the same.

In a value for money (VFM) audit the auditor assesses three main areas.

Economy

- The economy of a business is assessed by looking at the inputs to the business (or process), and deciding whether these are the most economical that are available at an acceptable quality level.

Efficiency

- The efficiency of an operation is assessed by considering how well the operation converts inputs to outputs.

Effectiveness

- The effectiveness of an organisation is assessed by examining whether the organisation is achieving its objectives. To assess effectiveness there must be clear objectives for the organisation that can be examined.

More on VFM audit

A VFM audit is 'an investigation into whether proper arrangements have been made for securing economy, efficiency and effectiveness in the use of resources'. It is an audit into the '3 Es' in an item or operation.

- **Economy** means obtaining the required resources at the lowest cost. There would be a lack of economy, for example, if there was overstaffing in a particular department or if an excessive price was paid for materials of the required quality. It is important to remember that economy does not mean achieving the lowest cost possible: it means keeping costs within acceptable limits for obtaining resources of the desired quality.

- **Efficiency** means using the minimum quantity of resources to achieve a given quantity and quality of output. Efficiency can be measured either in terms of:
  - maximising the output for a given quantity of input, such as the maximum quantity of services provided per employee or per £1 spent, or
  - achieving a given quantity of output with the minimum resources possible.
- **Effectiveness** exists when the output from a system achieves its intended aims and objectives.

Managers are responsible for achieving economy, efficiency and effectiveness in the operations for which they are responsible. A VFM audit provides a check to confirm that management is fulfilling this responsibility properly.

VFM audits have commonly been associated with auditing in the public sector, but they are applicable in any type of organisation, in the public or private sectors.

Problems with VFM audits

There are several problems with conducting a VFM audit.

- It might be **difficult to measure outputs**, particularly in government services. For example, the output from an education system can be measured in many different ways, both in terms of the numbers educated and the quality of education. In the health service, outputs might be measured in terms of the numbers of patients treated; on the other hand, successful preventive medicine would be measured in terms of reductions in the numbers of patients treated for particular conditions.
- The **objectives of the activity might be difficult to establish**, particularly in the public sector. For example, what are the objectives of the police service? If an activity has several different objectives, the problem is then how to decide their priorities. For example, the objective of the police force might be to maintain public order, arrest criminals, deter criminals, and so on.
- **The focus must be EITHER on economy and efficiency OR on effectiveness**. It is difficult to report on both issues simultaneously because costs can almost always be reduced by cutting back on the quality of service, while outputs can almost always be improved by spending more.

- **Quality might be ignored when economy and efficiency are measured**. For example, a government might succeed in reducing the costs of secondary education, but only by making schools overcrowded and by lowering the standards of the education provided. VFM tends to focus more on economy and efficiency because those are much easier to measure than effectiveness.

Test your understanding 3 – Government authority

A local government authority has a library service. As an auditor who has been asked to carry out a value for money audit on the service, discuss the issues of economy, efficiency and effectiveness that you might be looking at.

Social and environmental audit

Environmental audit

An environmental audit is defined as:

'A management tool comprising a systematic, documented, periodic and objective evaluation of how well organisations, management, and equipment are performing, with the aim of contributing to safeguarding the environment by facilitating management control of environmental practices, and assessing compliance with company policies, which would include meeting regulatory requirements and standards applicable.'

It is possible that an 'accounting' trained auditor could be asked to perform one of these audits but it is unlikely that they would be able to perform the task with the proper competence. The auditor is unlikely to have the necessary skills and therefore it would be professionally wrong to accept the assignment.

Social audit

The social audit would look at the company's contribution to society and the community. The contributions made could be through:

- Donations.
- Sponsorship.
- Employment practices.

- Education.

- Health and safety.

- Ethical investments, etc.

A social audit could either confirm statements made by the directors, or make recommendations for social policies that the company should perform.

Environmental reporting

The environmental report that is included in the annual report by many companies is sometimes accompanied by an 'auditors' statement'.

The environmental report produced by companies will normally contain information about:

- Sustainability.

- Targets achieved.

- Compliance with regulations.

- Emissions.

- Industrial legacies.

- Obtaining ISO 14001 (environmental management systems).

Many companies conduct an internal audit on these matters, and then have the audit verified by external assessors. It is possible that the external auditor could be asked to be an external assessor, however, it is more likely with environmental matters that the person will be an appropriately qualified environmental assessor.

Test your understanding 4 – Brandol PCT

Brandol Primary Care Trust (PCT) is a government funded health trust charged with meeting the non-hospital primary health care needs of the Brandol Community. Facilities it runs include:

- General Practitioner (GP) surgeries and Heath Centres

- Pre and Post Natal Services

- A network of district nurses

- Dental services

- Limited supported for chiropody services
- Out-of hours emergency doctor and dental services
- A network (limited) of hospices.

Brandol is a community on the Norfolk/Suffolk border. It is a predominantly rural community, with few large urban areas. The average age of the predominantly white community is increasing. This is accelerated by the out-migration of many youngsters raised in the region. It is also an attractive retirement area. More recently this ageing trend has started to reverse slightly, reflecting a large influx of young eastern European men moving to the UK for work on vegetable and fruit farms.

Brandol has recently spent a significant amount of money up-grading its midwifery services, which are now ranked some of the best in the country. The recommended ratio of midwives to mothers is 1 to 30. In Brandol this ratio is 1 to 15. The PCT has a less impressive record in providing support for the elderly and there is a chronic shortage of care home and hospice places. A private network of care homes and hospices has been contracted to supply care to patients, but this has increased costs per patient by about 50%.

In a recent survey of staff wages Brandol was shown to paying the 4th highest average salary to its GP's and the 8th highest average salary to its midwives (there are 45 PCTs in the country). As a result it has not experienced significant recruitment problems.

Brandol is also striving to improve the information it provides to patients. Its leaflets and websites are now available in Urdu, Hindi, Spanish and French.

Required:

(a) Explain what is meant by a value for money audit and identify areas of potential weakness for the PCT. Make recommendations for how these weaknesses can be overcome.

(b) Explain what is meant by an environmental and social audit using examples relevant to the PCT.

Management audit

A management audit is sometimes called an **operational audit.**

A management audit is defined by CIMA as 'an objective and independent appraisal of the effectiveness of managers and the corporate structure in the achievement of the entities' objectives and policies'.

- Its aim is to identify existing and potential management weakness and recommend ways to rectify them.'

- This type of audit would require the use of very experienced staff who understand the nature of the business.

More on management audit

The **objectives of a management audit** might be:

- re-focusing resources towards 'mission-critical' objectives

- improving efficiency (improving work flows, eliminating unnecessary activities, eliminating duplicated activities, etc)

- improving the effectiveness of management support tools (such as improvements in controls, automated system support etc)

- assessing the appropriate levels of service for an activity or operation

- identifying cost savings

- identifying opportunities to enhance revenue

- improvements in governance.

The **elements of a management audit** might include:

- a review of policies and procedures

- a general review of workloads, work methods and work flows

- an evaluation of systems and processes

- a review of management practices

- a review of resource utilisation

- a detailed cost analysis.

The **findings of a management audit** might focus not so much on compliance with policies and procedures, but on:

- a lack of technical competence or knowledge of the business amongst managers, and insufficient management training

- an unwillingness to delegate

- regular failure to achieve standards or targets

- inadequate management information systems

- poor communications within or between departments

- poor management/staff relationships

- an absence of clear leadership

- a failure by management to make good decisions.

Systems-based audit

A systems-based audit is an audit of internal controls within an organisation. Although the term refers to any type of system, it is often associated with the audit of accounting systems, such as the sales ledger system, purchase ledger system, receipts and payments, fixed asset records, stock records and so on.

The aim of such an audit is to identify weaknesses in the system (weaknesses in either the controls or in the application of controls, such that there is a risk of material inaccuracy in financial records and statements, or a risk of fraud). More will be seen of systems-based audit in the next chapter.

A systems-based audit would take the following steps:

- Identify the objectives of each system

- Identify the procedures

- Identify why the system might not meet its objectives

- Identify ways to manage the above

- Identify if current controls are adequate

- Report on the above.

Test your understanding 5 – Types of audit

BK is a company specialising in the sale of carpets and floor coverings to sports clubs, sports halls and social centres around the country. It obtains its carpeting and other materials directly from suppliers in Eastern Asia.

When it provides new carpeting to a customer, BK also undertakes to remove and dispose of the old carpeting or floor covering, but charges a fee for the service. The old carpets are taken to waste disposal sites or occasionally burned.

You have recently been appointed as an internal auditor to the company, and you are discussing your plan of work for the next 12 months with the finance director. The following points arise in your discussion.

- The work of the internal audit section has so far been largely restricted to audits of elements of the financial accounting system, although there have been occasional management audits. You suggest that it might be appropriate to carry out some value for money audits.

- The board of directors has come under pressure from its major shareholders to publish an annual Social and Environmental Report for inclusion in the annual report and accounts. You suggest that it might be appropriate to check and verify the contents of this report before publication.

- There has been considerable publicity in the national press recently about the use of child labour and slave labour in certain parts of the country from which BK purchases its carpets. The finance director expresses the view that BK benefited from low purchase costs for carpets and floor coverings, but he would be disappointed if BK's suppliers were associated with these labour practices.

- The Finance Director informs you that your predecessor as internal auditor resigned from the company after a dispute with the executive director concerning a department where the auditor had carried out a management audit. Apparently, the internal auditor had criticised the director and his department severely for lax controls and inefficiency. The director had argued that the internal auditor had not discussed any of the criticisms before preparing the report, had been deceitful in asking questions and was probably not qualified to do the audit work. On being told that the auditor was a CIMA member, you express the view that this seemed to be a matter where the Institute's Ethical Guidelines should have been followed.

Required:

(a) Explain the difference between a value for money audit of the accounts department and an audit of the accounting system.

(b) As the internal auditor, discuss how you might plan a social and environmental audit of the company and what you would consider to be the main social and environmental risks facing BK.

(c) From the information available about the dispute between the previous internal auditor and the executive director, advise how CIMA's Ethical Guidelines might have been relevant to the way in which the auditor acted, or ought to have acted.

Test your understanding 6 – SPM

SPM is a manufacturer and distributor of printed stationery products that are sold in a wide variety of retail stores around the country. There are two divisions: Manufacturing and Distribution. A very large inventory is held in the distribution warehouse to cope with orders from retailers who expect delivery within 48 hours of placing an order.

SPM's management accountant for the Manufacturing division charges the Distribution division for all goods transferred at the standard cost of manufacture which is agreed by each division during the annual budget cycle. The Manufacturing division makes a 10% profit on the cost of production but absorbs all production variances. The goods transferred to Distribution are therefore at a known cost and physically checked by both the Manufacturing and the Distribution division staff at the time of transfer.

The customer order process for SPM's Distribution division is as follows:

- SPM's customer service centre receives orders by telephone, post, fax, email and through a new on-line Internet ordering facility (a similar system to that used by Amazon). The customer service centre checks the creditworthiness of customers and bundles up orders several times each day to go to the despatch department.

- All orders received by the despatch department are input to SPM's computer system which checks stock availability and produces an invoice for the goods.

- Internet orders have been credit checked automatically and stock has been reserved as part of the order entry process carried out by the customer. Internet orders automatically result in an invoice being printed without additional input.

- The despatch department uses a copy of the invoice to select goods from the warehouse, which are then assembled in the loading dock for delivery using SPM's own fleet of delivery vehicles.

- When SPM's drivers deliver the goods to the customer, the customer signs for the receipt and the signed copy of the invoice is returned to the despatch office and then to the accounts department.

- SPM's management accountant for the Distribution division produces monthly management reports based on the selling price of the goods less the standard cost of manufacture. The standard cost of manufacture is deducted from the inventory control total which is increased by the value of inventory transferred from the manufacturing division. The control total for inventory is compared with the monthly inventory valuation report and while there are differences, these are mainly the result of write-offs of damaged or obsolete stock, which are recorded on journal entry forms by the despatch department and sent to the accounts department.

Due to the size of inventory held, a physical stocktake is only taken once per annum by Distribution staff, at the end of the financial year. This has always revealed some stock losses, although these have been at an acceptable level. Both internal and external auditors are present during the stocktake and check selected items of stock with the despatch department staff. Due to the range of products held in the warehouse, the auditors rely on the despatch department staff to identify many of the products held.

Required:

(a) Advise the board and the audit committee of SPM as to its responsibilities for internal control and for its relationship with both internal and external auditors.

(b) Advise the board about the role of internal and external audit and recommend an internal audit plan for SPM's Distribution division that is based on the risk assessment identified in (b) above.

6 Chapter summary

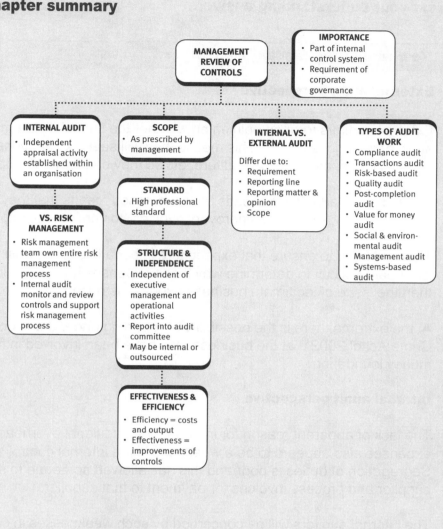

MANAGEMENT REVIEW OF CONTROLS

IMPORTANCE
- Part of internal control system
- Requirement of corporate governance

INTERNAL AUDIT
- Independent appraisal activity established within an organisation

VS. RISK MANAGEMENT
- Risk management team own entire risk management process
- Internal audit monitor and review controls and support risk management process

SCOPE
- As prescribed by management

STANDARD
- High professional standard

STRUCTURE & INDEPENDENCE
- Independent of executive management and operational activities
- Report into audit committee
- May be internal or outsourced

EFFECTIVENESS & EFFICIENCY
- Efficiency = costs and output
- Effectiveness = improvements of controls

INTERNAL VS. EXTERNAL AUDIT

Differ due to:
- Requirement
- Reporting line
- Reporting matter & opinion
- Scope

TYPES OF AUDIT WORK
- Compliance audit
- Transactions audit
- Risk-based audit
- Quality audit
- Post-completion audit
- Value for money audit
- Social & environmental audit
- Management audit
- Systems-based audit

Test your understanding answers

Test your understanding 1 – SHD

External audit perspective

External auditors form an opinion on whether the financial statements show a true and fair view. This means they will seek explanations for any unusual items, areas of expenditure, etc so they can form their opinion.

The fact that variable overheads have increased means that they will require evidence (such as approved invoices) to verify these expenses .

They will need to ensure that expenditure is bona fide to the business. If it appears difficult to determine why these expenses have been incurred, then the issue of legitimate business expense is raised.

At the extreme there is the possibility of reporting under the Proceeds of Crime Act of 2002 that the business may have been involved in fraud or money laundering.

Internal audit perspective

The lack of apparent reason for incurring the additional overhead expenses also appears to be a weakness in the internal control systems. Segregation of duties is poor and this has allowed someone to set up a supplier and process invoices for payment to that supplier.

The internal auditors will be concerned by such weaknesses in control and seek to rectify the situation.

They may also notice the increase in expenditure and question the efficient use of resources on the development projects.

Test your understanding 2 – Snarl plc

It is important to remember the following points.

- Not all internal audit work is concerned with the audit of the accounting and financial system. The internal auditors might also audit operational and compliance controls, which are not of direct relevance to the external auditors.

- The purpose of internal audit is to provide support to management, by helping to provide evidence of the effectiveness of the internal control and risk management system. The purpose of the external auditors is to fulfil a statutory requirement (the external audit) and report to the shareholders. Since the internal auditors serve management and the external auditors serve the shareholders, it cannot be assumed that their main areas of concern should be the same.

The audit committee should agree the annual audit plan with the external auditors (taking the views of the finance director into consideration), and the audit fee. The audit committee should also review and assess the annual internal audit plan.

If the work of the internal audit section overlaps with the work of the external auditors then it is certainly worth raising the suggestion. If there is scope to reduce the cost of the external audit without compromising the quality of either the external audit or internal audit work, the opportunities should be identified and taken.

Test your understanding 3 – Government authority

There is no one 'correct' answer here, but the audit might look at:

Economy. The purchase cost of books and other items, the cost of maintaining library premises, whether there is overstaffing in the library services department.

Efficiency. The audit might look at efficiency in the use of books and other items, such as the rate at which books are used or borrowed, or the average cost per book borrowed.

Effectiveness. Measuring effectiveness depends on the government authority's policy for the library service. It might be measured in terms of the percentage of the local population (within age groups or other social groups) that borrow books from the library each month or year.

(a) **Value for money audit**

A value for money audit involves considering the three dimensions of economy, efficiency and effectiveness. Each of these relates to slightly different aspects of an organisation's performance. Economy looks at the inputs to an organisation and considers whether these have been acquired at the lowest possible cost for a given quantity/quality. Efficiency considers the nature of the conversion process of inputs into output, whereas effectiveness considers the extent to which an organisation has achieved its strategic objectives. These three issues interact and may in some circumstances conflict. Buying the lowest cost inputs may mean that the conversion process becomes more problematic and efficiency is reduced. Value for money audits are part of the work of an internal audit department.

Weaknesses

Brandol PCT appears to have a number of potential weaknesses with regard to economy. The PCT is currently 'paying the 4th highest average salary to its GPs and the 8th highest average salary to its midwives'; this would seem to suggest that it is not acquiring inputs at the lowest possible cost. Of course in doing this it may be acquiring staff of a higher calibre and this may be benefiting its efficiency. However, given that there are 45 PCTs we would expect that it ought to be somewhere in the middle.

To be certain it would have been helpful to have had some information about the highest and lowest pay rates. For example, if there were only a matter of a couple of hundred pounds between the highest and lowest pay rates then the position in the table would be largely immaterial and it may be that by paying a little extra it has secured higher quality staff and thus has performed well with regard to economy. However, the fact that 'it has not experienced significant recruitment problems' would seem to suggest that it probably is paying substantially more than other PCTs.

The most obvious recommendation would be to ensure that future appointments are not as generous with regard to pay. It would be difficult to try to reduce the pay of current appointments as this could create legal issues for the PCT; although over the longer-term it may be possible to achieve this by ensuring that future pay increases are below the national average. It would need to be recognised that this solution may have adverse effects on morale and motivation and thus impact on the quality of the service provided.

Other recommendations might include suggesting that midwives are encouraged to re-train to work with the elderly. In practice this is unlikely to work as midwifery requires a higher level of nursing skills and there is unlikely to be much willingness for midwives to transfer in this way. The already existing pay differential is likely to be to the advantage of midwives and a transfer of midwives to geriatric services would thus result in a higher cost for the elderly support services. This works against the need for economy.

There would also appear to be a weakness with regard to the input cost of the care homes and hospice service as the new method of supply 'has increased costs per patient by about 50%'. However, it could be argued that this is really a weakness with regard to efficiency as it relates to the conversion process of inputs to output. In this case the chosen mechanism for the supply of the service could be argued to be inappropriate and that which is creating the inefficiency. A possible recommendation for this weakness would be for the PCT to investigate the cost of provision of an in-house system of care homes and hospices. This would involve substantial capital expenditure and the feasibility of funding for such provision would need to be investigated.

Brandol PCT would appear to be inefficient with regard to the current supply of its midwifery services as 'the recommended ratio of midwives to mothers is 1 to 30', whereas Brandol has a ratio of 1 to 15. Although this obviously makes Brandol PCT appear favourable to a potential user, it does suggest that inputs are not being converted into output in the best possible fashion. Midwifery resources are not being utilised in the best possible way. Various recommendations could be made.

One possibility is redundancies within the midwifery. The costs involved in doing this would need to be investigated. Again it may be possible that some midwives could be encouraged to take early retirement. The possibility of sharing service provision with neighbouring PCTs that have a higher ratio than the recommended ratio could also be investigated. In the longer-term natural wastage would reduce the ratio but this could be a lengthy process.

Assuming that the goal of the PCT is the provision of healthcare services to the local community there are very obvious weaknesses with regard to the effectiveness of this PCT. It has failed to recognise the demographic change in its client base and has an inappropriate mix of services. Currently it is not really meeting the needs of an ageing population. Nor has it recognised that it has an 'influx of young Eastern European men' working in the agricultural sector which tends to have higher incidence of accidents.

The information that it provides to patients seems to fail to meet the language needs of the population as no leaflets are written in any Eastern European languages. If these weaknesses are to be addressed then Brandol will need to alter the direction in which its resources go with more resources being directed towards the provision of care homes and hospices and less resources within the midwifery sector. GP services will probably need to be maintained, although there may be some necessity for more out of hours emergency doctor services given the influx of migrant workers. Recommendations with regard to information provision might controversially include abandoning the production of leaflets in foreign languages and printing only in English but maintaining and increasing (to include Eastern European languages) the provision of foreign language information on the website as this is a relatively lower cost option.

(b) **Environmental audits** are concerned with attempting to reduce the impact that an organisation has on the environment. In the case of Brandol such an audit would involve areas such as:

- the monitoring of emissions.

- auditing the extent to which the current service providers were lit by lower usage energy lighting, and how effective their heating and air conditioning systems are. The purpose of this would be to minimise its carbon emissions.

- how the PCT disposed of waste. Of particular concern here might be 'sharps' disposal.

- its employment policies and how these affected the distances that its employees travelled to work as this would also have an environmental impact.

- the extent to which an organisation recycles and this may be relevant to the PCT.

- environmental concerns from procedures for sterilisation of any equipment. Where this is conducted off-site there is likely to be an impact on the local environment.

Social audits consider the impact of an organisation on the local community and society. Such an audit would consider issues including:

- the extent to which employment policies encouraged local employment.

- the extent to which the PCT makes its resources available to the local society. This might include the extent to which grounds and facilities were made available to the local community. It would also include the extent to which the PCT was involved in the local community with regard to education in healthcare services. This could include visits to local schools to raise the profile of particular health issues. In the case of Brandol this might also include visiting local farms to make migrant workers aware of specific health issues and increase healthcare education.

- the extent to which the PCT provides support and assistance to local community voluntary groups. For example, the local community may provide volunteer transport facilities for the elderly to GPs, the extent to which the PCT assisted and was involved in this process would form part of a social audit report. Again the PCT may assist in the provision of resources for local charities conducting something like a 'fun run' and this would also be recorded in a social audit report.

Test your understanding 5 – Types of audit

Key answer tips

To tackle part (a) you will need to start by defining the types of audit being discussed, and then draw out what is different about them. There will be no marks for explaining similarities.

Part (b) is a straightforward requirement focusing on the specific type of audit and risks. Even if you are not too familiar with the detail of social and environmental audits you can still earn some marks by tackling this from the perspective of planning any audit.

Part (c) is more challenging since you will not be able to rely on text-book theory. Simply repeating CIMA's ethical principles will not be enough here – you need to think wider as to how they may assist in this situation.

(a) A value for money audit is an audit of economy, efficiency and effectiveness (the '3Es'). The audit investigates an aspect of operations, such as the work done in a particular department, or the work carried out to perform a particular activity (in more than one department). The aim of the audit is to establish the objective or objectives of the operations, and consider:

– whether the objectives are being successfully achieved, and if not what the reasons might be;

– whether the operations are being performed in a cost-efficient manner, or whether there is unnecessary and wasteful spending on items of expense;

– whether operations are being performed efficiently.

A value for money (VFM) audit of the accounts department might therefore look at issues such as:

– staffing levels in the department, and whether these are too high (resulting in low productivity);

– whether customers pay on time, or whether the debt collection staff give customers too much time to pay, and whether bad debt levels are high. (Poor debt collection procedures and high irrecoverable debts would indicate a lack of effectiveness);

– whether the department has spent too much on its computer equipment (resulting in poor economy).

A VFM audit might also investigate part of the accounts department that are not subject to an 'accounting audit', such as the management accounts and the capital expenditure appraisal procedures. For example, a VFM audit might assess the value that is provided by the current management accounting control system (in terms of what it achieves, and whether it does its work efficiently and economically), and whether the benefits justify the costs incurred.

In contrast, an audit of the accounting system would be concerned with the reliability of the accounting records and whether the assets of the company are being properly safeguarded. The audits will therefore consider the reliability of internal controls, and whether the auditors can rely on the effectiveness of those controls. The focus is therefore entirely different. An audit of the accounts is not particularly concerned with efficiency or economy.

(b) An audit needs to be conducted against a clear set of standards or targets. Since the company intends to publish an annual Social and Environmental Report, it has to decide the criteria against which its performance and policies should be measured.

The key issues should be established. The board of directors should have some idea of what these issues are, but guidance can be obtained if necessary from the company's shareholders, or from external agencies that have been established to assist companies to prepare Social and Environmental Reports (or Sustainability Reports). These sources include the UN's Global Research Initiative sustainability reporting guidelines.

The aspects of social and environmental and responsibility that might need to be covered by the report – and audited – include environmental issues (pollution, waste, sustainable supplies of raw materials) and work-related issues (human rights, working conditions, pay, employee education, avoiding discrimination at work, and so on).

A social and environmental audit should be planned within the framework of the company's policies for social and environmental matters and targets for achievement. An audit can then assess whether the policies are being applied and whether progress is being made towards the stated targets (which could be either quantitative or qualitative targets).

From the information available, two social and environmental risks are apparent. It is not clear how serious they are, but if they could affect the short-term or long-term value of the company, they should be disclosed in the Social and Environmental Report. (In the UK, listed companies may be required in the future to disclose significant risks, including risks relating to social and environmental issues, in their annual Operating and Financial Review.) The two issues that seem apparent are:

– Environmental issues relating to the disposal of old carpets and floor covering. BK currently burns some old materials and disposes of the rest using methods that are not stated. There is an immediate risk that BK is in breach of the law by burning the materials (air pollution and possibly other pollution) and might also be in breach of the laws on disposals of materials. Checking on compliance with the laws should be an element of a social and environmental audit. The company might also be affected by further legal restrictions on disposals (and recycling) of used items.

– There are also human rights issues in connection with the possible use of child labour or slave labour by suppliers. Although BK is not directly responsible for the labour policies of its suppliers, a socially responsible policy would be to influence suppliers to adopt different labour policies or switch to different suppliers. If BK is using suppliers who use child labour or slave labour, there will be a risk to the company's reputation. This could have an impact on sales of the company's services.

(c) From the information available about the dispute, it is not clear whether or not the internal auditor acted ethically.

– The CIMA Ethical Guidelines state that an accountant should act with integrity, and should be honest and straightforward in carrying out his or her work. There is a suggestion that this might not have been the case. The executive director accused the auditor of being 'deceitful'. It would also appear that the auditor did not discuss his findings or his concerns with the director or anyone else in the department subject to audit. This would have been inappropriate behaviour, because it would have lacked integrity. An internal auditor is required to look for weaknesses in systems, management and controls, but should discuss issues with the individuals concerned and be straightforward in doing so.

– The Ethical Guidelines also require an accountant to act with objectivity, and to be intellectually honest and fair. It is not clear whether the auditor acted in this way, or whether perhaps a personal dislike of the director might have affected his opinions and biased his judgements. The Ethical Guidelines require an accountant to show professional competence and due care in his work. The director has accused the auditor of not being qualified for the work. Without further information, this cannot be assessed any further.

– It is also possible that the internal auditor was subjected to strong pressure from the director and others in the department to give a favourable audit report, when a more critical report would be appropriate. If this was the situation and the auditor was under pressure from the director, he would have been the victim of an ethical conflict of interest. The CIMA Guidelines recommend that in such circumstances, the accountant should report the problem to his superior. However, since the target of the auditor's criticism was a director of the company, it is quite possible that his superior also felt a conflict of interest and inability to stand up to such a senior person.

When an accountant is unable to resolve a conflict of interest by referring the problem to a superior (or the superior's boss), the CIMA Guidelines state that there may be no alternative to resignation. It is possible that this is what happened in this particular case.

In conclusion, from the limited information available, it is not clear who was 'at fault', the director or the accountant (or both of them). However, with more information, it would be possible to judge the matter by reference to the CIMA Ethical Guidelines.

Test your understanding 6 – SPM

(a) The board is responsible for the company's system of internal control and for reviewing its effectiveness. An internal control system is designed to manage rather than eliminate the risk of failure to achieve business objectives, and can only provide reasonable but not absolute assurance against material misstatement or loss. The board should maintain a sound system of internal control to safeguard shareholders' investment and the company's assets, and should establish formal and transparent arrangements for considering how they should apply financial reporting and internal control principles and for maintaining an appropriate relationship with the company's auditors. The board or an audit committee need to satisfy themselves that there is a proper system and allocation of responsibilities for the day-to-day monitoring of financial controls but they should not seek to do the monitoring themselves.

The audit committee (or a separate risk committee) should review and approve the scope of work of the internal audit function; ensure that the internal audit function has access to the information it needs and the resources necessary to carry out its function; approve the appointment or termination of the head of internal audit and meet the external and the internal auditors at least annually, without management being present, to discuss the scope of work of the auditors and any issues arising from the audit.

When reviewing management reports on internal control, the board should consider the significant risks and assess how they have been identified, evaluated and managed; assess the effectiveness of internal controls in managing the significant risks, having regard to any significant weaknesses in internal control; consider whether necessary actions are being taken promptly to remedy any weaknesses and consider whether the findings indicate a need for more exhaustive monitoring of the system of internal control.

The audit committee should review with the external auditors their findings and should in particular discuss major issues that arose during the audit and have subsequently been resolved, and those issues that remain unresolved; review key accounting and audit judgements and review levels of error identified during the audit, obtaining explanations from management and the external auditors as to any errors that remain unadjusted.

(b) External auditors cannot be relied on to provide assurance of stock accuracy. This is a role for management and in particular for internal audit. The board and the audit committee should recognise its responsibility for providing adequate controls. At the very least, SPM's management accountant and its internal auditors should have identified the weakness in control and brought this to the attention of the board.

An audit is a systematic examination of the activities of an organisation, based primarily on investigation and analysis of its systems, controls and records. It is intended to objectively evaluate evidence about matters of importance, to judge the degree of correspondence between those matters and some criteria or standard and to communicate the results of that judgement to interested parties.

Internal audit is an independent appraisal function established within an organisation to examine and evaluate its activities and designed to add value and improve an organisation's operations. The main role of internal audit is to provide assurance that the main business risks are being managed and that internal controls are operating effectively.

Risk-based internal auditing is linked directly with risk management. It begins with business objectives and focuses on those risks identified by management that may prevent the objectives from being achieved. Internal audit assesses the extent to which a robust risk management process is in place to reduce risks to a level acceptable to the board. It provides assurance to the board that the risk management processes which management has put in place are operating as intended; that the risk management processes are part of a sound design; that management's response to risks are adequate and effective in reducing those risks to a level acceptable to the board and that a sound framework of controls is in place to mitigate those risks which management wishes to treat. Internal auditors should focus on matters of high risk and where significant control deficiencies have been found, to identify actions taken to address them.

For SPM's Distribution division, the internal audit aim will be based on a risk assessment of the likelihood and consequences of unreported stock losses, whether caused by fraud or other loss.

An audit plan needs to be determined, commencing with a preliminary survey to obtain background information about the area to be audited, and to judge the scope and depth of audit work to be undertaken, based on the complexity of the area to be audited. The survey will identify the objectives, scope and timing of the audit and the audit resources (staff days, other costs, skills and experience) required.

Analytic review is the audit technique used to help analyse data to identify trends, errors, fraud, inefficiency and inconsistency. Its purpose is to understand what has happened in a system, to compare this with a standard and to identify weaknesses in practice or unusual situations that may require further examination.

The main methods of analytic review of relevance to this scenario include flowcharting systems and procedures and obtaining narrative explanations from staff. While this would provide background information, the main form of assurance will come from physical inspection of inventory against computer records and may also involve the re-calculation and reconciliation of stock movements to check accuracy and the physical testing of how the Distribution system is operating. This could be supplemented by benchmarking reported stock losses with similar organisations.

The audit should provide an understanding of the system or process; identify strengths and weaknesses and a comparison between the system or process in operation with that documented in formal manuals and procedures. The evaluation will be based on the use of internal control questionnaires to provide assurance that controls are adequate.

If stock theft is occurring, the weakness in systems due to the lack of separation of duties provides an opportunity. Personnel policies and supervision may influence dishonesty, and employment or social conditions among the workforce may influence motive. Internal audit needs to review the risk of dishonesty and motive as well as the opportunity provided by weak systems. There may be warning signals such as backlogs of work, holidays not being taken, extravagant lifestyles, missing audit trails.

The likely results of such an audit approach are three-fold. First, there would be an independent check on the accuracy of the physical stock, uncontaminated by the expertise of the Distribution staff. This would identify whether the reported financial results were accurate. Second, there would be a systematic review of systems and processes in use that would be the basis for recommendations for improved internal control. Third, a better understanding of the risk of fraud will be obtained and controls can then be revised to manage this risk.

Audit process

Chapter learning objectives

Lead	Component
C1. Discuss the importance of management review of controls.	(a) Discuss the importance of management review of controls.
C2. Evaluate the process and purposes of audit in the context of internal control systems.	(c) Recommend action to avoid or solve problems associated with the audit of activities and systems.
	(d) Recommend action to improve the efficiency, effectiveness and control of activities.

Specific areas of indicative syllabus content of relevance here are the following:

- Major tools available to assist with a review and audit process (e.g. audit planning, documenting systems, internal control questionnaires, sampling and testing)

- Operation of internal audit, the assessment of audit risk and the process of analytical review, including different types of benchmarking, their use and limitations

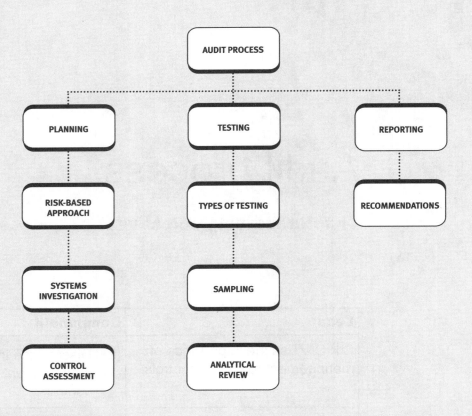

1 The audit process

Introduction

This chapter looks at a typical audit process as it would be carried out by the internal auditor to audit a company's systems or processes. A key point to consider when going through this process is the problems that might be encountered when attempting to audit these different areas.

The audit process

The audit process can be summarised in the following diagram:

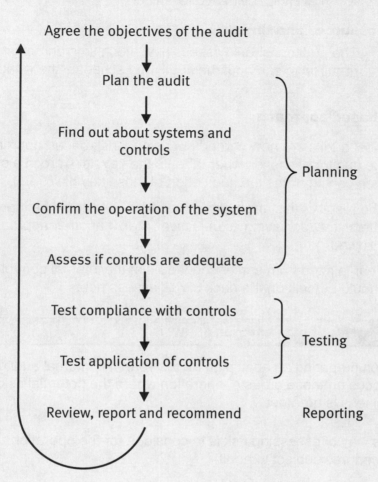

2 Audit planning

Audits should be planned. There should be an audit programme for each financial year, in which the internal auditors set out which activities or operations they will audit, and what the purpose of the audit will be in each case.

- **Objectives of the audit**
  - For example, to check whether the internal controls within a particular operation are adequate and are applied properly.

- **Conduct of the audit**
  - The auditors need to decide what information they need and what investigations they need to carry out.

- Decisions have to be made about:
  - how to collect and record evidence, and
  - how much evidence to collect

- **Resources and timing**
  - The auditors should assess how much time and effort will be required to carry out the audit, and schedule the work accordingly.

Risk-based approach

- Most audits are now carried out using a risk-based approach, whereby the auditor assesses whereabouts the key risks are in a system, and then concentrates the audit effort at those key risks.

- The result of this approach is that the audit should be more efficient and effective at achieving its objectives than if another approach were followed.

- Bear in mind from earlier chapters that the internal control system should be built on the back of risk assessments.

Annual audit plan and risk analysis

When preparing an audit plan for the year, the internal auditors should try to focus on those areas of operation where the potential risk to the business is greatest.

One way of assessing risk is to consider, for the operations or procedures subject to audit:

- the inherent risk, and
- the quality of control.

Inherent risk is the risk in the activity or operation, ignoring the controls in the system. For example, a cash based business such as a market stall or a taxi business is inherently risky due to possible theft or mis-declaration of tax payable.

Inherent risk relates both to the severity and the incidence of the risk, i.e.:

- the potential loss if an adverse situation or event arises, and the probability that an adverse situation or event will arise.

The size of the inherent risk will depend on a variety of factors, such as:

- the size of the operations unit, or the size of the expenditure budget

- the nature of the assets used or handled (e.g. systems involving the handling of cash or payments to suppliers have high inherent risk, due to the opportunities for fraud or loss)

- the extent to which procedures are computerised.

The **quality of control** is the perceived quality of the existing controls for the activity. Confidence in the quality of control will be affected by:

- the apparent effectiveness of management and supervision

- pressures on management to achieve targets

- changes in the system activities and procedures

- changes in key personnel

- a high staff turnover

- a rapid expansion in operations and the volume of transactions handled

- the length of time since the last audit of the activity was carried out. Confidence in the quality of controls will diminish over time without fresh reassurance from another audit that the controls are still effective.

The activities which should be given priority for audit are those where the inherent risk is high and the quality of control is low.

Audit risk

This is the risk that the auditors might give an inappropriate opinion on something which they tested i.e. they say that a process is well controlled when in fact it is out of control. Using the example of auditing the financial statements, audit risk has three components elements:

Inherent risk. This is the risk that an amount in the financial statements (for an asset or liability, or a transaction) might be stated as a materially incorrect amount, ignoring the existence of existing internal controls.

Control risk. This is the risk that the existing controls are not sufficient to prevent or detect a material mis-statement of a value in the financial statements.

Detection risk. This is the risk that the auditors' substantive tests will not reveal a materially incorrect amount in the financial statements, if such an error exists.

Materiality

The term 'materiality' is often used in the context of financial reporting. An item in the financial statements is material if its omission or a misstatement of its value would be likely to influence a user of the financial statements. However, materiality cannot be specified mathematically, because it has a qualitative as well as a quantitative aspect.

Materiality should also be considered in relative terms. For example, the risk of valuing an asset incorrectly by $100,000 would be material in the context of a company with assets of $1 million, but far less material in the context of a company with assets of $100 million.

3 Systems investigation and documentation

The auditors should document the system or operation subject to audit, and document their findings or judgements. They will need to ascertain what the system is and also the controls that operate over the system.

Ascertaining systems

The auditor could use the following sources and methods to ascertain how the systems operate:

Flowcharts	These could be examined or created from discussions with staff who use and operate systems.
Interviews/ Questionnaires	The staff who operate the system can describe how they use it. This has the advantage over other existing system documentation as it identifies how the staff use the system even if this is out of line with the proper procedures.
Systems documentation	The auditor can research the documentation of the system when it was produced to identify how the system operates. Documentation tends to be best for computerised systems as they will have gone through a proper systems development approach and also they tend to be least well understood by users.
Observation	The operation of the system can be observed.

Ascertaining controls

To specifically assess the controls in systems an auditor could use standard control questionnaires. These documents are structured so as to identify all key internal controls and also enable the auditor to assess the quality of the controls.

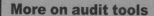

More on audit tools

Flowcharts

Flowcharts might be used to record:

- the sequence of activities and checks within an operation or procedure
- which individuals carry out each procedure or check.

The advantages of flowcharting the stages in an operation are that:

- a flowchart is more often effective at presenting information in an understandable form than a narrative description
- if there are weaknesses in the controls within an operation, these might be easier to identify by studying a flowchart.

Questionnaires

A questionnaire is a list of questions for which the auditor needs to finds answers in order to gather the information or evidence he needs. The questions should be specific, and should ideally call for a 'Yes' or 'No' answer, although room should be left on the form for additional comments to be added if required.

The answers to the questions help the auditor both to:

- establish the facts, and
- identify potential control weaknesses.

4 Control assessment

Once auditors have ascertained what the controls are they need to make an assessment of the internal controls and whether they will achieve their objectives.

Example of controls

A company has a small accounting department, in which the same individual is made responsible for accounts payable and also for carrying out the bank reconciliation checks. Ideally, these tasks should be segregated, because there is a risk that the individual might be making out cheques to his or her personal bank account, and the fraud would not be identified by the bank reconciliation process.

To overcome this weakness in the control system, a number of controls might be applied, such as:

- requiring that all cheques are signed by hand by a senior manager in the company, instead of signed automatically

- a review by the individual's supervisor of all bank reconciliations

- a periodic listing from the company's bank of all the payments out of the company's bank account in the period, for review by a senior manager.

5 Audit testing

Having made an assessment of the existing controls and identified the areas of greatest risk the auditor will move onto the testing.

Auditors need to carry out tests, to ensure that procedures are performed correctly, and that controls to prevent or detect errors are adequate and applied effectively.

Types of testing

Compliance testing (test of controls):

The test of controls should be carried out to ensure that the controls identified at the planning stage operate as they should.

If the controls are not being complied with then there will be a material weakness in the control system and the result could be serious errors or fraud and the business objectives may not be achieved.

The results of the compliance testing should indicate whether:

- the controls are effective, or
- the controls are ineffective in practice, even though they appeared adequate 'on paper'.

Substantive testing (test of balances or transactions):

Substantive testing, on the other hand, does not look at the controls in the system – it rather concentrates on the output and ensuring that the output is as expected.

Substantive testing is normally associated with financial systems but can also be used for non-financial systems.

The purpose of the substantive tests is either to:

- confirm that the controls are effective
- where the controls are ineffective, to establish the apparent consequences.

For example, an audit of a quality control system would give the following types of testing:

Substantive test	Monitor the number of quality control failures as a proportion of good output.
Compliance test	Observe the functioning of the quality control staff to ensure they are checking output.

In the exam, students should concentrate on using words like **reconcile, analyse, observe, monitor or sample** at the beginning of any sentence that recommends an audit test. Try to avoid the word 'check' since that can be construed as vague, unless you explain fully what you are checking for and why.

Test your understanding 1 – Compliance testing

Company X has recently employed John. John went through the company's interview process – after submitting his curriculum vitae and filling in the standard application form, he attended two interviews (one individual and one group). He was then offered the job and asked to start the following Monday.

John has been at X for a month now and his manager is not happy with his work. He is frequently late in to the office, and he frequently makes mistakes in the tasks he is given.

His manager has heard a rumour that the qualification he stated on his application form is false, which could explain his poor work.

Required:

Discuss the problem at X and suggest controls that should be in place to prevent this occurrence.

Detail appropriate compliance tests the internal auditor should perform on the recruitment process to ensure that this does not happen in the future.

Test your understanding 2 – Audit testing

Recommend some compliance and substantive tests that could be undertaken by an auditor to check whether errors are occurring in payroll processing. Staff are paid weekly in cash. The objective of the audit is to ensure that:

(i)   payments are only made to genuine employees.

(ii) all deductions from pay are calculated correctly.

(iii) employees are paid only for hours worked.

(iv) deductions are paid over to the appropriate authorities.

6 Sampling

With any audit testing it will probably be necessary to undertake some form of sampling.

Sampling is testing a proportion of a population to gain assurance about the population as a whole.

Audit sampling

The application of audit procedures to less than 100% of the items within an account balance or class of transactions to obtain and evaluate evidence about some characteristic of the items selected in order to form a conclusion on the population.

Risks that occur with sampling

As soon as an auditor decides to sample a population, there are risks that are brought into the audit:

Sampling risk	This is the risk that the auditor's conclusion, based on the results of the sample, may be different from the result that would have been obtained had all items in the population been tested. (This risk can never be removed if sampling is done.)
Non-sampling risk	This is the risk that the auditor may use inappropriate procedures, or misinterpret evidence that the test results give. As a result the auditor would fail to recognise an error. (This risk is avoidable if auditors use the appropriate procedures.)

7 Analytical review

Analytical review is arguably the most important test available to the auditor as they can be used in the audit of most items – both financial and non-financial – and can be used at various points in the audit process.

Definition

Analytical review is the examination of ratios, trends and changes in the business from one period to the next, to obtain a broad understanding of the results of operations, and to identify any items requiring further investigation.

When the results appear abnormal the auditors will investigate more closely to find out the cause(s) by performing further work.

Ratios

During the audit of any part of the financial statements, analytical review often involves the calculation of ratios, such as:

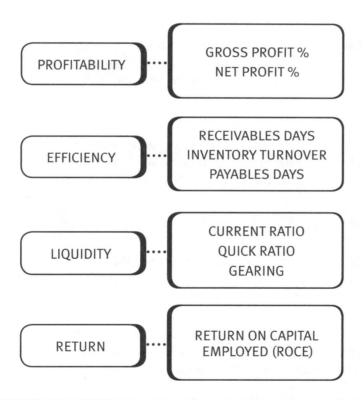

Nature of analytical review

Comparisons of information could be with:

Examples

	20X1	20X1	20X0
• Prior periods/anticipated results	Actual	Budget	Actual
Number of new products launched	9	11	10

• Predictive estimates   Depreciation for year = 15% × y/e cost

• Similar industry info   Staff turnover v industry average

Uses of analytical review

Analytical review will be used at all stages of the audit.

Planning	They will be used to identify risks, and therefore help in deciding the level of testing, and its nature and timing.
Substantive testing	Analytical review is a very important substantive procedure that can provide sufficient audit evidence in some areas. In practice in the audit of financial information, expenses in the income statement, accruals and prepayments are all audited by substantive analytical procedures.
Overall review	The procedures are used to conclude whether the area being tested is consistent with the auditors' knowledge of the business entity and the expected results.

More on analytical review

In order to use analytical procedures effectively you need to be able to create an expectation. It will be difficult to create an expectation if operations are significantly different from last year, more so if the changes haven't been planned for. If the changes were planned, we can compare the actual with the forecast. It will also be difficult to use analytical procedures if there have been lots of one-off events in the year as there will be nothing to compare them with.

Test your understanding 3 – Car dealership

You are an internal auditor for a car dealership with a number of branches. You have responsibility for looking at where efficiency gains could be made. From the following information, recommend, with reasons, which region you would look at first.

	North	South	East	West
Number of salesmen	16	12	10	24
Total sales value in the last month (£000)	2,700	2,520	2,320	2,400
Number of sales orders	180	156	160	190
Number of sales discussions	660	364	432	740

8 Audit reporting

Audit report

The final stage of an audit is the audit report. In an internal audit assignment the audit report does not have a strict structure, however, it would be expected to feature a number of different parts:

- The objectives of the audit work.
- A summary of the process undertaken by the auditor.
- The results of tests carried out.
- The audit opinion (if an opinion is required).
- Recommendations for action.

When giving recommendations auditors must always ensure that the recommendations are practical and cost-effective.

The auditor will need to consider whether the residual risk will be reduced by the recommendation. If it will not, the recommendation is not worthwhile.

- The internal auditor should have a process of post-implementation review to ensure that recommendations have been actioned by management.

Test your understanding 4 – Barcol

Barcol employs 25 sales representatives, each with a defined geographical area to cover. Each salesman is supplied with a company car that is changed every three years. At the end of each month, every salesman is required to submit an expenses claim with supporting vouchers for petrol, car repairs and maintenance, parking fees, hotel accommodation and subsistence, entertainment of clients and so on. Each claim is submitted to the deputy chief accountant, who inspects them to ensure that the claims are supported by receipts. He resolves any queries with the salesman concerned and then draws up cheques for each salesman, for signature by a company director.

Last year, total salesmen's expenses were $351,000 and the company made a pre-tax profit of $1,900,000.

Required:

(a) Discuss any weaknesses in the system for dealing with salesmen's expenses, and recommend improvements.

(b) Explain the use of compliance tests and identify some tests that might be carried out on the system.

(c) Explain the use of substantive tests and identify some tests that the auditor might carry out on salesmen's expenses.

9 Chapter summary

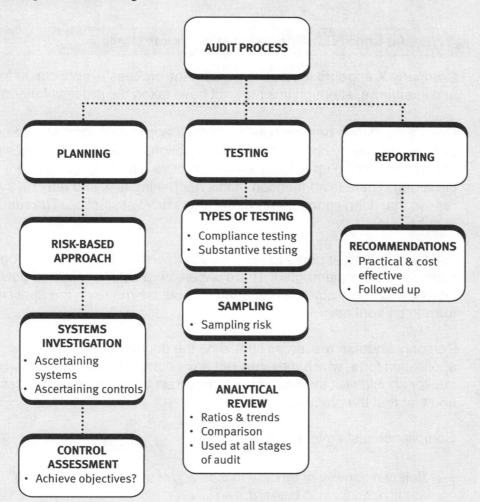

AUDIT PROCESS

PLANNING

TESTING

REPORTING

RISK-BASED APPROACH

TYPES OF TESTING
- Compliance testing
- Substantive testing

RECOMMENDATIONS
- Practical & cost effective
- Followed up

SYSTEMS INVESTIGATION
- Ascertaining systems
- Ascertaining controls

SAMPLING
- Sampling risk

CONTROL ASSESSMENT
- Achieve objectives?

ANALYTICAL REVIEW
- Ratios & trends
- Comparison
- Used at all stages of audit

Test your understanding answers

Test your understanding 1 – Compliance testing

Company X appears to have a recruitment 'process' – application forms and interviews, although this may not have taken the process far enough.

Once a candidate has been selected their application form should be verified, usually by checking their qualifications to actual certificates (not copies) and taking up references (usually two – one work and one personal). There is no mention of this happening at X and may be the reason that John cannot perform the job to any satisfaction. The rumour may be true.

John's start date appears to be too soon to enable the aforementioned controls to be implemented. There should be a sufficient period between interview and any start date to enable all claims made on the application form to be verified.

Personnel/human resources should be the department to verify the application form, which they may not have done. Therefore the internal auditor should visit the department, ascertain the recruitment process and test that the process is adhered to.

Compliance tests might include:

- Select a sample of employee files and test to see whether the application form is present.

- From the application forms, trace the references taken up.

- Check that the references were positive i.e. that previous employers found the staff punctual, trustworthy, etc.

- From the application forms, trace the copies of certificates (taken from the originals) which back up any qualifications stated.

- Qualifications could be further tested by contacting the relevant body to ascertain whether they have record of said employee.

The controls at X appear to be ineffective since the process does not cover these vital activities. Alternatively these activities might be part of X's personnel process, and the personnel staff have not followed them. Either way the personnel staff need to be reprimanded and further controls implemented to prevent future occurrences.

Test your understanding 2 – Audit testing

Compliance tests

- Look for evidence of the approval of new workers, such as a formal instruction to the payroll department.
- Check that the timesheets are all approved by a supervisor.
- Check that all overtime has been approved.
- Observe the wages payout to ensure:
  - wages are only collected by the person being paid;
  - all staff sign for their wages.
- Ensure that a PAYE/NIC control account is reconciled and reviewed each month by an appropriate manager.

Substantive tests

- Take a sample of timesheets and re-calculate wages and deductions.
- Perform a reconciliation of total hours worked to gross pay and compare month by month.
- Check a sample of payments to the pay rate records to ensure they are being used correctly.
- Re-perform the PAYE/NIC control account for a month to ensure it has been done correctly.

Test your understanding 3 – Car dealership

A number of performance ratios could be calculated across the different regions to compare performance:

	North	South	East	West
Sales value per salesman (£)	168,750	210,000	232,000	100,000
Sales discussions per salesman	41	30	43	31
Average orders per discussion	0.27	0.43	0.37	0.26
Average value per order (£)	15,000	16,200	14,500	12,600

From the above performance measures it can be seen that the West region is the most inefficient. In all measures this region is at or very near the bottom performance criteria which indicates there should be room for efficiencies. This region should be selected for audit.

Test your understanding 4 – Barcol

(a) Weaknesses in the current system

Since the expenses system involves payments of cash, a major control risk must be the possibility of overpayments, possibly due to fraud.

–   There is no check that the expenditures were actually incurred in the pursuit of company business. Salesmen might claim for private expenditures.

–   There is no proof that some of the expenditures were incurred at all by the salesmen. It is possible that claims might be submitted for expenditures occurred by other people, such as members of the salesmen's family.

–   The deputy chief accountant could easily perpetrate a fraud, either acting alone or in collusion with a salesman.

Recommendations for improvements

–   Expense claims should be submitted initially to the manager of the sales representatives. The manager should check the details of the claim against the work programme of the individual for the month. Checks should be carried out to ensure that the expenses for hotel accommodation and subsistence and parking fees are consistent with the salesman's itinerary, and that claims for entertainment of clients are consistent with the salesman's actual client meetings. The claims for petrol expenses should be checked against the approximate distances travelled by the salesman on business, to ensure that the cost per mile for petrol is reasonable. Expense claims by each salesman should be countersigned by the sales manager, to confirm that this check has been completed.

–   To reduce the risk of fraud by the deputy chief accountant, the director should check that each cheque for payment is supported by a countersigned expense claim form, and that each claim form has all the supporting receipts.

(b) Compliance tests

Compliance tests seek to find out whether the existing controls are being properly applied. For salesmen's expense claims, the best approach to compliance testing might be to obtain documentary evidence.

A sample of claims should be checked to ensure that:

- each claim is supported by receipts
- the total of the claim has been added up correctly
- the amount actually paid was the same as the total amount of the claim.

(c) **Substantive tests**

In the case of audits of financial systems and activities, substantive tests seek to provide audit evidence about the completeness, accuracy and validity of the transactions, and the amounts relating to those transactions that are included in the accounting records and financial statements.

Here, substantive tests might take the form of:

Analytical review. Comparing total salesmen's expenses in previous years, both in total and as a percentage of sales revenue, to check whether the total amount of expenses in the current year appears to be consistent with previous years.

Detailed tests of transactions, such as:

- verifying that the salesmen are all legitimate employees of the company
- taking a sample of claims and checking whether specific items of expense are valid, for example that the salesman's claims for hotel accommodation and subsistence were incurred in his sales area
- taking a sample of claims and checking whether the claims for petrol/mileage are consistent with the total number of miles travelled by the car, as evidenced by car service records.

Financial risk

Chapter learning objectives

Lead	Component
D1. Evaluate financial risks facing an organisation	(a) Evaluate financial risks facing an organisation
D2. Evaluate alternative risk management tools	(a) Evaluate appropriate methods for managing financial risks
	(b) Evaluate the effects of alternative methods of risk management
	(c) Recommend risk management strategies and discuss their accounting implications

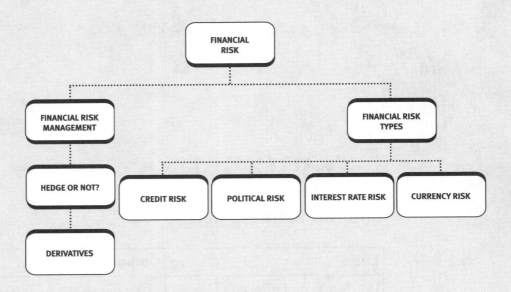

1 Overview of financial risk

Financial risk is *'a risk of a change in a financial condition such as an exchange rate, interest rate, credit rating of a customer, or price of a good'*.

Types of financial risk

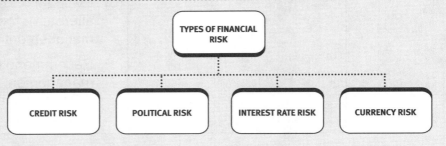

Political risk is not necessarily a financial risk but is included here because often financial risk is from the perspective of foreign business activities. Political risk is essentially to do with the wider risks of foreign direct investment.

2 Credit risk

Credit risk is the risk of non-payment or late payment of receivables. Credit risk will always exist in businesses that make credit sales and therefore it needs to be managed.

Management of credit risk

The most common methods used to manage and control credit risk are:

- Strong **credit control procedures**, including:
  - policies regarding credit checks
  - credit limits and terms
  - debt collection activities such as aged debtor analysis, statements and reminders.

- **Insuring** against the risk – it is possible to take out credit risk guarantees to act as insurance against debtor default.

- **Debt factoring without recourse** – the debts can be sold to a factoring business but without the obligation to buy back those debts in the event of default.

3 Political risk

Political risk is the risk faced by an overseas investor, that the host country government take adverse action against, after the company has invested.

It can take different forms and the threats (financial and non-financial) can include:

- Risk of confiscation or destruction of overseas assets
- Commercial risks because foreign governments discriminate against overseas firms e.g. quotas, tariffs, other taxes
- Restricted access to local borrowings
- Insisting on resident investors or a joint venture with a local company
- Restrictions on repatriating cash (capital or dividends)
- Restrictions on conversion of the currency
- Rationing the supply of foreign currency
- Exchange rate volatility due to political actions
- A minimum number of local nationals to be employed
- Price fixing by the government
- Minimum percentage of local components to be used
- Invalidating patents
- Claiming compensation for past actions

More on sources of political risk

Whilst governments want to encourage development and growth they are also anxious to prevent the exploitation of their countries by multinationals.

Whilst at one extreme, assets might be destroyed as the result of war or expropriation, the most likely problems concern changes to the rules on the remittance of cash out of the host country to the holding company.

Exchange control regulations, which are generally more restrictive in less developed countries. For example:

- rationing the supply of foreign currencies which restricts residents from buying goods abroad

- banning the payment of dividends to foreign shareholders such as holding companies in multinationals, who will then have the problem of blocked funds.

Import quotas to limit the quantity of goods that subsidiaries can buy from its holding company to sell in its domestic market.

Import tariffs could make imports (from the holding company) more expensive than domestically produced goods.

Insist on a minimum shareholding, i.e. that some equity in the company is offered to resident investors.

Company structure may be dictated by the host government – requiring, for example, all investments to be in the form of joint ventures with host country companies.

Discriminatory actions

- **Supertaxes** imposed on foreign firms, set higher than those imposed on local businesses with the aim of giving local firms an advantage. They may even be deliberately set at such a high level as to prevent the business from being profitable.

- **Restricted access to local borrowings** by restricting or even barring foreign owned enterprises from the cheapest forms of finance from local banks and development funds. Some countries ration all access for foreign investments to local sources of funds, to force the company to import foreign currency into the country.

> • **Expropriating assets** whereby the host country government seizes foreign property in the national interest. It is recognised in international law as the right of sovereign states provided that *prompt consideration at fair market value in a convertible currency* is given. Problems arise over the exact meaning of the terms prompt and fair, the choice of currency, and the action available to a company not happy with the compensation offered.

Management of political risk

Companies cannot prevent political risk, but they should seek to minimise it whenever the risk appears significant.

Before undertaking a foreign direct investment, a company needs to assess its exposure to political risk by:

- Using political ranking tables such as Euromoney magazine tables;

- Evaluating the country's macro-economic situation – balance of payments, unemployment levels, per capita income, inflation, exchange rate policy, rate of economic growth;

- Evaluating the current government's popularity, stability and attitude to foreign investment, together with the attitude of opposition parties;

- Looking at the historical stability of the political system;

- Looking at changing religious and cultural attitudes;

- Taking advice from the company's bank (if there is a representative office in the overseas country), the British embassy in the overseas country, and the Department of Trade and Industry (DTI).

Some methods of minimising risks are as follows:

- Prior negotiation (concession agreements and planned divestment)

- Structuring investment (local sourcing of materials and labour)

- Entering into foreign joint ventures

- Obtaining agreements and contracts with overseas government

- Using local financing

- Plans for eventual ownership/part-ownership by foreign country's investors.

More on managing political risk

Joint ventures. A company might go into a joint venture with one or more partners. A joint venture can reduce risk because:

- if each joint venture partner contributes a share of the funding for the venture, the investment at risk for each partner is restricted to their share of the total investment (although, the upside is reduced because each party has less invested in this potentially lucrative venture)

- if a local company is selected as a joint venture partner, the likelihood of winning major contracts in the country might be much greater. Some governments have made the involvement of a local company in a joint venture a condition of awarding contracts to consortia involving a foreign company

- the local venture partner has a better understanding of the local political risks and can manage them more effectively than a foreigner would be able to. Also the government might be less inclined to act against the interests of the local venture partner.

Pre-trading agreements. Prior to making the investment, agreements should be secured if possible with the local government regarding rights, remittance of funds and local equity investments and (where appropriate) the award of government contracts to businesses.

Gaining government funding. In some situations, it might be possible to gain government funding for a project or contract, with the government being either a customer, a backer or a partner for the deal. If government funding can be obtained:

- the government will have an interest in the transaction reaching a successful conclusion

- there should be little or no risk of exchange control regulations preventing the withdrawal of profits from the country.

Local finance. A company might try to obtain local finance for an investment in a particular country. The availability of local finance might depend on the state of the banking and capital markets in the country concerned. The major advantage of local finance is that it creates liabilities in the foreign currency, and so reduces:

- translation exposures: assets in the foreign currency can be offset against liabilities in the same currency

- transaction exposures, in the sense that interest costs will be payable in the foreign currency and can be paid from income in the same currency.

Raising finance locally might also help to maintain the interest of the local government in the success of the business, and there is less risk that the assets will be confiscated.

Planning for the eventual part-ownership or full ownership of the business by locals. Target dates might be set in advance of making the investment for the eventual part-ownership or full ownership of the business by local people. The transfer of ownership should be extended over a long-term, partly to ensure that a satisfactory return on investment is obtained but also to encourage the local government to understand the long-term benefits of foreign investment.

4 Interest rate risk

Interest rate risk is the risk of gains or losses on assets and liabilities due to changes in interest rates. It will occur for any organisation which has assets or liabilities on which interest is payable or receivable.

Interest rates and LIBOR

Non-financial organisations normally have many more interest-bearing liabilities than interest-bearing assets. These include bank loans and overdrafts, and issues of bonds or debentures. As a general rule:

* interest on bank loans and overdrafts is payable at a **variable rate** or **floating rate**, with the interest set at a margin above a benchmark rate such as the base rate or the London Inter Bank Offer Rate (LIBOR)

* interest on most bonds, debentures or loan stock is at a **fixed rate**.

When interest is at a floating rate, the amount of interest payable in each period is set by reference to the benchmark interest rate on a specific date, such as the starting date for the interest period. For example, suppose that a company has a bank loan on which it pays interest every six months at 50 basis points above LIBOR. (100 basis points = 1%, therefore 50 basis points = 0.50%.) At the start of an interest period, the six-month LIBOR rate might be, say, 4.75%: if so, the company would pay interest at the end of the six months at 5.25% for the six-month period. If LIBOR moves up or down, the interest rate payable every six months will go up or down accordingly.

(**Note:** LIBOR is the London Interbank Offered Rate. It is a money market rate at which top-rated banks are able to borrow short-term in the London sterling or eurocurrency markets. There are LIBOR rates for major traded currencies, including the US dollar, euro and yen, as well as sterling.)

Exposure to interest rate risk

The exposure to interest risk will depend on the amount of interest bearing assets or liabilities that it holds and the type that these are (floating or fixed rate).

Types of interest rate risk exposure

- **Floating rate loans:** If a company has floating rate loans, changes in interest rates alter the amount of interest payable or receivable. This directly affects cash flows and profits and the risk therefore is quite obvious.

- **Fixed rate loans:** If a company has fixed rate loans interest rate risk still exists. Even though interest charges themselves will not change, a fixed rate can make a company uncompetitive if its costs are higher than those with a floating rate and interest rates fall. (Remember interest rate risk can be about assets or liabilities – an asset that pays a fixed rate of interest will be worth less if interest rates rise.)

More on fixed rate exposure

Companies with fixed rate borrowings are also exposed to interest rate risk, because by paying a fixed rate of interest on its liabilities, a company runs the risk that:

- if interest rates fall, it will be unable to benefit from the lower rates available in the market, because it is committed to paying fixed rates, and

- competitor organisations might have floating rate liabilities, and so will benefit from lower interest costs, and so improve their profitability and competitive strength.

The same, of course, is true in reverse for a company that has fixed or floating rate deposits/investments.

Measuring exposure to interest rate risk

Floating rate loans

Interest risk exposure is the *total amount of floating rate assets and liabilities*. The higher the value of loans the greater the exposure to changes in interest rates.

Fixed rate loans

This is measured by the *total amount of fixed rate assets or liabilities together with average time to maturity and average interest rate*. Longer periods of tie-in at fixed rates could be beneficial, or more costly, to businesses depending on what market rates are and also what the future expectations of interest rate changes are. It is expectations that determine risks.

Illustration of interest rate risk exposure

Block has the following liabilities at 1 January Year 1:

- Bank loans £400 million, interest at LIBOR + 50 basis points

- £50 million floating rate bonds, interest at LIBOR + 25 basis points

- £200 million 6.5% bonds, redeemable 30 June Year 3

- £350 million 6% bonds, redeemable 30 September Year 4

Interest rate exposure:

The company has floating rate liabilities of £450 million and fixed rate liabilities of £550 million.

Average interest rate of fixed rate liabilities:

£200m × 6.5%	£13m
£350m × 6%	£21m
£550m of loans with	£34m of interest = 6.18% average rate

The average interest rate would be compared to other companies in the same industry to ascertain whether it was higher or lower, whilst bearing in mind the general expectation of movement in the base rate. For example, if Block's average rate is higher than the competitors and the base rate is expected to fall, then it will be deemed more risky because Block will pay more interest in the future compared to its competitors.

Average time to maturity of fixed rate liabilities:

£200m × 2.50 years	500.00
£350m × 3.75 years	1,312.50
	1,812.50
1, 812.50 /£550m	3.30 years average remaining life

Time to maturity creates a separate measure of exposure. Again Block's average time to maturity will be compared to its competitors. If the time to maturity is longer than the competitors and rates are expected to fall then Block is more risky since it has tied itself in to longer term fixed rate borrowings, paying out too much interest and possibly incurring a redemption penalty if it tried to restructure its debt.

Test your understanding 1 – G Plc

G Plc has the following fixed rate liabilities at 30 June 20X4:

£50m of 6% debentures, repayable on 30 June 20X7

£400m of 7% debentures, repayable on 30 June 20X9

Required:

Calculate the following for G Plc:

- total interest risk exposure for fixed interest securities
- the average interest rate, and
- the average time to maturity.

Discuss G Plc's interest risk exposure.

Refinancing

Refinancing risk is associated with interest risk because it looks at the risk that loans will not be refinanced or will not be refinanced at the same rates.

The reasons for this could include:

- Lenders are unwilling to lend or only prepared to lend at higher rates.
- The credit rating of the company has reduced making them a more unattractive lending option.
- The company may need to refinance quickly and therefore have difficulty in obtaining the best rates.

5 Currency risk

Currency risk is the risk that arises from possible future movements in an exchange rate. It is a two-way risk, since exchange rates can move either adversely or favourably.

Currency risk affects any organisation with:

- assets and/or liabilities in a foreign currency

- regular income and/or expenditures in a foreign currency

- no assets, liabilities or transactions that are denominated in a foreign currency. Even if a company does not deal in any currencies, it will still face economic risk since its competitors may be faring better due to favourable exchange rates on its transactions.

Currency risk can be categorised into three types: economic, transaction and translation exposure.

Economic risk

Economic risk is any change in the economy, home or abroad, which can affect the value of a transaction before a commitment is made i.e. payment or receipt.

A company may not have any transactions in a foreign currency i.e. it buys and sells in its home currency, but it is still affected by economic risk.

This can be due to several factors:

- Competitive position – even if a company trades wholly in its own currency, other companies can cause it to lose money in the form of reduced sales. For example, if a competitor company trades (either buys or sells) abroad where the currency is more favourable – cheaper for supplies, or allows a higher price for sales, then the competitor will be more profitable. Conversely, if the exchange rates are adverse for the competitor, they would be less profitable.

- Elasticity of demand – exchange rates can make a company's products more or less expensive. When an exchange rate makes the product more expensive, say, the demand for that product will probably fall. However, if the product is available at a lower price from another company, who perhaps trades in a different currency which enables the product to be made and sold more cheaply, then demand does not fall but transfers to that other company. Therefore the home company has lost sales, is less profitable and shareholder returns will fall.

- Pricing – competitor's product prices will affect a company's ability to raise their prices and affect their competitive position. For example, Scottish sheep farmers are exposed to economic risk when New Zealand lamb comes onto the market more cheaply in October / November. (Lambing in the UK occurs around March). The Scottish sheep farmers have to reduce their prices through October / November to maintain their volume of sales.

In effect, economic risk is the variation in the value of the business (i.e. the present value of future cash flows) due to unexpected changes in the economy.

Management of economic risk

One way the risk can be reduced is to diversify globally, meaning that a company can reduce its risk by having operations located all over the world or by doing business with other companies located in other parts of the world. This is portfolio theory – the idea of reducing risk by 'not having all your eggs in one basket'. This can be broken down into:

Diversification of production and sales

If a firm manufactures all its products in one country and that country's exchange rate strengthens, then the firm will find it increasingly difficult to export to the rest of the world. Its future cash flows and therefore its present value would diminish. However, if it had established production plants worldwide and bought its components worldwide (a policy which is practised by many multinationals, e.g. Ford) it is unlikely that the currencies of all its operations would revalue at the same time. It would therefore find that, although it was losing on exports from some of its manufacturing locations, this would not be the case in all of them. Also if it had arranged to buy its raw materials worldwide it would find that a strengthening home currency would result in a fall in its input costs and this would compensate for lost sales.

Diversification of suppliers and customers

Similarly a company could diversify its supplier and customer base so that if the currency of, say, one supplier strengthens, purchasing could be switched to a cheaper supplier.

Diversification of financing

When borrowing internationally, firms must be aware of foreign exchange risk. When, for example, a firm borrows in Swiss francs it must pay back in the same currency. If the Swiss franc then strengthens against the home currency this can make interest and principal repayments far more expensive. However, if borrowing is spread across many currencies it is unlikely they will all strengthen at the same time and therefore risks can be reduced.

Borrowing in foreign currency is only truly justified if returns will then be earned in that currency to finance repayment and interest. International borrowing can also be used to hedge the adverse economic effects of local currency devaluations. If a firm expects to lose from devaluations of the currencies in which its subsidiaries operate it can hedge this exposure by arranging to borrow in the weakening currency. Any losses on operations will then be offset by cheaper financing costs.

Note that diversification (of any type) will not necessarily help in extreme circumstances e.g. during a global recession.

Marketing

A way of managing economic risk is quite simply to have a very good marketing ploy that enables you to convince your customers that your product is the one to buy despite it being more expensive!

More on economic risk

Economic risk is the possibility that the value of the company (the present value of all future post tax cash flows) will change due to unexpected changes in future economies (which includes exchange rates). The size of the risk is difficult to measure as economies can change significantly and unexpectedly. Such changes can affect firms in many ways:

- Imagine a UK company had an investment in South East Asia during the late 1990s. They would have suffered some economic risk due to the economic downturn in that part of the world at that time. An economic downturn can reduce trade and have an impact on foreign currency exchange rates. This means that the UK company's investment might be worth less upon first glance. However, the wider implications might include the fact that the factory makes goods for export. Then the downturn might reduce costs. Meanwhile if the competition are manufacturing in the 'booming' West and costs are higher (material and wage inflation) then the Asian subsidiary may have the competitive advantage. Therefore, the economic downturn may not be wholly downside risk.

- Suppose a UK company invests in a subsidiary in Africa. The currency of the African country depreciates each year for several years. The cash flows remitted to the UK are worth less in sterling terms each year, causing a reduction in the investment value.

- A French company buys raw materials that are priced in US dollars. It converts the raw materials into a finished product which it exports to Japan. Over several years the euro appreciates against the dollar but depreciates against the yen. The euro value of the French company's income increases while the US dollar cost of its materials decreases, resulting in an increase in value of the company's cash flows.

- Insisting on dealing in only the home currency may affect the foreign demand for its products if the pound appreciates or their relationship with suppliers if the pound weakens.

- Consider a UK company exporting goods or services to Spain, in competition with (say) US companies. In this case, if the US dollar weakens relative to the euro (even if the pound remains unchanged against the euro), it will become cheaper for the Spanish customers to import those goods and services from the US supplier if the order is denominated in the foreign currency. Even if the order is denominated in euros (the Spanish currency) the euro price from the US supplier might not convert into enough sterling to make it worthwhile for the UK company.

- Deciding to acquire resources, say equipment in Italy, with a view to supplying goods or services to the UK market. In this case the company's costs are in euros with expected revenues in sterling. If sterling were to weaken against the euro, the costs of the operation could become uneconomic.

However, many of the above examples are not as straightforward as they might first seem, due to the compensating actions of economic forces. For example, if the exchange rate of a South American country depreciates significantly, it is probably due to high inflation. If the South American subsidiary of a UK company increases its prices in line with inflation in South America, its cash flows in the local currency will increase. However, these will be converted at a depreciating exchange rate to produce (theoretically) a constant sterling value of cash flows. Alternatively, if the subsidiary does not increase its prices, it may increase its sales volume by selling at a lower price. Therefore the subsidiary / group has not 'lost out'.

Measurement of economic exposure

Although economic exposure is difficult to measure it is of vital importance to firms as it concerns their long-run viability. Economic exposure cannot be ignored as it could lead to reductions in the firm's future cash flows or an increase in the systematic risk of the firm, resulting in a fall in shareholder wealth.

There are a very limited number of factors that can be observed to attempt to quantify economic exposure, which include the price elasticity of demand for products. For example, as prices rise demand usually falls, but the rate at which it falls and the resulting cashflows will impact on the value of a company. The price rise could be due to a change in the exchange rate.

Economic risk

Imagine a fictitious airport, XL, in country X with the £ as its currency.

XL services passengers that live in its own country (20%) and passengers that travel from other countries (80%).

90% of the travellers passing through XL are holiday makers while the other 10% travel for business purposes.

The fuel bought by the airlines passing through XL is mainly bought in the US where the currency is the $.

Why is the company exposed to currency risk?

Passenger numbers will be affected by the strength of the £:

- Only 20% of passengers live in the UK and travel within the country on internal flights. The other 80% will be exposed to foreign currency movements making their trips more or less expensive. For example, a holiday maker from the UK will find a holiday in the US more expensive if the £ weakens against the $ and may choose not to travel. Similarly passengers from outside the UK may choose other destinations if the £ strengthens against their home currency.

- Most passengers are travelling on holiday so they have a much wider choice of destinations than business travellers. A business person may have to go to a particular country because that is where the customer or supplier is based. In theory, 90% of XL's customers could change their travel plans and that could reduce demand for XL's routes.

- Movements in the value of the £ could affect interest rates and that may also prevent holiday makers from travelling due to the increase in the cost of their mortgage.

- If the £ weakens against the $, say, then fuel, for example, may become more expensive. This could force the airlines to raise prices which might reduce passenger numbers or the number of flights.

How can the risks you have identified be managed?

The first step is to always consider whether there are any natural hedges. For example, a strong £ would give holiday makers from country X more spending money when they travel abroad. However, that will also increase the airlines' costs when converted to their home currency and so fares may increase. These factors might offset each other.

Once the airport has established the overall impact of the strengthening or weakening of the £ the next step would be to hedge that risk. For example, if the strengthening was discovered to be bad then the airport might borrow in $ to create a hedge.

It would also be worth diversifying the routes covered by the airlines. It might be worth offering airlines that travel to popular destinations a discount for flying from XL. The cost of the discount could be viewed as an investment in managing currency risk.

Transaction risk

This is the risk related to buying or selling on credit in foreign currencies. There is a danger that, between the time of the transaction and the date of the cash flow, exchange rates will have moved adversely. This risk, unlike the translation risk, actually affects the cash flows of the business.

Illustration of transaction risk

A UK company purchases goods on six months' credit from a US supplier for US$150,000. At the time of the transaction, the exchange rate was £1/US$1.8000 and the expected payment for the purchase was £83,333 (US$150,000/1.8000).

However, suppose that the exchange rate changes in the next six months, and the dollar strengthens in value to £1/US$1.5000. The company must acquire the US$150,000 to make the payment, and if it buys this dollar currency at the exchange rate when the date of the payment is due, the actual cost will be £100,000. This is £16,667 more than originally expected. The UK company has been exposed to a transaction liability in US dollars for six months, and as a result of the dollar increasing in value during that time, an unexpected 'loss' of £16,667 arose.

The exchange rate might have moved the other way. If the exchange rate when the payment was due had changed to £1/US$2.0000, with the dollar falling in value, it would cost only £75,000 to acquire the dollars to make the payment. This is £8,333 less than originally expected, therefore there would be a 'profit' of £8,333 on the favourable exchange rate movement.

Test your understanding 2 – H plc (1)

H plc (a UK company) expects to make the following transaction in six months' time:

- US$100,000 purchases from US suppliers.

Exchange rates are as follows:

Dollar rate today	US$1/ £0.5556

Dollar rate in six months	US$1/ £0.5420

Required:

Calculate the payment required in sterling if H plc makes the payment now or in six months time.

Management of transaction risk

This will be covered in detail in the next chapter.

Translation risk

This arises when a company has assets or liabilities denominated in foreign currencies. The risk is that exchange rate volatility will cause the value of assets to fall or liabilities to increase resulting in losses to the company.

More on translation risk

The financial statements of overseas subsidiaries are usually translated into the home currency in order that they can be consolidated into the group's financial statements. Note that this is purely a paper-based exercise – it is the translation not the conversion of real money from one currency to another.

Settled transactions

When a company enters into a transaction denominated in a currency other than its functional currency (which could be the home currency or that of its parent), that transaction must be translated into the functional currency before it is recorded. The transaction will initially be recorded by applying the spot rate. However when cash settlement occurs the settled amount will be translated using the spot rate on the settlement date. If this amount differs from that used when the transaction occurred, there will be an exchange difference which is taken to the income statement in the period in which it arises.

Unsettled transactions

The treatment of any 'foreign' items remaining on the statement of financial position at the year end will depend on whether they are classified as monetary or non-monetary.

Monetary items include cash, receivables, payables and loans, and they are re-translated at the closing rate (year-end spot).

Non-monetary items include non-current assets, inventory and investments, and are not re-translated but left at historic cost.

For example, if a company has a foreign subsidiary which includes property, plant and equipment this will be valued at the date it was acquired (or revalued). However, if these assets were acquired using a loan, then the loan is translated at the closing rate (current spot) which could be very different to the spot when the assets were bought. This gives rise to currency risk because the assets and liabilities no longer offset each other. (This is covered by the 'temporal method' in International Accounting Standard (IAS) 21.)

The reported performance of an overseas subsidiary in home-based currency terms can be severely distorted if there has been a significant foreign exchange movement.

Any foreign exchange gains or losses are recorded in equity. They are unrealised and will only become realised when the subsidiary is sold.

Unless managers believe that the company's share price will fall as a result of showing a translation exposure loss in the company's accounts, translation exposure should not normally be hedged. (The company's share price, in an efficient market, should only react to exposure that is likely to have an impact on cash flows.)

However, research shows that company directors do spend (in some people's opinion – waste) money hedging translation risk. The management of translation risk is often considered to be dysfunctional behaviour.

Management of translation risk

Any change in parity will affect reported profits (and hence earnings per share), total assets, borrowings, net worth (and hence gearing) but – to repeat – it will not have affected the measured cash flow in the period being reported on.

Academic theory argues that translation risk, of itself, need not concern financial managers, but in practice, there are two strong arguments in favour of the relevance of translation risk:

(1) Although it does not affect the value of the entity as a whole, it can affect the attribution of that value between the different stakeholders. Higher gearing may lead to higher interest rates being charged on bank loans, either directly in accordance with clauses in borrowing agreements or indirectly as a result of the company's credit rating being reduced. The banks benefit at the expense of the equity investors in the business. If the treasurer is pursuing an objective of maximising shareholder wealth, he will want to manage this risk.

(2) If the accounts are being used 'beyond their design specification', for example as the basis for calculating bonus payments for directors and senior managers, then there is a temptation to protect the current year's figures, even though it is known that doing so has a long-term cost. This is comparable to pulling profit into the current year, knowing that it will both reduce next year's profit and result in tax being paid earlier than necessary.

The former is a good reason, the latter is often the real reason for managing translation risk.

Test your understanding 3 – RED

RED is a successful company manufacturing electronic equipment. Until recently, most of its sales were to customers in its domestic market, with just a few export sales. Recently, however, the board of directors of RED have approved a new export-led strategy for growth. The company is planning to grow sales and profits substantially by targeting new markets in other countries.

The targeted markets are:

- the US and countries in Western Europe;
- countries with developing economies.

The finance director of RED is concerned about the large amount of working capital required to finance the increase in trade. He has estimated that for every $1 of working capital needed to finance domestic sales, the company will need $2.50 to finance the same volume of export sales. He has also expressed concerns about the lack of experience of the credit assessment team in the accounts department in carrying out credit assessments on customers in other countries. He believes that credit risks will be much higher with customers in the new markets.

The risk management committee of RED will consider various risks associated with export sales at its next meeting, and as management accountant you have been asked to provide a discussion paper for the meeting.

Required:

Prepare a discussion paper for the meeting in which you:

(a) explain why credit risks might be higher with export sales;
(b) recommend methods of reducing these credit risks;
(c) discuss other risks associated with an export sales strategy, that the company should evaluate, control and monitor.

Test your understanding 4 – Equip

Equip plc is a major exporter of agricultural equipment to Australia, New Zealand and throughout Europe. All production facilities are in the United Kingdom. The majority of raw materials and tools are also sourced in the United Kingdom, with a few imports from Eire, priced in sterling. Major competitors are based in the United States and Germany. There are plans to set up a manufacturing subsidiary in Australia, funded in part by an Australian dollar loan to be taken out by Equip plc. The new manufacturing facility would be used to source the Australian and New Zealand markets.

Required:

(a) Describe the potential currency exposures faced by this company before setting up the manufacturing subsidiary.

(b) Consider the effects of setting up the new manufacturing subsidiary in Australia with respect to the following:

    (i) Will any of the exposures identified in (a) above be reduced?

    (ii) What new currency exposures will the group face?

Test your understanding 5 – Political risk

A UK company is planning to build and operate a factory in West Africa.

Required:

Discuss the potential political risks that may arise and recommend risk mitigation strategies that could be implemented to bring these risks to a satisfactory level.

Test your understanding 6 – KS

KS is a company that makes the majority of its sales on credit to both home and overseas customers and as such is exposed to credit risk.

Required:

(a) A description of what credit risk is and a company's maximum exposure to it.

(b) A critical evaluation of the methods that could be used to assess credit risk – both quantitatively and qualitatively.

(c) A description of the methods that could be used by a business to reduce exposure to credit risk, and any particular problems associated with them.

Test your understanding 7 – Economic risk

R is a large retail organisation that imports goods from Australia for sale in its home market, where the currency is the R$. The directors of R are aware that the company is subject to significant economic exposure to movements on the AUS $ because any appreciation of the AUS $ will increase the cost of goods for resale. R has attempted to create a partial hedge against this by placing all of its cash reserves in a AUS $ bank account. That way the losses associated with any increase in cost prices will be partially offset by a gain on the bank account. The directors are concerned that the translation gains and losses on the AUS$ bank balance are visible to shareholders, whereas the offsetting of economic exposure is not and so their hedging policy may be misunderstood. The AUS bank account has a balance of AUS$30m. The exchange rate is presently R$3 to AUS$1.

Required:

(a) Advise the directors on the matters that they would have to consider in order to determine the extent of R's economic exposure.

(b) Evaluate the validity of the directors' concern that "the translation gains and losses on the AUS$ bank balance are visible to shareholders, whereas the offsetting of economic exposure is not and so their hedging policy may be misunderstood".

6 Chapter summary

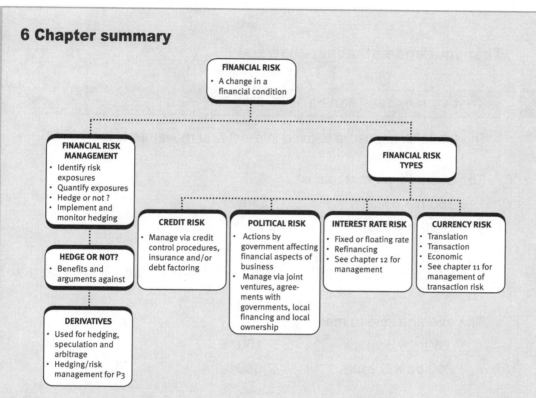

FINANCIAL RISK
- A change in a financial condition

FINANCIAL RISK MANAGEMENT
- Identify risk exposures
- Quantify exposures
- Hedge or not ?
- Implement and monitor hedging

HEDGE OR NOT?
- Benefits and arguments against

DERIVATIVES
- Used for hedging, speculation and arbitrage
- Hedging/risk management for P3

FINANCIAL RISK TYPES

CREDIT RISK
- Manage via credit control procedures, insurance and/or debt factoring

POLITICAL RISK
- Actions by government affecting financial aspects of business
- Manage via joint ventures, agreements with governments, local financing and local ownership

INTEREST RATE RISK
- Fixed or floating rate
- Refinancing
- See chapter 12 for management

CURRENCY RISK
- Translation
- Transaction
- Economic
- See chapter 11 for management of transaction risk

Test your understanding answers

Test your understanding 1 – G Plc

The total risk exposure to fixed interest rate movements is £450m.

The average interest rate is:

£50m × 6%	£3m
£400m × 7%	£28m
_____	_____
£450m of loans with	£31m of interest = 6.89% average rate

The average time to maturity:

£50m × 3 years	150
£400m × 5 years	2,000
	_____
	2,150
2,150/£450m	4.78 years average remaining life

The average interest rate would be compared to other companies in the same industry to ascertain whether it was higher or lower, whilst bearing in mind the general expectation of movement in the base rate. For example, if G Plc's average rate is lower than the competitors and the base rate is expected to fall, then it will be deemed less risky because G will pay less interest in the future compared to its competitors.

Time to maturity creates a separate measure of exposure. Again G Plc's average time to maturity will be compared to its competitors. If the time to maturity is shorter than the competitors and rates are expected to rise then G is more risky since it has tied itself in to shorter term fixed rate borrowings and new loans taken out (if required) will probably have a higher interest rate.

Test your understanding 2 – H plc (1)

Value of transaction at original rates

	£
US$100,000 purchases @ 0.5556	55,560 payment

Value of transaction at future rates

US$100,000 purchases @ 0.5420	54,200 payment

The amount saved by paying in six months time is £1,360. This saving arises due to the exchange rate moving in your favour.

Do not forget that you would have had approximately £55,000 in the bank for six months longer, earning interest which makes this an even better option.

Test your understanding 3 – RED

Key answer tips

Part (a) requires you to consider the risk / return trade-off; a business will be willing to take higher risks as long as it obtains a higher return. Export sales are more risky, and you will need to give examples here of why this is the case.

In answering part (b) ensure that you explain your recommendations clearly and show how they will reduce the risks established in part (a). You may find it helpful to plan your answers to parts (a) and (b) together since this will ensure you generate as many ideas as possible.

Part (c) is quite open, allowing you to use some common sense as opposed to text-book knowledge.

(a) Credit risks can be higher with export sales than with domestic sales, for several reasons.

It might be more difficult to obtain information about customers in other countries in order to check their credit status. Information should be easier to obtain from European countries, where the services of a credit reference agency can be used, than from developing countries. When credit information is not available, decisions about granting credit are likely to involve an acceptance of greater-than-usual risk.

When customers are in countries where economic conditions are difficult, perhaps in developing countries, customers might have financial difficulties. They would therefore be a higher credit risk.

There can be problems with late payment, when goods are delayed in shipment. Customers are usually reluctant to pay for goods until they have been delivered or at least are in transit. Delays in shipment are therefore likely to result in delays in payment.

Many customers need to be 'chased' for payment. It is easier to chase customers in the same country than it is to chase customers in other countries, due to difficulties with language and time differences.

When a customer refuses to pay, there could be problems with taking legal action. If a customer is in another country, the difficulties will include a lack of knowledge of the local legislative system.

(b) Since credit risks can be higher with export sales, it is important to take measures to restrict the risk and keep it within acceptable limits.

RED might consider the following options:

For sales to countries where credit reference agencies operate, the services of a credit reference agency might be used to obtain information on the credit status of potential customers. In developing countries, the trade section of the embassy might be able to provide assistance in obtaining information about credit conditions in the country.

The company should develop clear policies and procedures on granting credit and collecting payments. The staff involved in granting credit and in chasing customers for payment should be given training in how to apply these policies and procedures. The policies and procedures, and the internal controls that are applied to credit checking and debt collection, should be reviewed and re-assessed regularly, and adjusted where weaknesses are identified

It might be possible to agree to a secure method of settlement of debts for exports to developing countries. With export trade to many countries, documentary credits are a commonly-used method of payment. The exporter is required to deliver a specified set of documents to a bank representing the importer: these documents typically include shipping documents, insurance documents, an invoice and a letter of credit. If the documents are all in order, the buyer agrees to make the payment, usually by means of a term bill of exchange drawn on the buyer's bank that gives the buyer a suitable period of credit. The bill of exchange, since it is a bank bill (and which might be confirmed by a second bank in the exporter's country), should be a fairly low credit risk. It is a promise by the bank to make the payment on the due date. If the exporter needs earlier payment, the bill can be discounted.

Letters of credit are much less common for sales to countries with an advanced economy. For sales to customers in Western Europe, RED might be required to give credit on normal trade terms. The credit risk might be reduced if RED used the services of an export factor. The factor would undertake to collect debts on behalf of RED. If the service is a without-recourse factoring service, the factor would also make the credit checks on the customer, and would effectively insure RED against the credit risk.

RED might consider the possibility of export credit insurance, although the premiums can be expensive.

(c) There are significant business risks in an export-led sales growth strategy.

Due to cultural differences, customers in other countries might have different needs and requirements from the products they buy. RED would therefore need to consider whether its products need to be adapted and altered to meet country-specific needs.

Similarly, due to cultural differences there could be difficulties in adapting to the business practices of the targeted countries.

Other business risks include the potential difficulties in building up good relationships with customers in distant countries. It might be necessary to negotiate agreements with a local agent or 'partner' for the storage and distribution of products locally. These will need to be managed carefully, and operational difficulties are likely to arise.

Inevitably, there will be risks of loss or damage to goods during shipment, but it is standard business practice to insure the goods against loss and damage (with either the seller or the buyer paying the insurance cost).

If RED agrees to invoice customers in their domestic currency, or in another foreign currency (such as US dollars or euros) foreign exchange risk would arise on transactions. However, these risks could be hedged using forward foreign exchange contracts.

In some developing countries, there might possibly be political risks. A government might take action, for example, to restrict foreign currency payments by residents to foreign suppliers.

A developing country might experience severe economic difficulties for a time: this has been the experience in the past, for example, of several countries in South and Central America. For a company exporting to such countries, there will be a risk that an economic downturn could disrupt export sales.

Test your understanding 4 – Equip

(a) *Transaction risk:*

Sales revenue denominated in Australian dollars, New Zealand dollars euros, other.

Economic risk:

Purchase costs denominated in sterling but sourced from Eire.

Price pressure from competitors in the United States and Germany (this will be affected by the currency cost base of these companies).

Translation risk:

Minor as Equip Plc has no foreign subsidiaries – just retranslation of year-end currency debtors.

Overall assessment:

Mismatch of sterling cost base versus exposed sales revenue.

(b) (i) Reduction in exposure:

- Australian dollar transaction risk.

- Australian dollar economic risk.

- Exposure from competitors is not eliminated.

(ii) New exposures, to the extent that they do not net out:

- Translation risk from incorporating subsidiary accounts.

- Translation risk arising from the Australian dollar debt.

- Transaction risk as a result of the Australian dollar dividend payments to the UK.

The end result will depend on the success of the Australian operation, the actual figures involved and any increase in local sales that may naturally result from a greater presence in Australia. For example, exposure to New Zealand dollars could increase if sales to New Zealand were to increase.

Test your understanding 5 – Political risk

By entering into another country, the UK company is exposing itself to significant political risk.

Political risk arises due to political interference in either the company's own country of operation, or any country it chooses to expand into.

It can also be generated by neighbouring countries if West Africa could be affected. If, for example, the UK company intends to ship goods from WA then these ships may become a target by the pirates with a cost in the form of lost goods in transit and delays in production.

West Africa's political risk can be viewed from different levels of government:

Local government

Local political risk arises from the influence of local councils or state governments. It manifests itself in the decisions made by local government that may negatively affect the factory (such as business rates increases, or indirect taxation). Ideally, the UK company should try to source a representative from the local government on to the factory project.

National government

Government decisions will also impact upon the factory. For example, the National government may have offered tax incentives for the first few years of the project but might increase taxes or even introduce new streams of taxation such as green taxes in later years. They may also take punitive measures such as penalising businesses they see as operating incorrectly (e.g. low wages), or businesses operating at odds with their specified aims and objectives.

International government

International bodies such as the UN can also be a source of political risk for businesses if they find out about activities of which they disagree e.g. low wages.

Although the new factory might serve both parties aims and objectives now, there may come a point in time in the future where the respective governments of the UK & West Africa disagree on an issue, which could have serious repercussions for the UK company in the long run.

In addition, if West Africa had a relatively new government this would also be a concern, insofar that if their term in office was short any future government may reverse the decisions taken by their predecessors.

Political risk also covers legal and compliance risk to an extent. The UK company should ascertain whether there are any additional laws in West Africa of which they should be aware. The use of local lawyers should help.

Mitigation strategies

Mitigating political risk is never easy, as governments tend to be far more powerful than individual companies. However, there are some methods of reducing the risk. One such method would be for the UK company to invite locals (employees, local government) to become part owners in the factory.

Another option is for it to provide the foreign government with details of an eventual exit strategy that will leave the business in the hands of locals.

Neither of these strategies may be acceptable to the UK company.

Test your understanding 6 – KS

Definition of credit risk

- Credit risk is the risk of bad debts on receivables, i.e. the customer or borrower failing to pay the amount due – it occurs whenever a business gives credit.

- Maximum exposure to credit risk is normally the total value of receivables, but if on some receivables the risk has been transferred it is reduced by the amount of the receivables transferred.

- The exposure of a business to credit risk will depend on the risk culture and the nature of the customers dealt with.

Methods to evaluate credit risk

Quantitative:

Expected values

- A common way calculating a figure for credit risk is the use of expected values.

- Expected value methods require the evaluation of the potential level of bad debt and the probability of that level occurring. An 'average' or 'expected' bad debt level can then be calculated:

Problems of expected values

A number of problems exist with expected values:

(i) There is no indication of range – this could be addressed by also giving volatility figures.

(ii) The amount on its own is a fairly meaningless assessment of credit risk. To make it more useful it should perhaps be:

- monitored over time to ensure that credit risk is not increasing

- compared to industry averages – if the average bad debt in the industry is 1% but a company is running at 2.3% the company has a problem with its credit risk.

(iii) It is very often difficult to decide the inputs into the expected value calculations – it the inputs are based on judgement the result (which can appear to be accurate is not really, it is based on judgement.

(iv) The actual level of bad debt will not be the expected value.

(v) Expected value calculations do not lead well into risk management decisions. Qualitative methods can be better for this.

Qualitative:

Risk maps

The risk map plots risks onto a matrix in a way that prioritises the risks for the business. Credit risk could be one of the risks that is plotted onto the risk map.

Once risks have been plotted onto the risk map the business can decide risk management strategy. Obviously the high impact, high probability risks are dealt with first, with the low impact, low probability last. It may be decided that the low, low risks do not need to be controlled.

Judgement by management

Risk could be assessed by the management using judgement to decide which are the most important risks. The management will then take management action.
Danger with this approach – that management will be biased and therefore the decision might be better by a combination of a number of managers.

However it can be a good method in that management feel very involved and therefore they will be committed to risk management actions.

Reductions in credit risk

A number of methods exist to try to reduce credit risk:

Good controls

Set up very good internal controls over credit policies and debtor collection:

- Obtain references and credit ratings before a credit limit is given to a customer

- Ensure that all credit sales over a set level are approved

- Have policies to quickly follow up any late payments, and put non-payers in the hands of solicitors

- Offer prompt payment discounts to encourage early payments.

Insurance

It is possible to insure against default by customers and therefore transfer the risk to the insurance company. The insurance policy will require the payment of premiums and the higher the chance of bad debt, the greater the insurance premiums will be.

It is common to insure against overseas sales as these present higher credit risk and therefore the insurance premium becomes more worthwhile.

Governments have sometimes offered insurance against overseas credit sales cheaply as an inducement to business to export.

Factoring

Debt factoring is basically the sale of debtors to a factoring company. The business informs all its customers to pay the factoring company and the factor takes over full responsibility for the management and the collection of the debts.

Debt factoring can be done in two ways:

Recourse Under recourse debt factoring the factor does not take the bad debt risk. This can still be of benefit because the factor may get better collection rates than the business. This factoring will also be cheaper than non-recourse.

Non-recourse The factoring company accepts the bad debt risk and therefore the business factoring has got rid of the credit risk. This method will be more expensive however.

Avoid the risk

A company can always reduce credit risk by not entering into credit sales.

This would only be a viable policy for a customer where the risk of default is so great that it is not worth making sales. To have this as a policy for the business for all customers would almost certainly be damaging to the business as a whole.

Test your understanding 7 – Economic risk

(a) Economic exposure is generally difficult to measure, but an understanding can be obtained by identifying the factors that will lead to economic exposure. Generally, these boil down to identifying the effects of changes to cost prices and selling prices, both for the entity itself and for its competitors. R's purchase prices may be affected by movements in the AUS$. The actual effects may not be linear because R's Australian suppliers may not pass on the full effects of the currency movement. The suppliers may believe that the market for these products is sensitive to price rises and so the suppliers may choose to absorb some of the increased cost themselves. The likelihood of that happening will be determined in part by the availability of similar goods from economies that are not bound by the AUS$.

Currency movements may force R to raise its selling prices to customers. That makes the elasticity of demand for R's products important. It may be that prices are inelastic and that consumers are willing to buy just as much even if the price rises slightly. R's competitors may also buy products priced in AUS$ and that will reduce R's problem to an extent because all competing products will be affected in the same manner.

(b) The financial statements will show the gains and losses arising on R's currency holdings. The shareholders may be concerned that the company's assets are exposed in this way and that they are risking a serious loss if the AUS$ declines against the R$. The economic exposure that is being hedged will be apparent from the fact that the company will generate less revenue and make less profit when the AUS$ is high. This will not appear anywhere as a single, visible item or disclosure in the financial statements.

The shareholders could be forgiven for believing that the only exposure is with respect to the AUS$ balance. There is nothing to prevent the directors from explaining their strategy to the shareholders. It does not matter that there is a lack of symmetry in accounting for the different currency exposures provided the shareholders accept this explanation. This is, however, a complicated area and it would be legitimate for the directors to worry that the shareholders will misunderstand. If the shareholders believe that the directors' policy is misguided then it could undermine their confidence in the board. Technically, the directors are supposed to pursue the maximisation of shareholder wealth and so they should always act in accordance with the shareholders" best interests. It would be dishonest to leave the company exposed to a manageable risk for no good reason simply because the shareholders may misinterpret the directors' behaviour.

12

Currency risk management

Chapter learning objectives

Lead	Component
D2. Evaluate alternative risk management tools.	(a) Evaluate appropriate methods for managing financial risks.
	(b) Evaluate the effects of alternative methods of risk management.
	(c) Discuss exchange rate theory and the impact of differential inflation rates on forecast exchange rates.
	(d) Recommend risk management strategies and discuss their accounting implications.

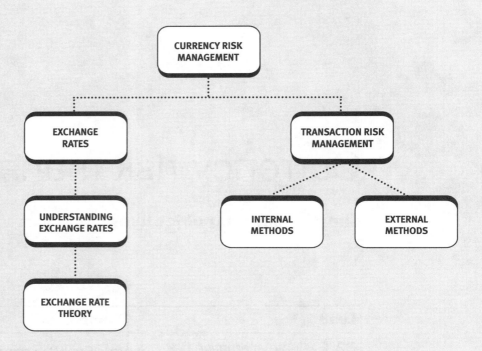

1 Understanding exchange rates

The foreign exchange, or forex, market is an international market in national currencies. It is highly competitive and virtually no difference exists between the prices in one market (e.g. New York) and another (e.g. London).

Exchange rates

An exchange rate is expressed in terms of the quantity of one currency that can be exchanged for one unit of the other currency - it can be thought of as the price of a currency. For example:

US$1/£0.6667

This means that £0.6667 will buy US$1, i.e. the price of a US$ is £0.6667. Hence:

- to convert from US$s to £s you must multiply by 0.6667
- to convert from £s to US$s you must divide by 0.6667.

(**Note:** This could also be stated as US$1 = £0.6667, or US$1: £0.6667. You may see any of these expressions in exam questions. By convention exchange rates are expressed (and rounded) to four decimal places, though this may not always be the case for information provided in questions.)

Spot rate

This is the rate given for a transaction with immediate delivery. In practice this means it will be settled within two working days.

Inverting exchange rates

Exchange rates may also be expressed the other way round, i.e. the US\$s are expressed in terms of £s instead of vice versa.

> e.g. the above spot rate US\$1/£0.6667

may be expressed in terms of US\$s to £s by dividing the rate into 1,

> i.e. $1 \div 0.6667 = 1.5000$

Therefore an equivalent illustration of the rate is:

> £1/US\$1.5000

Spread

Banks do not operate wholly for the greater good; in fact they wish to make a profit out of the deal. This means that they need to earn a **margin** or **spread** on the deal, as well as commission and fees.

> e.g. £1 = US\$1.5500 – 1.4500

- the rate at which the bank will sell the variable currency (US\$s) in exchange for the base currency (£s) is US\$1.4500. (i.e. the rate at which it will buy £s).
- the rate at which the bank will buy US\$s in exchange for £s is US\$1.5500. (i.e. the rate at which it will sell £s).

The key to understanding our (the company's) position is to identify that the bank always wins, hence in the example above the bank buys £ LOW and sells £ HIGH.

Illustration of spread prices

The rate quoted is £1/US\$ 1.4330 – 1.4325.

Company A wants to buy US\$100,000 in exchange for sterling.

Company B wants to sell US\$200,000 in exchange for sterling.

What rate will the bank offer each company?

Company A wants to buy US$100,000 in exchange for sterling (so that the bank will be selling US$s and buying £s):

- If we used the lower rate of 1.4325, the bank would sell dollars for £69,808

- If we used the higher rate of 1.4330, the bank would sell dollars for £69,784.

Clearly the bank would be better off selling dollars (and buying sterling) at the lower rate of 1.4325.

Company B wants to sell US$200,000 in exchange for sterling (so the bank would be buying US$s and selling £s):

- If we used the lower rate of 1.4325, the bank would buy dollars for £139,616

- If we used the higher rate of 1.4330, the bank would buy dollars for £139,567

The bank will make more money buying dollars (and selling sterling) at the higher rate of 1.4330.

Test your understanding 1 – Spread

Assume that the spread is £1/US$ 1.5500 – 1.4500. Consider the situations of three UK-based companies:

(a) A Ltd imports goods from Texas to the value of US$100,000. Payment is cash on delivery; what is the cost in sterling of this purchase?

(b) B plc exports goods to California valued at US$50,000. Receipt of payment is immediate on delivery of the goods; what is the value of sterling received?

(c) C Ltd wishes to buy a product from US that is for sale in the UK at £12 each; at what dollar price must it purchase the product?

Cross rates

You may not be given the exchange rate you need for a particular currency, but instead be given the relationship it has with a different currency. You will then need to calculate a **cross rate.**

For example, if you have a rate in £1/US$ and a rate in £1/€, you can derive a cross rate for €1/US$ by dividing the £1/US$ rate by the £1/€ rate.

Illustration of cross rate calculation

A French company is to purchase materials costing US$100,000. You have the following information:

£1/US$	1.9000
£1/€	1.4500

What is the value of the purchase in euros?

Solution

The solution could be calculated in two stages:

(1) Convert the purchase into sterling:

US$100,000/1.9000 = £52,632

(2) Convert the sterling value into euros

£52,632 × 1.4500 = €76,316

However, an easier alternative, particularly if there are a number of transactions to convert, is to calculate a cross rate:

The €1/US$ rate will be 1.9000/1.4500 = 1.3103

The value of the transaction is therefore:

US$100,000/1.3103 = €76,318

Test your understanding 2 – Cross rates

A US company has to pay €100,000 for a machine. You have the following information:

£1/€1.5300

£1/US$1.8700

Required:

What is the cost of the machine in dollars?

2 Exchange rate theory

Forecasting exchange rates

A company may wish to forecast exchange rates for a number of short-term and long-term reasons. These may include:

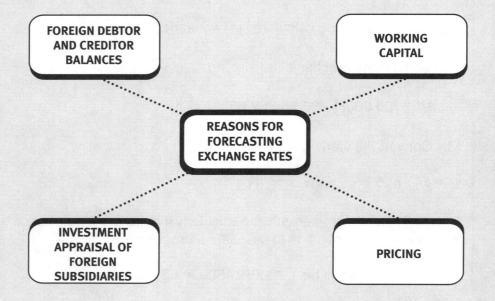

More on forecasting exchange rates

- **Foreign debtor and creditor balances** – Our balances in other currencies may change dramatically over the short-term in terms of sterling. If we are unable to forecast with some degree of certainty we open ourselves up to potentially very damaging exchange rate losses.

- **Working capital** – For a company with subsidiaries overseas it is important to be able to forecast movements in exchange rates over the medium-term to better facilitate the funding of those balances.

- **Pricing** – Movements in exchange rates may force the company to revise its pricing strategy in an individual country. This may be in response to a movement in the exchange rates between the country of manufacture and that of sale. Alternatively it is possible that an exchange rate movement favouring a competitor may also lead to a revision of prices.

- **Investment appraisal of foreign subsidiaries** – A longer-term forecast of exchange rate movements will be needed to identify the impact on a NPV analysis of the economic risks of a project.

- In the short-term rates may fluctuate due to market sentiment and **speculation** which are not easily explained theoretically, over the longer-term more fundamental factors take effect.

- If we could forecast exchange rates with some degree of accuracy this would reduce the transaction risk faced by a company, and may allow it to minimise hedging costs.

Why exchange rates fluctuate

Changes in exchange rates result from changes in the demand for and supply of the currency. These changes may occur for a variety of reasons including:

Speculation

Speculators enter into foreign exchange transactions with a view to making a profit from their expectations of the currency's future movements. If they expect a currency to devalue, they will short sell the currency with the hope of buying it back cheaply at a future date.

Balance of payments

Since currencies are required to finance international trade, changes in trade may lead to changes in exchange rates. In principle:

- demand for imports in the US represents a demand for foreign currency or a supply of dollars

- overseas demand for US exports represents a demand for dollars or a supply of the currency.

Thus a country with a current account deficit where imports exceed exports may expect to see its exchange rate depreciate, since the supply of the currency (imports) will exceed the demand for the currency (exports).

Any factors which are likely to alter the state of the current account of the balance of payments may ultimately affect the exchange rate.

Government policy

Governments may wish to change the value of their currency. This can be achieved directly by devaluation / revaluation, or via the foreign exchange markets (buying of selling their currency onto the markets).

Capital movements between economies

There are also **capital movements between economies**. These transactions are effectively switching bank deposits from one currency to another. These flows are now more important than the volume of trade in goods and services.

Thus supply/demand for a currency may reflect events on the capital account. Several factors may lead to inflows or outflows of capital:

- changes in *interest rates*: rising (falling) interest rates will attract a capital inflow (outflow) and a demand (supply) for the currency

- *inflation rates*: asset holders will not wish to hold financial assets in a currency whose value is falling because of inflation.

These forces which affect the demand and supply of currencies, and hence exchange rates, have been incorporated into a number of formal models.

We shall consider three related theories that together should give some insight into exchange rate movements:

(1) Purchasing power parity theory (PPPT)

(2) Interest rate parity theory (IRPT)

(3) The International Fisher Effect

Purchasing power parity theory (PPPT)

This theory suggests the rate of exchange will be directly determined by the relative rates of inflation suffered by each currency. If one country suffers a greater rate of inflation than another its currency should be worth less in comparative terms.

The basis of PPPT is the *'Law of One Price'*:

- identical goods must cost the same regardless of the currency in which they are sold.

- if this is not the case then **arbitrage** (buying at the lower price, selling at the higher price) will take place until a single price is charged. Remember this is where a commodity that appears cheap is bought by many traders. The sellers then realise that they can put up their price due to the commodities popularity. Demand will then fall at this higher price and potential profits have been competed away. However, imagine that this commodity has to cross a countries border – it would be easy to cross the border from, say Switzerland to France to buy cheaper groceries. If many Swiss did this it might affect the Swiss Franc / Euro exchange rate. However it is much more difficult to make the same saving if you live in the UK even if you believe that the £ / Euro is out of line.

PPPT

A company is going to buy a non-current asset at a cost of US$30 million. If the current rate is £1/US$1.5000 this would mean that in sterling terms it would cost **£20 million.**

What would be the prices in one year in each country given that the inflation rate in the US is 8% and in the UK is 5%?

The US market			The UK market
Year 0 (now)	US$30m	(£1/US$1.5000)	£20m
Inflation	8%		5%
Year 1	US$32.4m		£21m

What is the effective exchange rate in one year's time?

We can divide the US price by the UK price to calculate the revised exchange rate:

$$\text{Rate} = \frac{32.4}{21.0} = 1.5429$$

 Rule: The country with the higher inflation will suffer a fall (depreciation) in their currency.

The PPPT formula gives:

$$\text{Future spot rate} = \text{Current spot rate} \times \frac{1 + i_f}{1 + i_h}$$

i_f rate of inflation in the foreign country

i_h rate of inflation in the home country

spot rate in terms of 1 unit of home currency / foreign currency (e.g. £1/US$)

In the above illustration, the future spot rate would be calculated by

$$1.5000 \times \frac{1.08}{1.05} = 1.5429$$

Test your understanding 3 – Future spot rates

The dollar and sterling are currently trading at £1/US$1.7200.

Inflation in the US is expected to grow at 3% pa, but at 4% pa in the UK.

Predict the future spot rate in a year's time.

> ### Problems with PPPT in practice
>
> - Is the law of one price justified? In many markets it is apparent that the suppliers or manufacturers charge what the market will bear, this differing from one market to another.
>
> - The costs of physically moving some products from one place to another mean that there will always be a premium in some markets in relation to another.
>
> - Differing taxation regimes may dramatically affect the costs of a product in one market to that in another.
>
> - Manufacturers may be able to successfully differentiate products in each market to limit the amount of arbitrage that occurs.

Is PPPT a good predictor of future spot rate?

PPPT certainly does explain the reasoning behind much of the movements in exchange rates but is not a very good predictor of exchange rates in the short- to medium-term.

Reasons for this include:

- Future inflation rates are only an estimate and often cannot be relied upon to be accurate.

- The market is dominated by speculation and currency investment rather than trade in physical goods.

- Government intervention in both direct (e.g. management of exchange rates) and indirect ways (e.g. taxation policies) can nullify the impact of PPPT.

Interest rate parity theory (IRPT)

This theory is based on very similar principles to that of PPPT.

The IRPT claims that the difference between the spot and the forward exchange rates is equal to the differential between interest rates available in the two currencies.

The **forward rate** is a future exchange rate, agreed now, for buying or selling an amount of currency on an agreed future date.

IRPT

An investor has US$5 million to invest over one year in either dollars (US$) or sterling (£). His options are to:

- Invest in dollars at the prevailing dollar interest rate of 10.16% or,
- Convert the dollars to sterling at the prevailing spot rate (£1/ $1.5000) and invest in sterling at 7.1%.

The one-year forward rate is £1/US$1.5429.

Analysing the options open to this investor:

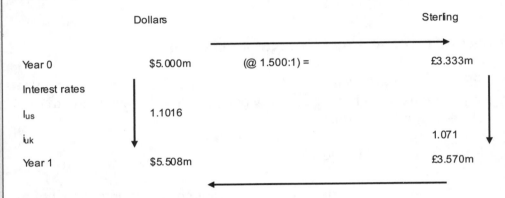

In one year US$5.508 million must equate to £3.570 million, so what you gain in extra interest you lose in an adverse movement in exchange rates. The effective exchange rate is

$$\text{Exchange rate} = \frac{5.508}{3.570} = 1.5429$$

which equals the forward rate for one year. The forward rate moves to bring about interest rate parity between the currencies.

Rule: IRPT predicts that the country with the higher interest rate will see the forward rate for its currency subject to a depreciation.

The IRPT formula gives:

$$\text{Forward rate} = \text{Current spot rate} \times \frac{1 + \text{ints}_f}{1 + \text{ints}_h}$$

Where

> ints$_f$ money risk-free rate of interest for the foreign currency
> ints$_h$ money risk-free rate of interest for the home currency
> spot rate in terms of 1 unit of home currency / foreign currency (e.g. £1/US$)

Test your understanding 4 – Future spot

A treasurer can borrow in Swiss francs at a rate of 3% pa or in the UK at a rate of 7% p.a. The current rate of exchange is £1/10SF.

What is the likely rate of exchange in a year's time?

More on IRPT

The interest rate parity model shows that it may be possible to predict exchange rate movements by referring to differences in nominal exchange rates. If the forward exchange rate for sterling against the dollar was no higher than the spot rate but US nominal interest rates were higher, the following would happen:

- UK investors would shift funds to the US in order to secure the higher interest rates, since they would suffer no exchange losses when they converted $ back into £.

- The flow of capital from the UK to the US would raise UK interest rates and force up the spot rate for the US$.

The IRP theory holds because of **arbitrage** (discussed earlier). Arbitrageurs actively seek out anomalies in the exchange rate market. They buy and sell currency to make a profit (buy at a low price and sell at a high price, as with any commodity). If many arbitrageurs do this, the exchange rate alters (differences in supply and demand will alter the price), the exchange rate moves and the anomaly then disappears. Nick Leeson at Barings Bank used to be an unsuccessful arbitrageur!

Is IRPT applicable to determining forward rates?

The only limitation on the universal applicability of this relationship will be due to government intervention. These may arise in a number of ways including the following:

- **Controls on capital markets** – The government may limit the range and type of markets within their financial services system.

- **Controls on currency trading** – These may be in the form of a limit on the amount of currency that may be taken out of a country or the use of an 'official' exchange rate that does not bear any relation to the 'effective' rate at which the markets wish to trade.

- **Government intervention in the market** – The government may attempt to control or manipulate the exchange rate by buying or selling their own currency.

The International Fisher Effect

The International Fisher Effect claims that the interest rate differentials between two countries provide an unbiased predictor of future changes in the spot rate of exchange.

- The International Fisher Effect assumes that all countries will have the same real interest rate, although nominal or money rates may differ due to expected inflation rates.

- Thus the interest rate differential between two countries should be equal to the expected inflation differential.

- Therefore, countries with higher expected inflation rates will have higher nominal interest rates, and vice versa.

The Fisher effect

As seen in your earlier studies, the Fisher effect looks at the relationship between interest rates and inflation. Inflation is the difference between the real return on investment (real interest) and the nominal return (nominal interest rate). The relationship between the nominal rate of interest, the real rate of interest and inflation can be expressed by the formula:

[1 + nominal rate] = [1 + real rate] × [1 + inflation rate]

Example

One-year money market interest rates in the UK are 5.06%. Inflation in the UK is currently running at 3% per annum.

The real one-year interest rate in the UK can be calculated as follows:

[1.0506] = [1 + real rate] × [1.03]
[1 + real rate] = 1.0506/1.03 = 1.02
Real rate = 0.02 or 2% per year.

The nominal or market interest rates in any country must be sufficient to reward investors with a suitable real return plus an additional return to allow for the effects of inflation.

Test your understanding 5 – Parity relationships

US$1/€0.9050

Interest rates p.a. on short-term government securities

US treasury	6.0%
Eurozone	4.5%

Inflation rates

US	2.0%
Eurozone	1.3%

Required:

Calculate using the parity relationships (PPPT and IRPT) the theoretically correct forward rates. Determine the reasons for a difference between the two, if one arises.

Arbitrage

Arbitrage is the simultaneous purchase and sale of a security in different markets with the aim of making a risk-free profit through the exploitation of any price differences between the two markets. (CIMA Official Terminology)

(The purchase and sale does not necessarily have to be a security. It could be as simple as buying apples in one market and selling them in another at a higher price.)

Arbitrage is mainly used by **speculators** rather than as a hedging tool.

Arbitrage differences are short-term. When other traders see differences in the price of a commodity they will exploit them and the prices will converge. The differences will disappear as equilibrium is reached.

Some kinds of arbitrage are completely risk-free—this is pure arbitrage. For instance, if Euros are available more cheaply in London than in New York, arbitrageurs can make a risk-free profit by buying euros in London and selling an identical amount in New York. Opportunities for pure arbitrage have become rare in recent years, partly because of the globalisation of financial markets and immediate access to information via the use of the internet. This enables almost anyone (who understands what they are doing) to trade and potentially make a profit.

More on arbitrage

For example, imagine you bought and sold fruit and vegetables on a market stall. One day asks for a kilo of apples. You don't have any apples but you know where you can get some. Having ascertained that the customer will pay up to £1 per kilo, you contact a friend who has apples on another market stall. They are selling at £0.90 per kilo. You offer to buy the kilo of apples at £0.90, collect them from the other market stall, and sell them for £1 making £0.10 profit. If enough customers ask for apples, eventually the friend will realise that there is an increased demand for apples, which appear to be in short supply, and they will increase their price. This effectively eliminates the opportunity for arbitrage profits.

The same principle can be applied to any commodity but is commonly used by 'day-traders' with exchange rates. They look for an apparently 'cheap' currency and then sell it quickly, at a profit, to someone who needs it.

Margaret is a day-trader (based in the UK) looking for arbitrage opportunities on the currency market. On 1st June she thinks she has spotted a difference in the market for US dollars.

She can buy US$ 2 for euros 1.50. She can buy one euro for £0.80. She can sell dollars for US$ 1.50 /£1. She has £100,000 available to invest for the purpose of making a profit.

Margaret converts her £ in to euros: £100,000 / 0.80 = E125,000

Margaret then converts her euros into dollars: (E125,000 / 1.5) × 2 = $166,667

Margaret now sells the dollars: $166,667 / $1.50 = £111,111

Margaret has made a risk-free profit of £11,111.

3 Financial risk management

The stages in the financial risk management process are essentially the same as in any risk management process:

(1) identify risk exposures

(2) quantify exposures

(3) decide whether or not to hedge

(4) implement and monitor hedging program.

Stage 1 and 2 was covered in chapter 3.

Hedge or not ?

Hedging can involve the reduction or elimination of financial risk by passing that risk onto someone else. Or internal hedging techniques involve reducing risk by creating an offsetting position that has a tendency to cancel any risks.

Benefits of hedging

- hedging can provide certainty of cash flows which will assist in the budgeting process

- risk will be reduced, and hence management may be more inclined to undertake investment projects

- reduction in the probability of financial collapse (bankruptcy)

- managers are often risk-averse since their job is at risk. If a company has a policy of hedging it may be perceived as a more attractive employer to risk-averse managers.

Arguments against hedging

- shareholders have diversified their own portfolio, thus further hedging by the business may harm shareholders' interests

- transaction costs associated with hedging can be significant

- lack of expertise within the business, particularly with regards to use of derivative instruments

- complexity of accounting and tax issues associated with the use of derivatives.

Derivatives

A derivative is a financial instrument whose value depends on the price of some other financial asset or underlying factor (such as oil, gold, interest rates or currencies).

The directors of an organisation will decide how to use derivatives to meet their goals and to align with their risk appetite.

Derivatives have the following uses:

- **Hedging**: used as a risk management tool to reduce / eliminate financial risk.

- **Speculation**: used to make a profit from predicting market movements.

- **Arbitrage**: used to exploit price differences between markets. (This will be short-term only. If a commodity appears to be cheap, demand will increase which will push up the price. Hence the price differential, where a gain could be made in the past, has now closed.)

For the purposes of this subject we are interested in the hedging use of derivatives.

Treasury function

The treasury function exists in every business, though in a small business it may be absorbed into the accounting or company secretarial work.

The **main functions** of treasury are:

- managing relationships with the banks – regarding the investment of surplus cash or making arrangements to allow deficits of cash, or to arrange hedging.

- working capital and liquidity management – to ensure that sufficient but not excessive amounts of cash are available on a daily basis to fund inventory, payables and receivables.

- long-term funding management – providing cash for longer term investments such as non-current assets or arranging mortgages / debentures.

- currency management – dealing with all currencies which will entail both internal and external hedging techniques, sourcing currencies, managing foreign currency bank accounts.

More on the treasury function

Organisational structure

The treasurer has the capacity to make large gains or losses in a short period of time, particularly when trading in financial derivatives. As a result it is important to define and carefully monitor the responsibility and authority associated with treasury.

There are a number of differing structures for the treasury activity within a business. The two key debates are discussed below.

Profit centre or cost centre

Should the treasury activities be accounted for simply as a cost centre, or as a profit centre in its own right (making profit out of trading activities)?

Advantages of operating as a profit centre, as opposed to cost centre include:

- a market rate is charged to business units throughout the entity, making operating costs realistic

- the treasurer is motivated to provide services as efficiently and economically as possible.

The main disadvantages are:

- the profit concept brings the temptation to speculate and take excessive risk

- management time can be wasted on discussions about internal charges for the treasury activities

- additional administrative costs will be incurred.

Centralised or decentralised

Many large companies operate a centralised treasury function, which has merits and limitations.

Risks associated with centralised treasury include:

- a lack of motivation towards managing cash in the subsidiaries, since any cash that is received is swept up to head office to be managed from the group's perspective.

- the risk that, should head office commit some error in their treasury operations, the financial health of the whole group could be placed in jeopardy.

Risks associated with decentralised activity are:

- that one company might pay large overdraft interest costs, while another has cash balances in hand earning low interest rates

- the risk of not generating the profits for the group that would be earned if the group funds were actively managed by a treasury operation seeking profits rather than individual executives just seeking to minimise costs.

Corporate treasury policies

Marks and Spencer

Marks and Spencer 'operates a centralised treasury function to manage the Group's funding requirements and financial risks in line with the Board approved treasury policies and procedures, and delegated authorities. … Group Treasury also enters into derivative transactions, principally interest rate and currency swaps and forward currency contracts. The purpose of these transactions is to manage the interest-rate and currency risks arising from the Group's operations and financing. It remains Group policy not to hold or issue financial instruments for trading purposes, except where financial constraints necessitate the need to liquidate any outstanding investments. The treasury function is managed as a cost centre and does not engage in speculative trading. The principal risks faced by the Group are liquidity/funding, interest rate, foreign currency risks and counterparty risks.

(a) **Liquidity/funding risk**

The risk that the Group could be unable to settle or meet its obligations as they fall due at a reasonable price.

The Group's funding strategy ensures a mix of funding sources offering flexibility and cost effectiveness to match the requirements.

(b) **Counterparty risk**

Counterparty risk exists where the Group can suffer financial loss through default or non-performance by financial institutions.

Exposures are managed through Group treasury policy which limits the value that can be placed with each approved counterparty to minimise the risk of loss. The counterparties are limited to the approved institutions with secure long-term credit ratings A+/A1 or better assigned by Moody's and Standard & Poor's respectively, unless approved on an exception basis by a Board director. Limits are reviewed regularly by senior management.

(c) **Foreign currency risk**

Transactional foreign currency exposures arise from both the export of goods from the UK to overseas subsidiaries, and from the import of materials and goods directly sourced from overseas suppliers.

Group treasury hedge these exposures principally using forward foreign exchange contracts progressively covering up to 100% out to 18 months. Where appropriate hedge cover can be taken out longer than 18 months, with Board approval. The Group is primarily exposed to foreign exchange risk in relation to sterling against movements in US dollar and euro.

(d) **Interest rate risk**

The Group is exposed to interest rate risk in relation to the sterling, US dollar, euro and Hong Kong dollar variable rate financial assets and liabilities.

The Group's policy is to use derivative contracts where necessary to maintain a mix of fixed and floating rate borrowings to manage this risk. The structure and maturity of these derivatives correspond to the underlying borrowings and are accounted for as fair value or cash flow hedges as appropriate.

Capital policy

The Group's objectives when managing capital are to safeguard its ability to continue as a going concern in order to provide optimal returns for shareholders and to maintain an efficient capital structure to reduce the cost of capital.

In doing so the Group's strategy is to maintain a capital structure commensurate with an investment grade credit rating and to retain appropriate levels of liquidity headroom to ensure financial stability and flexibility. To achieve this strategy the Group regularly monitors key credit metrics such as the gearing ratio, cash flow to net debt see (note 29) and fixed charge cover to maintain this position. In addition the Group ensures a combination of appropriate committed short-term liquidity headroom with a diverse and smooth long-term debt maturity profile.

During the year the Group maintained an investment grade credit rating of Baa3 (stable) with Moody's and BBB- (stable) with Standard & Poor's, and through the successful tender of £200m of existing short-dated bonds in conjunction with a new £400m 10 year bond issue extended the average fixed debt maturity by one year to ten years and increased short-term liquidity by £200m.

In order to maintain or re-align the capital structure, the Group may adjust the number of dividends paid to shareholders, return capital to shareholders, issue new shares or sell assets to reduce debt.

Marks and Spencer Plc, Annual Report 2010.

4 Currency risk management

There are several methods of managing exposure to currency risk. As a general rule the simplest and most convenient methods are used by any business.

The methods can be split as follows:

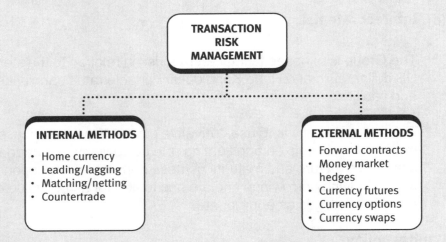

The differences between internal and external hedging can be very significant:

• Internal hedging is often more effective for dealing with economic risk;

• Internal hedging is often cheaper and simpler to understand;

• External hedging is popular with treasury departments because of the excitement of setting up any transactions.

5 Internal hedging

If a company wants to remove transaction risk, it is possible to hedge this internally in a number of ways, including:

• Invoice in home currency.

• Leading and lagging payments.

• Offsetting – matching, netting and pooling.

• Countertrade.

More on internal hedging techniques

Invoice in home currency

If a UK business invoices in pounds and only accepts invoices from suppliers in pounds then it partly removes currency risk. The currency risk is transferred to the customer or supplier. However economic risk is not removed - the value of the business will still fall if the overseas competition are 'winning' with their overseas trade in foreign currencies.

This method does give some very practical business issues:

*   The customers and suppliers may not be prepared to accept all the currency risk and therefore they will not trade with the business.

*   The other parties may not be prepared to accept the same prices and will require discounts on sales or premiums on purchases.

*   There are other ways of hedging risks that mean that the risk of transacting in foreign currency is acceptable.

Leading and lagging

This is a method of trying to makes gains on foreign currency payments.

Leading is making a payment before it is due, and lagging is delaying a payment for as long as possible. This is effective if the company has a strong view about the future movements in the exchange rate.

For example, a company has to make a $100,000 payment to a US supplier. The payment is due in two months' time but could be paid immediately or delayed until three months' time. Sterling is expected to depreciate in value against the dollar over the next three months. In this case the company would want to pay as early as possible and therefore lead. To check this, consider that if the rate went from $:£ 2.0000 to $:£ 1.5000, the payment in £ would go from £50,000 to £66,667. The company would obviously want to only pay £50,000.

Problems with leading and lagging include:

*   Early payment will cost a company in interest foregone on the funds that have been disbursed early;

- The payee will not be happy that payment may become overdue, especially if the currency is expected to fall;

- It requires the company to take a view on exchange rates i.e. speculate. There is a risk that the company will be wrong.

Offsetting

Matching

This technique involves matching assets and liabilities in the same currency. Financing a foreign investment with a foreign loan would reduce the exposure to exchange risk since as the rate changes favourably on one it would move adversely on the other.

Netting

Netting normally involves the use of foreign currency bank accounts. If a company knows it will be both receiving and paying in foreign currency, it can reduce exchange risk by using the foreign receipts to cover the foreign payments. The netting will work best if the dates of the receipt and payment are as near together as possible.

In a group, netting can be done across the group by a treasury function. This would mean that if one subsidiary is making foreign payments and another subsidiary is taking foreign receipts, the group can net the two off.

Pooling

Pooling is a system of managing cash. When a business has several bank accounts in the same currency, it might be able to arrange a system with its bank(s) whereby the balances on each bank account in the same currency are swept up into a central account at the end of each day, leaving a zero balance on every account except the central account. Overdraft balances and positive cash balances are all swept up into the central account maximising interest earned and minimising any bank charges or interest payable.

This does not provide a system for hedging against FX risk, but can be an efficient system for cash management. It avoids overdraft costs on individual bank accounts, and it enables the treasury department to make more efficient use of any cash surpluses.

For an efficient system of cash pooling, there needs to be a centralised cash management system. The current organisation allows each subsidiary to operate their own cash management system. Pooling can be organised by each subsidiary. However, it might be even more efficient if subsidiaries operating in the same currencies shared the same pooling system, hence it is best operated by a central treasury function.

Countertrade

This involves parties exchanging goods and services of equivalent value. It is the old fashioned bartering and avoids any type of currency exchanges. However the tax authorities do not like this method – if cash does not change hands it is difficult to establish the value of the transaction and any related sales tax payable. For this reason, countertrade is not very common since it can lead to disputes with the tax authorities and take up management time.

Matching

A company wishes to fund a $1m investment and uses a $1m loan. The exchange rate is $1.8:£1 on the date the investment is made, but sterling strengthens to $2:£1 six months later.

The company has matched its assets and liabilities:

Investment (asset)

At acquisition ($1m / 1.8) = £555.6k

Six months later ($1m / 2) = £500k

Loan (liability)

At acquisition ($1m / 1.8) = £555.6k

Six months later ($1m /2) = £500k

Whether at acquisition or six months later, the asset and the loan are worth the same as each other.

Netting

Division A is due to receive $1m on Friday. Division B has a payable of $700,000 due on the same day.

Because the receipt is at the same time as the payment, the company should use the receipt of $1m to pay their supplier $700,000. This would minimise any transaction costs arising from buying $700,000 from the bank.

The $300,000 left could be kept in a $ bank account for later $ payments, saving on further transaction costs in later months, or it could be converted into the home currency (now, or at some time in the future when rates are more favourable).

6 External hedging

If a company wants to remove transaction risk it is also possible to hedge this externally in a number of ways including:

- Netting centres;
- Forward contracts;
- Money market hedges;
- Futures;
- Options;
- Swaps.

7 Netting centres

Multilateral netting is a treasury management technique used by large companies to manage their intercompany payment processes, usually involving many currencies. Netting can yield significant savings from reduced foreign exchange trading.

A netting centre collates batches of cashflows between a defined set of companies and offsets them against each other so that just a single cashflow to or from each company takes place to settle the net result of all cashflows.

The netting process takes place on a cyclical basis, typically monthly, and is managed by a central entity called the netting centre.

Although netting centres are occasionally used to net off cashflows in just one currency, it is more usual for a netting centre to manage cashflows in several currencies. In a multiple currency netting system, each company's cashflows are converted to an equivalent amount in the company's base currency, so that the company still has only a single net position to settle in that currency.

A netting centre is typically used by a multinational company that has many production and sales divisions in a number of countries. Direct billing in many currencies by each company can lead to excessive foreign exchange trading, in which individual companies may be both buying and selling the same currencies many times over. The objective of using a netting centre is to reduce the overall foreign exchange volume traded and thereby cut the amount of foreign exchange spread paid by the company to manage all the currency conversions.

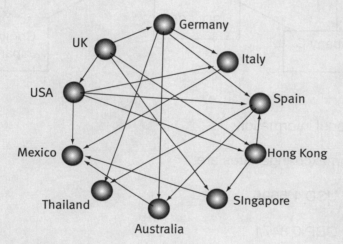

Without netting, each company settles its receipts and payments directly and individually with each of the other companies.

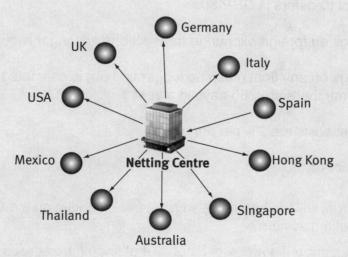

After using a netting centre, each company pays or receives a single local currency balance to or from the netting centre.

Netting centres

A group of companies have the following inter-company cash flows for the next month:

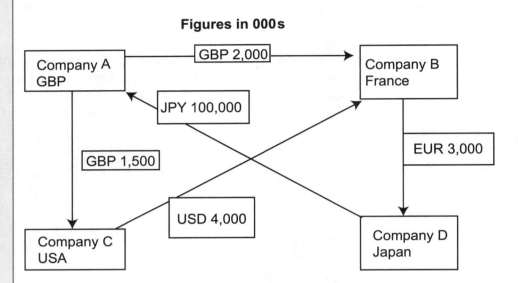

Figures in 000s

Additional information:

Foreign exchange rates are:

GBP / USD 1.5695

EUR / GBP 0.8471

GBP / JPY 125.81

Cost of transfers is GBP 30.

Savings on foreign exchange transactions no longer required is 1%.

Savings on any float (cash no longer tied up) is estimated at 3 days. (Assume there are 365 days in a year.)

Interest costs are 2% per annum.

Required:

(a) What will the annual savings be from introducing a multilateral netting system?

(b) Describe the areas of a policy that should be agreed on before introducing a multilateral netting system.

Solution

(a) **Step 1: Translate all receipts and payments into the base (home) currency – in this case GBP**

France (€) : €3,000,000 × 0.8471 = £2,541,300

US ($) : $4,000,000 / 1.5695 = £2,548,582

Japan (Y) : Y100,000,000 / 125.81 = £794,849

Step 2: Tabulate individual company receipts and payments in GBP

	A	B	C	D	Total
	GBP	EUR	USD	JPY	
A				794,849	794,849
B	2,000,000		2,548,582		4,548,582
C	1,500,000				1,500,000
D		2,541,300			2,541,300
	3,500,000	2,541,300	2,548,582	794,849	9,384,731

Step 3: Tabulate net payments/receipts and any cashflows eliminated

	Pays	Receives	Net (paid)/received	Flows eliminated
A	(3,500,000)	794,849	(2,705,151)	794,849
B	(2,541,300)	4,548,582	2,007,282	2,541,300
C	(2,548,582)	1,500,000	(1,048,582)	1,500,000
D	(794,849)	2,541,300	1,746,451	794,849
	(9,384,731)	9,384,731	0	5,630,998

Step 4: Calculate any savings

Payments / receipts reduce from 5 to 4 saving: £30.00

The float of £9,384,731 saves 2% interest that would otherwise be lost, for 3 days (time saving):

£9,384,731 × 2% × 3/365 days = £1,542.70

Reduction in foreign exchange conversions:

£5,630,998 × 1% = £56,309.98

Total monthly saving = £30.00 + £1,542.70 + £56,309.98 = £57,882.68

Annual saving = £694,592.16

(b) For netting to be successful participants must agree on a number of issues such as:

- Currencies – Which currencies will be used for invoicing? They may be the buyer's, the seller's or a third currency.

- Credit period – Ideally all participants should have the same credit periods but there may be variations for those participants who are long or short of funds.

- Settlement dates – The netting settlement dates and the netting cycle timetable must be known by all the participants and adhered to. Netting periods must also be decided e.g. weekly, monthly etc.

- Exchange rates – The exchange rates to be used in the netting must be agreed. Will it be spot or forward rates, mid at 11-00 am or some budgeted in-house rate? Rates should be 'arms length' as there would be potential tax issues otherwise.

- Conflict resolution – Multilateral netting may be payment driven, receivables driven or both. Either way disagreements will arise as to who owes what to whom so a process for sorting these issues out so that the items may be included in the netting will need to be in place. If not resolved then items may have to be pulled from the netting process.

- Management – will it be a bespoke system or bank managed.

8 Currency forward contracts

A forward contract is an agreement to buy or sell a specific amount of foreign currency at a given future date using an agreed forward rate.

This is the most popular method of hedging exchange rate risk. The company is able to fix in advance an exchange rate at which a transaction will be made.

The risk is taken by the bank who are better able to manage their exposure. A proportion of their exposure will normally be avoided by writing forward contracts for opposite trades on the same day.

Illustration of currency forward contract

It is now 1 January and Y plc will receive US$10 million on 30 April.

It enters into a forward exchange contract to sell this amount on the forward date at a rate of £1/US$1.6000. On 30 April the company is guaranteed £6.25 million (US$10 million / 1.6000).

The transaction risk has been removed (if the receipt arrives on time).

Features and operation

Forward contracts are a commitment, and as a result they have to be honoured even if the rate in the contract is worse than the rate in the market.

Forward contract rates are often quoted at a **premium** or **discount** to the current spot rate.

- A discount means that the currency being quoted (the dollar) is expected to fall in value in relation to the other currency (sterling). If a currency falls in value then you need more of that currency to buy a single unit of the other, i.e. we need more dollars to buy a single pound.

- A discount is often to referred to as 'dis', a premium as 'prem'.

- These can be quoted in cents (i.e. US$0.01) and shown as 'c' in the quote.

In most exam questions you can use the following rule for obtaining a forward rate from the spot rate:

- add a forward discount to the spot rate ('**add:dis**')

- subtract a forward premium from the spot rate.

(**Note:** This rule is only applicable where the exchange rate is quoted as 'amount of foreign currency to a home currency unit'.)

(Also note that discounts and premiums derive from the interest rate parity formula, in theory.)

Remember that you will need to be aware of whether the premium or discount is quoted in, say, dollars or cents. It would usually be cents. There are 100 cents in a dollar. (Similarly there are 100 cents in a euro.) This affects how you add or deduct the discount or premium in terms of decimal places.

For example, if the dollar was currently 1.5000 and there was a premium of 0.5 c (c means cents, and there are 100 cents in a dollar so this is half a cent) this makes the forward rate 1.4950 (1.5000 − 0.0050).

Test your understanding 6 – Forward contract

Calculate the forward contract bid and offer prices in the following situation:

(i)	The current spot rate is	£1=US$1.5500 − 1.4500
	and, one month forward rate is quoted at	0.55 − 0.50 cdis
(ii)	The current spot rate is	£1=€1.7150 − 1.6450
	and, one month forward rate is quoted at	0.68 − 0.75 cpm

Test your understanding 7 – EEFS

EEFS Ltd (a UK company) sold goods to the value of US$2.0 million. Receipt is due in 90 days.

The current spot rate is £1 = US 1.5430 − 1.5150.

There is a three-month discount forward of 2.5 cents − 1.5 cents.

Required:

Calculate the amount of sterling that EEFS Ltd will receive under the forward contract.

Advantages and disadvantages

The advantages of forward contracts are that they:

- Are simple, and so have low transaction costs;
- Can be purchased from a high street bank;
- Fix the exchange rate;
- Are tailored, so are flexible to amount and delivery period.

The disadvantages are that there is:

- A potential credit risk since the company is contractually bound to sell a currency, which it may not have received from its customer;
- No upside potential.

More on disadvantages of forward contracts

There are two key disadvantages of forward contracts:

It is a **contractual commitment** which must be completed on the due date.

This means that if a payment from the overseas customer is late, the company receiving the payment and wishing to convert it using its forward exchange contract will have a problem. The existing forward exchange contract must be settled, although the bank will arrange a new forward exchange contract for the new date when the currency cash flow is due.

To help overcome this problem an '**option date' forward exchange contract** can be arranged. This is a forward exchange contract that allows the company to settle a forward contract at an agreed fixed rate of exchange, but at any time between two specified dates. If the currency cash flow occurs between these two dates, the forward exchange contract can be settled at the agreed fixed rate.

It is **inflexible.** It eliminates the downside risk of an adverse movement in the spot rate, but also prevents any participation in upside potential of any favourable movement in the spot rate. Whatever happens to the actual exchange rate, the forward contract must be honoured, even if it would be beneficial to exchange currencies at the spot rate prevailing at that time.

9 Money market hedges (MMH)

The money markets are markets for wholesale (large-scale) lending and borrowing, or trading in short-term financial instruments. Many companies are able to borrow or deposit funds through their bank in the money markets.

Instead of hedging a currency exposure with a forward contract, a company could use the money markets to lend or borrow, and achieve a similar result.

Since forward exchange rates are derived from spot rates and money market interest rates (see IRPT earlier in this chapter), the end result from hedging should be roughly the same by either method.

Features and operation

The basic idea of an MMH is to create assets and liabilities that 'mirror' the future assets and liabilities.

Rule: The money required for the transaction is exchanged at today's spot rate, and is then deposited / borrowed on the money market to accrue to the amount required for the transaction in the future.

Note: Interest rates are used for the depositing / borrowing. The rates are usually quoted per annum. If you require a six monthly rate then you simply divide by 2. If you require a quarterly rate, then divide by 4.

Money market interest rates

Money market interest rates are available for any length of borrowing or deposit period, up to about one year. Banks quote rates for standard periods, such as overnight, one week, one month, three months, six months and one year.

Two rates are quoted:

- The **higher** rate is the interest rate that the bank will **charge on loans**.

- The **lower** rate is the interest rate that the bank will **pay on deposits**.

All rates are quoted on an annual basis.

Example

A London bank quotes the following interest rates on US dollars:

1 month

US$ LIBOR   3¼ – 3 ⅛

In the above example, suppose that a company wanted to borrow US dollars for one month. The bank would charge 3¼% per annum.

For the purpose of your examination, you can assume that the rate for one month is one-twelfth of the rate for one year; therefore in this example, the actual interest for one month would be 3¼%/12 = 0.270833%. If the company borrowed, say, US$1 million for one month, it would repay the loan plus interest of US$2,708.33 at the end of the loan period.

Characteristics

- The basic idea is to avoid future exchange rate uncertainty by making the exchange at today's spot rate instead.

- This is achieved by depositing/borrowing the foreign currency until the actual commercial transaction cash flows occur:

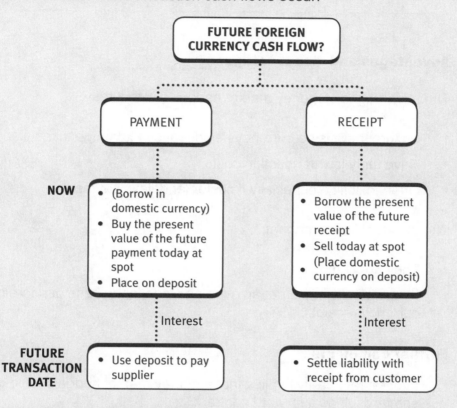

Test your understanding 8 – DD Ltd (1)

DD Ltd (a UK company) is required to make a payment of €1.3 million in six months' time. The company treasurer has established the following rates going forward:

Spot rate	£1 = €1.5095 – 1.5050
Six month	£1 = €1.5162 – 1.4895

Money market rates (pa):

	Loan	Deposit
Euro	4.0%	2.5%
Sterling	4.6%	3.1%

Required:

(a) What is the cost of using a money market hedge?

(b) What is the cost of using a forward contract hedge?

Test your understanding 9 – DD Ltd (2)

Re-perform the forward contract and MMH assuming the business will receive €1.3 million in six months' time.

Advantages and disadvantages

The advantages of money market hedges are that they:

- Ensure there is no currency risk because exchange takes place today.

- Have fairly low transaction costs.

- Offer flexibility (especially if customer delays payment).

The disadvantages are that:

- They are complex.

- It may be difficult to get an overseas loan in the case of a foreign currency receipt.

Further comments

- Interest rate parity implies that a money market hedge should give the same result as a forward contract.

- This approach has obvious cash flow implications which may prevent a company from using this method, e.g. if a company has a considerable overdraft it may be impossible for it to borrow funds now.

Test your understanding 10 – Marcus

Marcus, based in France, has recently imported raw materials from the USA and has been invoiced for US$240,000, payable in three months' time.

In addition, it has also exported finished goods to Japan and Australia.

The Japanese customer has been invoiced for US$69,000, payable in three months' time, and the Australian customer has been invoiced for A$295,000, payable in four months' time.

Current spot and forward rates are as follows:

€1/US$

Spot:	0.9850 – 0.9830
Three months' forward:	0.9545 – 0.9520

A$1/ €

Spot:	1.8920 – 1.8890
Four months' forward:	1.9540 – 1.9510

Current money market rates (per annum) are as follows:

US$:	10.0% – 12.0%
A$:	14.0% – 16.0%
Euro:	11.5% – 13.0%

Required:

Show how the company can hedge its exposure to FX risk using:

(i)   the forward markets;

(ii) the money markets;

and in each case, determine which is the best hedging technique.

10 Currency futures

In essence this form of hedging is very similar to the use of a forward contract. The critical difference is that, whereas using a forward contract requires the preparation of a special financial instrument 'tailor-made' for the transaction, currency futures are standardised contracts for fixed amounts of money for a limited range of future dates.

Features and operation

Futures are derivatives contracts and as such can be traded on futures exchanges. The contract which guarantees the price (known as the futures contract) is separated from the transaction itself, allowing the contracts to be easily traded.

Denomination

Futures contracts are limited to a small range of currencies and are typically denominated in terms of dollars (US$). There are also markets in euro (€) denominated futures contracts but this is relatively new and much less common.

Given US$ denominated currency futures, we would simply know them in terms of the other currency, i.e. the £1/US$ future will be known as £ contracts or €1/US$ futures are known as € contracts.

Futures are standardised contracts for standardised amounts. For example, the Chicago Mercantile Exchange (CME) trades sterling futures contracts with a standard size of £62,500. Only whole number multiples of this amount can be bought or sold hence they rarely cover the exact foreign currency exposure.

Process

There is a three step process which can be followed to answer a futures question:

Step 1: Set up

Set up the hedge by addressing 3 key questions:

- Do we initially buy or sell futures?

To decide whether to buy or sell futures, the simplest way is to follow this rule: identify the currency of the futures contract (e.g. £) and then do the same to the futures that you intend to do to that currency (e.g. buy or sell).

- Which expiry date should be chosen?

Settlement takes place in three-monthly cycles (March, June, September or December). It is normal to choose the first contract to expiry after the required conversion date.

- How many contracts?

Step 2: Contact exchange

Pay the initial margin. Then wait until the transaction / settlement date.

Margin: The futures exchange requires all buyers and sellers of futures to pay a deposit to the exchange when they buy or sell. This deposit is called an initial margin. This margin is returned when the position is closed out.

Step 3: Closing out

At the end of the contract's term the position is *closed out*. This means that on expiry of the contract the trading position is automatically reversed. Any profit or loss is computed and cleared, and the underlying commodity is retained by the trader.

The margin is refunded by the exchange.

The value of the transaction is calculated using the spot rate on the transaction date.

Concept

In essence we are hedging or speculating on the movement of the exchange rate on the futures market.

More on futures contracts

When a futures contact is bought or sold, the buyer or seller must deposit an **initial margin** with the exchange. If losses are incurred, the buyer or seller may be called on to deposit additional funds (**variation margin**) with the exchange. Equally, profits are credited to the margin account on a daily basis as the contract is 'marked to market'.

Most futures contracts are closed out before their settlement dates by undertaking the opposite transaction to the initial futures transaction, i.e. if buying currency futures was the initial transaction, it is closed out by selling currency futures.

Effectively a future works like a bet. If a company expects a US$ receipt in 3 month's time, it will lose out if the US$ depreciates relative to sterling. Using a futures contract, the company 'bets' that the US$ will depreciate. If it does, the win on the bet cancels out the loss on the transaction. If the US$ strengthens, the gain on the transaction covers the loss on the bet.

Ultimately futures ensure a virtual no win/no loss position.

Futures calculation illustration

It is 15 October and a treasurer has identified the need to convert euros into dollars to pay a US supplier US$12 million on 20 November. The treasurer has decided to use December euro futures contracts to hedge with the following details:

- Contract size €200,000.

- Prices given in US$ per euro (i.e. €1 = ...).

- Tick size US$0.0001 or US$20 per contract.

He opens a position on 15 October and closes it on 20 November. Spot and relevant futures prices are as follows:

Date	Spot	Futures price
15 October	1.3300	1.3350
20 November	1.3190	1.3240

Calculate the financial position using the hedge described.

Solution

Step 1	(1) Buy or sell initially?	(1) We need to sell € (to buy US$), so sell futures now.
	(2) Which expiry date?	(2) Transaction date is 20 November, so choose December futures (the first to expire after the transaction date).
	(3) How many contracts?	(3) Cover US$12m/1.3350 = €8.99 million, using €200,000 contracts, hence €8.99m / €0.2m = 44.9 – round to 45 contracts.
Step 2	Contact the exchange – state the hedge	Sell 45 December futures (at a futures price of €1/US$1.3350)

| Step 3 | Calculate profit/loss in futures market by closing out the position. | Initially: Sell at 1.3350

 Close out: Buy at 1.3240

 Difference is US$0.011 per €1 profit

 45 × €200,000 covered, so total profit is 0.011 × 45 × 200,000 = US$99,000 |
| Step 3 continued | Transaction at spot rate on 20 November:

 Need to pay US$12m less profit = US$11.901m, needed at spot rate of €1/US$1.3190 | Cost in € is €9,097,801 |

Ticks

A tick is the minimum price movement for a futures contract. Take for example a sterling futures contract for a standard amount of £62,500 in sterling. The contracts are priced at the exchange rate, in US dollars, and the tick size (minimum price movement) is US$0.0001.

If the price of a sterling futures contract changes from, say, US$1.7105 to US$1.7120, the price has risen US$0.0015 or 15 ticks.

The significance of a tick for futures trading is that every one tick movement in price has the same money value.

Take for example a sterling futures contract for a standard amount of £62,500: every movement in the price of the contract by one tick is worth US$6.25, which is £62,500 at US$0.0001 per £1.

Basis and basis risk

The current futures price is usually different from the current 'cash market' price of the underlying item. In the case of currency futures, the current market price of a currency future and the current spot rate will be different, and will only start to converge when the final settlement date for the futures contract approaches. This difference is known as the **'basis'**.

At final settlement date for the contract (in March, June, September or December) the futures price and the market price of the underlying item ought to be the same; otherwise speculators would be able to make an instant profit by trading between the futures market and the spot 'cash' market.

Most futures positions are closed out before the contract reaches final settlement. When this happens, there will inevitably be a difference between the futures price at close-out and the current spot market price of the underlying item. In other words, there will still be some basis.

Because basis exists, an estimate can be made when a hedge is created with futures about what the size of the basis will be when the futures position is closed.

Example

In February, a UK company wishes to hedge a currency exposure arising from a US dollar payment that will have to be made in May, in three months' time. The current spot exchange rate is US$1.5670 and the current June futures price is US$1.5530. The basis is therefore 140 points in February.

If it is assumed that the basis will decline from 140 points in February to 0 in June when the contract reaches final settlement (say four months later), we can predict that the basis will fall from 140 in February by 105 points (140 × 3 months/4 months) to 35 points in May, when it is intended to close the futures position.

Basis risk is the risk that when a hedge is constructed, the size of the basis when the futures position is closed out is different from the expectation, when the hedge was created, of what the basis ought to be.

In the example, when the futures position is closed in May, the actual basis might be, say 50 points, which is 15 points higher than expected when the hedge was constructed.

Test your understanding 11 – UK company

A UK company will receive US$2.5 million from an American customer in three months' time in February.

Currently:

Futures: £ contracts (£62,500)   December   £1/US$1.5830

March   £1/US$1.5796

Margins are US$1,000 per contract.

£1/US$ forward rates: Spot   1.5851 – 1.5842

One month   0.53 – 0.56 c pm

Three month   1.64 – 1.72 c pm

28 February:

Assume that the spot rate moves to 1.6510 – 1.6490

March futures have a price of 1.6513

Required:

Calculate the £ receipt using a forward contract and a future.

Test your understanding 12 – X Inc

X Inc imports goods to the US from Y plc in the UK. It pays in Sterling.

X is due to pay £650,000 in 30 days' time and is worried that the £ will strengthen against the US$ making the import more expensive.

Futures contracts are available on the Philadelphia exchange as follows:

Contract	Size
£	£62,500

Futures contract rate £1/US$1.5960
Spot rate is now   £1/US$1.5850

> **Required:**
>
> (a) Illustrate how X Inc would hedge its transaction risk on the futures market.
>
> (b) Comment on the hedge efficiency if, in 30 days' time, the spot rate is £1/US$1.6030 and the futures contract rate is £1/US$1.6120.

Advantages and disadvantages

The advantages of currency futures contracts are that they:

- Offer an effective 'fixing' of exchange rate;
- Have no transaction costs;
- Are tradable.

The disadvantages are that:

- A foreign futures market must be used for UK £ futures;
- They require up front margin payments;
- They are not usually for the precise tailored amounts that are required.

11 Currency options

A currency option is a right, but not an obligation, to buy or sell a currency at an exercise price on a future date.

If there is a favourable movement in rates the company will allow the option to **lapse**, to take advantage of the favourable movement. The right will only be **exercised** to protect against an adverse movement, i.e. the worst-case scenario.

Features and operation

As a result of this, options could look great, BUT they have a cost. Because options limit downside risk but allow the holder to benefit from upside risk, the writer of the option will charge a non-refundable **premium** for writing the option.

It is possible for the holder of the option to calculate the gains and losses on using options:

The gain if the option is exercised: this is the difference between the exercise price (option strike price) and the market price of the underlying item	X
Less: The premium paid to purchase the option	(X)
	X

There are two types of option:

*   A **call** option gives the holder the right to **buy** the underlying currency.
*   A **put** option gives the holder the right to **sell** the underlying currency.

Test your understanding 13 – UK exporter

A UK exporter is due to receive US$25 million in 3 months' time. Its bank offers a 3 month dollar put option on US$25 million at an exercise price of £1/US$1.5000 at a premium cost of £300,000.

Required:

Show the net £ receipt if the future spot is either US$1.6000 or US$1.4000

Illustration of currency options

A typical pricing schedule for the € currency option on the Philadelphia (US) exchange is as follows.

Strike price	CALLS			PUTS		
	Jun	Sept	Dec	Jun	Sept	Dec
115.00	1.99	2.25	2.47	0.64	1.32	2.12
116.00	1.39	2.03	2.28	1.00	1.56	–
117.00	0.87	1.55	1.81	1.43	2.22	–
118.00	0.54	1.08	1.30	–	–	–

*   Here, the options are for a contract size of €125,000 and prices (both strike price and premia) are quoted in US$ (cents) per €1.

- So to buy a call option on €125,000 with an expiry date of September and at a strike price of €1 = US$1.1700 would cost 1.55 cents per euro, or US$1,937.50.

- Similarly, the premium on a June put at a strike price of 115.00 (€1 = US$1.1500) would cost 0.64 cents per euro, or US$800.

The decision as to which exercise price to choose will depend on cost, risk exposure and expectations.

- In the exam it is unlikely that you will be given such a wide range of values – it is more likely to have just one call and one put option price.

Options hedging calculations

Step 1: Set up the hedge by addressing 4 key questions:

- Do we need call or put options?
- Which expiry date should be chosen?
- What is the strike price?
- How many contracts?

Step 2: Contact the exchange. Pay the up-front premium. Then wait until the transaction / settlement date.

Step 3: On the transaction date, compare the option price with the prevailing spot rate to determine whether the option should be exercised or allowed to lapse.

Step 4: Calculate the net cash flows – beware that if the number of contracts needed rounding, there will be some exchange at the prevailing spot rate even if the option is exercised.

In- and out-of the money options

The strike price for an option might be higher or lower than the current market price of the underlying item. For example, a call option might give its holder the right to buy £125,000 in exchange for US dollars at US$1.7900, and the current spot rate could be higher than US$1.7900, below US$1.7900 or possibly US$1.7900 exactly.

- If the exercise price for an option is more favourable to the option holder than the current 'spot' market price, the option is said to be **in-the-money**.

- If the exercise price for an option is less favourable to the option holder than the current 'spot' market price, the option is said to be **out-of-the-money**.

- If the exercise price for the option is exactly the same as the current 'spot' market price, it is said to be **at-the-money**.

An option holder is not obliged to exercise the option, and will never do so if the option is out-of-the-money. **An option will only ever be exercised if it is in-the-money**.

However, when an option is first purchased, or during the period before the expiry date, an option might be out-of-the-money.

Options that start out-of-the-money might become in-the-money if the market price of the underlying item changes. On the other hand, an option that starts out-of-the-money might stay out-of-the-money until expiry, and so will lapse without being exercised.

Test your understanding 14 – Currency options

Philadelphia SE £ Options   **£31,250 (cents per £1)**

Strike	...............Calls...............			...............Puts...............		
Price	Oct	Nov	Dec	Oct	Nov	Dec
1.540	4.40	–	5.12	–	0.37	0.88
1.550	3.40	3.83	4.39	–	0.56	1.16
1.560	2.49	3.09	3.73	–	0.81	1.49
1.570	1.61	2.47	3.12	0.11	1.06	1.88
1.580	0.88	1.88	2.84	0.38	1.47	2.09
1.590	0.68	1.40	2.57	0.88	2.00	2.33

A UK company will receive US$5 million from a US customer in December. The spot rate is £1/US$ 1.5848 – 1.5840 and the UK company is concerned that the US$ might weaken.

Required:

Using the data above show how traded £ currency options can be used.

Assume for the purposes of your illustration that the spot rate moves to either 1.6500 or 1.5000.

Test your understanding 15 – Pongo

Pongo plc is a UK-based import-export company. It has an invoice, which it is due to pay on 30 June, in respect of US$350,000. In addition it is due to receive US$275,000 from a US customer on 30 September.

The company wishes to hedge its exposure to currency risk on both transactions using currency options with an exercise price of US$1.50.

The current £1/US$ spot rate is 1.5230 – 1.5190.

Futures market contract size is £25,000.

Exercise price (£1/US$)	June contracts		September contracts	
	Calls	Puts	Calls	Puts
1.5000	6.80	12.40	8.00	13.40

Option premiums are in cents per pound.

Assume that it is now the 31st March.

Required:

Describe the action that the company will take in respect to both the payment and receipt if the spot rate is:

1.5200 – 1.5240 on the 30 June.

1.5250 – 1.5285 on the 30 September.

In each situation calculate the resultant cash flows.

Advantages and disadvantages

The advantages of currency options are that:

- They offer the perfect hedge (downside risk covered, can participate in upside potential).

- There are many choices of strike price, dates, premiums, etc.

- The option can be allowed to lapse if the future transaction does not arise.

The disadvantages are that:

- Traded sterling currency options are only available in foreign markets.

- There are high up-front premium costs (non-refundable).

The Black-Scholes model

Writers of options have to decide what level of premium to set, and for this they use complex option pricing models. These models are also used to calculate the fair value of an option at any given date (useful for financial reporting purposes).

In the exam you will not be expected to calculate option values, but you are expected to be aware of the factors that affect the option price. The most common option pricing model used is the Black-Scholes model.

The basic principle of the Black-Scholes model is that the market value, or price, of a call option consists of two key elements: Between these two elements there are five variables affecting the price of a call option.

Intrinsic value

This is the difference between the current price of the underlying asset and its option strike (exercise) price. For the market value of a call option to rise, one or both of the following variables must change:

- The intrinsic value of the option.
- The time value of the option.

(1) Current price of the underlying asset must increase.

(2) Strike price must fall (hence making it more likely that the option will be exercised, and so is worth something).

Time value

This reflects the uncertainty surrounding the intrinsic value, and is impacted by three variables:

(1) Standard deviation in the daily value of the underlying asset. The more variability that is demonstrated, the higher the chance that the option will be 'in the money' and so will be exercised.

(2) Time period to expiry of the option. A longer time period will increase the likelihood that the asset value increases and so the option is exercised.

(3) Risk free interest rates. Having a call option means that the purchase can be deferred, so owning a call option becomes more valuable when interest rates are high, since the money left in the bank will be generating a higher return.

Limitations of the Black-Scholes model

The basic form of the Black-Scholes model has been illustrated above. It is widely used by traders in option markets to give an estimate of option values, and more expensive scientific calculators include the model in their functions so that the calculations can be carried out very quickly.

However, the model in its basic form does suffer from a number of limitations:

- It assumes that the risk-free interest rate is known and is constant throughout the option's life.

- The standard deviation of returns from the underlying security must be accurately estimated and has to be constant throughout the option's life. In practice standard deviation will vary depending on the period over which it is calculated; unfortunately the model is very sensitive to its value.

- It assumes that there are no transaction costs or tax effects involved in buying or selling the option or the underlying item.

Certain of these limitations can be removed by more sophisticated versions of the model, but the basic model is complicated enough for the purposes of this text.

The discussion of the value of options does not just relate to currency options but is relevant to interest rate options and other assets or liabilities.

For example, a company may wish to purchase an option to buy a factory which is under construction. The company might pay a premium to the builder of the factory which entitles them to first option to buy the completed factory (not a commitment to buy). If in the following months the council, say, change the planning guidelines and no further developments can be constructed, then the option becomes very valuable if another company then wishes to build a factory in the same location because it could be sold on (subject to the builder's agreement) at a profit.

12 Currency swaps

A currency swap allows the two counterparties to swap different currencies.

A bank will usually set up the swap by identifying the potential swap partners and helping to set the terms of any legal agreement between the two parties. The bank will charge both companies a commission for doing this. From the company's point of view, the bank will probably know the potential swap partners credibility and therefore there should be less risk of default by one of the companies.

Test your understanding 16 – No hedging

Assume that you are the treasurer of a medium-sized manufacturing company which trades throughout Europe. At a recent meeting to discuss the company's policy on foreign exchange management, the managing director, a non-accountant, makes the following statements:

Statement 1. 'Translation risk is concerned only with the effect of exchange rate changes on financial statements and is mainly an accounting issue. There is no need to hedge this risk unless we are close to our foreign currency borrowing limits.'

Statement 2. 'Transaction risk can easily be hedged using the forward market although I am inclined either not to hedge at all or to use internal hedging methods as they are cheaper.'

Required:

(i)   In respect of statement 1, explain what the MD means when he says that there is no need to hedge unless the company is close to its foreign currency borrowing limits.

(ii) In respect of statement 2, comment on whether the MD is right to consider not hedging as an appropriate strategy, and discuss, briefly, three internal hedging techniques which the company could consider.

Test your understanding 17 – Arbitrage

A speculator can buy US$2 for £1, sell one euro for £0.80 and can sell dollars for US$1.50 / E1. There is £1,000,000 available to invest for the purpose of making a profit.

Required:

Calculate the possible profit using arbitrage opportunities.

Test your understanding 18 – IRPT

A dealer working for a major commercial bank which deals in international currencies finds the following quotations for US dollars to Swiss francs:

Spot $0.8313/SF1
Six months forward $0.8447/SF1

The annualised 6-month dollar interest rate is 5.33% and the annualised 6-month Swiss franc rate is 2.4%.

Interest rates are annualised by semi- (half-yearly) compounding.

The dealer is authorised to buy or sell up to US$5 million, or its equivalent in other currencies. Other relevant information is as follows:

Transaction costs for dealing in hard currencies are US$2,750 per transaction, paid at the end of the 6-month period.

The final profits, if any, are held in sterling.

Borrowing and lending can be done at the rates given above.

The current exchange rate for US$ to sterling is 2.00.

Required:

(a) Explain the term 'arbitrage profits' and discuss the reasons why such profits might be available in the scenario given above.

(b) Describe, with the aid of suitable calculations, the actions necessary for the dealer to take advantage of such possibilities.

Test your understanding 19 – NPV

PG plc is considering investing in a new project in Canada which will have a life of 3 years. The initial investment is C$150,000, including working capital. The net after-tax cash flows which the project will generate are C$75,000 per annum for year 1, 2 and 3. The scrap value of the project is estimated at C$50,000, net of tax.

The current spot rate for C$ against sterling is 1.7. Economic forecasters expect sterling to strengthen against the Canadian dollar by 5 per cent per annum over the next 3 years.

The company evaluates UK projects of similar risk at 14%.

Required:

(a) Calculate the NPV of the Canadian project using the following two methods:
  (i) convert the currency cash flows into sterling and discount the sterling cash flows at a sterling discount rate;
  (ii) discount the cash flows in C$ using an adjusted discount rate which incorporates the 12-month forecast spot rate;

and explain briefly the theories and/or assumptions which underlie the use of the adjusted discount rate approach in point (ii).

(b) The company had originally planned to finance the project with internal funds generated in the United Kingdom. However, the finance director has suggested that there would be advantages in raising debt finance in Canada.

You are required to discuss the advantages and disadvantages of matching investment and borrowing overseas as compared with UK-sourced debt or equity.

Wherever possible, relate your answer to the details given in this question for PG plc.

Test your understanding 20 – Netting, matching and pooling

BNM International is a multinational company, based in the UK, with subsidiaries operating in 14 different countries and 8 different currencies. There is a substantial amount of decentralisation of authority within the group and subsidiaries are treated as investment centres, for management reporting purposes. Each subsidiary operates its own cash management systems, although if additional capital is required, the subsidiary must apply to the central treasury unit in the Netherlands. This treasury unit is responsible for raising new capital for the group as a whole and for managing the group's debt.

In the past few months, there has been an increase in the volatility of exchange rates, and subsidiaries are reporting significant gains or losses on foreign exchange transactions. At a recent meeting of the finance committee, it was suggested that the foreign exchange risk needed to be kept under control, and that techniques such as netting, pooling and matching would help to reduce the risk.

A dissenting view at the meeting was that since exchange rates fluctuate up and down, gains and losses usually cancel each other out: the FX risk was therefore immaterial.

Required:

(a) Explain the factors that a group such as BNM International might take into consideration when deciding whether it should control its foreign exchange risks.

(b) Describe the following techniques:

    (i)   netting;

    (ii) matching;

    (iii) pooling.

    Advise the management of BNM as to whether any of these techniques would be appropriate for hedging foreign exchange risk.

(c) Recommend other methods that the group might use to manage its foreign exchange risk, if the board of directors has already decided on a policy of avoiding the use of financial derivatives for foreign exchange risk management.

(d) Discuss why the group might use a central treasury department to raise capital for the group, instead of delegating the responsibility for raising their own capital to the individual subsidiaries.

Test your understanding 21 – H plc (2)

H plc (a UK company) expects to make the following transactions in six months' time:

- US$100,000 purchases from US suppliers.

- US$20,000 sales to US customers.

- €50,000 sales to French customers.

Current exchange rates are as follows, but the company expects the pound to strengthen against the dollar by 5% and against the euro by 3% in the next year:

Dollar rate: US$1/£0.5556
Euro rate: €1/£0.6711

Required:

Calculate the potential gain or loss H plc would make, assuming the company's predictions are correct.

Test your understanding 22 – Gymbob (1)

Gymbob plc is a national chain of gyms listed on the UK Stock Market. It was set up nearly twenty years ago, and has 40 branches nationwide each having essentially the same facilities – a dry side including a gym with running machines, cross trainers, rowing machines and weights, and a wet side including a swimming pool, sauna, spa pool, and steam room. There are daily classes for both the wet and dry side activities, held by various full-time and freelance instructors.

Much of the equipment in the gym area is starting to look outdated and, with the advent of many newer competitors, the management feel there needs to be significant investment. It is now early January, and a deal has been struck with a US supplier to replace many of the running and rowing machines across all 40 gyms. It will cost around $3 million, and payment is to be made in dollars in three months' time. Information gathered in respect of exchange rates and interest rates is detailed below:

Exchange rates today $/£1:
Spot 1.8023 – 1.8188
One month forward 2.1–2.4 c pm
Three months' forward 2.3–2.5 c pm

Interest rates (annual):
£ 4.25% – 3.75%
$ 3.25% – 2.75%

Sterling currency futures are trading at 1.8100. Each futures contract is for £62,500.

Required:

Calculate the £ payment that Gymbob will expect to pay in 3 months if it:

(a) hedges the risk using the forward market;

(b) hedges the risk using the money market;

(c) hedges the risk using currency futures, assuming the market price for March futures in March is 1.8000 and the spot rate is 1.7900.

Test your understanding 23 – Martha Inc.

Martha Inc is a US-based company importing German sausage for sale in its speciality delicatessens throughout the USA. It is September now and Martha Inc needs to make a payment of €9,000,000 in three months' time for a large quantity of sausages they imported over the last three months.

Currently the exchange rate is 0.825 – 0.875 €/$. The three month Euro interest rate is 8 – 10% per annum, and the US interest rate is 7 – 9% per annum.

Required:

(a) Explain the exchange rate risks facing the US importer.

(b) Show how this risk may be hedged using a money market hedge, and calculate the cost of the imported goods in dollars to the US importer if the money market hedge is used.

(c) Explain how the exchange rate risk may be hedged using December Euro futures, the current price is $ 1.25/€. The contract size for the Euro futures is €250,000. Assume that the spot rate and the futures market rate for $/€ are the same in December. Calculate the effective cost to the US company in dollars if the spot rate at the time of payment in December is: (i) $ 1.23 /€, (ii) $ 1.27 /€.

(d) Explain the problems faced when hedging with currency futures.

Test your understanding 24 – Options

Required:

(a) Explain the five input variables involved in the Black-Scholes pricing model and discuss how a decrease in the value of each of these variables is likely to change the price of a call option.

PS is a medium-sized UK-based company that trades mainly in the United Kingdom and the United States. In the past, PS has not hedged its currency risks but movements in the exchange rate have recently become more volatile. Assume it is now 30 September. The company expects net cash inflow in US dollars (sales receipts less purchases) on 31 December, that is US$2,350,000.

The current quoted spot rate of exchange is US$1.4180–1.4220 to the £1.

The US$ discount on the 3-month forward rate of exchange is 0.36–0.46 cents.

Option prices (**cents per pound**, payable on purchase of the option, contract size £31,250):

September contracts:

Exercise price $	Calls	Puts
1.41	2.28	1.69
1.42	1.77	2.19
1.43	1.36	2.68

Assume there are three months from now to the expiry of the September contracts.

The company is risk averse and plans to hedge the risk using either a fixed forward contract or a European currency option. Ignore transaction costs.

Required:

(b) Recommend, with reasons, the most appropriate methods for PS to use to hedge its foreign exchange risk for the next three months. Your answer should include appropriate calculations to support your recommendation.

13 Chapter summary

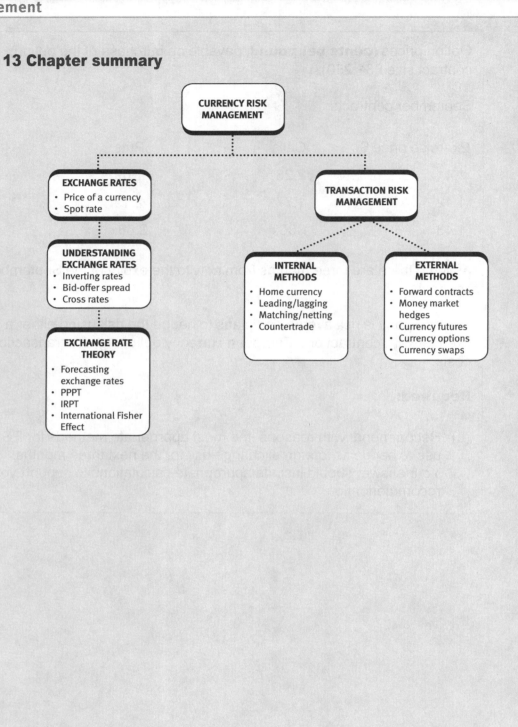

Test your understanding answers

Test your understanding 1 – Spread

(a) A Ltd will need to sell £ and buy US$ and therefore the bank is buying £ and selling US$. The bank always buys £ low and sells £ high and therefore the rate is £1/US$1.4500.

Cost is therefore US$100,000 ÷ 1.4500 = £68,966.

(b) B plc is receiving US$ and therefore the bank will buy US$ and sell £. The rate is therefore £1/US$1.5500.

Receipt is therefore US$50,000 ÷ 1.5500 = £32,258.

(c) C Ltd is importing goods and therefore needs to sell £ and the bank needs to buy £. The rate is therefore £1/US$1.4500.

The product must therefore cost £12 × 1.4500 = US$17.40.

Test your understanding 2 – Cross rates

The US$1/€ cross rate will be calculated as:

1.5300/1.8700 = 0.8182 i.e. US$1/€0.8182.

The cost of the machine is therefore:

€100,000 / 0.8182 = US$122,220

Test your understanding 3 – Future spot rates

$$1.7200 \times \frac{1.03}{1.04} = US\$1.7035$$

Test your understanding 4 – Future spot

$$10 \times \frac{1.03}{1.07} = SF9.6262$$

Test your understanding 5 – Parity relationships

PPPT

$$\text{Future spot rate} = 0.9050 \times \frac{1 + 0.013}{1 + 0.02}$$

$$= €0.8988$$

IRPT

$$\text{Forward rate} = 0.9050 \times \frac{1 + 0.045}{1 + 0.06}$$

$$= €0.8922$$

The rates are similar, but not identical under the two different forecasting methods.

Using the Fisher Effect, the real rate of interest can be found in both US and Eurozone.

US:

$(1 + m)$ $= (1 + r)(1 + i)$
$(1+ 0.06)$ $= (1 + r)(1 + 0.02)$
Hence r $= 3.9\%$

Eurozone:

$(1 + m)$ $= (1 + r)(1 + i)$
$(1+ 0.045)$ $= (1 + r)(1 + 0.013)$
Hence r $= 3.2\%$

For the PPPT and the IRPT to give identical predicted rates, the International Fisher Effect must hold, which states that real rates of interest are identical in all countries. This is apparently not the case.

Other factors that may affect the prediction of exchange rates include:

- Transaction costs of shifting money and making investments.

- Lack of mobility of capital and goods, and the costs associated with this.

- Political intervention.

- Cultural differences between different countries.

- Central bank action.

- Trader activity.

- Key commodity prices (e.g. oil is priced in US dollars).

Test your understanding 6 – Forward contract

(i) **Add** a **discount** to get the forward rate.

Spot rate	1.5500	–	1.4500
Add discount	0.0055		0.0050
Forward rate	1.5555	–	1.4550

(ii) **Subtract** a **premium** to get the forward rate.

Spot rate	1.7150	–	1.6450
Subtract premium	(0.0068)		(0.0075)
Forward rate	1.7082	–	1.6375

Test your understanding 7 – EEFS

EEFS Ltd is expecting a receipt of US$, and therefore wishes to buy £ from the bank. The bank will sell £ high and therefore the rate is 1.5430 (current spot). The discount of 2.5c must be added to the rate thus giving a rate of 1.5680.

The sterling receipt is therefore US$2m ÷ 1.5680   £1,275,510

Test your understanding 8 – DD Ltd (1)

DD Ltd

(a) The money market hedge to pay € in six months' time requires DD Ltd to borrow in £, translate to € and deposit in €.

A payment of €1.3 million in six months (only 1.25% interest) will require a € deposit now of (€1,300,000 ÷ 1.0125) €1,283,951. This means that with a spot rate of 1.5050 the £ loan will need to be £853,124.

The loan of £853,124 will increase over the six months to the date of repayment by 2.3% and will therefore be £872,746.

The cost is therefore £872,746.

(b) The forward contract will use the six-month forward rate of 1.4895 for buying €.

The cost is therefore (€1,300,000 ÷ 1.4895) £872,776

There is virtually no difference between the two methods. This is expected because any significant difference would mean that profit could be made simply by converting one currency into another.

Test your understanding 9 – DD Ltd (2)

Under an MMH the company would borrow € now, translate into £ and deposit £ for six months.

The borrowing would be €1,300,000 ÷ 1.02	€1,274,510
This would translate now into €1,274,510 ÷ 1.5095	£844,326
By growth for interest for six months this becomes	£857,413

Forward contract

The forward contract would give:

€1,300,000 ÷ 1.5162	£857,407

Test your understanding 10 – Marcus

US$ Exposure

As Marcus has a US$ receipt (US$69,000) and payment (US$240,000) maturing at the same time (three months), it can match them against each other to leave a net liability of US$171,000 to be hedged.

(i) **Forward market hedge**

Buy US$171,000 three months' forward at a cost of:

US$171,000 / 0.9520 = €179,622 payable in three months' time.

(ii) **Money market hedge**

The money market hedge to pay US$ in three months' time requires Marcus to borrow in €, translate to US$ and deposit in US$.

A payment of US$171,000 in three months (only 2.5% interest) will require a US$ deposit now of (US$171,000 ÷ 1.025) US$166,829. This means that with a spot rate of 0.9830 the € loan will need to be €169,714.

The loan of €169,714 will increase over the three months to the date of repayment by 3.25% and will therefore be €175,230.

The cost is therefore €175,230.

In this case the money market hedge is a cheaper option.

A$ Receipt

Converting exchange rates to home currency

€1/A$

Spot:	0.5294 – 0.5285
Four months forward:	0.5126 – 0.5118

A$295,000 to be hedged.

(i) **Forward market hedge**

Sell A$295,000 four months' forward at a cost of:

A$295,000 / 0.5126 = €575,497 receivable in four months' time.

(ii) Money market hedge

The money market hedge to receive A$ in four months' time requires Marcus to borrow in A$, translate to € and deposit in €.

A receipt of A$295,000 in four months (only 5.33% interest) will be balanced with a A$ loan now of (A$295,000 ÷ 1.0533) A$280,072. This means that with a spot rate of 0.5294 the € deposit will need to be €529,037.

The deposit of €529,037 will increase over the four months to the date of repayment by 3.83% and will therefore be €549,299. In this case, more will be received in euros under the forward hedge.

Test your understanding 11 – UK company

Forward contract

$$\frac{US\$2,500,000}{(US\$1.5851 - US\$0.0164)} = £1,593,676$$

Futures

Time line

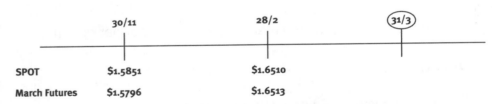

	30/11	28/2	31/3
SPOT	$1.5851	$1.6510	
March Futures	$1.5796	$1.6513	

Step 1: Set up – 30/11

- Downside risk will be if £ rises in value.
- Bet that £ will rise on futures market.
- Buy March £ futures
- No. of contracts =

$$\frac{\dfrac{US\$2.5m}{US\$1.5796}}{£62,500} = 25$$

Step 2: Contact exchange

- Buy 25 March futures contracts @ US$1.5796

- Deposit margin = $\dfrac{25 \times \text{US\$1,000}}{\text{US\$1.5842}}$ = (£15,781)

Step 3: Close out – 28/2

- Futures profit:

  Difference = 1.6513 – 1.5796 = 0.0717.

  Profit = 0.0717 × 25 × 62,500 = US$112,031

  + margin returned (US$25,000) = US$137,031

- Convert receipt & profit at spot = $\dfrac{\text{US\$2.5m} + \text{US\$137,031}}{\text{US\$1.6510}}$ = £1,597,233

Net futures position (net of initial margin payment)

= £1,597,233 – £15,781

= £1,581,452

With benefit of hindsight, the forward contract would have been a better choice.

Test your understanding 12 – X Inc

Time line

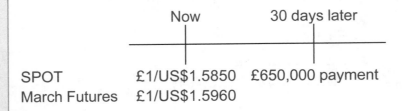

Now   30 days later

SPOT   £1/US$1.5850   £650,000 payment
March Futures   £1/US$1.5960

Step 1: Set up – now

- Downside Risk will be if £ rises in value.
- Bet that £ will rise on futures market.
- Buy £ futures
- No. of contracts.

$$\frac{£650,000}{£62,500} \approx 10 \text{ contracts}$$

- Tick value = $0.01c/£ × £62,500 = US$6.25 / Tick / Contract

Step 2: Contact exchange

- buy 10 futures contracts @ US$1.5960

Step 3: Close out – 30 days later

	US$
• Futures profit	
$\frac{US\$1.6120 - US\$1.5960}{US\$0.0001} = 160 \text{ ticks}$	
∴ 160 × US$6.25 × 10 =	10,000
• Convert payment at spot	
£650,000 × 1.6030	(1,041,950)
	(1,031,950)

If transaction had taken place at today's spot rate, it would have cost:

£650,000 × £1/US$1.5850 = US$1,030,250

It actually cost US$1,031,950 with the hedge, which is an additional US$1,700 more. So, the hedge is not perfect, but it has reduced the possible downside.

Test your understanding 13 – UK exporter

Dividing by the smallest £1/US$ rate gives the highest £ receipt – the premium is paid no matter what so it should be ignored for the purposes of determining whether to exercise the option.

Future spot US$1.6000 – exercise the option. US$25m / US$1.5000 = £16.67m less £300,000 premium gives a net receipt of £16.37m

Future spot US$1.4000 – abandon the option. US$25m / US$1.4000 = £17.86m less £300,000 premium gives a net receipt of £17.56m

Test your understanding 14 – Currency options

Time line

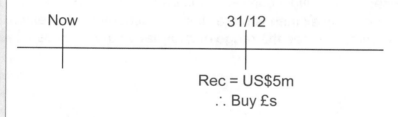

Step 1: Set up – now

* Right to buy £s in December.

* Use December call option

* Rate – US$1.590 as this is lowest premium.

   (**Note:** there are numerous ways to decide which price to select - just state your reasoning)

- No. of contracts =

$$\dfrac{\dfrac{US\$5m}{US\$1.590}}{£31,250} \approx 101$$

Step 2: Contact exchange

- Buy 101 December call options at exercise price of US$1.590.

- Pay premium $= \dfrac{101 \text{ contracts} \times £31,250 \times 2.57 \text{ cents}}{US\$1.5840}$

  $= £51,209.$

Step 3: December – potential outcomes:

(1) SPOT = US$1.6500

   – Use (exercise) options

(2) SPOT = US$1.5000

   – Use spot rate for conversion and options will lapse.

(**Tutorial note:** With multiple contracts and prices available, this question is more complex than you are likely to encounter in the exam, but it is good practice to see the range of information that may be presented.)

Test your understanding 15 – Pongo

30 June Payment of US$350,000

Time line

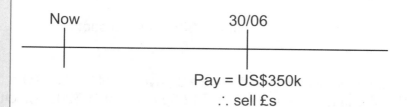

Now   30/06

Pay = US$350k
∴ sell £s

Step 1: Set up – now

- Right to sell £s in June.
- Use June put option
- Rate – US$1.5000
- No. of contracts.

$$\frac{\dfrac{US\$350{,}000}{US\$1.500}}{£25{,}000} \approx 9$$

Step 2: Contact the exchange

- Buy 9 June put options at an exercise price of US$1.5000.

- Pay premium $= \dfrac{9 \text{ contracts} \times £25{,}000 \times 12.40 \text{ cents}}{US\$1.5190}$

  $= £18{,}367$

Step 3: June – outcome

SPOT = US$1.5200

Do not use options:

Without the option, the payment would be $350,000 (at spot of $1.52000) = £230,263

If the option had been used it would involve a payment of 9 × 25,000 = £225,000 plus the unhedged amount of $12,500 at spot (1.5200) which equates to £8,224. A total payment of £233,224 – more than without the option.

Remember that options are only a type of insurance. They do not always have to be exercised (used).

Step 4: Determine net cash flows

	US$	£
Payments in real world	(350,000)	
Buy US$s and sell £s using options	337,500	(225,000)
Shortfall	(12,500)	
Buy at spot (12,500 ÷1.5200)	12,500	(8,224)
		(18,367)
Cost of option		
Net payments in £s		(251,591)

30 September Receipt of US$275,000

Time line

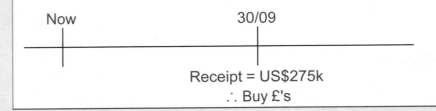

Now   30/09

Receipt = US$275k
∴ Buy £'s

Step 1: Set up – now

- Right to buy £s in September.
- Use September call option
- Rate – US$1.500
- No. of contracts.

$$\frac{\dfrac{US\$275,000}{US\$1.500}}{£25,000} \approx 7$$

Step 2: Contact the exchange

- Buy 7 September call options at an exercise price of US$1.5000.

$$\text{Premium} = \frac{7 \text{ contracts} \times £25,000 \times 8.00 \text{ cents}}{US\$1.5190}$$

$$= £9,217$$

Step 3: September – outcome:

SPOT = US$1.5285

- Use options:
- Buy 7 × 25 = £175,000
- Sell 175,000 × 1.5 = US$262,500.

Step 4: Determine net cash flows

	US$	£
Receipts in real world	275,000	
Buy £s and sell US$s using options	(262,500)	175,000
Surplus	12,500	
Sell at spot (12,500 ÷ 1.5285)	(12,500)	8,178
Cost of options		(9,217)
Net receipt in £s		173,961

Test your understanding 16 – No hedging

(i) **Statement 1**

It is generally assumed that translation risk is an accounting issue and has no effect on the economic value of the firm. As a consequence there is no need to hedge as there is no real risk, other than the possible effects on performance measures and ratios. However, if a multinational company has extensive borrowings in foreign currencies and has agreed and approved limits for these borrowings, a major change in exchange rates could have an impact on the company's ability to borrow and cost of capital. For example, assume a company has borrowings in sterling and US dollars. Its capital structure is as follows:

Equity £100m

Debt £20m

Debt US$66m = £40m (an implied exchange rate of 1.65)

Total £160m

If the US$/£ exchange rate falls substantially during the year to 1.4, the value of the debt in sterling rises to £47m. The gearing ratio has risen from 37.5% to over 40%, assuming no change in the other components of the capital structure. If the company has a maximum debt:debt 1 equity ratio of 40%, beyond which the UK shareholders and providers of debt will impose borrowing restrictions, the fall in the exchange rate has meant the company is now in breach of its debt contract. In reality this is unlikely to be a problem for most companies, although those with very heavy foreign currency-denominated borrowings may suffer. It is also unlikely that the other variables will remain the same.

(ii) **Statement 2**

Transaction risk arises from delays in foreign currency payments – the risk is that customers do not pay their foreign currency-denominated bills immediately and the exchange rate moves against the supplier in the period between invoice and payment.

Hedging is a risk-reduction technique and as such has a cost. It could be argued that company treasurers are not employed to take risks with shareholders' money unless the company has a stated objective of making profits by speculating on the foreign currency markets. As the company here is a manufacturing company it is reasonable to assume it has no expertise in foreign currency speculation.

Not hedging is a valid strategy, and carries no direct transaction cost, but it carries risk. It is up to the company's management to decide on the size of the risk and whether they should take that risk with shareholders' money.

Internal hedging techniques include:

- Invoicing in home currency – Risk is not avoided, but merely transferred to the customer.

- Multilateral netting – Appropriate for multinational companies or groups of companies with subsidiaries or branches in a number of countries. This is highly complicated and requires a sophisticated accounting system to monitor the currency movements.

- Leading and lagging – Involves changing the timing of payments to take advantage of changes in the relative value of currencies. This is easier said than done and overseas customers might not appreciate your strategy if it means deferring payment.

- Matching – 'Matching' receipts in one currency with payment obligations in the same currency. This is also difficult to arrange and has similar problems to multilateral netting.

Test your understanding 17 – Arbitrage

The speculator should convert £ in to $: £1,000,000 × $2 = $2,000,000

Convert dollars into euros: $2,000,000 / $1.50 = E1,333,333

Now sell the euros: E1,333,333 × 0.80 = £1,066,667

The speculator has made a risk-free profit of £66,667.

Test your understanding 18 – IRPT

(a) The expression 'arbitrage profits' relates to the gain made by exploiting differences in market rates, for instance interest rates and forward currency rates. If, for example, a forward currency rate is at a higher premium than is warranted by the differences in the respective local interest rates, then a profit can be made by borrowing in one currency and depositing in the other. Given the advanced state of communications, however, such simple differences are rarely available.

More recently, therefore, it has been applied to much more speculative positions, for example selling particular bonds forwards and buying others which, it is believed, will increase in price relative to the bonds sold (so they can be bought back leaving a net profit). The so-called 'hedge funds' build up big positions of this kind, but at considerable risk.

In the scenario provided, there is a possibility of profiting by entering into arbitrage, because the interest-rate differentials are not precisely matched by the premium implicit in the forward rates.

(b) The actions which would be necessary to take advantage of this are as follows:

(1) borrow $5 million at 5.33% p.a. for 6 months, at a cost of $133,250;

(2) buy $5 million of Swiss francs at 1.2029 per dollar, that is 6,014,500 Swiss francs;

(3) invest this amount at 2.4% p.a. for 6 months to earn 72,174 Swiss francs, bringing the total to 6,086,674 Swiss francs;

(4) sell this amount forward at 0.8447 to yield $5,141,414;

(5) pay off the original loan, which has accumulated to $5,133,250 to yield a gross profit of $8,164, or $2,664 net of the transaction costs (equivalent to £1,332 at today's exchange rate).

Test your understanding 19 – NPV

(a) **Calculations**

   (i) *Method 1*

Year	0	1	2	3
Cashflows	(150,000)	75,000	75,000	125,000
C\$ per £	1.700	1.785	1.874	1.968
£	(88,235)	42,017	40,021	63,516
14% DF	1.000	0.877	0.769	0.675
Discounted £	(88,235)	36,849	30,776	42,873

      NPV = £22,263

   (ii) *Method 2*

Year	0	1	2	3
Cashflows	(150,000)	75,000	75,000	125,000
19.7% DF	1.000	0.835	0.698	0.583
DCF in C\$	(150,000)	62,625	52,350	72,875

      NPV = C\$37,850 / 1.700 = £22,265

For the two approaches to yield the same NPV, the discount rate applied to the Canadian \$ cash flows needs to be the combination of the sterling discount rate (14% p.a.) and the projected strengthening of the pound (5% p.a.), that is 19.7% p.a. (1.14 × 1.05 being 1.197).

A forecast of a 5% p.a. strengthening of the pound against the dollar will, generally, be associated with UK inflation rates/interest rates being 5 percentage points per annum below the corresponding Canadian figures. It is surprising, therefore, to see that the Canadian cash flows are expected to be constant. It would be worth checking that they are nominal, and not inadvertently real.

(b) As the barriers to international trade come down, and globalisation becomes a reality, exchange rate risk management becomes a higher priority in financial management.

This particular project looks viable given the assumptions as regards future exchange rates. However, they are only forecasts and the actuals could turn out to be significantly different. If the pound were to strengthen by more than forecast, the value of the project to PG plc's shareholders would fall – and could even become negative. If PG plc's managers are sufficiently risk averse, they may wish to protect the company's cash flows against that possibility.

Borrowing Canadian dollars (as opposed to allowing UK borrowings to rise) would offer such protection in that, were sterling to strengthen, the number of pounds required to service/repay the loan would be fewer. Lower trading receipts, in other words, would be offset by lower financing payments. Covering the entire value of the project would mean borrowing its gross present value, but they could choose to hedge a proportion, so as to offset some of the risk.

The interest rate is likely to be different in the two countries – in the particular situation described, it could afford to be up to 5 percentage points per annum higher in Canada than in the United Kingdom before it adds to PG plc's costs. Interest payable is usually deductible in arriving at taxable profits, which could add further value. The other side of the coin, however, is that financing a project in the local currency could reduce its value if the currencies move in the opposite direction to that feared. In this case, for example, choosing not to borrow in Canada would be seen to have been the right move if sterling weakens against the dollar. It is most unlikely that additional UK equity would be raised for such a small (in the context of a plc) investment. It may, indirectly, affect the decision as to how much dividend to declare, but it is likely to be overwhelmed by other considerations.

Test your understanding 20 – Netting, matching and pooling

Key answer tips

This question is broken down into several sections, which is very helpful since it makes the requirements very clear. Manage your time well to ensure that you can attempt all parts.

Your answers to all sections need to relate back to BMN, the markets it is in and recent events.

(a) A company might decide not to control its foreign exchange risks for several reasons.

The risk might not be material. If the maximum loss that the group might expect to suffer is low, the benefits from control measures would also be small. Control measures would therefore be unnecessary.

If the group operates in different currencies whose value fluctuates up and down against other currencies, it might be considered that gains and losses on foreign exchange will cancel each other out, and the net risk is therefore immaterial.

Since BNM is based in the UK, its main currency might be sterling. If management took the view that the currencies in which it earns income are expected to strengthen against sterling, and the currencies in which it incurs expenditures are likely to weaken against sterling, it might choose not to hedge its FX exposures.

However, there are reasons why an international group should consider hedging its FX risk exposures. The exposures might be large, and if exchange rates are volatile, the risk might be significant. A risk-averse company would want to avoid losses (or gains) on foreign exchange that might have a significant effect on its reported profits. In extreme situations, the trading profits of a company might be eliminated by FX losses. This appears to be the situation that BNM is now in.

(b) (i) **Netting** is a process of using income in a currency to make payments in the same currency, so that the exposure is reduced to the net amount. For example, if a company expects to receive $400,000 and at about the same time make a payment of $500,000, it could use the income to make most of the payment, leaving a net exposure of just $100,000.

For netting to work successfully, there must be receipts and payments in the same currency at about the same time. Netting might therefore operate on a daily basis, a weekly basis or monthly basis, and would require efficient centralised control, possibly by the group treasury department.

Since receipts and payments do not occur on exactly the same days, there would also have to be currency bank accounts, for temporarily holding currency receipts until they are needed to make payments.

A problem for BNM is that the group has a decentralised management structure, and for netting to be effective, it would probably be appropriate for the cash flows of the subsidiaries to be netted. This will require centralised management.

(ii) **Matching** is a term that could be used to mean netting. It is also used to describe the practice of matching assets and liabilities, so that if a company or group has an asset in a particular currency, it should seek to have a matching liability in the same currency. Any translation loss on the asset would then be offset by a matching FX translation gain on the liability.

Translation gains or losses are features of financial reporting, rather than a cash flow matter.

However, financing assets with liabilities in the same currency can also reduce actual losses on foreign exchange movements. For example, a subsidiary that operates in US dollars might be financed largely by US dollar-denominated debt, so that income from trading (in dollars) can be used to make the interest payments and debt capital repayments in the same currency, avoiding FX risk.

The capital funding operations of BNM are the responsibility of the central treasury unit, and it should be expected that the unit will use matching principles when deciding on the appropriate currency for any new borrowing.

(iii) **Pooling** is a system of managing cash. When a business has several bank accounts in the same currency, it might be able to arrange a system with its bank(s) whereby the balances on each bank account in the same currency are swept up into a central account at the end of each day, leaving a zero balance on every account except the central account. Overdraft balances and positive cash balances are all swept up into the central account.

This does not provide a system for hedging against FX risk, but can be an efficient system for cash management. It avoids overdraft costs on individual bank accounts, and it enables the treasury department to make more efficient use of any cash surpluses.

For an efficient system of cash pooling, there needs to be a centralised cash management system. The current organisation allows each subsidiary to operate their own cash management system. Pooling can be organised by each subsidiary. However, it might be even more efficient if subsidiaries operating in the same currencies shared the same pooling system.

(c)   A common method of hedging foreign exchange exposures is forward exchange contracts. These can be used to fix the exchange rate for a future purchase or sale of a quantity of currency. In theory, each forward contract would relate to a specific future transaction in the currency, but in practice, large companies might buy or sell large quantities of currency forward without necessarily specifying which forward contracts apply to which trading transaction.

Similarly, a company might use the money markets to hedge its FX exposures, borrowing or depositing foreign currencies 'now' in anticipation of future receipts or payments. Money market hedging can effectively fix a forward rate for a future FX transaction.

(d)   An international group will benefit from raising debt capital centrally for several reasons.

If the central treasury has the responsibility for arranging borrowing for the group, a finance subsidiary could be used to raise capital, supported by a guarantee from the parent company of the group. Since debt would then effectively be guaranteed by the group as a whole, the credit rating for any bonds (or the interest rate on any bank loans) will be determined by the credit status of the group. It can therefore use the credit status of the group as a whole to borrow at lower rates of interest.

A centralised treasury department can raise capital in larger amounts than the individual subsidiaries. This might provide opportunities for the group to use different methods of borrowing that might not be appropriate for individual subsidiaries on their own. For example, the group as a whole might raise capital in the bond market when individual subsidiaries on their own would not require enough capital to make a bond issue worthwhile.

Raising capital centrally also allows the group to control its debt and capital structure more easily. If individual subsidiaries are allowed to raise capital on their own, without reference to head office, there would be a risk that the group will become excessively indebted, without proper controls being applied to debt risk management.

Test your understanding 21 – H plc (2)

The future exchange rates in six months will be:

US$1/£	0.5556 ÷ 1.025 (2.5% for six months)	0.5420
€1/£	0.6711 ÷ 1.015 (1.5% for six months)	0.6612

Value of transactions at original rates

	£
US$100,000 purchases @ 0.5556	(55,560) payment
US$20,000 sales @ 0.5556	11,112 receipt
€50,000 sales @ 0.6711	33,555 receipt
Net payment	(10,893)

Value of transactions at future rates

US$100,000 purchases @ 0.5420	(54,200) payment
US$20,000 sales @ 0.5420	10,840 receipt
€50,000 sales @ 0.6612	33,060 receipt
Net payment	(10,300)
Gain on strengthening of pounds:	**£593**

Test your understanding 22 – Gymbob (1)

(a) **Forward market**

1.8023
(0.0230)
———
1.7793
———

= £1,686,056

(b) **Money market hedge**

Invest y × 1.006875 = $3,000,000   (2.75%/4 = 0.006875)
y = $2,979,516

= £1,653,174

£1,653,174 × 1.010625   (4.25%/4 = 0.010625)
= £1,670,739

(c) **Futures contract**

= £1,657,459

Number of contracts

= 26.52, say 27 contracts

Sale price of sterling futures in January 1.8100
Purchase price of sterling futures in March 1.8000
Profit on future 0.0100
£62,500 × 27 × 0.0100 = $16,875

Dollars to pay supplier $3,000,000
Profit on futures contract ($16,875)
= $2,983,125
@ spot in March 1.7900
= £1,666,550

(Effective exchange rate = $1.8001)

Test your understanding 23 – Martha Inc.

(a) Martha Inc faces transaction risk in that the dollar will depreciate against the Euro so that the cost of the €9,000,000 import might increase over the payment period.

Martha Inc also faces translation risk in their accounts at the year-end should any Euro transactions still be outstanding.

In the longer term, Martha Inc may be exposed to economic risk – long-term transaction risk that could ultimately affect the value of the company.

(b) To hedge in the money market, Martha Inc should borrow a certain amount of dollars today which, when converted into Euros and invested in the Eurozone, would yield €9,000,000 to cover the payment in Euros.

Martha should invest X so that with interest accrued over the next 3 months in the Eurozone , they have €9,000,000.

The relevant interest rate is the Euro deposit rate of 8% (when we deposit we receive the lower rate of interest).

The three-monthly interest rate is 8% × 3/12 = 2%

Therefore the amount we should invest would be:

X × 1.02 = €9,000,000
X = €8,823,529

We need to buy these Euros on the spot market today at the prevailing €/$ exchange rate which is 0.825 – 0.875.

Because we are buying Euros we use the lower rate of 0.825 (meaning we will receive fewer Euros for a dollar, allowing the bank to make a profit).

This equates to 8,823,529/0.825 = $10,695,187. This is the amount of $ we need to borrow today in order to undertake this transaction.

Because we are borrowing $ we will be charged interest at the US lending rate for three months.

9% × 3/12 = 2.25%

Therefore, the actual cost of this transaction in $ is:

10,695,187 × 1.0225 = $10,935,829.

(c) The US company would buy December Euro futures to hedge the risk that the Euro will appreciate during the payment period.

Number of contracts required = €9,000,000 / €250,000 = 36 contracts.

Thus Martha Inc would buy 36 December Euro futures contracts at $1.25/€.

December 2005:

(i) If spot price = $1.23/€ and the futures price = $1.25/€, there will be a loss of (1.23 − 1.25) × 250,000 × 36 = ($ 180,000)

Dollar cost at spot = €9,000,000 × 1.23
= $11,070,000

Add loss from futures = $180,000
Net cost = $11,250,000

(ii) If spot price = $1.27/€ and the futures price = $1.25/€, there will be a profit of (1.27 − 1.25) × 250,000 × 36 = $180,000

Dollar cost at spot = €9,000,000 × 1.27
= $11,430,000

Less profit from futures = $180,000
Net cost = $11,250,000

(d) There are a number of problems regarding the use of currency futures. These include:

– The difficulty in achieving a perfect hedge due to:
  – Standardised contract sizes – where the needs of the company fall between two contract amounts and an unhedged amount is left.
  – Mismatch between spot market price and futures price where the exchange rate on the futures market is different from the rate available on the spot market.
  – The standardised delivery dates may not match the needs of the company.
  – Currency futures are also for a limited number of currencies only, which may not suit the needs of the company.

Test your understanding 24 – Options

(a) The Black-Scholes pricing model can be used to calculate the value of a European call option. The five input variables involved are:

- The price of the underlying instrument (current or spot market price).

- The exercise price (the price the holder of the option wishes to buy or sell the share at).

- The risk free interest rate (the rate typically paid on three-month treasury bills) (quoted as an annual rate and as a decimal number).

- The time to expiry of the option (quoted in years).

- The standard deviation of the underlying instrument's returns (i.e. the price volatility).

A decrease in the value of each of these factors will have the following effect.

- Current market price. As the current market price of the underlying item falls, the call option will fall in value. The option will become more out-of-the money, or less in-the-money. If the option is exercised, the option holder would be buying an underlying item that is worth less than previously.

- The exercise price. The lower the exercise price, the higher is the value of the call option. The option will become more in-the-money or less out-of-the-money, increasing the probability that the option holder will exercise the option.

- The risk-free interest rate. A reduction in the risk-free interest rate will reduce the value of a call option. The Black-Scholes model assumes that if a call option is purchased, the money saved by purchasing the option instead of purchasing the underlying item could be invested at the risk-free rate. A reduction in the risk-free rate makes purchasing the call option less attractive, because the interest income will be lower. This reduces the value of the option

There is an alternative view to the impact of a movement in interest rates. If interest rates fall the demand for interest bearing securities will fall. Hence, the demand for equities will rise and share prices will rise. On this basis the value of a call option on equities would increase. If you have explained this point instead of the one above you would still earn full marks.

- The time to expiry of the option. As the time to expiry of the option becomes less, the value of the option will fall. The 'time value' element of the option is reduced, and at expiry, the time value of a European option is zero.

- Volatility in the price of the underlying item. A reduction in the price volatility of the underlying item will reduce the value of an option. This is because lower volatility reduces the probability of extreme movements in price. As a consequence, there is a smaller probability that the option will be in-the-money at expiry (and a lower probability that it will be in-the-money by a large amount).

(b) **Fixed forward contract**

The forward rate for selling US$ in exchange for sterling is:

1.4220 + 0.0046 = 1.4266

The sterling proceeds in three months' time (to the nearest £1) would be:

= $2,350,000/1.4266 = £1,647,273

Option contracts

To hedge the currency risk, the company would buy sterling call options because it will be buying sterling (and selling US dollars).Of the three option prices available, two are in-the-money. PS would therefore be more likely to consider the option at 1.43 that is slightly out-of-the-money.

At a strike price of $1.43, the sterling equivalent of $2,350,000 is £1,643,357. Each option is for £31,250, therefore PS would want to buy 52.6 options (£1,643,357/£31,250).

This would be rounded up to 53 or down to 52 contracts.

If PS takes out 52 contracts, it would be exposed to currency risk on $26,250 of income. The option contracts would be for 52 × 31,250 × 1.43 = $2,323,750. The under-hedged amount is therefore $2,350,000 – $2,323,750 = $26,250). If the option contracts are exercised in December, the unhedged dollars would be sold at the spot rate.

The premium for the options would be £31,250 52 1.36 = $22,100. These dollars would be purchased at the spot rate on 30 September (= 1.4180) and the premium cost in sterling would therefore be $15,585.

The options will only be exercised if the spot rate on 31 December is worse than 1.43 (higher than 1.43). Suppose for example that the spot rate on 31 December is 1.44. The sterling receipts would be:

52 contracts at £31,250 =1,625,000

$26,250 sold at spot (1.44) = 18,229

Total income = 1,643,229

Less: Option premium cost (15,585)

Net receipts = 1,627,644

The forward contract will produce higher income if the US dollar weakens between 30 September and 31 December, and the options are exercised. However, exercising the options gives PS a 'worst possible' outcome. The financial benefit of options (compared with a forward contract) arises if the options are not exercised, and PS can sell the dollars at a more favourable spot rate. The 'breakeven point' at which the options would provide higher net income than a forward contract can be calculated as follows:

Income if forward contract is used 1, 647,273

Option premium cost 15,585

Total income 1,662,858

Dollar income $2,350,000

Breakeven rate: $2,350,000/£1,662,858 = $1.4132

If the spot rate falls below $1.4132, it would be more beneficial to buy call options than to arrange a forward contract.

The final decision will probably be based on views of movements of exchange rates in the future and a company's attitude to risk. PS is risk averse, which probably means that a fixed forward contract would be the better choice.

13

Interest rate risk management

Chapter learning objectives

Lead	Component
D2. Evaluate alternative risk management tools.	(a) Evaluate appropriate methods for managing financial risks.
	(b) Evaluate the effects of alternative methods of risk management.
	(d) Recommend risk management strategies and discuss their accounting implications.

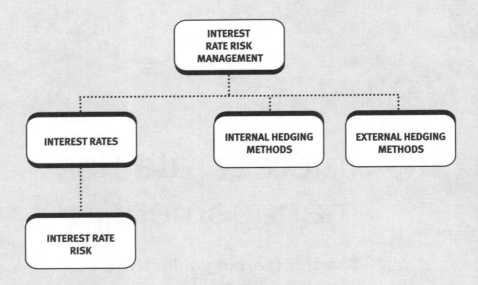

1 Interest rates

Lending and depositing rates

A bank will quote two interest rates to a customer – a lending rate and a depositing rate. The lending rate is always higher than the depositing rate because the bank wants to make a profit.

London Inter Bank Offer Rate (LIBOR)

This is the interest at which a major bank can borrow wholesale short-term funds from another bank in the London money markets.

- There are different LIBOR rates for different lengths of borrowing, typically from overnight to one year.

- Most variable rate loans are linked to LIBOR and therefore a loan at LIBOR + 2% (where LIBOR is 4.5%) would mean that the customer would pay interest at 6.5% on the loan.

LIBOR, LIBID and basis points

LIBOR

Each top bank has its own LIBOR rates, but an 'official' average of LIBOR rates is calculated each day by the British Bankers Association. The LIBOR rates that it publishes, the BBA LIBOR rates, are used as benchmark rates for some financial instruments, such as short-term interest rate futures.

LIBOR is important because London is the world's major money market centre. However, other financial centres have similar benchmark interest rates in their money market. For example, the banks of the eurozone produce an alternative benchmark rate of interest for the euro. This is called euribor, but it is similar in concept to euro LIBOR, with the only difference that the average rate is calculated daily from data submitted by a completely different panel of banks.

Most floating rate loans for companies are linked to LIBOR. For example, a company might borrow at 1.25% above LIBOR. In the language of the financial markets, 1% = 100 **basis points**, so a loan at 1.25% above LIBOR might be called a loan at LIBOR plus 125 basis points. If it pays interest every six months, the interest payable at the end of each period will be set with reference to the LIBOR rate at the beginning of the period.

LIBID

LIBID stands for the London Interbank Bid Rate. It is less important than LIBOR, but you might come across it. LIBID is the rate of interest that a top-rated London bank could obtain on short-term wholesale deposits with another bank in the London money markets. LIBID is always lower than LIBOR.

2 Interest rate risk and its management

The concept of interest rate risk is discussed in chapter 4. Along with the risk to cash flow and/or competitiveness, companies face the risk that interest rates might change in value (upside risk as well as downside risk), and between the point when the company identifies the need to borrow or invest and the actual date when they enter into the transaction. For example, a company might anticipate that they will need to borrow in the future but do not yet know exactly how much or when. If in the interim, interest rates rise the delayed decision will cause higher interest payments in the future.

Compared to exchange rates, interest rates are less volatile, but changes in them can still be substantial.

The term structure of interest rates provides an implicit forecast (according to market expectations) that is not guaranteed to be correct but is the most accurate forecast available.

Just like currency risk, interest rate risk management techniques can be split between internal and external methods.

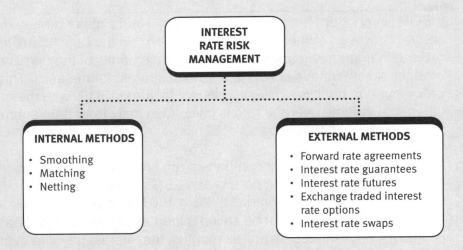

(**Note:** It is stated in the syllabus that numerical questions will not be set involving FRAs, IRGs, interest rate futures or options. Some numerical examples are given in this chapter, however, to clarify the explanations.)

3 Internal hedging

Internal (or operating) hedging strategies for managing interest rate risk involve restructuring the company's assets and liabilities in a way that minimises interest rate exposure. These include:

- **Smoothing** – the company tries to maintain a certain balance between its fixed rate and floating rate borrowing. The portfolio of fixed and floating rate debts thus provide a natural hedge against changes in interest rates. There will be less exposure to the adverse effects of each but there will also be less exposure to an favourable movements in the interest rate.

- **Matching** – the company matches its assets and liabilities to have a common interest rate (i.e. loan and investment both have floating rates).

- **Netting** – the company aggregates all positions, both assets and liabilities, to determine its net exposure.

Marks and Spencer's funding and interest rate hedging policy

The Group's funding strategy is to ensure a mix of financing methods offering flexibility and cost effectiveness to match the requirements of the Group … Interest rate risk primarily occurs with the movement of sterling interest rates in relation to the Group's floating rate financial assets and liabilities. Group policy for interest rate management is to maintain a mix of fixed and floating rate borrowings. Interest rate risk in respect of debt on the balance sheet is reviewed on a regular basis against forecast interest costs and covenants. A number of interest rate swaps have been entered into to redesignate fixed and floating debt.

4 External hedging

To manage the risk of interest rates moving before an agreed loan or deposit date, the following techniques can be used:

	Over-the-counter (OTC) instruments	Exchange traded instruments
'Fixing' instruments	Forward rate agreements (FRAs)	Interest rate futures
'Insurance' instruments	Interest rate guarantees (IRGs), (sometimes called caps / floors or options)	Interest rate options

'Fixing' instruments lock a company into a particular interest rate providing certainty as to the future cashflow, whilst 'insurance' instruments allow some upside flexibility in the interest rate i.e. the company can benefit from favourable movements but are protected from adverse movements.

OTC instruments are bespoke, tailored products that fit the companies needs exactly. Exchange traded instruments are ready-made and standardised.

These will be discussed in more detail in the following sections.

5 Forward rate agreements (FRAs)

An FRA is a forward contract on an interest rate for a future short-term loan or deposit. An FRA can therefore be used to fix the interest rate on a loan or deposit starting at a date in the future.

It is a contract relating to the level of a short-term interest rate, such as three-month LIBOR or six-month LIBOR. FRAs are normally for amounts greater than £1 million.

Features and operation

An important feature of an FRA is that the agreement is independent of the loan or deposit itself.

- It is about the rate of interest on a **notional** amount of principal (loan or deposit) starting at a future date.

- A receipt or payment will be made at the start of the loan period that will compensate for interest rate changes between the forward rate agreement and the market rate for the loan.

For example, a company may need a loan starting in five months time on 1 June to last for three months. The treasurer will be concerned that between now and taking out the loan, interest rates will increase.

- The treasurer will arrange an FRA, which means that he will enter into an agreement with a bank to fix the interest rate on a three month loan starting in five months' time.

- On the settlement date (1 June) the seller pays the purchaser (the treasurer) if interest rates have risen.

Therefore a **borrower**, wishing to hedge against an increase in interest rates, will **buy** an FRA. The profit on the FRA will compensate them for the extra interest cost of the loan.

Terminology

In the terminology of the markets, an FRA on a notional three-month loan/deposit starting in five months time (such as in the example) is called a '5–8 FRA' (or '5v8 FRA').

Pricing

FRA's will be priced according to the current bank base rate and future expectations of its movements. The bank will try to predict the interest rate at the date of inception of the borrowing and over its duration, and add on a profit margin. The bank will expect to make a profit for the risk they are taking in lending a company money and therefore any FRA will be priced at some amount above the base rate for a borrower. The amount above the base rate will depend on several factors including the banks attitude to their estimated interest rate (how sure they are in their prediction) and also the reputation of the company they are lending to.

Hedging using FRAs

Hedging is achieved by a combination of an FRA with the 'normal' loan or deposit.

Borrowing (hence concerned about interest rate rises)

- The firm will borrow the required sum on the target date and will thus contract at the market interest rate on that date.

- Separately the firm will **buy** a matching FRA from a bank or other market maker and thus receive compensation if rates rise.

Depositing (hence concerned about a fall in interest rates)

- The firm will deposit the required sum on the target date and will thus contract at the market interest rate on that date.

- Separately the firm will **sell** a matching FRA to a bank or other market maker and thus receive compensation if rates fall.

In each case this combination effectively fixes the rate.

Settlement of FRAs

When an FRA reaches its settlement date, the buyer and seller must settle the contract.

- If the fixed rate in the agreement (the FRA rate) is higher than the reference rate (LIBOR), the buyer of the FRA makes a cash payment to the seller. The payment is for the amount by which the FRA rate exceeds the reference rate.

- If the fixed rate in the agreement (the FRA rate) is lower than the reference rate (LIBOR), the seller of the FRA makes a cash payment to the buyer. The payment is for the amount by which the FRA rate is less than the reference rate.

Illustration of hedging using FRAs

A company wishes to borrow £10 million in six months' time for a three-month period. It can normally borrow from its bank at LIBOR + 0.50%. The current three-month LIBOR rate is 5.25%, but the company is worried about the risk of a sharp rise in interest rates in the near future.

A bank quotes FRA rates of:

3 v 9:	5.45	–	5.40 %
6 v 9:	5.30	–	5.25%

Required:

(a) How should the company establish a hedge against its interest rate risk using an FRA?

(b) Suppose that at settlement date for the FRA, the LIBOR reference rate is fixed at 6.50%. What will be the effective borrowing rate for the company?

Solution

(a) The company wants to fix a borrowing rate, so it should buy an FRA on a notional principal amount of £10 million. The FRA rate is for a 6 v 9 FRA, and the FRA rate is therefore 5.30% (you will have to buy from the bank at the higher rate - remember the bank always wins !).

(b) At settlement date interest rates have risen and the reference rate is higher than the FRA rate. The FRA will therefore be settled by a payment to the FRA buyer of 1.20% (6.50% − 5.30%).

	%
Actual interest rate on three-month loan	(7.00)
(LIBOR + 0.50%)	
Gain on FRA	1.20
Effective interest cost	(5.80)

This effective interest cost is the FRA rate of 5.30% plus the 0.50% margin above LIBOR that the company must pay on its borrowing.

Test your understanding 1 – Cooper plc (1)

It is 31 October and Cooper plc is arranging a six-month £5 million loan commencing on 1 July, based on LIBOR. Cooper wants to hedge against an interest rate rise using an FRA. The current LIBOR is 8%.

(a) If LIBOR turned out to be 9% on 1 July, evaluate the use of the FRA.

(b) If LIBOR on 1 July was 5%, re-evaluate the FRA.

6 Interest rate guarantees (IRGs)

An IRG is a contract with a bank fixing a maximum / (minimum) borrowing / (lending) rate on a notional loan for a stated period from a stated future date, in exchange for an up front fee.

IRGs are sometimes referred to as **interest rate options** or **interest rate caps / floors**.

Features and operation

They are over-the-counter instruments arranged directly with a bank and have a maximum maturity of one year.

Decision rules

If there is an adverse movement	If there is a favourable movement
↓	↓
Exercise the option to protect	**Allow the option to lapse**

IRGs are more expensive than the FRAs as one has to pay for the flexibility to be able to take advantage of a favourable movement.

Test your understanding 2 – Cooper plc (2)

It is 31 October and Cooper plc is arranging a six-month £5 million loan commencing on 1 July, based on LIBOR. Cooper wants to hedge against an interest rate rise using an IRG. The current LIBOR is 8%.

The IRG fee is 0.25% p.a. of the loan.

(a) If LIBOR turned out to be 9% on 1 July, evaluate the use of the IRG.

(b) If LIBOR on 1 July was 5%, re-evaluate the IRG.

---

7 Interest rate futures (IRFs)

IRFs are similar in principle to forward rate agreements in that they give a commitment to an interest rate for a set period.

They are tradable contracts and operate for set periods of three months, and terminate in March, June, September and December.

As with currency futures, the futures position will normally be closed out for cash and the gain or loss will be used to offset changes in interest rates.

There are two types of IRFs:

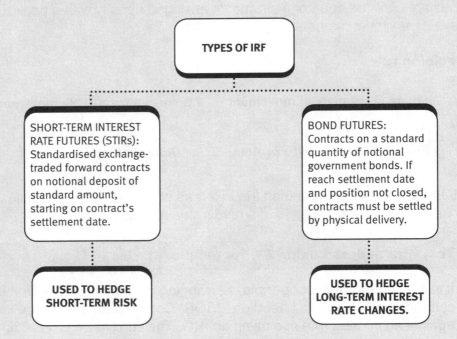

TYPES OF IRF

SHORT-TERM INTEREST RATE FUTURES (STIRs): Standardised exchange-traded forward contracts on notional deposit of standard amount, starting on contract's settlement date.

BOND FUTURES: Contracts on a standard quantity of notional government bonds. If reach settlement date and position not closed, contracts must be settled by physical delivery.

USED TO HEDGE SHORT-TERM RISK

USED TO HEDGE LONG-TERM INTEREST RATE CHANGES.

(**Note:** These notes concentrate on STIRs which are more common.)

Features and operation

The future operates by the customer making a commitment to effectively deposit or borrow a fixed amount of capital at a fixed interest rate. The notional sterling deposit/loan on the LIFFE (London futures exchange) is £500,000.

Pricing

The future is priced by deducting the interest rate from 100.

- if the interest rate is 5% the future will be priced at 95.00.
- the reason for this is that if interest rates increase, the value of the future will fall and vice versa if interest rates reduce.

Gains and losses on STIRs are calculated by reference to the interest rate at the date of close out. The difference between the futures price at inception and close will be the gain or loss.

Futures hedging calculations

Companies can hedge using futures by buying or selling a number of futures contracts that cover a loan period and value.

- Most companies use futures to hedge **borrowings** and therefore hedge against an increase in the interest rate.
- To do this the company **sells** futures.

IRFs are complicated by a number of factors including:

- Contract sizes and standard contract lengths (3 months).
- Margins/deposits payable at the start of the hedge.
- Speculators – who dominate the market.

More information on hedging with IRFs

Hedging against the risk of a rise in interest rates with STIRs

If a company plans to borrow short-term in the future and wants to create a hedge against the risk of a rise in interest rates before then:

- It should set up a position with futures that will give it a profit if interest rates go up. The profit from futures trading will offset the higher interest cost on the loan, when it is eventually taken out.
- On the other hand, if the interest rate goes down, the effect of the hedge will be to create a loss on the futures position, so that the benefit from borrowing at a lower interest rate on the actual loan, when it is taken out, will be offset by the loss on the futures position.

This hedge is created by **selling** short-term interest rate futures.

The **futures position should be closed** when the actual loan period begins, by buying an equal number of futures contracts for the same settlement date.

- **If interest rates have gone up, the market price of futures will have fallen**. A profit will be made from futures by having sold at one price to open the position and then buying at a lower price to close the position. The profit should offset the increased interest rate.
- **If interest rates have gone down, the price of futures will have risen**. A loss will be made from futures by having sold at one price to open the position and then buying at a higher price to close the position. The loss should offset the lower interest rate.

The company should have eliminated any downside or upside risk, and be paying the interest rate it wanted.

Imperfect hedge with IRFs

One problem is that futures are for a **standard size** of contract, whereas the amount of the loan or deposit to be hedged might not be an exact multiple of the amount of the future contract's notional deposit.

For example, suppose that a company wishes to hedge against the risk of a rise in the three-month LIBOR rate for a three-month loan of US$9,250,000. Futures could be sold to hedge the exposure, but the number of contracts sold would have to be either 9 or 10 (notional deposit = $1 million per contract). However, the unhedged amount is likely to be small (perhaps immaterial) in comparison to the hedged amount.

A second problem is the existence of **basis risk**: the future rate (as defined by the future prices) moves approximately but not precisely in line with the cash market rate.

The current futures price is usually different from the current 'cash market' price of the underlying item. In the case of interest rate futures, the current market price of an interest rate future and the current interest rate will be different, and will only start to converge when the final settlement date for the futures contract approaches. This difference is known as the **'basis'**.

At final settlement date for the contract (in March, June, September or December) the futures price and the market price of the underlying item ought to be the same; otherwise speculators would be able to make an instant profit by trading between the futures market and the spot 'cash' market (arbitrage).

Most futures positions are closed out before the contract reaches final settlement. When this happens, there will inevitably be a difference between the futures price at close-out and the current market price of the underlying item. In other words, there will still be some basis.

FRAs vs. STIRs

Short-term interest rate futures are an alternative method of hedging to FRAs. They have a number of similarities.

- Both are binding forward contracts on a short-term interest rate.
- Both are contracts on a notional amount of principal.
- Both are cash-settled at the start of the notional interest period.

FRAs have the advantage that they can be tailored to a company's exact requirements, in terms of amount of principal, length of notional interest period and settlement date.

However, futures are more flexible with regard to settlement, because a position can be closed quickly and easily at any time up to settlement date for the contract.

Given the efficiency of the financial markets, the difference between the two in terms of effective interest rate is unlikely to be large.

Hedging with bond futures

Bond futures might be used to hedge the risk of a change in the price of bonds over the next few months. They can be particularly useful to bond investors for hedging against the risk of a rise in long-term interest rates and a fall in bond prices.

Suppose that an investment institution has a quantity of UK government bonds and its financial year-end is approaching. It would like to secure the value of its bond portfolio and hedge against the risk of a rise in long-term interest rates and fall in bond prices over the next few months.

It can do this with bond futures. As with hedging with STIRs, a hedge is constructed so that if interest rates move adversely, an offsetting gain will be made on the bond futures position. For a bond investor, a hedge can be constructed whereby if interest rates go up and bond prices fall, there will be a loss on the bond portfolio but an offsetting gain on the bond futures position.

Bond futures fall in value when interest rates go up. **For a bond investor, the required hedge is therefore to sell bond futures.** If the interest rate goes up, both the bonds and the bond futures will fall in value. The futures position can be closed by buying futures at a lower price than the original sale price to open the position. The gain on the futures position should match the loss in the value of the bonds themselves.

8 Exchange traded interest rate options

The future and options market provides a product that can cap interest rates for borrowers like an IRG.

This option gives its buyer the right to buy or sell an interest rate future, at a specified future date at a fixed exercise rate, i.e. to effectively have the 'right to bet' on an interest rate increase as shown on the futures market.

Because they are an option as opposed to a commitment, they require the option holder to pay the writer of the option a **premium**.

Features and operation

The characteristics of an option are:

- They fix the interest on a notional amount of capital (either for borrowers where put options are used, or for lenders where call options are used).
- They are for a given interest period (e.g. six months) starting on or before a date in the future.

(**Note**: Interest rate options are only options on interest rates and not an option to take a loan. The loan is taken quite independently of the option.)

Given that these are options to buy or sell futures, all the futures information is still valid, for example:

- The standard size of the contracts, i.e. £500,000, $1,000,000, etc.
- The duration of the contract, i.e. 3 month contracts.
- Maturity dates end of March, June, September and December.

(Standard contracts are only for exchange traded options. It is possible to purchase a bespoke option – variable contract sizes and dates, provided a willing counterparty can be found.)

A **call** option gives the holder the right to **buy** the futures contract.

A **put** option gives the holder the right to **sell** the futures contract.

You always buy the option – buy the right to buy or buy the right to sell.

Cash market	Deposits	Loan
Futures market	Buy futures contacts	Sell futures contracts
Options market	Buy calls	Buy puts

Collars

- Premiums can be reduced by using a collar.

- Simultaneously buying a put and selling a call option creates a collar, hence a cap and floor is created but premium is saved.

- For example:

	%
Cap at 5.75%, pay a premium	(0.77)
Floor at 5.25%, receive a premium	0.16
Net cost	(0.61)

- The premium saved comes at the expense of giving up the benefits of any interest rate falls below the floor value.

More on collars

- A company buys an option to protect against an adverse movement whilst allowing it to take advantage of a favourable movement in interest rates. The option will be more expensive than a futures hedge. The company must pay for the flexibility to take advantage of a favourable movement.

- A collar is a way of achieving some flexibility at a lower cost than a straight option.

- Under a collar arrangement, the company limits its ability to take advantage of a favourable movement. It buys a cap (a put option) as normal but also sells a floor (a call option) on the same futures contract, but with a different exercise price.

- The floor sets a minimum cost for the company. The counterparty is willing to pay the company for this guarantee of a minimum income. Thus the company gets paid for limiting its ability to take advance of a favourable movement if the interest rate falls below the floor rate. The company does not benefit therefore the counterparty does.

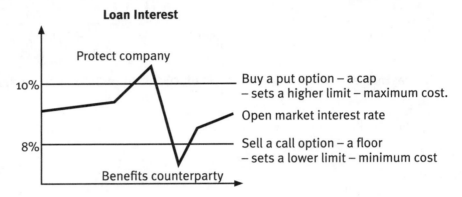

- It involves a company arranging both a minimum and a maximum limit on its interest rates payments or receipts. It enables a company to convert a floating rate of interest into a semi-fixed rate of interest.

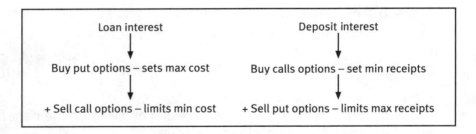

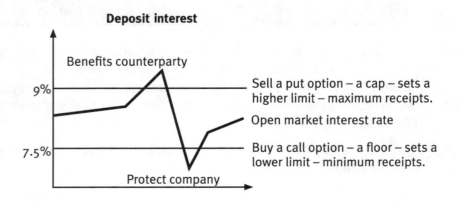

9 Interest rate swaps

An interest rate swap is an agreement whereby the parties agree to swap a floating stream of interest payments for a fixed stream of interest payments and vice versa. There is no exchange of principal.

Features and operation

- In practice interest rate swaps are probably the most common form of interest rate hedge used by companies because they can hedge loans of anywhere between a year and 30 years and therefore are used for long-term borrowings.

- In this chapter we only consider the 'plain vanilla' swap of fixed or floating rate (or vice versa) without any complications that can occur in practice.

- The companies involved in a swap can be termed 'counterparties'.

- Some banks specialise in swaps and therefore they have become a tradable instrument.

- In practice banks often act as counterparties and attempt to hedge their risk by having a large number of positions in the fixed and floating rate markets.

The following diagram summarises the operation of a swap:

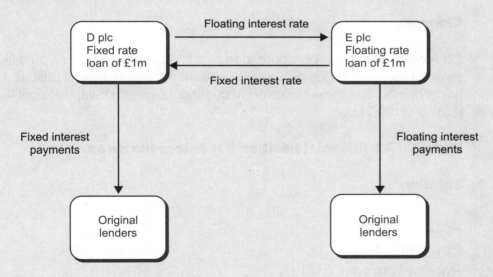

In practice the way the payments are made is that a net payment is made from D plc to E plc depending on the difference in the fixed and floating interest rates.

This type of swap will only work if one company wants a fixed rate whilst another company wants a variable rate.

Swaps utilising intermediaries

Calculations involving quoted rates from intermediaries

In practice a bank normally arranges the swap and will quote the following:

- The 'ask rate' at which the bank is willing to receive a fixed interest cash flow stream in exchange for paying LIBOR.

- The 'bid rate' that they are willing to pay in exchange for receiving LIBOR.

- The difference between these gives the bank's profit margin and is usually at least 2 basis points.

Note: LIBOR is the most widely used benchmark or reference rate for short-term interest rates worldwide, although the swap could relate to Euribor, say.

The bank will usually set up the swap by identifying the potential swap partners and helping to set the terms of any legal agreement between the two parties. The bank will charge both companies a commission (profit margin) for doing this. From the companies point of view, the bank will probably know the potential swap partners credibility and therefore there should be less risk of default by one of the companies.

Example

Co A currently has a 12-month loan at a fixed rate of 5% but would like to swap to variable. It can currently borrow at a variable rate of LIBOR + 12 basis points. The bank is currently quoting 12-month swap rates of 4.90 (bid) and 4.95 (ask).

Show Co A's financial position if it enters the swap.

Solution

	Co A
Actual borrowing	(5.00%)
Payment to bank	(LIBOR)
Receipt from bank (bid)	4.90%
Net interest rate after swap	**(LIBOR + 0.10%)**
Open market cost – no swap	(LIBOR + 0.12%)
Saving	2 basis points

Interest rate swap calculation

Company A wishes to raise $10 million and to pay interest at a floating rate, as it would like to be able to take advantage of any fall in interest rates. It can borrow for one year at a fixed rate of 10% or at a floating rate of 1% above LIBOR.

Company B also wishes to raise $10 million. They would prefer to issue fixed rate debt because they want certainty about their future interest payments, but can only borrow for one year at 13% fixed or LIBOR + 2% floating, as it has a lower credit rating than company A.

Calculate the effective swap rate for each company – assume savings are split equally.

Solution

(**Note:** Sometimes the question will tell you which company is currently borrowing which type of finance (fixed or variable). If this isn't given, you will need to use the first two steps to establish which company has the comparative advantage.)

Step 1: Identify the type of loan with the biggest difference in rates.

- Answer: Fixed (difference of 3% (13% vs. 10%) as opposed to just 1% for variable)

Step 2: Identify the party that can borrow this type of loan the cheapest.

- Answer: Company A
- Thus Company A should borrow fixed, company B variable, reflecting their **comparative advantages**.

(**Note:** All swap questions will start from step 3.)

Step 3: Interest difference

	A		B		TOTAL
Now:	10	+	LIBOR + 2	=	LIBOR + 12
Want:	LIBOR + 1	+	13	=	LIBOR + 14
			Difference		2

- 'Now' refers to the loan that the companies will take out.
- 'Want' refers to the type of interest payments that they desire to have, and the cost that they would have to pay if they arranged it themselves.
- The difference is shared equally between the companies.

Step 4: Possible swap

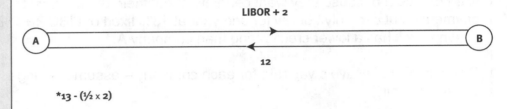

LIBOR + 2

A   B

12

*13 - (½ × 2)

Note: there are many ways of setting up the terms of a swap to achieve the required results

- both companies get the type of interest they desire, and
- save their share of the difference calculated above.

The method used here is:

(1) company B pays off ALL of company A's variable rate interest (LIBOR + 2% in this case)

(2) company A then pays to B interest equivalent to its own fixed rate (13%) less share of the difference (½×2%=1% in this case).

Step 5: Check

	A	B
	%	%
Pay own interest	(10.00)	(LIBOR + 2)
Receive	12.00	LIBOR + 2
Pay	(LIBOR + 2)	(12.00)
Net interest	(LIBOR)	(12.00)

Both companies achieved what they wanted, so the swap works.

Advantages of using swaps

- As a way of managing fixed and floating rate debt profiles without having to change underlying borrowing.

- To take advantage of expected increases or decreases in interest rates.

- To hedge against variations in interest on floating rate debt, or conversely to protect the fair value of fixed rate debt instruments.

- A swap can be used to obtain cheaper finance. A swap should result in a company being able to borrow what they want at a better rate under a swap arrangement, than borrowing it directly themselves (this is known as the 'theory of **comparative advantage**').

Disadvantages of using swaps

- Finding a swap partner can be difficult, although banks help (for a fee) in this respect these days.

- Creditworthiness of your swap partner – default on an interest payment may be a worry but, again, using a bank to credit check the swap partner beforehand should alleviate this concern.

- Interest rates may change in the future and your company might be locked into an unfavourable rate.

Test your understanding 3 – Company A and B

Company A can borrow at 10.75% fixed or LIBOR variable, but wants fixed. Company B can borrow at 11.25% fixed or LIBOR + 1% variable, but wants variable. The bank would charge a fee of 5 basis points to each company to arrange a swap. A requires a 10 basis point advantage before they will enter into a swap.

Required:

Demonstrate whether a swap is viable and suggest possible terms for such a swap.

Test your understanding 4 – Interest rate hedging

Assume you are the Treasurer of AB, a large engineering company, and that it is now May 20X4. You have forecast that the company will need to borrow £2 million by the end of September 20X4 for at least 6 months. The need for finance will arise because the company has extended its credit terms to selected customers over the summer period. The company's bank currently charges customers such as AB plc 7.5% per annum interest for short-term unsecured borrowing. However, you believe interest rates will rise by at least 1.5 percentage points over the next 6 months. You are considering using one of three alternative methods to hedge the risk:

- forward rate agreements; or

- interest rate futures; or

- an interest rate guarantee (a borrower's option or short-term cap).

You can purchase an interest rate cap at 7% per annum for the duration of the loan to be guaranteed. You would have to pay a premium of 0.1% of the amount of the loan. As part of the arrangement, the company will agree to pay a 'floor' rate of 6% per annum.

Required:

Discuss the features of each of the three alternative methods of hedging the interest rate risk and advise on how each might be useful to AB, taking all relevant and known information into account.

Test your understanding 5 – Swaps

You are contacted by AB's bank and informed that another of the bank's clients, a smaller company in the same industry, is looking for a swap partner for a similar amount of borrowing for the same duration. The borrowing rates applicable to AB and RO are as follows:

	Floating	Fixed
AB	LIBOR + 0.3%	7.5%
RO	LIBOR + 0.5%	8.5%

Required:

(a) Comment briefly on why swaps may be used.

(b) Recommend how the two companies could co-operate in a swap arrangement to their mutual benefit, including the option of changing the type of loan normally preferred. Support your recommendation with appropriate calculations.

(c) Discuss the advantages and disadvantages of arranging a swap through a bank rather than negotiating directly with a counterparty.

Test your understanding 6 – QW (1)

Assume that you are treasurer of QW plc, a company with diversified, international interests. The company wishes to borrow £10 million for a period of three years. Your company's credit rating is good, and current market data suggests that you could borrow at a fixed rate of interest of 8% per annum or at a floating rate of LIBOR + 0.2% per annum. You believe that interest rates are likely to fall over the next three years, and favour borrowing at a floating rate.

Your company's bankers are currently working on raising a three-year loan for another of their customers, ER plc. This company is smaller and less well known than QW plc, and its credit rating is not as high. ER plc could borrow at a fixed rate of 9.5% per annum or a floating rate of LIBOR + 0.5%. ER plc has indicated to the bank that it would prefer a fixed-rate loan. Your bankers have suggested you engage in a swap which might benefit both companies. The bank's commission would be 0.2% of the benefits to the two parties. Your counterpart in ER plc suggests that the commission fees and swap benefits should be shared equally.

Assume that interest is paid at the end of each twelve-month period of the loan's duration and that the principal is repaid on maturity (i.e. at the end of three years).

Required:

Write a report to the board which:

(i) describes the characteristics and benefits of interest rate swaps compared with other forms of interest rate risk management, such as forward-rate agreements and interest rate futures

(ii) explains the course of action necessary to implement the swap being considered with ER plc, and calculates and comments on the financial benefits to be gained from the operation.

Test your understanding 7 – Gymbob (2)

Gymbob plc is a national chain of gyms listed on the UK Stock Market. It was set up nearly twenty years ago, and has 40 branches nationwide each having essentially the same facilities – a dry side including a gym with running machines, cross trainers, rowing machines and weights, and a wet side including a swimming pool, sauna, spa pool, and steam room. There are daily classes for both the wet and dry side activities, held by various full-time and freelance instructors.

The directors of Gymbob have heard of a rival gym chain being put up for sale for £20 million. Gymbob would be very keen to acquire their competitor, since the gyms are well patronised and in locations that complement Gymbob's current portfolio. Gymbob would be able to raise most of the purchase price in cash or by liquidating investments, but would still need to borrow £5 million. It is anticipated that, all going well, they would need to borrow the £5 million in 3 months' time for only a one-year period. Current interest rates are 7% for this type of loan, and Gymbob's directors would not want to pay more than this since they have other commitments. They are considering the use of a forward rate agreement, interest rate future or an interest rate option.

Required:

Explain how each of the three interest rate hedging alternatives might be useful to Gymbob.

10 Chapter summary

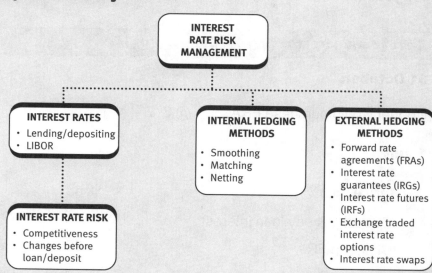

Test your understanding answers

Test your understanding 1 – Cooper plc (1)

31 October:

Cooper would purchase FRA $_{8-14}$ @ 8%

1 July:

		% pa
(a)	**LIBOR = 9%**	
	Cooper will pay loan interest	(9.00)
	Claim on FRA	1.00
	Net interest	(8.00)

		% pa
(b)	**LIBOR = 5%**	
	Pay loan interest	(5.00)
	Pay out on FRA	(3.00)
	Net interest	(8.00)

Remember that the point of an FRA is to manage future risk. In reality there is no point in looking at the past to see whether rates rose or fell. Perhaps the only worthwhile reason for doing this would be to measure the ability of the Treasury department in guessing what will happen to interest rates.

Test your understanding 2 – Cooper plc (2)

31 October:

Cooper would purchase IRG_{8-14} @ 8%

1 July:

(a) **LIBOR = 9%**

	% pa
Cooper will pay loan interest	(9.00)
Pay fee	(0.25)
Claim on IRG	1.00
Net interest	(8.25)

(b) **LIBOR = 5%**

	% pa
Pay loan interest	(5.00)
Pay fee	(0.25)
Net interest	(5.25)

Note: When LIBOR has fallen the IRG allows Barden to take advantage of the lower interest rates. BUT the fee is still paid !

Remember again that the point of an IRG is to manage future risk. In reality there is no point in looking at the past to see whether rates rose or fell. Perhaps the only worthwhile reason for doing this would be to measure the ability of the Treasury department in guessing what will happen to interest rates.

Test your understanding 3 – Company A and B

Step 1: Interest difference

	A	B	TOTAL
Now:		LIBOR + 11.25	= LIBOR + 11.25
Want:	10.75 +	LIBOR + 1	= LIBOR + 11.75
		Difference	0.50

- 'Now' refers to the loan that the companies will take out.
- 'Want' refers to the type of interest payments they desire to have, and the cost that they would have to pay if they arranged it themselves.
- The difference is shared equally between the companies, unless otherwise specified.

Step 2: Possible swap

* 10.75 − (½ × 0.50)

Tutorial note: There are many ways of setting up the terms of a swap to achieve the required results

- both companies get the type of interest they desire, and
- save their share of the difference calculated above.

The method used here is:

(1) company B pays off ALL of company A's variable rate interest (LIBOR in this case).

(2) company A then pays to B interest equivalent to its own fixed rate less share of the difference (net 10.50% in this case).

Step 3: Check

	A	B
	%	%
Pay own interest	(LIBOR)	(11.25)
Receive	LIBOR	10.50
Pay	(10.50)	(LIBOR)
	———	———
	(10.50)	(LIBOR + 0.75)
Fees	(0.05)	(0.05)
	———	———
Net interest	(10.55)	(LIBOR + 0.80)
	———	———

Both companies achieved what they wanted:

- A has a saving of 20 basis points (required a 10 basis point advantage)

- B has a saving of 20 basis points

so the swap works.

Test your understanding 4 – Interest rate hedging

With all three methods of hedging interest rate risk, a time limit has to be decided for the period of the hedge. With a Forward Rate Agreement (FRA) or an interest rate guarantee (option/cap), the time limit must be specific, with an agreed settlement date or expiry date, say six months exactly from the contract/transaction date. With futures, the hedge would be for six months from any date up to the settlement date for the futures, which in this question would probably be September.

It is assumed here that the required hedge is for exactly six months in all three cases.

FRA

An FRA is an over-the-counter instrument that can be arranged with a bank, fixing the interest rate on a notional principal amount for a given period of time, in this case six months. The notional six-month interest period would start from an agreed date in September, in four months' time, so the FRA would be a 4v10 FRA. FRAs are only available for quite large principal amounts (at least $1 million) and can be arranged up to about two years into the future.

A company wishing to fix an interest rate for borrowing should buy an FRA. Here, AB should buy a 4v10 FRA on a notional principal amount of £2 million. The bank would specify an interest rate for the FRA, which might be about 7.5% in this case.

The FRA is not an agreement to borrow the funds required. AB must arrange to borrow the £2 million separately. AB will borrow £2 million at the current market rate of interest in September, whatever this happens to be. The FRA would be settled by:

- a payment from the bank to AB if the benchmark interest rate (here probably the six-month LIBOR rate) is higher than the FRA rate; or

- a payment from AB to the bank if the benchmark rate is lower than the FRA rate.

The hedge works because the interest payment on the actual borrowing plus or minus the settlement amount for the FRA should fix the overall effective borrowing cost for AB. For example, if the interest rate does rise by 1.5 percentage points to 9% and AB borrows at this higher rate, it would receive a payment under the FRA agreement worth the equivalent of about 1.5%, thereby reducing the net borrowing cost to about 7.5% (depending on the actual rates that apply).

Interest rate futures

Short-term interest rate futures are exchange-traded instruments. A short sterling future is a notional three-month deposit of £500,000, traded on LIFFE.

A company wishing to fix a rate for borrowing should sell interest rate futures. Since AB wants to hedge the borrowing cost for £2 million for six months, it should sell 8 futures [(£2 million/£500,000) × (6 months/3 months)] and set up a 'short hedge'. It could sell either September or December futures, depending on when the interest period will begin, and when the September futures contract expires during the month.

The interest rate is in the price of the future. Prices are quoted at 100 minus the interest rate, so if AB were to sell September futures, say, at 92.50, this would 'fix' its borrowing rate at 7.5%. As the future approaches settlement date, if the interest rate has risen to 9%, the market price of September futures should have moved to about 91.00. AB could then close its position by buying 8 September futures, and making a profit of 1.50 (150 points) on each contract of its futures dealing. A profit of 150 points on 8 futures would be worth £15,000 (150 points × 8 × contracts £12.50 per point). This is equivalent to interest at 1.5% on £2 million for six months.

AB would borrow £2 million at the market rate. If this is 9%, the net borrowing cost would be 9% less the value of the profit on futures trading (1.5%) giving a net effective interest cost of 7.5%.

Since interest rate futures are only available in standardised amounts and dates, they are less flexible than FRAs, and so possibly less attractive to AB.

Interest rate guarantee

This is a type of borrower's option but with characteristics of an interest rate collar. Unlike an FRA or futures which are binding contracts on both parties, it is not a binding commitment on the option holder. If AB buys this instrument at a cap strike price of 7% (and a notional principal amount of £2 million for six months), for expiry in September, it will exercise its option if the interest rate at expiry is higher than 7%. It will then receive the interest value of the difference (on £2 million for six months) between the actual interest rate (six-month LIBOR) and the cap rate of 7%.

However, in this case, if the interest rate falls below 6%, the option counterparty (a bank) will exercise a floor option, and require AB to pay the difference between the actual interest rate and 6%.

As a result, AB is able to fix the benchmark interest rate between 6% and 7%. So if AB can borrow at, say, LIBOR + 0.50%, the interest rate guarantee would fix its actual borrowing cost between 6.5% and 7.5%, plus the cost of the guarantee.

Arranging this guarantee would cost £2,000 (0.1% of £2 million), which is equivalent to interest of 0.2% on £2 million for six months. The premiums payable on interest rate guarantees can be expensive and must be paid up-front, which can be compared to an FRA on which no premium is payable.

Usefulness of the instruments to AB

All three instruments can help AB to hedge against the risk of a rise in interest rates.

FRAs and futures are binding contracts, so that the hedge effectively fixes the borrowing cost. The interest rate guarantee is a form of option, so that AB can benefit from lower interest rates if they are between 6% and 7%. However, the guarantee has to be paid for.

All three instruments are arranged for a fixed amount and a fixed borrowing period, which means that a hedge might not be perfect. For example, if it turns out that AB needs to borrow £2.5 million for seven months starting in five months' time, none of the hedges would be perfect.

Test your understanding 5 – Swaps

(a) Interest rate swaps can have several uses.

   – They can be used by companies to arrange fixed rate borrowing, when direct access to fixed rate funding (the bond markets) is not possible, for example, if the company is too small or would not have a sufficiently good credit rating.

   – Occasionally, they can be used to obtain lower cost borrowing, through interest rate arbitrage. This opportunity exists in the case of RO and AB.

   – They can be used to alter the proportions of fixed and variable rate funding in a company's debt mix without the expense of redeeming existing debt and issuing new debt in its place, and so can be used to manage exposure to risk from possible future interest rate movements.

(b) AB is a larger company than RO, so we see that AB has cheaper borrowing rates in both the floating rate as well as the fixed rate market. However, while RO only has to pay 0.2% more in the floating rate market, it has to pay a full 1.0% more for fixed rate debt. This creates an opportunity to reduce their combined borrowing costs by 0.8% (1% – 0.2%).

AB has a comparative advantage in the fixed rate market, since it is cheaper by 1% than RO, compared to just 0.2% in the floating rate market. So, the companies could co-operate to their mutual benefit if:

- AB borrows at a fixed rate and swaps into floating rate; and
- RO borrows at a floating rate, where it can borrow comparatively more favourably than at a fixed rate (only 0.2% more), and swap into a fixed rate.

The opportunity for arbitrage is 0.8%, which means that if they share this equally, both will borrow 0.4% more cheaply than if they borrowed directly at a floating rate in the case of AB or at a fixed rate in the case of RO.

A swap could be arranged as follows:

- AB borrows in the fixed rate market at 7.5% and pays LIBOR to RO.
- RO borrows in the floating rate market at LIBOR + 0.5% and pays a fixed rate of 7.6% to AB.

The net effect is as follows:

AB pays 7.5% to the bank, receives 7.6% from RO and pays LIBOR to RO which equates to LIBOR – 0.1%.

RO pays LIBOR + 0.5% to the bank, receives LIBOR from AB, and pays 7.6% to AB which equates to a payment of 8.1%.

These net borrowing rates are each 0.4% less than AB could borrow at a floating rate or RO could borrow at a fixed rate.

(c) In practice, most swaps are arranged through banks that run a 'swaps book'. There are several advantages in dealing with a bank rather than directly with another company.

- In dealing with a bank, there is no problem about finding a swaps counterparty with an equal and opposite swapping requirement. The bank will arrange a swap to meet the specific requirements of each individual customer, as to amount and duration of the swap.

- In dealing with a bank, the credit risk is that the bank might default, whereas in dealing directly with another company, the credit risk is that the other company might default. Banks are usually a much lower credit risk than corporations.

– Banks are specialists in swaps, and are able to provide standard legal swaps agreements. The operation of the swap is likely to be administratively more straightforward.

The significant drawback to using a bank is that the bank will want to make a profit from its operations. In practice, it will generally do this by charging different swap rates for fixed rate payments and fixed rate receipts on different swaps. In terms of the RO and AB situation, where there is a credit arbitrage opportunity of 0.8%, if a swaps bank were to be used to arrange a separate swap with each company, it might take a profit of, say, 0.2%, leaving just 0.6% of benefit to be shared between RO and AB.

Test your understanding 6 – QW (1)

REPORT

To: The Board of QW plc
From: The Treasurer
Date: XX-XX-XX
Subject: Interest rate swaps

(i) A swap is an agreement between two parties to exchange the cash flows related to specific underlying obligations. In an interest rate swap, the cash flows are the interest payments arising on principal amounts. For example, company A might have outstanding borrowings of £1m with annual interest fixed at 10%, whilst company B has borrowings of £1m with annual interest paid at a floating rate of LIBOR + 1%.

If company A and company B agree on an interest rate swap, they agree to take on the other's interest obligations, so that company B will pay fixed annual interest of £100,000 pa, while company A will now pay floating interest of LIBOR + 1% on £1m. Such a swap might be entered into if company A thought that interest rates were going to fall, while company B thought they would rise.

A forward rate agreement (FRA) is a contract in which two parties agree on the interest rate to be paid for a period of time starting in the future, for example for a three-month period starting in six months' time. The contract is settled in cash; exposure is limited to the difference in interest rates between the FRA agreed rate and the actual rate, based on the notional agreed principal.

An interest rate futures contract is a standardised form of FRA traded on an investment exchange. Each contract is for a specified nominal amount of a specified financial instrument on a specified date.

The advantages of swaps compared to other forms of interest rate risk management are as follows:

– Swaps allow a company to restructure its capital profile without the expense of actually redeeming existing borrowings. Fixed borrowings can be changed to floating rate, or floating to fixed, without incurring the transaction costs and possible redemption penalties associated with actual redemption.

– Using the principle of comparative advantage, companies with different credit ratings can reduce their cost of borrowing, by borrowing at different costs in different markets.

– Swaps can offer access to capital markets for companies which would not normally be allowed to participate due to their low credit rating, by swapping borrowings with a company with a higher credit rating.

(ii) We (QW plc) could borrow at a fixed 8%, while ER plc borrows at a floating LIBOR + 0.5%, and then swap the interest obligations. Total interest paid by both parties is LIBOR + 8.5%.

The alternative is for us to borrow at a floating LIBOR + 0.2%, while ER plc borrows at a fixed 9.5%. Total interest then paid by both parties is LIBOR + 9.7%.

Clearly the swap is advantageous, since total interest is 1.2% less than the alternative. The bank's commission is 0.2%, leaving 1% (or £100,000) as the net benefit to be shared between the two companies. ER plc has opportunistically proposed that the net benefit should be shared equally between the two companies. Since our credit rating is better than ER's, it would be fairer for us to receive more than 50%, though this is a matter for negotiation.

As a final point, it should be noted that, if we are confident that interest rates are going to fall over the next three years, it will probably be better to take out floating rate borrowings from the start, rather than take out fixed rate borrowings and swap these for floating rate. We would not have to share the benefits of falling interest rates with any third party or pay the swap's commission payment to the bank. The decision therefore depends on how confident we are that interest rates will fall as expected. Please contact me again if I can be of any further help to you in this or any other matter.

Test your understanding 7 – Gymbob (2)

Forward rate agreements offer Gymbob the facility to fix the future interest rate on borrowings for a specified period. For example, if Gymbob entered into an FRA with a bank in 3 months' time one year at a guaranteed 7%, then if the interest rate rose the bank would have to pay Gymbob the difference. On the other hand, if the interest rate fell, Gymbob would still have to pay the bank the difference. No matter which way the interest rate moved, Gymbob would pay 7%.

FRAs do not involve any actual lending of the principal sum of £5 million. This can be done with the same or a different bank, or other lender.

FRAs are usually for at least £1 million, and can be arranged for up to 2 or 3 years in the future, so FRAs appear to be a suitable way for Gymbob to manage interest rate exposure.

Interest rate futures are binding contracts between seller and buyer to take delivery of a specified interest rate commitment on an agreed date at an agreed price. They can be used to protect against interest rate rises and are available for a maximum of 1 – 2 years.

Futures contracts are sold now in the expectation that, as interest rates rise the contract value will fall, and they can then be purchased at a lower price, generating a profit on the futures deal. The profit compensates for the actual rises in interest rates experienced by companies that have borrowed funds from banks and elsewhere. If the interest rate moves in the opposite direction to that expected, a futures loss will occur, but this will be offset by cheaper interest costs in the market.

All contracts require a small initial deposit or margin.

Futures should allow Gymbob to hedge successfully against increases in the interest rate, although a perfect hedge is rare.

Interest rate options such as caps, floors and collars guarantee that the interest rate will not rise above, or fall below, an agreed fixed level during a specified time period commencing sometime in the future. The interest rate protection for Gymbob is similar to that given by an FRA.

However, options involve the payment of a premium to the seller of the option, whether or not the option is exercised. No premium is payable with an FRA.

Also, whilst protecting downside risk (an interest rate rise), Gymbob can take full advantage of favourable interest rate movements.

For example, if interest rates fall, the option is left to lapse and Gymbob will borrow the £5 million from the market at the lower rate. However, if rates rose, then Gymbob would exercise the option to guarantee a maximum cost of 7%.

However, the premium involved with an option can be prohibitively expensive. A way to lower this would be to take out a collar (a cap and a floor).

Reporting on financial instruments

Chapter learning objectives

Lead	Component
D2. Evaluate alternative risk management tools.	(d) Recommend risk management strategies and discuss their accounting implications.

Specific areas of indicative syllabus content of relevance here are the following:

- Principles of valuation of financial instruments for management and financial reporting purposes (IAS 39), and controls to ensure that the appropriate accounting method is applied to a given instrument.

- Quantification and disclosure of the sensitivity of financial instrument values to changes in external conditions.

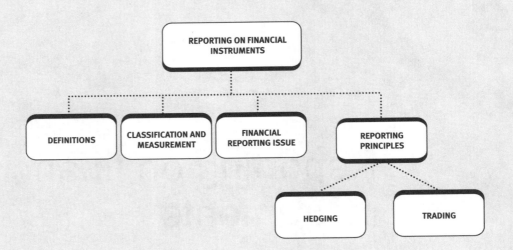

1 Definitions

There are specific accounting provisions that relate to the use of derivatives and other financial instruments. In the context of this syllabus it is important that you are aware of the accounting and reporting implications of the risk management techniques that may be utilised in a business (and have been discussed in previous chapters).

Firstly, some definitions of key terms:

Financial instruments

A financial instrument is 'any contract that gives rise to both a financial asset of one enterprise and a financial liability or equity instrument of another enterprise' (IAS 32). They include forward contracts (and FRAs) and derivatives, such as futures, options and swaps.

Financial asset

A financial asset is created where a company enters into an agreement 'now' with another party creating a contractual right that will (or might) lead to cash receipts in the future.

Financial liability

A financial liability is created where the agreement creates a contractual obligation that will (or might) lead to cash payments in the future.

Derivatives

Derivatives are a type of financial instrument whose value depends on the price of another asset or underlying factor. These would include futures, options and swaps.

Under IAS 39 (*Financial Instruments: Recognition and Measurement*), which is soon to be replaced by IFRS 9, derivatives are defined as any instruments with three features:

- They derive their value from another underlying item.

- They require little or no initial net investment (low cost).

- They are settled at a future date.

Recap of cashflows with financial instruments

To understand the concept of forward contracts and derivatives creating rights or obligations, it is helpful to consider the nature of the cash flows with each type of contract or instrument.

- With a **forward exchange contract**, an agreement is made on the contract transaction date to exchange a fixed quantity of one currency for a fixed quantity of another currency at a specified future date.

- With an **FRA**, an agreement is made to exchange an amount of cash at a future settlement date for the difference between an FRA rate and a reference interest rate such as LIBOR, on a notional principal amount.

- With an **option**, the holder has a right that will be exercised at a future date if it is beneficial for the holder. An in-the-money option, or an option that might be in-the-money by its expiry date, has a value to its holder. It is also a liability to the option writer/seller. An out-of-the-money option is one not worth exercising by the option holder.

- A **swap** is a contract for the exchange of cash flows over the term of the swap. Exchanges of cash in the past are irrelevant to current value, but a swap that has not yet reached the end of its term represents a series of expected future cash inflows and future cash outflows. If the value of the expected future inflows exceeds the value of the expected future outflows, the swap has a value that should be recognised as an asset. On the other hand, if the value of future outflows exceeds the value of future inflows, the swap is a liability.

- A **future** is a contract for the future sale or purchase of a quantity of an item, and as long as a futures position remains open, it will give rise to future cash receipts or payments, depending on the future movement in the futures price. At a reporting date, a future will already have resulted in some cash flows (initial margin and variation margin paid or withdrawn). However, there will be more cash flows in the future until the position is closed or reaches settlement.

2 Financial reporting issue

Management and all stakeholders of a company need to be aware of the financial rights and obligations facing the business that will create cash flows in the future. There are three reporting standards that deal with financial instruments:

- IAS 32 deals with presentation
- IAS 39 deals with recognition and measurement (soon to be IFRS 9)
- IFRS 7 deals with disclosures

This increased disclosure is part of a general move towards fair value accounting, and in the context of the global financial crisis, accounting for financial instruments has taken on increased significance. It has led to:

- instruments which may have been off-balance sheet previously now having to be recognised, and
- changes in value of financial instruments now being recognised in the income statement.

Problems with increased disclosure

- any volatility in the instruments or their underlying factors (e.g., exchange rates) will directly impact profit in that it too may be more volatile leading to a volatile share price
- measurement of fair value can be highly subjective, and may be out-of-date by the time the financial statements are in use.

3 Reporting principles

Forward contracts and derivative instruments create rights or obligations in the future, and these can be valued.

You will not be required to measure a derivative instrument in the examination, but you should understand the **principles** of valuation.

Measuring the value of a forward contract or derivative, and reporting value in the statement of financial position, depends on whether the instruments are used to create a hedge for a risk exposure.

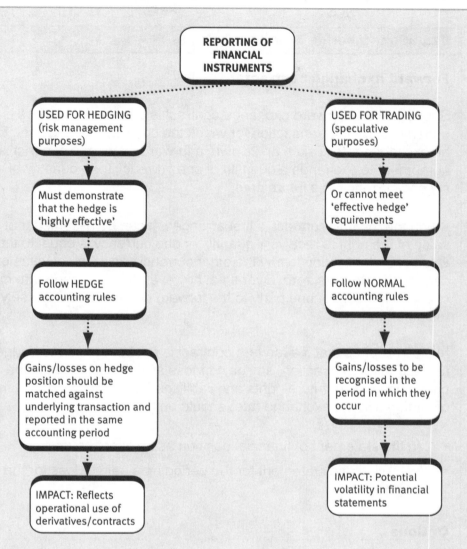

Hedge effectiveness

IAS 39 provides detailed conditions that the company must meet if a hedge is deemed to be 'effective'. The company must:

- Fully document the hedge at its inception.
- Test throughout the life of the hedge that it is effective.
- Justify that any future transactions hedged are highly probable (assumed by accounting profession as >90% certain).

Valuations ignoring hedging

Forward exchange contracts

Suppose that a forward exchange contract is arranged, but there is no underlying trading transaction for which the contract is being used to fix an exchange rate. Taken on its own, a forward exchange contract is an agreement to exchange a quantity of one currency for a quantity of a second currency at a future date.

When the forward contract is first arranged, it can be assumed that the value of the right to receive a quantity of one currency is equal to the value of the obligation to pay the other currency, and the net value of the contract is therefore zero. Over time, however, the exchange rate might change, in favour of one party to the forward contract and adversely for the other party.

IAS 39 requires that if a forward contract is not being used to hedge a future trading transaction, any gain or loss arising as a result in the changing value of future rights and liabilities (i.e. in this case, as a result of changes in the exchange rate) should be reported:

- in the statement of financial position as an asset or liability

- in the income statement for the period as a gain or loss for the period.

Options

Options have a value that can be measured using the Black-Scholes pricing model. For an option holder, the maximum cost or liability is the option premium, paid when the option is bought. It could increase in value over time (and for the option writer, there could be an increasing liability).

The value of an option that has not yet reached expiry should be reported as an asset in the statement of financial position of the option holder and a liability in the statement of financial position of the option writer. If the option is not being used to hedge an underlying transaction, the gain or loss should be reported in the income statement for the period.

Swaps

The value of a swap at any time is the difference between the present value of expected future cash receipts and the present value of expected future cash payments. When a swap is first transacted, the present values of expected future receipts and payments should be the same, and the swap should have a value of zero.

However, the value of a swap will change over time:

- The value of an interest rate swap, in which one party pays a fixed rate and the other pays a floating rate, will change if the floating rate goes up or down. A fall in the floating rate creates benefits for the payer of the floating rate (receiver of the fixed rate) and creates future obligations for the payer of the fixed rate (receiver of the floating rate). This is because the cash flows exchanged between the two parties to the swap will change.

- Similarly, the value of a currency swap will change if the exchange rate between the two currencies changes. The value of the interest in one currency will rise or fall relative to the value of the interest payments in the other currency.

Futures

The changing value of positions in futures up to closure of a position or settlement date for the contract is easily measured by the changes in the daily futures price. A daily settlement price is announced each day by the futures exchange for each contract, and this can be used to measure gains or losses on a position. (The futures exchange uses the daily settlement price to decide how much variation margin might be required from investors to cover the losses on their positions during the day.)

If futures are bought or sold for speculative purposes, gains or losses on open positions should be reported in the income statement.

FRAs

An FRA is a contract on an interest rate. When it is first arranged, it should have a zero value to both the buyer and the seller. However, if the reference rate for the FRA is different from the FRA rate, there will be a cash exchange between the buyer and seller at settlement.

At the statement of financial position date, an FRA that has not yet reached settlement will be either a future right or a future obligation, depending on the difference between the FRA rate and the reference interest rate, and so whether a cash receipt or cash payment is expected at settlement.

If an FRA is not used to hedge an underlying transaction, IAS39 requires that any such gain or loss should be recognised in the income statement for the period and in the statement of financial position.

Hedge accounting

IAS 39 recognises three types of hedge:

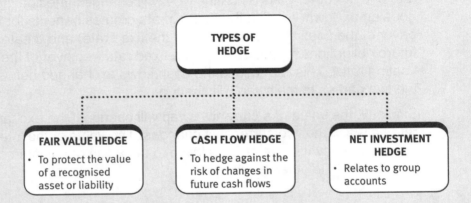

Fair value hedging

- The hedging instrument should be re-measured at fair value. All gains or losses in its value should be included in the income statement for the period.

- The hedged portion of the hedged item should also be re-measured at fair value, with all gains or losses reported in the income statement for the period.

In this way, gains or losses in the fair value of the hedged item will be offset by losses or gains on the hedging instrument, in the period when the changes in value occur.

Cash flow hedging

- The hedging instrument should be re-measured at fair value. All gains or losses in its value should be taken to equity, but not reported in the income statement.

- When the hedged transaction is settled the gain or loss that was previously taken to equity can be recycled to the income statement.

In this way, the gain or loss on the hedging instrument will be reported in the income statement in the same period as the transaction for which it is a hedge.

Examples of valuations of hedging treatments

Fair value hedges

For example, if a lender has made a fixed rate loan to a customer at 6% interest, but interest rates subsequently increase, the lender suffers a reduction in the real value of their loan (the discounted cash flows at market rate are lower than the original value of the loan). To hedge this they could enter an interest rate swap, swapping fixed for floating rate interest.

Under normal accounting rules:

Loan asset   At cost on the statement of financial position .

Interest swap   At fair value on the statement of financial position with gains or losses going to income statement (means that the profits are volatile making users perceive risk).

Under hedge accounting rules:

Loan asset   At fair value with gain/loss going to income statement.

Interest swap   At fair value with opposite gain/loss going to income statement.

If the hedge is perfectly effective the gains and losses would offset each other.

Cash flow hedges

For example, a company expects to pay $100,000 in six months' time for a new machine from a US supplier. To hedge they enter into a forward contract.

Under normal rules:

Future sale   Not recognised until sale occurs.

Forward contract   At fair value with gains or losses in income statement. This means that the income statement will recognise the gains and losses on the forward contract earlier than the sale is recognised, resulting in profit volatility.

Under hedging rules:

Future sale   Not recognised until sale occurs.

Forward contract   At fair value but gains and losses go to equity. The gain/ loss is transferred against the income statement only when the sale is made.

If the hedge is perfectly effective the sale value recognised will be at the forward contract rate following the commercial intention of the company.

Net investment hedges

These are special rules for foreign subsidiaries financed by foreign loans. The reason for using the foreign liability to fund a foreign asset is that commercially there is a gain on one and a loss on the other that offset.

Under normal rules:

Subsidiary   Gains and losses in equity.

Loan   Gains and losses in the income statement.

Under hedging rules:

Subsidiary   Gains and losses in equity.

Loan   Gains and losses in equity.

The benefit of hedge accounting is not having volatility in the income statement.

Test your understanding 1 – Bank

A bank makes a £100 million fixed rate loan to a customer. The interest is swapped for floating rate interest on £100 million and the hedge should be perfectly effective. At inception the swap has zero fair value.

One year later the interest rate has increased which has had the following impact:

Fair value of the loan has reduced to £95 million.

The interest swap is an asset of £5 million.

Required:

Describe the impact on the financial statements for the following situations:

(a) The swap is not designated as a hedge.
(b) The swap is designated as a hedge.

Test your understanding 2 – QW (2)

Assume that you are treasurer of QW plc, a company with diversified, international interests. You have been in post for twelve months, having been recruited from a large financial institution. You have a keen interest in using financial derivatives (such as futures and options) to both manage risk and generate revenue. Some board members have expressed concern that your activities may be involving the company in unnecessary risk.

Required:

Explain the meaning and use of financial derivatives in general terms, and the advantages and disadvantages of their use for companies such as QW plc.

4 Chapter summary

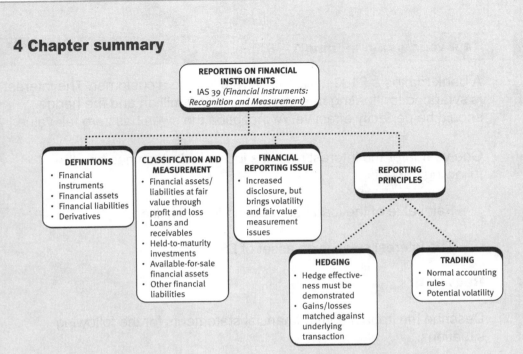

REPORTING ON FINANCIAL INSTRUMENTS
- IAS 39 (*Financial Instruments: Recognition and Measurement*)

DEFINITIONS
- Financial instruments
- Financial assets
- Financial liabilities
- Derivatives

CLASSIFICATION AND MEASUREMENT
- Financial assets/liabilities at fair value through profit and loss
- Loans and receivables
- Held-to-maturity investments
- Available-for-sale financial assets
- Other financial liabilities

FINANCIAL REPORTING ISSUE
- Increased disclosure, but brings volatility and fair value measurement issues

REPORTING PRINCIPLES

HEDGING
- Hedge effectiveness must be demonstrated
- Gains/losses matched against underlying transaction

TRADING
- Normal accounting rules
- Potential volatility

Test your understanding answers

Test your understanding 1 – Bank

(a) **Not a hedge**

The loan would be included in the accounts at amortised cost as a loan or receivable.

The swap would be recognised on the statement of financial position at fair value with gains and losses going to the income statement. The result would be that £5 million income would be recognised in the income statement for the year.

(b) **A hedge**

The loan would be revalued to fair value, and the swap would be recognised at fair value. The impact is that the loan makes a £5 million loss and the swap a £5 million gain which gets offset in the income statement.

On the statement of financial position the assets would be reflected as:

Loan asset	£95m
Interest swap	£5m

Test your understanding 2 – QW (2)

A 'derivative' is a financial instrument that derives its value from the price or rate of some underlying item. Underlying items include equities, bonds, commodities, interest rates, exchange rates, and stock market and other indices. Financial derivatives therefore include futures contracts, options, forward contracts, interest rate and currency swaps, interest rate caps, collars and floors, forward interest rate agreements, commitments to purchase shares or bonds, note issuance facilities and letters of credit. There are three main ways in which a company such as QW plc can use derivatives:

- Hedging
- Arbitraging
- Speculating

Hedging uses derivatives to reduce risk exposure. For example, if we are a UK company due to receive $100,000 in two months' time, we can take out a derivatives contract to sell $100,000 forward. This eliminates our exchange risk, but at the cost of the contract and the downside of no longer being able to benefit from exchange rate movements in our favour. Risk-averse managers would favour hedging as many risks as possible. Arbitraging uses derivatives to benefit from temporary price anomalies to create riskless profits. If, say, US dollars could be bought for $1.6 to the £ in one currency market and sold for $1.7 to the £ in another, then one could buy the underlying currency, take out a short derivative position for the same number of dollars, and enjoy riskless sterling profits.

Speculating uses derivatives to create profits from unhedged positions. For example, if I believe that sterling will weaken against the dollar, I could buy dollars forward. At the maturity date, I sell the dollars into sterling at the then spot rate and make a profit, since the dollars are worth more pounds than was expected by the market. This type of speculation increases the company's risk exposure. If I buy dollars forward and am wrong about sterling weakening, there is the possibility of unlimited losses.

QW plc has diversified international interests, so the hedging of certain risks may well be practicable and appropriate. Arbitrage opportunities occur rarely, so can probably be ignored. Whether you wish the company to earn potential profits by speculating on derivatives depends on the board's attitude to risk. Financial derivatives have had a bad press in recent years, with some companies suffering large losses. What is important is that you see derivatives as a means of managing risk exposures; by taking out appropriate derivative contracts, a company can either reduce or increase its risk as it wishes. They are therefore a valuable tool in the treasurer's arsenal of financial instruments.

Information strategy, systems and technology

Chapter learning objectives

Lead	Component
E1. Evaluate the benefits and risks associated with information-related systems.	(a) Advise managers on the development of information management (IM), information systems (IS) and information technology (IT) strategies that support management and internal control requirements.
	(b) Evaluate IS/IT systems appropriate to an organisation's needs for operational and control information.

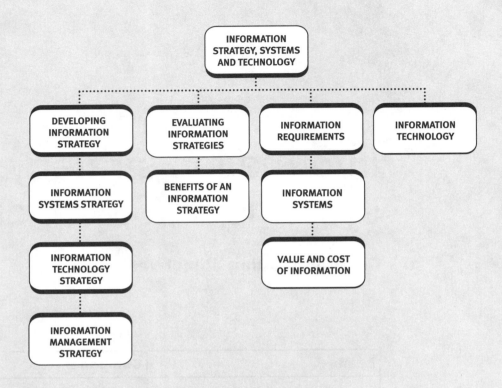

1 Developing an information strategy

A key factor in companies controlling and monitoring the risks they face is being able to provide the information to managers to run the business. Companies therefore need information systems and an information strategy.

The reason companies now refer to and talk about 'information strategy' as opposed purely to information systems is that information is being identified as a key strategic resource, arguably the most valuable resource businesses create and have. Because of its value it is worth having a good plan to structure the information provision, ensure it meets the needs of the business and secure and control it.

Information strategy

The company needs to develop a plan to link its business and information strategies, and the model below shows how this can be done.

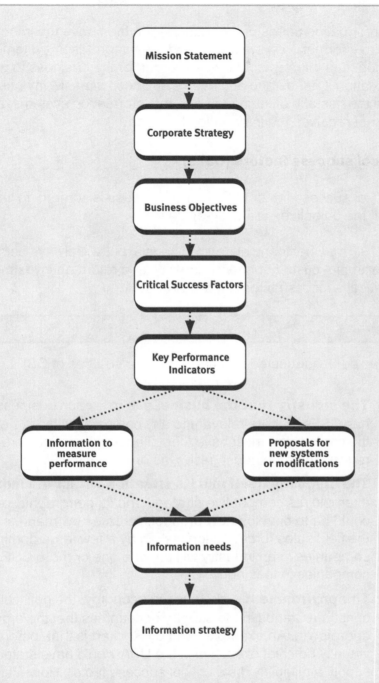

The corporate strategy will be set first and this will drive information needs and information systems. The link between the corporate strategy and the information needs is often established by considering 'critical success factors' (CSFs) for the organisation.

The organisation will need information on the key performance indicators (KPIs) to ensure that the CSFs are being achieved and, as a result, that the business aims are being achieved.

The information needs of the organisation then drive the information strategy and the information systems created. The information systems should be developed in this 'top down' way in order for the business to get the information it needs and achieve its business aims. Many businesses have made the mistake of letting IT drive the information systems, and managers have not received the information they need.

Critical success factors (CSFs)

A critical success factor (CSF) for a business is something 'that must go right if the objectives are to be achieved'.

The CSF may be financial or non-financial but will always be at a high level. For example, customer service, quality, and return on investment might all be critical success factors for a business.

Sources of CSFs

It has been suggested that there are four sources of CSFs:

- **The industry that the business is in** – each business or industry has CSFs that are relevant to any company within it. For example, the car industry must have 'compliance with pollution requirements regarding car exhaust gases' as one of its CSFs.

- **The company itself and its situation within the industry** – for example, its competitive strategy and its geographic location. CSFs could be to develop new products, create new markets or to support the field sales force. Actions taken by a few large dominant companies in an industry will provide one or more CSFs for small companies in that industry.

- **The environment** – such as the economy, the political factors and consumer trends in the country or countries that the organisation operates in. An example used by Rockart is that, before 1973, virtually no chief executive in the USA would have stated 'energy supply availability' as a critical success factor. However, following the oil embargo in 1973 many executives monitored this factor closely.

- **Temporal (short-term) organisational factors** – these are areas of company activity that are unusually causing concern in the short-term because they are unacceptable and need attention. For example, cases of too little or too much inventory might classify as a CSF for a short time during recession.

Many CSFs will require new systems to be developed or improvements made to existing systems. Other CSFs will require improved information to monitor performance of key indicators which measure the achievement, or otherwise, of success factors and objectives. This may require further development of information systems.

Performance indicators

A performance indicator (PI) is an objective stated in such a way that progress towards the achievement of a critical success factor can be measured.

More on PIs

The PIs should be:

Specific   Expressed clearly and precisely.

Measurable   Capable of quantification.

Achievable   Realistically achievable by the organisation.

Relevant   To the critical success factor that is being measured.

Time-constrained   By when?

Test your understanding 1 – KPI

Recommend KPIs that can be used to support the CSFs below:

- Maintain overall gross profit of 40%
- Increase customer satisfaction
- Be the most innovative company in our industry

2 Information strategy components

The information strategy is the overall plan a business has to create and develop its information systems.

Information strategy is usually broken up into three parts:

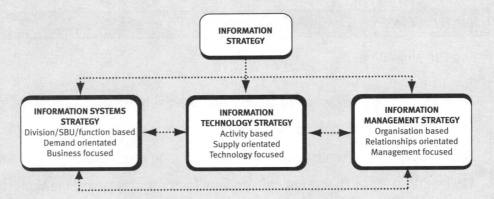

The three strategies link as shown in the diagram.

The term **information systems strategy** is normally used to cover all three.

The differences between the three components are summarised below:

- **IS strategy** looks at the way in which information systems in various parts of the organisation are organised.
- **IT strategy** looks at the technology infrastructure of the systems.
- **IM strategy** considers how the systems support management processes.

More on IS strategy

Information systems (IS) strategy is concerned with identifying the information requirements of the organisation. IS strategy must ensure that the information required by the organisation, to help it achieve its strategic objectives, is:

- acquired
- retained
- shared, and
- made available for use.

It relates to all aspects of information, and all areas of activity (financial and non-financial; strategic, tactical and operational; human resources, operations, sales and marketing, research and development; internal and external information, and so on). It is concerned with answering the questions, for all aspects of activity at all levels within the organisation:

- What information is required? and

- Where might it come from?

IS strategy should be demand-oriented, in the sense that answers to the question 'What information is required?' should focus on the demands of the business managers for information. IS strategies must also be business-driven and capable of delivering tangible benefits, for example increased productivity, enhanced profits, and perhaps a reduction in the workforce.

Traditional organisational structures that divide business functions are not suitable as a basis for IS strategy development in a 'process-oriented' business environment. Client-server technologies have the capability to integrate business functions. This results in a blurring of the divisions found in the old functional-based organisation structure and demands a different way of conceptualising organisations and their associated business processes and information requirements.

More on IT strategy

Information technology can be defined as 'the use of computers, microelectronics and telecommunications to help us produce, store, and send information in the form of pictures, words or numbers, more reliably, quickly and economically'.

Information technology (IT) strategy is concerned with what specific IT systems are needed to meet the demands for information within the organisation, in terms of:

- system networks and communication systems

- hardware, and

- software.

IT systems should be developed or adapted so that they are capable of obtaining, processing, summarising and reporting the information required by the organisation. The IT systems must also be consistent with the requirements for the storage and availability of data and information to users.

IT strategy is about the delivery of workable solutions to business problems – the practical application of information technology to the organisation. It is described as activity-based, supply-oriented and technology-focused and is seen as the technology framework or architecture that drives, shapes and controls the IT infrastructure. In other words, it considers what technologies are available, and which of these would be most suitable for meeting the information requirements of the organisation.

More on IM strategy

Information management (IM) strategy is concerned with the management of the information that is gathered by the organisation, and how it is stored and made available for access by users. It is therefore concerned with matters such as:

- the use of databases, and the type of databases used
- data warehousing
- back-up facilities for data storage
- data security issues
- archiving.

The IM strategy should ensure that information that has been provided through IT systems is made available to the individuals who need it. From an economic perspective, it should also be concerned with making the information available in the most efficient way but at the least cost. IM strategy might therefore promote the elimination of data duplication.

Information management is also concerned more broadly with:

- planning – ensuring that the IS and IT strategies are integrated with the other strategic plans and objectives of the organisation
- organisation – this involves issues such as decentralisation or centralisation of the IT function, the formation of steering committees, management education and training, IT reporting procedures and the responsibilities of IT managers
- control – control issues relate to the assessment of the performance of IT systems and controls over IT costs (and benefits). Key aspects are performance measurement and investment appraisal of IT
- technology – is related to managing the priorities for IT strategy, e.g. the design and development of new methodologies for IT, security practices and data management techniques.

3 Benefits of an information strategy

The benefits of an information strategy include:

- Achievement of **goal congruence** between the information systems objectives and the corporate objectives. Failure of computer systems to work can result in the failure of some organisations to function at all e.g. Amazon and eBay.

- The organisation is more likely to be able to create and sustain **competitive advantage**. The company's computer system will likely impact on the customer these days, if they order over the internet or rely on order information for a delivery date.

- The high levels of expenditure on information systems will be more focused on **supporting** key aspects of the **business**.

- **Developments in IT can be exploited** at the most appropriate time – which is not always when they are first available.

- Computers are often of strategic importance in a company. Having an information strategy is a **costly** business and unmanaged development can lead to costly mistakes.

- IT affects all levels of **employees and management**. Having a plan that can be communicated to these employees should ensure that they 'buy-in' to the ideas within it and efficiency will be increased more quickly.

4 Evaluating information strategies

In the exam you could be asked to evaluate the information strategy and systems developed by a business.

The key feature of the strategy is that it should support business needs and managers and be an integral part of the overall business strategy and therefore if it does not achieve this it is a poor strategy.

A more structured evaluation approach could be:

(1) Identify the objectives of the organisation and the CSFs.

(2) Identify objectives for risk management and control.

(3) Identify key information requirements of managers.

(4) Establish information currently available and assess whether information provision is adequate.

(5) Identify alternative strategies and the beneficial information they would provide.

(6) Evaluate whether the technology used by the organisation is the best and most appropriate available (IT strategy assessment).

(7) Assess whether the information is managed and controlled in the best way for the organisation (IM strategy assessment).

(8) Evaluate whether the information strategy is appropriately controlled in the organisation and ensure that there are clear lines of responsibility for it.

In the exam there is likely to be a scenario littered with IT issues in a company where the information systems are not working optimally. Think about your own place of work:

- How old is your computer system?

- Is it slow to process information?

- Is the information well laid out, superfluous, have errors in it?

- Do you have a good IT support department that can resolve any issues quickly and to your satisfaction?

There are many other issues which you could probably think of since you probably use a computer each day at work - always try to relate your own experiences to the scenario given in the exam.

5 Information requirements of managers

Levels of management

The various levels of management that exist within an organisation may be illustrated by Anthony's Triangle:

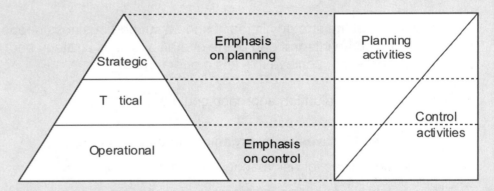

The different levels of management within an organisation will take different types of decision and will require different information to take those decisions. The information systems of the organisation must meet the information needs of all of these different levels.

More on management levels

In general terms, each level of management will be involved in specific activities:

Level	Activity
Strategic	Involved with monitoring and controlling the organisation as a whole, making decisions on areas such as opening of new shops and factories or investment in new product line.
Tactical	Responsible for implementing the decisions of strategic managers and ensuring that the different divisions or departments within the organisation are operating correctly.
Operational	Controlling the day-to-day operations of the organisation, reporting queries or problems back to tactical management for decisions as necessary.

The two key activities of management are therefore:

Planning	Planning refers to setting the strategic direction of the company. This involves a significant degree of risk as strategic decision makers are effectively determining what the company will do in the context of a risky external environment.
Control	Control refers to monitoring the activities of the company – with the internal control systems checking that those activities are being carried out correctly. While control strategy is set by strategic management, the implementation and monitoring is a more junior activity.

Good information

The information received by management needs to be of a certain standard to be useful in internal control, risk management and monitoring.

The information should meet the criteria of 'good' information:

- **A**ccurate
- **C**omplete
- **C**ost-beneficial
- **U**ser-targeted
- **R**elevant
- **A**uthoritative
- **T**imely
- **E**asy to use

Information needs of managers

Information is required to enable managers at all levels to plan and control their responsible activities. Information must be provided to enable managers to make timely and effective decisions.

Management level	*Information needs*
Strategic management	- Business markets
	- Suppliers
	- Customers
	- Competitors
	- Stock market
	- Technology
	- Politics
	- Environmental issues.

Tactical management	• Tactical planning information
	• Targets
	• Production
	• Plant capacity
	• Budgets
	• Purchasing
	• Operating expenses
	• Manpower levels.
Operational management	• Primary activities
	• Work scheduling
	• Work force
	• Immediate resources.

Information characteristics

Strategic and operational information – characteristics

Information characteristic	Strategic	Operational
Time period	Information can be both historical (enabling management to learn from what has happened in the past) and forecast.	Operational information must be actual historical information.
Timeliness	Generally speaking, the timeliness of information is not crucial as decisions are taken over a series of weeks or months. Significant changes, such as the acquisition of a competitor, will normally be reported quickly to senior management.	Information must be immediately available

Objectivity	Strategic decision making will require a mixture of objective and subjective information. Building long-term plans needs future information, which incorporates subjective forecasts of what is likely to happen.	The highly structured and programmable decisions made at the operational level need information that is both objective and quantifiable. The comparatively junior level at which decisions are made requires strict guidelines to be set and disqualifies subjective data as a basis for this level of decision.
Quantifiability	Strategic decision making needs both qualitative and quantitative information, although attempts will often be made to quantify apparently qualitative data. This enables such data to be incorporated into the kind of mathematical models often used in the building of strategic plans.	
Accuracy	There is no demand for information to be completely accurate, it will often be rounded to the nearest thousand.	Information must be accurate to the nearest £ or $ – as it relates to low level or detailed decision making.
Certainty	By its very nature, future information is subject to uncertainty. Strategic planners must be capable of adjusting to the limitations of the data.	Information will have little or no uncertainty as it relates to historical recording of actual events, e.g. individual sales.
Completeness	Strategic planners will often need to work with only partial information, using assumptions and extrapolations to try to build as complete a picture as possible.	The sort of decisions to be made at this level are highly predictable, which enables the information needed to be specified and an appropriate information system built. This will ensure that a complete set of information is available when it is needed.

Breadth	A wide variety of data are needed for strategic planning. It must cover the whole gamut of the organisation's operations and can come in various forms.	Information will be focused on the specific decisions being made – any other data are irrelevant and potentially distracting.
Detail	It is unnecessary to have a great deal of detail when building a strategic plan, and detail is likely to be distracting and confusing. Aggregated and summarised data are most commonly used by senior management.	Information will be detailed to enable the manager to make decisions about individual items, e.g. the number of items to order.

Tactical information – characteristics

Just as tactical decision making forms a link between strategic and operational management, the information it requires has some of the characteristics of each.

Forecast and historical data are both required, although historical data are not needed as immediately as it is for operational decisions. Information is largely objective and quantitative but the greater experience of middle managers making tactical decisions makes this less important than for operational information.

For each of the other information qualities – accuracy, certainty, completeness, breadth and detail – tactical information occupies the mid-point between strategic and operational information.

6 Information systems to support management

To meet their information needs, managers use information systems, of which there are a number of different types. The different types of system meet the different information needs of the different managers.

The main systems can be summarised in the following diagram:

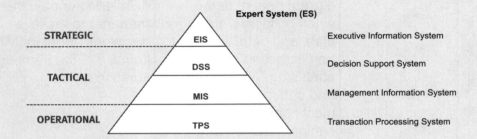

As a basic idea the systems towards the top of the tree will support the strategic decisions and they will use the data from systems in the levels below.

Definitions of information systems

Transaction Processing System (TPS)

- This is the system that records historic information and it represents the simple automation of manual systems.

- The TPS routinely captures, processes, stores and outputs the low level transaction data. This system is very important – data input incorrectly will effect every report produced using it, giving management mis-information and hence they will make poor decisions.

Management Information System (MIS)

- A management information system is defined as 'a system to convert data from internal and external sources into information, and to communicate that information in an appropriate form to managers at all levels and in all areas of the business to enable them to make timely and effective decisions'.

Decision Support System (DSS)

- A decision support system is defined as a 'computer based system which enables managers to confront ill-structured problems by direct interaction with data and problem-solving programs'.

- They are computer systems which are used as an aid in making decisions when presented with semi-structured or unstructured problems. Their aim is to provide information in a flexible way to aid decision making.

Executive Information System (EIS) / Executive Support System (ESS)

- An executive support system (ESS) or executive information system (EIS) is an interactive system that allows executives to access information for monitoring the operations of the organisation and scanning general business conditions. It gives executives ready access to key internal and external data.

Enterprise Resource Planning System (ERPS)

- An enterprise resource planning system is comprised of a commercial software package that promises the seamless integration of all the information flowing through the company – financial, accounting, human resources, supply chain and customer information.

- This is achieved by holding the data for all transaction and management information systems on a common database.

Expert Systems (ES)

- An expert system is defined as 'a computerised system that performs the role of an expert or carries out a task that requires expertise'.

- The system holds expert/specialist knowledge and allows non-experts to interrogate a computer for information, advice and recommended decisions.

Strategic Enterprise Management System (SEMS)

- A strategic enterprise management system assists management in making high-level strategic decisions.

- Tools such as activity-based management (ABM) and the balanced scorecard are applied to the data to enable the strategic goals of the organisation to be worked towards.

Information system types

System	Purpose	Features	Example(s)
Transaction processing system.	Captures and stores transaction data.	Batch, on-line or real time processing.	• Sales order processing. • Accounting system.
Management information system.	Integrated system for supporting operations and decision making.	Data gathered from TPS. Pre-determined output format.	• Databases. • Reporting systems.
Enterprise resource planning system.	Integration of information across the company.	Commercial software package installed on a Database Management System.	• Customer relationship management (CRM). • Balanced scorecard performance reporting.
Decision support system.	Manipulation of information to support decision making.	User-friendly style and assists with unstructured problems.	• Budgeting on a spreadsheet.
Executive information system.	Present selected / focused information for senior executives.	Highly visual and incorporates internal and external data.	• Executive performance 'dashboard'.

Expert system.	Present decision options to 'non-expert' users.	Modify its knowledge database in accordance with its own results.	• Tax advice. • Legal advice. • Selection of training methods.
Strategic enterprise management system.	Assists with strategic decision making.	Incorporates tools such as ABM.	• Significant investment decisions. • Acquisition decisions.

More on TPS

A transaction processing system (TPS) records all of the daily routine transactions that take place within an organisation, relating to a particular aspect of operational activities. A TPS is used primarily by clerks and operations staff that either input or maintain the data on the system.

After the data have been captured by the TPS, the MIS and other systems can then use it. There will often be direct links from the TPS to the MIS, which effectively summarises data from the TPS to show totals for weeks, months or even years. The summarisation process allows trends to be established and helps with strategic planning.

Examples of transaction processing systems are given below:

- **Sales/marketing system**. The sales and marketing systems within an organisation will cover not only the recording of individual sales transactions, but also more detailed information about the whole sales system including market research, sales promotion, pricing and new product details.

- **Manufacturing/production systems**. Manufacturing and production systems record details of the goods being manufactured from the initial order through to the completion of the final products. Specifically, the system will record details of purchasing, shipping/receiving, and production system operations.

- **Finance/accounting systems**. Book-keeping systems record transactions relating to sales, expenditure, assets and liabilities, and cash receipts and payments data. Some organisations also maintain cost accounting systems.

- **Human resources systems**. Human resources systems capture data relating to the employees of the organisation, with specific emphasis on areas such as personnel records, training and benefits payable.

The transaction processing system is normally characterised by the use of one of the following methods of processing:

- **Batch.** Information is collated into batches and then input onto the system in one batch. This method allows batch controls but information on the system is out-of-date.

- **On-line.** On-line systems allow users to enter information continuously, but the processing is performed at periodic intervals, such as the end of each day. Again the information on the system is out of date but it does give the benefit of continuous input to users.

- **Real time.** On this type of system, input and processing are done continuously. As a result the information is up to date but the system may be more expensive to operate and require higher specification of hardware than batch or on-line systems.

More on MIS

Types of MIS

There are four broad types of MIS:

- **Database systems**. These systems process and store information, which becomes the organisation's memory.

- **Direct control systems**. Systems to monitor and report on activities such as output levels, sales ledger and credit accounts in arrears.

- **Enquiry systems**. Which are based on databases, which provide specific information such as the performance of a department or an employee.

- **Support systems**. Systems that provide computer-based methods and procedures for conducting analyses, forecasts and simulations.

Features of a management information system

Management information systems can be distinguished from other information systems within an organisation:

- They provide support for structured decision making at all management levels.

- They provide on-line access to the transaction processing systems of the organisation, to give summary information on the performance of the organisation.

- They provide an internal rather than external focus, with detail being provided internally about the organisation itself, rather than externally-generated information about competitors or the overall economic environment.

- If required, they can provide more detailed information about the organisation's operations, or individual transactions, through a 'drill down' facility.

- An MIS produces relatively simple summary reports and comparisons, and does not contain the more detailed mathematical models or statistical techniques found in a DSS, for example.

Management information systems can be found in almost any organisation above a small size. A few examples are given below:

- **Car manufacturing**. Systems to summarise sales of motor vehicles to assist in trend analysis and hiring of new workers.

- **Firm of accountants**. Summarising work performed on different audit engagements to assist in fee negotiation.

- **Training company**. Provision of details of students booked on to different courses to indicate the size of lecture rooms required and number of lecturers for each subject.

- **Manufacturing company**. Provision of stock ageing analysis to determine the amount of stock provision in the financial statements.

More on ERPS

ERP systems offer:

- on-line/real-time information throughout all the functional areas of an organisation

- standardisation of data across the entire organisation

- common data files for all functions, thereby saving duplication.

ERP software providers offer ERP packages for areas of the business such as human resources, finance and accounting, customer data, supplier data, manufacturing, sales and distribution. Each ERP software provider may also offer different functions for different industries.

ERP Systems are installed on a Database Management System. Once installed, the user only enters data at one point, and the information is transferred automatically to other modules in the system. In effect, ERP systems integrate the different processes or functions in a business (manufacturing, inventory control, sales, distribution, accounting, human resources, etc) into a common, centralised data pool that facilitates data sharing and eliminates information redundancy.

Because they are enterprise-wide, ERP systems can be useful for extracting performance data relating to cross-functional or multi-functional activities, such as:

- supply chain management
- activity-based costing
- balanced scorecard performance reporting.

More on DSS

'A decision support system ... provides access to (mostly) summary performance data, using graphics to display and visualise the data in a very easy to use fashion (frequently with a touch screen interface), and with a minimum of analysis for modelling beyond the capability to 'drill down' in summary data to examine components' (Wallis).

The DSS does not make the decision, it merely assists in going through the phases of decision making:

- Gathering information and identification of situations requiring decisions.
- Design of possible solutions.
- Choice of solution.

The system sets up various scenarios and the computer predicts the result for each scenario by using a process of 'what if' analysis.

A decision support system will have the following characteristics:

- To provide support for decision making, especially for semi-structured or unstructured decision making.
- To provide support for all stages within the decision-making process.
- To provide support for decisions that are inter-dependent as well as for those that are independent.

- To support a variety of decision-making processes.
- To be user friendly.

A decision support system will include the following tools:

- Spreadsheets.
- Expert systems.
- 4GLs. (4th generation languages – a form of query language).
- Databases.
- Statistical programs.

There are three basic elements to the DSS:

- Language sub-system which is likely to be non-procedural (does not require significant programming ability to use).
- Problem processing sub-system which includes spreadsheet, graphics, statistical analysis.
- Knowledge sub-system which includes a database function.

More on EIS / ESS

An ESS has been described as 'a system for total business modelling' and its purpose is to monitor reality and facilitate actions that improve business results. The data for an ESS must be on-line and updated in real-time, in order to ensure its integrity for decision making at a senior management level.

It incorporates a workstation programmed to minimise the procedures for obtaining management information. It may have access to external databases such as news and stock exchange databases, in order to gain up-to-date information that may have an impact on the organisation.

The need for executive information systems comes from:

- the way in which executives use and demand information. When a senior manager asks for certain information, providing the information often leads to a demand for more information about something different or something extra.
- the shortcomings of management information systems. Most management information systems produce large, standard printed reports at fixed intervals, which executives rarely use because the reports do not help to answer the questions that concern them.

The key features of this system include the ability to:

- Call up summary data from an organisation's main system, e.g. summary income statement, statement of financial position, etc.

- Analyse the summary data to a more detailed level, e.g. analysis of the stock figure shown in the statement of financial position.

- Manipulate summary data, e.g. rearrange its format, make comparisons with similar data.

- Set up templates so that information from different areas of the business is always summarised in the same format.

- Perform 'what if' analysis operations.

More on ES

An expert system is a software system with two basic components: a knowledge base and an inference engine. The knowledge base is a structured database which stores the knowledge and experience of a number of experts. The inference engine makes it possible to draw on the knowledge base in an organised way. The system mimics an expert's reasoning process within a limited context.

The user accesses the system through a user-friendly graphical user interface (GUI) and asks questions of the system, or is prompted with questions by the system. The operating software or 'inference engine' then uses a mixture of rule-based logic and 'fuzzy logic' to infer a solution from the knowledge base.

There are many examples of expert systems in such areas as:

- law (e.g. how does a piece of complex legislation apply to a specific company?)

- taxation (e.g. how does a particular tax planning technique apply to a particular set of facts?)

- banking (e.g. should credit be granted to a new applicant?)

- medicine (e.g. what diagnosis best fits a set of symptoms?).

Non-experts can use this type of software to draw 'expert' conclusions from information input into the system. Experts can also use the software in order to confirm (or at least test) their own opinions against those offered by the system. This might speed up the decision-making process by giving less qualified managers the tools to draw conclusions or it might enhance the consistency of decision making across the organisation (e.g. reducing the scope for personal subjectivity in the decisions made by senior bank lending officers).

7 Value and cost of information

Cost-benefit analysis (CBA) can be used to assess the expected costs and benefits of the system design to be recommended. It is often called a method for 'system justification' – if the system is justified, then it will be recommended.

(This section does not relate solely to IT projects but to all projects a business could undertake – be prepared in the exam to discuss a cost-benefit analysis from more than an IT viewpoint.)

The **net value of information** in decision-making situations could be calculated as:

- the difference in the values of outcomes in a decision with and without the information, minus
- the cost of obtaining the information.

In other words a manager will make a decision based upon the information currently known. If additional information is available, which makes the manager take a different decision, then the value of that information is:

- the savings or profits made as a result of taking the different decision
- adjusted for the cost of obtaining the information, which may be:
    - a cost arising from preparing the information internally
    - the cost of purchasing the information from external sources
    - the cost of the delay to the decision whilst the information is prepared.

Cost of information

The cost of information could be classified under three general headings:

(a) The cost of **designing and setting** up the system that produces the information including:
    - systems design
    - systems testing
    - capital costs of equipment (e.g. IT equipment)
    - installation
    - training.

(b) The **day-to-day running** costs of the system providing the information, including:

- staff salaries

- supplies (paper, disks, etc)

- other running expenses such as premises costs and security costs.

(c) **Storage** costs including:

- hardware costs

- retrieval costs

- security costs.

Assessing the value and cost of information

Assessing the value of information

In order to assess the value of information, the following questions can be asked:

- What information is provided?

- What is it used for?

- Who uses it?

- How often is it used?

- What benefit is achieved by using it?

- Is it used as often as it is provided?

- What other relevant information is available that could be used instead?

Unfortunately, the value of information is not always easy to quantify in terms of benefits obtained. An alternative approach might therefore be to assess the consequences of not having the information, taking into account the quantity of the information and its availability (e.g. on-line), accuracy, level of detail and other information qualities.

Budgeting and IS/IT costs

The description of cost-benefit analysis above assumes that there are identifiable IT projects whose costs and benefits can be estimated and evaluated. In practice, although some new projects can be evaluated in this way, much spending on IT does not take the form of spending on identifiable new projects. A considerable amount of spending is incurred on maintaining, expanding and upgrading existing systems.

This type of spending, particularly IT running costs but also some capital expenditure (e.g. on new PCs and printers) is included within the normal budgeting process. Where an organisation uses an incremental approach to budgeting, annual IT spending could be agreed simply by taking spending for the previous year and adding a percentage for anticipated growth and cost inflation.

There is clearly a risk that when IT costs are budgeted in this way, they could easily grow more quickly than necessary and get out of control. For example:

- New PCs, laptops or other equipment might be purchased without due consideration to the benefits as well as the cost.

- Systems upgrades might be purchased in the same way, when an upgrade is not necessary.

- Spending on system maintenance, such as providing protection against software viruses, or 'cleaning up' systems affected by viruses, might escalate without the costs being adequately monitored and controlled.

Budgeting for IT costs might benefit from:

- a zero-based budgeting approach, although this will depend on whether the organisation uses ZBB for all its budgeting

- an activity-based budgeting approach, where the costs of IT activities (and cost drivers for those activities) are identified and used as the basis for budgeting.

The use of IT systems and services might also be controlled through a system of charging for the use of central IT systems.

8 Information technology

The system to deliver information to management must have the following attributes:

- the system must produce material in an appropriate way to enable informed decision-making.

- the system must process the required volumes of data within the required timescales, with adequate controls and efficient use of resources.

- to avoid being stuck with outdated technology and solutions, the system should be sufficiently adaptable to people's varied and changing needs and behaviour.

- the system should capitalise on the best of people and of machines to obtain the optimum mix of human intuition and machine reliability and speed.

The most common complaints levelled at information systems are the lack of decision orientation and the lack of flexibility. The unsatisfactory systems are those that deny people the access to take decisions in the way they wish to.

Networks

Many IS/IT systems within an organisation are network systems, linking users to common files, processing capabilities and shared equipment (e.g. printers).

A **local area network** (LAN) links terminals, servers and other equipment by cable, allowing them to communicate with each other. A typical system might consist of a mainframe computer with microcomputers as intelligent terminals, with a range of peripheral equipment.

A **client/server network** is a method of allocating resources in a LAN so that computing power is distributed among the personal computers in the network, but some shared resources (programs and files, etc) are centralised in a file server.

A **client-based application** in a local area network resides on a personal computer workstation and is not available for use by others on the network. Client-based applications do not make sharing common data easy, but they are resistant to the system-wide failure that occurs when a server-based application becomes unavailable if the file server crashes.

A **wide area network** (WAN) differs from a local area network mainly by size and communication technology. Whereas equipment items in a LAN are linked by cable, items in a WAN are linked through communication systems where modems are required for the transmission of data. WANs are also generally much larger than LANs, and can cover the entire organisation and its information users.

Intranets, extranets and e-commerce

Intranets

An intranet is a private network within an organisation that includes connections through one or more gateway computers to the outside Internet.

- The main objective of an intranet is to make information flow more freely by sharing company information and computing resources among employees. This means making files and programs more widely available to those who need them, but preventing access to those who do not.

- The intranet allows users access to the external information sources of the Internet, as well as the internal information sources of system databases and other files.

- An intranet can also be used to provide an e-mail system or other messaging systems for the organisation.

- It is usually cheaper than a WAN with dedicated lines/communication links.

Extranets

An extranet is a private, secure extension of the enterprise via a corporate intranet. It allows the organisation to share part of its business information or operations with suppliers, customers, and other business partners using the Internet. Organisations can use an extranet to:

- exchange large volumes of data using Electronic Data Interchange (EDI)

- share product catalogues exclusively with wholesalers or those 'in the trade'

- collaborate with other organisations on joint development efforts

- jointly develop and use training programmes with other companies

- provide or access services provided by one company to a group of other companies, such as on-line banking applications managed by one company on behalf of affiliated banks

- share news of common interest exclusively with partner companies.

E-commerce

E-commerce is commercial activity conducted over electronic networks, usually the Internet, which leads to the purchase or sale of goods and/or services. Buying goods electronically is also known as 'e-procurement'.

- On a business to business basis, the two parties are often known to each other and business is conducted across extranets. Electronic Data Interchange (EDI) is the electronic exchange of business documents (purchase orders, invoices, application forms, etc) from one organisation's computer system to another organisation's computer system in standard data formats.

- In the business to consumer sector, e-commerce is carried out over the public Internet. Companies can advertise their products or services on a website, and invite customers to place orders electronically using secure credit card/debit card payment systems. Orders placed via a website can be confirmed electronically by e-mail to the customer.

Test your understanding 2 – JLP

JLP is a large multinational organisation which sells electronic goods. It has branches in 105 countries and sales in billions of pounds each year. To try and improve its vertical integration and preserve its supply chain, JLP has just purchased a small manufacturer of computer components. Although this company – WR – is very profitable, it is run without any real corporate planning. The Directors of JLP believe that they can improve the profitability and growth prospects of the company, while reducing the costs of suppliers to the manufacturing plants that JLP operates. Following the purchase, all but two of the members of the Board at WR took early retirement.

Required:

You are the (CIMA-qualified) Finance Director, a member of the new management team at WR. Your knowledge of strategy matters has led you to have some concerns for the situation of WR and JLP.

Prepare a report to the two remaining Board members, discussing the reasons why any company must have an IT strategy.

Test your understanding 3 – SP (1)

SP plc is considering investing in the building of a new hotel in Dubai. The hotel is to be 'state of the art', and SP's management is hoping that it will be the first 6-star hotel in the world. It is expected that the richest people in the world will want to holiday here and the hotel will, therefore, command a premium price.

Many of the facilities in the hotel will involve computerisation. For example, the booking system – via the telephone or internet, the internal telephone system, and the availability of the internet in every suite. The cost of these facilities is thought to be around $7 million because the server will be housed in a separate building on the edge of the hotel grounds.

The management of SP have over 200 other hotels around the world to oversee. Over the past 10 years, their management information has become increasingly difficult to collate due to the size of the group and the diversity of activities that each hotel undertakes. The finance director is now trying to convince the other directors to invest in an Enterprise Resource Planning System (ERPS) to hopefully overcome some of these problems.

Required:

Advise the board on how an Enterprise Resource Planning System might benefit the management of SP, and explain the costs involved.

Test your understanding 4 – Printing company

Some time ago, a printing company designed and installed a Management Information System that met the business needs of a commercial environment which was characterised at that time by:

- a unitary structure with one profit centre

- central direction from senior managers

- 100% internal resourcing of ancillary services

- the employment exclusively of permanent full-time employees

- customers holding large inventories who accepted long delivery times

- most of the work concerned with long print runs for established large publishing houses.

A radical change in the business environment has resulted in the following outcomes:

- the development of a divisionalised structure with four profit centres that utilise each others services

- empowerment of team leaders and devolved decision making

- considerable outsourcing of activities

- a significant proportion of the employees work part-time and/or on temporary contracts

- customers now commonly operate JIT systems requiring immediate replenishment of inventories

- the typical customer requires specialist low volume but complex high value printing.

Required:

Recommend the significant changes in the Management Information Systems that would probably be required to meet the needs of this new situation. Explain the reasons for your recommendations.

Test your understanding 5 – Intranets

RBT manufactures tractors, harvesting machinery and similar farm equipment. It operates from one integrated office and factory near the capital of the country in which it is based. Due to restricted demand and the cost of manufacture of individual items, all equipment is manufactured to specific orders from clients. No inventories of finished goods are maintained although inventories of spare parts are available for sale.

The farm equipment is sold to farm owners by one of 20 sales representatives. The general procedure for making a sale is for the representative to visit the farm owner to discuss the owner's requirements. Basic price and model specification information are obtained from printed manuals that the representative carries. The representative then telephones the RBT office and confirms with production staff that the order can be made, checks the price and receives an estimated delivery date. An order confirmation is written out and the representative moves on to the next appointment. The farmer pays for the equipment on receipt.

As the country in which RBT operates is large, representatives cannot often visit RBT's office, so their price and model specification manuals may be out of date. The Board of RBT is considering the introduction of a new information system. Each representative will be given a portable PC. Information on such things as products and prices will be kept on an Intranet and downloaded by telephone line when needed by the representative. Access to production managers and sales representatives will also be made via the Intranet. The voice telephone system will be discontinued and e-mail is thought to be unnecessary.

Required:

(a) Evaluate the proposed use of the Intranet within the RBT Company showing whether it would provide an appropriate communication channel for the sales representatives. Suggest ways in which any problems you have identified with the new systems may be resolved.

(b) Identify and evaluate any information systems that can be used to provide clients with information on the progress of their orders with RBT while they are being manufactured.

Test your understanding 6 – HZ

The HZ hospital has recently invested in the most up-to-date computer systems to assist its doctors in making assessments of patients' illnesses. Two of the software packages now available to doctors are:

- a Management Information System which provides information on the medical history of each patient. It includes detailed factual information on past illnesses and any recurring symptoms as well as the patient's name, address and other personal information.

- an Expert System which is used to assist in the diagnosis of current illnesses. The Expert System is linked to the MIS to obtain details on each patient's medical history. From this information, and symptoms of the current illness, the Expert System provides an initial diagnosis, which the doctor uses in making his recommendation for the treatment of the patient. The diagnosis is stated in terms of probabilities of what the illness could be, rather than giving definite conclusions. Both systems are accessed and updated via a series of on-line terminals located at key points around the hospital. All terminals are linked directly to a central file server; there are no external communications links due to the sensitive nature of the information being held.

Required:

(a) Explain the differences in the characteristics of information being provided by the two systems.

(b) Describe three general conditions, which must exist in order for an Expert System to be appropriate.

(c) Describe three advantages of using Expert Systems (other than speed and accuracy).

Test your understanding 7 – Supply Co.

SupplyCo has recently acquired a new enterprise resource planning (ERP) system from a well-known supplier. The ERP system automates the tasks involved in performing a business process, from order fulfilment, which involves taking an order from a customer, shipping it and invoicing the customer. Previously, that order took a mostly paper-based journey from in-basket to in-basket around the company, often being keyed and re-keyed into different computer systems along the way.

With ERP, when customer service takes an order, all the necessary information to complete the order is available. This includes the customer's credit rating, the order history, inventory levels and delivery schedules. Everyone in the company sees the same information, from a single database. As each department carries out its function, the ERP system automatically routes the customer order to the next department. However, SupplyCo is faced with the problem that the ERP software does not support an important business process. There are two solutions to this problem: change the way the company does business to fit the package, or modify the package to fit the business.

Required:

(a) Compare and contrast strategies for information systems (IS), information technology (IT) and information management (IM). Discuss how an ERP system can be seen from the perspective of each of IS, IT and IM strategies.

(b) Discuss the IT-related risks that could be faced by SupplyCo in using an ERP system and recommend the control strategies that would be appropriate for an ERP environment.

(c) Advise SupplyCo as to whether it should change the way it does business to fit the ERP package, or modify the ERP package to fit its business needs. Recommend how management should go about deciding which solution to implement.

Test your understanding 8 – SN plc

SN plc provides a large range of insurance services and advice to clients ranging from private individuals to large corporate organisations. The sales staff are supported by a wide range of information systems, which are designed to be user-friendly. The systems are regularly reviewed to ensure that the information requirements of the professional staff are being met by those systems.

The information systems are maintained and upgraded by a team of trainers; sales personnel are not involved in the design of systems because this would result in a loss of chargeable time. The actual process of maintaining the information system is outlined in Figure A.

Figure A: Maintaining SN plc's information systems

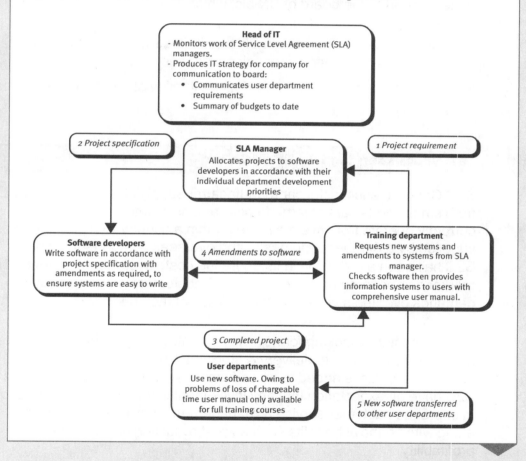

Other relevant information

- Costs of training and IT department are allocated to the different user departments in accordance with staff numbers in those departments. The costs of the IT department include software development and all costs relating to the SLA managers.

- The IT staff work in the main development centre, which is located on a university campus for reasons of cost and accessibility to a supply of trained programmers.

- The IT department has a reputation within the company for not meeting user requirements in a timely manner.

Required:

Write a report to the board of SN plc, which

(a) explains the weaknesses in SN plc's infrastructure for maintaining the information systems for sales staff; and

(b) produces specific recommendations to alleviate those weaknesses.

Test your understanding 9 – B2C Cars

B2C Cars is a successful car manufacturer supplying a range of cars from small sports cars to large family saloons & hatch backs. They currently operate from five main sites within a country with parts being supplied by a number of domestic and overseas component suppliers. B2C has seen a reduction in its operating costs over recent years as the market has become more competitive & customers have increasing demands over the style e.g. colour & finish of their purchase.

B2C is constantly looking for new ways of integrating technology into its activities from design to delivery & stock control to manufacture to ensure that value is added to these functions. The senior management of B2C have an expectation that any investment in technology should result in improved customer service & management information provision along with financial benefits such as cost reduction & improved profitability.

Required:

Using B2C as your example, illustrate how the following types of system may be integrated into the organisation, along with a description of the benefits that B2C will achieve if the investment is made:

- Transaction Processing Systems
- Management Information Systems
- Decision Support Systems
- Executive Information Systems
- Expert Systems.

Test your understanding 10 – Cost benefit

A systems analyst must be prepared to carry out both cost-benefit calculations & risk analysis as part of the proposal for a new computer system.

Required:

(a) Describe two methods for demonstrating the costs and benefits of such a system over a period of time.

(b) Explain the specific problems associated with the measurement of information systems costs and benefits.

(c) Explain the factors you would take into account when undertaking a risk analysis of the costs and benefits of a proposed computer project.

Test your understanding 11 – ZX

ZX is a pharmaceutical company which specialises in the development and marketing of new drugs. On average, the company spends $100 million each year (about 10% of turnover) on research and brings five new drugs to the market each year.

Before any drug can be licensed for use, the country's Drug Administration Unit (DAU) undertakes a detailed review. This review takes up to 15 months, with several thousand pages of material on the drug being submitted to the DAU by ZX. Most of the time for the review is taken up by DAU employees finding specific information in the paper documentation supplied by ZX, and occasionally requesting duplicate copies of missing or mislaid documents.

Prior to the review, and to comply with DAU requirements, information on each drug has to be prepared and checked through a quality control process at ZX. The process involves preparation and the checking of drugs and review material in four separate stages in offices in different geographical locations. Each group of employees reports to a central manager in the company's Head Office. To ensure completeness of processing of information on each drug, tasks are arranged and completed in a strict order. Although some tasks could be run in parallel, this does not happen. Processing of this information is slow. Further delays result from teams occasionally duplicating work or waiting for reports, which are subsequently found to be lost in the internal mail at ZX.

Work may also be duplicated between ZX and other pharmaceutical companies in the market. Sharing information between different pharmaceutical companies might avoid duplication of work and save money.

There is considerable pressure on ZX to decrease the overall time taken to place new drugs on the market.

This pressure comes from two sources:

- the Board of ZX which recognises that every week saved in the R&D process and review will generate up to $1 million each year in extra revenue for the organisation; and

- customers – particularly for new HIV and cancer drugs.

Required:

(a) Evaluate the current system at ZX showing where the use of an Intranet would help to meet the expectations of customers and the Board.

(b) Discuss the limitations of using an Extranet to share information between different pharmaceutical companies.

Test your understanding 12 – RBT

RBT manufactures tractors, harvesting machinery and similar farm equipment. It operates from one integrated office and factory near the capital of the country in which it is based. Due to restricted demand and the cost of manufacture of individual items, all equipment is manufactured to specific orders from clients. No inventories of finished goods are maintained although inventories of spare parts are available for sale.

The farm equipment is sold to farm owners by one of 20 sales representatives. The general procedure for making a sale is for the representative to visit the farm owner to discuss the owner's requirements. Basic price and model specification information are obtained from printed manuals that the representative carries. The representative then telephones the RBT office and confirms with production staff that the order can be made, checks the price and receives an estimated delivery date. An order confirmation is written out and the representative moves on to the next appointment. The farmer pays for the equipment on receipt.

As the country in which RBT operates is large, representatives cannot often visit RBT's office, so their price and model specification manuals may be out of date.

The Board of RBT is considering the introduction of a new information system. Each representative will be given a portable PC. Information on such things as products and prices will be kept on an Intranet and downloaded by telephone line when needed by the representative. Access to production managers and sales representatives will also be made via the Intranet. The voice telephone system will be discontinued and e-mail is thought to be unnecessary.

Required:

(a) Evaluate the proposed use of the Intranet within the RBT Company showing whether it would provide an appropriate communication channel for the sales representatives. Suggest ways in which any problems you have identified with the new systems may be resolved.

(b) Identify and evaluate any information systems that can be used to provide clients with information on the progress of their orders with RBT while they are being manufactured.

9 Chapter summary

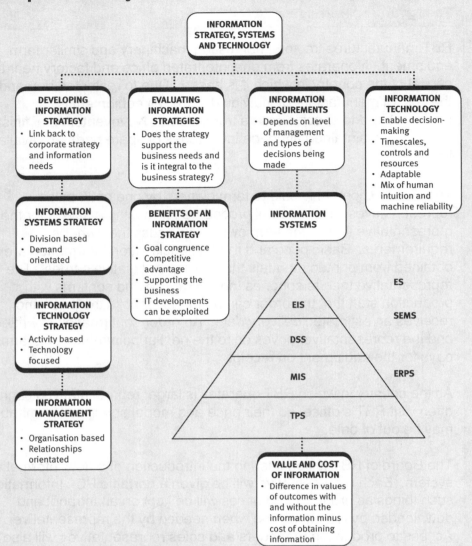

Test your understanding answers

Test your understanding 1 – KPI

40% gross profit

40% gross profit per month

40% gross profit by product

Customer satisfaction

Number of repeat orders increases each month

Value of repeat orders increases each quarter

Innovation

Number of new products launched increases each year

Number of patents applied for increases each quarter.

Test your understanding 2 – JLP

Report

To: Board of WR
From: Finance Director
Date: Today
Title: The significance of IT strategies for WR

WR has undergone significant changes in recent times with the purchase by JL, and is being placed under a lot of pressure to meet cost reduction targets set by the new parent.

To date WR has not operated a formal corporate planning process. In fact, WR has been extremely successful, and it has been felt in the past that such a process would inhibit the development of the company. In order for the company to continue to be successful, and to meet the requirements of the parent company, WR will benefit from the introduction of some formalised strategic planning processes. A particular area of concern is the information strategy.

Reasons why WR and JLP should work together to prepare an information strategy include:

(1) Goal congruence – as JLP and WR have recently merged, it is important that the new senior planners consider the two organisations' IT requirements to ensure that any decisions are compatible and in line with each other. It seems as if WR has had little investment in IT, owing to the lack of corporate planning in the past – for example, the decision to adopt a particular hardware or software platform in WR must be the same as JLP to enhance the transfer of information between the two companies. As the reason behind the purchase of WR was to improve the supply chain, greater return will be made on the investment if parallel planning of IT takes place between the two businesses.

(2) Costs – of IT can be high especially with the use of new and unproven technology. Planning for the use of IT over the long term can help to set budgets and forecasts, improving the overall cash flow of the business. Cost planning will also have a direct result on the profitability of both organisations, enabling JLP to achieve the expected returns from the WR purchase and supply chain benefits.

(3) Supporting the business strategy – JLP has used IT to enhance its performance, enabling it to become an international retailer of electronic goods. This strategy would enable JLP to retain its position and enhance its dominance in the market with the inclusion of WR. The decision to purchase technology and implement within both businesses will improve the ability to achieve profitability owing to its support of the business strategy.

(4) **Create new opportunities** – IT can be used to enhance the performance of vertical integration as the time between the order and delivery can be shortened, reducing the need to hold stocks. As JLP is unlikely to receive all the products that it requires from WR, this system can be integrated with the systems of other suppliers, enabling them to reduce the need to hold supplier stocks and reduce their dependence on a small number of suppliers.

(5) **Future planning** – both organisations should recognise not only the effect of IT strategy on their current position but also how the development of such technologies can be integrated with new ones across all areas of the business. Owing to the enhanced compatibility of systems, investment in one area may have benefits in a number of others. As technology continues to improve, JLP can make the most of these changes and integrate them into its business structure.

(6) **Education** – all the board members but two have left WR, implying that they were unhappy about the merger and the differences in management style. The strategy process creates an opportunity for the senior staff of both companies to get together and develop a plan for the integration of systems. The remaining two board members will be able to review the systems currently in place in JLP and see how they could be incorporated into WR to improve performance.

Test your understanding 3 – SP (1)

An Enterprise Resource Planning System (ERPS) is a software package that brings together information, both internal and external, financial and non-financial, for the purpose of producing custom-designed reports for management covering many different strategic and tactical activities. The ERPS will probably collate its information from many transaction processing systems, as well as outside sources such as customers and suppliers via data warehouses. The ERPS will help to integrate data flows, and access to information over the whole of the hotel chain's activities. For example it can be used to assist in activity based costing, balanced scorecard performance analysis, strategic planning, and customer and supplier management.

SP will be investing in an ERP system in the hope that it will integrate and optimise business processes. Benefits that might accrue will include:

- Reduced external consultancy – Much of SP's external information may have been collated by external consultants who may be partly/wholly dispensed with now.

- Reduced staffing – The directors and managers will probably have many staff whose job it is to try to collate the information which the ERPS will now do automatically. Several of these staff may be relieved of their roles, saving their salaries.

- Better information – The whole purpose of the ERPS is the production of faster, more accurate and increased amounts of information so that the managers can run SP more efficiently, make better decisions and hopefully more profit. There may be the possibility of increasing revenues or the cutting of costs by using the ERPS.

The introduction of an ERP system is not without its costs. These include:

- Software licences – ERPS can be bought ready-written, which is much faster to get into use than having a specialist package written.

- Hardware – It is possible that a more powerful server will be required due to the increasing amounts of information that need warehousing.

- Consultancy – Initially, SP will require help to get the new ERPS up and running. A consultancy with experience of implementing ERPS, and especially in the hotel industry, should be appointed.

- Backfill staff – This will include finding suitable temporary staff to cover for those seconded onto the ERPS project.

- Capital costs – ERP systems are not cheap, and in conjunction with any new hardware required, a loan may be taken out and hence interest costs may be incurred.

- Implementation costs – These will include training costs for the users of the ERPS. The ERPS will require testing also, to ensure that the information that it produces is accurate.

- Additional support – Extra IT staff may be required to oversee the use of the ERPS.

- Maintenance – Finally, as with any computer system, maintenance will be required. This could be in the form of corrective, perfective or adaptive maintenance.

Clearly, in order for the ERPS to be worthwhile implementing, the benefits should outweigh the costs. Evidence to date from companies that have implemented ERP systems has shown that the costs expected spiralled well above expectations (61% higher on average). Obviously SP should think carefully before deciding to go ahead with this project.

Test your understanding 4 – Printing company

The change from a unitary to a divisionalised structure

Each division or profit centre will require its own accounting information and other management information. The accounting system must therefore provide for the recognition of revenues and costs of individual divisions.

There is now a requirement to assess the performance of each division, and the management information system must therefore provide performance reports containing both quantitative and qualitative, and financial and non-financial information

Since each division is a profit centre, the system must provide for a system of transfer pricing for goods or services provided by each division to the other divisions. Ideally, the management information system will provide benchmarking data, whereby the performance of each division can be compared with the available performance data about similar printing operations in other (rival) companies.

Change from central direction to empowerment of divisional managers

The management information must be capable of providing information to the divisional managers that they need to make decisions. The system should allow each division to extract the data it requires from the company's files for analysis and reporting to management. In addition, local managers should have access to other sources of data external to the company. This might simply be internet access.

Whereas divisional managers will need access to more management information and operational data, the management at head office will need less detailed information. Reports to head office management will monitor the performance of each profit centre, and will also be more strategic in nature. Reports to head office managers will therefore need to be re-designed.

Since authority has been delegated to divisional level and below, new control systems will be required to meet the requirements of the newly-empowered team leaders, as well as the requirements of senior management.

To ensure consistency in control throughout the company, there should be some standardisation in the nature of the control systems and control information.

The change from internal sourcing of ancillary services to outsourcing

The management information system needs to identify the responsibilities for outsourcing. If outsourcing decisions are taken at divisional level, the costs must be allocated to the division concerned. If outsourcing decisions are taken at head office, individual managers at head office should be made accountable, through a control reporting system.

The information system should maintain a file of external service providers (e.g. approved contractor lists). There should also be a control reporting or monitoring system to ensure that only contractors on the approved list are used.

It will probably also be necessary to establish a system for recording both the costs and the quality and amount of services provided by external suppliers. Outsourcing reports can then be provided to show the total cost and amount of outsourcing, and the cost of individual services. Comparisons between different service providers, and comparisons over time can be reported, for costs, volumes of service and quality.

Use of part-time and temporary employees

The implications for the management information system of using part-time and temporary employees are likely to relate mainly to hours worked and the costs of labour. When all staff are full-time employees, the management information system might report costs per employee. However, when part-time staff are used, it is more appropriate to report costs per labour hour or costs per activity.

Management should also monitor the costs of the various types of employee, to ensure that inefficiencies do not occur. Management reports are therefore likely to include an employee cost report that analyses the costs of each type of employee.

Other aspects of management information might also be affected, such as information relating to the employees themselves (availability in the case of part-time staff, contract termination dates for temporary staff, training records, and so on).

Customers adopting JIT systems

When customers adopt a JIT purchasing system, the supplier becomes responsible for ensuring that customer orders can be met either immediately or very quickly. This has implications for the inventory system of the printing company, and for its production scheduling systems. The information system must be able to recognise JIT customers, and respond instantly to their orders.

This might involve maintaining inventories to meet demand, or immediate scheduling of a print run to satisfy the order.

Change from long print runs to high-value low-volume production

The change in the character of customer orders has several important implications for the company's management information systems and order processing systems. First, the order processing system must be capable of handling complex orders. Secondly, there must be a reliable system for measuring the costs of these orders: an entirely different cost and management accounting system might be necessary, based on job costing rather than batch process costing. In addition, due to the complexity of the work, it might be appropriate to analyse overheads differently, perhaps using an ABC costing system. The information system should then be able to estimate prices for customers, if a cost-plus pricing system is appropriate, and also to compare actual and expected job costs for control purposes.

It is also probable that customers for high-value printing will insist on high quality printing, and the management information system should therefore be capable of providing control information about quality standards, and also the costs of achieving those quality standards.

Test your understanding 5 – Intranets

Key answer tips

The requirement "evaluate" is a high level verb requiring you to look at the value of something. It is often helpful to consider advantages and disadvantages of an idea when tackling this requirement. Your answers to both parts (a) and (b) of this question need to utilise information from the scenario to score high marks. Points that do not relate to RBT will not be rewarded, particularly if they are inappropriate suggestions for this type of organisation.

(a) **Intranet**

An intranet is an internal company information system where a wide variety of internal information can be posted for access by staff members. Internal information often includes company news, telephone directories, standard forms, copies of rules and procedures, and so on. In this case of the system under consideration by RBT, the intranet would hold up-to-date information on products and prices, so that sales representatives can download this information to their laptops from a customer's premises and other remote locations.

Advantages

The proposed new system has the following advantages over the old system:

–   More regularly updated information

An intranet site is very easy and cheap to update, and product and price information can be kept fully up-to-date by head office. The downloaded product information will therefore be much more up-to-date than the old printed materials, and a better customer service can be provided. All the latest products would be made available to customers and customers would always be given the correct prices.

–   Reduced costs of producing price lists/brochures

Regular price lists and brochures will no longer be required, and the production and printing costs of paper-based products should be reduced.

Disadvantages

The intranet site has the following disadvantages compared with the old system:

–   Slower communication with the production department

Since the telephone system will be discontinued, the sales people will not have access to production staff to resolve any queries or difficulties with customers. This would be a serious weakness in the system. Good communications between sales and production staff must be maintained.

Solutions

Possible solutions to this problem include:

(i) *E-mail system*

E-mail might provide an efficient way for sales representatives to communicate directly with the production staff, although controls would need to be in place to ensure that the production staff responds promptly to e-mail queries they receive.

(ii) *Maintain telephone access*

Voice telephone access offers immediate communication. A salesperson can get in contact with a member of the production staff and get an immediate reply. Maintaining telephone access for certain queries would be a useful way of ensuring very quick communication where needed.

(iii) Access to production scheduling system

Allowing salespeople access to the production scheduling system over the intranet would allow them to estimate a delivery date themselves thus reducing the need for direct contact between production and sales.

 – Less personal communication with production department

The intranet is a very impersonal way to communicate with people. It does not allow for two-way conversation, whereas personal contact may be required to resolve difficult issues.

Solution

Both e-mail and a voice telephone system are more personal forms of communication than the intranet. The voice telephone system in particular allows a two-way conversation to take place so that more difficult issues can easily be resolved.

– *Rejection of new technology*

The sales people may dislike the new technology that they are required to use. At present they do not use IT significantly in their work, and so new skills may be required. Many new systems also have 'teething problems' on implementation, which may also make users dislike the new system.

Solutions

(i) *Training*

Training will be required so people know how the system works and can get the best use from it.

(ii) *Consultation*

Consulting users early in the development process is an excellent way of getting user buy-in to the new system. It will also ensure the system is practical from a day-to-day usage point of view.

(iii) *Testing*

Testing systems well prior to implementation will help avoid the teething problems which may be encountered, particularly if the end users are involved since they know better than anyone else the way the system will be used in practice.

— Up-front costs

The proposed new system will require significant up-front costs both in terms of developing the new systems and training staff. Given the relatively small number of sales representatives (just 20) the investment may not be financially justified.

Solution

A cost-benefit analysis can be undertaken to ascertain whether the costs of the investment are justified.

(b) **Information systems – order progress**

Manufacturing system – order tracking

As part of the manufacturing process, progress on orders will need to be recorded. The information recorded will include work done, work still to do and the expected completion date. This information might already exist within the current system or it may need to be input into a database which can be accessed by clients.

EDI or extranet

Using electronic data interchange the customer would be able to log on to RBT's systems to directly access the production data.

An extranet is an extension of an intranet. External parties are allowed to log onto the intranet site and use it to access sections of the intranet. The intranet site would need to be connected to the manufacturing system/database so that up-to-date information was available.

Advantages

(1) Clients could access information themselves. This could save staff time and resources in RBT, since there will be fewer customer queries to deal with.

(2) An extranet would be relatively easy to provide if the manufacturing system is already linked to the intranet for the benefit of the salespeople.

(3) Other information could also be provided to customers (such as past order information, account balances and so on).

Disadvantages

(1) There would be a loss of personal contact with customers. The salesperson would not have as many opportunities to make contact with customers in order to build an ongoing relationship. As a consequence, they might identify fewer sales opportunities or find it harder to make a sale because they are less trusted by the customer.

(2) External parties would be accessing internal systems. There is a danger that hackers will get into parts of the system that are confidential, and a risk that important information is stolen or damaged. It could also increase the possibility of viruses being brought in which could damage internal systems.

Internet

Alternatively the RBT could put tracking information on a database which is connected to the company's web site. Clients would then be able to access their information through this site.

Advantages

(1) Labour cost savings, as described for an extranet.

(2) Customers will be familiar with the internet and so find it easier to use than an extranet or internal system accessed via EDI. It also means they will not have to dial in directly to the company's internal network, saving them time and effort.

(3) There is less opportunity for hackers or viruses to enter the internal systems using a web site on the internet, since they are not directly accessing internal systems.

(4) Other information could also be provided to customers on the internet site.

Disadvantage

The company may not currently have an internet site. This could be a significant extra expense, in terms of designing, creating and maintaining the site.

Test your understanding 6 – HZ

(a) **The characteristics of information** provided by the Management Information System (MIS) and the Expert System (ES) in the HZ hospital are different in every respect. The management information system provides information on the medical history of each patient. It includes factual information on past illnesses and any recurring symptoms as well as the patient's name, address and other personal information. An expert system is used to diagnose an illness. The differences in the characteristics of the information provided by the two systems can be explained under the following five headings: accuracy, completeness, timeliness, reliability, and security and control.

(i) In terms of **accuracy** of information, the MIS should be accurate and give a true reflection of the medical history of a particular patient. It is the basic record-keeping system for the hospital's patients. It holds the records for each patient including details of past illnesses and symptoms, and has the ability to produce reports either on statistical or individual bases.

The hospital uses the MIS to automate the record-keeping and, instead of writing out patients' notes to be kept in a paper-based file, this information is input to the computer system to create an electronic file. The expert system is unlikely to be as accurate or precise as the MIS. It does not have records and data but comprises a knowledge base and an inference engine, which is a rule set from which the likelihood of illnesses can be inferred. It is used to provide several diagnoses with a range of probabilities and precision can only be increased by entering more symptoms or details about the patient or the illness.

(ii) The MIS must be **complete and up-to-date**. The system depends on inputs made to it following a patient's visit to hospital. The doctor may input information during the consultation with the patient and any medication prescribed would be recorded. The ES depends on being updated to reflect the latest research findings or expert opinion. There is a very good chance of it being incomplete and out of date and not representing a complete body of knowledge. Also, if the knowledge base was created by the hospital, i.e. the software framework purchased and the information (knowledge) input locally, then there is no guarantee that all the necessary information will be present.

(iii) **Timeliness**. The MIS produces information quickly with typical response times of a few seconds. Most MIS are record-based within a hierarchical or relational database, both types being able to display records quickly at the touch of a button. In comparison, the ES is very slow because it may need to consider many different combinations of symptoms, rules and information before it can perform a diagnosis. If the patient is showing unusual symptoms, the ES may take a lot longer relatively (i.e. minutes rather than seconds) before it can respond, particularly. This obviously depends on the sophistication of the inference engine and the speed and capacity of the processors used.

(iv) **Reliability**. MIS data is only reliable if it has been input correctly. Even if the information is incomplete, the doctor can see from the screen where the gaps are and, with the patient's help, it should be possible to obtain a good indication of their history. The MIS can therefore offer a degree of assurance that there is control over matching the patient to the information. In the case of the ES the information should never be considered 100% reliable because the doctor or consultant will not know if all the relevant information has been input.

For example, some completely different illnesses are identified by similar symptoms. It is very difficult to diagnose appendicitis because the symptoms are similar to stomach problems, constipation problems and pregnancy problems. When the ES creates its diagnostic inference, it will only pick up the information present and could therefore present a faulty diagnosis.

(v) **Security** and control procedures are much easier with the MIS than the ES. When the records are input, the operating system controls the processing and the information can be prevented from corruption by the database management system (DBMS). It is more difficult with an ES because of the potential size of its knowledge base and the complexities of its rule-based inference engine. With the hospital ES, there is also a link to the historical records within the MIS. If a link is missing, or a piece of information is incorrect, then the processing could take the completely wrong path towards its goal. The only way this could be tested is by completing every single diagnostic/symptom combination. This would not help because it would create almost an infinite number of possibilities.

(vi) **General conditions for the application of an expert system**

Three of the conditions that should be present if a particular domain of knowledge warrants the building of an expert system are:

(i) The expert is capable of explaining how decisions are made in all situations, and the decisions that are reached are consistent. If the expert might reach different conclusions given the same data, or the decision is taken on 'feel', then an expert system is not appropriate. It should be noted that some experts may find it difficult to explain how a decision has been made because their experience enables them to reach a conclusion automatically. An example of this would be in the diagnosis of why a car will not start. The conclusion may be reached that 'the starter motor is jammed'. Although the decision may be instant, it is the result of a series of logical thoughts and therefore is suitable for an expert system. 'The make and model of the car is XYZ, the engine makes a particular noise, the engine does not turn over, therefore the probability is high that the car has a jammed starter motor'. In the situation where the expert finds it difficult to rationalise their conclusion, a skilled knowledge engineer is required to help design the system.

(ii)   The expertise that is the basis of the expert system is rare and in demand. This often manifests itself in the situation that the expert is always busy answering the questions of others and cannot do his or her own job properly. In many situations the 'users' are themselves experts in an associated field but sometimes need to augment their knowledge with specialised information. Doctors who are GPs may need to find out if a particular combination of drugs may react together to give bad side effects, or they may need to find out information about a rare speciality. Lawyers or accountants may need to consult about a complex and/or specialised category of law.

(iii)   The problem must be one that is worth solving and it must cost less to develop the system than the cost of non-experts making the wrong decision. Examples include:

– when decisions are taken by non-experts ('should a customer be allocated a credit card'); or

– when the cost of making a bad decision is so horrendous that the right decision is vital (this often occurs in legal situations).

(c) **Three advantages of using expert systems**

(i)   An expert system may enable a person training in a job to be immediately useful. Expert systems themselves are useful training aids, and if the trainee makes decisions based on the output from an expert system, then the manager can be assured that the right decision is reached despite the trainee's inexperience. This situation is particularly beneficial when there is a high turnover of staff in a particular job. A telephone sales operation is an example of when this benefit is important.

(ii)   The expert is released from the mundane task of answering 'routine' queries to work where their expertise is of more value.

(iii)   The process of building an expert system can provide significant advantages in understanding the problems to be solved. By going through the disciplines that are vital in building a knowledge base, then the expert is often able to understand their own decision making better, and sometimes to eradicate bad habits that may have crept in to their work.

Test your understanding 7 – Supply Co.

(a) Information systems (IS) strategies are focused on the business unit, enabling it to satisfy (internal or external) customer demand strategy. IS strategies determine the long-term information requirements of an organisation, providing an 'umbrella' for different information technologies that may exist. Information technology (IT) strategies are supply-oriented, focused on activities and the technology needed to support those activities. IT strategy defines the specific systems that are required to satisfy the information needs of the organisation, including the hardware, software and operating systems. Information management (IM) strategies are management focused at the whole organisation level. IM strategy will ensure that information is being provided to users, is securely stored and backed up and that redundant information is not produced.

Enterprise resource planning (ERP) systems integrate data flow across the organisation. They capture transaction data for accounting purposes, operational data, customer and supplier data, all of which are made available through data warehouses against which custom-designed reports can be produced. ERP systems are a development of older-style materials requirement planning (MRP), manufacturing resource planning (MRPII) and distribution resource planning (DRP) systems. ERP system data can be used to update performance measures in a Balanced Scorecard system and can be used for activity-based costing, shareholder value, strategic planning, customer relationship management and supply chain management.

From an IS perspective, ERP takes a whole supply chain view from supplier to customer, obtaining all of the information needs of SupplyCo, including customer, product, supplier, inventory, distribution, and so on and provides the foundation data for all business processes. From an IT perspective, the particular vendor selected and the hardware platform utilised for ERP will depend on the volume of business, extent of distributed processing, Internet access requirements (e.g. for EDI or EFTPOS), and so on. An ERP is likely to be used in larger organisations with substantial transaction and user volume. From an IM perspective, the shared data available on an ERP need to be accessible by all users, subject to information security policies and the need for business continuity. The complexity and scale of an ERP system will dictate its importance to the organisation and the reliance the organisation will place on secure and reliable IM strategy.

(b) An IT environment has risks that are particular to the technology and structures adopted for business. File structures in modern relational databases can be very complex as files have multiple purposes and methods of access. Also, real-time processing of data takes place, causing a greater risk for deliberate or accidental error. As much data entry takes place automatically, less documentation is evident, and this has implications for auditability and security. The dependence of SupplyCo on its ERP system will also dictate sophisticated business continuity procedures.

Security controls are aimed at preventing unauthorised access, modification or destruction of stored data. Integrity controls ensure that data are accurate, consistent and free from accidental corruption. Contingency controls operate so that a back-up facility and a contingency plan can be implemented to restore business operations as quickly as possible.

To address these risks, controls should exist over personnel, physical and logical access to systems, business continuity, and transaction input, processing and output. The extent of controls implemented will depend on a risk assessment process involving the likelihood/consequence of risk occurring and the organisation's risk appetite.

Personnel controls include those over recruitment, training, supervision, termination and separation of duties. Logical access controls provide security over unauthorised access to data through password authorisation. Facility controls include having a secure location from physical risk and controlling physical access to systems, remote or otherwise. Business continuity planning or disaster recovery planning takes place in order to recover information systems from critical events after they have happened.

Input controls are designed to detect and prevent errors during transaction data entry to ensure that the data entered are complete and accurate, such as through authorisation, verification and reasonableness checks. This is particularly important in an ERP environment where transactions update files that are accessed by multiple users for different purposes. Processing controls ensure that processing has occurred according to the organisation's requirements and that no transactions have been omitted or processed incorrectly. These can take place through control totals, standardisation and balancing procedures. Output controls ensure that input and processing activities have been carried out and that the information produced is reliable and distributed to users, such as transaction lists, exception reports, distribution lists and forms control.

(c) If SupplyCo changes the way it does business to fit the ERP package, it may impair its competitive advantage if it is providing something different to its competitors. If the company fits the package, companies will tend to be isomorphic (see institutional theory) with each other, with the computer system defining the way business processes are conducted for all companies using that system. This is dangerous as competitive advantage is likely to be eroded in pursuit of fitting in with a standard system, particularly when only two to three computer suppliers are likely to offer a suitable ERP product. Change is also likely to meet resistance from employees, suppliers or customers as there will be 'taken-for-granted' ways of doing things that will now need to be altered. However, cost efficiency may dictate that there is a need to change a business process as, according to value chain principles, the cost of providing a benefit must be less than what the customer is prepared to pay for the added value.

If SupplyCo modifies the ERP package to fit the business this is likely to be an expensive option. Changing standard software involves a significant financial cost, increases implementation time and is likely to result in 'bugs' in the system. It could also result in unforeseen control problems that have been removed from the standard system but emerge in the modified system. Upgrading to the supplier's next version of the software is also likely to be much more difficult. Introducing a system as sophisticated as an ERP system requires a reconsideration of business processes. Companies that have merely automated existing business processes sometimes find that they have missed an opportunity to re-examine fundamental business processes and modify them to enhance their competitive advantage.

The ERP should be seen as a source of value. To release this value a rigorous business analysis is needed including addressing all existing business processes. Only by carrying out such a process with a cost-benefit analysis can a judgement be made about whether the package should be modified or whether business processes should be changed to fit the package.

Test your understanding 8 – SN plc

Report

To   Board of SN plc
From   Management accountant
Subject   Information system maintenance
Date   May 20XX

As requested in the board minutes of March this year, I have reviewed the systems for providing information to the company's professional sales staff. Specific weaknesses are identified and recommendations made to show how those weaknesses can be alleviated.

Lack of joint design committee

There appears to be no overall control of the design and maintenance of information systems being used by the professional sales staff. The functions of specifying the information systems, overall authorisation of each system, writing each system and final implementation are all carried out by different departments with little or no ongoing contact. The lack of control may mean that projects become late, are cancelled or lack the necessary prioritisation, to the overall detriment of the company.

Implementing a joint design committee with representatives from all interest groups would help to maintain an appropriate project schedule and maintain overall control of the information systems.

IT department maintained in a separate physical location

Having the IT department in a separate location has some advantages, most notably being that programmers do not become involved personally with answering users' minor queries when they should be working on other projects. However, there are significant disadvantages to this arrangement, including lack of contact with users and trainers, difficulty in monitoring the work of the department and the appearance that the IT department is not interested in completing projects in a timely fashion. The scenario notes that the IT department is seen to be complacent.

Locating the IT department in one of the company's main buildings would help to provide more visibility for the department as well as making contact easier. Directing ongoing queries from users regarding software to a specific Help Desk will also help staff in the IT department to focus on the task of writing new programs rather than answering minor queries from users.

Lack of direct user input

User input is essential for most projects to ensure that any revised or new system actually meets the requirements of those users. In SN plc, user input is not obtained until a new system is ready for implementation. At this stage, there is a danger that any revised system will be rejected by the users, either because it does not fully meet their requirements or because the users feel that they do not own the IT system, because they have not been involved in its development.

The main method of ensuring that user requirements are met is to involve users in system design from initial specification through to implementation. Setting up the joint design committee would help to achieve this objective.

Lack of a review to ensure the project meets company strategy

Although the head of IT produces the overall IT strategy for SN plc, there does not appear to be a check to ensure that any new information system projects are in alignment with this strategy. While this may not be an issue in some situations, there is a danger that a new system may be implemented which cannot be supported by the company's IT strategy. For example, a system may request information from a centralized database when the company's overall strategy is to move to decentralised databases linked via an Intranet.

To avoid this problem, the head of IT must review all project specifications to ensure that there are no conflicts with the IT strategy of SN plc. If any conflicts are found, then appropriate changes must be made to the project, at the design stage, to ensure that the delivered systems are congruent with the company's overall TT strategy.

No ownership of data, therefore no responsibility for update

The main users of the information systems are not involved in the development process, and as noted below, receive little training on how to use the systems. This approach makes it very difficult for the users to take ownership of the information systems. It is likely that the users will feel that the systems are imposed on them and there will be little or no incentive to use those system or ensure that the data on them are actually up-to-date.

Users must be given some incentive to accept the new information systems. This can be achieved either by involving them in the development process, by providing more detailed training, or explaining the benefits of the new systems in more detail.

Lack of user training

The only training provided for users is the provision of a user manual. Given that sales staff tend to be very busy, it is unlikely that they will be able to find the time to work through a user manual, either to understand what any new system can do, or to resolve queries on the use of that system. There is also the danger that the system will be used incorrectly, resulting in incorrect or inaccurate data being maintained on that system. This will result in incorrect sales decisions being taken which may result in financial loss to the company if incorrect advice is given.

It is essential that appropriate training be introduced as soon as possible to ensure that information systems are used correctly and to avoid financial loss to SN plc. Appropriate rotation of staff in user departments will be needed to ensure that the company's operations can continue while training takes place.

Test your understanding 9 – B2C Cars

Transaction Processing Systems

- These systems are routine and deterministic and are responsible for processing large volumes of scheduled information through functional operations.

- It is likely that B2C Cars already have this type of information system in operation as they are the first to be developed and can support functions such as stock, sales and accounting.

- For example all stock systems will be linked to a centralised ordering system, as soon as items/parts reach a predetermined reorder level an automated search of all potential suppliers will take place using a system such as an Extranet or Electronic Data Interchange (EDI).

- The system will seek out the lowest cost supplier who is likely to deliver in the shortest lead time and place an order on the supplier system.

- The impact of using this kind of system for B2C is that it will give the opportunity to efficiently operate just-in-time (JIT) where stock holding is very low as part/item replacement can be made very quickly, therefore reducing the associated costs of holding stock.

- In addition BS may decide to set an Electronic Funds Transfer system where direct payment is made to the supplier as soon as the delivery is made, this will reduce the time and costs associated with the reconciliation of orders and delivery and also increases the power of purchasing as B2C becomes the preferred customer.

Management Information Systems

- An MIS is a rigid summarised reporting system summarising information from the TPS.

- Again it is likely that B2C already have a number of MIS which report on the existing transaction systems such as movements in stock and sales, performance by model etc; these systems will alert management to changes in these levels, therefore enabling them to take appropriate action.

- For example, by combining exception reporting and data mining the management of B2C would be able to determine the best selling cars by region, which would improve the ability to the target market and direct promotions at specific groups.

- MIS only provide the answers to structured type questions such as which items are out of stock or which model is the highest selling; using this information management would explore comparisons helping to establish trends, etc.

- It is vital that the TPS is 100% accurate as subsequent systems such as the MIS are based upon its information provision, therefore any errors provided by the TPS would be amplified within the MIS.

Decision Support Systems

- A DSS is a system which has the ability to integrate reporting facilities with the inclusion of variables; often a DSS would incorporate software such as a spreadsheet, enabling managers to create budgets and forecasts.

- B2C Cars would find it necessary to be able to forecast potential sales in the future and this would be achieved through the application of judgement/intuition to past transactions.

- For example, management would extract a summary of sales by model and apply a variable (perhaps a %) which would denote the potential change, therefore giving the opportunity to forecast sales based on knowledge in the past. This would be vital for the setting of reorder levels of stock.

- The development of these forecasts and budgets would enable management to explore alternatives and complete sensitivity or 'what if ...' analysis e.g. if sales of model X increase by 2%, what is the impact on the cost of sales, ordering requirements and can the manufacturing capacity of the factory meet this increase?

- A decision support system would generally support the requirement of middle managers who are required to make semi-structured decisions.

Executive Information Systems

- This type of system will support senior managers in making long-term decisions in relation to capital investment in new technology or plant and machinery or changes in design, i.e. launch a new model.

- An EIS incorporates flexible forecasting with extraction from a TPS, in addition to information from external sources such as competitors and trade associations.

- The EIS will present this information in a summarised format e.g. graphs, and has the ability to overlay the information from these sources to ease comparison.

- The main feature of the EIS is the opportunity to 'drill down' i.e. explore the detail in relation to the output. For example, if sales are falling in a particular region the system would be able to extract information (given parameters) to offer management the detail as to why these results may be occurring.

- An additional feature of the EIS is that it must be easy to use for senior management and incorporate a range of user-friendly features such as icons, on-line help, colour, etc; although these are now common in many of the systems described above, it should be noted that they are a prerequisite of an EIS.

Expert Systems

- These systems are designed to replace the need to employ experts; the user is able to gain access to the advice through the interaction with the system. Examples of use include tax advice and insurance quotations.

- An expert system is based upon a knowledge base, user interface, inference engine (the software which combines the knowledge an user requirements) and the knowledge acquisition program (ability for knowledge to be added, i.e. for the system to learn).

- B2C may have an opportunity to develop an expert system in a number of areas and these include:
    - Maintenance of equipment and robotics on production lines; engineers input details of the fault and the system provides a diagnosis and instructions.

    - Customisation of requirements; customers may require different styles and finishes, these needs could be entered via the interface and a price/delivery, etc could be provided.

- The impact of the use of this type of IS is the reduction in cost (in particular the creation and distribution of knowledge); this knowledge also becomes a tangible asset within the organisation which can be shared.

- The last example, whereby customers can specify needs and quickly obtain the price of this requirement, may become a competitive advantage.

Test your understanding 10 – Cost benefit

(a) Cost-benefit analysis techniques

Techniques of cost-benefit analysis fall into two main categories: those that ignore the time value of money (TVM), and those that take into account the TVM. First, we will consider two techniques, which do not take into account the TVM.

Payback period – this method measures the number of years taken by the project to recoup the initial investment. Obviously, the shorter the payback period the better. Companies use this method frequently because it is easy to apply and comprehend. Use of the payback period does, however, have a number of drawbacks. The determination of the cut-off period is essentially an arbitrary decision. The payback period ignores cash flows, which occur after the cut-off date; it also ignores the timing of cash flows within the payback period itself. As a result, viable projects may easily be rejected.

In its favour, the payback period does allow for risk and uncertainty by attempting to recover the initial outlay in as short a period as possible.

Return on investment – using this method, the benefits of the project are expressed as a return on investment in terms of a rate per year.

This technique assumes that the investment is repaid over its economic life in a straight-line way. As with the payback period method, it is easy to apply and comprehend but it, too, does not take into account the time value of money. It does, however, provide a useful indicator; organisations obviously seek to invest scarce resources where they will derive the highest return.

Discounted cash flow (DCF) methods take into consideration the time value of money. We will consider the two principal DCF methods of project appraisal: Net Present Value (NPV) and Internal Rate of Return (IRR).

Net Present Value – this method takes the discounted present value of the future cash flows generated by the project, less the initial outlay. If the NPV is equal to, or greater than, zero the project should be considered as it will at least attain the required rate of return; when greater than zero it will enhance the value of the firm. When using this method to compare projects the one with the largest NPV should be selected.

Internal Rate of Return – this method identifies the rate of return, which produces an NPV of zero for the project. If the IRR of a project is greater than the firm's required rate of return (usually the cost of capital), it should proceed with the project.

(b) **Measurement of information systems costs and benefits**

Costs – some categories of costs associated with a computer system can be quite precisely ascertained, while others are less easily defined. The main costs related to information systems are those of building the system, installation costs, and operational and maintenance costs.

The costs associated with building the system include staff costs (the average salaries for all levels of staff participating in the project; lost time due to sickness, holidays etc; staff training where the use of new software or hardware is necessary, and travel expenses incurred when making associated trips to suppliers etc) and computer-related costs (computer time incurred during system development, and any new equipment which may need to be bought). Many of these costs cannot be accurately defined, but can only be estimated.

The cost of installing the system, which may include recruitment and training, commissioning and installation, conversion of files, user training, parallel running or phased implementation etc, may be easier to quantify. Operating and maintenance costs, (usually contributing to as much as 70% of the total cost of the system) would include the costs of financing the system, maintenance contracts, etc. These costs are often predetermined, and therefore their measurement is less problematic.

Benefits – tactical benefits are those, which enable the company to continue functioning in the same way, but at a lower level of costs, or with increased profits. These can be moderately straightforward to define, although the accuracy of any estimation will be determined by the effectiveness of the new system, and its ability to accomplish the required functions. Strategic benefits are those that enable the company to enter new markets, either offering a new product/service or reaching new customers, or both. These are of fundamental importance, yet are so difficult to predict, or quantify.

The improved system will enable better use to be made of information, which should enhance decision-making and the productivity of managers. Monitoring and quantifying these could present difficulties.

The information system may help in attracting new customers and retaining existing ones; and it should improve stock and credit control. Again, attempts to quantify and classify these benefits may be problematic.

(c) **Risk analysis of the costs and benefits**

The majority of investments are exposed to at least some element of risk. It may be categorised as systematic (factors that affect all organisations) or unsystematic (events that affect one project).

Most managerial decisions involve an element of uncertainty, and are therefore subject to some level of risk. Identifying, and being able to quantify, the risk factor is of great consequence.

Management want to have their vulnerable assets identified, their security requirements outlined, and protective measures delineated. The costs of safeguarding against risks can then be balanced against the estimated costs, which would be incurred if the event took place. The project may be affected by prices that are higher than anticipated.

This may be caused by:

(i) bankruptcy of hardware suppliers;

(ii) high turnover of staff on the project team;

(iii) technology not meeting expectations;

(iv) opportunity being lost;

(v) unforeseen problems with contractors, unions etc;

(vi) inadequacies in the project team;

(vii) instability in the economic environment;

(viii) unforeseen costs/overheads;

(ix) inadequate information from the users with regard to their needs of the system.

The project may equally be affected by anticipated benefits, which do not emerge:

(i) the users may experience difficulties or apprehension in adopting the new system; delays or disruption may ensue as a result;

(ii) projected increases in the market share may not occur;

(iii) the system may not be capable of performing at the level estimated, resulting in lower productivity than predicted;

(iv) the benefits derived from the information being produced by the new system may not be discernible.
Risk assessment often involves scenario-based methodologies, which may involve preparing three scenarios: worst case, best case, and expected case.

Test your understanding 11 – ZX

(a) Both ZX's Board and potential customers would like new drugs to reach the market place quicker than they currently do. The information systems should support this aim and enable information to be processed and accessed quickly and efficiently.

An intranet is a private network operating within an organisation that potentially makes information flow more freely by bringing the same information and computing resources to all staff wherever they are located. This means making company information more available to those who need to have the rights to it, but less widely available to those who do not.

There are several problems in the existing system that an intranet might help resolve.

(i) Finding specific items of data takes employees a long time, mainly due to the volume of information. There could be many reasons for this – the referencing of documents could be poor, the physical access to documents could be difficult etc. If the documents were put into an electronic format, searching could be achieved by using a specific search program. Manual request for copies of documents could be eliminated as the entire information base could be accessed from any location.

(ii) The difficulties of accessing data and sending data to and from many different locations is therefore overcome by using an intranet.

(iii) Searches can be more rigorous and sophisticated by using electronic methods. For instance references to specific drugs could be found, or documents containing combinations of issues could be found and then accessed.

(iv) Delays and wasted time due to teams duplicating work, having to finish one process before starting another, and reporting back to a central project manager can be minimised if an intranet were used. Information flows are quicker and the manager can maintain control by viewing documents as work progresses, in real time, which might well enable tasks to run concurrently.

(v) The problem of documents being lost in the post could be eliminated (although electronic documents can also be lost unless proper procedures are in place to prevent it). Document transfers are almost instantaneous using the intranet, however the network must be robust enough to suffer from minimal down time and the appropriate backup, archiving and disaster recovery procedures must be in place as with any other vital computer installation.

(vi) An extranet is a private, secure extension of an enterprise via its intranet. It allows the business to share part of its business information or operations with others using the Internet. In ZX's case this means that access rights are provided on specific drugs on the company database for third parties to access (but presumably not amend).

There are several limitations of using an extranet for this purpose.

(i) Firstly, there is the issue of loss of competitive position. Whilst sharing knowledge could result in faster development times, there is usually great competitive advantage to be gained by being first on the market with a new drug.

(ii) Secondly, the data may be considered confidential and therefore unavailable for sharing with others. For example, test results may include references to individuals and contain personal data – to share such information may involve breaching confidentiality agreements.

(iii) Thirdly there may be lack of trust between organisations – if ZX gives all its information to a third party, how does it know that this other organisation is reciprocating and giving ZX all its information.

(iv) Finally systems may be incompatible between organisations making electronic information exchange impossible in computer form. This problem is becoming less common in practice. Of course, the first three limitations are not exclusive to information exchanged using an extranet; however, because of the ease in which large volumes of data can be exchanged or accessed electronically, these problems can be exacerbated in the extranet situation.

Test your understanding 12 – RBT

(a) **Intranet**

An intranet is an internal company information system where a wide variety of internal information can be posted for access by staff members. Internal information often includes company news, telephone directories, standard forms, copies of rules and procedures, and so on. In this case of the system under consideration by RBT, the intranet would hold up-to-date information on products and prices, so that sales representatives can download this information to their laptops from customer's premises and other remote locations.

Advantages

The proposed new system has the following advantages over the old system:

(1) **More regularly updated information**

An intranet site is very easy and cheap to update, and product and price information can be kept fully up-to-date by head office. The downloaded product information will therefore be much more up-to-date than the old printed materials, and a better customer service can be provided. All the latest products would be made available to customers and customers would always be given the correct prices.

(2) **Reduced costs of producing price lists/brochures**

Regular price lists and brochures will no longer be required, and the production and printing costs of paper-based products should be reduced.

Disadvantages

The intranet site has the following disadvantages compared with the old system:

(1) **Slower communication with the production department**

Since the telephone system will be discontinued, the sales people will not have access to production staff to resolve any queries or difficulties with customers. This would be a serious weakness in the system. Good communications between sales and production staff must be maintained.

Solutions

Possible solutions to this problem include:

(i) *E-mail system*

E-mail might provide an efficient way for sales representatives to communicate directly with the production staff, although controls would need to be in place to ensure that the production staff respond promptly to e-mail queries they receive.

(ii) *Maintain telephone access*

Voice telephone access offers immediate communication. A salesperson can get in contact with a member of the production staff and get an immediate reply. Maintaining telephone access for certain queries would be a useful way of ensuring very quick communication where needed.

(iii) *Access to production scheduling system*

Allowing salespeople access to the production scheduling system over the intranet would allow them to estimate delivery date themselves thus reducing the need for direct contact between production and sales.

(2) Less personal communication with production department

The intranet is a very impersonal way to communicate with people. It does not allow for two-way conversation, whereas personal contact may be required to resolve difficult issues.

Solution

Both e-mail and a voice telephone system are more personal forms of communication than the intranet. The voice telephone system in particular allows a two-way conversation to take place so that more difficult issues can easily be resolved.

(3) Rejection of new technology

The sales people may dislike the new technology that they are required to use. At present they do not use IT significantly in their work, and so new skills may be required. Many new systems also have 'teething problems' on implementation, which may also make users dislike the new system.

Solutions

(i) *Training*

Training will be required so people know how the system works and can get the best use from it.

(ii) *Consultation*

Consulting users early in the development process is an excellent way of getting user buy-in to the new system. It will also ensure the system is practical from a day-to-day usage point of view.

(iii) *Testing*

Testing systems well prior to implementation will help avoid the teething problems which may be encountered, particularly if the end users are involved since they know better than anyone else the way the system will be used in practice.

(4) Up-front costs

The proposed new system will require significant up-front costs both in terms of developing the new systems and training staff. Given the relatively small number of sales representatives (just 20) the investment may not be financially justified.

Solution

A cost benefit analysis can be undertaken to ascertain whether the costs of the investment are justified.

(5) Information systems – order progress

Manufacturing system – order tracking

As part of the manufacturing process, progress on orders will need to be recorded. The information recorded will include work done, work still to do and the expected completion date. This information might already exist within the current system or it may need to be input into a database which can be accessed by clients.

EDI or extranet

Using electronic data interchange the customer would be able to log on to RBT's systems to directly access the production data.

An extranet is an extension of an intranet. External parties are allowed to log onto the intranet site and use it to access sections of the intranet. The intranet site would need to be connected to the manufacturing system/database so that up-to-date information was available.

Advantages

(1) Clients could access information themselves. This could save staff time and resources in RBT, since there will be fewer customer queries to deal with.

(2) An extranet would be relatively easy to provide if the manufacturing system is already linked to the intranet for the benefit of the salespeople.

(3) Other information could also be provided to customers (such as past order information, account balances and so on).

Disadvantages

(1) There would be a loss of personal contact with customers. The salesperson would not have as many opportunities to make contact with customers in order to build an ongoing relationship. As a consequence, they might identify fewer sales opportunities or find it harder to make a sale because they are less trusted by the customer.

(2) External parties would be accessing internal systems. There is a danger that hackers will get into parts of the system that are confidential, and a risk that important information is stolen or damaged. It could also increase the possibility of viruses being brought in which could damage internal systems.

Internet

Alternatively the RBT could put tracking information on a database which is connected to the company's web site. Clients would then be able to access their information through this site.

Advantages

(1) Labour cost savings, as described for an extranet.

(2) Customers will be familiar with the internet and so find it easier to use than an extranet or internal system accessed via EDI. It also means they will not have to dial in directly to the company's internal network, saving them time and effort.

(3) There is less opportunity for hackers or viruses to enter the internal systems using a web site on the internet, since they are not directly accessing internal systems.

(4) Other information could also be provided to customers on the internet site.

Disadvantage

The company may not currently have an internet site. This could be a significant extra expense, in terms of designing, creating and maintaining the site.

16

Information management

Chapter learning objectives

Lead	Component
E1. Evaluate the benefits and risks associated with information-related systems.	(c) Evaluate benefits and risks in the structuring and organisation of the IS/IT function and its integration with the rest of the business.

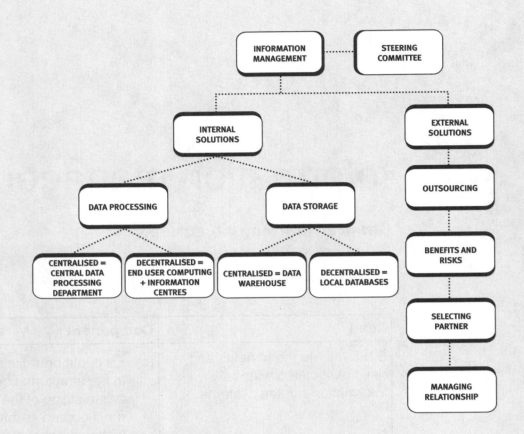

1 Organising the IT function

The previous chapters considered the structure and development of information strategy and the types of information systems that might be available to business managers to assist them in their duties.

This chapter considers how the business could structure its information provision to those managers, i.e. the information management. It also looks at some of the practical issues that have to be addressed with these different solutions.

The issues are split between internal and external solutions. The **internal solutions** are:

(i) Central data processing (all computer access from one point).

(ii) End-user computing and information centres.

(iii) Databases and data warehouses.

The **external solution** discussed is outsourcing or facilities management.

Steering committees

Due to the strategic importance of IS/IT and the high level of spend that many companies make in this area, steering committees are usually established to decide on the provision of the information services.

Membership of the steering committee

A steering committee would normally be structured with the following groups represented:

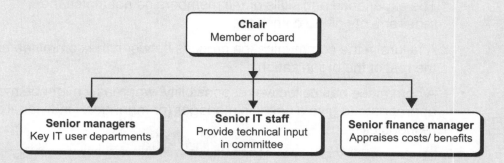

Purpose of the steering committee

The purpose of the steering committee is to:

* Plan, monitor and control IS/IT/IM strategy.

* Identify and analyse IS/IT risk.

* Consider the competitive issues raised by IT.

* Ensure that IS/IT programmes achieve their specified objectives, in line with organisational policy and objectives.

* Make resource decisions and IT funding decisions.

* Plan for future systems developments.

More on the steering committee

Other activities of the steering committee include:

* providing leadership at senior level for the exploitation and management of IT

* ensuring that resource allocation decisions are effective

* approving the terms of reference for IT project teams for new systems developments

* monitoring the progress of the various systems development projects.

The approval of new systems developments could be the responsibility of a steering committee at either corporate or divisional level within the organisation.

Several problems could arise with ensuring that steering committees are effective in fulfilling their responsibilities:

- The experience and skills of the members do not match the requirements of the committee.

- A failure in the communication process between the committee and the rest of the organisation.

- A committee has collective responsibility, whereas it might be more appropriate to give a specific manager (or managers) individual responsibility.

2 Internal solutions

This section will consider two aspects of information management:

- Data processing (collection and processing of data and information)
  - centralised: central data processing department, or
  - decentralised: end-user computing.
- Data storage (where data are held within an organisation)
  - centralised: data warehousing, or
  - decentralised: local databases.

Central data processing department

In the early stages of computerisation, many organisations set up large data processing departments that ran all their computer operations. In some cases this was the only practical way of running and controlling IT, as the IT system was dependent on a large central computer and personal computers were rare.

Advantages and disadvantages

Advantages of this type of structure:

- IT specialism could be retained at the centre
- control of the system was straightforward.

Disadvantages:

- users would not get the applications they required
- the department was expensive to run.

End-user computing and information centres

In the 1980s PCs became a very common business tool and this led to the development of end-user computing. Users were empowered to directly use the computer systems without the need for a large data processing department.

Distributed processing is appropriate in a situation where the organisation has several geographical locations, linked over a communications network. It may be carried out:

- using terminals connected to a remote central computer, or
- with local computers, which may be:
    - independent of each other, or
    - linked to form a network.

Advantages and disadvantages

Advantages:

- improved user satisfaction because individual managers
    - are able to schedule their own processing
    - have more control over the database
- the organisation can 'down-size' the IT function, leading to cost savings in the business.

Disadvantages:

- the organisation could lose the ability to develop or maintain major systems
- the organisation loses the knowledge of key staff, again leading to difficulties repairing and modifying systems
- the controls over the information systems are relaxed
- external consultants are required and these are expensive to employ.

Information centres

Because of the problems with end-user computing, information centres began to be developed, firstly by IBM but subsequently by other companies.

An information centre is a part of the IT department that is established to support end-users in developing their own information systems.

More on information centres

An information centre or service centre is a department within an organisation whose function is to provide help and assistance to other departments and individuals using the computer systems of the organisation.

The services that might typically be offered by the information centre would include:

- Evaluation of hardware and software on behalf of users, to ensure that compatibility and performance levels are acceptable.
- Direct assistance with development projects.
- Prototype development, where this is beyond the expertise of users.
- User training.
- Advice on controls that are necessary for the system.
- Maintenance of a corporate database.
- Maintenance of the end-user systems.
- Development of major IT systems centred on the corporate server.

It responds to the organisation's need to control technology by:

- establishing hardware standards, and specifying what users must buy if they are adding equipment to their system
- approving a range of suppliers of hardware
- establishing software, testing and documentation standards
- becoming a central point for the release of updated software
- ensuring data integrity in the databases
- enforcing security procedures, such as file back-ups and virus checking.

A service centre will probably include a help desk.

Help desks

In an organisation with distributed processing systems, there is a serious practical problem about how to provide support in situations where a user suffers a computer malfunction, due to a hardware fault, a software fault or (perhaps most often) because the user has input an inappropriate command to the system. The user will need help in sorting out the problem, but it is usually impossible to have expert IT staff at every site to provide assistance. Having an IT expert at every location where there are computer terminals would be a waste of scarce IT staff resources, as well as far too expensive.

A help desk is a centralised IT support service that users can contact whenever something goes wrong and a user 'can't get the computer to do what he wants' or 'the computer isn't working properly'. The initial contact by the user in difficulty to the help desk could be by telephone or e-mail.

The IT expert answering help desk calls or messages will try to deal with the problem by telephone or e-mail, giving the user instructions about what to do to resolve the problem. If this fails to deal with the problem, either:

- the help desk centre will send an individual to visit the user's premises and investigate the problem on site, or

- an IT expert in the help centre will use remote diagnostic software that takes control of the user's computer without the expert leaving his desk. The expert can then use the software to investigate the problem and try to correct it.

Some organisations have their own in-house help desk, whereas others outsource the service to an outside organisation.

Databases

Under a traditional distributed system, each local area would have a database containing data required for local operations. This data would not be stored at the central location.

Data warehousing

Data warehousing is defined as 'the concept of integrating data from disparate internal and external sources centrally within the organisation such that the database thus established can be used for flexible reporting and analysis'.

Data warehousing is a very valuable tool if an organisation wants to

- set up an effective executive information system
- introduce an enterprise resource planning system.

IT structure

An effective data warehouse will need a particular IT structure in order to operate. The structure will be set-up on the basis of a distributed (or client-server) architecture, but with a very controlled data storage system.

For data warehousing to be effective, however, all data would be stored centrally, with local branches only storing the applications that use the data. The knock-on effect of this is that communication lines between the central data store and local branches will probably need to be permanent and dedicated.

Advantages of data warehousing (as opposed to local databases):

- Lower volumes of data are held.
- Lower storage costs.
- Easy to amend data, and only one piece of data needs amendment.
- Users have confidence they are using up-to-date data.
- Data management is improved as it is practical to employ database administrators.
- Controls over data are improved.
- More consistency is achieved in decision making.

Disadvantages of data warehousing:

- Most of the departments will require new hardware and software before they can use the data warehouse.
- Almost all staff who want to use the new system will need training.
- The data will either need to be analysed and 'cleansed' before it can be integrated into a warehouse. This will not be easy, quick or cheap to achieve.
- Data needed by individual locations may not be collected and stored by the central data function, and reporting requirements may differ.
- If the database fails or is damaged then the organisation processes stop, hence effective back-up arrangements are vital.
- Response times may be slower (however, for some data items the central store will be able to respond more quickly).

3 External solution

Outsourcing IT services means obtaining some or all IT services from an external supplier, rather than having them provided internally by the organisation's own IT staff.

Reasons for outsourcing:

- Many organisations regard IS/IT as a 'non-core' aspect of their business. They therefore choose to outsource this function and focus internal resources on the core elements of the business.

- In most countries there is a shortage of IT specialists, and organisations that do not specialise themselves in IT could have serious difficulty in recruiting and retaining IT staff.

- Outsourcing can be used to fill temporary gaps created by in-house IT job vacancies.

- Even if an organisation could recruit IT specialists, it might not have sufficient valuable IT-related work to make use of these specialist staff in a cost-effective way. Outsourcing is therefore often considered a much cheaper option.

Outsourcing can range from buying in occasional services from external providers to total outsourcing, known as **facilities management**.

Total outsourcing (facilities management)

With total outsourcing, an organisation (the 'host') outsources most or all of its IT function – system development, and systems operations and maintenance (hardware and software):

- to **one** external service provider

- at an agreed 'service level'

- over a fixed period of time, usually several years

- with an agreed cost formula for the payments for services provided.

What generally happens is that the facilities management provider charges a fixed fee for a pre-specified number of services, known as the 'baseline'. The host organisation is then guaranteed that the costs for this baseline will be fixed over the contract duration – typically five to ten years.

- The facilities management provider manages the organisation's IT facilities, even though the physical elements of the IT (computers, etc) might be on the host's premises.

- The host organisation might retain a small core of internal staff to oversee the management of the contract with the external supplier.

Other outsourcing approaches

Multiple/selective sourcing

With multiple/selective sourcing, an organisation enters into agreements with a range of suppliers for the external provision of IT services. It may draw up framework contracts, whereby it can then buy the selected service or equipment from one of the suppliers with a degree of competition, since each supplier would quote a price based on the same framework agreement. These types of contracts are unlikely to last for more than five years, although successful contract relationships may lead to renewal.

Many organisations choose a selective approach, and outsource selected services to individual external suppliers. For example, they might retain high-level IT services in-house, such as IS/IT systems development, and outsource routine IT services such as payroll or a help desk service for basic IT systems such as e-mail or word processing.

Where an IS function finds that it does not have the necessary resources it will place contracts with service providers. The following list of services is a fair representation of the kinds of services that a typical IS function will place contracts for:

- training on packaged software
- support on packaged application packages
- specialist management of communications networks
- user requirements studies
- maintenance of hardware
- operating system support.

Joint venture/strategic alliance sourcing

With joint venture/strategic alliance sourcing, an organisation enters into a joint venture with an IT supplier:

- on a shared risk/reward basis, and
- for a specific purpose, such as the development of a software package or an item of IT equipment that is seen as having widespread application across other organisations.

The concept of a joint IT venture is that if the IT firm and the user organisation develop the software or hardware item jointly, they will then share in its more widespread commercial exploitation. Joint ventures might involve setting up a jointly owned company that competes on the open market.

Insourcing

With insourcing, the organisation retains its own IT department, but buys in ('insources') IT management or technical resources to meet peak demands in IS development work. Insourcing is similar to body shop outsourcing, but on a larger scale.

For example, a UK company might specify the requirements for a major new IT system and then contract out the writing of the system (and possibly also the maintenance and system support) to an offshore company, say in India, where IT staff costs are much lower.

The obvious benefit of insourcing can be lower system development costs. The problems can be difficulties with project management and communication, when the IT firm is in a different part of the world and a different time zone.

Benefits of outsourcing

The major advantages are as follows:

- Cost and efficiency savings as the information systems are run by experts, giving economies of scale. Additionally using external services can be much cheaper than employing in-house IT staff and not using them fully or efficiently.

- Short-term responsiveness improved because outsourcers can provide a quicker service.

- Flexibility since using external IT providers allows an organisation to buy in services as and when it needs them.

- To overcome skills shortages required to carry out the full range of IT activities.

- Control of information provision through the contract (i.e. redress if the outsourcer fails to deliver).

- Allows the organisation to focus on core activities.

Risks of outsourcing

- Loss of in-house expertise and IT knowledge since no experts are employed by the company. This may limit knowledge of what the systems might be able to deliver.

- Financial constraints as the company is tied into one outsourcer.

- Difficulties in agreeing and enforcing contract terms.

- Loss of control of information provision, and therefore a failure to get the information required.

- Lack of co-ordination between departments because systems are not seen as integrated.

- Risk of system loss if the outsourcer fails.

- Dependency on supplier for the quality of service provision.

- Risk of a loss of confidentiality, particularly if the external supplier performs similar services for rival companies.

- A loss of competitive advantage (if information systems are a core competence, they must not be outsourced).

More detail on some outsourcing benefits and risks

The benefits of outsourcing

The potential benefits of outsourcing will depend on the extent to which IT services are outsourced. Some of the advantages include:

- To achieve **savings in costs**. The main perceived benefit of outsourcing is reduced cost. Using external services can be much cheaper than employing in-house IT staff and not using them fully or efficiently.

- To **overcome skills shortages**. The IS/IT function of the organisation may not have all the resources necessary to carry out the full range of IT activities required. In many cases, the IS/IT requirements of the organisation might not justify an in-house IT department, particularly in the areas of systems development. Facilities management specialists will have a larger pool of technical staff than the organisation. This will effectively eliminate the risk of all skills being lost simultaneously.

- **Flexibility**. Using external IT providers allows an organisation to be flexible in its choice of IT services. It can buy in services as and when it needs them.

- An argument that has been used in favour of outsourcing (largely by firms of management consultants) is that organisations should **focus on their core skills** and activities where they have a clear competitive advantage over rival firms, and sub-contract non-core activities. Outsourcing frees up management time, and allows management to concentrate on those areas of the business that are most critical.

The risks of outsourcing

There are a number of problems with outsourcing, including:

- When an organisation outsources its IT services on a large scale (total outsourcing), the **chain of command is effectively broken**. The organisation has a contract with the external supplier and therefore has no direct management control.

- A further difficulty is that the organisation's **goals and objectives** will be different from those of the external suppliers providing the outsourced services. For example, the organisation might be interested in ensuring that it's IS/IT function remains dynamic, and responds to changes in IT technology and changes in its information systems requirements. The external supplier, on the other hand, might be more interested in stability and minimal change, in order to keep costs under control and avoid the risks that inevitably arise with system changes and upgrades.

- Once a company has handed over its computing to another company under a long-term service agreement, it is **locked into the arrangement**. Should the service of the facilities management provider be unsatisfactory, leading to a cancellation of the contract, the organisation will be faced with the large expense of having to take the work in-house or arrange a new contract with an alternative supplier.

- Organisations embarking on outsourcing contracts to develop major new systems often find that the **actual costs are significantly higher than the expected costs**, due to a failure to anticipate the time and the difficulties in writing and testing the system to the client organisation's satisfaction. This is an area where the management accountant should be able to contribute usefully, by applying sensible forecasts and suitable risk analysis to the evaluation of the capital expenditure proposal.

Selecting an FM partner

In selecting an FM partner a business will need to go through a tendering process and this process needs to be carried out correctly. The following summarises the way that a tendering process might be done to select a partner.

Invitation to tender

Suppliers are sent an invitation to tender document. This document defines what needs to be done to achieve the system objectives and acts as a basis for the supplier presentation/proposal.

The invitation to tender also sets the rules for the response and the form that the response should take.

Contents of an invitation to tender include:

- Information about the organisation.
- Information about the system requirements gathered from investigation and analysis.
- Information required from the supplier.

More detail on an invitation to tender

The contents of an invitation to tender include:

Information about the organisation:

- Description of business.
- Number of employees, location.
- Future likely changes in organisation.
- Organisation structure.
- Current hardware and software.

Information about the system requirements gathered from investigation and analysis:

- Statement of business objectives and system.
- Description of what the system comprises: hardware, software, communications.
- Number of users accessing system.
- Required response rate.
- Current input, output, processing and storage volumes.
- Service, maintenance and training requirements.

Information required from the supplier:

- Description of supplier business: products and services offered.
- Size and geographical breakdown.
- Current customer base.
- Third party references.

- Experience of similar systems.

- System proposal.

- Utilisation and implementation proposals.

- Suggested timescale for supply and implementation.

- Proposals for training, maintenance and after sales service.

- Cost and payment term.

Evaluating supplier proposals

Once proposals are received from potential suppliers, they must be compared with what was requested in the tender document and the best one selected. The steering committee is likely to play a key role in this process.

The criteria for the evaluation might include:

Technical performance	This examines if the supplier proposals tally with the system requirements specified in the tender document.
Cost	Are all suppliers within budget?
Customer support	How good is the service offered by the supplier?

Once validated, tenders must be evaluated and ranked. Tenders may well have different strengths and weaknesses, with no one offer providing the perfect solution.

To maintain good relations with suppliers, a letter should be sent to unsuccessful suppliers, thanking them for their applications but stating that unfortunately they have been unsuccessful on this occasion.

Managing outsourcing relationships

When an organisation decides to enter into an outsourcing arrangement, and having decided which services to outsource, it needs to:

- negotiate a contract with the service provider, and

- when the contract has been agreed, manage the relationship with the service provider.

When a contract is negotiated with an external provider of IT services, the ideal outcome is an agreement that benefits both parties and encourages them to develop a constructive relationship throughout the term of the agreement.

The **service level agreement** with a supplier is a key element of the contract, and must specify points such as:

- which of the host organisation's computer systems are covered, and which items of equipment

- if the supplier agrees to provide help desk facilities, the agreement has to specify whether the help desk service will be:
    - by e-mail only
    - by e-mail and telephone only
    - by e-mail and telephone, with site visits as required.

- performance standards that the supplier should meet, such as:
    - a minimum percentage of the time that the system must be operating properly and fully functional ('system up-time')
    - a minimum response time for requests for service or assistance.

- deadlines for the completion of tasks (e.g. payroll processing to be completed by the last Friday in each month, or target dates for the completion of system development projects).

Contract negotiation issues

Various contract negotiation issues are set out in the table below:

Problem to negotiate	Contract response
Difficulty of maintaining performance service levels	Include in contract measures on the following and set sliding scale penalties for size and frequency of failing to meet parameters: • availability (uptime percentage) • quality (response time, % of work completed to schedule, time to initiation) • response to requests for new services and capabilities • keeping up-to-date in hardware and software.
Inappropriate contract timescale	Make contract term short if major architectural change is expected. Five years is typically long enough to gain benefits without making contract onerous.

Difficulty in protecting software entitlement	Payment must cover where the software is running (make extra licence payment at start and end of outsourcing contract) unless vendor already holds licence.
Loss of copyright on own software run by vendor	Explicit contract clauses must cover: • ownership of software • software security • software confidentiality.
Loss of copyright on software vendor develops as part of outsourcing	Before development, make explicit in the contract the trade-off between value of the product, its exclusivity and cost of development, leading to copyright held by either the outsource client, the outsource vendor or jointly held.
Difficulty of transferring to a new vendor	To avoid becoming dependent on IS elements to which the vendor has exclusive rights, the outsource client should only use: • what they own • what they have rights to • what is publicly available • what is easily replaced.
Client organisation might wish to discontinue the contract before the end of the contract period, because the IT services are no longer required	Contract to include a clause providing for early termination, subject to suitable notice and termination payments.
Difficulty of grouping/separating IS applications or functions	To increase flexibility, split contracts for logically separate services, e.g. data centre management from local equipment support. Closely connected services should be covered in one contract to increase service quality.

Impossibility of regaining original in-house staff	Outsourcing should be viewed as a semi-permanent decision and plans to regain staff should not be relevant. Outsourcing contracts should not prevent re-hiring of staff at contract end.
Loss of staff who are familiar with the client organisation's systems	The supplier should agree to create sufficient documentation of the client's systems so that sufficient knowledge is preserved in the event of loss of key personnel.

Discontinuation

At the end of a service agreement, if the client organisation wishes to switch to a different supplier, or take the IS/IT services back in-house, there could be difficulties including:

- If there have been changes to the system software during the period of the agreement with the supplier, who has the rights to the new software, the supplier or the client organisation? Clearly, the client organisation must insist in the contract on having rights to use the software for its systems, and to give other external suppliers the rights to use and upgrade the software.

- If the system is moved from one computer system/network to the system/network of a different supplier, there could be problems with the changeover, due to incompatibility between the systems. There is a risk that the 'old' supplier, having been informed that its services will no longer be required, will want to avoid any obligations to ensure a smooth handover to the new supplier. Arrangements for the handover to a new supplier must therefore be written into the original service agreement, so that the obligations are contractual.

- There is the need to protect the security of the client's data. The contract terms should therefore provide that at the end of the contract period the outsource organisation should hand over data files and back-ups, and destroy all other files (e.g. out-of-date files and copies). The client organisation might require the right to send in an auditor to check that this has been done.

Test your understanding 1 – SI

The SI organisation builds and sells computers in 35 different countries. A customer can order a computer by telephone, mail order or the internet. The computer is then built to the customer's specification using parts manufactured by SI or supplied from one of 86 different suppliers. The completed computer is then shipped to the customer and installed by SI technicians. The whole process takes between five and seven days.

Following installation, the customer is given access to the country-specific support system of SI. This comprises a country-specific internet site containing detailed information on installation, errors with SI computers, and answers to Frequently Asked Questions. The errors database is the same as that used by SI staff, so customers are effectively being given access to SI's own systems. Technical staff are also available to provide human assistance if customers cannot find the answer to a query within the other support systems.

Databases are maintained in each country, and contain information on the different customers, types of computer sold, queries raised and solutions to those queries, along with standard accounting and financial data.

No other computer manufacturer provides this type of service. Most other manufacturers prefer to sell computers via retail stores on the assumption that customers wish to 'try out' the computers prior to purchase. This strategy of differentiation from competitors has provided SI with a substantial market share, along with significant profits. Customers are prepared to pay for the enhanced service. SI's distribution costs are slightly less than those of its competitors although selling prices are the same, providing additional contribution for SI.

SI organisation structure

Within each country, the SI organisation is run as a separate company. Each company has its own unique information system, resulting in a range of hardware, software and database formats being used. Although this is unusual, the philosophy of SI has been to allow each country to establish systems to meet its own individual requirements. This has resulted in an extremely successful SI company in each country, at the expense of worldwide compatibility.

Similarly, local suppliers supply parts for SI computers, so the SI company in that country can form good working relationships with the suppliers. Again, this has worked to the benefit of SI, as the quality of parts supplied has consistently exceeded expectations and resulted in fewer hardware failures in SI computers compared to other brands.

Each SI company is therefore run as a separate business unit. The head office of SI is located on a small island close to Western Europe. Budgets for each SI company are set after discussions with head office. Apart from this, as long as each company meets budget, no other intervention by SI's head office is considered necessary.

There is a centralised R&D unit, which provides model specifications for new SI computers to all locations. This unit employs 75 research and development specialists.

Their main activities include:

- research into existing SI products in order to make them more reliable and economical to run

- amending existing SI products, incorporating minor design changes such as larger hard disks or additional RAM

- reviewing current developments in computing

- building and testing new products

- providing specifications for new SI computers to the individual SI companies in each country.

Information is provided by the R&D unit on a regular basis to sales and other departments in SI. However, the information flow is one way. The R&D unit does not have access to the sales staff or databases within each SI company.

Recent developments

In the last few years, the sales pattern of SI has shifted significantly away from individual customers purchasing one or two computers, to larger organisations purchasing up to 1,000 computers at a time. These requirements cannot always be met by the production capacity in one SI company, so orders are transferred to other SI companies in other countries. This transfer of production to different countries has led to an increase in exchange risk for individual companies but there is no overall exchange risk policy for the group. Individual company management make decisions about whether to hedge risks or not.

Many customers also request additional support, including 24-hour telephone hotlines and access to worldwide databases of errors and information, which SI currently cannot provide. The Chief Executive of SI recently made a decision to provide this support, effectively authorising a worldwide network to be put in place to link all SI companies. All accounting, customer, financial, support and similar databases are to be linked within one year. Failure to meet this target may result in significant loss of sales if the larger corporate customers move to other suppliers. This investment is to be financed by loans against which the chief executive believes should be hedged. The loans will be a mixture of short- and long-term, but will all be raised in the UK.

Required:

(a) Evaluate the current use of IT within the SI organisation, clearly identifying:

    (i) the strengths and weaknesses of the decentralised systems; and

    (ii) the problems of integrating the systems into one worldwide system.

(b) Describe the risks that SI faces in the way it currently operates the centralised R&D unit.

Test your understanding 2 – DS

The directors of DS are not satisfied with the GDC Ltd Facilities Management Company, which was contracted two years ago to run the IT systems of the company. At that time, the existing in-house IT development and support department was disbanded and all control of IT systems handed over to GDC Ltd. The appointment of GDC Ltd was relatively rushed, and although an outline contract was agreed no detailed service level agreement was produced.

Over the last few weeks, the number of complaints received from staff regarding the service has been increasing and the provision of essential management reports has not been particularly timely.

A recent exchange of correspondence with GDC Ltd failed to resolve the matter. Staff at GDC Ltd recognised the fall in standards of service, but insisted that it had met its contractual obligations. DS's lawyers have confirmed that the following are key features of DS's contract with GDC Ltd Facilities Management Company:

- The contract can be terminated by either party with three months' notice.

- GDC Ltd will provide IT services for DS, the service to include:
  - purchase of all hardware and software
  - repair and maintenance of all it equipment
  - help desk and other support services for users
  - writing and maintaining in-house software
  - provision of management information
  - price charged to be renegotiated each year but any increase must not exceed inflation, plus 10%.

Required:

(a) Explain, from the point of view of DS, why it might have received poor service from GDC Ltd, even though GDC Ltd has met the requirements of the contract.

(b) Recommend the courses of action now available to DS relating to the provision of IT services. Comment on the problems involved in each course of action.

Test your understanding 3 – GDS

GDS is a small listed manufacturing company that has experienced difficulties in retaining qualified and experienced staff for the production of all its management accounting information. It has been approached by CMA, a professional accounting firm that has proposed to carry out a full outsourcing of the accounting function. This will include:

- Backflushing of all labour and materials transactions as a result of the manufacturing process.

- Maintenance of inventory records for raw materials and finished goods.

- Processing of all sales invoicing and purchase invoices.

- Production of monthly management reports and end of year financial reports.

- Interpretation and advice to management based on the financial information.

This information will be processed on computer and access to all data will be available on GDS' own premises via an extranet. The payment of suppliers and non-creditor expenses, receipt of customer payments, maintenance of cash books and all payroll transactions will be retained in-house and carried out by GDS' own staff although the daily cash payment and receipt records will be processed by CMA. The cost savings for GDS in existing staff more than compensate for the cost of outsourcing the accounting function to CMA.

Required:

(a) Compare and contrast the advantages and disadvantages of outsourcing generally.

(b) Advise GDS in relation to the outsourcing of the accounting function to CMA specifically.

(c) Recommend the methods by which a decision to outsource could be best controlled by GDS.

Test your understanding 4 – LDS

Library Direct Services (LDS) is an organisation providing data to central and local government personnel. It maintains a database of:

- all laws, both statute and case law

- reports of proceedings in central government

- comparative data on the services provided by local government in each region of the country and

- some comparative data on services provided in different countries.

LDS allows access to this database 24 hours a day, 365 days a year. LDS is contractually obliged to provide this information within 30 minutes of receiving a request. All requests are received by telephone or email.

The existing database is accessed via command line input at DOS, which the database administrators can use quickly and efficiently. Any perceived or actual decrease in the usefulness of the database will mean that the administrators are unlikely to accept the system.

Over the years, a number of small but significant modifications have been made to the original 'off-the-shelf' database software. It is essential to retain these if the database is to be used, although the programmer who made these changes has left the company and has not been replaced. Program changes are not fully documented.

LDS is now asking for tenders from database suppliers to upgrade the database to Windows functionality. This is likely to involve rewriting the database itself, and implementing a new database management system. LDS needs to make a decision on which company to choose to make this change for them. For budgetary reasons, any proposed change must be completed within the next six months.

Required:

(a) Suggest six questions that LDS can use to help evaluate potential suppliers for the systems changes contract explained above. Explain why each of these questions is relevant to the specific circumstances of LDS.

(b) Discuss whether LDS might benefit from outsourcing the maintenance of the database as well as the development. The alternative option would be to train existing database support staff in the operation of the new database.

4 Chapter summary

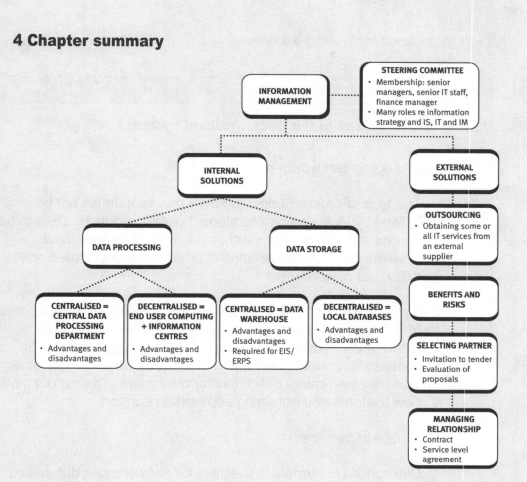

Test your understanding answers

Test your understanding 1 – SI

(a) (i) Weaknesses of the decentralised systems

Changing sales pattern

The type of orders SI now receives can sometimes not be fulfilled by local companies alone. Instead, production has to be shared with companies in other countries. Decentralised systems will make this means of order fulfilment increasingly difficult to co-ordinate.

It may also mean that what the customer views as a single order of identical computers may actually be fulfilled with slightly different configurations of computer, depending on which SI company produced each batch that makes up the whole order. This may well cause difficulties for customers in rolling out their new systems and obtaining appropriate support.

Range of formats

Differences in formats, especially for software and databases, will make it difficult to compile consolidated information (for example accounting information) needed to manage the business as a whole.

It will also make it difficult for companies that are co-operating on a large order to share information.

Economies of scale

It is argued that the use of local suppliers for computer parts results in higher quality, but it no doubt also means that much smaller orders are placed with suppliers than truly reflects SI's global requirements, and therefore economies such as volume discounts are not obtained. It would be better to identify the highest quality suppliers and place global orders with them.

Since each company is likely to have the same overall pattern of costs and activities, there may well be many other areas of business activity where similar economies could be obtained.

Centralised stockholding may also bring about significant economies: at present each company will have its own small storage facilities, whereas a larger central warehouse in a country where such space was cheapest could bring significant savings. (However, lead time is very short, and if JIT procedures are used this may not be a major issue.)

Duplication and inconsistency

Duplication of information (and duplication of effort in creating and inputting it) is particularly likely to arise in the case of the customer support databases. For instance, 'frequently asked questions' are, by definition, frequently asked! They will not be significantly different from country to country, yet individual companies may be giving inconsistent advice, or may not know about a better solution to a customer's query identified by another company.

Duplication no doubt occurs in other areas: for instance, a customer may have global offices and will therefore have multiple accounts, one for each SI company that it does business with. Much better understanding of the needs of such large customers would result if sales databases were amalgamated.

Lack of flexibility

Staff and other resources cannot easily and quickly be moved between locations because of local differences. This means that staff shortages are more difficult to manage and may limit career development opportunities in SI as a whole.

Strengths of the decentralised systems

Containing local difficulties

Problems in one country, such as a strike or an earthquake, or something more minor such as a server breakdown or a database corruption, will only affect operations in that one country, not the company as a whole.

Autonomy

Managers typically like as much autonomy as possible. Local managers will have the best understanding of local difficulties and how to solve them. This is generally thought to improve motivation.

Supply chain management (SCM)

If supplies are obtained locally, this should result in shorter lead times and stronger influence over the quality of supplies.

Customer relationship management (CRM)

The importance of speaking the local language and understanding the local culture should not be underestimated, and it is undeniable that local management and local facilities are likely to result in faster, better customer service, both in terms of delivery of the product and provision of support services.

Genuine local differences

Certain differences in customers' requirements may arise from local conditions such as mains voltage, or local legislation ranging from health and safety requirements to government prescriptions on the format of data submitted to it.

Language, of course, affects fundamental matters such as which version of an operating system is installed and how keyboards are laid out.

None of these issues could easily be addressed by centralised systems.

(ii) **Problems of integrating into one worldwide system**

Lack of standards

As the question itself acknowledges, it is unusual that each company still has its own unique information system. This situation was very widespread a few years ago but the fact that it persists at SI flies in the face of global trends towards open systems.

On the face of it, it appears that it may be difficult, at least in the short term, to amalgamate existing systems because of different formats in hardware, software and data itself.

The SI organisation will either need to impose a single set of standards to be used globally (in which case it needs to decide and obtain agreement on which set of standards to impose), or it will need to purchase and implement a variety of sophisticated middleware and make extensive use of XML to convert data to common formats. The former is contentious and highly error-prone and the latter is not cheap, nor easy, nor quick to implement.

Change management issues

Change needs to be sensitively handled if motivation is not to suffer. SI companies in each country have been extremely successful to date and it is likely to be difficult to persuade staff and management that there is any need to change, especially if they perceive the new worldwide system to be inferior to the one they are used to.

Internal competition and goal congruence

We are not given any information about competition between separate companies, but no doubt each country thinks that its own way of doing things is best, and each company has a strong instinct for self-preservation.

Individual companies may refuse to share information in the belief that knowledge is power.

If resistance to change is very strong, staff may even refuse to use the new system and continue with the systems they have already, in the genuine belief that this is in the best interests of the company as a whole.

Training

Training in the new systems must be provided as required, and this may be expensive, especially as the training material will need to be adapted for each country to ensure that it properly reflects differences between each old individual system and the new global one.

Cultural differences

Certain aspects of business operation are undeniably subject to differences in local culture, and it will be difficult to accommodate these in a single worldwide system for supply chain management and customer relationship management.

Language differences are the obvious example, but there are also significant differences in business customs and the degree of formality with which business is conducted in, say, the UK and the USA, as opposed to Eastern European countries, the Middle East and the Far East. That means that global sales procedures and the information held about customers may need to be very different in different countries.

CRM and SCM

Some customers and most suppliers are likely to resent having to deal with a centralised sales and purchase system which takes no account of previous good relationships between individuals sharing a local culture.

Interdependence

As mentioned already, at present problems can be contained within the local area where they occur. With a single worldwide system, however, any future problem may affect the operations of the entire business, worldwide.

This could manifest itself in many different ways: If a server crashes then no-one in the worldwide company will be able to find the information they need, and likewise customers may not be able to get the support they need. If a supplier goes out of business, deliveries to all customers, worldwide, could be delayed. If a central warehouse is flooded, SI's entire stocks will be damaged. And so on!

(b) The centralised R&D unit operates as a support function to all the businesses in the group but it is structured to only provide information and not to receive information from the user businesses. This gives a number of risks to SI, as follows:

Unresponsive to business

One of the major problems and risks is that the R&D function will be unresponsive to the business needs. Particular users may have needs for certain types of system or particular functions, and these may not be met by the R&D department. This will damage the reputation of the business and may allow competitors to 'steal a march' by developing products better suited to client needs.

Demotivational to users

The locations may feel detached from the R&D function as they are unable to provide feedback to the unit. This may result in the locations being resentful and not supporting the systems suggested by the R&D function, or it could result in locations finding alternative support to provide them with developments that better support their needs.

There could also be cost implications for SI if the locations do not use the developments that R&D generate. SI is paying for a department that is not providing the best benefit it could.

Too technical

Without feedback from the business there is a danger that the R&D departments will be too technical in their solutions. The R&D staff will be very technically capable and therefore interested in developing products that are technically the best available. These products, however, may not be cost effective for SI or desired by the different businesses.

Inappropriate work

It may be that the R&D department is incurring significant cost and time maintaining and improving products that are not wanted by customers. If this is the case, SI is not getting value for money as the R&D staff would be better employed developing the products required by customers. It would be very difficult for the department to do a proper cost/benefit analysis without external information from the businesses.

Test your understanding 2 – DS

(a) **Reasons for poor service**

It is not clear from the scenario whether GDC Ltd inherited a system that was already running or whether they were involved in any of the system design and development. From the point of view of DS, there are many reasons why it may have received poor service, even though the terms of the contract have been fulfilled.

The terms are as follows:

Purchase of all hardware and software

GDC may have a preference for hardware and software that they are familiar with, and this may not be a suitable fit to the existing system. Unfortunately, hardware and software become obsolete very quickly and GDC Ltd may not have been replacing it fast enough to keep up with the demands of the company. It could be that they have bought software to upgrade the system, e.g. moved from Windows 95 to NT, and they have no staff trained sufficiently to maintain it. A similar situation could have occurred with networking and routing equipment. Problems can occur that are very difficult to sort out without available expertise.

Repair and maintenance of all IT equipment

This is a tall order for any company. When the equipment was purchased, DS should have arranged maintenance service through the manufacturers themselves. There could easily be a misunderstanding over the type of maintenance required from GDC Ltd. Are they supposed to fix faults when they occur or do regular maintenance checks to ensure the smooth running of the equipment?

Help desk and other support services for users

Users often have an inadequate understanding of existing systems and develop unrealistic expectations. This means that they may generate unreasonable and unmanageable volumes of requests for change. GDC Ltd might suffer from high programmer turnover rates. Their employees may not have the necessary skills or motivation. Many programmers prefer development work to maintenance work and may be reluctant to get involved in help desk support.

Writing and maintaining software

There are two main areas of software maintenance:

- changes to the specification, requiring the software to be changed
- bug fixes or rectifying deficiencies so that the system performs as originally specified.

There are three types of maintenance activity:

- **corrective**, where behaviour or performance fails to be as specified due to faulty implementation
- **adaptive**, where a change in the environment has not been anticipated, and causes a departure from the specification. Adaptive changes may arise from:
  - changes in the law
  - alterations in taxation regulations
  - changes forced by technical advances by competitors
  - improvements in hardware within the company
  - the evolution of new standards and procedures
- **perfective**, where some feature is enhanced though it was within the tolerances of the specification, e.g. the program may be made more user-friendly, or the processing speed may be increased.

Since the contract is vague and the scope so large, there are bound to be areas of poor service from GDC Ltd.

Provision of management information

Unless the type, content and timing of the management report required is specified, then there is ample scope for poor service. A new person at GDC Ltd may be responsible for producing the reports and he or she may not know the full routine. The report may have been left in the wrong place, or delivered to the wrong person first. However, the problem may not be due to a fault at GDC Ltd. To obtain essential management reports, the information must be kept up-to-date by the staff at DS. If the employee responsible for maintaining the database is sick or the files containing the data get damaged or corrupted, then the production of reports is likely to be delayed.

(b) **Options available to DS**

There are several options available to DS

The first is to re-write the contract with the help of GDC Ltd so that there is some flexibility but no vague areas and each party knows what is expected from them. This could be done through negotiation while the existing contract is still running. The problem with this course of action is that DS are locked into the current arrangement and GDC Ltd will be aware of the problems it could cause by giving three months' notice and leaving DS. They would be in a very strong position to increase the price substantially or restrict their commitment to DS in any negotiations that might take place.

The second would be to obtain help in re-writing the contract, and when satisfied, give GDC Ltd three months' notice and ask them, and other facilities management companies, to tender for the new contract. The problem with this course of action is that DS might just be trading-in one company that is giving poor service for another that they do not know. There is no guarantee that service standards will always be as expected.

The third option would be to revert to an in-house IT development and support department solution. This would require a lot of effort and expense, and if new staff have to be recruited there will be a long period before they could understand the system and be in a position to do what GDC Ltd are already doing.

Test your understanding 3 – GDS

(a) Outsourcing enables organisations to concentrate on their core activities while sub-contracting support activities to those organisations who are specialists. The main advantages of outsourcing are more effective budgetary control through the ability to predict costs; improved quality and service from a specialist supplier; relieving the organisation of the burden of managing specialist staff, especially where there is little promotional opportunity and/or high staff turnover and keeping up-to-date with changing techniques and practices.

The main disadvantages of outsourcing are the difficulty that may be experienced in obtaining a service level agreement that clearly identifies the obligations of each party; the loss of flexibility and inability to quickly respond to changing circumstances as the function is no longer under organisational control; the risk of unsatisfactory quality and service, or the failure of the supplier; poor management of the changeover or of the outsource supplier; increasing costs charged by the outsource supplier over time and the difficulty of changing the outsourced supplier or returning to in-house provision.

(b) Outsourcing the management accounting function is at first an appealing proposition, especially given the difficulties experienced by GDS in retaining qualified and experienced staff. Routine management accounting tasks are increasingly being carried out by computer systems, interpreting and managing detailed accounting information is increasingly decentred to non-accountants located in business units, and the more flexible use of budgets and non-financial performance measures in many organisations has led to a shift in the ownership of accounting reports from accountants to business managers. This supports the potential for outsourcing the accounting function.

Recent research has suggested a change in the way management accounting is used in organisations, from a traditional monitoring and control perspective to a more business- and support-oriented perspective. For example, the CIMA report on Corporate Governance: History, Practice and Future viewed the role of management accountants in corporate governance as providing the information to the chief executive and the board which allows their responsibilities to be effectively discharged. CIMA's Risk Management: A Guide to Good Practice suggested that management accountants can have a significant role to play in developing and implementing risk management and internal control systems within their organisations.

However, while this might be seen as conflicting with the outsourcing of the accounting function, given GDS' difficulties, they are unlikely to be obtaining consistently reliable and timely advice for management. Hence, outsourcing might provide a better quality of advice.

(c) To ensure that the outsourced accounting provision is cost-effective, it should be subject to a competitive bidding process and a comprehensive service level agreement needs to be formulated which sets out the rights and obligations of both parties. The preferred bidder's business references and credit worthiness need to be scrutinised in detail. A legal agreement needs to be drawn up addressing the ownership and privacy of the data.

The risk of outsourcing can be partly offset by retaining some in-house expertise to monitor and work with the outsource supplier, although given the difficulty GDS experiences already, this may not be possible. An alternative may be for an independent internal auditor to monitor their work and for the outsource supplier to accept this involvement and that of GDS' external auditor.

The maintenance of access to data by GDS will be beneficial for GDS management and will provide assurance that data are being processed in a timely manner. An implant from the outsource supplier working within GDS might also alleviate day-to-day problems, although this may not be practical given the size of GDS. However, regular visits by the outsource supplier and the maintenance of a strong working relationship over time will prove beneficial to both parties. Risk can be reduced by building a strategic partnership between both companies as opposed to a short-term supplier–contractor relationship. The board of GDS or its audit committee should monitor the outsource supplier's performance in terms of quality, reliability and cost of the service being provided compared with the service level agreement.

Test your understanding 4 – LDS

(a) LDS will need to consider a number of factors before deciding on the selection criteria for the supplier to carry out this systems change. The type of questions that should be put to potential suppliers are as follows:

(1) **Do they have the necessary skills?**

The rather antiquated system being used by LDS has been changed, and there is insufficient documentation. This means a virtual rewrite is required from initial system analysis through programming to implementation. This may compromise one of the criteria, i.e. the full support of administrators may not be obtained for what is, basically, a new system. It will therefore be essential that the supplier has the necessary skills to deal with all aspects of this systems change.

(2) **Are they efficient?**

Suppliers need to be assessed in terms of both time and quality. LDS is working to a six-month timetable. This is the total amount of elapsed time available, and is not very long given the size of the problem. There is a natural order of analysis, design, build, test and implement, and throwing more resources at a project of this nature may just result in diminishing returns without timescales being met. Quality is equally important, as a firm can give the impression of being efficient by delivering on time, but to an inferior standard. The system change required will need a very high level of efficiency, due to both the short timescales and the level of accuracy needed.

(3) **Do they have the experience?**

This is a specialised field. The database consists of legal information which must be accurate. There is also the requirement for 24-hour access, together with a contractual service-level agreement. Therefore, the supplier should ideally have experience of similar applications requiring such a degree of accuracy and availability. Relevant experience will obviously help to speed up the systems change.

(4) **Are they reliable?**

Do they have a successful 'track-record' of previous work, or are there outstanding claims for non-compliance or non-delivery, or, worse still, consequential loss? LDS cannot afford to take risks with such an application and, given the constraints that exist on this systems change, they must satisfy themselves that the supplier will achieve what they say they can deliver. Also, it will increase the confidence of LDS in the supplier if previous work of a similar nature could be examined, i.e. LDS should ask the supplier to provide details of similar contracts, so that the clients can be contacted to ascertain their level of satisfaction with the supplier.

(5) **Is their cost reasonable?**

Given the constraints of this application, it is unlikely that LDS will secure a fixed-price contract, but rather one based on 'time and materials'. There will be a very real need to ensure that the scope does not 'drift', particularly if the administrators do not like the look of the new Windows front-end. It is unlikely that this systems change will be cheap, and anyway LDS may not want to select the cheapest supplier because of the factors mentioned above. With all developments of this nature, the three major aspects to be considered are time, cost and quality, and success is achieved by finding the right balance between these aspects.

(6) **Are they financially stable?**

The last thing LDS wants is for a supplier to go out of business part-way through the development. Although it is possible to specify an escrow agreement (whereby the program code is lodged with a third party), the sheer disruption caused in obtaining a replacement supplier would not only dramatically increase costs, but also extend timescales to an unacceptable level. Appropriate financial analysis should therefore be carried out on the potential supplier before selection.

In conclusion, this is an ambitious project to carry out in such a timescale, and potential suppliers will need to be fully evaluated over the complete range of technical, commercial and financial competencies in order to minimise the risks to LDS.

(b) The decision to outsource the maintenance has advantages and disadvantages to LDS that must be considered. LDS will then need to make a decision whether it is in the best interest of the organisation to outsource. The factors that need to be considered in this are financial and non-financial.

Advantages

Some of the main advantages of the outsourcing decision are as follows:

(i) The outsourcer may have better knowledge and expertise in the running of the database, and therefore be in a better position to maintain the database. This would be especially true if the outsourced maintenance provider were the company that originally developed the database.

(ii) It may be cheaper for LDS to outsource as it will save training costs, and also the outsourcer will be servicing and maintaining the databases in other companies so they will be able to obtain economies of scale.

(iii) The cost is variable. If in the outsourcing contract it is specified that a fee is only paid if the maintenance service is required, the cost becomes variable and dependent on usage. If LDS use their own staff, the cost will be fixed. With a new database this could mean that relatively little maintenance is required and therefore it will be cheaper.

(iv) If the outsourcer fails to provide the service that they have promised, it may be possible to seek redress through legal action. This would not be possible if the maintenance service is run internally by LDS.

(v) It allows LDS to concentrate on their business of providing support to central and local government rather than having to concentrate on IT support.

Disadvantages

The above points indicate that there are advantages to outsourcing, but it should be borne in mind that there are disadvantages as well.

(i) As LDS's business is providing data, support of the database is a core activity and therefore it is high risk to give that function to an outside party. There is a danger that LDS might lose control of the support, and that could mean that they cannot service the demands of local and central government.

(ii) There is a danger that the outsourcer will provide a minimum level of service because their main focus is making a profit. The profit incentive could motivate the outsourcer to cut costs and reduce levels of service.

(iii) Once an outsourcing contract has been entered into, the company will lose all expertise internally. This could make it very difficult for LDS to revert back to supporting their systems in the future, and, as such, they could be tied into the outsourcer. LDS therefore could, for example, find in difficult to combat price increases from the outsourcer.

(iv) It may be more expensive as LDS is having to pay the outsourcer's profit as well as the cost of services.
These arguments make the decision difficult but LDS have to make it. In the case of LDS, because of their current lack of knowledge and the fact that they are outsourcing development of the new database, outsourcing maintenance may well be a good idea (and cheaper for them) provided they can build security on service levels and prices into the contract.

Risks and control of information systems

Chapter learning objectives

Lead	Component
E1. Evaluate the benefits and risks associated with information-related systems.	(d) Recommend improvements to the control of IS. (e) Evaluate specific problems and opportunities associated with the audit and control of systems which use IT.

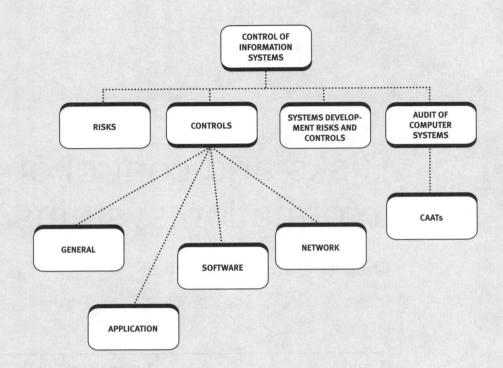

1 Risks

Computer systems have unique risk and control issues that need to be addressed by business. As with any risk factor the company needs to make an assessment of the risks and decide on the appropriate level of control to reduce the risks to an acceptable level.

Risks to a computer system

A risk to a computer system could be anything that prevents the managers getting the information they need from the system at the time that they need it.

Risks to information processing facilities may arise from:

- Dissatisfied employees might deliberately modify or destroy information in the system.
- A hacker or industrial spy might break into the system.
- Viruses or malicious software could be introduced.
- Accidental mistakes could be made on input to the system.
- Inadequate security of the hardware or data.
- Faults in the hardware system.

Such risks result in the loss of information (or the loss of its integrity or confidentiality), business disruption and a loss of time and money.

Further detail on risks

Information security

Risks to information security can be categorised as follows:

Risks	Description
Risk of hardware theft	This risk might seem fairly obvious, but the theft of computer hardware is common.
Physical damage to hardware and computer media (disks, etc)	Physical damage can be caused by: • malicious damage • poor operating conditions causing damage to equipment and magnetic files • natural disasters, such as fire and flooding.
Damage to data	Data can be damaged by hackers into the system, viruses, program faults in the software and faults in the hardware or data storage media. Software, particularly purpose-written software, can become corrupted. Programs might be altered by a hacker or computer fraudster. Alternatively, a new version of a program might be written and introduced, but contain a serious error that results in the corruption or loss of data on file.
Operational mistakes	Unintentional mistakes can cause damage to data or loss of data; for example, using the wrong version of computer program, or the wrong version of a data file, or deleting data that is still of value.
Fraud and industrial espionage	This can lead to the loss of confidentiality of sensitive information, or the criminal creation of false data and false transactions, or the manipulation of data for personal gain.

Data protection legislation

Some countries give individuals the right to seek compensation against an organisation that holds personal data about them, if they suffer loss through the improper use of that data. In the UK, for example, rights are given to 'data subjects' by the Data Protection Act. There could be a risk that an organisation will improperly use or communicate personal data about individuals, in breach of the legislation.

Erroneous input

Many information systems, especially those based on transaction processing systems and with large volumes of input transactions, are vulnerable to mistakes in the input data.

- Some input items might be overlooked and omitted. Other transactions might be entered twice.

- There might be errors in the input data, particularly where the data is input by humans rather than by electronic data transfer. For example, in a system relying on input via keyboard and mouse, data accuracy depends on the ability of the operator to input the data without making a mistake.

Where input errors are high, the integrity of the data and information becomes doubtful.

Hacking

Hacking is the gaining of unauthorised access to a computer system. It might be a deliberate attempt to gain access to an organisation's systems and files, to obtain information or to alter data (perhaps fraudulently).

Once hackers have gained access to the system, there are several damaging options available to them. For example, they may:

- gain access to the file that holds all the user ID codes, passwords and authorisations

- discover the method used for generating/authorising passwords

- interfere with the access control system, to provide the hacker with open access to the system

- obtain information which is of potential use to a competitor organisation

- obtain, enter or alter data for a fraudulent purpose

- cause data corruption by the introduction of unauthorised computer programs and processing on to the system (computer viruses)

- alter or delete files.

Viruses

A virus is a piece of software that seeks to infest a computer system, hiding and automatically spreading to other systems if given the opportunity. Most computer viruses have three functions – avoiding detection, reproducing themselves and causing damage. Viruses might be introduced into a computer system directly, or by disk or e-mail attachment.

Viruses include:

- trojans – whilst carrying on one program, secretly carry on another
- worms – these replicate themselves within the systems
- trap doors – undocumented entry points to systems allowing normal controls to be by-passed
- logic bombs – triggered on the occurrence of a certain event
- time bombs – which are triggered on a certain date.

Risks and benefits of internet and intranet use

Many organisations have intranet systems or use the Internet directly. Using an intranet or the Internet has obvious advantages, but also creates substantial risks.

The advantages of intranets and the Internet

- Employees have ready access to vast sources of external data that would not otherwise be available. Using external information can help to improve the quality of decision making.
- Organisations can advertise their goods and services on a website, and provide other information that helps to promote their image.
- Organisations can use the Internet to purchase goods or supplies, saving time and money. For example, the Internet is used regularly by businesses to purchase standard items such as stationery, and to reserve hotel rooms and purchase travel tickets.
- The Internet/intranet provides a means of operating an e-mail system. Communication by e-mail is fast and should remove the requirement for excessive quantities of paper. Using e-mails might also reduce the non-productive time spent by employees on the telephone.

- Intranets create the opportunity for more flexible organisation of work. For example, employees who are away from the office can access the organisation's IT systems and files through the Internet. Similarly, employees can work from their home but have full access to the organisation's systems.

The disadvantages of intranets and the internet

There are disadvantages with using intranets and the Internet.

- E-mail systems can become inefficient if too many messages are sent and users have to look through large amounts of 'junk mail' to find messages of value.

- E-mails can be disruptive, especially if a prompt appears on an individual's computer screen whenever a new message is received.

- Senders of e-mails often expect an immediate reply to their messages, and a delay in responding can create bad feelings and ill-will.

- Employees might waste too much time looking for information on the Internet, when the value of the information is not worth the time spent looking for it.

- Without suitable controls, employees might spend large amounts of time on the Internet or exchanging e-mails for their personal benefit, rather than in carrying out their work responsibilities.

The greatest problem with using intranets and the Internet, however, is the vulnerability of the organisation's IT systems to:

- unauthorised access by hackers, including industrial spies

- the import of viruses in attachments to e-mail messages and other malicious software.

2 Controls in an information systems environment

To combat the types of risks discussed above companies will put in place control procedures. These must be assessed for cost effectiveness and should reduce risk to an acceptable level.

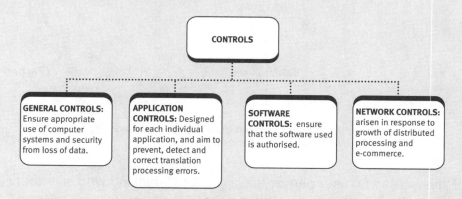

Alternative control classification

There are a number of different ways in which controls can be classified in an IT environment.

An alternative to the classification described above is:

- **Security controls**: controls designed to ensure the prevention of unauthorised access, modification or destruction of stored data.

- **Integrity controls**: controls to ensure that the data are accurate, consistent and free from accidental corruption.

- **Contingency controls**: in the event that security or integrity controls fail there must be a back-up facility and a contingency plan to restore business operations as quickly as possible.

3 General controls

Personnel controls

Recruitment, training and supervision needs to be in place to ensure the competency of those responsible for programming and data entry.

Logical access controls

Security over access is often based on a logical access system. This is illustrated by the following diagram:

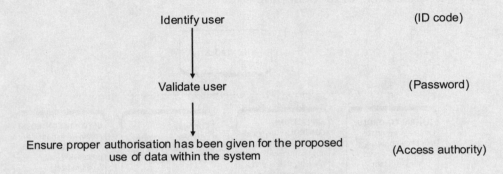

Passwords and user names are a way of identifying who is authorised to access the system, and granting access to the system, or to specific programs or files, only if an authorised password is entered. There may be several levels of password, with particularly sensitive applications protected by multiple passwords.

Problems with passwords

Password systems can only be effective if users use them conscientiously. There are several inherent problems with a password system:

- Authorised users may divulge their password to a colleague.

- Many passwords may have associations with the user so that a hacker can discover them by experimentation.

- Passwords are often written down close to the computer (e.g. pinned to the notice board inside the office) and so easily discovered.

To protect passwords and user numbers against discovery, a number of precautions should be adopted:

- Users should be required to change their passwords regularly.

- Passwords should be memorable but not obviously related to a user's private life.

- Users should be encouraged never to write down their passwords.

- There should be strict controls over passwords – they should never be 'lent' or written down where they can be easily seen.

- There should be automatic sentinel or watchdog programs to identify when a password has been keyed incorrectly.

Access logging

The system will produce regular reports including a system access report and various pre-determined exception reports. The effectiveness of these reports is determined by:

- The frequency of report production.
- The follow up of detected breaches in security.

Audit trail

An audit trail consists of a record or series of records that allows the processing of a transaction or an amendment by a computer or clerical system to be identified accurately, as well as verifying the authenticity of the transaction or amendment, including the identity of the individuals who initiated and authorised it.

Audit trails are also used to record customer activity in e-commerce on a company's website. The audit trail records the customer's initial access to the website, and then each subsequent activity (purchasing and payment, confirmation of order and delivery of the product). The audit trail can be used to deal with any subsequent enquiry or complaint from the customer. In some cases, 'audit trails' can be used to track down hackers into a system. A hacker might sometimes unknowingly leave a trail of where he came from, for example through records in the activity log of the hacker's Internet service provider.

Facility controls

Physical access

There are various basic categories of controlling access to sensitive areas. These include:

- security guards in buildings
- working areas to which access is through a locked door or a door with an ID card entry system or entry system requiring the user to enter a personal identification code (PIN number)
- using safes and lockable filing cabinets
- closed circuit TV used to monitor what is happening in a particular part of a building – this may be backed up by security video cameras
- doors automatically locked in the event of a security alarm.

Additionally, procedural controls to protect files and output include:

- disks should not be left lying around on desks and working surfaces
- computer printout and disks should be shredded or otherwise destroyed before being thrown away.

Location of IT facilities

It is imperative that the location of the system is considered, and hence all equipment is located so as to protect against:

- Fire
- Flood
- Smoke
- Food
- Drinks
- Power failure
- Environment.

Business continuity

Business continuity planning (**disaster recovery planning**) takes place in order to recover information systems from business critical events after they have happened. It involves:

- Making a risk assessment
- Developing a contingency plan to address those risks.

More on disaster recovery plans

An unexpected disaster can put an entire computer system out of action. For large organisations, a disaster might involve damage from a terrorist attack. There could also be threats from fire and flood damage. A disaster might simply be a software or hardware breakdown within a system.

Disaster recovery planning involves assessing what disasters might occur that would pose a serious threat to the organisation, and trying to ensure that alternative arrangements are available in the event that a disaster occurs.

In the case of a computer system for a clearing bank, this would mean having an entire back-up computer system in place that could be brought into operation if a disaster puts the main system out of action.

Not all organisations have extensive disaster recovery plans. Certainly, however, back-up copies of major data files should be kept, so that in the event that the main files are destroyed, the data can be re-created with the back-up files.

System back-ups

All files containing important information should be backed up on a regular basis. Backing up provides protection against the loss or corruption of data due to:

- faults in the hardware (e.g. hard disk)
- the accidental deletion of a file by a computer operator
- damage to a data file by a hacker.

A back-up is simply a copy of the file. If the original file is lost or becomes corrupt, the back-up can be substituted in its place, and the master file can be re-created.

There will be some loss of data if the input to the system since the most recent back-up copy of the file was made.

- However, if back-ups are made regularly, the loss of data should be limited. If there are paper records of input transactions since the most recent back-up copy was made, the file can be brought up to date by re-inputting the data.
- Some systems provide back-up copies of both master files and transaction data files, and copies of these files can be used to re-create an up-to-date master file if the original master file is lost or corrupted.

Back-up copies might be stored on the same physical computer file as the original file, but this is risky, since damage to the physical file will result in the loss of the back-up as well as the main file.

Back-up files might be created by copying them on to a disk or tape. Where security is important, any such back-up copies should be held in a secure place, such as a safe.

To counter the risk of damage to a file due to a fire or similar disaster at the premises where the IT system is located, a back-up copy might be taken off-site and held somewhere else.

4 Application controls

These are controls to ensure that data are correctly input, processed and correctly maintained, and only distributed to authorised personnel.

Application controls are specific to each application, but can be grouped as follows:

Input controls:

- Checking and authorising source documents manually.
- The use of batch controls.
- Pre-numbered forms.

Processing controls:

- Computer verification and validation checks.
- Error detection controls such as
  - control totals
  - balancing.

Output controls:

- Monitoring of control logs.
- Physical checking of output.

More on input controls

Some controls over the completeness and accuracy of the data to the system can be written into the system design as controls by the program.

Software controls might be applied to:

- ensure the completeness of input data
- improve the accuracy/correctness of input data.

Controls over the completeness of input. This is only possible if there is a way of checking how many transactions should be processed, or whether a transaction has been omitted. Within accounting systems, examples of completeness checks might be:

- in a payroll system, checking that the number of payroll transactions processed is exactly equal to the number of employees on the payroll file

- in a sales invoicing system, where all invoices are numbered sequentially, to ensure that no invoices have been omitted from processing. (Altering an invoice should be dealt with by raising a credit note to reverse the original invoice and issuing a new invoice.)

Controls over the accuracy of input: In computer systems, software validation checks might be written into the software to identify logical errors in the input. Examples of data validation checks might be:

- Existence checks: if a particular item of data must have a code 1, 2 or 3, a data validation check can be carried out on the input to make sure that the value entered is 1, 2 or 3, and if any other value is entered, the input will not be accepted.

- Reasonableness check or range check: this is a logical check to ensure that the value of an item input to the system is a reasonable value. For example, a system might carry out a reasonableness check that the value of a sales order is not in excess of, say, $50,000.

- Check digit verification: Some codes used in a computer system, such as customer identity codes or inventory codes, include a check digit. A check digit allows the program to check that the entire code is valid, and that there is no error in the input digits for the code.

- Controls over the authorisation of input: Manual controls include requiring the signature of an authorised individual on the authorisation document (e.g. a document giving approval to make a payment). Within a computer system, authorisation is granted by the input of an appropriate user name/password.

5 Software controls

Software control prevents making or installing unauthorised copies of software. Illegal software is more likely to fail, comes without warranties or support, can place systems at risk of viruses and the use of illegal software can result in significant financial penalties.

Software can be controlled by:

- Buying only from reputable dealers.
- Ensuring that the original disks come with the software.
- Ensuring that licences are received for all software.
- Retaining all original disks and documentation.

6 Network controls

Risks on networks

The increase in popularity of the LAN (local area network) has brought concerns in relation to system security. A LAN allows for many more breaches of security than does a single computer.

The main areas of concern are:

- Tapping into cables.
- Unauthorised log in.
- Computer viruses.
- File copying.
- File server security.

Controls

Controls must exist to prevent unauthorised access to data transmitted over networks and to secure the integrity of data.

Methods include:

- Firewalls.
- Flow.
- Data encryption.
- Virus protection.

More on network controls

Firewalls: A firewall will consist of a combination of hardware and software located between the company's intranet (private network) and the public network (Internet). A set of control procedures will be established to allow public access to some parts of the organisation's computer system (outside the firewall) whilst restricting access to other parts (inside the firewall).

Flow: This regulates movement of data from one file to another. Channels are specified along which information is allowed to flow, i.e. confidential/non-confidential, and these are linked by authority levels.

Data encryption: Encryption is a technique of disguising information to preserve its confidentiality. It is disguised during processing/storage. In essence it is a method of scrambling the data in a message or file so that it is unintelligible unless it is unscrambled (or decrypted).

Virus protection: It is extremely difficult to protect systems against the introduction of computer viruses. Preventative steps may include:

- control on the use of external software (e.g. checked for viruses before using new software)

- using anti-virus software, regularly updated, to detect and deal with viruses

- educating employees to be watchful for viruses being imported as attachment files to e-mail messages.

Legislation surrounding information systems

Data Protection Act (DPA)

The DPA was needed to protect individuals against the misuse of personal data. This was necessary due to:

- Easy interrogation of large files.

- Speed of response (less control).

- Interrogation from outside.

- Entire files can be copied or transmitted in seconds.

- Computer systems can be cross-linked to obtain personal profiles.

- Individuals' records can be selected easily through the search facilities.

Registration

All users of computers who are intending to hold personal data are required to register and supply the following details:

- Name and address of data user.

- Description of, and purpose for which, data are held.

- Description of source data.

- Identification of persons to whom it is disclosed.

- Names and non-UK countries to which transmission is desired.

- Name of persons responsible for dealing with data subject enquiries.

If an organisation fails to register, this is a criminal offence, although compensation is through a civil action.

Key principles

The DPA has the following key principles:

- Personal information shall be obtained and processed fairly and lawfully.

- Personal data shall be held and used only for specified purposes.

- Personal data shall be adequate, relevant and not excessive in relation to those specified purposes.

- Personal data shall not be used or disclosed in a manner incompatible with those specified purposes.

- Personal data shall be accurate and kept up to date.

- Personal data should not be kept for longer than is necessary.

- A data subject is entitled to be informed and is:
  - entitled to access
  - entitled to have data corrected or erased.

- A data user is responsible for the security and protection of data held against unauthorised access, alteration, destruction, disclosure or accidental loss.

Exemptions to the Act

Data subjects are not entitled to see their personal data if it is held for:

- Law enforcement purposes.

- Revenue purposes.

- Statistical and research purposes.
- Regulating provision of financial service (covered by Consumer Credit Act 1974).
- Legally privileged reasons.
- Back-up security reasons.
- Social work.
- Medical purposes.

The following are exempt from the provisions of the Act:

- Manual records.
- Payroll, pension, test preparation, etc.
- Data held which is crucial to the interests of the state:
  - Crime
  - Tax
  - National security.
- Data held relating to personal household.

Computer Misuse Act 1990

Computer crime is defined as 'any fraudulent behaviour connected with computerisation by which someone attempts to gain dishonest advantage' (Audit Commission). Computer crime was enshrined within the Computer Misuse Act 1990.

Objectives

The key objective of the Act was to make crimes of 'hacking' and the theft of data.

Unfortunately the Act does not provide a definition of:

- Computer.
- Program.
- Data.

Criminal offences

The Act created three new criminal offences:

- Unauthorised access, e.g. by employee who exceeds authority – minor offence (Magistrates Court) – penalty six months imprisonment/fine/both.

- Unauthorised access with intent to commit and then facilitate the commission of a further offence, e.g. divert funds – serious offence – penalty five years imprisonment/fine/both.

- Knowingly causing an unauthorised modification of the contents of any computer with the intention of interfering with the operation of that computer, preventing access to a program or data, or interfering with the operation of the program or the reliability of the data - includes introducing a virus to a system – penalty five years imprisonment/fine/both.

7 Systems development

The systems development life cycle SDLC)

The systems development life cycle is assumed knowledge at this level. However, there were six stages within the SDLC, with several activities involved:

- Planning – project initiation document, project quality plan, work breakdown structure, budget;

- Analysis – get to the root of the problem via user involvement in the form of interviews and questionnaires, complaints review;

- Design – prototyping;

- Development – build the system which has been agreed on;

- Implementation – staff training, file conversion, documentation, testing;

- Review – post completion audit/review on quality , cost, timescale.

Systems development risks

The development of new computer systems, designed and written for a specific user organisation, is a high-risk venture. It is widely recognised that many new purpose-written systems fail, for several reasons:

- They fail to satisfy the user's real requirements: the system was specified incorrectly.

- They do not provide the data processing or information for which they were designed, or to the quality expected.

- The system was therefore designed and programmed incorrectly.

- They cost much more to develop and run than expected. The system is therefore less efficient than expected.

8 Controls

Controls

Controls should be built into the system development process to reduce these risks. These controls should be implemented at all stages of the systems development life cycle (SDLC).

Examples of systems development controls	
Control	**Comments**
Approval of an outline system specification by the user/IT steering committee.	The proposed system must be specified in terms of what it is expected to provide to the user, in terms of data processing and information quality, and should evaluate the expected costs and benefits. A system should not progress to detailed system design without formal authorisation. By giving formal approval to the system design, the user confirms the objectives of the system.
System designed in detail, using system design standards. The system is fully documented. A detailed system design is produced.	The documentation provides a source for checking in the event of problems with the system. By giving approval to the detailed system design, the user confirms that the programming work should begin.
Programs written using programming standards. All programs fully documented.	The documentation provides a source for checking in the event of problems with the system.
Systems and program testing.	The systems analysts and programmers should carry out their own tests on the programs and the system as a whole, to satisfy themselves that the system objectives have been met.
User testing.	Before the system 'goes live', it should be tested by the user. Before accepting the system for implementation, the user must be satisfied that it meets the planned objectives.

Development timetable and cost control.	The project development should be completed on time and within the budgeted cost. A management/project team should be given the responsibility for monitoring the progress of the project (e.g. using critical path analysis techniques) and its costs.
Control over implementation.	The implementation of the new system should be carefully planned and monitored. There are three methods of implementing a new system: • To introduce the system initially in one area or department, as a pilot test. Implement the system universally if the pilot test is successful, and after initial 'teething troubles' have been identified and resolved. • To introduce the new system by running it in parallel with the old system, until the new system is operating successfully. Parallel running can be expensive, because it involves running two systems at the same time. However, it should be less risky than an immediate changeover. • To make the changeover from old system to new system immediately and in full, without pilot testing or parallel running.
Monitoring the new system: audit of new systems.	A new system should be monitored, with a view to checking that it has been successful and has achieved its objectives. The success of a system should also be assessed in terms of: • user satisfaction levels and level of system use • actual costs and benefits.

Changeover methods

- **Direct changeover** – This is where the old system is switched off and the new system is switched on. This is appropriate when the two systems are very different or it is too expensive to run two systems. Although this method is cheap, it is also risky since if the new system doesn't work properly then the company might be unable to revert to their old system quickly. (Also, staff trust of the new system would be lost.)

- **Parallel running** – The old and new systems are run together for a period of time, until it feels safe to switch the old system off. This method will be costly (inputting data twice and possibly employing more staff to do this), however, it will be less risky than direct changeover.

- **Pilot changeover** – This is where one part of the business changes over first. When the system operates correctly there, the rest of the business will changeover. The pilot department or division could be using direct or parallel changeover. Again, this is a safer method of changeover as only one part of the business will be affected if anything goes wrong. However, when the system is rolled out across the rest of the company there may be different problems in each location and the IT teams resources will be stretched.

- **Phased changeover** – This involves bringing in the new system one part of the business at a time, say, by department or division. It differs from pilot changeover in that all departments or divisions are staggered with respect to receiving the new system. The downside of this is that this method is time-consuming. However, this method is less risky as should there be a problem in any particular department or division, the IT staff are able to deal with the problems one at a time.

Post-implementation review

A post-implementation review should establish whether the objectives of a project have been met.

When appraising a new system after changeover, comparison should be made between predicted and actual performance (variance analysis). This might include:

- Throughput speeds;
- Number of errors or queries;
- Cost of processing;
- Amount of downtime.

The review would also need to cover whether users' needs had been met.

The review should not be performed too soon after the new system goes live, or 'teething problems' and lack of user familiarity will distort the results.

Recommendations should be made where appropriate to improve the system's future performance.

The review should also make wider recommendations on improving systems development and project planning and management processes.

Criminal records bureau

The objective of the Criminal Records Bureau (CRB) is to widen access to criminal records so that employers could make better informed recruitment decisions, especially in relation to the protection of children and vulnerable adults. The CRB is a Public Private Partnership with Capita plc which operates a call centre, inputs applications for checking, collects fees, develops and maintains the IT infrastructure and issues disclosures. Planning for the CRB commenced in 1999 and live access began in March 2002, seven months later than planned caused by problems in business and technical development and the decision to conduct more extensive testing prior to live operations.

There were weaknesses in the business assumptions made by Capita. In particular, the assumption that 70–85 per cent of people would apply by telephone to a call centre or on-line was incorrect and not based on adequate research with potential users, 80 per cent of whom preferred paper applications. However, data entry screens had been designed for input from a telephone call, not from paper forms, and Optical Character Recognition (OCR) systems did not have the capacity to handle the volume of paper applications. Also, systems had been designed around receipt of individual applications and could not cope when batched applications were received. The processes were also unable to cope with the volume of errors and exceptions on paper applications.

Since June 2003 the CRB has met service standards in terms of turnaround times and backlogs have been eliminated. A House of Commons Report concluded that 'the key to running a complex, Greenfield operation with a private sector partner is to work together as a team to solve operational problems'.

Source: House of Commons, Criminal Records Bureau: Delivering Safer Recruitment? (HC266), 2004

9 Audit of computer systems

In the case of computer systems, audits are carried out:

- to check whether the system is achieving its intended objectives, and
- in the case of accounting systems, to check that the information produced by the system is reliable.

Problems of auditing computer systems

Auditing computer systems gives some different problems and some new opportunities to auditors to test systems. There are several problems for the auditor of computer systems that do not occur with 'manual' systems, including:

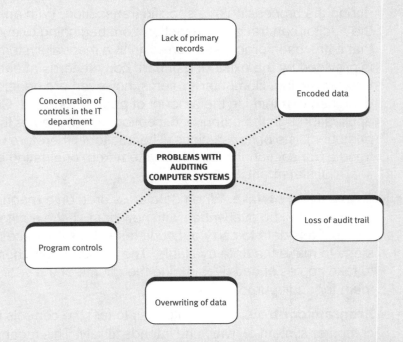

More on problems with auditing

There are several problems for the auditor with computer systems that do not occur with 'manual' systems. These include:

- **Concentration of controls** in the IT department. In large computer systems, many of the controls over data are concentrated in the central IT department. This can be a potential weakness in the control system, because of the risk of an accidental or deliberate corruption of data or programs, of which the user departments are not aware.

- A **lack of primary records**. In some computer systems, a document originating a transaction might not be created. For example, in an on-line system a customer order received by telephone might be keyed into the system. The system might then generate a despatch document and an invoice, and update the inventory and customer files. The auditor would not be able to trace these documents back to a paper sales order.

- **Encoded data**. When data are entered into a computer system and encoded, there is a risk of error in the input details. Auditors need to consider the effectiveness of program controls, such as data validation checks (including check digit checks) to prevent the acceptance of incorrect data by the system, especially changes to standing data on a master file.

- A **loss of audit trail**. Ideally, in an accounting system, there should be an audit trail providing evidence of the file updating that occurs during the processing of a specific transaction. With an audit trail, the auditor can trace a transaction from beginning to end, to confirm that it has been processed correctly. In a manual system, evidence is provided by the existence of hard copy records at each stage of the transaction. Computer systems, however, are generally designed to minimise the amount of paper produced. Control is applied through the output of exception reports, rather than the printout of lists of transactions. The auditor is therefore unable to trace a transaction through the system from originating document to financial statement.

- **Overwriting of data**. When data are stored on a magnetic file, it will eventually be overwritten with new data. If the auditor needs some of this data to carry out audit tests, it will be necessary to take steps to make the data available. The auditor might therefore need to take copies of data files during the course of the year, and retain them for audit purposes.

- **Program controls.** The auditor has to test the controls in the computer system on which he intends to rely. This means that he must test the controls written into the computer programs. To do this, it will be necessary to use computer-assisted audit techniques.

Errors

Additionally, when auditors audit computer systems they need to be aware of the types of errors that occur in the systems. The characteristics of errors are:

- No one-off errors unless deliberate amendment of individual items.
- Systematic errors which repeat across all transactions.
- Higher danger that input errors will not be detected.

Audit approach

The audit approach for computer auditing is often summarised in one of two ways:

- through the computer; or
- round the computer.

Round the computer

Under this approach the auditor does not attempt to understand the operation of the computer system, but rather treats it as a 'black box'. To audit the system, the auditor matches up inputs to predicted outputs to ensure that the outputs are being processed correctly.

The approach is good in that it does not require a high level of expertise of IT in the audit teams, but it is only suitable if the following conditions are met:

- Computer processing is relatively simple
- Audit trail is clearly visible
- A substantial amount of up-to-date documentation exists about how the system works.

Problems with auditing round the computer include:

- Computer files and programs are not tested, hence there is no direct evidence that program is working as documented
- If errors are found it may be impossible to determine why they have happened
- All discrepancies between predicted and actual results must be fully resolved and documented no matter how small (this is because controls are being tested).

Through the computer

This approach actually interrogates the computer files and computer controls and relies much more on the processes that the computer uses.

The auditor follows the audit trail through the internal computer operations and attempts to verify that the processing controls are functioning correctly. The computer controls are directly tested and the accuracy of computer-based processing of input data is verified.

To audit through the computer requires more expertise and a longer set-up time; however, the results can be of very good quality.

This approach utilises different computer-assisted audit techniques (CAATs) such as test data and audit software, discussed below.

10 Computer-assisted audit techniques (CAATs)

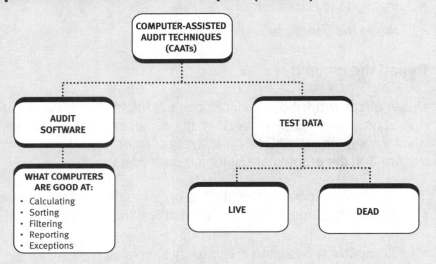

Computer-assisted audit techniques are methods of using a computer to carry out an audit of a computer system. There are two main categories of CAAT:

- audit software, such as audit interrogation software
- test data.

Audit interrogation software

Audit software consists of computer programs used by auditors to interrogate the files of a client. Normally the client's data files are input into the audit software program on the auditor's computer, and the auditor can then test those files. Examples of what audit software can do include:

- Extract a sample according to specified criteria
  - Random
  - Over a certain amount
  - Below a certain amount
  - At certain dates
- Calculate ratios and select those outside the criteria
- Check calculations (for example, additions)
- Prepare reports (budget vs. actual)
- Produce letters to send out to customers suppliers
- Follow items through a computerised system
- Search for underlying relationships and check for fraud.

Packages are generally designed to:

- read computer files
- select information
- perform calculations
- create data files, and
- print reports in a format specified by the auditor.

Audit software enables large volumes of data to be processed very quickly and accurately. The main drawback of audit software is that it can take a long time to set up the systems with the client data, and it will require expertise.

Further examples of the use of audit software

An audit program can carry out rapid checks on large volumes of data and extract information for further investigation by the auditor. For example:

- an audit program can check all the balances on accounts in the receivables ledger, to ensure that no individual customer has a balance above a specified credit limit

- a program can check records for reasonableness, for example by checking that the maximum discount allowed to a customer is, say, 50%

- a program can carry out a statistical analysis, for example an analysis of inventory movements, to identify slow-moving items

- a program can carry out a random selection of transactions for detailed manual checking by the auditors

- audit software can extract information from different files or databases, and search for underlying relationships in the file data. For example, a comparison of accounts payable data with the file for contracts placed with suppliers might reveal an unusually large number of orders placed with the same contractor by the same individual, raising suspicions of bribery.

CAATs and fraud detection

Audit software includes a variety of routines for identifying transactions where there could be a suspicion of fraud, such as:

- comparing the home addresses of employees with the addresses of suppliers, to identify employees who are also suppliers

- searching for duplicate cheque numbers

- analysing the sequence of transactions to identify missing invoices or cheques

- identifying suppliers with more than one supplier code or more than one mailing address

- finding several suppliers all with the same address

- listing payments for transactions that fall just within the spending authorisation limit of the individual who has authorised the payment.

Benefits and weaknesses of CAATs

Benefits of CAATs	Examples
CAAT's force the auditor to rely on programmed controls during the audit. Sometimes it may be the only way to test controls within a computer system, therefore enables the auditor to test program controls.	Credit limits within a system can only be changed by the accountant. A computer assisted check will test that this is the case.
Large number of items can be tested quickly and accurately.	Checking the depreciation charged on each asset would be quicker with a computer assisted program than manually.
CAAT's test original documentation instead of print outs, therefore the authenticity of the document is more valid this way.	Actual wages will be tested instead of paper copies.

After initial set-up costs, using CAATs are likely to be cost-effective, as the same audit software can be used each year as long as the system doesn't change.	Examples of use or audit tests (1) Calculation checks (2) Reviewing lists of old or outstanding items and investing those specifically (3) Detecting for unreasonable items (4) Detecting violation of the system rules (5) New analysis (6) Completeness checks (7) Selects samples (8) Identifying exception reporting facilities.
Allow the results from using CAATs to be compared with 'traditional' testing.	If the two sources of evidence agree then this too will increase the overall audit confidence.

Weaknesses of CAATs	Recommendations
CAAT's will be limited depending on how well the computer system is integrated. The more integrated the better the use of CAAT's. For example, the invoices should be computer generated and then processed through the accounts system to feed in to the financial statements.	Ensure understanding of the system to assess whether audit software will be relevant for the company. Need to assess whether there is a need for the audit software.
It takes time to design CAATs tests therefore, may not be cost-effective if the auditor is dealing with a bespoke system, as there may be a lot of set-up costs. The reason for this is it takes time to write specific test data or to program the audit software to the needs of the client.	A cost-benefit analysis from the audit point of view should be carried out prior to deciding to use the audit software.
If the company you are auditing cannot confirm all system documentation is available, then the auditors will be unable to do the tests effectively due to lack of understanding.	Do not use audit software until these have been identified.
If there is a change in the accounting year, or from the previous year, then the audit software will have to be reset and designed, therefore may be costly.	A cost-benefit analysis from the audit point of view should be carried out prior to deciding to use the audit software.

Test your understanding 1 – Audit software

Recommend how audit software could be used in the audit of a mail-order company concerned that deliveries are not being invoiced and that stock files are not being updated.

Embedded audit facilities

Embedded audit facilities might be written into a program, particularly in on-line/real-time systems. These facilities can carry out automatic checks or provide information for subsequent audit, such as:

- extracting and storing information for subsequent audit review, with sufficient details to give the auditor a proper audit trail

- identifying and recording items that are of some particular audit interest, as specified by the auditor.

Test data

Test data can be used by inputting the data into the system and checking whether it is processed correctly. The expected results can be calculated in advance, and checked against the actual output from the system. The auditors might include some invalid data in the tests, which the system should reject.

It will only be used if the auditor is intending to do a 'test of controls' audit, and it must be considered cost effective.

Live data = test data are processed during a normal production run.

Dead data = test data are processed outside the normal cycle.

The stages involved in using test data are:

(1) Gain a thorough understanding of how the system being tested is supposed to work and the controls that are included in it.

(2) Devise the test data set. This should be a set of data containing both valid and invalid items. The controls in the system should identify the invalid items.

(3) Run the test data. This can be 'live' (within the normal processing at the client), or 'dead' (outside the normal processing). Live runs give more reliable results but are more risky to operate.

(4) Evaluate the results. It is important that the auditor fully evaluates the results of the test data and does further work if unexpected results occur.

Risks with test data

Risks	Controls
Damage to the system as the system is tested to its limits.	Ensure auditors understand the system and have software support.
Corruption of the systems data if test data are not properly removed.	Ensure process for data removal.
System down time if 'dead' data used.	Establish when system can be used with minimum disruption to the business.

Examples of test data

Tests	Reason for the test
Revenue	
Input an order into the client's system that would cause a customer to exceed their credit limit	The order should not be accepted, or should raise a query whether you are sure you wish to proceed. If this happens then the auditors will have confidence the system is working properly
Input a negative number of items on an order	Ensures only positive quantities are accepted
Input incomplete customer details	The system should not process the order unless all information is completed
Input an excessive amount	There are reasonable checks in the system to identify possible input errors. A warning should appear on the screen confirming the number

Tests	Reason for the test
Purchases	
Raise an order from a supplier not on the preferred supplier list	A query should be raised as to whether you want to proceed with this transaction
Process an order with an unauthorised staff ID	The system should reject the process altogether or send the request through to an appropriate person for authorisation
Try and make changes to the supplier standing data using the ID of someone who is not authorised to do so	The system should reject the process altogether or send the request through to an appropriate person for authorisation
Payroll	
Try and set up a new employee up on the payroll system using an unauthorised ID	The system should reject the process altogether or send the request through to an appropriate person for authorisation
Try and make employee changes of detail using an unauthorised ID	The system should reject the process altogether or send the request through to an appropriate person for authorisation
Make an excess change, for example increase someone's salary by $1,000,000 by someone authorised	The system should have parameters in place to question this amount, and maybe reject it due to it being outside the normal range

Test your understanding 2 – Money transfer

Recommend some controls that a bank could put in place over an interbank money transfer system.

Test your understanding 3 – Doyle

The DOYLE Company runs trains in the North American continent, on a network from the Atlantic to the Pacific coast. Income is in the region of $2,000 million with operating profit at approximately 5%. The company operates over 3,750 trains each day hauling freight between 250 major cities and 300 mines, quarries and forests.

Recently, the company invested in some train management software to assist in determining which track each train should take between different locations, minimising delays caused by having too many trains using the same tracks. DOYLE can now offer an east coast to west coast delivery of 63 hours, which compares favourably with 60 hours for driving the same distance. A courier company, CGK, is now considering using DOYLE services for long haul freight rather than sending 120 trucks each day on the coast-to-coast route. However, DOYLE must guarantee reliability of its service to be able to obtain the contract.

One of the main problems facing DOYLE, is lack of certainty about the weather. For example, on one bad day last winter, 72 trains were stranded in a severe snowstorm for 3 days. Weather information is currently collated by 4 staff from over 200 different sources including radio, weather station reports and local media including newspapers. However, conflicting information and lack of timely input mean that over 40,000 trains are delayed due to inclement weather each year including snow, flooding and high winds. Receiving prior warning of inclement weather could allow DOYLE to route trains away from inclement weather.

A new weather forecasting system has just come onto the market offering weather forecasts accurate to within a 2 km area. The cost of the system is $500,000 per month. It is estimated that installing the system will enable DOYLE to half the number of train delays caused by inclement weather.

Required:

(a) Identify and explain any risks affecting DOYLE, noting whether the new software will help mitigate those risks.

(b) Explain the benefits to include in a cost benefit analysis for the purchase of the new software.

(c) Assuming that the purchase goes ahead, recommend an appropriate IT system for receiving and displaying the weather related information.

Test your understanding 4 – AMROM

The AMROM organisation provides insurance products including household, car and personal insurance to individuals. Although the company maintains a website, this is used to provide information on services only; the directors of AMROM are convinced that people much prefer to talk to a 'real' person when purchasing insurance products rather than complete a form online. For this reason, the company employs 500 experience sales staff who operate from a call centre in a large city in North America.

A typical sale of products is as follows:

- A potential customer telephones AMROM, having either viewed insurance products on the web site or identified AMROM through its other marketing activities.

- A sales representative identifies which insurance products are needed by the potential customer and completes an online form under instruction of an Expert System with the customer's details. Many input fields have default values which the representative does not have to amend, while others have checks built into the program to guard against incorrect data entry. For example, the number of years driving field cannot exceed the age of the customer less 17 years.

- Customer details are analysed by the Expert System and then stored in AMROMs relational database.

- The Expert System provides the sales representative with an insurance quote, which is presented to the customer.

- The customer either accepts or declines the quote.

- Acceptance of the quote means that customer details are recorded on the main database at AMROMs head office with an invoice being sent to the customer to pay the premium due. The invoice also contains details input to AMROMs computer system.

- If details are subsequently found to be incorrect, then the customer telephones AMROM and the incorrect data in the database is overwritten with the new data.

- On receipt of payment, customer details are transferred to a AMROMs data processing storage centre in another city via a VPN link.

Required:

(a) Identify and discuss any audit problems with the AMROM computer systems, suggesting, where possible, methods of overcoming those problems.

(b) Data is transferred to an off-site location using a VPN link. Discuss the risks affecting data when it is transferred between two locations in this way and explain the controls that can be used to minimise those risks.

(c) Briefly explain the concept of data mining and show how this can be of use to AMROM.

Test your understanding 5 – ARG

ARG is an international airline operator, based in a central European country. It maintains a fleet of approximately 350 aircraft, and its core activity is to provide passenger and freight services to over 200 destinations worldwide.

ARG maintains offices in each country to which its aircraft fly. Each office provides the following services.

Information provision on the airline services offered by ARG, including flight times and destinations serviced by ARG. Access to ARG's passenger and freight booking system for customers who wish to book either passenger or freight carriage services with ARG.

Each office also has access to ARG's confidential internal data systems, which provide information on aircraft location, servicing history and the company's personnel. The latter includes salary details as well as staff locations.

Systems specification – to support its core business activity, ARG recently invested in a high-speed international wide area network (WAN). This system enabled ARG to transfer large volumes of data relating to its operations between its 200 offices world-wide with a minimum of delay. The systems specification for the new ARG system was rigorous.

The specification included the following requirements:

- The basic infrastructure of the WAN, including such items as the cabling and communication hardware, had to have an expected life of ten years.

- Computer chips and other similar system elements had to be upgradeable as technology improved.

The entire system had to be easily upgradeable, with a fixed capital amount being allocated for this upgrade each year. System upgrades were not to exceed this capital amount under any circumstances.

ARG also assumed that its WAN infrastructure and its core business as an international airline operator would remain unchanged for the next ten years. Very few equipment suppliers were willing to provide this level of commitment to the system. Finally, a small but financially stable company called AP Ltd successfully tendered for the contract, even though some of AP Ltd's systems were not industry standard.

Systems implementation – the actual systems changeover and implementation were performed with few problems. The staff at ARG were able to use the new system efficiently within one week of implementation.

It should be noted that the Board of ARG made the decision to invest in the WAN on the basis that the company must be at the forefront of the use of technology to support its core business activities. This strategy is seen as being essential to produce a sustainable competitive advantage in the airline industry.

Post-implementation review – in the three months since the system was, installed ARG has seen significant increases in productivity and levels of customer service. The investment has therefore been judged to be a success.

During the post-implementation review of the system, it was found that the WAN had considerable excess capacity to take additional network traffic. ARG's initial forecast showed that it would use only one third of the capacity of the network in its first two years of operation. Even optimistic forecasts of network traffic growth indicate that this excess capacity would not be used by ARG for at least another seven years. The board of ARG therefore asked the IT Director to consider ways of providing additional revenue to the company from this excess capacity.

After detailed consideration of the problem the IT Director reported back to the board. The main proposal was to make this excess capacity available to other companies which required a WAN but either did not have the money, or the strategy, to build a WAN for themselves. Should the proposal be accepted, then it is expected that these other companies would require:

A guarantee of the level of service that they can expect from ARG, including access rights to the WAN and delivery times of information across the network.

Internet access to transfer data to customers and receive information back from customers.

A guarantee of data security both from non-ARG WAN users and from the staff of ARG itself.

The IT Director considers that ARG could provide this service, whilst at the same time making a positive contribution to profits. The board has therefore decided to accept the IT Director's proposal and make the required investment to provide the additional services noted above. This decision was made against the advice of a minority of Board members who saw potential conflicts between the core business strategy and the IT strategy of ARG.

Required:

(a) Explain why large companies should have an IT strategy. You should make reference to ARG's situation in your explanation.

(b) Evaluate the potential dangers and benefits, both to ARG and to its potential WAN users, of providing Internet access.

(c) Advise how ARG can provide adequate data security to the companies which are paying to use its WAN. You should consider the potential security problems posed by other WAN customers, by ARG's airline customers and by the employees of ARG itself.

Test your understanding 6 – Marlborough Conferences

Marlborough Conferences organises conferences and exhibitions that specialise in IT subjects. Recent conferences have dealt with multimedia, the business opportunities presented by the Internet, and business software.

Marlborough Conferences has its own website with address http://www.marlcon.com. This site receives about 200 hits per day from browsers using many different Internet service providers. In addition to containing information about Marlborough's own activities the site also contains hyperlinks to related sites that may be of interest to visitors. Some of the links are maintained free of charge as a service provided by Marlborough. However, for others Marlborough charges a fee to include the link in its site.

Visitors to Marlborough's site may go there directly by entering the site address into their web browser software. However, many reach the site by carrying out a search using keywords. Marlborough ensures that the keywords 'conference', 'exhibition', 'computer', 'hardware', 'software' and 'IT' could lead web browsers to their site.

Required:

(a) Describe the business opportunities that a presence on the Internet and accessing the Internet could offer Marlborough.

(b) Identify the dangers that may exist if Marlborough's own employees are allowed access to the Internet from Marlborough's IT system.

Test your understanding 7 – SP (2)

SP plc is considering investing in the building of a new hotel in Dubai. The hotel is to be 'state of the art', and SP's management is hoping that it will be the first 6-star hotel in the world. It is expected that the richest people in the world will want to holiday here and the hotel will, therefore, command a premium price.

Many of the facilities in the hotel will involve computerisation. For example, the booking system – via the telephone or internet, the internal telephone system, and the availability of the internet in every suite. The cost of these facilities is thought to be around $7 million because the server will be housed in a separate building on the edge of the hotel grounds.

The management of SP have over 200 other hotels around the world to oversee. Over the past 10 years, their management information has become increasingly difficult to collate due to the size of the group and the diversity of activities that each hotel undertakes. The finance director is now trying to convince the other directors to invest in an Enterprise Resource Planning System (ERPS) to hopefully overcome some of these problems.

Required:

Explain the importance of information security to SP, and recommend the main controls necessary to ensure that the computer systems and the information they hold are secure.

Test your understanding 8 – Risk management

(a) Explain what is meant by the term 'risk management' when applied to information systems.

(b) Explain how risks in information systems can be classified, and the various approaches that might be taken to manage information system risk.

(c) Explain four factors that could result in information system failure.

(d) Explain four measures that could be used to assess systems success.

11 Chapter summary

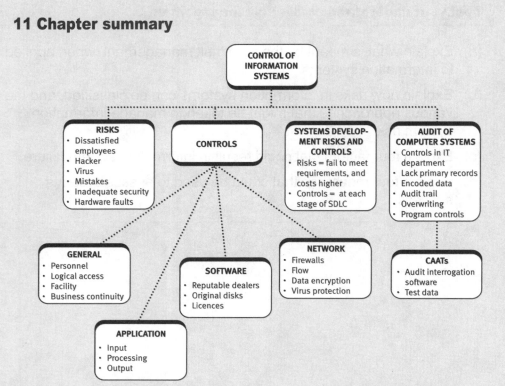

CONTROL OF INFORMATION SYSTEMS

RISKS
- Dissatisfied employees
- Hacker
- Virus
- Mistakes
- Inadequate security
- Hardware faults

CONTROLS

SYSTEMS DEVELOP-MENT RISKS AND CONTROLS
- Risks = fail to meet requirements, and costs higher
- Controls = at each stage of SDLC

AUDIT OF COMPUTER SYSTEMS
- Controls in IT department
- Lack primary records
- Encoded data
- Audit trail
- Overwriting
- Program controls

GENERAL
- Personnel
- Logical access
- Facility
- Business continuity

SOFTWARE
- Reputable dealers
- Original disks
- Licences

NETWORK
- Firewalls
- Flow
- Data encryption
- Virus protection

CAATs
- Audit interrogation software
- Test data

APPLICATION
- Input
- Processing
- Output

Test your understanding answers

Test your understanding 1 – Audit software

Possible use of audit software:

- Sequence checks on delivery note file and invoice file.

- Computer can check that every delivery results in an amendment to the invoice file and the stock file (with list produced of every exception).

- Exception reports generated of zero value invoices and non-invoiced deliveries.

- Calculation checks on all invoices to ensure in line with price lists.

- Check on agreement of deliveries against order files.

Test your understanding 2 – Money transfer

Interbank transfers are a very high risk area for a bank as the sums involved could be significant, and in addition there could be a loss of reputation if errors occur.

Controls might include:

- Physical controls over access to computer systems that perform very high value transfers.

- Logical access controls for any staff making transfers.

- Logs of all money transfers.

- Strong network security – firewalls, passwords, etc to prevent hacking.

- Encryption of the transfers to prevent eavesdropping on the lines.

- Dual input of the amounts and bank accounts numbers – possibly forward and reverse entry (e.g. CHARLES and SELRAHC).

- Authorisation of all transfers over a set limit by supervisor staff.

- Dual input by different people for transfer to be made.

Test your understanding 3 – Doyle

(a) **Income risk – new customer**

The new contract with CGK appears to be dependent on DOYLE being able to guarantee the reliability of trains across the continent. While the weather forecasting system will remove some train delays, others will remain. Initially therefore, investment would appear to be appropriate as this will decrease train delays.

However, it is not clear how many delays occurred on the long haul coast to coast route, so the effect of obtaining the weather information may be marginal. It is also not clear what penalty clauses are being levied by CGK is response of late delivery. The number of delays avoided can then be estimated and quantified to provide a benefit in the purchase decision.

Environmental risk

The new weather forecasting does not decrease environmental risk for DOYLE as inclement weather will still occur. However, it does provide a method of mitigating that risk and should be considered because of this.

Reputation risk

There is a risk to the reputation of DOYLE should too many trains be delayed, for whatever reason. DOYLE may attract an image of being unreliable, making it very difficult to obtain new customers such as CGK or retain existing customers. Use of the new software will help to minimise this risk as trains should be more reliable.

Technology risk

There is technology risk involved in the new system, simply because it is new and potentially untested. So while the technology creates an opportunity for DOYLE, it also creates a risk of technology failure and the consequent poor publicity associated with this. Careful contract negotiation will be required to ensure that this risk is minimised, and ensure that DOYLE is appropriately compensated should the technology fail.

(b) **Factors to include in a cost benefit analysis on the new software**

Intangible benefits

Minimise risk of incorrect/incompatible information

Weather information is currently collated from many different sources. There is the possibility of errors occurring for two reasons:

Firstly, the information from the different sources may not be compatible. In this situation it is not clear which set of information should be used and there is the risk that the wrong information will be relied upon.

Secondly, the 4 people collating the information may be suffering from information overload. As information is being provided from many sources, some important detail may be missed, resulting in incorrect decisions being taken.

Obtaining the weather information from one source should remove any inconsistency, as well as limit the possibility of information overload. Unfortunately, it is not clear what value can be placed on this enhanced decision making. There will be some intangible benefit.

Tangible benefits

Time saved on trains/disruption to schedules

Routing trains away from inclement weather will limit the possibility of delays as well as overall disruption to schedules. Presumably if one train is late, then the next assignment for that particular train will also be delayed. Even with the new train management software, it will take time to get all trains back on schedule again. Late deliveries will also result in worsening customer relations.

Being able to remove some of the delays will decrease the amount of rescheduling time as well as helping to maintain customer goodwill.

Cost saving – staff

If the new system is installed, then it appears that the 4 staff collating weather information will no long be required. Salaries and other costs such as pension scheme contributions will be avoided.

Overtime payments

Ensuring that trains run on time will have other quantifiable effects on costs such as decreased overtime payments as staff will not have to work such long hours (e.g. not being stuck in snowdrifts!).

(c) An appropriate IT system to access and display real-time weather information will include:

Broadband or similar permanent Internet connection to receive high volume of data. A permanent connection is required because updated weather information will be sent frequently to the company throughout each day. A broadband link is necessary because the amount of data to be transferred will be large; weather data will include pictures which tend to have large file sizes.

PC with fast processor. High processing speed is required firstly to receive the large amounts of data from the weather forecast supplier. Presentation of graphical data also requires more processing power than text, for example, again making a fast processor important.

Large flat screen monitor. The weather information will be detailed and may cover significant geographical area. A large screen with high resolution will be required. Provision of flat screen should also reduce glare and eye strain for users as well as taking up less desk space.

An appropriate pointing device to indicate areas on screen, perhaps for zooming in on for more detailed information.

Large hard disk. It is likely that historical information will need to be accessed, possibly to try and identify trends in weather patterns or review decisions on train routing to identify whether alternative decisions could have been made. Given the relatively large size of graphical files, large online storage will be required. The data mining facility may be provided by the information provider, limiting the need for storing historical information.

Test your understanding 4 – AMROM

(a) **Audit problems with AMROM computer system**

Audit problems with AMROMs insurance sales system include:

Lack of primary records

'Orders' for insurance quotes are received over the telephone only. This means that there is no actual paper record of the details being input into the computer system. An invoice is generated by the system; however, there is no way that an auditor can trace this back to an original to obtain initial approval for the order.

Input errors

There is a risk of input errors being made. The customer cannot see what data is being entered into the computer system by the sales representative, which may result in errors due to misunderstanding. Similarly, the sales representative may make other input errors – many of the fields have default values entered into them – the representative may not notice that a default has been used when this should have been amended.

The auditor will find it very difficult to input is correct when they are subject to human error and not audited or checked by the customer directly.

Validation controls

Many of the input controls are provided by the Expert System. For example, one rule is used to ensure that the number of years driving quoted by a customer cannot exceed the customer's age less 17 years (the legal driving age in the UK – or 15 years in the USA). As these controls are centralised in the Expert System, and the auditor may not have full knowledge of this system, then testing the controls to ensure they are effective will be difficult.

Use of test data may help, but it may be difficult, if not impossible, to check every combination of input rule that the Expert System is designed for.

Loss of audit trail

Auditors like to be able to trace a transaction through an accounting system from beginning to end. In many computer systems this is difficult because the audit trail is not clear. In the case of AMROMs systems, it may be no clear trail from the initial input into the relational database, or evidence to show how the Expert System reached a particular decision regarding how a particular insurance quote was decided.

The loss of visible audit trail may be overcome by using Computer Assisted Audit Techniques (CAATs). Specifically, some form of embedded audit software may be able to monitor inputs and decisions from the Expert System, providing an audit trail between the two. Failing this, details of specific inputs can be saved for later re-input as test data to confirm the Expert System is providing consistent decisions.

Overwriting of data

Where customer information requires amendment, this is over-written in the database with the new data. This appears to mean that the 'old' data is lost, so it will not possible to check either the old data or whether amendments are complete and accurate (again there is a telephone call to make the amendment with no written record being produced).

Retaining old data may be difficult. It may be necessary to retain some form of file with details of amendments made, although how this can be linked to the database is unclear.

(b) The risks of data transfer include:

- Loss of data between the two computers. It is possible that data sent from one computer does not arrive at the destination computer.

- Copying of data en-route. Copying electronic data may be difficult to identify because the original data is normally unchanged. Copying may occur as a deliberate act of industrial espionage by a competing company (hopefully not), or by a hacker attempting to obtain personal details perhaps as part of an identity theft scheme.

– Corruption of data en-route. Corruption can occur due to hardware and/or software failures, or simply resulting from 'noise' on the communication link.

– Human error can also cause loss or corruption of data. Also, human error may result in an operational mistake – an operator may simply forget to transfer the data, assuming that some form of human intervention is necessary to provide data transfer.

Controls that can be implemented to overcome these risks include:

– Encryption of data – effectively coding the data so if it is intercepted during transmission, the data cannot be understood until it has been decoded. Use of one-way encryption, keeping the decryption key safe at the receiving computer will guard against accident or deliberate interception of data.

– Providing each message with a unique number prior to transmission. Numbers will be monitored at the receiving computer and any omissions accounted for. This will help to ensure all messages are received.

– Sending a message digest (an electronic summary of the message) which is duplicated on receipt from the full received message. The two digests should be identical. If they are, then this confirms that the message has integrity and has not been amended, deliberately or otherwise, on route.

Note: The question asked for risks associated with the data in transit, not risks within the hardware transfer system itself such as hackers being able to access computer systems.

(c) Data mining is the analysis of data to unearth unsuspected or unknown relationships, patterns or associations in data. It involves the use of analytical techniques to review data (normally held on a data base or in a data warehouse) to discover these relationships.

Within AMROM, data mining may be useful to identify relationships in data such as:

One event being correlated with another event (sequences) such as successful purchase of home insurance being followed by purchase or car insurance. AMROM could send email or paper mail to customer following one purchase to encourage them to purchase other products.

Events being linked (associations) such as purchase of car insurance and breakdown insurance at the same time. Sales consultants can be instructed to offer breakdown insurance to customers requesting car insurance.

Profiling customers who make specific types of purchases (classification). AMROM may be able to identify specific socio-economic groups who purchase insurance from the company and then target other non-customers in that group with promotional material.

Test your understanding 5 – ARG

(a) Strategic planning is particularly important in the following circumstances:

   – There are long timescales – for example, in developing new systems.

   – There is heavy capital expenditure – for example, on new equipment.

   – The success of the organisation is at stake – for example, in gaining competitive advantage.

Here are three examples of how ARG could make strategic use of IT.

   – By monitoring how many bookings are made for a flight, fares could be continually adjusted to maximise revenue. If a flight is well booked early on, few seats need to be released for cheap fares. If a flight has few bookings it would be worth reducing fares to attract marginal revenue.

   – Code sharing with other airlines can give passengers a better, more comprehensive service.

   – In the light of bookings, assigning different aircraft to flights to control costs.

IT will be so fundamental to the success of ARG that without a successful IT strategy its success will be at risk.

(b) The **main potential dangers** are as follows:

Internet access would mean that individuals accessing ARG's network via the Internet could create many problems. These problems can range from inadvertent mistakes to malicious damage or corruption of information and files. For example, in the case where the local office had allowed access to the passenger booking system, there is a risk that individuals might be able to make bookings and/or cancel them at will. This is potentially an extremely dangerous situation and the entire operation of ARG could be put at risk if these accesses are not properly controlled.

The Internet contains material that can be offensive and it can be an offence to be in possession of such material, so if ARG staff download any such files, then this could present problems for ARG. ARG WAN users could access such material by accident or design. Also, business operations could be disrupted, which may result in ARG's staff accessing the Internet via the WAN and wasting time looking at irrelevant information that may be of interest to them personally, but not of much commercial value to the company.

Internet security is not as comprehensive as it could be and it is possible to download virus-contaminated material. The first conviction in the UK, under the Computer Misuse Act, was in respect of an individual who introduced viruses onto the Internet. Hacking generally is a problem, which, as a minimum, results in an unauthorised disclosure, but can also be far worse if data are manipulated leading to all sorts of misleading information.

The cost of using the Internet over prolonged periods of time can be expensive particularly if staff fail to log off, for example. So it is important that access to the Internet is controlled and appropriate standards followed.

The **benefits of Internet access** fall into two main areas:

Marketing

By providing information about ARG via a World Wide Web (WWW) site, 'visitors' to the site can see the range of services offered, the prices, schedules, etc. ARG can effectively use the pages contained within the site to market its services by providing additional information to encourage sales. Similarly, third party users of the WAN could also create WWW sites for marketing and information purposes. It is important to keep such information updated, however, as the WWW is subject to advertising regulation standards like any other media.

Transactions

In its simplest form, the Internet can be used to exchange e-mail although this can be extended to the electronic exchange of trading information between businesses and individuals. The Internet could be used by travel agents, e.g. to effect reservations with ARG's offices. Again, the third-party users could also use this facility to handle such things as purchase orders and invoices, etc. As the volume of business conducted over the Internet is expected to rise considerably over the next few years (US research indicates $45 billion for the year 2000) then there is a real advantage to be gained by having the necessary infrastructure in place to support this activity.

The security aspects of the Internet are continually being improved and many of the dangers should disappear over time. The trading and business aspects of the Internet will become increasingly important to all businesses and ARG would be at the forefront of applying this technology.

(c) It would be essential that security controls are put into place in order to minimise the risk of virus or hacking.

Passwords

Passwords would be used to verify a user on the system. This would relate both to ARG employees and to its external WAN customers. When anyone logged into the system their user code and password would have to be verified before admission to the system.

Encryption

Because some of the data being transferred by ARG to its other offices is highly confidential and because of the guarantee of security it is offering to its WAN customers, they would probably have to set up encryption facilities. Data would be encrypted before transmission to ensure that if the transmission was intercepted it would be difficult for anyone to read the data.

Firewalls and gateways

At each gateway into another system firewalls would have to be put into place to stop unauthorised access between systems. ARG employees should not have access through the network to the other WAN customers' systems and vice versa.

Partitioning controls

If ARG and its WAN customers are going to trade through the Internet then it will be necessary that they partition off their databases. The product, stock or booking systems that would be available for viewing and booking by customers should be completely separate to the management information systems of ARG and its WAN customers. Partitioning controls will need to be put into place to ensure that customers cannot gain access to company management systems.

Test your understanding 6 – Marlborough Conferences

(a) A presence on the Internet or accessing the Internet could offer Marlborough Conferences the following opportunities:

- More customers might become aware of Marlborough's existence and activities through Marlborough appearing as the result of a key word search. This could lead to an increase in business. The customers could be of several types: those who want to run conferences, those who want stands at exhibitions, those who want to attend exhibitions or attend conferences as delegates.

- Information about forthcoming events can be published on the Internet. This information is available internationally and could be used as initial publicity. More expensive printed material could be sent on request. This should reduce overall publicity costs.

- Transactions can be completed over the Internet. For example, the purchase of tickets and the booking of places on conferences.

- Including hypertext links to other organisations could be a source of revenue for Marlborough. Effectively, Marlborough's website is providing advertising space for other organisations.

- Feedback can be received from clients.

- Information about competing or similar organisations can be obtained from their websites.

- A web address can give the impression of an up-to-date, technically advanced business.

(b) The dangers of allowing employee access to the Internet include:

- Employees spending too much time 'surfing the net' instead of getting on with their jobs. This can waste employees' time and connection costs.

- Employees could download virus-infected material which could endanger the whole IT system.

- Employees could download illegal material.

- There is a possibility that information could be divulged which would allow outsiders to hack into the company's system.

Test your understanding 7 – SP (2)

Information security is about protecting the systems and data of an organisation from loss caused by human error, fraud, theft or hacking. Information security needs to be based on a risk assessment, and controls should be put in place to mitigate those risks.

The main elements of information security are that SP should have:

- a security policy to allocate responsibility for the information and systems in the hotel.

- a management structure with roles defined and documented, covering authorisation of purchases of software and hardware, and systems to prevent unauthorised access to data. In particular, the staff using the booking system would have access to clients' details and credit card information. This needs to be protected by employing reputable staff and by having supervision at all times.

- an asset register of all hardware and software owned by the hotel.

- systems in place and monitored to minimise risks from error, fraud, theft or hacking. All staff should be fully trained to be able to use the systems, reducing the number of errors that might occur. Systems should be protected against attack from viruses and malicious software, and should have anti-virus software, intruder detection systems and firewalls in place. This is particularly relevant since bookings will be taken over the internet and there is an internet connection in every suite. Customers may unwittingly cause a virus problem.

- controls to restrict access and provide physical security against fire and theft, e.g. passwords, locks on doors, security cameras and fire extinguishers. There should be systems access controls over physical access, passwords and authentication of remote users.

All systems should be developed in accordance with standards, tested and documented.

Change control systems should be in place to control all development and maintenance work thereafter.

SP should develop a continuity/disaster-recovery plan to cover all information systems, including backup, offsite fireproof storage of data and alternative hardware, software and building site requirements for recovery.

Adequate insurance should be taken out.

SP should also be aware of their legal obligations, and should comply with relevant legislation over data protection and computer misuse.

Test your understanding 8 – Risk management

(a) Risk management when applied to an information system is the management process of ensuring that the risks to the system are removed or kept within acceptable levels. The process involves identifying and assessing the risks, deciding on appropriate controls for those risks and implementing those controls, and monitoring actual performance of the information system to ensure that the risks have been suitably controlled. Where appropriate new controls should be introduced or existing controls improved.

(b) **Classifying and managing risk**

Risks can be classified in various ways.

- Risks can be classified as risks to the achievement of strategic, financial or operational objectives.

- Alternatively, risks could be classified as risks from ineffective system design and testing, risks from inefficient operations and financial risks.

- Risks might also be categorised according to their potential severity and the probability that an adverse outcome will occur, so that they can be mapped and priorities assigned to them.

The sub-categories of risk might include:

- Ineffective system design and testing

- Delays in systems development, delaying the implantation of the system.

- Inadequate system testing, to check that the system meets user needs.

- Excessive software faults.

- Failure of the system to provide suitable information (reliable or relevant information).

- Inappropriate technology for the system, given user requirements.

Inefficient operations

- Bottlenecks in the system, resulting in processing delays.

- Frequent breakdowns.

- Inadequate use of the system.

- Inadequate security in the system, with unauthorised access from hackers, the release of confidential information or damage to data or software from viruses and worms etc.

Financial risks

- Cost over-runs on system design.

- Cost over-runs for hardware.

- Cost over-runs for system operations.

- Failure of the system to deliver the expected financial benefits.

Approaches to risk management

There are various ways in which the risk from information systems might be managed.

Risk avoidance

Risks can be avoided by not having such extensive or complex information systems. However, the risks of not having IS might be even greater than the risks of having them.

Risk transfer

Some risk can be transferred to others more able to handle it, such as a specialist supplier of software. This might reduce the risk that the system will be designed inefficiently. It might also be possible to transfer some of the financial risk by persuading a supplier to agree to a fixed price contract.

Risk reduction

Some risks can be reduced, using a variety of risk control methods.

- Internal controls should be implemented for the operations of IS/IT systems, such as management and supervision controls, the use of anti-virus software, security controls, system design controls, and so on.

- Some risks, particularly to hardware damage or loss, might be insurable.

- The risks of bottlenecks on system operations, or the risks of system down-time can be reduced by investing in more hardware and communication links.

(c) **Information systems failure**

Possible reasons why systems could fail relate to the system risks described earlier. They include the following:

(1) The design of the system fails to reflect the information needs of the user, due to lack of planning, poor user involvement in the design and planning process or inappropriate hardware and software specifications. Users will be reluctant to use the system if it does not meet their specific needs or allow them to carry out their jobs effectively. User involvement is a key requirement for systems success.

(2) The data used by the system may be inaccurate or incomplete, caused by incorrect data input or incorrect processing. If data or information produced by an IS cannot be trusted by the user, it will not be used.

(3) Systems may also fail because development costs exceed budget. In some instances, development may be stopped before the system is complete because predicted future costs are considered unacceptable.

(4) The system itself may not operate particularly well, due to delays in processing or hardware and software faults.

(d) **Measures of systems success**

(1) *Level of use*

If the system is used as intended, this indicates that it is acceptable to the user. However, actual levels and frequency of use would need to be compared with the planned or expected levels of use.

(2) *User satisfaction*

Users can be asked to express their satisfaction or dissatisfaction with the system, for example by means of interviews and questionnaires.

(3) *Achievement of systems objectives*

Probably the most important measurement of systems success is whether the new system achieves or exceeds its original objectives. It is important for the project team to review the original objectives set at the planning stages of the project and compare actual operational performance and outcomes with expected performance or outcomes.

(4) *Financial benefit*

Although the actual costs of the system up to and including the actual implementation are normally quite easy to ascertain and monitor, on-going costs, in particular intangible costs and benefits are not as easy to monitor. Improved performance, increased staff morale, improved skill levels are all potential areas of benefit, but measuring their financial impact is difficult.

18

How to prepare for the exam

Chapter learning objectives

HOW TO PREPARE FOR THE EXAM

Section A of the Performance Strategy exam accounts for 50% of the paper, and it relates to a pre-seen case study which is common to all three Strategic Level papers. It is vital that you study the pre-seen material carefully before the exam. This chapter explains how you should prepare for the exam and what you should do with the pre-seen material.

1 Introduction

About two months before the May or November exam sittings for the strategic level, a pre-seen case study will be released by CIMA.

It will be background information regarding a particular company in an industry which should be reasonably familiar to everyone. The case study is typically about seven pages long and includes information that would be useful when answering a range of unknown questions on any of the three strategic level papers – E3, P3 and F3.

The case study question is for 50 marks (50% of the exam). Since the exam is 3 hours long with 20 minutes reading time, you should spend one and a half hours only on answering the case study question.

No questions will be asked at this stage. They will be disclosed on the day of the exam.

Preparing for the exam

This chapter explains how to use the pre-seen information, starting from the moment you receive it and going through to the exam day. Towards the end of the chapter, you will find the real CIMA pre-seen material for the May 2010 and September 2010 exams, some detailed analysis of it, and then a question and answer based on it.

The idea is that if you follow the process through right to the end of the chapter, this should give you an invaluable practice run which you can repeat when the real pre-seen material is released.

2 Two months before the exam

Initial reading

You should start by reading the pre-seen case study several times to assimilate the large amount of information.

While reading, keep asking yourself the question

"If I were the management accountant in this organisation, what would I be interested in?"

Further research

Students are expected to research the industry and gain a wider knowledge which they can demonstrate in an exam question. This can be achieved in several ways:

- Research on the Internet – try to think of a similar real world company and look on its website. In particular the financial statements will be useful.

- Swap ideas and information with friends who are also sitting the exam. You may be lucky enough to have someone in your peer group who works in that industry. (Don't worry that they might fare better than you in the exam. The examiners have commented that those who do work in the industry specified in the case study appear to fare no better than others.) Industries so far have included electronics and an airport.

- Speak to your colleagues and managers at work.

- Discuss with your training provider if you are enrolled on a course covering these exams.

- Watch the television and read quality newspapers which may cover the industry or a similar company in the months preceding the exam.

Objectives of your reading and research

While it important to understand the organisation in the pre-seen, and the industry in which it operates, you shouldn't spend too long researching the industry. In previous exams, all the information needed to answer the question has been contained within the pre-seen and the unseen information received on the exam day.

Your key objectives at this stage of the process should be:

- to analyse the context of the case organisation – what industry is it in? (with DEF airport in November 2010, several students seemed to think that DEF was an airline, rather than an airport – lack of awareness)

- to analyse the current position of the case organisation (perhaps using SWOT)

- to identify and analyse key issues facing the case organisation

- to identify key issues from the pre-seen and consider how they might be developed in the unseen and the requirement – consider each chapter of this text and try to think how the examiner might fit that particular topic into the case study, and how it could be examined.

3 One month before the exam

Question practice

Students are expected to be able to answer a range of questions based on this scenario in all of the three strategic level papers. The only way to achieve this is to practise as many potential questions as possible.

Past questions and answers are available on the CIMA website for:

- The Specimen exam paper released when the case study question was launched;
- The May 2010/September 2010 real exam;
- The November 2010/ March 2011 real exam;
- The May 2011 real exam.

Your training provider will also have produced several practice papers covering other areas of the syllabus which may be tested.

While attempting these practice questions, you should start to think about how best to tackle the exam paper in its entirety.

It has been found by the P3 examiner that students who fare best seem to be those who tackle the case study question first, and the section B questions second. However, in paper F3 students who attack the Section A case study first sometimes get bogged down in the detail of the calculations.

By practising a few mock papers you will find which order best suits you for each paper. The critical point in all papers is that you must allocate time carefully and strictly.

For any question you attempt, you should always write down (on the exam paper possibly) the time you should start and stop that question. You should further break this down into what time to finish each individual requirement so that you have covered the whole paper at the end of the three hours.

4 The night before the exam

Last minute preparation

On the night before the exam, you should re-read the case study scenario fully and try to separate in your mind the real CIMA material from the practice scenarios you may have attempted in the previous weeks – you must make sure that you don't get confused in the exam and bring in fictional scenarios which you have seen during your revision.

Then, get a good night's sleep to ensure you are alert and ready for the exam.

5 The day of the exam

Unseen material

On the day of the exam, further unseen material will be supplied by CIMA along with the question paper. The unseen material tends to be about two further pages of information. (You will also receive a clean copy of the case study pre-seen material in the exam.)

There are commonly 3 or 4 requirements on each exam paper, which may be further broken down into parts (i), (ii), etc.

The requirements are likely to cover a range of topics across the syllabus.

Time management

For each mark available you have 1.8 minutes available. So for a 10 mark requirement you should spend no longer than 18 minutes answering it.

Remember to write down your start and stop times for each question / requirement.

There is a law of diminishing returns when answering exam questions – you will probably score the first half of the available marks in the early minutes of your answer. The last few minutes will probably score far fewer as you may have gone off on a tangent or be waffling. Stop! Move on to the next requirement where you will start to score rapidly once again.

Planning

For E3 and P3 your answer will probably be predominantly written although some calculations may be required that you will then need to discuss. In F3 the split between calculations and discussion is more even.

Planning your answers is absolutely critical if the requirement is for a large number of marks.

Most students can write a coherent answer for a requirement of, say, 5 marks. But when the requirement is larger than this many students will ramble, or move away from the actual question asked.

It is recommended that in your answer booklet, possibly on the middle two pages (which you could pull out, but need to put back at the end of the exam) you should plan your answer to each requirement.

Try considering:

- Information from the pre-seen material;
- Information from the unseen material;
- Technical topics from your study text;

- Past exam questions you may have done which might just cover the same topic if you are lucky (but be careful if they are slightly different not to answer the question you had earlier rather than the one asked in the exam);

- Common sense.

Writing up your answer

Write up your answer once your plan is complete. Remember that your plan should be very brief, so that you don't waste time rewriting it out in full without adding very much.

As you use points on your plan tick them off. Do not obliterate them since if you fail to use all of them in the time allowed, markers are allowed to consider whether any further marks are available within them for a marginal candidate.

The layout of your answer needs to be professional. Use full English sentences and avoid notes. Never use the word etcetera. This indicates that you know more but that you can't be bothered to tell the examiner!

Other exam tips

- Leave plenty of space between each requirements answer (possibly start a fresh page for each) so that you can go back to add to your answer later if need be.

- You can answer the requirements in any order, however, you should clearly mark which is (a), (b), (c) or (d), or part (i), (ii) etc.

- Keep looking at your watch to ensure that you do not run over your allocated time. Stop when you are supposed to. Many students think 'just two more minutes' and the next time they look at their watch ten minutes have passed. This can mean that whole requirements are not attempted later which is a recipe for failure.

- It is unlikely, but you may have time at the end of the exam to review what you have written. You should really make time to do this, but few students do since they think it is better to keep writing. At the end of the day, there is no negative marking, and therefore the more you write the more possible marks you might get.

- As a rough guide, a student with average sized writing might score about 6 marks per page, so aim to write about 2 sides for a ten mark requirement. (This includes the use of headings, and spacing between each point made.)

- Underline your headings and any key words which you are sure will gain marks (but don't go wild underlining everything).

- Use a black or blue biro. Never use red or green biro or highlighter pens anywhere in your answer booklet. Pencil can be used for diagrams.

- Leave plenty of space between different requirements in the answer booklet, so that you can add to your answer later if necessary. This also makes your answer much tidier and more professional.

6 Practice exam – Pre-seen material

The pre-seen information below is the real CIMA pre-seen case study for the May 2010 and September 2010 exams. It describes an electronic components manufacturer called Aybe.

Follow the steps above in order to prepare yourself for a requirement based on this pre-seen material and the following unseen material.

Read the pre-seen material first, prepare some analysis of it and compare this with our analysis in the next section. Then, when you feel that you are ready to spend 90 minutes attempting the question, start to look at the unseen material.

Pre-seen material – Aybe

Background

Aybe, located in Country C, was formed by the merger of two companies in 2001. It is a listed company which manufactures, markets and distributes a large range of components throughout Europe and the United States of America. Aybe employs approximately 700 people at its three factories in Eastern Europe and supplies products to over 0.5 million customers in 20 countries. Aybe holds stocks of about 100,000 different electronic components.

Aybe is regarded within its industry as being a well-established business. Company Ay had operated successfully for nearly 17 years before its merger with Company Be. Company Ay can therefore trace its history back for 25 years which is a long time in the fast moving electronic component business.

The company is organised into three divisions, the Domestic Electronic Components division (DEC), the Industrial Electronic Components division (IEC) and the Specialist Components division (SC). The Domestic and Industrial Electronic Components divisions supply standard electronic components for domestic and industrial use whereas the Specialist Components division supplies components which are often unique and made to specific customer requirements. Each of the three divisions has its own factory in Country C.

Composition of the Board of Directors

The Board of Directors has three executive directors, the Company Secretary and five non-executive directors. The Chairman is one of the five independent non-executive directors. The executive directors are the Chief Executive, Finance Director and Director of Operations. There is also an Audit Committee, a Remuneration Committee and a Nominations Committee. All three committees are made up entirely of the non-executive directors.

Organisational structure

Aybe is organised along traditional functional/unitary lines. The Board considers continuity to be a very important value. The present structure was established by Company Ay in 1990 and continued after the merger with Company Be. Many of Aybe's competitors have carried out structural reorganisations since then. In 2008, Aybe commissioned a review of its organisational structure from a human resource consultancy. The consultants suggested alternative structures which they thought Aybe could employ to its advantage. However, Aybe's Board felt that continuity was more important and no change to the organisational structure took place.

Product and service delivery

Customers are increasingly seeking assistance from their component suppliers with the design of their products and the associated manufacturing and assembly processes. Aybe's Board views this as a growth area. The Board has recognised that Aybe needs to develop web-based services and tools which can be accessed by customers. The traditional method of listing the company's range of components in a catalogue is becoming less effective because customers are increasingly seeking specially designed custom made components as the electronics industry becomes more sophisticated.

Financial data

Aybe's historical financial record, denominated in C's currency of C$, over the last five years is shown below.

Year ended 31/12	2009 C$m	2008 C$m	2007 C$m	2006 C$m	2005 C$m
Revenue	620	600	475	433	360
Operating profit	41	39	35	20	13
Profit for the year	23	21	16	9	5
Earnings per share (C$)	0.128	0.117	0.089	0.050	0.028
Dividend per share (C$)	0.064	0.058	0	0	0

Extracts from the 2009 financial statements are given at Appendix A. There are currently 180 million ordinary shares in issue with a nominal value of C$0.10 each. The share price at 31 December 2009 was C$0.64. No dividend was paid in the three years 2005 to 2007 due to losses sustained in the first few years after the merger in 2001.

Aybe's bank has imposed an overdraft limit of C$10 million and two covenants: (i) that its interest cover must not fall below 5 and (ii) its ratio of non-current liabilities to equity must not increase beyond 0.75:1. Aybe's Finance Director is comfortable with this overdraft limit and the two covenants.

The ordinary shareholding of Aybe is broken down as follows:

	% holding at 31/12/09
Institutional investors	55
Executive directors and company secretary	10
Employees	5
Individual investors	30

The Executive Directors, Company Secretary and other senior managers are entitled to take part in an Executive Share Option Scheme offered by Aybe.

Performance Review

Aybe's three divisions have been profitable throughout the last five years. The revenue and operating profit of the three divisions of Aybe for 2009 were as follows:

	DEC division C$m	IEC division C$m	SC division C$m
Revenue	212	284	124
Operating profit	14	15	11

Financial objectives of Aybe

The Board has generally taken a cautious approach to providing strategic direction for the company. Most board members feel that this has been appropriate because the company was unprofitable for the three-year period after the merger and needed to be turned around. Also, most board members think a cautious approach has been justified given the constrained economic circumstances which have affected Aybe's markets since 2008. While shareholders have been disappointed with Aybe's performance over the last five years, they have remained loyal and supported the Board in its attempts to move the company into profit. The institutional shareholders, however, are now looking for increased growth and profitability.

The Board has set the following financial objectives which it considers reflect the caution for which Aybe is well known:

(i)   Dividend payout to remain at 50% of profit for the year.

(ii) No further equity shares to be issued over the next five years in order to avoid diluting earnings per share.

Capital budget overspends

Aybe has an internal audit department. The Chief Internal Auditor, who leads this department, reports directly to the Finance Director. Investigation by the Internal Audit department has revealed that managers with responsibility for capital expenditure have often paid little attention to expenditure authorisation levels approved by the Board. They have justified overspending on the grounds that the original budgets were inadequate and in order not to jeopardise the capital projects, the overspends were necessary.

An example of this was the building of an extension to the main factory at the DEC division that was completed in 2009 at a final cost of nearly C$3 million which was almost 50% over budget. The capital budget for the extension was set at the outset and the capital investment appraisal showed a positive net present value. It subsequently became apparent that the site clearance costs and on-going construction expenditure were under-estimated. These estimates were provided by a qualified quantity surveyor who was a contractor to Aybe. The estimates supplied by the quantity surveyor were accurately included in Aybe's capital investment appraisal system which was performed on a spreadsheet. However, no regular checks were carried out to compare the phased budgeted expenditure with actual costs incurred. It came as a surprise to the Board when the Finance Director finally produced the capital expenditure project report which showed the cost of the extension was nearly 50% overspent.

Strategic development

Aybe applies a traditional rational model in carrying out its strategic planning process. This encompasses an annual exercise to review the previous plan, creation of a revenue and capital budget for the next five years and instruction to managers within Aybe to maintain their expenditure within the budget limits approved by the Board.

Debates have taken place within the Board regarding the strategic direction in which Aybe should move. Most board members are generally satisfied that Aybe has been turned around over the last five years and were pleased that the company increased its profit in 2009 even though the global economy slowed down. Aybe benefited from a number of long-term contractual arrangements with customers throughout 2009 which were agreed in previous years. However, many of these are not being renewed due to the current economic climate.

The Board stated in its annual report, published in March 2010, that the overall strategic aim of the company is to:

"Achieve growth and increase shareholder returns by continuing to produce and distribute high quality electronic components and develop our international presence through expansion into new overseas markets."

Aybe's Chief Executive said in the annual report that the strategic aim is clear and straightforward. He said "Aybe will strive to maintain its share of the electronic development, operational, maintenance and repair markets in which it is engaged. This is despite the global economic difficulties which Aybe, along with its competitors, has faced since 2008. Aybe will continue to apply the highest ethical standards in its business activities."

In order to facilitate the achievement of the strategic aim, Aybe's Board has established the following strategic goals:

(1) Enhance the provision of products and services which are demanded by customers.

(2) Invest in engineering and web-based support for customers.

(3) Maintain the search for environmentally friendly products.

(4) Pursue options for expansion into new overseas markets.

The Board has also stated that Aybe is a responsible corporate organisation and recognises the social and environmental effects of its operational activities.

Concern over the rate of growth

Aybe's recently appointed Director of Operations and one of its Non-Executive Directors have privately expressed their concern to the Chief Executive at what they perceive to be the very slow growth of the company. While they accept that shareholder expectations should not be raised too high, they feel that the Board is not providing sufficient impetus to move the company forward. They fear that the results for 2010 will be worse than for 2009. They think that Aybe should be much more ambitious and fear that the institutional shareholders in particular, will not remain patient if Aybe does not create stronger earnings growth than has previously been achieved.

Development approaches

The Board has discussed different ways of expanding overseas in order to meet the overall strategic aim. It has, in the past, been reluctant to move from the current approach of exporting components. However the Director of Operations has now begun preparing a plan for the IEC division to open up a trading company in Asia. The DEC division is also establishing a subsidiary in Africa.

APPENDIX A

Extracts of Aybe's Income Statement and Statement of Financial Position

Income statement for the year ended 31/12/09

	C$m
Revenue	620
Operating costs	(579)
Finance costs	(4)
Profit before tax	37
Income tax expense	(14)
Profit for the year	23

Statement of financial position at 31/12/09

	C$m
ASSETS	
Non current assets	111
Current assets:	
Inventories	40
Trade and other receivables	81
Cash and cash equivalents	3
	124
Total assets	**235**
EQUITY AND LIABILITIES	
Equity:	
Share capital	18
Share premium	9
Other reserves	8
Retained earnings	75
Total equity	110
Non current liabilities	
Bank loan (8% interest, repayable 2015)	40

Current liabilities

Trade and other payables	73
Current tax payable	8
Bank overdraft	4
Total current liabilities	85
Total liabilities	125
Total equity and liabilities	**235**

End of pre-seen material

7 Analysis of the pre-seen material

Introduction

Now that you have had chance to read the pre-seen material, you should do some further research into the industry and try to pick out key themes which might form the basis of the exam questions.

You will find below:

- a SWOT analysis on Aybe

- stakeholder analysis

- quantitative analysis

- a consideration of potential examinable P3 topics.

Before reading this information, try to do your own analysis first and then compare your analysis to the information below.

The examiners have commented that students really need to do their own analysis. Simply copying analysis from your tutors or colleagues will not necessarily help you to understand the pre-seen properly.

Aybe pre-seen analysis – SWOT

Strengths

- Steady financials – growth in revenue and margins

- Seems to comply with Governance "best practice" (e.g. many NEDs although should have executive input to nominations committee)

- Share option plan should motivate directors

Weaknesses

- Board lacks ambition
- Aybe may have outgrown its functional structure
- Restrictive bank covenant limits financing opportunities
- Poor MIS (e.g. Board surprised about capex overspend)
- Poor budgetary control processes

Opportunities

- Expansion into Asian and /or African markets
- Enhance CRM – especially for specialist components division
- Develop website and e-business – especially for managing customer relationship
- Switch manufacturing to be closer to markets or to cheaper countries
- Improve information systems
- Sell a division

Threats

- Increasing competitive pressure
- Further loss of major customers
- High risk of takeover as shareholders may become dissatisfied
- Risk of breaching covenant
- Political risks – e.g. Eastern European country, African target
- Currency and interest rate risks.

Aybe pre-seen analysis – Stakeholders

Key stakeholders

- Institutional Shareholders (since privatisation) are becoming dissatisfied with current levels of growth and returns
- Major customers may threaten to move their business elsewhere

Aybe pre-seen analysis – Quantitative analysis

Divisions

- IEC contributes the most to both revenue and profit and SC the least
- Operating margins are DEC 6.6%, IEC 5.6% and SC 8.9%

Overall company profitability

- Fairly steady and unexciting
- Average revenue growth of 14.6% p.a. since 2005
- Operating margin has grown from 3.6% in 2005 to 6.6% (41/620) in 2009
- ROCE = 41/150 = 27.3% (no comparisons)

Liquidity

- Current ratio = 124 / 85 = 1.46
- Quick ratio = (81+3) / 85 = 0.99
- Receivables days = 81/620 × 365 = 48 days – seems high
- Payables days using operating costs = 73/579 × 365 = 46 days
- Inventory days using operating costs = 40/579 × 365 = 25 days
- Length of operating cycle = 25 + 48 – 46 = 27
- All fairly unexciting except Aybe has low cash reserves

Investor ratios

- Market capitalisation = 180m × 0.64 = C$115.2m
- Eps growth of 9.4% in 2009
- Dividend payout ratio set at 50% in 2008 and 2009
- Gearing based on book value of debt/equity = 40 / 110 = 36% which seems low enough. Slightly lower if you use market values.

Aybe Case Study – Key examinable issues for paper P3

Note: It is important that in the real exam you fully incorporate the new unseen information into your answers and do not rely too much on your analysis of the pre-seen. However, based on the pre-seen the following potential issues can be identified.

Corporate governance

Aybe is a listed company. Its listed status immediately brings to mind the various aspects of corporate governance, particularly those surrounding the board of directors, board committees and directors' remuneration (all mentioned in the pre-seen). The company appears to be compliant with many elements of governance codes (with a minor exception of a lack of executive directors on the nominations committee), but be prepared to discuss the requirements of any aspect.

Institutional shareholders may exercise their power and challenge the board's strategic direction – it appears that the risk appetite of the board does not reflect that of those holding 55% of the shares.

Risks and controls

It is common in the section A question to be asked to identify risks in a situation, and move onto control recommendations. There are numerous risks facing Aybe including currency risk, cultural risk (both arising from multinational operations), risk surrounding the capture of customer requirements and associated IT security, and the risks connected with its proposed overseas expansions. Any changes to the business or its operations will bring additional risks, so keep a lookout for these in the unseen case.

Management accounting controls

Information is provided regarding the capital budgeting process, and the apparent poor control over budget overspends. An assessment of the feedback control system in place may be required, possibly with recommendations for improvement.

Information requirements

The SC division of Aybe will require complete and accurate information regarding customer requirements. There is discussion of the introduction of web-based services, which may bring benefits to the business, but will also bring significant risks to IT security. It may, therefore, be a useful exercise to consider how this information requirement may be met and how the risks may be mitigated.

Financial risks

As already mentioned Aybe is exposed to currency risk, and may increase this exposure with further expansion. Additionally the business will face interest rate risk connected with its bank loan and overdraft usage. Discussion of financial risk, and evaluation of appropriate management techniques may be required.

8 Sample unseen material

Note: You should only read this unseen information and the associated question when you have already read and analysed the Aybe pre-seen material in detail. For maximum benefit (to simulate the time you will have in the real exam), you should aim to spend 10 minutes reading the unseen material and the requirement, and then 90 minutes preparing and writing up your answer.

Unseen material for the Aybe Case Study

Director of Operations' proposals

The most recent meeting of the Board of Directors of Aybe was dominated by discussions regarding the profitability of the business, following concerns recently expressed by some of the major institutional investors and Board members.

The Director of Operations reported that he had completed proposals to open a trading company in Asia. This, he said, would enable Aybe to exploit the lucrative potential of the developing economies.

The new director also put forward the following suggestions to the Board for consideration to improve the business' profitability and growth.

The company should look to expand its product range and diversify from purely component level products to complete systems. Examples were provided of systems such as a security solution utilising the latest online technology to give remote access to CCTV systems, fire alarm and voice evacuation solutions for large office blocks.

The Director of Operations pointed out that the large, and growing, number of installation companies in the market are looking for cost-effective systems. Aybe's knowledge and experience in electronics and manufacturing, along with their reputation and established client base, would give them a stepping stone to develop these markets.

The Board should investigate the possibility of offshoring production (moving business activity out of the original country of operation) by opening a factory in Asia or Africa to take advantage of lower labour rates and less onerous employment legislation in these countries. Aybe would continue with its Eastern European facilities and use the new plant for the expanded 'complete systems' range of products.

The company should move forward with the development of web-based services, including amongst these an e-commerce facility (permits customers to make purchases via the website). These new services should include the following functionality:

A specific website for each division (all branded to Aybe) linked to a data warehouse. This would combine the entire product range across the three divisions, and would be cross-referenced to allow customers to access the full product range through any gateway.

A bespoke system-design service for both the proposed range (as per suggestion (1) above), and for circuit-board level design. This service would have a minimum order requirement.

Full on-line ordering services with payment facilities permitting debit or credit card payment for one-off or low-volume users, and account facilities for larger established customers.

Board members' opinions

The Chief Executive, whilst broadly supportive of these suggestions, expressed a number of concerns:

The scale of the projects, if all undertaken at once, would mean a substantial drain on resources, both financially and in the amount of management time required.

The diversification, whilst in similar industries to their current business, was still very different to Aybe's existing core competencies of mass production and quality.

With particular regard to the idea of the Asian trading subsidiary, offshoring production carried with it a significant number of risks. These would need to be adequately assessed before any decision was reached.

The other Board members continued to discuss the proposals. One of the non-executive directors expressed a concern regarding the large amount of capital expenditure required. Given Aybe's previous record of not keeping tight control of budgets he felt that this could become a major problem. He advised that any such investment proposals would have to be closely reviewed and monitored by the Audit Committee.

It was also pointed out that the website would need to be extremely sophisticated to deliver the required functionality, and that Aybe had little experience in such areas. It was therefore likely that, at minimum, the development and implementation of such a system would need to be outsourced. This matter, it was agreed, should be dealt with by the IT Steering Committee.

Views regarding risk

The Director of Operations responded to some of these concerns as the discussion at the Board meeting grew more heated.

He was adamant that the diversification proposals would both reduce risk and attract new investment to Aybe. It was his opinion that "to not take risks was frankly worse than excessive risk-taking", and he added that the Board should "get out their comfort zone" before the institutional investors replaced all Board members.

The Board meeting concluded with only one decision reached; the company would progress with the proposed website immediately. The Director of Operations was requested to put a full analysis of his proposals, including a complete net present value (NPV) assessment, to the next Board meeting.

Sample

Required:

(a) (i) Discuss the opinions regarding risk taking expressed by the Director of Operations, and the benefits of diversification that he alludes to.

    (ii) Analyse the Chief Executive's concerns regarding the diversification and offshoring proposals. Your answer should cover both the risks specific to diversification and any other risks you feel appropriate.

(b) Following the Board's decision to pursue the website project, they will be looking to outsource the design, build and maintenance of both the site and data warehouse. It is intended that a tender process to select the appropriate outsource partner will be initiated within the next two months.

    (i) Describe the risks of outsourcing this project and make recommendations to minimise those risks.

    (ii) Advise how Aybe should approach the tender and selection process.

(c) The non-executive director who chairs the Audit Committee has expressed some concerns regarding the role, responsibilities and membership of the IT Steering committee and project team during the design, development and implementation of the new website and data warehouse for Aybe.

Advise this non-executive director on:

(i) The role of the IT Steering Committee and the responsibilities of each of its individual members.

(ii) The role of the project team.

Test your understanding answers

Key answer tips

This question focuses on the risks facing Aybe from diversification, offshoring and outsourcing – all common business practices. It then moves onto consider some specific roles in IT. It will be important throughout your answer to relate your points to the situation facing this business.

Part (a) requires you to focus on the opinions and concerns expressed by two Board members. Ensure that you establish what they have discussed from the scenario before commencing your answer. Diversification is a risk response strategy, but in itself brings additional risks to a business – this is the key to the discussion that has arisen.

Part (b) covers the popular area of outsourcing. You should have some points of theory in hand to assist in your answer to the two parts of the question. Be careful to answer both sections of part (b)(i) – risks and recommendation for their minimisation.

Part (c) is relatively theoretical, but you can earn additional marks for illustrating your points in the context of the case provided. Use the mark allocation to guide you as to the number of points that you need to make (one point will earn one mark in this section).

(a) (i) **Risk taking**

There is generally a trade off between a company's need to take risks to remain competitive and its risk appetite. Whilst Aybe has pursued a low risk strategy for some time their competitive advantage and profitability have suffered accordingly.

The Director of Operations is correct in his view that to generate higher returns a business may have to take more risk. This can be necessary in order to be competitive. Conversely, not accepting risk tends to make a business less dynamic, and implies a 'follow the leader' strategy.

This appears to be the situation that Aybe has got itself into, with the Board unwilling to take chances and grow the business in an aggressive manner. The institutional investors' growing impatience for improved returns necessitates a change in approach.

Incurring risk also implies that the returns from different activities will be higher —such benefits being the return for accepting risks. Benefits can be financial, such as decreased costs, or intangible, such as better quality information.

In both cases, these will lead to the business being able to gain competitive advantage. This can sometimes be referred to as 'entrepreneurial risk'.

Benefits of diversification

Diversification can reduce risk to a business through the stabilisation of revenue flows.

By diversifying operations, as one arm of the business performs badly the other arms of the business will perform well thus taking up the slack and maintaining a stable income stream.

Further, by diversifying internationally Aybe should have operations in countries at different points of the economic cycle thus minimising economic risk.

A well-diversified operation giving stable revenue streams is hence more likely to attract investors than a company with unstable revenue flows or a dependence on one area. This is the crux of the opinion expressed by the Director of Operations.

However, for this to be effective a negative correlation is needed between the different business areas. If both products are affected by the same conditions then the business will simply magnify the effects as now two operations will perform badly at the same time.

For this reason unrelated diversification is more appropriate as a pure risk management tool. Aybe are proposing to move into a related area which is potentially a natural progression for the business but less ideal for risk management purposes.

(ii) **Risks from diversification**

Aybe will face a number of risks specific to the diversification proposals. These include:

Skill set

Although the Director of Operations has stated that Aybe have considerable expertise in electronics and design services, this is at component level. It is very likely that Aybe do not have the knowledge or experience of the installation industry.

Whilst there are some similarities there are also significant differences between component design and the design of complete systems and this may require expertise, and management skills, that the business does not currently have.

Investor dissatisfaction

Investors are more than capable of diversifying their own portfolios and do not need Aybe to do it on their behalf. If an investor wants to invest in both component wholesalers and installation they can do it themselves by buying shares in the different companies.

It could also be argued that investors would expect companies to perform better by sticking to their core competencies.

Risks related to the offshoring proposal

By building a new factory in either Asia or Africa Aybe will be exposing itself to a number of additional international risks.

Culture

The cultures in both Africa and Asia are very different to the European manufacturing base that Aybe is familiar with. There will be different working practices, religious issues which could lead to products, services or business practices being unacceptable in the target country.

Failure to adequately understand cultural differences will lead to the project failing.

Litigation

As with culture, a lack of understanding of local laws could easily lead to the company being sued for breaches. Some countries have a highly developed legal culture and often there is a presumption in favour of the domestic litigant.

Goods in transit

There will be considerable traffic of components between Aybe's operations which could result in losses from either accident or theft. Piracy is now common in Africa and can certainly not be discounted.

Further hold ups in Customs can also delay production.

Political

Certain African states are extremely unstable and Aybe run the risk of finding an administration favourable to foreign business could change overnight resulting in the loss of the operation, or higher taxes, or restrictions on repatriation of profits.

Reputation

Offshoring operations is often controversial since the home country residents may view this as jobs that have been created elsewhere, leading to unfavourable publicity.

Further, whilst some employment laws are less onerous there are certain working practices which will also affect Aybe's reputation. The use of child labour in factories, poverty level wages, excessive working hours which may well be acceptable in the target countries will nonetheless be unacceptable to both Aybe's clients and some investors.

Financial risk

Aybe might be venturing into geographical locations where the currencies are fairly volatile. This therefore begs the question as to whether the operations will be paid in local currencies; if this is the case exchange rate fluctuations will cause uncertainty in the cash flows.

(b) (i) **Risks of outsourcing**

There are several risks that Aybe may encounter if it chooses to outsource the design, build and maintenance of its new website and data warehouse. These include:

Suitable system

There is significant risk that the outsource partner may try to sell an off-the-shelf solution which will not have all the facilities required by Aybe. Or it may have additional, expensive functionalities which are not required by Aybe.

For example, it will be crucial that Aybe can accurately capture the information required by their clients for bespoke design services and that the system ensures clients give all required information.

Costs

Projects of this nature have a tendency to overrun the time predictions. Additionally the annual costs may start to rise above the level expected as the outsource partner knows it will be difficult to change the company. The power it has as the supplier allows them to increase charges above those anticipated.

Control

Aybe will not have control of the website, but any issues or problems will be their responsibility and will reflect badly on their brand. Should there be serious security issues around client data, especially account details then Aybe will held responsible.

It is Aybe's reputation at stake if the system fails to work as proposed or if there are issues around slow loading and response times or regular service outages.

Confidentiality

The outsource partner will have access to confidential data regarding Aybe's business such its client list, products and products under development.

Locked into one partner

Aybe will be handing over the provision and maintenance of the site to the outsource partner. If the partner's services or the system operation prove to be unsatisfactory, then Aybe will incur significant expense in changing partner.

It may well be that the outsourcer holds all system diagrams and software for the system and will be unwilling to release any codes in the event of the contract being terminated – effectively holding Aybe to ransom.

Outsourcer partner stability

If the partner were to fail as a business then Aybe would be left with no back-up for the site and potentially no information or source codes if these are owned by the partner. This could leave Aybe with a system that no other company can maintain.

Recommendations to minimise the risks

Most of the above risks can controlled by a suitable service level agreement which would layout the following points:

- Agreed annual cost increases.
- Performance levels (for system downtime, response times, support hours).
- A confidentiality agreement.
- Ownership of the elements of the system i.e. the system documents, source codes, information stored and the hardware.
- Early exit terms – notice periods, penalty clauses etc.
- Penalties for sub standard performance.
- The financial stability of any potential partner should be thoroughly investigated as part of the tender process.
- It will be essential to provide and agree on a full detailed specification for the system at the outset of negotiations and a continuous audit should take place to ensure that the service level agreement is being adhered to.

Tutorial note: An acceptable alternative presentation to your answer to (b) (i) would be to show risks and the appropriate recommendations together rather than under two separate headings.

(ii) **Tender and selection**

Aybe will need to follow a formal tender process, inviting applications from a number of potential suppliers. This should then be followed up by a thorough evaluation of supplier proposals, against criteria that the business (and ultimately the Board) have determined.

Identify potential suppliers

Aybe could advertise for expressions of interest through a variety of trade journals across Europe which specialise in contracts of this nature, either as an advert or via a press release. Alternatively, Aybe could research the market to shortlist potential partners.

Invitation to tender

Once the shortlist is complete invitations to tender can be sent. This document defines what needs to be done to achieve the system objectives and acts as a basis for the supplier presentation/proposal.

This would include the following information about Aybe:

- Description of business, products and client base.

- Number of employees and business location(s).

- Future likely changes in organisation. It will be crucial to bear in mind the potentially large upheaval if the Director of Operations' diversification proposals are eventually accepted.

- Organisation structure.

- Current hardware and software. Information would also be provided about the system requirements, gathered from investigation and analysis:

- Statement of business objectives from the system.

- Description of what the system comprises: hardware, software, communications.

- Predicted input, output, processing and storage volumes.

- Service, maintenance and training requirements. It is critical that Aybe get this absolutely right and in sufficient detail so that the tenderer cannot leave out critical requirements, or add in elements that are not needed.

Information is also requested from the supplier at this stage. This may include:

- Description of supplier business: products and services offered.

- Size and geographical breakdown.

- Current customer base (Aybe need to be sure that the partner can deal with customers of their size).

- Third party references. It is essential to get references from current clients (due diligence required).

- Bank reference – would help to assess stability.

- Accountants' reference and at least three years accounts. Again this will aid investigation into the provider's stability.

— Experience of similar systems.

— System proposal.

— Utilisation and implementation proposals.

— Suggested time scale for supply and implementation.

— Proposals for training, maintenance and after sales service.

— Cost and payment terms.

Tutorial note: A lot of detail has been given here for completeness. Use the mark allocation in the question to guide you to the amount of detail required; you could assume ½ mark for each example of the type of information to be requested.

Evaluate proposals and supplier selection

The proposals will then be evaluated on the basis of how closely they meet the original specification and then weighted on Aybe's priorities.

These priorities could include:

— Cost and payment terms

— Training and support

— Response times

— Any other factors that differentiate a particular supplier

Once the partner is selected then the Service level Agreement (SLA) needs to written, agreed and signed. As discussed this is Aybe's most effective control against non-performance hence may require significant time and legal costs to finalise.

(c) (i) **Role of IT Steering Committee**

An IT Steering Committee involves a broad range of people from the business and IT in the information systems and information technology decisions of the company. It will monitor the Information Systems strategy, risks and competitive issues and plan for future systems developments and costs. The members would include:

— A director – to chair the committee and provide Board level representation and involvement. Bearing in mind the limited number of directors on Aybe's Board this would seem to be a role for the Director of Operations.

–   Senior Managers from key departments, who will know the information needs of their sections of business. They will be involved in requirements analysis, requirements specification, testing and potentially sponsoring specific projects / implementations.

–   Senior IT representation (IT Manager) – to provide the technical expertise and advice.

–   IT staff will advise on the systems and costs, provide options for the new system. They also are managing existing developments so will be able to ensure integration and appropriate time scales and will also be able to highlight risks involved.

The issue for Aybe is how much expertise they have at the moment and whether additional staff need recruiting, or existing staff need additional training.

A senior finance manager to include the financial perspective and ensure that costs and benefits are appropriately considered. Their role will include investment appraisal of any major implementations.

(ii)   **Role of the project team**

The project team will be involved in delivering the actual system and will need to carry out a number of activities.
Initially they should ensure that the design of the system is suitable and covers all aspects of the company's requirements by:

–   identifying the information needs of the business (requirements capture)

–   tracking requirements from capture through design, development and testing.

The team should ensure that all users are considered – probably by involving a range of users in identifying information needs. They will then move onto identify potential options for the system, and perform cost-benefit analysis of the various options to reach their recommendations.

The project team along with the steering committee will then be responsible for the tender selection, carrying out the following activities:

– produce tender request to send to potential providers

– review tenders submitted

– create short lists and select providers.

During implementation the project manager will arrange regular meetings with the outsource partner to ensure all project plans, designs and specifications are agreed and signed off prior to implementation.

The project team and internal audit will also monitor progress against contractual terms and provide status reports to the project steering committee, who will feed them into the IT Steering Committee.

The project manager should highlight any issues as they arise and ensure a managed outcome, and, in conjunction with internal audit they will also ensure suitable controls are in place to avoid cost overruns.

Section A-style practice question

1 Crashcarts

PRE-SEEN INFORMATION

Group structure

Crashcarts IT Consultancy is a £100 million revenue business with a head office in the UK and additional offices in Paris, Madrid and one recently opened in Chicago. The group has the following divisional structure:

- *Consultancy division.* This division is structured on a regional basis with business units as follows:
    - Central and Western Europe
    - Eastern Europe
    - North America
    - Emerging markets (covers South East Asia and India).

    The division provides a range of IT and business change/business process re-engineering consultancy services to clients. Over the history of the group, clients have spanned all sectors and sizes, from small local businesses to large blue-chip organisations.

- *Support division.* This division primarily provides outsourcing services to businesses, and is structured on a product basis as follows:
    - Technical IT support
    - Project management
    - Development
    - Value-added services (discussed in more detail below).

Background

Crashcarts developed from a small partnership established 18 years ago by three former employees of a major international consultancy. They brought with them approximately 28 years of combined experience in consultancy and IT management. At first the business grew organically, with additional consultants being taken on when required to meet workload demands. The original business premises were rented office space in a provincial UK town.

After eight years in operation the company was employing 52 consultants across the UK on a full-time basis, with additional partners providing services where required. The activity was supported by a central team of 30 administration, finance, marketing and IT specialists, with all sales activities continuing to be driven by the three founding partners.

Growth in business continued to be impressive with the consultancy division gaining a reputation for providing world class IT consultancy services to blue chip clients, predominantly in the retail sector. In order to fund further expansion Crashcarts floated on the London Stock Exchange seven years ago. The group was subsequently restructured as described above.

Management structure

Crashcarts is run by a Board of Directors headed by the Chairman, who is one of the former managing partners. Up until two years ago he held the role of Chief Executive in the company. The other two founding partners hold the positions of Chief Executive Officer and Sales Director. The remaining board level positions are filled by people who have been recruited into the business in the three years, having been headhunted from other management consultancies.

The executive directors on the board are supported by three independent non-executive directors (NEDs) with backgrounds in IT development, retail banking and manufacturing. These NEDs provide a wide range of experience and support to the strategic development process. They also play a major part in the board sub-committees such as the remuneration and audit committee. All such committees are chaired by the Executive Chairman of the board.

Expansion plans

Since obtaining a listing on the London Stock Exchange, Crashcarts has followed an aggressive 'growth by acquisition' strategy whereby it has acquired a number of smaller consultancy businesses. This has led to its expansion into Europe and North America with business premises now being situated in both regions.

The support division is an area of relatively recent growth, having been set up just five years ago. Crashcarts' management felt that it was an obvious extension of their consultancy activities to move towards the outsource provision field for IT and related activities. To date this decision has proved extremely successful with the business winning many high profile contracts for provision of services to major clients.

Value added services

The newest business unit in the group is that of Value Added Services within the support division. This unit was established in 20X1 when Crashcarts acquired a new subsidiary named Crashcarts Call Centre. The purchase was completed for £2 million based on a P/E ratio of 8.

The call centre subsidiary provides two major services for its clients. First, it holds databases, primarily for large retail chains' catalogue sales, connected in real time to clients' inventory control systems. Second, its call centre operation allows its clients' customers to place orders by telephone.

UNSEEN INFORMATION

Further information is available about the new subsidiary, Crashcarts Call Centre.

Operations

The call centre subsidiary leases all of its hardware, software and telecommunications equipment over a five-year term. The infrastructure provides the capacity to process three million orders and ten million line items per annum. In addition, maintenance contracts have been signed for the full five-year period. These contracts include the provision of a daily backup facility in an off-site location.

For telephone orders the real-time system determines whether there is inventory available and, if so, a shipment is requested. The sophisticated technology in use by the call centre also incorporates a secure payment facility for credit and debit card payments, details of which are transferred to the retail stores' own computer system.

Crashcarts Call Centre is staffed by call centre operators (there were 70 in 20X2 and 80 in each of 20X3 and 20X4). In addition, a management team, training staff and administrative personnel are employed. Like other call centres, there is a high turnover of call centre operators (over 100% per annum) and this requires an almost continuous process of staff training and detailed supervision and monitoring.

Charging basis

The call centre charges each retail client a lump sum each year for the IT and communications infrastructure it provides. There is a 12 month contract in place for each client. In addition, Crashcarts earns a fixed sum for every order it processes, plus an additional amount for every line item. If items are not in inventory, Crashcarts earns no processing fee.

Performance

A summary of Crashcarts Call Centre's financial performance for the last three years:

	20X2	20X3	20X4
	£000	£000	£000
Revenue			
Contract fixed fee	400	385	385
Order processing fees	2,500	3,025	3,450
Line item processing fees	600	480	390
Total revenue	3,500	3,890	4,225
Expenses			
Office rent and expenses	200	205	210
Operator salaries and salary-related costs	1,550	1,920	2,180
Management, administration and training salaries	1,020	1,070	1,120
IT and telecoms lease and maintenance expenses	300	310	330
Other expenses	150	200	220
Total expenses	3,220	3,705	4,060
Operating profit	280	185	165

Non-financial performance information for the same period is as follows:

	20X2	20X3	20X4
Number of incoming calls received	1,200,000	1,300,000	1,350,000
Number of orders processed	1,000,000	1,100,000	1,150,000
Order strike rate (orders/calls)	83.3%	84.6%	85.2%
Number of line items processed	3,000,000	3,200,000	3,250,000
Average number of line items per order	3.0	2.9	2.8
Number of retail clients	8	7	7

Fixed contract income per client	£50,000	£55,000	£55,000
Income per order processed	£2.50	£2.75	£3.00
Income per line item processed	£0.20	£0.15	£0.12
Average number of orders per operator	15,000	15,000	15,000
Number of operators required	66.7	73.3	76.7
Actual number of operators employed	70.0	80.0	80.0

Question – Crashcarts – Risk management

Discuss the increase in importance of risk management to all businesses (with an emphasis on listed ones) over the last few years, and the role of management accountants in risk management.

Question – Crashcarts – Risk analysis

Advise the Crashcarts Call Centre on methods for analysing its risks.

Question – Crashcarts – Risk identification & quantification

Identify and quantify (using appropriate methods) the major risks facing Crashcarts, at both parent level and subsidiary level, arising from its expansion into the call centre business.

Question – Crashcarts – Management control systems & controls

Explain the components of a management control system and recommend the main controls that would be appropriate for the Crashcarts Call Centre.

Test your understanding answers

Question – Crashcarts – Risk management

Importance of risk management

Risk management should always be important, but it has gained wider recognition in recent years following the development of corporate governance frameworks in many countries, such as the Combined Code in the UK and the Sarbanes-Oxley legislation in the US.

In the UK, the Combined Code recognised the need for a sound system of internal control and risk management, and specified that it was a responsibility of the board of directors to carry out an annual review of the internal control and risk management systems. The basic view is that the objectives of a company should be to achieve a return for its shareholders consistent with the risk to which the shareholders wish to be exposed to achieve that return. Greater risk as well as lower returns can destroy shareholder value.

In the UK, the board of directors of a listed company should be responsible for maintaining a sound system of internal control, and for carrying out an annual review of the system of internal control. This review should cover all material controls, including financial, operational and compliance controls, and risk management systems.

However, it is the responsibility of executive management to devise the system of internal controls and to implement it. Such a system should include arrangements for identifying risks, implementing risk controls, monitoring performance and taking control measures where appropriate. The effectiveness of control systems depends to a very large extent on the quality of its information and communication systems.

Role of management accountant

The extent to which management accountants are involved in risk management will vary between different organisations, but the management accounting system is an essential element in the management information systems of an organisation. An essential feature of control systems is that targets need to be established, together with risk limits, and actual performance needs to be monitored and compared with these targets. This requires systems for planning and forecasting, and for monitoring performance through systems of feedforward control or feedback control.

Management accountants are closely involved in the design and implementation of such systems. For example:

- Within a system of budgeting and budgetary control, management accountants are involved in the preparation of budgets, and in monitoring actual performance against budget, or revised forecasts against budget, and reporting variances.

- Management accountants are often involved in the provision and analysis of information for strategic planning and control, including risk assessment (for example, through risk modelling and analysis of forecasts).

- Management accountants are often involved in the operation of systems for reporting non-financial performance, including reporting systems based on a balanced scorecard or Key Performance Indicators.

- In the role of internal auditors, management accountants are involved in monitoring the effectiveness of controls.

Question – Crashcarts – Risk analysis

Risk analysis methods

The Call Centre should establish methods for risk analysis within an organised control framework. To do this, it is necessary to identify the objectives of the Call Centre (for example, to achieve growth in annual profits), because risks need to be considered in the context of failing to achieve objectives. In addition, a management framework should be established, with individual managers or risk management committees given the responsibility for risk analysis.

A variety of methods should be used to identify and assess or measure risks. These include brainstorming by a group of managers, environmental analysis (PEST or SLEPT analysis), scenario analysis and modelling (for example, simulation or forecasting models). All recognisable risks should be considered. In the case of a Call Centre, these will include business continuity risks and breach of security risks, as well as commercial, business and financial risks.

Where possible, the analysis of risks should include an attempt to measure them, in terms of both the probability that they will occur and the potential losses or consequences when they do occur. A record should be kept of all the assessed risks, and risk mapping could also be used as a comparative analytical tool.

Question – Crashcarts – Risk identification & quantification

Risk identification

An appropriate method of identifying the major risks at both parent level and subsidiary level might be brainstorming.

Subsidiary risks

At the subsidiary level, it seems clear that the Call Centre is essentially a fixed cost operation. Variations in profit depend on controlling fixed costs and ensuring that there is sufficient revenue. Major risks that might be identified from the information provided are:

(1) excessive growth in annual fixed costs;

(2) a fall in operator productivity;

(3) the loss of a client (or several clients) at the yearend;

(4) a fall in the number of processed orders: this could be caused by either a fall in the total number of incoming calls received or a fall in the order strike rate (conversion of calls to processed orders);

(5) possibly, a fall in the number of line items for each order;

(6) resistance to further price increases from clients;

(7) problems with the computer system and back-up, such as a fraud.

The probability of each of these adverse events occurring might be assessed, and divided simply into 'likely' or 'not likely', as a first step towards risk mapping.

Parent company risks

At the parent company level, the risks would appear to be strategic, and therefore more difficult to measure. A brainstorming approach to risk identification could be used. Potential risks might include:

(1) The risks from diversifying into an unfamiliar business over which management at the parent company level has little or no experience.

(2) The different risk profile of the Call Centre business compared with the consultancy business might result in a change in the risk profile, and the market value, of the Crashcarts group.

(3) If any of the Call Centre clients are either clients of the consultancy business, or keen competitors of the consultancy business clients, there could be adverse consequences for customer relations.

(4) The parent company could be exposing itself to a greater risk to its reputation, if the Call Centre performs badly or attracts bad publicity.

(**Tutorial note:** This is not a exclusive list of all risks – other relevant and well-explained risks will be appropriate.)

Risk quantification

The risks for the parent company cannot be measured from the information available. However, some of the risks facing the subsidiary can be quantified.

Risk: fixed costs become excessive

Between 20X1 and 20X3, annual revenue increased by £725,000 but the total annual salaries and salary-related costs of operators, management and administration staff rose by £730,000. If salary costs continue to rise at a faster rate than annual income, annual profits will be eroded. Operating profit in 20X3 was equal to just 5% [165/(2,180 + 1,120)] of salary costs.

Risk: fall in processed orders

Since the business has few, if any, variable costs, profitability is affected directly by variations in revenue.

Revenue from each processed call:	£
Income per order processed	3.000
Income from line items (2.8 items × £0.12)	0.336
	3.336

The breakeven point for processed orders in 20X3 was therefore 49,460 orders (£165,000/£3.336 per order). This is 4.3% (49,460/1,150,000) less than the actual number of processed orders in the year.

The risks to the number of processed orders include:

- a fall in the total number of calls, which is possibly a low risk;

- a fall in the number of incoming calls that turn into actual orders, possibly due to a greater frequency in out-of-inventory responses from clients' inventory systems;

- a fall in the number of clients.

Risk: loss of a client

This is likely to be a major risk in terms of probability. It would also have a major effect on profitability. In 20X3, the average number of processed orders per client was about 164,000 (1,150,000/7). The loss of revenue would be, in terms of 20X3 revenue:

	£000
Loss of fixed contract income	55
Loss of revenue from processed orders (164,000 × £3.336)	547
Total loss of revenue	602

Although there would be some savings in fixed costs, it seems probable that the loss of a further client would damage profits significantly.

Risk: fall in operator productivity

In view of the rapid staff turnover, there is probably a fairly high risk of some loss in operator productivity. However, in 20X3, 80 operators were employed when only 76.7 operators were required.

The excess capacity might be due to the risk of sudden staff reductions, or the need to employ large numbers temporarily whilst new operators are being trained. However, on the basis of the figures available, productivity in 20X3 could have been worse by 4.3% [(80 − 76.7)/76.7] without affecting staffing requirement levels.

Since productivity has been unchanged for three years, the risk of such a fall is probably remote.

Risk: fall in line orders for each processed order

Income from processing line items was just £390,000 in 20X3. To reduce profitability significantly, there would have to be a very large fall in the average line entries per processed order. Although there has been some decline between 20X1 and 20X3, the probability of a large fall seems unlikely.

Conclusion

Each measured risk could be placed on a 2 × 2 risk map, with high/low likelihood on one axis and serious/not serious consequences on the other axis. This would indicate, for example, that the risk of a loss of a client is a major risk (high probability/major consequence) whereas the risk from a fall in productivity is a much smaller risk (fairly low probability/ probably a limited consequence). Other risks could be placed on the map in the same way. Management must then identify those risks that need the most urgent control measures or monitoring.

(**Tutorial note**: The extent of the quantified analysis you can provide for this part will depend on the time you have available. There is no single 'correct' answer to this question, but having selected the risks you wish to quantify, present your argument – and your figures – clearly.)

Question – Crashcarts – Management control systems & controls

(**Tutorial note**: Our solution provides the component elements in a diagram as well as in narrative form; however, a diagram is not essential, since it is not required specifically by the question)

Components of a management control system

A management control system might include elements of both feedforward control and feedback control.

- Feedback control involves a comparison of actual results with a plan, measuring differences or variances, investigating their causes and taking control action.

- Feedforward control involves using information about actual results or from external sources to revise forecasts for the future, comparing the revised forecast with the plan, measuring differences, investigate their causes and taking control measures as appropriate.

The components of these systems are illustrated in the simple diagram below:

The components are as follows:

(1) Outputs from the system are measured, to provide control information.

(2) In a feedback system, these measured outputs (actual results) are compared with the budget or plan, and differences or variances are measured.

(3) On the basis of this control information, the controller responsible for results takes suitable control measures to change inputs to the system.

(4) In a feedforward system, revised forecasts are prepared, using information from measured actual results or from other (external sources).

(5) On the basis of this information, the controller responsible takes suitable control measures.

(6) Where appropriate, the original plan is replaced with a revised plan or revised forecast as the basis for future control comparisons.

Main controls for the Call Centre

- There must be all necessary system and security controls in the Call Centre and the Call Centre's computer system, to minimise the risks of unauthorised access by hackers and the risks of system down-time.

- A major risk is the loss of a client, and controls should be applied that contain or reduce this risk. Control information might include client feedback (for example, information obtained from discussions with each client's management team), and measures of operator performance, in terms of quality of service to customers as well as speed and productivity. Control measures to ensure client and customer satisfaction might be applied by means of supervision and refresher training.

- Another potentially significant risk is a change in the total number of processed orders, both a fall in total calls for reasons other than the loss of a client and also an increase in calls due to a growth in business volume. Feedforward information can be provided at regular intervals, comparing the current forecast of total calls volume with the original plan. Where necessary, suitable control measures might be to reduce or increase operator staffing levels.

- Controls over salary levels should be applied through the annual salary review process.

- Operator productivity does not appear to be a major risk at the moment, but productivity (measured by orders taken per operator or line items processed per operator) could be checked by means of productivity and idle time measures. Improvements in productivity might be achieved through better training, supervision, or by reducing staff levels to reduce inactivity/ idle time.

Mock examination

Chapter learning objectives

The following mock examination is the Specimen Paper for P3, published at the launch of the most recent syllabus.

Pillar P

P3 – Performance Strategy

Specimen Examination Paper

Instructions to candidates

You are allowed three hours to answer this question paper.
You are allowed 20 minutes reading time **before the examination begins** during which you should read the question paper and, if you wish, highlight and/or make notes on the question paper. However, you will **not** be allowed, **under any circumstances**, to open the answer book and start writing or use your calculator during this reading time.
You are strongly advised to carefully read ALL the question requirements before attempting the question concerned (that is, all parts and/or sub-questions). The requirements for all questions are contained in a dotted box.
ALL answers must be written in the answer book. Answers or notes written on the question paper will **not** be submitted for marking.
Answer ALL compulsory questions in Section A on page 8.
Answer TWO of the three questions in Section B on pages 9 to 12.
Maths Tables are provided on pages 13 and 16.
The list of verbs as published in the syllabus is given for reference on page 17
Write your candidate number, the paper number and examination subject title in the spaces provided on the front of the answer book. Also write your contact ID and name in the space provided in the right hand margin and seal to close.
Tick the appropriate boxes on the front of the answer book to indicate which questions you have answered.

P3 – Performance Strategy

Power Utilities

Pre-seen Case Study

Background

Power Utilities (PU) is located in a democratic Asian country. Just over 12 months ago, the former nationalised Electricity Generating Corporation (EGC) was privatised and became PU. EGC was established as a nationalised industry many years ago. Its home government at that time had determined that the provision of the utility services of electricity generation production should be managed by boards that were accountable directly to Government. In theory, nationalised industries should be run efficiently, on behalf of the public, without the need to provide any form of risk related return to the funding providers. In other words, EGC, along with other nationalised industries was a non-profit making organisation. This, the Government claimed at the time, would enable prices charged to the final consumer to be kept low.

Privatisation of EGC

The Prime Minister first announced three years ago that the Government intended to pursue the privatisation of the nationalised industries within the country. The first priority was to be the privatisation of the power generating utilities and EGC was selected as the first nationalised industry to be privatised. The main purpose of this strategy was to encourage public subscription for share capital. In addition, the Government's intention was that PU should take a full and active part in commercial activities such as raising capital and earning higher revenue by increasing its share of the power generation and supply market by achieving growth either organically or through making acquisitions. This, of course, also meant that PU was exposed to commercial pressures itself, including satisfying the requirements of shareholders and becoming a potential target for take-over. The major shareholder, with a 51% share, would be the Government. However, the Minister of Energy has recently stated that the Government intends to reduce its shareholding in PU over time after the privatisation takes place.

Industry structure

PU operates 12 coal-fired power stations across the country and transmits electricity through an integrated national grid system which it manages and controls. It is organised into three regions, Northern, Eastern and Western. Each region generates electricity which is sold to 10 private sector electricity distribution companies which are PU's customers.

The three PU regions transmit the electricity they generate into the national grid system. A shortage of electricity generation in one region can be made up by taking from the national grid. This is particularly important when there is a national emergency, such as exceptional weather conditions.

The nationalised utility industries, including the former EGC, were set up in a monopolistic position. As such, no other providers of these particular services were permitted to enter the market within the country. Therefore, when EGC was privatised and became PU it remained the sole generator of electricity in the country. The electricity generating facilities, in the form of the 12 coal-fired power stations, were all built over 15 years ago and some date back to before EGC came into being.

The 10 private sector distribution companies are the suppliers of electricity to final users including households and industry within the country, and are not under the management or control of PU. They are completely independent companies owned by shareholders.

The 10 private sector distribution companies serve a variety of users of electricity. Some, such as AB, mainly serve domestic users whereas others, such as DP, only supply electricity to a few industrial clients. In fact, DP has a limited portfolio of industrial customers and 3 major clients, an industrial conglomerate, a local administrative authority and a supermarket chain. DP finds these clients costly to service.

Structure of PU

The structure of PU is that it has a Board of Directors headed by an independent Chairman and a separate Managing Director. The Chairman of PU was nominated by the Government at the time the announcement that EGC was to be privatised was made. His background is that he is a former Chairman of an industrial conglomerate within the country. There was no previous Chairman of EGC which was managed by a Management Board, headed by the Managing Director. The former EGC Managing Director retired on privatisation and a new Managing Director was appointed.

The structure of PU comprises a hierarchy of many levels of management authority. In addition to the Chairman and Managing Director, the Board consists of the Directors of each of the Northern, Eastern and Western regions, a Technical Director, the Company Secretary and the Finance Director. All of these except the Chairman are the Executive Directors of PU. The Government also appointed seven Non Executive Directors to PU's Board. With the exception of the Company Secretary and Finance Director, all the Executive Directors are qualified electrical engineers. The Chairman and Managing Director of PU have worked hard to overcome some of the inertia which was an attitude that some staff had developed within the former EGC. PU is now operating efficiently as a private sector company. There have been many staff changes at a middle management level within the organisation.

Within the structure of PU's headquarters, there are five support functions; engineering, finance (which includes PU's Internal Audit department), corporate treasury, human resource management (HRM) and administration, each with its own chief officers, apart from HRM. Two Senior HRM Officers and Chief Administrative Officer report to the Company Secretary. The Chief Accountant and Corporate Treasurer each report to the Finance Director. These functions, except Internal Audit, are replicated in each region, each with its own regional officers and support staff. Internal Audit is an organisation wide function and is based at PU headquarters.

Regional Directors of EGC

The Regional Directors all studied in the field of electrical engineering at the country's leading university and have worked together for a long time. Although they did not all attend the university at the same time, they have a strong belief in the quality of their education. After graduation from university, each of the Regional Directors started work at EGC in a junior capacity and then subsequently gained professional electrical engineering qualifications. They believe that the experience of working up through the ranks of EGC has enabled them to have a clear understanding of EGC's culture and the technical aspects of the industry as a whole. Each of the Regional Managers has recognised the changed environment that PU now operates within, compared with the former EGC, and they are now working hard to help PU achieve success as a private sector electricity generator. The Regional Directors are well regarded by both the Chairman and Managing Director, both in terms of their technical skill and managerial competence.

Governance of EGC

Previously, the Managing Director of the Management Board of EGC reported to senior civil servants in the Ministry of Energy. There were no shareholders and ownership of the Corporation rested entirely with the Government. That has now changed. The Government holds 51% of the shares in PU and the Board of Directors is responsible to the shareholders but, inevitably, the Chairman has close links directly with the Minister of Energy, who represents the major shareholder.

The Board meetings are held regularly, normally weekly, and are properly conducted with full minutes being taken. In addition, there is a Remuneration Committee, an Audit Committee and an Appointments Committee, all in accordance with best practice. The model which has been used is the Combined Code on Corporate Governance which applies to companies which have full listing status on the London Stock Exchange. Although PU is not listed on the London Stock Exchange, the principles of the Combined Code were considered by the Government to be appropriate to be applied with regard to the corporate governance of the company.

Currently, PU does not have an effective Executive Information System and this has recently been raised at a Board meeting by one of the non-executive directors because he believes this inhibits the function of the Board and consequently is disadvantageous to the governance of PU.

Remuneration of Executive Directors
In order to provide a financial incentive, the Remuneration Committee of PU has agreed that the Executive Directors be entitled to performance related pay, based on a bonus scheme, in addition to their fixed salary and health benefits.

Capital market
PU exists in a country which has a well developed capital market relating both to equity and loan stock funding. There are well established international institutions which are able to provide funds and corporate entities are free to issue their own loan stock in accordance with internationally recognised principles. PU is listed on the country's main stock exchange.

Strategic opportunity
The Board of PU is considering the possibility of vertical integration into electricity supply and has begun preliminary discussion with DP's Chairman with a view to making an offer for DP. PU's Board is attracted by DP's strong reputation for customer service but is aware, through press comment, that DP has received an increase in complaints regarding its service to customers over the last year. When the former EGC was a nationalised business, break-downs were categorised by the Government as "urgent", when there was a danger to life, and "non-urgent" which was all others. Both the former EGC and DP had a very high success rate in meeting the government's requirements that a service engineer should attend the urgent break-down within 60 minutes. DP's record over this last year in attending urgent break-downs has deteriorated seriously and if PU takes DP over, this situation would need to improve.

Energy consumption within the country and Government drive for increased efficiency and concern for the environment
Energy consumption has doubled in the country over the last 10 years. As PU continues to use coal-fired power stations, it now consumes most of the coal mined within the country.

The Minister of Energy has indicated to the Chairman of PU that the Government wishes to encourage more efficient methods of energy production. This includes the need to reduce production costs. The Government has limited resources for capital investment in energy production and wishes to be sure that future energy production facilities are more efficient and effective than at present.

The Minister of Energy has also expressed the Government's wish to see a reduction in harmful emissions from the country's power stations. (The term harmful emissions in this context, refers to pollution coming out of electricity generating power stations which damage the environment.)

One of PU's non-executive directors is aware that another Asian country is a market leader in coal gasification which is a fuel technology that could be used to replace coal for power generation. In the coal gasification process, coal is mixed with oxygen and water vapour under pressure, normally underground, and then pumped to the surface where the gas can be used in power stations. The process significantly reduces carbon dioxide emissions although it is not widely used at present and not on any significant commercial scale.

Another alternative to coal fired power stations being actively considered by PU's Board is the construction of a dam to generate hydro-electric power. The Board is mindful of the likely adverse response of the public living and working in the area where the dam would be built.

In response to the Government's wishes, PU has established environmental objectives relating to improved efficiency in energy production and reducing harmful emissions such as greenhouse gases. PU has also established an ethical code. Included within the code are sections relating to recycling and reduction in harmful emissions as well as to terms and conditions of employment.

Introduction of commercial accounting practices at EGC
The first financial statements have been produced for PU for 2008. Extracts from the Statement of Financial Position from this are shown in **Appendix A.** Within these financial statements, some of EGC's loans were "notionally" converted by the Government into ordinary shares. Interest is payable on the Government loans as shown in the statement of financial position. Reserves is a sum which was vested in EGC when it was first nationalised. This represents the initial capital stock valued on a historical cost basis from the former electricity generating organisations which became consolidated into EGC when it was first nationalised.

Being previously a nationalised industry and effectively this being the first "commercially based" financial statements, there are no retained earnings brought forward into 2008.

APPENDIX A

EXTRACTS FROM THE PRO FORMA FINANCIAL STATEMENTS OF THE ELECTRICITY GENERATING CORPORATION

Statement of financial position as at 31 December 2008

	P$ million
ASSETS	
Non-current assets	15,837
Current assets	
Inventories	1,529
Receivables	2,679
Cash and Cash equivalents	133
	4,341
Total assets	20,178
EQUITY AND LIABILITIES	
Equity	
Share capital	5,525
Reserves	1,231
Total equity	6,756
Non-current liabilities	
Government loans	9,560
Current liabilities	
Payables	3,862
Total liabilities	13,422
Total equity and liabilities	20,178

End of Pre-seen Material

SECTION A – 50 MARKS

[The indicative time for answering this section is 90 minutes]

ANSWER THIS QUESTION

Question One

Unseen material for Case Study

New investment

Following the privatisation of PU, the board are now considering the investment needed to retain and improve the productive capacity available to the company. Currently, PU operates 12 power stations which were all built over 15 years ago. Life expectancy for coal fired power stations is around 25 to 30 years. This means that all 12 power stations will need replacing within 10 to 15 years. This will be a significant capital cost for PU which will almost certainly have to be financed by borrowing or other forms of external investment.

Although the Asian country PU operates in does have coal reserves to fuel new coal fired power stations, the board are keen to investigate other methods of power generation such as gas, nuclear and more environmentally friendly alternatives such as wind and wave power. If coal fired power stations are built they will have to meet new environmental legislation in the Asian country, as well as global agreements to decrease the amount of Carbon Dioxide emissions from this type of power station. This will mean that the cost per power station will be higher in real terms than when the power stations were first built.

The non-executive directors in PU have recently identified that there is a lack of an effective Executive Information System for the Board. This means that board members cannot either monitor the current management and financial information produced within PU, or appraise new investment projects. One option to replace coal fired power stations is coal gasification. In this process, coal is mixed with oxygen and water vapour under pressure, normally underground, and then pumped to the surface where the gas can be used in power stations or converted into petrol and other similar fuels. The process has the benefit of significantly reducing carbon dioxide emissions although the technology is not widely used at present and not on any significant commercial scale.

One of the non-executive directors is aware that country Zee is a market leader in coal gasification processes. Country Zee is located in Africa; while Zee appears to be financially stable, there is some political unrest caused partly from ethnic divergence and issues of inequitable income distribution. Country Zee appears keen to retain its lead in this technology; at present the technology has only been made available to one other company in another country. The government of country Zee required this company to establish a subsidiary in Zee and manufacture the gasification equipment in Zee prior to export to the other country. This is the only method currently available to obtain the technology. To repeat the process, an initial investment will be required in Zee$, although the government guarantees to purchase the subsidiary at prevailing market prices in Zee after five years. A further requirement was that 80% of the workforce had to be drawn from the population of country Zee.

Environmental information

Legislation in the Asian country requires PU to provide environmental information each year on its activities, with specific reference to emissions of carbon dioxide from its power stations. This environmental information is collated at each power station and then forwarded to PU's head office for inclusion within PU's overall environmental report. Information from each power station is audited on a rotational basis by PU's internal audit department.

This year, power station N3 was part of the rotational audit. The internal audit department discovered significant discrepancies between the published emissions information and actual information obtained from the records maintained in the power station itself. The manager of the power station indicated that emissions were actually higher than expected due to faulty extraction filters fitted to the power station. Although PU's head office was aware of the problem, funds were not made available to rectify this. The matter was reported by the head of internal audit to the Managing Director with the recommendation that the emissions information was amended to show actual emissions.

Required:

Working as a consultant to the board of PU:

(a) The board of PU needs to assess methods of power generation in preparation for replacing the existing coal fired power stations. Advise the board how to develop an Information strategy to support this objective.

(12 marks)

(b) Evaluate the financial and other risks affecting PU if a subsidiary is established in Zee to manufacture coal gasification equipment.

(16 marks)

(c)

(i) PU's internal audit department may be asked to participate in the environmental audit of PU.

Explain the term "environmental audit" and evaluate the attributes that PU's internal audit department should have prior to carrying out this work.

(8 marks)

(ii) There is a discrepancy in environmental returns from power station N3. Recommend the actions (apart from reporting to the Managing Director) that the internal audit department of PU should undertake regarding this situation.

(8 marks)

(d) Discuss the extent to which false reporting of environmental information is a source of risk to PU and explain control mechanisms that may be used to avoid false reporting.

(6 marks)

(Total for question One = 50 marks)

End of Section A
Section B starts on page 9

SECTION B

[The indicative time for answering this section is 90 minutes]

ANSWER *TWO* OF THE THREE QUESTIONS – 25 MARKS EACH.

Question Two

The Y company produces a range of dairy products such as yoghurts, cream and butter from one factory. The main ingredient for these products is milk, which is obtained from 27 different dairy farms (fields where cows are allowed to graze and produce milk) within a 60 km radius of the factory. Y requires that milk must be delivered within 6 hours of being obtained from the cows and that the farms themselves use "organic" principles (farming without using manmade pesticides, growth hormones etc.). Transportation systems in Y's country are good and milk is rarely delivered late.

Each farm provides a quality certificate on each batch of milk produced confirming adherence to these standards (this is important to Y although customer satisfaction surveys show Y products are sold on taste, not sourcing of ingredients).

In Y's factory, yoghurt is produced in batches. The inputs to each batch such as milk, fruit, *appropriate* bacteria and other ingredients, are recorded in the batch database showing the source of that ingredient, that is the specific farm. During production, Y's quality control department tests each batch for purity (lack of contamination from *harmful* bacteria etc) and acceptable taste, with the results being recorded in the quality control database. Any batches not meeting quality standards are rejected and destroyed. Y's costing systems have maintained a 5% failure rate in production for the last 6 years which is now well in excess of the industry average.

On completion of each batch, the quality control department again undertakes purity control and taste testing. Batches are rejected where standards are not met; a further 2% failure rate is expected at this stage.

Batches of yoghurt etc are packed on Y's premises and then despatched for sale via retail outlets such as supermarkets; Y does not sell direct to the consumer. However, Y has an excellent brand name resulting from innovative advertising and high product quality. Product reviews in magazines and news websites have always been favourable meaning that Y does not need to pay much, if any, attention to customer feedback.

Required

(a) Evaluate the control systems in Y for the manufacture of yoghurt, recommending improvements to those systems where necessary.

(12 marks)

(b) Explain the process of risk mapping and construct a risk map for Y. Discuss how risk mapping can be used within the Y organisation.

(13 marks)

(Total for Question Two = 25 marks)

Question Three

A is a small company based in England. The company had the choice of launching a new product in either England or France but lack of funding meant that it could not do both. The company bases its decisions on Expected Net Present Value (ENPV) and current exchange rates. As a result of this methodology, and the details shown below, it was decided to launch in England (with an ENPV of £28,392) and not France (with an ENPV of £25,560).

England		France	
	Probability		Probability
Launch Costs		**Launch Costs**	
£145,000	0·1	£190,000	1·0
£120,000	0·9		
Annual Cash Flows		**Annual Cash Flows**	
£65,000	0·4	£90,000	0·5
£42,000	0·4	£70,000	0·2
£24,000	0·2	£30,000	0·3

Required:

(a) Discuss the risks associated with each launch option. Advise how these risks may be managed by the company.

(12 marks)

(b) Company A wishes to raise 3 year £500,000 floating rate finance to fund the product launch and additional capital investments. Company A has a choice between:

Alternative A: floating rate finance at LIBOR + 1·2% or

Alternative B: fixed rate finance at 9·4%, together with an interest rate swap at a fixed annual rate of 8·5% against LIBOR with a swap arrangement fee of 0·5% flat payable up front

Required:

(i) Discuss the potential benefits and hazards of interest rate swaps as a tool for managing interest rate risk.

(8 marks)

(ii) Ignoring the time value of money, calculate the total difference in cost between the two alternative sources of finance available to Company A.

(5 marks)

(Total for part (b) = 13 marks)
(Total for question Three = 25 marks)

Question Four

X is an organisation involved in making business-to-business sales of industrial products. X employs a sales team of 40 representatives and assigns each a geographic territory that is quite large. Sales representatives search for new business and follow up sales leads to win new business, and maintain contact with the existing customer base.

The sales representatives spend almost all their time travelling to visit clients. The only time when they are not doing this is on one day each month when they are required to attend their regional offices for a sales meeting. Sales representatives incur expenses. They have a mobile telephone, a fully maintained company car and a corporate credit card which can be used to pay for vehicle expenses, accommodation and meals and the cost of entertaining potential and existing clients.

The performance appraisal system for each sales representative is based on the number and value of new clients and existing clients in their territory. All sales representatives are required to submit a weekly report to their regional managers which gives details of the new and existing clients that they have visited during that week. The regional managers do not get involved in the daily routines of sales representatives if they are generating sufficient sales. Consequently, sales representatives have a large amount of freedom.

The Head Office Finance department, to whom regional managers have a reporting relationship, analyses the volume and value of business won by sales representatives and collects details of their expenses which are then reported back monthly to regional managers. At the last meeting of regional managers, the Head Office Finance department highlighted the increase in sales representatives' expenses as a proportion of sales revenue over the last two years and instructed regional managers to improve their control over the work representatives carry out and the expenses they incur.

Required:

(a) Explain what an internal control system is, how it relates to the control environment and its likely costs, benefits and limitations.

(8 marks)

(b) Discuss the purposes and importance of internal control and risk management to the X company and recommend action that should be taken to overcome any perceived weaknesses identified in internal control and/or risk management systems.

(12 marks)

(c) Recommend how substantive analytical procedures could be used in the internal audit of X's sales representatives' expenses.

(5 marks)

End of Question Paper

MATHS TABLES AND FORMULAE

AREA UNDER THE NORMAL CURVE

This table gives the area under the normal curve between the mean and a point Z standard deviations above the mean. The corresponding area for deviations below the mean can be found by symmetry.

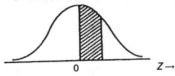

$Z = \dfrac{(x - \mu)}{\sigma}$	0.00	0.01	0.02	0.03	0.04	0.05	0.06	0.07	0.08	0.09
0.0	.0000	.0040	.0080	.0120	.0159	.0199	.0239	.0279	.0319	.0359
0.1	.0398	.0438	.0478	.0517	.0557	.0596	.0636	.0675	.0714	.0753
0.2	.0793	.0832	.0871	.0910	.0948	.0987	.1026	.1064	.1103	.1141
0.3	.1179	.1217	.1255	.1293	.1331	.1368	.1406	.1443	.1480	.1517
0.4	.1554	.1591	.1628	.1664	.1700	.1736	.1772	.1808	.1844	.1879
0.5	.1915	.1950	.1985	.2019	.2054	.2088	.2123	.2157	.2190	.2224
0.6	.2257	.2291	.2324	.2357	.2389	.2422	.2454	.2486	.2518	.2549
0.7	.2580	.2611	.2642	.2673	.2704	.2734	.2764	.2794	.2823	.2852
0.8	.2881	.2910	.2939	.2967	.2995	.3023	.3051	.3078	.3106	.3133
0.9	.3159	.3186	.3212	.3238	.3264	.3289	.3315	.3340	.3365	.3389
1.0	.3413	.3438	.3461	.3485	.3508	.3531	.3554	.3577	.3599	.3621
1.1	.3643	.3665	.3686	.3708	.3729	.3749	.3770	.3790	.3810	.3830
1.2	.3849	.3869	.3888	.3907	.3925	.3944	.3962	.3980	.3997	.4015
1.3	.4032	.4049	.4066	.4082	.4099	.4115	.4131	.4147	.4162	.4177
1.4	.4192	.4207	.4222	.4236	.4251	.4265	.4279	.4292	.4306	.4319
1.5	.4332	.4345	.4357	.4370	.4382	.4394	.4406	.4418	.4430	.4441
1.6	.4452	.4463	.4474	.4485	.4495	.4505	.4515	.4525	.4535	.4545
1.7	.4554	.4564	.4573	.4582	.4591	.4599	.4608	.4616	.4625	.4633
1.8	.4641	.4649	.4656	.4664	.4671	.4678	.4686	.4693	.4699	.4706
1.9	.4713	.4719	.4726	.4732	.4738	.4744	.4750	.4756	.4762	.4767
2.0	.4772	.4778	.4783	.4788	.4793	.4798	.4803	.4808	.4812	.4817
2.1	.4821	.4826	.4830	.4834	.4838	.4842	.4846	.4850	.4854	.4857
2.2	.4861	.4865	.4868	.4871	.4875	.4878	.4881	.4884	.4887	.4890
2.3	.4893	.4896	.4898	.4901	.4904	.4906	.4909	.4911	.4913	.4916
2.4	.4918	.4920	.4922	.4925	.4927	.4929	.4931	.4932	.4934	.4936
2.5	.4938	.4940	.4941	.4943	.4945	.4946	.4948	.4949	.4951	.4952
2.6	.4953	.4955	.4956	.4957	.4959	.4960	.4961	.4962	.4963	.4964
2.7	.4965	.4966	.4967	.4968	.4969	.4970	.4971	.4972	.4973	.4974
2.8	.4974	.4975	.4976	.4977	.4977	.4978	.4979	.4980	.4980	.4981
2.9	.4981	.4982	.4983	.4983	.4984	.4984	.4985	.4985	.4986	.4986
3.0	.49865	.4987	.4987	.4988	.4988	.4989	.4989	.4989	.4990	.4990
3.1	.49903	.4991	.4991	.4991	.4992	.4992	.4992	.4992	.4993	.4993
3.2	.49931	.4993	.4994	.4994	.4994	.4994	.4994	.4995	.4995	.4995
3.3	.49952	.4995	.4995	.4996	.4996	.4996	.4996	.4996	.4996	.4997
3.4	.49966	.4997	.4997	.4997	.4997	.4997	.4997	.4997	.4997	.4998
3.5	.49977									

Present value table

Present value of $1, that is $(1+r)^{-n}$ where r = interest rate; n = number of periods until payment or receipt.

Periods (n)	Interest rates (r)									
	1%	2%	3%	4%	5%	6%	7%	8%	9%	10%
1	0.990	0.980	0.971	0.962	0.952	0.943	0.935	0.926	0.917	0.909
2	0.980	0.961	0.943	0.925	0.907	0.890	0.873	0.857	0.842	0.826
3	0.971	0.942	0.915	0.889	0.864	0.840	0.816	0.794	0.772	0.751
4	0.961	0.924	0.888	0.855	0.823	0.792	0.763	0.735	0.708	0.683
5	0.951	0.906	0.863	0.822	0.784	0.747	0.713	0.681	0.650	0.621
6	0.942	0.888	0.837	0.790	0.746	0.705	0.666	0.630	0.596	0.564
7	0.933	0.871	0.813	0.760	0.711	0.665	0.623	0.583	0.547	0.513
8	0.923	0.853	0.789	0.731	0.677	0.627	0.582	0.540	0.502	0.467
9	0.914	0.837	0.766	0.703	0.645	0.592	0.544	0.500	0.460	0.424
10	0.905	0.820	0.744	0.676	0.614	0.558	0.508	0.463	0.422	0.386
11	0.896	0.804	0.722	0.650	0.585	0.527	0.475	0.429	0.388	0.350
12	0.887	0.788	0.701	0.625	0.557	0.497	0.444	0.397	0.356	0.319
13	0.879	0.773	0.681	0.601	0.530	0.469	0.415	0.368	0.326	0.290
14	0.870	0.758	0.661	0.577	0.505	0.442	0.388	0.340	0.299	0.263
15	0.861	0.743	0.642	0.555	0.481	0.417	0.362	0.315	0.275	0.239
16	0.853	0.728	0.623	0.534	0.458	0.394	0.339	0.292	0.252	0.218
17	0.844	0.714	0.605	0.513	0.436	0.371	0.317	0.270	0.231	0.198
18	0.836	0.700	0.587	0.494	0.416	0.350	0.296	0.250	0.212	0.180
19	0.828	0.686	0.570	0.475	0.396	0.331	0.277	0.232	0.194	0.164
20	0.820	0.673	0.554	0.456	0.377	0.312	0.258	0.215	0.178	0.149

Periods (n)	Interest rates (r)									
	11%	12%	13%	14%	15%	16%	17%	18%	19%	20%
1	0.901	0.893	0.885	0.877	0.870	0.862	0.855	0.847	0.840	0.833
2	0.812	0.797	0.783	0.769	0.756	0.743	0.731	0.718	0.706	0.694
3	0.731	0.712	0.693	0.675	0.658	0.641	0.624	0.609	0.593	0.579
4	0.659	0.636	0.613	0.592	0.572	0.552	0.534	0.516	0.499	0.482
5	0.593	0.567	0.543	0.519	0.497	0.476	0.456	0.437	0.419	0.402
6	0.535	0.507	0.480	0.456	0.432	0.410	0.390	0.370	0.352	0.335
7	0.482	0.452	0.425	0.400	0.376	0.354	0.333	0.314	0.296	0.279
8	0.434	0.404	0.376	0.351	0.327	0.305	0.285	0.266	0.249	0.233
9	0.391	0.361	0.333	0.308	0.284	0.263	0.243	0.225	0.209	0.194
10	0.352	0.322	0.295	0.270	0.247	0.227	0.208	0.191	0.176	0.162
11	0.317	0.287	0.261	0.237	0.215	0.195	0.178	0.162	0.148	0.135
12	0.286	0.257	0.231	0.208	0.187	0.168	0.152	0.137	0.124	0.112
13	0.258	0.229	0.204	0.182	0.163	0.145	0.130	0.116	0.104	0.093
14	0.232	0.205	0.181	0.160	0.141	0.125	0.111	0.099	0.088	0.078
15	0.209	0.183	0.160	0.140	0.123	0.108	0.095	0.084	0.079	0.065
16	0.188	0.163	0.141	0.123	0.107	0.093	0.081	0.071	0.062	0.054
17	0.170	0.146	0.125	0.108	0.093	0.080	0.069	0.060	0.052	0.045
18	0.153	0.130	0.111	0.095	0.081	0.069	0.059	0.051	0.044	0.038
19	0.138	0.116	0.098	0.083	0.070	0.060	0.051	0.043	0.037	0.031
20	0.124	0.104	0.087	0.073	0.061	0.051	0.043	0.037	0.031	0.026

Cumulative present value of $1 per annum, Receivable or Payable at the end of each year for n years $\frac{1-(1+r)^{-n}}{r}$

Periods	Interest rates (r)									
(n)	1%	2%	3%	4%	5%	6%	7%	8%	9%	10%
1	0.990	0.980	0.971	0.962	0.952	0.943	0.935	0.926	0.917	0.909
2	1.970	1.942	1.913	1.886	1.859	1.833	1.808	1.783	1.759	1.736
3	2.941	2.884	2.829	2.775	2.723	2.673	2.624	2.577	2.531	2.487
4	3.902	3.808	3.717	3.630	3.546	3.465	3.387	3.312	3.240	3.170
5	4.853	4.713	4.580	4.452	4.329	4.212	4.100	3.993	3.890	3.791
6	5.795	5.601	5.417	5.242	5.076	4.917	4.767	4.623	4.486	4.355
7	6.728	6.472	6.230	6.002	5.786	5.582	5.389	5.206	5.033	4.868
8	7.652	7.325	7.020	6.733	6.463	6.210	5.971	5.747	5.535	5.335
9	8.566	8.162	7.786	7.435	7.108	6.802	6.515	6.247	5.995	5.759
10	9.471	8.983	8.530	8.111	7.722	7.360	7.024	6.710	6.418	6.145
11	10.368	9.787	9.253	8.760	8.306	7.887	7.499	7.139	6.805	6.495
12	11.255	10.575	9.954	9.385	8.863	8.384	7.943	7.536	7.161	6.814
13	12.134	11.348	10.635	9.986	9.394	8.853	8.358	7.904	7.487	7.103
14	13.004	12.106	11.296	10.563	9.899	9.295	8.745	8.244	7.786	7.367
15	13.865	12.849	11.938	11.118	10.380	9.712	9.108	8.559	8.061	7.606
16	14.718	13.578	12.561	11.652	10.838	10.106	9.447	8.851	8.313	7.824
17	15.562	14.292	13.166	12.166	11.274	10.477	9.763	9.122	8.544	8.022
18	16.398	14.992	13.754	12.659	11.690	10.828	10.059	9.372	8.756	8.201
19	17.226	15.679	14.324	13.134	12.085	11.158	10.336	9.604	8.950	8.365
20	18.046	16.351	14.878	13.590	12.462	11.470	10.594	9.818	9.129	8.514

Periods	Interest rates (r)									
(n)	11%	12%	13%	14%	15%	16%	17%	18%	19%	20%
1	0.901	0.893	0.885	0.877	0.870	0.862	0.855	0.847	0.840	0.833
2	1.713	1.690	1.668	1.647	1.626	1.605	1.585	1.566	1.547	1.528
3	2.444	2.402	2.361	2.322	2.283	2.246	2.210	2.174	2.140	2.106
4	3.102	3.037	2.974	2.914	2.855	2.798	2.743	2.690	2.639	2.589
5	3.696	3.605	3.517	3.433	3.352	3.274	3.199	3.127	3.058	2.991
6	4.231	4.111	3.998	3.889	3.784	3.685	3.589	3.498	3.410	3.326
7	4.712	4.564	4.423	4.288	4.160	4.039	3.922	3.812	3.706	3.605
8	5.146	4.968	4.799	4.639	4.487	4.344	4.207	4.078	3.954	3.837
9	5.537	5.328	5.132	4.946	4.772	4.607	4.451	4.303	4.163	4.031
10	5.889	5.650	5.426	5.216	5.019	4.833	4.659	4.494	4.339	4.192
11	6.207	5.938	5.687	5.453	5.234	5.029	4.836	4.656	4.486	4.327
12	6.492	6.194	5.918	5.660	5.421	5.197	4.988	7.793	4.611	4.439
13	6.750	6.424	6.122	5.842	5.583	5.342	5.118	4.910	4.715	4.533
14	6.982	6.628	6.302	6.002	5.724	5.468	5.229	5.008	4.802	4.611
15	7.191	6.811	6.462	6.142	5.847	5.575	5.324	5.092	4.876	4.675
16	7.379	6.974	6.604	6.265	5.954	5.668	5.405	5.162	4.938	4.730
17	7.549	7.120	6.729	6.373	6.047	5.749	5.475	5.222	4.990	4.775
18	7.702	7.250	6.840	6.467	6.128	5.818	5.534	5.273	5.033	4.812
19	7.839	7.366	6.938	6.550	6.198	5.877	5.584	5.316	5.070	4.843
20	7.963	7.469	7.025	6.623	6.259	5.929	5.628	5.353	5.101	4.870

Formulae

Annuity

Present value of an annuity of £1 per annum receivable or payable for n years, commencing in one year, discounted at $r\%$ per annum:

$$PV = \frac{1}{r}\left[1 - \frac{1}{[1+r]^n}\right]$$

Perpetuity

Present value of £1 per annum, payable or receivable in perpetuity, commencing in one year, discounted at $r\%$ per annum:

$$PV = \frac{1}{r}$$

Growing Perpetuity

Present value of £1 per annum, receivable or payable, commencing in one year, growing in perpetuity at a constant rate of $g\%$ per annum, discounted at $r\%$ per annum:

$$PV = \frac{1}{r-g}$$

LIST OF VERBS USED IN THE QUESTION REQUIREMENTS

A list of the learning objectives and verbs that appear in the syllabus and in the question requirements for each question in this paper.

It is important that you answer the question according to the definition of the verb.

LEARNING OBJECTIVE	VERBS USED	DEFINITION
Level 1 - KNOWLEDGE What you are expected to know.	List State Define	Make a list of Express, fully or clearly, the details/facts of Give the exact meaning of
Level 2 - COMPREHENSION What you are expected to understand.	Describe Distinguish Explain Identify Illustrate	Communicate the key features Highlight the differences between Make clear or intelligible/State the meaning or purpose of Recognise, establish or select after consideration Use an example to describe or explain something
Level 3 - APPLICATION How you are expected to apply your knowledge.	Apply Calculate/compute Demonstrate Prepare Reconcile Solve Tabulate	To put to practical use Ascertain or reckon mathematically To prove with certainty or to exhibit by practical means Make or get ready for use Make or prove consistent/compatible Find an answer to Arrange in a table
Level 4 - ANALYSIS How you are expected to analyse the detail of what you have learned.	Analyse Categorise Compare and contrast Construct Discuss Interpret Prioritise Produce	Examine in detail the structure of Place into a defined class or division Show the similarities and/or differences between Build up or compile Examine in detail by argument Translate into intelligible or familiar terms Place in order of priority or sequence for action Create or bring into existence
Level 5 - EVALUATION How you are expected to use your learning to evaluate, make decisions or recommendations.	Advise Evaluate Recommend	Counsel, inform or notify Appraise or assess the value of Propose a course of action

Performance Pillar

Strategic Level Paper

P3 – Performance Strategy

Specimen Paper

Wednesday Morning Session

The Examiner's Answers – Specimen Paper
P3 – Performance Strategy

SECTION A

Answer to Question One

Requirement (a)

Business strategy
In this situation, the business strategy has been clearly defined; that is the coal fired power stations need to be replaced and the board will require information on the power generation options available the relevant merits, costs etc. of each alternative. The Information Strategy must therefore support this business strategy. In terms of Anthony's generic IT strategies, system development will follow the Business Led "leg".

Information strategy
The Information strategy will therefore need to focus on the specific information required by the board to enable an informed investment decision to be made. Information requirements will focus on the strategic level information. In this situation information requirements will include:

- Analysis of the different power generation options or coal, gas, nuclear and wind/wave including costs and benefits of each option.

- Feasibility of each option for PU taking into account existing knowledge base, resources available (eg funds) etc.

- Feasibility of each option in terms of establishing that power generation system within the Asian country. For example, the availability of gas (as compared to coal) or regions with sufficient wind for turbines must be considered.

Initially the information strategy must be to obtain and start to analyse this data; this may involve the recruitment of a management accountant with appropriate skills to obtain the data. Development of the strategy can then be divided into three specific sections:

Information Systems Strategy
The IS strategy will determine the actual systems required to provide the strategic information. The need for an information specialist has already been noted. However, there will also be information collection requirements in terms of obtaining internal and external information. The information requirements list identifies the need for data from PU's existing accounting systems (costs of running coal fired power stations) as well as external links to obtain data on other power generation methods (use of the Internet / access to providers of power stations etc will be essential). Consideration will also be required of future information needs and where appropriate, planning carried out to ensure that those needs will be met.

Information Technology Strategy
The IT strategy will determine the actual hardware and software requirements to provide the information identified in the IS strategy. As information is being provided to the board, provision of systems capable of detailed graphical output as well as ability to analyse different financial options quickly would be expected. Large computer systems, significant processing power and storage are expected.

Information Management Strategy
The IM strategy will determine how the information collected is provided to users and protected or backed up securely as required. IT infrastructure must ensure links from the information specialists to the board as well as offsite backup of data. A further consideration will be security of information produced for the decision. While external links will be necessary to collect data, information on alternatives will be sensitive and only accessible by the board of PU. Provision of data via a secure firewall to the board EIS, possibly with no other external access for security, will maintain information integrity.

Costs
Finally, the cost of the strategies must be determined and a budget agreed by the board ready to establish the necessary information systems to analyse the investment decision.

Requirement (b)

Economic risks
Economic risk is the risk that exchange rate movements might reduce the international competitiveness of a company and/or that the company's future cash flows may be reduced by adverse exchange rate movements.

Economic risk can affect PU in two ways:

- Firstly, as parts for the gasification process would have to be manufactured in Zee, PU would have to transfer funds to Zee to pay for that manufacture. If the currency of Zee appreciates over time then PU would have to remit additional funds to pay to continue to obtain the same quantity of manufactured items.

- Secondly, PU would be required to establish a subsidiary in Zee. The government of Zee indicate that the subsidiary can be sold after the gasification equipment is manufactured. However, if the currency of Zee depreciates against the Asian country then the value of that investment will fall. PU will therefore make a loss when the subsidiary is sold.

Translation Risk
This is the risk that an organisation will make exchange losses when the accounting results of foreign subsidiaries are translated back into the home currency.

If PU establishes a subsidiary in Zee, then that subsidiary would be consolidated into PU's financial statements each year. The rate used will be the date of the statement of financial position. Translation losses will mean that the value of the subsidiary will fall over time, showing a lower value in the financial statements of PU. While this has no effect on cash flow until the subsidiary is sold (see economic risk above) any fall in value could still affect the investor's attitudes to PU and may make it more difficult for PU to raise additional funds if subsidiary values fall significantly.

Transaction Risk
This is the risk that an organisation will be subject to exchange gains on losses where goods are imported or exported and the settlement date for the contract for import or export is at some future date. The risks it that the exchange rate changes between import/export and the receipt/payment of monies for those goods.

If PU establishes a subsidiary in Zee, then goods will be sent to Zee and/or back to PU's home country. Where exchange rate movements are expected, either PU or the subsidiary could delay payment/receipt for those goods if that exchange rate movement is favourable for that entity.

Exchange rate changes will also affect any internal transfer prices which may mean monitoring of these changes to ensure that the transfer price does not become uncompetitive compared to third party suppliers.

Political risk
Political risk is simply the risk that political action affects the position and value of a company. Various political risks could affect PU as follows:

- Firstly, PU will be required to employ a given percentage of workers from within Zee. There is a risk that sufficient employees with appropriate skills may not be found, limiting the ability of PU to manufacture gasification equipment. Alternatively, higher wages will have to be paid to attract workers with the necessary skills. Late delivery of equipment will have a financial impact on PU due to late start date for the projects and delaying income streams results from the sale of fuel.

- Secondly, political uncertainty could result in workers striking, again delaying manufacture and installation of equipment. PU may incur costs for late delivery / installation of equipment.

- Thirdly, additional export controls could be imposed on PU, limiting ability to transfer equipment from Zee to its Asian home country. Although this is unlikely due to Zee wanting to encourage investment, the risk could still crystallise with a change in government, for example. PU could be adversely affected financially if equipment has to be manufactured outside of Zee, especially where contracts are given to a third party. Alternatively, PU may have to pay higher taxes perhaps in the form of export duties, which again will have a financial impact on the company.

Product risks
Product risks include produces not meeting specific legislative requirements, potential breach of copyright through to the product not performing as specified.

Product risk can affect PU in various ways including:

- Firstly, the coal gasification process has not, as yet, been developed on a large commercial scale. There is a risk therefore that the process does not work as specified in the Asian country. The financial impact on PU may be significant unless appropriate insurance has been obtained or indemnities from the government of Zee.

- Secondly, the process may work, but not as expected. The gasification process itself may be unstable and cause environmental or other damage in the Asian country. PU may incur rectification costs unless again appropriate insurance or indemnities have been obtained.

Trade and credit risk
Trade and credit risk relate to a business trading in more than one jurisdiction.
PU will be effectively buying the gasification equipment from another jurisdiction (Zee). Risks in this category which will have a financial impact on PU should be limited to risk of damage or loss of equipment in transit not met by insurance. PU will be purchasing from its own subsidiary which will limit the possibility of other risks such as default in payments. However, transaction risk will also need to be considered as noted above.

Requirement (c)(i)

An environmental audit is, according to CIMA, a systematic, documented, periodic and objective evaluation of how well an entity, its management and equipment are performing with the aim of helping to safeguard the environment by facilitating management control of environmental practices and assessing compliance with entity policies and external compliance with entity policies and external regulations.

In terms of PU, the main focus of the audit will be the power stations with specific focus on the carbon dioxide emissions those stations produce. The importance of monitoring and limiting these emissions is important not only from the Asian countries legislation but also from global agreements to limit this "greenhouse gas" in the future.

Prerequisites for the internal audit department of PU which may be involved in an environmental audit of PU include:

Skills and experience
Staff in the department will need appropriate skill and experience in conducting audits. This does not necessarily mean they need to be qualified accountants, but they must be able to understand the process of internal audit and apply this to the work being carried out. Of vital importance is the ability to recognise errors and discrepancies identified as part of their work.

Knowledge of subject material
Staff must be aware of the criteria being used as part of the audit. In this situation, they must understand the environmental legislation, the standards to be adhered to and then the reporting requirements within that legislation.

They must also then be able to obtain the relevant information from within PU, compare this to the environmental standards.

Organisational standing
The internal audit department itself must be sufficiently independent to be able to produce reports without bias that will be acted on by the board of PU. In this situation, the department must report to the audit committee of PU. As the audit committee will comprise non-executive directors, they can ensure that the reports of internal audit are acted on and appropriate disclosure of any discrepancies is made.

Requirement (c)(ii)

Actions that the internal audit department of PU should undertake regarding falsification of environmental returns from power station N3 include:

Report to the audit committee
The internal audit report must clearly state the work carried out and the findings in respect of the false reporting and therefore opinion on that report. The responsibility of internal audit technically ceases when the report is made to the audit committee although the head of internal audit may also want to ensure appropriate action is taken in respect of the report by the committee.

Remedial actions – previous reports
The integrity of previous environmental reports is called into question as the N3 power station information is incorrect this year. Internal audit may decide to review prior year reports from N3 to ensure they are correct.

Review of results from other power stations
Following on from the above point, reports from other power stations where reported emissions are better than expected could also be audited, even if they are not part of the standard rotational audit this year. This additional work will help to determine whether the N3 power station report was an isolated case or more endemic across the whole of PU.

Remedial actions – control systems
The internal audit department could also recommend additional control procedures to try and avoid false reporting in the future. One option would be to increase internal audit work on the reports to review all reports annually rather than on a rotational basis. Alternatively, another responsible official could be tasked with checking and signing off the environmental report from each power station. While the latter would not remove false reporting, some collusion would now be necessary to perpetrate the false report.

Requirement (d)

False reporting of environmental information in PU is potentially a source of risk because:

- Environmental reports will be inaccurate. This will potentially undermine the integrity of other reports from PU and may provide adverse publicity for the company.

- Breach of environmental legislation may result in monetary fines being levied against PU. Again, imposition of a fine may result in adverse publicity for PU.

- False reporting may be indicative of an inappropriate management attitude to risk and control within PU. If false reporting is effectively condoned in one area (the MD being in agreement with the report) then staff may see this as an excuse to produce false reports in other areas. The whole control and reporting system within PU could be undermined.

Control mechanisms that could be used to avoid false reporting include:

- Use of an internal audit department (as PU have at present) as both a check on the accuracy of reporting as well as a deterrent against false reporting; the fact that internal audit may identify false reports should deter false reporting initially.

- Management setting the appropriate "tone" within the organisation. The MD condoning the false reporting is obviously not appropriate in this respect.

- Contracts of employment clearly stating that ethical principles are important and breach of principles will result in disciplinary action.

- For important positions such as board membership or managers of power stations, ensuring that the post holder is a member of a professional organisation (such as CIMA) where members are expected to follow ethical principles.

SECTION B

Answer to Question Two

Requirement (a)

Inputs

Y obtains the milk and other ingredients for its products from farms within a 60 km radius of its main processing factory. The milk etc. needs to be assessed for quality (freshness and organically produced) prior to entering the production process. At present, Y relies on a statement of quality from each individual farm. While the farms reputation and future sales would be decreased should the quality certificate be incorrect, there is no independent check on the quality of input. This weakness can be overcome in two ways:

- Firstly, an independent company can be appointed to verify the accuracy of the quality certificate produced by each farm. Milk delivered to Y needs to be produced by "organic" cows. In the UK, companies such as the Soil Association (in South Africa AFRISCO) provide this service. As the verifier is independent of the farm, their report can be trusted to confirm the organic quality.

- Secondly, Y can perform quality control checks on milk received before it enters the production processes. Assessing quality during the production process may be too late as whole batches of product will have to be destroyed, and it may not be possible to identify the precise farm that the milk or other ingredient was derived from due to mixing of inputs during processing.

Processing – quality control

During manufacture, Y's quality control department tests products for contamination from bacteria as well as meeting expectations regarding taste and flavour. Any batches of product not meeting quality control standards are rejected. However, information on the reasons for rejection are them simply stored as independent records in a database; there is no attempt to feedback reasons for quality deviations into the processing system to either amend inputs or identify where potentially contaminated batches of input were obtained.

Given that inputs into each batch of production are recorded on one database, and quality control reports on another, information concerning quality failures can be easily matched by comparing database records. Providing this matching would help Y improve product quality by identifying farms where poor quality milk was obtained, and by identifying how the product mix can be improved to enhance taste.

Processing – batch rejection rate

A 5% batch rejection rate is expected during production. It is not clear how the 5% figure was derived or whether this rate is "achieved" within Y. Ideally, rejection rates should be below 5% with feedback from quality control providing reasons for batch failure which can be used to minimise batch failures in the future. The discrepancy compared to industry average would support this view. As the 5% rejection figure has not been amended for 6 years, it appears this feedback control is lacking. Implementing the control as part of quality management would reduce rejection rates, allowing the rejection rate to be set at a lower target in future budgeting periods. Overall production costs would also fall with fewer rejected batches.

Output

Testing of outputs from Y production systems appears to be satisfactory. All batches are tested and again batches rejected where quality control standards are not met. As with processing, the lack of feedback control means batch quality may not be improved over time. The main weakness with output controls is lack of use of customer feedback. In this respects, Y is a closed system in that comments from customers are not used to enhance product taste or quality. Although Y does have a good brand name, this does not mean that either existing products cannot be changed or that new products (such as new yoghurt flavours) cannot be suggested by customers. Providing some formal feedback mechanism via the company's website help Y to ensure that its products continue to be aligned to customer requirements. In other words, Y's quality systems should be "open" to external suggestions and improvements.

Requirement (b)

Risk mapping is a method of determining the potential importance and impact of risks on an organisation. The map can be constructed as a 2 x 2 or 3 x 3 matrix, depending on the level of detail required. In some situations, even larger maps will be necessary.

In the map below, the Y axis shows the severity or potential impact of a risk on Y with the X axis showing how likely that specific risk is to actually occur.

- High likelihood, high impact risks are risks which will have a significant impact on the business and are likely to occur. Risks is this category must be monitored closely and either control systems put in place to ensure those risks do not occur or that any potential damage is mitigated as far as possible.

- High likelihood, low impact risks, while likely to occur, will not necessary have a significant effect on the company. These risks require monitoring to ensure they do not move into the high severity category.

- Low likelihood, high impact risks will have a significant effect on the company, show they actually occur. Again, control systems will be required to ensure that the risks are monitored and action taken should it appear that the risk will crystallise.

- Finally, low likelihood, low impact risks are unlikely to have any significant impact on the company and are normally ignored.

In Y, a risk map can be constructed as follows:

		Likelihood	
		High	**Low**
Impact	**High**	• Batches of product pass quality control which should fail. Although quality control tests appear good, releasing sub-standard food has risks of causing illness and consequent adverse publicity. • Adverse impact on brand name causes loss of sales.	• Late delivery of milk – production is disrupted and possible loss of quality of product. • Customers change tastes – unlikely in the short term but lack of analysis of customer feedback means Y may not amend product in line with customer expectations. • Products are considered not to be "tasty" by consumers – Y's main selling point is taste. Potential loss of market share.
	Low	• Milk does not have quality certificate (less important to Y's customers.	• Insufficient inputs are obtained (has contracts with a range of farms).

Risk maps can be used within Y as follows:

- Firstly, to provide a framework around which risks applicable to Y can be analysed. This will specifically show the "hi:hi" category risks – as in those for which a risk response must be determined.

- Secondly, to ensure that appropriate controls and risk management systems are in place to mitigate the impact of any risks actually crystallising. The main risk not sufficiently well covered is that customers may change "taste" causing demand to fall for Y's products.

- Thirdly, to recommend improvements to internal control systems to mitigate risks where control systems are poor. Within Y, there is a need to actively monitor customer feedback to ensure products do continue to meet customer "tastes".

___

SECTION C

Answer to Question Three

Requirement (a)

There are two types of risks faced by A in making its launch decision. The first set of risks relate to the market conditions, strategic implications and cash flow risks of the two alternative locations. The second set of risks relates to the limitations of the methodology chosen for decision- making.

Overseas expansion

The risks associated with expanding overseas are very different to the risks of focusing on the domestic market. There are issues of cultural understanding, language, exchange rate risk, and broader market knowledge that all need to be taken into account in the decision process. Some of these risks can be reduced by additional market research and changes in company strategy such as the use of a joint venture arrangement. Others may be more difficult to eradicate and the potential threat they pose to cash flows needs to be incorporated into decision making.

Expansion opportunities – home or overseas marketplace

By launching in the UK rather than France, A's decision ignores the broader strategic considerations, and their associated risks, with the result that the company forfeits potential expansion opportunities. These opportunities may not appear financially viable over the time frame used for the investment decision, but may be important for the long term development of the business. In the absence of additional information, if A is assumed to be a UK based company, then a UK launch simply means that it is expanding its position within the domestic market place. This may bring good short term growth levels for the business, but may not offer the longer term potential of a move into Europe, which could open up a significant range of new opportunities.

This risk is difficult to mitigate as A will never know the results of the alternative investment decision, had it been made. Risk mitigation will focus on ensuring that A has a balanced project portfolio, minimising the risk to A overall of one country providing less than acceptable returns, or one type of project providing less than acceptable returns.

Exchange rate risk

In purely financial terms France seems to pose less risk because the launch costs appear certain, but this is not actually true in reality. There is a risk that the exchange rate will change between the date of the decision and the date at which the costs are incurred, but this could be managed relatively easily by the use of a forward contract that would fix the exchange rate.

Cash flow risk

The exchange rate risk extends to affect the cash flows throughout the life of the product. Even a small change in the exchange rate can reverse the project rankings in terms of their ENPV.

The risk can be better understood via the application of sensitivity analysis on the NPV using different exchange rate scenarios, and the resulting exchange rate uncertainties can be managed via the use of a range of different hedging tools. These may include both internal and external hedging, such as netting, forward contracts, futures, or currency swaps. The exchange rate risk implicit in the launch in France may be regarded as significantly affecting the project's risk profile relative to the UK launch, and consideration must be given as to whether this additional risk is acceptable to the Board of Directors.

Product margin not achieved

The relative risk for the UK is that the contribution margin is comparatively low, which leaves limited scope for price cutting if the launch is not successful. This is counterbalanced by the fact that the probability schedule indicates that higher rather than lower sales levels are the most likely, but even these are not certain.

The risk of low margins can be managed by detailed market research to evaluate the price elasticity of demand for the product. It may be that the net contribution could be increased by raising prices (and margins) in combination with lower sales volumes.

Project risk – discount rate used

One possible approach to dealing with different levels of risk across projects would be to adopt different discount rates with a higher rate being applied to the project perceived as carrying the greater expected risks. This method creates a problem insofar as each additional risk has to be allocated a value in terms of a discount rate adjustment and this requires the use of subjective judgement. Additionally, a discount rate adjustment may not be necessary for some of the risks, such as exchange rate volatility because these may be managed via the use of hedging tools.

An alternative approach, as used in this case, is to use a common discount rate for both France and the UK. The final choice is then made by subjectively comparing the resulting ENPVs. Making this type of judgement is also difficult, however, because the ENPV for the UK is just £2,832 higher than that for France.

NPV calculations

The NPV calculations are based on expected costs and expected contribution levels. In practice it is unlikely that the expected values will ever be realised, which means that there is a possibility that the ENPV for the UK may actually be lower than expected or even lower than in France. Furthermore, the cash flow forecasts are based upon just four years of data, whilst the effective product life may be much longer. As a result, the decision may be based upon incomplete information.

There is a limit to how far this risk can be mitigated as the future is uncertain. Attempting to ensure that the cash flow forecasts are as accurate as possible by having them prepared and reviewed by competent professional staff will help.

Requirement (b)

Interest rate swaps are a useful tool for the management of interest rate risk because they allow a company to switch between fixed and variable rate loans, and therefore take a position on the future direction of interest rates. For example, a company may believe that interest rates have "bottomed out" and hence choose to swap its variable rate loans for fixed rate ones set at the current low interest rate level. In making this swap, the company is affirming its belief that future rates will rise ie taking a position.

In many but not all cases, swaps are used to obtain funding at a lower rate than that available elsewhere, but they can also be used beneficially to manage future cash flow patterns. If, for example, a company is operating in a market where its incoming cash flows are uncertain, it may wish to use a swap to ensure that it has fixed rate commitments that are wholly predictable. In so doing, it minimises uncertainty of outgoings even if it cannot eliminate the uncertainty in respect of incoming cash.

Interest rate swaps may also be used to manage interest rate risk in respect of investments rather than borrowings. In such cases a swap may be useful in enhancing the returns via speculation on interest rate movements. One such example would be a decision to swap a variable rate for a fixed rate investment in the belief that interest rates will fall.

A key advantage of interest rate swaps is that because they are an over the counter product, they can be tailored to meet the specific needs of the company, in terms of both their duration and value. Where the swap is arranged without the use of an intermediary, transaction costs are also kept to a minimum, although this also results in a disadvantage because it creates a counterparty credit risk. In the absence of an intermediary, there is no guarantee that the counterparty will fulfil their part of the contract, although this credit risk can be minimised by seeking a credit rating on the counterparty before agreeing to a swap.

Another disadvantage of swap arrangements is that the binding nature of the agreement means that a company may find itself unable to take advantage of changing interest rates that move in its favour. This problem is reinforced by the lack of a secondary market for swaps which means that it is difficult if not impossible to liquidate a contract.

Alternative A
Pay annual interest of: (LIBOR + 1·2%)
Alternative B:
Pay interest on borrowing of: (9·4%)
Pay interest under swap of: (LIBOR)
Receive interest under swap of: 8·5%
So pay net annual interest of: (LIBOR + 0·9%)

Annual interest saving   0·3%
Total interest saving over 3 years   0·9%
Less arrangement fee   (0·5%)
Net total cost saving   0·4%, that is £2,000

Answer to Question Four

Requirement (a)

Internal control system and the control environment

Internal control is the whole system of financial and other internal controls established in order to: provide reasonable assurance of effective and efficient operation; internal financial control; and compliance with laws and regulations. While the internal control system includes all the policies and procedures, the control environment is the overall attitude, awareness and actions of directors and management regarding internal controls and their importance to the organisation and encompassing management style, corporate culture and values.

A system of internal control will reflect its control environment and include: control activities; information and communication processes; and processes for monitoring the effectiveness of the internal control system. The system of internal control should be embedded in the operations of the company and form part of its culture; be capable of responding quickly to evolving risks; and include procedures for reporting immediately to appropriate levels of management any significant control failings or weaknesses.

Costs, benefits & limitations

The costs of internal control will comprise the time of regional managers and any opportunity costs resulting from this plus costs associated with introducing and operating new systems and reports. However, it is difficult to differentiate between internal controls and policies and procedures that are simply good business practice, e.g. human resource practices and accounting procedures. A cost of internal control may be restrictions on the flexibility, creativity and responsiveness of the organisation.

The benefits of internal control may be difficult to identify but can be largely considered to be an improvement in the efficiency and effectiveness by which sales representatives use their time to win business, and the improved management of costs associated with their activities. These are largely concerned with eliminating both waste and fraud. Losses incurred from ineffective internal control can be estimated based on their level compared to targets or by benchmarking representatives against each other or by observing the trend over time. To the extent that effective internal control provides assurance to external auditors it can be used in negotiations to reduce the external audit fee.

A system of internal control cannot eliminate: poor judgement in decision-making; human error; the deliberate circumvention of control processes (especially where collusion occurs); the overriding of, or lack of emphasis on, controls by senior management; and unforeseeable circumstances.

Requirement (b)

Internal control and risk management systems are established in an organisation in order to ensure that activities are carried out in accordance with the policies and procedures of the organisation and any risks of those policies and procedures not being followed is mitigated as far as possible.

In X, there appear to be two key risks that need to be considered:

- the lack of control over the activities of sales representatives that may result in them not spending their time efficiently and effectively on business activities; and

- the incurrence of costs that are unauthorised or unnecessary.

The first results in paying salaries for representatives but obtaining inadequate or inappropriate efforts from them. This has both a financial and an opportunity cost. The second results in excessive financial costs. Both are largely a problem of agency in which there is information asymmetry between the sales representative and regional manager. There is also an issue of moral hazard in which there is the potential for 'shirking' behaviour. Implementing appropriate internal control and risk management systems will help to ensure that these risks are avoided.

From the scenario, it would appear that these risks are not being appropriately monitored, due to the lack of internal controls identified by the Finance Director. The risks of not spending contracted time with the company and incurring unauthorised costs is compounded by factors such as:

- Lack of direct control over sales representatives; sales managers attend their office infrequently and overall performance is not monitored unless sufficient sales are not generated.

- There is a performance imperative to visit new and existing clients (the main focus of the sales representatives reports) which may mean expenditure is incurred on unnecessary visits (such as frequent visits to small clients),

- The reporting regime for expenses is to the finance department and then back to regional managers; the finance department may not have the knowledge to determine whether expenses are unreasonable. The delay in reporting back to regional managers also means that by the time expenses are queried, they have already been paid.

- In other words, prior to the approach by Finance to regional managers, there appears to have been no assessment, reporting or mitigation of risk in X. This is an internal control weakness which must be rectified by implementing appropriate internal controls to mitigate the possibility of loss being incurred by X.

The controls that should be introduced should include an appropriate mix of financial controls, non-financial quantitative controls, and non-financial qualitative controls. Appropriate controls will have to be implemented to overcome each weakness, and then the control tested to ensure that it works.

For example, in relation to expenses, initial authorisation should be by the regional managers, cross referencing expense claims with clients visited. Only then should the claim be sent to the finance department for payment.

Implementing the appropriate controls then mitigates the risks already identified above, ensuring that company resources are being used to achieve company objectives.

Requirement (c)

Substantive analytical procedures involves the examination of ratios, trends and changes, between periods, to obtain a broad understanding of financial position and the results of operations. It can help to identify any items requiring further investigation. It is an important audit technique used to identify errors, fraud, inefficiency and inconsistency. Its purpose is to understand what has happened in a system, to compare this with a standard and to identify weaknesses in practice or unusual situations that may require further examination.

Appropriate substantive analytical procedures for X may include:

- Ratio analysis of sales expenses to sales revenue with comparisons over time and between regions and sales representatives. Benchmarking data may be available from other sources or internally developed from identified best practice;

- Review, by sales representative, the proportions of new and existing business generated;

- Compare data, by representative, on the loss of customers.

Index

Index

Index

Index

Index

Index